Upper Level Review

Table of Contents

To be used in conjunction with the Fall 2011 and Spring 2012 semesters

Constitutional Law

CONSTITUTIONAL LAW

TABLE OF CONTENTS

PART ONE: POWERS OF THE FEDERAL GOVERNMENT

I. THE JUDICIAL POWER

A. ARTICLE III
The federal government is a government of limited powers, which means that for federal action to be legitimate, it must be authorized. The Constitution is the instrument that authorizes the federal government to act. Thus, whenever a question involves action by an entity of the federal government, the action will be valid only if it is authorized by the Constitution. The Constitution authorizes a federal court system in Article III, which provides that federal courts shall have judicial power over all *"cases and controversies"*:

1. Arising under the Constitution, laws, or treaties of the United States;

2. Of admiralty and maritime jurisdiction;

3. In which the United States is a party;

4. Between two or more states;

5. Between a state and citizens of another state;

6. Between citizens of different states;

7. Between citizens of the same state claiming lands under grants of different states; and

8. Between a state or citizens thereof and foreign states, citizens, or subjects.

B. POWER OF JUDICIAL REVIEW

1. **Review of Other Branches of Federal Government**
    The Constitution does not explicitly state that the Supreme Court may determine the constitutionality of acts of other branches of government. However, judicial review of other branches of the federal government was established in *Marbury v. Madison,* 5 U.S. 137 (1803) (per Marshall, C.J.); the Constitution is "law" and it is the province and duty of the judiciary to declare what the law is.

    a. **Separation of Powers and Finality of Court Decisions**
        The Constitution separates governmental powers among the branches of government. This separation of powers doctrine prohibits the legislature from interfering with the courts' final judgments.
        Example: The Supreme Court inferred a limitations period under an ambiguous federal securities law. Because new Supreme Court rulings generally apply to all pending cases, the limitations period imposed by the Court resulted in the dismissal of many pending cases as time-barred. Congress amended the securities law to provide (i) a different limitations period and (ii) a special motion for reinstating the cases dismissed as time-barred by the Supreme Court's ruling. The Supreme Court held

that the statute providing for the reinstatement of the dismissed cases violated the separation of powers doctrine under the Constitution. [Plaut v. Spendthrift Farm, Inc., 514 U.S. 211 (1995)]

1) Caution
When determining whether federal legislation impairs the finality of a decision of the United States Supreme Court, be careful to scrutinize the facts. For example, states have limited power to regulate interstate commerce, while the federal government has plenary power to do so. Thus, a decision that a state lacked the power to enact a particular regulation of commerce does not necessarily prevent Congress from adopting a regulation similar to the state regulation that was struck down. There is no interference with the finality of the Court's decision, because of the difference in standards.

2. Federal Review of State Acts
Federal review of state acts (executive, legislative, or judicial) was established by the Marshall Court in a series of decisions. Clear basis exists here in the Supremacy Clause of Article VI, which states that the Constitution, Laws, and Treaties of the United States take precedence over state laws and that the judges of the state courts must follow federal law, anything in the constitution or laws of any state to the contrary notwithstanding. [Fletcher v. Peck, 10 U.S. 87 (1810)]

C. FEDERAL COURTS
Only the actions of Article III courts are the subject of our outline, but you should know that there are two types of federal courts.

1. Article III Courts
Article III courts are those established by Congress pursuant to the provisions of Article III, Section 1. Although Congress has plenary power to delineate the jurisdictional limits, both original and appellate, of these courts, it is bound by the standards of judicial power set forth in Article III as to subject matter, parties, and the requirement of "case or controversy." Thus, Congress cannot require these courts to render advisory opinions or perform administrative or nonjudicial functions.

2. Article I Courts
Congress has created certain other courts, however, by way of implementing its various legislative powers; *e.g.,* United States Tax Court, courts of the District of Columbia. Judges of such Article I courts do not have life tenure or protection from salary decrease as do Article III court judges. Article I courts are sometimes vested with ***administrative as well as judicial*** functions, and the congressional power to create such "hybrid" courts has been sustained by the Supreme Court. [Glidden v. Zdanok, 370 U.S. 530 (1962)]

a. Limitation
Congress may not take cases of the type traditionally heard by Article III courts and assign jurisdiction over them to Article I courts. [Northern Pipeline Construction Co. v. Marathon Pipeline Co., 458 U.S. 50 (1982)—broad grant of jurisdiction to bankruptcy courts, including jurisdiction over contract claims, violates Article III]

D. JURISDICTION OF THE SUPREME COURT

1. Original (Trial) Jurisdiction

Under Article III, Section 2, the Supreme Court has original jurisdiction "in all cases affecting Ambassadors, other public Ministers and Consuls, and those in which a State shall be a Party." This provision is self-executing: Congress may *neither restrict nor enlarge* the Supreme Court's original jurisdiction, but Congress may give concurrent jurisdiction to lower federal courts and has done so regarding all cases except those between states.

2. Appellate Jurisdiction

Article III, Section 2 further provides that "in all other Cases before mentioned [*i.e.,* arising under the Constitution, Act of Congress, or treaty], the Supreme Court shall have appellate jurisdiction, both as to Law and Fact, with such Exceptions, and under such Regulations as the Congress shall make."

a. Statutory Application of Appellate Jurisdiction

Congress has provided two methods for invoking Supreme Court appellate jurisdiction: *appeal* (where jurisdiction is mandatory), and *certiorari* (where jurisdiction is within the Court's discretion). Very few cases fall within the Court's mandatory appeal jurisdiction; thus, appellate jurisdiction is almost completely discretionary.

1) Writ of Certiorari (Discretionary)

The Supreme Court has complete discretion to hear cases that come to it by writ of certiorari. A case will be heard if four justices agree to hear it. The following cases may be heard by certiorari:

a) Cases from the *highest state courts* where (i) the constitutionality of a federal statute, federal treaty, or state statute is called into question; or (ii) a state statute allegedly violates federal law [28 U.S.C. §1257]; and

b) All cases from *federal courts of appeals* [28 U.S.C. §1254].

2) Appeal (Mandatory)

The Supreme Court must hear those few cases that come to it by appeal. Appeal is available only as to decisions made by three-judge federal district court panels that grant or deny injunctive relief. [28 U.S.C. §1253]

b. Limitations on Statutory Regulation

Ex parte McCardle, 74 U.S. 506 (1868), has been read as giving Congress full power to regulate and limit the Supreme Court's appellate jurisdiction. However, *possible* limitations on such congressional power have been suggested:

1) Congress may eliminate certain avenues for Supreme Court review as long as it does not eliminate all avenues. For example, in *McCardle,* two statutes had allowed the Supreme Court to grant habeas corpus to federal prisoners. The Supreme Court upheld the constitutionality of the repeal of one of the statutes because the other statute remained as an avenue for Supreme Court habeas corpus review.

2) Although Congress may eliminate Supreme Court review of certain cases within the federal judicial power, it must permit jurisdiction to remain in *some* lower federal court.

3) If Congress were to deny *all* Supreme Court review of an alleged violation of constitutional rights—or go even further and deny a hearing before any federal judge on such a claim—this would violate due process of law.

E. CONSTITUTIONAL AND SELF-IMPOSED LIMITATIONS ON EXERCISE OF FEDERAL JURISDICTION—POLICY OF "STRICT NECESSITY"

Even if a federal court has jurisdiction over the subject matter of a case, it still might refuse to hear the case. Whether the court will hear the case (*i.e.,* whether the case is justiciable) depends on whether a "case or controversy" is involved, and on whether other limitations on jurisdiction are present.

1. No Advisory Opinions

The Supreme Court's interpretation of the "case and controversy" requirement in Article III bars rendition of "advisory" opinions. Thus, federal courts will not render decisions in *moot* cases, *collusive* suits, or cases involving challenges to governmental legislation or policy whose enforcement is neither actual nor threatened.

a. Compare—Declaratory Judgments

Federal courts can hear actions for declaratory relief. A case or controversy will exist if there is an actual dispute between parties having adverse legal interest. Complainants must show that they have engaged in (or wish to engage in) specific conduct and that the challenged action poses a *real and immediate danger* to their interests. However, the federal courts will not determine the constitutionality of a statute if it has never been enforced and there is no real fear that it ever will be. [Poe v. Ulman, 367 U.S. 497 (1961)—anticontraceptive law not enforced for 80 years despite open public sales]

2. Ripeness—Immediate Threat of Harm

A plaintiff generally is not entitled to review of a state law before it is enforced (*i.e.,* may not obtain a declaratory judgment). Thus, a federal court will not hear a case unless the plaintiff has been harmed or there is an immediate threat of harm.

3. Mootness

A federal court will not hear a case that has become moot; a *real, live controversy* must exist *at all stages of review*, not merely when the complaint is filed. [*See, e.g.,* De Funis v. Odegaard, 416 U.S. 312 (1974)—dismissing as moot a white law student's challenge to state's affirmative action program, since the student, although originally passed over for minority applicants with allegedly poorer records, had been admitted to law school while litigation was pending, was about to graduate by the time the case reached the Supreme Court, and would receive the same law degree whether or not the affirmative action program was invalidated]

a. Exception—Capable of Repetition But Evading Review

Where there is a reasonable expectation that the same complaining party will be subjected to the same action again and would again be unable to resolve the issue because of the short duration of the action (*i.e.,* where the controversy is capable of

repetition yet evading review), the controversy will not be deemed moot. [*See* Weinstein v. Bradford, 423 U.S. 147 (1975)]

Examples: 1) Issue concerns events of short duration (*e.g.,* pregnancy, elections, divorce actions); and

2) Defendant voluntarily stops the offending practice, but is free to resume it.

b. Class Actions

A class representative may continue to pursue a class action even though the representative's controversy has become moot, as long as the claims of others in the class are still viable. [United States Parole Commission v. Geraghty, 445 U.S. 388 (1980)]

c. Distinguish Ripeness

Ripeness and mootness are related concepts in that the court will not hear a case unless there is a live controversy. Ripeness bars consideration of claims *before* they have been developed; mootness bars their consideration *after* they have been resolved.

4. Standing

The Supreme Court will not decide a constitutional challenge to a government action unless the person who is challenging the government action has "standing" to raise the constitutional issue. A person has standing only if she can demonstrate a concrete stake in the outcome of the controversy.

a. Components

A plaintiff will be able to show a sufficient stake in the controversy only if she can show an *injury in fact*—caused by the government—that will be *remedied* by a decision in her favor (*i.e.,* causation and redressability).

1) Injury

To have standing, a person must be able to assert that she is injured by a government action or that the government has made a clear threat to cause injury to her if she fails to comply with a government law, regulation, or order. Some *specific injury* must be alleged, and it *must be more* than the merely theoretical injury that all persons suffer by seeing their government engage in unconstitutional actions.

Example: A Communist Party member would have standing to challenge a statute making it a crime to be a member of the Communist Party because the member's freedom of association is directly infringed, but a non-Party member would have no standing.

a) Injury Need Not Be Economic

The injury does not always have to be economic. In some cases, the Court has found that an individual is harmed because the alleged illegal act or unconstitutional action has an impact on the person's well-being.

Example: Law students were allowed to challenge an Interstate Commerce Commission rate-setting policy on the ground that such policies discouraged recycling and thereby diminished the quality of each student's physical environment. If the ICC

rate-setting policy violated congressional statutes, the elimination of those rate-setting policies would have an impact on the students' physical environment. [United States v. SCRAP, 412 U.S. 669 (1973)]

2) Causation

There must be a causal connection between the injury and the conduct complained of—*i.e.,* the injury must be traceable to the challenged conduct of the defendant and not be attributable to some independent third party not before the court.

Example: Plaintiffs claiming that a municipality's zoning policies prevented low income persons from finding housing in the municipality were denied standing because they failed to show a substantial probability that they would be able to afford housing in the municipality even absent the zoning policies. [Warth v. Seldin, 422 U.S. 490 (1975)]

3) Redressability

In determining whether a litigant has a sufficient injury to establish standing, courts ask whether a ruling favorable to the litigant would eliminate the harm to him. If a court order declaring a government action to be illegal or unconstitutional (and ending that government action) would not eliminate the harm to the litigant, then that individual does not have the type of specific injury that would grant him standing to challenge the government action.

Examples: 1) The Supreme Court held that mothers do not have standing to challenge the government's refusal to enforce criminal laws that would require the fathers of their children to pay child support. The enforcement of the criminal laws against a father who is guilty of nonsupport would not necessarily result in the father's providing support to the mother and her children.

2) Indigents have no standing to challenge an Internal Revenue Service policy that allows hospitals to receive favorable tax treatment even though they refuse to provide free or subsidized care for indigents. The indigents could not demonstrate that a different IRS policy would cause hospitals to provide them with free care.

b. Common Standing Issues

1) Congressional Conferral of Standing

Congress has no power to completely eliminate the case or controversy requirement, because the requirement is based in the Constitution. [*See* United Food & Commercial Workers Union Local 751 v. Brown Group, Inc., 517 U.S. 544 (1996)] However, a federal statute may create new interests, injury to which may be sufficient for standing.

2) Standing to Enforce Government Statutes—Zone of Interests

In some instances a plaintiff may bring suit to force government actors to conform their conduct to the requirements of a specific federal statute. Even in such cases,

the person must have an "injury in fact." Often, the Court asks whether the injury caused to the individual or group seeking to enforce the federal statute is within the "zone of interests" that Congress meant to protect with the statute. If Congress intended the statute to protect such persons, and intended to allow private persons to bring federal court actions to enforce the statute, the courts are likely to be lenient in granting standing to those persons.

Example: Persons who sold data processing services to private businesses had standing to challenge a ruling by the Comptroller of Currency that allowed national banks to make data processing services available to other banks and bank customers. These plaintiffs had an injury in fact because the Comptroller's ruling would hurt their future profits. The plaintiffs were determined to be within the "zone of interests" protected by the federal statutes limiting the authority of the Comptroller and national banks.

3) Standing to Assert Rights of Others
To have standing, the claimant must have suffered or may presently suffer a direct impairment of his *own* constitutional rights. A plaintiff may, however, *assert third-party rights* where he himself has suffered injury and:

(i) *Third parties find it difficult to assert their own rights* (the NAACP was permitted to assert the freedom of association rights of its members in attacking a state law requiring disclosure of membership lists because its members could not file suit without disclosing their identities) [NAACP v. Alabama, 357 U.S. 449 (1958)]; or

(ii) *The injury suffered by the plaintiff adversely affects his relationship with third parties*, resulting in an indirect violation of their rights (a vendor of beer was granted standing to assert the constitutional rights of males under 21 in attacking a state law prohibiting sale of beer to them but not to females under 21) [Craig v. Boren, 429 U.S. 190 (1976)].

a) Limitation—Family Law Issues
A divorced father sought to challenge on First Amendment grounds, on behalf of his daughter, the saying of the Pledge of Allegiance at her public school because the Pledge includes the words "under God." A state court order gave the girl's mother final authority over decisions regarding the girl's health, education, and welfare. The mother objected to the lawsuit, and neither the mother nor the daughter objected to the Pledge. The Court held that the father lacked standing to bring the claim. [Elk Grove Unified School District v. Newdow, 542 U.S. 1 (2004)]

4) Standing of Organizations
An organization (unincorporated association, corporation, union, etc.) has standing to challenge government action that causes injury to *the organization itself.* An organization also has standing to challenge government actions that cause an injury in fact to *its members if* the organization can demonstrate the following three facts:

(i)   There must be an *injury in fact to the members* of the organization that would give individual members a right to sue on their own behalf;

(ii) The injury to the members must be *related to the organization's purpose*; *and*

(iii) *Neither the nature of the claim nor the relief requested requires participation of the individual members* in the lawsuit.

[Hunt v. Washington Apple Advertising Commission, 432 U.S. 333 (1977)]

Example: The All Dentist Association ("ADA") is composed entirely of dentists; its purpose is to promote the professional well-being of dentists. Assume that most ADA members make between $100,000 and $200,000 per year. The ADA would not have standing to challenge a change in the federal income tax rates that will disadvantage all persons making between $100,000 and $200,000 on the basis that the statute deprives all persons (in the income category) of property without due process, because that claim is not related to the organization's purpose—the representation of dentists as such. But the ADA probably could bring a lawsuit challenging a state regulation of dental practices if the regulation injures ADA members, as long as the injury to ADA members does not vary.

5) No Citizenship Standing

As stated above, if an injury is too generalized, there can be no standing. Thus, people have no standing merely "as citizens" to claim that government action violates federal law or the Constitution. Congress cannot change this rule by adopting a statute that would allow persons to have standing merely as citizens (where they otherwise have no direct, personal claim) to bring suit to force the government to observe the Constitution or federal laws. [Lujan v. Defenders of Wildlife, 504 U.S. 555 (1992)]

6) Taxpayer Standing

a) Generally No Standing to Litigate Government Expenditures

A taxpayer, of course, has standing to litigate her tax bill (*e.g.,* whether she really owes X dollars). However, people generally do not have standing as taxpayers to challenge the way tax dollars are spent by the state or federal government, because their interest is too remote.

b) Exception—Congressional Measures Under Taxing and Spending Power that Violate Establishment Clause

There is an exception to the general rule: A federal taxpayer has standing to challenge federal appropriation and spending measures if she can establish that the challenged measure:

(i)   Was enacted under *Congress's* taxing and spending power (*see* II.A.2., 3., *infra*); and

(ii) Exceeds some specific limitation on the power.

To date, the only limit that the Supreme Court has found on the taxing power is the Establishment Clause. (*See* XXII.D., *infra*.)

Note: The measure challenged must arise under the taxing and spending power. Thus, there was no standing to challenge a federal government transfer of surplus property under the Property Clause that allegedly violated the Establishment Clause. [Valley Forge Christian College v. Americans United for Separation of Church and State, 454 U.S. 464 (1982)] Neither was there standing to challenge expenditures of executive branch general funds that allegedly violated the Establishment Clause. [Hein v. Freedom From Religion Foundation, 551 U.S. 587 (2007)]

7) **Legislators' Standing**
Legislators may have standing to challenge the constitutionality of government action if they have a sufficient "personal stake" in the dispute and suffer sufficient "concrete injury." [Raines v. Byrd, 521 U.S. 811 (1997)]

Example: A state's lieutenant governor cast the deciding vote to break a tie in the state senate. Legislators who had voted against the prevailing position had standing to challenge the right of the lieutenant governor to vote because his vote completely nullified theirs and caused the specific legislative enactment to go into effect. [Coleman v. Miller, 307 U.S. 433 (1939)]

Compare: Members of Congress had **no** standing to challenge the Line Item Veto Act authorizing the President to cancel (veto) certain spending and tax law measures that are part of a bill that he signs into law. *Rationale:* Rather than causing a "personal" and "concrete" injury, the challenged statute caused only a type of "institutional" injury to all members of Congress equally. [Raines v. Byrd, *supra*]

8) **Assignee Standing**
An assignee of a legal claim has standing even if the assignee has agreed to remit any proceeds recovered from the litigation back to the assignor, if this is done pursuant to an ordinary business agreement made in good faith. [Sprint Communications Co., L.P. v. APCC Services, Inc., 554 U.S. 269 (2008)—a paid collection agent has standing to bring the claims of an assignor even though the collection agent will submit any recovery back to the assignor]

5. **Adequate and Independent State Grounds**
The Supreme Court will hear a case from a state court only if the state court judgment turned on federal grounds. The Court will refuse jurisdiction if it finds *adequate and independent* nonfederal grounds to support the state decision.

a. **"Adequate"**
The nonfederal grounds must be "adequate" in that they are fully dispositive of the case, so that even if the federal grounds are wrongly decided, it would not affect the outcome of the case. Where that is the case, the Supreme Court's review of the federal law grounds for the state court's decision would have no effect on the judgment rendered

8. Eleventh Amendment Limits on Federal Courts

The Eleventh Amendment is a jurisdictional bar that modifies the judicial power by prohibiting a federal court from hearing a private party's or foreign government's claims against a state government. [*See* Hans v. Louisiana, 134 U.S. 1 (1890)]

a. What Is Barred?

The Eleventh Amendment's jurisdictional bar extends to the following:

(i) Actions against state governments *for damages*;

(ii) Actions against state governments for injunctive or declaratory relief *where the state is named as a party*;

(iii) Actions against state government officers where the effect of the suit will be that *retroactive damages* will be paid from the state treasury or where the action is the functional equivalent of a *quiet title action* that would divest the state of ownership of land; and

(iv) Actions against state government officers *for violating state law*.

1) Compare—Sovereign Immunity

The Court has also held that the following are barred by the doctrine of *sovereign immunity:*

a) Suits against a state government in state court, even on federal claims, without the defendant state's consent [Alden v. Maine, 527 U.S. 706 (1999)—provision in federal Fair Labor Standards Act creating a private cause of action in state courts against state employers who violate the Act violates sovereign immunity]; and

b) Adjudicative actions against states and state agencies before federal administrative agencies [Federal Maritime Commission v. South Carolina State Ports Authority, 535 U.S. 743 (2002)].

b. What Is Not Barred?

1) Actions Against Local Governments

The Eleventh Amendment protects only state governments. Local governments (*e.g.,* cities or counties) are not protected.

2) Actions by the United States Government or Other State Governments

Actions by the United States Government or other state governments are not barred.

3) Bankruptcy Proceedings

The Eleventh Amendment does not apply to federal laws that are exercises of Congress's Article I power to create bankruptcy laws, and thus does not bar actions of the United States bankruptcy courts that have a direct impact on state finances. [Tennessee Student Assistance Corp. v. Hood, 541 U.S. 440 (2004); Central Virginia Community College v. Katz, 546 U.S. 356 (2006)]

c. **Exceptions to Eleventh Amendment**

1) **Certain Actions Against State Officers**
The Supreme Court allows the following actions to be brought against *state officials* despite the Eleventh Amendment:

a) **Actions Against State Officers for Injunctions**
A federal court may enjoin a state officer to refrain from future actions that violate federal law or to take prospective actions to comply with constitutional mandates. [*Ex parte* Young, 209 U.S. 123 (1908)]

b) **Actions Against State Officers for Monetary Damages from Officer**
A federal court may hear an action for damages against a state officer for violations of *federal law if* the monetary damages are to be paid out of the officer's own pocket. *Rationale:* By acting outside the scope of federal law, the officer is stripped of his representative capacity—the action is not one against a state, but rather is against an individual.

c) **Actions Against State Officers for Prospective Payments from State**
A federal court may hear an action for damages against a state officer where the effect of the action will be to force the state to pay money in the future to comply with the court order. [*Ex parte* Young, *supra*] However, federal court jurisdiction is barred if the action will result in retroactive damages to be paid from the state treasury. [Edelman v. Jordan, 415 U.S. 651 (1984)]

Example: P sues the State Commissioner of the Department of Public Welfare for failing to comply with federal welfare regulations. The federal court can order future compliance with the federal regulations, even if this will result in costing the state a large amount of money in the future. However, the federal court cannot award back payments of amounts previously improperly withheld, because the order would require payment from the state treasury for retroactive relief. [Edelman v. Jordan, *supra*]

2) **Congressional Removal of Immunity Under the Fourteenth Amendment**
Congress can remove the states' Eleventh Amendment immunity under its power to *prevent discrimination under the Fourteenth Amendment.* For example, the Equal Pay Act—based on the Fourteenth Amendment—can serve as a basis for federal suits against a state by its employees. [Fitzpatrick v. Bitzer, 427 U.S. 445 (1976)]

a) **Compare—Article I Powers**
Unlike its power under the Fourteenth Amendment, Congress's legislative powers under Article I (*see* II., *infra*) do *not* include the power to abrogate state immunity under the Eleventh Amendment. [Seminole Tribe of Florida v. Florida, 517 U.S. 114 (1996)] However, the Supreme Court has held that states may not assert sovereign immunity in proceedings arising under the bankruptcy law. [Central Virginia Community College v. Katz, *supra*]

d. **Summary**

For most bar exam questions, a key principle to remember is this: The Eleventh Amendment will prohibit a federal court from hearing a claim for damages against a state government (although not against state officers) unless:

1) The state has consented to allow the lawsuit in federal court;

2) The plaintiff is the United States or another state; or

3) Congress has clearly granted federal courts the authority to hear a specific type of damage action under the Fourteenth Amendment (*e.g.*, under a civil rights statute).

II. LEGISLATIVE POWER

A. ENUMERATED AND IMPLIED POWERS

The Constitution grants Congress a number of specific powers, many of which are enumerated in Article I, Section 8. It also grants Congress auxiliary power under the Necessary and Proper Clause.

1. **Necessary and Proper "Power"**

The Necessary and Proper Clause grants Congress the power to make all laws necessary and proper (*i.e.,* appropriate) for carrying into execution *any* power granted to *any* branch of the federal government.

Example: Congress has the power to charter banks since that power is appropriate to executing Congress's enumerated powers to tax, borrow money, regulate commerce, etc. [McCulloch v. Maryland, 17 U.S. 316 (1819)]

Note: The Necessary and Proper Clause is not itself a basis of power; it merely gives Congress power to execute specifically granted powers. Thus, if a bar exam question asks what is the best source of power for a particular act of Congress, the answer should not be the Necessary and Proper Clause, standing alone.

a. **Limitation**

Congress cannot adopt a law that is expressly prohibited by another provision of the Constitution.

2. **Taxing Power**

Congress has the power to lay and collect taxes, imposts, and excises, but they must be uniform throughout the United States. [Art. I, §8] Capitation or other direct taxes must be laid in proportion to the census [Art. I, §9, cl. 4], and direct taxes must be apportioned among the states [Art. I, §2, cl. 3].

a. **Uniformity**

Requirement of uniformity in the levy of indirect taxes (generally, this means any kind of "privilege" tax, including duties and excises) has been interpreted by the Court to mean *geographical uniformity* only—*i.e.*, identical taxation of the taxed Article in every state where it is found. [Fernandez v. Wiener, 326 U.S. 340 (1945)]

b.   **Direct Taxes—Must Be Apportioned**

A "direct" tax (imposed directly on property or on the person) has seldom been employed by Congress because of the cumbersome ***apportionment requirement***; taxes on income from real or personal property were initially held "direct" by the Court, but the resulting need for apportioning such taxes was obviated by the Sixteenth Amendment (income tax amendment).

c.   **Export Taxes Not Permitted**

Neither Congress nor the state can tax exports to foreign countries.

d.   **Taxes Are Generally Valid**

Absent a specific restriction such as those above, be very hesitant to rule against a tax measure on the exam. A tax measure will be upheld if it bears some ***reasonable relationship to revenue production*** or if Congress has the ***power to regulate*** the taxed activity.

Example: Special excise tax levied on dealers in illegal narcotics is valid because it raises revenue. [United States v. Doremus, 249 U.S. 86 (1919)]

3.   Spending Power

Congress may spend to "provide for the common defense and general welfare." [Art. I, §8] This spending may be for ***any public purpose***—not merely the accomplishment of other enumerated powers. However, nonspending regulations are not authorized. Remember that the Bill of Rights still applies to this power; *i.e.,* the federal government could not condition welfare payments on an agreement not to criticize government policies.

a.   **Regulation Through Spending**

Note that Congress can use its spending power to "regulate" areas, even where it otherwise has no power to regulate the area, by requiring entities that accept government money to act in a certain manner (*i.e.,* attaching "strings" to government grants). (*See* VI.A.2.b., *infra.*)

4.   Commerce Power

Article I, Section 8, Clause 3 empowers Congress to "regulate commerce with foreign nations and among the several states, and with the Indian tribes."

a.   **Definition of Commerce**

1)   **Includes Basically All Activity Affecting Two or More States**

Chief Justice Marshall, in *Gibbons v. Ogden,* 22 U.S. 1 (1824), defined commerce as "every species of commercial intercourse . . . which concerns more states than one" and included within the concept virtually every form of activity involving or affecting two or more states.

2)   **Includes Transportation or Traffic**

The Court has consistently regarded transportation or traffic as commerce, whether or not a commercial activity is involved.

Example: Interstate transportation of liquor for personal consumption, women for immoral purposes (not necessarily prostitution), and

interstate transportation of stolen motor vehicles are all interstate commerce.

a) Vehicular Transportation Not Required
Any *transmission across state lines*, such as electricity, gas, telegraph, telephone, TV, radio, and mail transmission (including educational materials and sale of insurance), will constitute interstate commerce.

b. "Substantial Economic Effect"
The Supreme Court has sustained congressional power to regulate any activity, local or interstate, that either in itself *or in combination with other activities* has a *"substantial economic effect upon,"* or *"effect on movement in,"* interstate commerce.

Example: The classic case is the Court's holding that Congress can control a farmer's *production* of wheat *for home consumption*. [Wickard v. Filburn, 317 U.S. 111 (1942)] *Rationale:* Cumulative effect of many instances of such production could be felt on the supply and demand of the interstate commodity market.

1) Power Not Unlimited
The Supreme Court has recently made clear that the power of Congress to regulate commerce, although very broad, does have limits so as not to obliterate the distinction between what is national and what is local. To be within Congress's power under the Commerce Clause, a federal law must either:

(i) *Regulate the channels* of interstate commerce;

(ii) *Regulate the instrumentalities* of interstate commerce and persons and things in interstate commerce; or

(iii) *Regulate activities that have a substantial effect* on interstate commerce.

a) Intrastate Activity
When Congress attempts to regulate *intrastate* activity under the third prong, above, the Court will uphold the regulation if it is of *economic or commercial activity* and the court can conceive of a *rational basis* on which Congress could conclude that the activity *in aggregate* substantially affects interstate commerce. [Gonzales v. Raich, 545 U.S. 1 (2005)—upholding regulation of intrastate cultivation and use of marijuana (permitted by state law for medicinal purposes) because it was part of a comprehensive federal program to combat interstate traffic in illicit drugs] However, if the regulated intrastate activity is noncommercial and noneconomic, it cannot be regulated under the Commerce Clause unless Congress can factually show a *substantial economic effect* on interstate commerce. [*See, e.g.,* United States v. Lopez, 514 U.S. 549 (1995)—federal statute barring possession of a gun in a school zone is invalid; United States v. Morrison, 529 U.S. 598 (2000)—federal civil remedy for victims of gender-motivated violence is invalid]

5. **War and Related Powers**

Article I, Section 8 gives Congress the power to declare war, raise and support armies, provide for and maintain a navy, make rules for the government and regulation of the armed forces, and organize, arm, discipline, and call up the militia. Of course, several other congressional powers may have direct or indirect application to military purposes: tax and spending power, commerce power, Senate's treaty consent power, maritime power, investigatory power, etc.

a. **Economic Regulation**

1) **During War**

Regulatory power of Congress, especially in economic matters and mobilization of troops, in support of war effort is *pervasive* (although theoretically limited by the Bill of Rights); thus, the Court has sustained national price and rent control, as well as conscription and regulation of civilian/military production and services.

2) **Postwar**

To a considerable extent, this pervasive regulatory power may be validly extended into post-wartime periods both to *remedy wartime disruptions* [*e.g.,* Woods v. Miller, 333 U.S. 138 (1948)—rent controls] and to cope with *"cold war" exigencies*. Legislation in the field of veterans' rights and limitations thereon may be extended indefinitely as long as veterans or their relatives may survive.

b. **Military Courts and Tribunals**

The constitutional basis of courts of military justice (trial and review of offenses by military personnel, including courts-martial and reviewing agencies and tribunals) is not Article III, but rather Article I, Section 8, Clause 14 (congressional power to make rules for government and regulation of armed forces), buttressed by the Necessary and Proper Clause.

1) **Judicial Review**

The regular federal (or state) courts have *no general power to review* court-martial proceedings. However, in habeas corpus cases, the Article III courts, including the Supreme Court, may make a limited inquiry into the military court's jurisdiction of the person and offense or the validity of the court's legislative creation.

2) **Court-Martial of Enemy Civilians and Soldiers Permitted**

Military courts may try enemy civilians as well as enemy military personnel, at least during wartime.

a) **Suspension of Habeas Corpus for Enemy Combatants**

Congress does not have the power to deny habeas corpus review to all aliens detained as enemy combatants absent a meaningful substitute for habeas corpus review. A meaningful substitute would allow prisoners to (i) challenge the President's authority to detain them indefinitely, (ii) contest the military commission's findings of fact, (iii) supplement the record on review with exculpatory evidence discovered after the military commission's proceedings, and (iv) request release. [Boumediene v. Bush, 553 U.S. 723 (2008)]

3) Court-Martial of American Soldiers Permitted
Military courts have jurisdiction over *all* offenses (not just service connected offenses) committed by persons who are members of the armed services, both when charged and at the time of the offense. [Solorio v. United States, 483 U.S. 435 (1987), *overruling* O'Callahan v. Parker, 395 U.S. 258 (1969)]

4) Court-Martial of American Civilians Generally Prohibited
The Supreme Court has denied Congress the power to authorize the court-martial trial of American civilians as long as actual warfare has not forced courts to shut down, even though martial law has been declared [*Ex parte* Milligan, 71 U.S. 2 (1866)]; even though the civilians accused may have been members of the armed forces when committing the alleged offense [Toth v. Quarles, 350 U.S. 11 (1955)] or are dependents of military personnel accompanying the latter overseas [Reid v. Covert, 354 U.S. 1 (1957)] or are civilian employees of the military forces at overseas bases and installations; such trials by court-martial violate the Fifth and Sixth Amendments, particularly the right to trial by jury.

c. **Calling Forth the Militia**
Under the Militia Clauses [Art. I, §8, cl. 15, 16], Congress has the power to authorize the President to order members of National Guard units into federal service—even in circumstances that do not involve a national emergency (*e.g.,* for training outside of the United States). The President need not obtain the consent of the governor of a unit's home state to call it into such service. [Perpich v. Department of Defense, 496 U.S. 334 (1990)]

6. Investigatory Power
The power to investigate to secure information as a basis for potential legislation or other official action (such as impeachment or trying impeachments) is a well-established implied power. It is a *very broad power*, in that an investigation need not be directed toward enactment of particular legislation, but the following limitations on its use do exist.

a. **Authorized Investigation**
The investigatory inquiry must be expressly or impliedly authorized by the congressional house concerned, *i.e.,* by statute or resolution creating or directing the investigating committee or subcommittee.

b. **Witnesses' Rights**

1) Fifth Amendment
The privilege against compulsory self-incrimination (the Fifth Amendment) is available to witnesses, whether formal or informal, unless a statutory immunity co-extensive with the constitutional immunity is granted.

2) Relevance
Written or oral information elicited by the investigative body must be "pertinent" to the subject of the inquiry.

3) Procedural Due Process
Witnesses are generally entitled to procedural due process, such as presence of

counsel and right of cross-examination; but it is not yet clear whether such rights are constitutionally required or whether some of them are required merely by house rule or statute.

c. Enforcement of Investigatory Powers
Congress can hold a subpoenaed witness in contempt for refusing to appear or answer before Congress.

7. Property Power
Congress has the power to "dispose of and make all needful rules and regulations respecting the territory or other property belonging to the United States." [Art. IV, §3] Many other congressional powers (war, commerce, postal, fiscal, etc.) obviously would be unworkable if the ancillary *power to acquire and dispose of property of all kinds*—real, personal, and intangible—were not also implied from the main grants.

Example: The Property Clause empowers Congress to even protect wildlife wandering onto federally owned lands. [Kleppe v. New Mexico, 426 U.S. 529 (1976)]

a. No Limits on Disposition of Property
There is no express limitation on Congress's power to dispose of property owned by the United States. The power extends to all species of property, such as leasehold interests and electrical energy, as well as ordinary realty and personalty. Moreover, disposal may involve direct competition with private enterprise and has never been invalidated on that ground.

b. Eminent Domain
Acquisition of property for a public purpose by eminent domain is indirectly recognized by the Fifth Amendment: ". . . nor shall private property be taken for public use, without just compensation." Federal taking must be for the purpose of *effectuating an enumerated power* under some other provision of the Constitution.

8. No Federal Police Power
Congress has no general police power (*i.e.*, power to legislate for the health, welfare, morals, etc., of the citizens). Thus, on the bar exam the validity of a federal statute cannot rely on "the police power." However, Congress can exercise police power-type powers as to the District of Columbia pursuant to its power to legislate over the capital [Art. I, §8, cl. 17] and over all United States possessions (*e.g.*, territories, military bases, Indian reservations) pursuant to the property power.

9. Bankruptcy Power
Article I, Section 8, Clause 4 empowers Congress "to establish uniform laws on the subject of bankruptcies throughout the United States." This power has been interpreted by the Supreme Court as nonexclusive; *i.e.*, state legislation in the field is superseded only to the extent that it conflicts with federal legislation therein.

10. Postal Power
Article I, Section 8, Clause 7 empowers Congress "to establish post offices and post roads."

a. Exclusive
The postal power has been interpreted as granting Congress a postal monopoly. Neither

private business nor the states may compete with the Federal Postal Service absent Congress's consent. [Air Courier Conference of America v. American Postal Workers Union, 498 U.S. 517 (1991)]

b. Scope of Power
Congress may validly classify and place **reasonable restrictions** on use of the mails, **but may not deprive** any citizen or group of citizens of the general mail "privilege" or regulate the mail in such a way as to abridge freedom of speech or press (except under valid standards, such as "obscenity") or violate the ban of the Fourth Amendment against unreasonable search and seizure.

11. Power Over Citizenship
Article I, Section 8, Clause 4 empowers Congress "to establish a uniform rule of naturalization."

a. Exclusion of Aliens
Congress's power to exclude aliens is broad.

1) Nonresident Aliens
Aliens have no right to enter the United States and **can be refused entry** because of their political beliefs. [Kleindienst v. Mandel, 408 U.S. 753 (1972)]

2) Resident Aliens
Resident aliens are entitled to **notice and hearing** before they can be deported.

b. Naturalization and Denaturalization—Exclusive Control of Congress
Congress has exclusive power over naturalization and denaturalization. The Supreme Court has held that this grant gives Congress plenary power over aliens (*see* XVIII.D.2.a., *infra*).

1) No Loss of Citizenship Without Consent
Under the Fourteenth Amendment, Congress may not take away the citizenship of any citizen—native-born or naturalized—without his consent.
Example: The Court held unconstitutional a statute that provided for loss of citizenship upon voting in a foreign election. [Afroyim v. Rusk, 387 U.S. 253 (1967)]

a) Proof of Intent
A citizen's intent to relinquish citizenship may be expressed by words or conduct—and Congress may provide that such intent may be proven by a preponderance of the evidence. [Vance v. Terrazas, 444 U.S. 252 (1980)]

2) Rights of Children of Citizens
A person born in another country to United States citizen parents does not have a constitutional right to become a United States citizen. Congress can grant citizenship to children born abroad conditioned on their return to live in the United States within a specified period of time or for a specified number of years. Such a child who fails to return to the United States loses his grant of citizenship because he has failed to meet the statutory condition precedent to his final grant of citizenship.

12. **Admiralty Power**

Although congressional power to legislate in maritime matters is not expressed in the Constitution, the Supreme Court has implied it from the exclusive jurisdiction given the federal courts in this field by Article III, Section 2, supported by the Necessary and Proper Clause of Article I, Section 8.

a. **Exclusive Power**

The congressional power is plenary and exclusive, except to the extent that Congress may leave (and has left) some maritime matters to state jurisdiction.

b. **Navigable Waterways**

The federal admiralty power attaches to all navigable waterways—actually or potentially navigable—and to small tributaries that affect navigable waterways. The federal maritime power is not limited to tidewaters or interstate waters.

13. **Power to Coin Money and Fix Weights and Measures**

Congress has the power to coin money and fix the standard of weights and measures under Article I, Section 8, Clause 5.

14. **Patent/Copyright Power**

Congress has the power to control the issuance of patents and copyrights under Article I, Section 8, Clause 8.

B. DELEGATION OF LEGISLATIVE POWER

1. **Broad Delegation Allowed**

Congress has broad discretion to delegate its legislative power to executive officers and/ or administrative agencies [Schechter Poultry Corp. v. United States, 295 U.S. 495 (1935)], and even delegation of rulemaking power to the courts has been upheld [Mistretta v. United States, 488 U.S. 361 (1989)].

Example: Congress can delegate the power to establish sentencing guidelines for criminal cases to a sentencing commission located in the federal courts and made up, in part, of federal judges, as long as the tasks delegated do not undermine the integrity of the judiciary or usurp the powers of the other branches. [Mistretta v. United States, *supra*]

2. **Limitations on Delegation**

a. **Power Cannot Be Uniquely Confined to Congress**

To be delegable, the power must not be uniquely confined to Congress; *e.g.,* the power to declare war cannot be delegated, nor the power to impeach.

b. **Clear Standard**

It is said that delegation will be upheld only if it includes intelligible standards for the delegate to follow. However, as a practical matter almost anything will pass as an "intelligible standard" (*e.g.,* "upholding public interest, convenience, or necessity").

c. **Separation of Powers Limitations**

While Congress has broad power to delegate, the separation of powers doctrine restricts Congress from keeping certain controls over certain delegates. For example, Congress

cannot give itself the power to remove an officer of the executive branch by any means other than impeachment (*e.g.,* if Congress delegates rulemaking power to an executive branch agency (*e.g.,* the FCC), it may not retain the power to fire the agency head). (*See* III.B.1.b.2)a), *infra.*) Similarly, Congress cannot give a government employee who is subject to removal by Congress (other than by impeachment) purely executive powers. (*See* III.B.1.b.2)b), *infra.*)

Example: A federal statute transferred the authority to control two D.C. area airports from the federal government to a local authority. However, the statute reserved to a review board a veto power over the local authority's decisions. The review board was comprised of nine members of Congress. The statute violates the separation of powers doctrine in one of two ways: (i) If the review board's power is considered to be legislative, the statute created an unconstitutional legislative veto (*see* D., *infra*). (ii) If the review board's power is considered to be executive, the separation of powers doctrine prohibits members of Congress from exercising it. [Metropolitan Washington Airports Authority v. Citizens for Abatement of Aircraft Noise, 501 U.S. 252 (1991)]

d. Important Liberty Interests
If the delegate interferes with the exercise of a fundamental liberty or right, the burden falls upon the delegate to show that she has the power to prevent the exercise of the right and her decision was in furtherance of that particular policy.

Example: In *Kent v. Dulles,* 357 U.S. 116 (1958), the Secretary of State was required to issue a passport to a Communist because he could not show that Congress gave him the power to encroach upon the fundamental right to travel simply because the applicant was a Communist.

e. Criminal vs. Civil Punishment
The legislature may delegate its authority to enact regulations, the violation of which are crimes, but prosecution for such violations must be left to the executive and judicial branches. [*See* United States v. Grimaud, 220 U.S. 506 (1911)] However, agencies may enact and impose civil penalties (*i.e.,* fines labeled as civil fines) without prosecution in court. [Helvering v. Mitchell, 303 U.S. 391 (1938)]

C. THE SPEECH OR DEBATE CLAUSE—SPECIAL IMMUNITY FOR FEDERAL LEGISLATORS
Article I, Section 6 provides that "For any speech or debate in either House [members of Congress] shall not be questioned in any other place."

1. Persons Covered
The immunity extends to aides who engage in acts that would be immune if performed by a legislator. [Gravel v. United States, 408 U.S. 606 (1972)]

Note: The Speech or Debate Clause does ***not extend to state legislators*** who are prosecuted for violation of federal law. [United States v. Gillock, 445 U.S. 360 (1980)]

2. Scope of Immunity
Conduct that occurs in the regular course of the legislative process and the motivation behind that conduct are immune from prosecution.

a. **Bribes Excluded**

Taking of a bribe is not an act in the regular course of the legislative process and is therefore actionable. [United States v. Brewster, 408 U.S. 501 (1972)]

b. **Speeches Outside Congress**

Speeches and publications made outside Congress are not protected.

c. **Defamatory Statements**

Republication in a press release or newsletter of a defamatory statement originally made in Congress is not immune. [Hutchinson v. Proxmire, 443 U.S. 111 (1979)]

D. CONGRESSIONAL "VETO" OF EXECUTIVE ACTIONS INVALID

A legislative veto is an attempt by Congress to overturn an executive agency action *without* bicameralism (*i.e.,* passage by both houses of Congress) or presentment (*i.e.,* giving the bill to the President for his signature or veto). Legislative vetoes of executive actions are invalid. [Immigration & Naturalization Service v. Chadha, 462 U.S. 919 (1983)] The legislative veto usually arises where Congress delegates discretionary power to the President or an executive agency. In an attempt to control the delegation, Congress requires the President or agency to present any action taken under the discretionary power to certain members of Congress for approval. If they disapprove, they veto the action and that is the final decision on the action. This is unconstitutional, because, to be valid, legislative action (the veto) must be approved by both houses and presented to the President for his approval (*see* III.B.3., *infra*). In *Chadha,* the Court also noted that the legislative veto violates the implied separation of powers requirements of the Constitution.

Examples: 1) Congress granted to the Immigration & Naturalization Service ("INS") the power to deport or suspend from deportation illegal aliens. INS decisions to suspend deportations had to be submitted to Congress. Either house could pass a resolution overriding the decision. This legislative veto provision is unconstitutional. [Immigration & Naturalization Service v. Chadha, *supra*]

2) By statute, Congress grants to the President the power to send military troops into combat, without Congress's prior approval, whenever the United States or its territories are attacked. The statute, however, reserves in Congress the power to force the President to withdraw the troops. The statute does not provide for presidential veto of Congress's decision to withdraw. The decision in *Chadha* suggests that this statute is unconstitutional.

III. THE EXECUTIVE POWER

A. VESTED IN PRESIDENT

The entire "executive power" is vested in the President by Article II, Section 1 of the Constitution. Various executive functions may be and are delegated within the "executive branch" by the President or by Congress.

B. DOMESTIC POWERS

1. **Appointment and Removal of Officers**

   a. **Appointment**
      Under Article II, Section 2, the President is empowered "with the advice and consent of the Senate" to appoint "all *ambassadors*, other *public ministers* and consuls, *judges of the Supreme Court*, and all *other officers of the United States*, whose appointments are not herein otherwise provided for . . . but the Congress may by law vest the appointment of such inferior officers, as they think proper, in the President alone, in the courts of law, or in the heads of departments."

      1) **Appointment of "Independent Counsel" (Special Prosecutor)**
         A special prosecutor with the limited duties of investigating a narrow range of persons and subjects (*e.g.*, to investigate alleged misconduct of a government employee) is an inferior officer. Therefore, under the Appointment Clause, Congress is free to vest the power to appoint a special prosecutor in the judiciary. [Morrison v. Olson, 487 U.S. 654 (1988)]

      2) **No Appointments by Congress**
         Although Congress may appoint its own officers to carry on *internal legislative tasks* (*i.e.*, its staff), it may not appoint members of a body with administrative or enforcement powers; such persons are "officers of the United States" and must, pursuant to Article II, Section 2, be appointed by the President with senatorial confirmation unless Congress has vested their appointment in the President alone, in federal courts, or in heads of departments. [Buckley v. Valeo, 424 U.S. 1 (1976)]

   b. **Removal**
      As to removal of appointees, the *Constitution is silent* except for ensuring tenure of all Article III judges "during good behavior."

      1) **By President**
         Under the Court's decisions, the President probably can remove high level, purely executive officers (*e.g.*, Cabinet members) at will, without any interference from Congress. However, after *Morrison v. Olson, supra*, it appears that Congress may provide statutory limitations (*e.g.*, removal for good cause) on the President's power to remove all other executive appointees.

      2) **By Congress**

         a) **Limitation on Removal Power**
            Congress cannot give itself the power to remove an officer charged with the execution of laws except through impeachment. A congressional attempt through legislation to remove from government employment specifically named government employees is likely to be held invalid as a bill of attainder.

         b) **Limitation on Powers of Removable Officers**
            Congress cannot give a government employee who is subject to removal from office by Congress any powers that are truly executive in nature. For this reason, Congress could not give to the Comptroller General (who could be removed from office not only by impeachment but also by a joint resolution of Congress)

the function of establishing the amount of automatic budget reductions that would be required if Congress failed to make budget reductions necessary to insure that the federal budget deficit did not exceed a legislatively established maximum amount. [Bowsher v. Synar, 478 U.S. 714 (1986)]

2. Pardons

The President is empowered by Article II, Section 2, "to grant reprieves and pardons for offenses against the United States, *except in cases of impeachment*." This power has been held to apply before, during, or after trial, and to extend to the offense of criminal contempt, but not to civil contempt, inasmuch as the latter involves the rights of third parties. The pardon power *cannot be limited by Congress*, and includes power to commute a sentence on any conditions the President chooses, as long as they are not independently unconstitutional. [Schick v. Reed, 419 U.S. 256 (1974)]

3. Veto Power

a. Congress May Override Veto by Two-Thirds Vote

Every act of Congress must be approved by the President before taking effect, unless passed over his disapproval by two-thirds vote of *each house*. [Art. I, §7]

b. President Has Ten Days to Veto

The President has 10 days (excepting Sundays) to exercise his veto power. If he fails to act within that time:

(i) The bill becomes law if Congress is still in session; or

(ii) The bill is automatically vetoed if Congress is not in session (a "*pocket veto*"). [Pocket Veto Case, 279 U.S. 655 (1929)]

Note: Brief recesses during an annual session create no pocket veto opportunity. [Wright v. United States, 302 U.S. 583 (1938)]

c. Line Item Veto Unconstitutional

The veto power allows the President only to approve or reject a bill in toto; he cannot cancel part (through a line item veto) and approve other parts. *Rationale:* The President's veto power does not authorize him to amend or repeal laws passed by Congress. [Clinton v. City of New York, 524 U.S. 417 (1998)]

4. Power as Chief Executive

The President's power over internal (*i.e.*, within the United States) affairs as the chief executive is unclear. Clearly the President has some power to direct subordinate executive officers, and there is a long history of presidents issuing executive orders. Perhaps the best guide for determining the validity of presidential actions regarding internal affairs can be based on Justice Jackson's opinion in *Youngstown Sheet & Tube v. Sawyer*, 343 U.S. 579 (1952):

(i) Where the President acts with the express or implied authority of Congress, his authority is at its maximum and his actions likely are valid;

(ii) Where the President acts where Congress is silent, his action will be upheld as long as the act does not take over the powers of another branch of the government or prevent

another branch from carrying out its tasks [*see, e.g.,* United States v. Nixon, I.E.7.b.2), *supra*—President's invocation of executive privilege was invalidated because it kept federal courts from having evidence they needed to conduct a fair criminal trial]; and

(iii) Where the President acts against the express will of Congress, he has little authority and his action likely is invalid.

Example: Hamdan was captured in the Afghanistan war, sent to Guantanamo Bay, and then tried for war crimes by a military commission that had been created by an Executive Order issued after the 9/11 terrorist attack. Citing Justice Jackson's *Youngstown* concurrence, the Court held that the military commission could not proceed, because the executive order authorizing the commission went beyond the limitations that Congress had placed on the President. The Court found that the Executive Order was authorized by an act of Congress that was interpreted as limiting the President's power to convene commissions to those that comply with the Constitution, laws, and rules of war, and that the commission here violated the laws and rules of war in several respects (*e.g.,* it did not require a sufficient showing of the facts justifying the commission's jurisdiction; it did not provide the accused and his attorney sufficient access to the evidence). [Hamdan v. Rumsfeld, 548 U.S. 557 (2006)]

a. No Power to Impound
It follows from the above that the President has no power to refuse to spend appropriated funds when Congress has expressly mandated that they be spent. [Kendall v. United States, 37 U.S. 524 (1838)]

C. POWER OVER EXTERNAL AFFAIRS

1. War
Although lacking the power to declare or initiate a "formal" war, the President has extensive military powers (essentially an external field, although applicable to civil war as well and to many domestic affairs caught up in military necessities).

a. Actual Hostilities
The President may act militarily under his power as ***commander in chief*** of the armed forces and militia (when federalized), under Article II, Section 2, in actual hostilities against the United States without a congressional declaration of war. But ***Congress*** may limit the President under its power to enact a ***military appropriation every two years***. (A military appropriation may not be for more than two years.)

b. Military Government
This power includes the establishment of military governments in occupied territories, including military tribunals.

2. Foreign Relations
The President's power to represent and act for the United States in day-to-day foreign relations is paramount. He has the power to appoint and receive ambassadors and make

treaties (with the advice and consent of the Senate), and to enter into executive agreements. His power is broad even as to foreign affairs that require congressional consent. No significant judicial control has been exercised over this power.

3. Treaty Power

The treaty power is granted to the President "by and with the advice and consent of the Senate, provided *two-thirds of the Senators* present concur." [Art. II, §2, cl. 2]

a. Supreme Law

Like other federal law, treaties are the "supreme law of the land." Any state action or law in conflict with a United States treaty is invalid (regardless of whether it is a state law or a state constitutional provision).

1) Self-Executing vs. Non-Self-Executing Treaties

Some treaties are expressly or impliedly self-executing (*i.e.*, they are effective without any implementation by Congress). Others are not effective unless and until Congress passes legislation to effectuate their ends. If a treaty is not self-executing, it is not treated as the supreme law of the land until Congress acts to effectuate it, but the treaty itself can serve as an independent basis for Congress's power to adopt the required legislation (*i.e.*, Congress need not point to one of its enumerated powers, such as the commerce power, as the basis for the legislation).

a) President Has No Power to Implement Non-Self-Executing Treaties

Based on the *Youngstown* analysis (B.4., *supra*), the President generally does not have any independent power to issue a "memorandum" ordering compliance with a non-self-executing treaty that has not been the subject of effectuating legislation by Congress. [Medellin v. Texas, 552 U.S. 491—President had no power to enforce provisions of the Vienna Convention (a non-self-executing international treaty) by issuing a memorandum requiring states to grant habeas corpus petitions to reconsider convictions of criminals who are foreign nationals and who were not informed at the time of their arrest of their right to notify their consulate of their detention]

2) Conflict with Congressional Acts

Valid treaties are on a "supremacy parity" with acts of Congress; a conflict between an act of Congress and a treaty is resolved by order of adoption—*the last in time prevails*.

3) Conflict with Constitution

Treaties are not co-equal with the Constitution. For example, no treaty (or executive agreement) could confer on Congress authority to act in a manner inconsistent with any specific provision of the Constitution. [Reid v. Covert, 354 U.S. 1 (1957)]

b. Other Limitations

Other substantive limitations on the treaty power have not been judicially established; but in one case the Court expressed in dictum the view that a treaty could not upset the basic structure of the United States's federalism, or wield a power barred to the national government by the Constitution, or cede any part of a state to a foreign nation without the state's consent. The Court has *never held a treaty unconstitutional* (*Reid v. Covert,*

supra, invalidated an executive agreement for violating the Fifth Amendment), but it is conceivable that the treaty power extends only to subjects plausibly bearing on our relations with other countries.

4. Executive Agreements

The President's power to enter into agreements (*i.e.,* executive agreements) with the heads of foreign countries is not expressly provided for in the Constitution; nevertheless, the power has become institutionalized. Executive agreements can probably be on any subject as long as they do not violate the Constitution. They are very similar to treaties, except that they do not require the consent of the Senate.

a. Conflicts with Other Governmental Action

Executive agreements that are not consented to by the Senate are not the "supreme law of the land." Thus, *conflicting federal statutes and treaties* will prevail over an executive agreement, regardless of which was adopted first. However, executive agreements prevail over conflicting state laws.

b. Example—Power to Settle Claims of United States Citizens

The President, with the implicit approval of Congress, has power to settle claims of United States citizens against foreign governments through an executive agreement. [Dames & Moore v. Regan, 453 U.S. 654 (1981)]

D. EXECUTIVE PRIVILEGE/IMMUNITY

1. Executive Privilege

The executive privilege is not a constitutional power, but rather is an inherent privilege necessary to protect the confidentiality of presidential communications.

a. Extent of the Privilege

Presidential *documents and conversations* are *presumptively privileged*, but the privilege must yield to the need for such materials as evidence in a criminal case to which they are relevant and otherwise admissible. This determination must be made by the trial judge after hearing the evidence.

1) National Security Secrets

Military, diplomatic, or sensitive national security secrets are given great deference by the courts.

2) Criminal Proceedings

In criminal proceedings, presidential communiques will be available to the prosecution, where a need for such information is demonstrated. [United States v. Nixon, B.4., *supra*]

3) Civil Trials

The Court has avoided ruling on the scope of executive privilege in a civil case. Nevertheless, in *Cheney v. United States District Court*, 542 U.S. 367 (2004), the Court noted that the need for information in a criminal case is "weightier," and the Executive's withholding of information in a civil trial would not impair the judiciary's ability to fulfill its responsibility to resolve cases as much as in a criminal

trial. Thus, it appears that an Executive branch decision to withhold information will be given more deference in a civil trial than in a criminal trial.

    4)   **Screening Papers and Recordings of Former President**
    A federal statute requiring the Administrator of General Services to screen presidential papers is valid, notwithstanding the privilege. [Nixon v. Administrator of General Services, 433 U.S. 425 (1977)]

    5)   **Screening by Judge in Chambers**
    The court will determine in an *in-camera* inspection which communications are protected and which are subject to disclosure.

2.   **Executive Immunity**

    a.   **Absolute Immunity for President**
    The President has *absolute immunity from civil damages* based on any action that the President took within his *official responsibilities* (even if the action was only arguably within the "outer perimeter" of presidential responsibility). [Nixon v. Fitzgerald, 457 U.S. 731 (1982)] However, the President has *no* immunity from private suits in federal courts based on *conduct that allegedly occurred before taking office.* [Clinton v. Jones, 520 U.S. 681 (1997)] *Rationale:* The immunity is intended only to enable the President to perform his *designated functions* without fear of personal liability.

    b.   **Immunity May Extend to Presidential Aides**
    Presidential aides share in this immunity only if they are exercising discretionary authority for the President in "sensitive" areas of national concern, such as foreign affairs. Other aides are entitled only to a qualified immunity (a "good faith" defense). [Harlow v. Fitzgerald, 457 U.S. 800 (1982)]
    Example: The Attorney General does not share the President's absolute immunity for authorizing a warrantless wiretap on "national security" grounds. The Attorney General would have a defense to a lawsuit regarding such a wiretap if it was shown that he was able to act in good faith because his actions were not violating clearly established or well-settled statutory or constitutional rights. [Mitchell v. Forsyth, 472 U.S. 511 (1985)]

E.   **IMPEACHMENT**

    1.   **Persons Subject to Impeachment**
    The President, Vice President, and all civil officers of the United States are subject to impeachment.

    2.   **Grounds**
    The grounds for impeachment are treason, bribery, high crimes, and misdemeanors.

    3.   **Impeachment by the House**
    A *majority vote* in the House is necessary to invoke the charges of impeachment.

    4.   **Conviction by the Senate**
    A *two-thirds vote* in the Senate is necessary to convict.

PART TWO: THE FEDERAL SYSTEM

IV. RELATIVE SPHERES OF FEDERAL AND STATE POWER

A. EXCLUSIVE FEDERAL POWERS

1. **Power of States Expressly Limited**
   Some powers are exclusively federal because of express constitutional limitation on or prohibition of the states' exercise thereof—such as the treaty power, coinage of money, and duty on imports.

2. **Inherent Federal Powers**
   Others are exclusively federal in view of their nature—such as declaration of war, federal citizenship, naturalization, and borrowing money on the credit of the United States. Any state exercise of these powers would basically subvert the federal system. On the exam, ***do not*** allow states to take actions that might touch upon ***foreign relations***.

   Examples: 1) In *Zschernig v. Miller,* 389 U.S. 429 (1968), the Court held invalid state statutes that sought to withhold the proceeds of local decedents' estates from heirs living in nations that (i) discriminate against Americans in their probate laws, (ii) impede the transmission of funds to the United States, or (iii) confiscate property inherited by their citizens. The Court concluded that such laws are so potentially disruptive of a nationally conducted foreign policy that they are invalid notwithstanding the traditional commitment of probate law to the states.

   2) California adopted an act to aid Holocaust victims that, among other things, required any California insurer that sold insurance policies in Europe between 1920 and 1945 to disclose certain information about those policies. The President of the United States also entered into an agreement with Germany regarding Holocaust victims' claims and informed California that its law would impede the effectiveness of that agreement. Nevertheless, California announced that it would enforce its law. Several insurance companies and a trade association brought suit to enjoin enforcement of the act. *Held:* The act interferes with the President's power over foreign affairs and is preempted on that ground. [American Insurance Association v. Garamendi, 539 U.S. 396 (2003)]

B. EXCLUSIVE STATE POWERS
Whereas the federal government has only those powers granted to it by the Constitution, the state governments are governments of "unlimited" powers, having all powers not prohibited to them by the Constitution. This is recognized by the Tenth Amendment, which provides that all powers not delegated to the federal government by the Constitution are reserved to the states (or to the people). However, given the expansive interpretation of federal powers (*e.g.,* the commerce power; *see* II.A.4., *supra*), little state power is exclusive.

C. CONCURRENT FEDERAL AND STATE POWER—SUPREMACY CLAUSE
Most governmental power is concurrent, belonging to both the states and the federal government. Thus, it is possible for states and the federal government to pass legislation on the same subject matter. When this occurs, the Supremacy Clause provides that the federal law is supreme, and the conflicting state law is rendered void.

1. **Actual Conflict Between State and Federal Laws**

    A valid act of Congress or federal regulation supersedes any state or local action that actually conflicts with the federal rule—whether by commanding conduct inconsistent with that required by the federal rule, or by forbidding conduct that the federal rule is designed to foster.

    Example: Federal law [42 U.S.C. §1983] gives state and federal courts jurisdiction to hear claims for violations of federal rights committed by persons acting under color of state law. New York determined that the majority of suits seeking money damages from corrections officers under section 1983 are frivolous and therefore divested its trial courts of jurisdiction to hear such cases. *Held:* The state's policy of shielding corrections officers from suits under section 1983 violates the Supremacy Clause. State courts must hear federal claims. They may apply their own procedural rules as they do to state claims, but they cannot exclude a class of federal claims from being heard in state court. [Haywood v. Drown, 129 S. Ct. 2108 (2009)]

2. **State Prevents Achievement of Federal Objective**

    The conflict need not relate to conduct; it is sufficient if the state or local law interferes with achievement of a federal objective. This is true even if the state or local law was enacted for some valid purpose and not merely to frustrate the federal law.

    Example: A purpose of the federal bankruptcy laws is to give bankrupts a fresh start, free of their old debts. A state law providing for suspension of the driver's license of persons who have failed to pay off auto accident judgments, regardless of the judgment debtor's discharge in bankruptcy, interferes with the federal objective and will fail. [Perez v. Campbell, 402 U.S. 637 (1971)]

3. **Preemption**

    A state or local law may fail under the Supremacy Clause, even if it does not conflict with federally regulated conduct or objectives, if it appears that Congress intended to "occupy" the entire field, thus precluding *any* state or local regulation.

    a. **Express Preemption**

        Federal law may expressly preempt state law. Note, however, that an express preemption clause will be narrowly construed. [*See* Altria Group, Inc. v. Good, 129 S. Ct. 538 (2009)]

        Example: A federal law [15 U.S.C. §1334(b)] provides that: "no requirement or prohibition based on smoking and health shall be imposed under state law with respect to the advertising or promotion of any cigarettes" that are labeled in conformity with federal law. A smoker brought a state law consumer fraud claim against a cigarette company, claiming that the company's advertisements that its cigarettes were "light" and contain less tar and nicotine were fraudulent. The cigarette company argued that its advertisements were in conformity with federal law and, therefore, the state law claim was preempted by the federal law. *Held:* The state law claim is not preempted. The state consumer protection law is based on a duty not to deceive rather than on smoking or health, and the federal law preempts only state laws based on smoking or health. [Altria Group, Inc. v. Good, *supra*]

b. Implied Preemption

If the federal law does not specifically indicate whether state law should be preempted, the courts will try to deduce Congress's intent. For example, if the federal laws are comprehensive or a federal agency is created to oversee the area, preemption will often be found. However, the Supreme Court has stated that in all preemption cases, especially any involving a field traditionally within the power of the states (*e.g.,* regulations involving health, safety, or welfare), it will start with the *presumption* that the historic state police powers are *not* to be superceded unless that was the *clear and manifest purpose of Congress.* [Wyeth v. Levine, 129 S. Ct. 1187 (2009)]

Example: A person who was injured by a prescription drug that was improperly administered brought a state law tort suit against the drug's manufacturer, claiming that the drug's label did not provide adequate warnings. The label was approved by the Food and Drug Administration ("FDA") pursuant to its power to regulate prescription drugs. The drug company claimed that the state tort action was preempted. *Held:* Congress did not intend to preempt the state court action here. The Court held that while Congress enacted the legislation here to protect consumers, it did not provide a remedy for consumers injured by unsafe drugs. Also Congress had not enacted an express preemption provision within the statute for prescription drugs although it did enact an express preemption provision for medical devices. Moreover, there is no conflict between the FDA approval of a warning label and the state tort failure to warn claim here because the FDA regulation allowed companies to strengthen warnings without preapproval and, thus, the company was free to provide stronger warnings. [*See, e.g.,* Wyeth v. Levine, *supra*]

D. ABSENCE OF FEDERAL AND STATE POWERS

Some powers are denied to both Congress and the states. For example, the Supreme Court has held that the Qualifications Clauses [Art. I, §2, cl. 2; §3, cl. 3], setting the qualifications to serve in Congress, are exclusive and cannot be altered by Congress or the states. [United States Term Limits, Inc. v. Thornton, 514 U.S. 779 (1995)—state-imposed term limit for members of Congress invalidated; *and see* Cook v. Gralike, 531 U.S. 510 (2001)—state law instructing each member of its congressional delegation to support a constitutional amendment for term limits, and providing that failure to do so be noted on the ballot, was held invalid because it imposes a substantive qualification rather than regulates the "manner" in which elections are held]

E. INTERSTATE COMPACT CLAUSE

The Constitution provides that states may enter into agreements or compacts with other states upon the consent of Congress. [Art. I, §10, cl. 3] However, not all agreements between states are "compacts" requiring congressional consent. The Compact Clause reaches only interstate agreements that *increase the political power* of the states at the expense of federal supremacy (*e.g.,* an agreement whereby one state cedes territory to another state). [*See* United States Steel Corp. v. Multistate Tax Commission, 434 U.S. 452 (1978)—congressional consent not required for multistate tax compact because the compact does not give member states any powers they could not exercise in its absence] The Supreme Court has the power to interpret such compacts—the member states do not have final authority over interpretation. [West Virginia *ex rel.* Dyer v. Sims, 341 U.S. 22 (1951)]

F.   FULL FAITH AND CREDIT CLAUSE
The Full Faith and Credit Clause provides that "full faith and credit shall be given in each state to the public acts, records, and judicial proceedings of every other state." By virtue of the Clause, if a judgment is entitled to full faith and credit, it must be recognized in sister states (*i.e.*, a party who loses a case in New York generally may not relitigate it in New Jersey; the New Jersey courts are bound by the New York ruling). However, not every decision is entitled to full faith and credit. There are three requirements:

(i)   The court that rendered the judgment must have had *jurisdiction over the parties and the subject matter*;

(ii)   The judgment must have been *on the merits*; *i.e.,* on the substance of the plaintiff's claim rather than on a procedural issue, such as improper venue or running of the statute of limitations; and

(iii) The judgment must be *final*.

Although the Clause itself governs only recognition of state judgments in sister states, a federal statute provides for recognition of state judgments in federal courts as well.

V.   INTERSOVEREIGN LITIGATION

A.   SUITS BY THE UNITED STATES AGAINST A STATE
The United States may sue a state without its consent.

B.   SUITS BY STATE AGAINST UNITED STATES—UNITED STATES MUST CONSENT
Public policy forbids a state from suing the United States without its consent. Congress can pass legislation that permits the United States to be sued by a state in given situations.

C.   FEDERAL OFFICER AS DEFENDANT

1.   Limitation
Suits against a federal officer are *deemed to be brought against the United States* itself *if* the judgment sought would be satisfied out of the public treasury or would interfere with public administration and, therefore, are not permitted.

2.   Specific Relief Against the Individual Officer
Specific relief against an officer as an individual will be granted if the officer acted ultra vires:

a.   Beyond his statutory powers; or

b.   The valid power was exercised in an unconstitutional manner.

D.   SUITS BY ONE STATE AGAINST ANOTHER
One state may sue another state without the latter's consent. The Supreme Court has *exclusive original jurisdiction*.

VI. INTERGOVERNMENTAL TAX AND REGULATION IMMUNITIES

A. FEDERAL TAXATION AND REGULATION OF STATE OR LOCAL GOVERNMENTS

The Tenth Amendment provides that powers not delegated to the United States by the Constitution, nor prohibited to the states, are reserved to the states. This reservation of power is often cited as a restriction on Congress's power to regulate the states.

1. Tax or Regulation Applying to State and Private Entities—Valid

The Supreme Court will not likely strike down on Tenth Amendment grounds a tax or regulation that subjects states or local governments to regulations or taxes that apply to *both* the public sector and the private sector. It has held that in such cases, the states' interests are best protected by the states' representation in Congress. [Garcia v. San Antonio Metropolitan Transit Authority, 469 U.S. 528 (1985)]

Example: Congress can require state and local governments to follow the provisions of the Federal Fair Labor and Standards Act requiring minimum wages for all employees. [Garcia v. San Antonio Metropolitan Transit Authority, *supra*]

2. Tax or Regulation that Applies Only to States

However, the Tenth Amendment does limit Congress's power to regulate the states alone by requiring the states to act in a particular way. Congress may not compel states to enact or enforce a regulatory program. [New York v. United States, 505 U.S. 144 (1992)—federal statute requiring states to either regulate radioactive waste or take title to it is beyond Congress's power] Similarly, if Congress passes a tax that does not apply to private businesses but merely taxes state government entities, there is a possibility that the Court would use the Tenth Amendment to prohibit the tax.

a. Exception—Civil Rights

Congress *may* use its power under the Fourteenth and Fifteenth Amendments to restrict state activities that it determines would violate the civil liberties of persons within the state.

Examples: 1) Congress may invalidate state laws establishing a literacy test as a prerequisite to voting in state elections. [Oregon v. Mitchell, 400 U.S. 112 (1970)]

2) Congress may restrict changes in state voting laws that have the effect of diminishing the voting power of racial minorities even though the change in state law was not purposeful racial discrimination that would violate Section 1 of the Fifteenth Amendment. [Rome v. United States, 446 U.S. 156 (1980)]

b. Exception—Spending Power Conditions

Congress may also "regulate" states through the spending power by imposing explicit *conditions on the grant of money to state or local governments*. Such conditions will not violate the Tenth Amendment merely because Congress lacked the power to directly regulate the activity that is the subject of the spending program.

Example: A federal law that would withhold 5% of the federal highway funds otherwise allocable to a state if the state did not set a 21 years' minimum age for the drinking of alcohol has been upheld. [South Dakota v. Dole, 483 U.S. 203 (1987)]

3. **Commandeering State Officials**

The Supreme Court has held that the Tenth Amendment prohibits Congress from adopting a statute that "commandeers" state officials by *requiring states to regulate their own citizens*. [Printz v. United States, 521 U.S. 898 (1997)—striking portions of a federal gun law that required state law enforcement officers to collect from gun dealers reports regarding prospective handgun purchasers and to conduct background checks on them] However, the Court has allowed Congress to *regulate the states by prohibiting them from performing certain acts*. [*See* Reno v. Condon, 528 U.S. 141 (2000)—upholding federal act that bars states (as well as private resellers) from disclosing personal information required on drivers' license applications]

B. STATE TAXATION AND REGULATION OF FEDERAL GOVERNMENT

1. **No Direct Tax on Federal Instrumentalities**

A state tax levied directly against the property or operation of the federal government without the consent of Congress is invalid.

2. **Nondiscriminatory, Indirect Taxes**

Nondiscriminatory, indirect taxes on the federal government or its property are permissible if they *do not unreasonably burden* the federal government.

Examples: 1) State income taxes on salaries of federal employees are valid. However, a state tax that imposes a higher tax on federal employees (or retired federal employees) than on state or local government employees (or retired employees) would violate the principle of intergovernmental tax immunity, unless Congress had approved this discriminatory tax. [Davis v. Michigan Department of Treasury, 489 U.S. 803 (1989)]

2) Private contractors, *acting as purchasing agents* for the federal government, cannot be compelled to pay state sales or use taxes on materials purchased on behalf of the federal government. However, state sales or use taxes are valid where the contractor is working for the federal government on a "cost-plus" basis. These extra costs are not characterized as direct taxes.

3. **State Regulation of Federal Government**

The states have no power to regulate the activities of the federal government unless Congress consents to the regulation. Thus, instrumentalities and agents of the federal government are immune from state regulations relating to performance of their federal functions.

Examples: 1) A state may not require a post office employee to obtain a state driver's license in order to drive a mail truck. [Johnson v. Maryland, 254 U.S. 51 (1920)]

2) A state may not require a contractor to obtain a state license to build facilities on an Air Force base, located within the state, pursuant to a government contract. [Leslie Miller, Inc. v. Arkansas, 352 U.S. 187 (1956)]

VII. PRIVILEGES AND IMMUNITIES CLAUSES

A. INTRODUCTION

There are two Privileges and Immunities Clauses: the Fourteenth Amendment Privileges or

Immunities Clause and the Interstate Privileges and Immunities Clause of Article IV. The Fourteenth Amendment clause protects attributes of United States citizenship and is rarely applicable. The Article IV provision prevents some discrimination by states against nonresidents, and is usually more relevant on the bar exam.

B. ARTICLE IV—PRIVILEGES OF STATE CITIZENSHIP

Article IV, Section 2, the Interstate Privileges and Immunities Clause, provides that "[t]he Citizens of each state shall be entitled to all Privileges and Immunities of citizens in the several states." Thus, it prohibits discrimination by a state against nonresidents.

1. Corporations and Aliens Not Protected

Corporations and aliens are *not citizens* of a state for purposes of the Privileges and Immunities Clause.

2. Only "Fundamental Rights" Protected

The Interstate Privileges and Immunities Clause does not prohibit all discrimination by a state in favor of its own citizens, but only when the denial concerns "fundamental rights"— *i.e.,* those involving important *commercial activities* (such as pursuit of a livelihood) or *civil liberties*. For example, the following have been struck down:

a. *Statute charging nonresident commercial fishermen substantially more for commercial fishing license* than resident commercial fishermen ($2,500 vs. $25) [Toomer v. Witsell, 334 U.S. 385 (1948); *cf.* Baldwin v. Montana Fish & Game Commission, 436 U.S. 371 (1978)—vast difference between resident and nonresident *recreational* hunting license constitutional since no essential commercial activity involved];

b. *Statute giving resident creditors priority* over nonresident creditors as to assets of foreign corporations in receivership proceedings [Blake v. McClung, 172 U.S. 239 (1898)];

c. *Statute or court rule requiring state residency to be licensed* to practice law within the state [Supreme Court of Virginia v. Friedman, 487 U.S. 59 (1988)];

d. *State income tax only on nonresidents* who earn money within the state [Austin v. New Hampshire, 420 U.S. 656 (1975)]; and

e. *State law requiring private sector employers to give hiring preference to residents* absent a closely related substantial justification (*see* below) [Hicklin v. Orbeck, 437 U.S. 518 (1978)], but states *may* require a person to be a resident to hold *government employment* [McCarthy v. Philadelphia Civil Service Commission, 424 U.S. 645 (1976) (per curiam)].

3. Substantial Justification Exception

A state law discriminating against nonresidents may be valid if the state has a substantial justification for the different treatment. In effect, it must show that nonresidents either cause or are part of the problem it is attempting to solve, and that there are *no less restrictive means* to solve the problem.

Example: The Court held that a city ordinance requiring 40% of employees of contractors and subcontractors working on city construction projects to be city residents was an apparent violation of the Article IV Privileges and Immunities Clause because it gave a preference in private sector employment to city residents. However, the Court found that it could not make a final determination as to *whether the preference was justified* in this case because the record from the lower courts did not allow it to evaluate the city's argument that the preference was necessary *to counteract grave economic and social ills* in urban environments caused by spiraling unemployment and declines in the population base of such cities. [United Building & Construction Trades Council v. Mayor of Camden, 465 U.S. 208 (1984)]

4. Note—Relationship to Commerce Clause

Although the Article IV Privileges and Immunities Clause and the Commerce Clause may apply different standards and produce different results, they tend to mutually reinforce each other. Consequently, they both have to be considered in analyzing bar exam questions.

C. FOURTEENTH AMENDMENT—PRIVILEGES OF NATIONAL CITIZENSHIP

The Fourteenth Amendment Privileges or Immunities Clause prohibits states from denying their citizens the privileges and immunities of national citizenship, such as the right to petition Congress for redress of grievances, the right to vote for federal officers, the right to enter public lands, the right to interstate travel, and any other right flowing from the distinct relation of a citizen to the United States Government.

1. Corporations Not Protected

Corporations are *not citizens* of the United States and are *not protected*.

2. Bill of Rights Not Included

The *Slaughterhouse Cases,* 83 U.S. 36 (1873), held that the fundamental rights protected against federal abuse (first 10 Amendments) are *not privileges or immunities of national citizenship* within the meaning of the Fourteenth Amendment; nor are such other basic rights as the right to live, work, and eat. Thus, the guarantees of the Bill of Rights are protected from state action only by the Due Process and Equal Protection Clauses of the Fourteenth Amendment.

3. Right to Travel and the Privileges and Immunities Clause

The right to travel, which is protected by the Fourteenth Amendment, includes the right of newly arrived citizens to enjoy the same privileges and immunities as are enjoyed by other citizens of the state.

Example: A California statute limiting the welfare benefits of first year residents was held unconstitutional under the Fourteenth Amendment Privileges or Immunities Clause. The statute provided that citizens who had lived in California for less than one year could receive only the benefits they would have received in their prior state of residence. The Court noted that the right to travel includes the right to be treated equally in a new state of residence. [Saenz v. Roe, 526 U.S. 489 (1999)]

PART THREE: STATE REGULATION OR TAXATION OF COMMERCE

VIII. REGULATION OF FOREIGN COMMERCE

A. LIES EXCLUSIVELY WITH CONGRESS

For all practical purposes, the power to regulate foreign commerce lies exclusively with Congress. "Foreign" commerce has been held to include traffic on the high seas, even though both terminal ports are within the United States. [Japan Line, Ltd. v. County of Los Angeles, 441 U.S. 434 (1979)]

B. MINOR EXCEPTIONS WHERE STATE REGULATION PERMITTED

The Supreme Court, however, has recognized a few minor exceptions; thus, the states are free to regulate local aspects of port pilotage and navigation of ships in foreign commerce (*e.g.,* aspects such as safety of handling); and in one case the Court permitted state regulation of excursion boat traffic between Detroit and a Canadian island (state barred racial discrimination among boat passengers) since no Canadians or Canadian products or services were involved. [Bob-Lo Excursion Co. v. Michigan, 333 U.S. 28 (1948)]

IX. REGULATION OF INTERSTATE COMMERCE

A. REGULATION OF COMMERCE BY CONGRESS

As already seen, Congress's power over interstate commerce is "plenary" and pervasive. However, the power is ***nonexclusive***—it is shared with the states to some degree.

1. Power of Congress to Supersede or Preempt State Regulation

Recall that the Supremacy Clause makes federal law supreme. (*See* IV.C., *supra*.) Thus, if a state law regulating commerce conflicts with a federal law, the state law will be void. Moreover, if Congress desires, it may preempt an entire area of regulation, thus preventing states from making any laws concerning the area preempted. (*See* IV.C.3., *supra*.)

2. Power of Congress to Permit or Prohibit State Regulation

Although Congress's commerce power is nonexclusive, the states' power to regulate interstate commerce is restricted by the negative implications of the Commerce Clause, even absent federal legislation—the states generally may ***not*** discriminate against interstate commerce. (*See* below.) Nevertheless, Congress is not so restricted; it may allow the states to adopt legislation that would otherwise violate the Commerce Clause.

Example: A state imposed a 3% tax on out-of-state insurance companies for all premiums received from insuring residents of the state. No similar tax was placed on in-state insurance companies. Although such a tax would ordinarily be held invalid under the Commerce Clause—because it discriminates against interstate commerce—the tax here was upheld because Congress had adopted an act permitting the states to regulate insurance in any manner, as long as the state regulation did not conflict with a federal statute specifically regulating insurance. [Prudential Insurance Co. v. Benjamin, 328 U.S. 408 (1946); *and see* Northeast Bancorp, Inc. v. Board of Governors, 472 U.S. 159 (1985)]

Note: As indicated above, Congress may also prohibit the states from adopting legislation that would otherwise be permitted under the Commerce Clause.

a. **Limitation**
While Congress may permit states to adopt regulations that would otherwise violate the Commerce Clause, such consent will not obviate other constitutional objections to the regulation. Thus, Congress may not give states the power to restrict civil liberties. (*See* X.A.1.b.2)a), *infra.*)

B. **STATE REGULATION OF COMMERCE IN THE ABSENCE OF CONGRESSIONAL ACTION**
If Congress has not enacted laws regarding the subject, a state or local government may regulate local aspects of interstate commerce if the regulation:

(i) Does *not discriminate* against out-of-state competition to benefit local economic interests; and

(ii) Is *not unduly burdensome* (*i.e.,* the incidental burden on interstate commerce does not outweigh the legitimate local benefits produced by the regulation).

If either test is not met, the regulation will be held void for violating the Commerce Clause (sometimes called the "*Dormant Commerce Clause*" or "*Negative Commerce Clause*" under such circumstances).

1. **Discriminatory Regulations**

a. **Generally Invalid**
State or local regulations that discriminate against interstate commerce to protect local economic interests are almost always invalid.

b. **Examples**

1) **Regulations Protecting Local Businesses**
Laws designed to protect local businesses against interstate competition generally will be invalidated.
Examples: 1) A state cannot place a surcharge on out-of-state milk to make that milk as expensive as (or more expensive than) milk produced in the state.

2) A state cannot exempt local businesses or products from taxation or regulation that it seeks to apply to out-of-state businesses or products that come into the state.

3) A law requiring all locally produced solid waste to be processed at a local waste processing business was held to violate the Commerce Clause because it was a trade barrier against competition from out-of-state waste processors. [C&A Carbone, Inc. v. Town of Clarkstown, 511 U.S. 383 (1994)]

2) Regulations Requiring Local Operations

If a state law requires a business to perform specific business operations in the state to engage in other business activity within the state, the law will normally be held invalid as an attempt to discriminate against other states where the business operations could be performed more efficiently.

Example: If a state required all businesses that produce melons in the state and all businesses that purchase melons from local producers to wrap or package the melons in the state (before the melons were exported from the state), the law would be invalid as an attempt to force businesses to locate their packaging operations in the state.

3) Regulations Limiting Access to In-State Products

A state law that makes it difficult or impossible for out-of-state purchasers to have access to in-state products (other than products owned by the state itself) is likely to be held invalid.

Examples: 1) A state cannot prohibit in-state owners of "ground water" from selling and exporting the water they own to persons in other states.

2) A state cannot require in-state companies to sell products at a lower price to in-state residents than to out-of-state residents.

4) Regulations Prohibiting Out-of-State Wastes

A state may not prohibit private landfill or waste disposal facilities from accepting out-of-state garbage or waste or surcharge such waste [Philadelphia v. New Jersey, 437 U.S. 617 (1978); Chemical Waste Management v. Hunt, 504 U.S. 334 (1992)] unless Congress authorizes such discrimination [New York v. United States, VI.A.2., *supra*—federal statute allowing states to impose surcharge on certain out-of-state nuclear wastes upheld]. This rule applies even to hazardous wastes. [Oregon Waste Systems, Inc. v. Department of Environmental Quality, 511 U.S. 93 (1994)]

c. Exceptions

1) Necessary to Important State Interest

A discriminatory state or local law may be valid if it furthers an important, noneconomic state interest (*e.g.,* health or safety) and there are ***no reasonable alternatives*** available.

Example: A state could prohibit the importation of live baitfish (such as minnows) into the state because the state could demonstrate that it had no other way of effectively avoiding the possibility that such baitfish might bring certain parasites into the state or, in other ways, have a detrimental effect on the state's wild fish population. [Maine v. Taylor, 477 U.S. 1138 (1986)] However, a state could not prohibit the export of live baitfish to out-of-state purchasers because the sale of such fish to out-of-state purchasers would not impair any interest of the state, except the interest of protecting local purchasers of baitfish from competition by out-of-state purchasers. [Hughes v. Oklahoma, 441 U.S. 322 (1979)]

2) **State as Market Participant**

The Commerce Clause does not prevent a state from preferring its own citizens when the state is acting as a market participant (*e.g.,* buying or selling products, hiring labor, giving subsidies).

Examples: 1) A state may purchase scrap automobiles from its citizens at a higher-than-market rate and refuse to pay nonresidents the same amount. [Hughes v. Alexandria Scrap Corp., 426 U.S. 794 (1976)]

2) Under the market participant exception to the Commerce Clause, a city may require that all construction *projects funded by the city* be performed by contractors using a workforce composed of at least 50% bona fide residents of the city. [White v. Massachusetts Council of Construction Employers, 460 U.S. 204 (1983)]

a) **Limitation—Interstate Privileges and Immunities Clause**

While a state or local government does not violate the *Commerce Clause* by preferring its own citizens while acting as a market participant, there is no market participant exception to the Interstate Privileges and Immunities Clause. Thus, a regulation that interferes with private sector employment, such as the one in example 2), above, may violate the Privileges and Immunities Clause unless the regulating entity can show a substantial justification for the regulation. (*See* VII.B.3., *supra.*)

b) **Limitation—"Downstream" Restrictions**

While a state may choose to sell only to state residents, it may not attach conditions to a sale that would discriminate against interstate commerce.

Example: Alaska violated the Commerce Clause when it imposed a contractual requirement on purchasers of state-owned timber that the timber be processed in Alaska before being shipped out of state. [South-Central Timber Development, Inc. v. Wunnicke, 467 U.S. 82 (1984)—plurality opinion]

3) **Favoring Government Performing Traditional Government Functions**

The Supreme Court applies a more lenient standard when a law favors government action involving the performance of a traditional government function (such as waste disposal). Discrimination against interstate commerce in such a case is permissible because it is likely motivated by legitimate objectives rather than by economic protectionism.

Examples: 1) A county flow control ordinance that favored a state-created public waste facility by requiring waste haulers to bring the wastes to the state facility rather than to private facilities is valid. [United Haulers Association, Inc. v. Oneida-Herkimer Solid Waste Management Authority, 550 U.S. 330 (2007)]

2) A state may exempt from state taxation interest on its own bonds and bonds of its municipalities while taxing bonds of other states and their subdivisions. [Department of Revenue of Kentucky v. Davis, 533 U.S. 328 (2008)—issuing debt securities to pay for

public projects is a "quintessentially public function" with a venerable history]

2. Nondiscriminatory Laws—Balancing Test

Sometimes a nondiscriminatory state or local law that regulates commerce may impose a burden on interstate commerce; *e.g.,* a state law regulating the size of trucks within that state may burden interstate commerce because interstate trucking operations will be subject to the law when their trucks enter the state. A nondiscriminatory law will be invalidated only if the burden on interstate commerce outweighs the promotion of legitimate (not discriminatory) local interests. This is a case-by-case balancing test. Thus, some regulations of trucks will be upheld, because they do not impose an undue burden on interstate commerce, whereas other truck regulations will be invalidated, because they would make it extremely difficult for interstate trucking operators to have their trucks travel into or through the state.

a. Less Restrictive Alternatives

In determining whether a nondiscriminatory state regulation of interstate commerce violates the Commerce Clause, a court will sometimes consider whether less restrictive alternatives are available.

Example: Although it is legitimate for a city to pass laws designed to ensure that milk products sold within the city are safe, a city cannot require those businesses that wish to sell milk in the city to have the milk processed (purified and placed in bottles) at a processing site close to the city. *Rationale:* The city has a variety of alternatives that impose less burden on interstate commerce.

b. Absence of Conflict with Other States

State and local laws regulating commerce are more likely to be upheld when there is little chance that states would have conflicting regulations of the same subject matter.

Example: A state could validly apply a state law prohibiting racial or gender discrimination in the hiring of personnel to an airline doing business in the state because the law was not discriminatory against out-of-state businesses, it promoted a legitimate interest, and no other state could validly require or permit racial or gender discrimination by airlines.

c. State Control of Corporations

A different standard may apply to statutes regulating the internal governance of a corporation adopted by the state of incorporation. Because of the states' long history of regulating the internal governance of corporations that they create, and because of their strong interest in doing so, even a statute that heavily impacts interstate commerce may be upheld.

Example: To protect shareholders of corporations incorporated in Indiana from hostile takeovers, the Indiana legislature adopted a "control share acquisition statute." The statute provided that once a person acquires shares that take him across a specified ownership threshold (*e.g.,* one-third ownership of all voting shares), he may not vote those shares unless the other shareholders consent. Even though most hostile takeover bids originate from outside the state, the Supreme Court found that the statute did not violate the Commerce Clause because its aim was to protect current

shareholders, it did not discriminate between takeover bidders based on their state of origin, and there is no chance that the state law would conflict with the laws of other states because the internal governance of a corporation is regulated only by the state in which the corporation is incorporated. [CTS Corp. v. Dynamics Corp. of America, 481 U.S. 69 (1987)]

C. TWENTY-FIRST AMENDMENT—STATE CONTROL OVER INTOXICATING LIQUOR

1. Intrastate Regulations
The Twenty-First Amendment, which repealed prohibition, gives state governments wide latitude over the importation of liquor and the conditions under which liquor is sold or used within the state. However, state liquor regulations that constitute only an economic preference for local liquor manufacturers may violate the Commerce Clause. The Commerce Clause prohibits both outright economic favoritism for local businesses and attempts to regulate out-of-state transactions in order to guarantee the competitive position of in-state businesses.

Examples: 1) A state law that prohibits out-of-state wineries from shipping wine directly to in-state consumers, but permitting in-state wineries to do so if licensed, discriminates against interstate commerce. [Granholm v. Heald, 544 U.S. 460 (2005)]

2) A state law that requires out-of-state distillers or sellers of alcoholic beverages to affirm that the price the distiller/seller is charging liquor retailers or wholesalers in the state is no greater than the price the distiller/seller is charging in other states violates the Commerce Clause. Such a price affirmation law directly interferes with and burdens interstate commerce. The Twenty-First Amendment does not authorize this type of state interference with commerce. [Brown-Forman Distillers Corp. v. New York State Liquor Authority, 476 U.S. 573 (1986); Healy v. The Beer Institute, Inc., 491 U.S. 324 (1989)]

2. Interstate Regulations
Transitory liquor (liquor bound for out-of-state destinations) is subject to the Commerce Clause. Thus, a state prohibition on transporting liquor through the state would probably be held unconstitutional as violating the Commerce Clause.

3. Federal Power
The Twenty-First Amendment does not prohibit Congress from controlling economic transactions involving alcoholic beverages under the federal commerce power. Thus, federal antitrust law can prohibit a practice of liquor dealers that has the effect of fixing minimum prices. [324 Liquor Corp. v. Duffy, 479 U.S. 335 (1987)] Similarly, as mentioned above, Congress may, without violating the Twenty-First Amendment, "regulate" liquor distribution by imposing conditions on the grant of federal funds given under the spending power. [South Dakota v. Dole, VI.A.2.b., *supra*]

D. BAR EXAM APPROACH
Whenever a bar exam question involves a state regulation that affects the free flow of interstate commerce, you should proceed as follows:

First, see if the question refers to **any federal legislation** that might be held either to: (i) **supersede** the state regulation or **preempt** the field, or (ii) **authorize** state regulation otherwise impermissible.

Second, if neither of these possibilities is dispositive of the question, ask if the state legislation either **discriminates** against interstate or out-of-state commerce or places an **undue burden** on the free flow of interstate commerce. If the legislation is discriminatory, it will be invalid unless (i) it furthers an important state interest **and** there are no reasonable nondiscriminatory alternatives, or (ii) the state is a market participant. If the legislation does not discriminate but burdens interstate commerce, it will be invalid if the burden on commerce outweighs the state's interest. Consider whether there are less restrictive alternatives.

X.   POWER OF STATES TO TAX INTERSTATE COMMERCE

A.   GENERAL CONSIDERATIONS

The same general considerations applicable to state regulation of commerce (*supra*) apply to taxation. Pursuant to the Commerce Clause, Congress has complete power to authorize or forbid state taxation affecting interstate commerce. If Congress has not acted, look to see whether the tax **discriminates** against interstate commerce. If it does, it is invalid. If it does not, assess whether the burden on interstate commerce outweighs the benefit to the state. Three tests must be met: (i) there must be a **substantial nexus** between the taxpayer and the state; (ii) the tax must be **fairly apportioned**; and (iii) there must be a **fair relationship** between the tax and the services or benefits provided by the state.

1.   Discriminatory Taxes

Unless authorized by Congress, state taxes that discriminate against interstate commerce violate the Commerce Clause. Such taxes may also be held to violate the Interstate Privileges and Immunities Clause (*see* VII.B., *supra*) if they also discriminate against nonresidents of the state [Austin v. New Hampshire, 420 U.S. 656 (1975)], as well as the Equal Protection Clause if the discrimination is not rationally related to a legitimate state purpose [WHYY, Inc. v. Borough of Glassboro, 393 U.S. 117 (1968)—denial of tax exemption solely because taxpayer was incorporated in another state is invalid].

a.   Finding Discrimination

1)   Tax Singles Out Interstate Commerce

If a state tax singles out interstate commerce for taxation, the Court ordinarily will not "save" the tax by finding other state taxes imposed only on local commerce (which might arguably eliminate the "apparent" discrimination against interstate commerce).

Example: The Supreme Court invalidated an Ohio statute that gave a tax credit against the Ohio motor vehicle fuel sales tax (paid by fuel dealers) for each gallon of ethanol sold as a component of gasohol if, but only if, the ethanol was produced in Ohio or in a state that granted a similar tax advantage to ethanol produced in Ohio. The Supreme Court found that this tax credit system constituted discrimination against interstate commerce. [New Energy Co. of Indiana v. Limbach, 486 U.S. 269 (1988)]

Note: However, state taxes that single out interstate commerce are considered **nondiscriminatory** if the particular statutory section or scheme **also** imposes the same type of tax on **local** commerce (*e.g.,* sales and use taxes, discussed *infra*).

2) Tax with In-State Subsidy

A seemingly uniform tax may be ruled to be discriminatory if the proceeds from the tax are "earmarked" for subsidies to in-state businesses.

Example: A state imposed a tax on all milk dealers, but the tax law provided that revenue from the tax would be put into a fund that would be used to pay subsidies to in-state dairy farmers. This assessment-subsidy system violates the Commerce Clause because it operates identically to a tax placed only on sales of milk produced outside the state. [West Lynn Creamery, Inc. v. Healy, 512 U.S. 186 (1994)]

b. Choosing the Proper Clause

While a state or local tax that discriminates against interstate commerce generally violates the Commerce Clause, the Clause is not always the strongest argument against the tax.

1) Interstate Privileges and Immunities Clause

If a state or local tax discriminates against a **natural person who is a nonresident**, the Article IV Interstate Privileges and Immunities Clause is the strongest argument against the tax's validity, because it is more direct than a Commerce Clause argument.

2) Equal Protection

a) Where Congress Approves the Discrimination

Although the Supreme Court normally uses the Commerce Clause to invalidate discriminatory legislation, it may also find that such discrimination violates the Equal Protection Clause. This is important where Congress has given the states the power to do something that would otherwise violate the Commerce Clause: Congress can give states the power to take actions that otherwise would violate the Commerce Clause, but it **cannot** approve state actions that would violate equal protection. Thus, if Congress has approved a type of state tax that discriminates against out-of-state businesses, that state tax will not be in violation of the Commerce Clause, but it might be found to be a violation of equal protection.

Example: In *Metropolitan Life Insurance Co. v. Ward,* 470 U.S. 869 (1985), the Court invalidated a state tax on insurance companies that imposed a higher tax on out-of-state insurance companies than was paid by in-state companies. The Court found that federal statutes exempted state regulation of insurance businesses from Commerce Clause restrictions but found that the tax violated equal protection because it did not relate to a legitimate interest of government (*i.e.,* the state does not have a legitimate interest in discriminating against out-of-state businesses simply to protect local economic interests from competition).

b) Taxes Based on Suspect Classifications or Infringing on Fundamental Rights

The Court may use equal protection analysis rather than Commerce Clause analysis to strike state taxes that are imposed on the basis of a *suspect classification* or that burden a *fundamental right*. A state tax system giving tax exemptions only to long-time residents of the state and denying a similar tax exemption to newer residents will be held to violate the Equal Protection Clause.

Example: The Court invalidated a state property tax provision that gave an exemption from the property tax only to those Vietnam-era veterans who had been residents of the state before May 1976. [Hooper v. Bernalillo County Assessor, 472 U.S. 612 (1985)]

2. Nondiscriminatory Taxes

The Court reviews nondiscriminatory state and local taxes affecting interstate commerce and balances the state need to obtain the revenue against the burden the tax imposes on the free flow of commerce—an approach similar to the one used for examining nondiscriminatory regulations to see whether they impose an undue burden on interstate commerce (*see* IX.B.2., *supra*).

a. Factors

The Court generally considers three factors in determining whether the nondiscriminatory tax is valid:

1) Substantial Nexus

A state tax will be valid under the Commerce Clause only if there is a substantial nexus between the activity or property taxed and the taxing state. Substantial nexus requires significant or substantial activity within the taxing state.

Examples: 1) A state in which a sale is made may force the seller to pay a sales tax if the seller has some significant contact with the state (*e.g.,* carries on business in the state). However, the state may not force the seller to pay a sales tax if its only contact with the state is the receipt of orders from sales representatives that may be accepted or rejected by the seller.

2) If an interstate seller solicits sales in a state by mail only, with orders shipped to the state by mail or common carrier, the substantial nexus required by the Commerce Clause is not present—the mere mailing of catalogs to the state and shipment by mail or common carrier is not significant activity within the state. [Quill Corp. v. North Dakota, 504 U.S. 298 (1992)]

2) Fair Apportionment

A state or local tax affecting interstate commerce will be valid under the Commerce Clause only if it is fairly apportioned according to a rational formula (*i.e.,* the tax should be based on the extent of the taxable activity or property in the state). Otherwise the activity or property would be subject to cumulative tax burdens.

Examples: 1) State A imposes a 1% tax on gross receipts of all businesses within the state. Harvester is located in State A but makes a number

of sales out of state. The tax is invalid as to Harvester's out-of-state sales since it potentially subjects those sales to cumulative burdens—the tax by the seller's state and a similar tax by the buyer's state—without apportioning the tax.

2) Chooch is a resident of State A. It owns railroad cars used in interstate commerce. The cars are in State A three months each year and State B three months each year. For a State B property tax on the railroad cars to be valid, it must fairly apportion the tax, so that the cars will not be subjected to a similar tax by State A, thus cumulating Chooch's tax burden.

Note: The taxpayer has the burden of proving an unfair apportionment.

3) **Fair Relationship**
A state or local tax affecting interstate commerce will be valid under the Commerce Clause only if the tax is fairly related to the services or benefits provided by the state.
Example: A state may levy a tax on passengers enplaning at a state airport if the tax is related to the benefits that the passengers receive from the state (*e.g.,* the airport facilities). [*See* Evansville-Vanderburg Airport Authority District v. Delta Airlines, Inc., 405 U.S. 707 (1972)]

B. **USE TAX**
Use taxes are taxes imposed on the users of goods purchased out of state.

1. **Permissible in Buyer's State**
Use taxes are not considered to discriminate against interstate commerce even though they single out interstate commerce for taxation (*i.e.,* they are imposed only on goods purchased outside the state), as long as the use tax rate is not higher than the sales tax rate. *Rationale:* The purpose of such a tax is to **equalize** the tax on in-state and out-of-state goods rather than to give in-state goods an advantage. [*See* Henneford v. Silas Mason Co., 300 U.S. 577 (1937)]

2. **State May Force Seller to Collect Use Tax**
Often, states force the user to come forward and pay the state the use tax owed. However, a state may force a nonresident, interstate seller to **collect** the use tax from the local buyer and remit it to the state *if* the seller has the substantial nexus required by the Commerce Clause. The substantial nexus requirement can be met if the seller engages in some **significant activity** in the buyer's state, *e.g.,* maintains offices there. Merely soliciting orders by mail and shipping orders into the state is not sufficient. [Quill Corp. v. North Dakota, A.2.a.1), *supra*]

C. **SALES TAXES**
Sales taxes are taxes imposed on the seller of goods for sales consummated within the state. They generally do not discriminate against interstate commerce; rather the issue usually involves whether there is a substantial nexus (*see* A.2.a.1), *supra*) between the taxpayer and the taxing state, or whether the tax is properly apportioned.

D. AD VALOREM PROPERTY TAXES

Ad valorem property taxes are taxes based on a percentage of the assessed value of the property in question. Such taxes are generally valid. However, a Commerce Clause issue arises when the property taxed moves in interstate commerce. Goods in transit are ***totally exempt*** from taxation. Once the goods come to a halt in a state (*i.e.,* obtain a ***taxable situs***), they may be taxed. Then, the issue usually revolves around whether the tax imposes an undue cumulative burden (*i.e.,* apportionment).

1. No Tax on Commodities in the Course of Interstate Commerce

Commodities in the course of interstate commerce are ***entirely exempt*** from local taxation—since each state could otherwise exact a toll as the goods passed through, imposing an intolerable burden on interstate commerce. [Standard Oil v. Peck, 342 U.S. 382 (1952)] Thus, states may not levy an ad valorem property tax on commodities being shipped in interstate commerce, even if the goods happen to be in the state on tax day.

a. When Is Property "in the Course of" Interstate Commerce?

Only property "in the course of" interstate commerce is immune from local property taxation.

1) When Does Interstate Transportation Begin?

Interstate transportation begins when (i) the cargo is delivered to an interstate carrier (the shipper thereby relinquishing further control), ***or*** (ii) the cargo actually starts its interstate journey. Goods merely being prepared for transit are ***not*** in the course of interstate commerce.

2) Effect of a "Break" in Transit

Once started, a shipment remains in the course of interstate commerce unless actually diverted. Breaks in the continuity of transit will not destroy the interstate character of the shipment, unless the break was ***intended to end or suspend*** (rather than temporarily interrupt) the shipment.

3) When Does Interstate Shipment End?

The interstate shipment usually ends when it ***reaches its destination***, and thereafter the goods are ***subject to local tax***.

b. No Apportionment Required

The validity of state taxes on goods in interstate commerce is strictly a Commerce Clause question; *i.e.,* either the goods are "in the course of" interstate commerce and exempt from tax or they are not. There is no need for apportionment.

2. Tax on Instrumentalities Used to Transport Goods Interstate

The validity of ad valorem property taxes on instrumentalities of commerce (airplanes, railroad cars, etc.) depends on (i) whether the instrumentality has acquired a ***"taxable situs"*** in the taxing state (*i.e.,* whether there are ***sufficient "contacts" with the taxing state*** to justify the tax), and (ii) since the physical situs of the instrumentalities may change from state to state during the year, whether the ***value*** of the instrumentality has been properly ***apportioned according to the amount of "contacts"*** with each taxing state. (The taxable situs ("nexus") is required by the Due Process Clause to establish the state's power to tax at all, and apportionment is required by the Commerce Clause to prevent an intolerable burden on interstate commerce.)

   a.   **Taxable Situs ("Nexus")**
   In general, an instrumentality has a taxable situs in a state if it receives *benefits or protection* from the state. [Braniff Airways v. Nebraska Board of Equalization and Assessment, 347 U.S. 590 (1954)—airplanes have taxable situs in nondomiciliary state where airline company owned no property but made 18 regularly scheduled flights per day from rented depot space, even though same aircraft did not land every day] Note that an instrumentality *may have more than one taxable situs*, upon each of which states can impose a tax subject to the required apportionment (*infra*).

   b.   **Apportionment Requirement**
   If an instrumentality has only one situs, the domiciliary state can tax at full value. If the instrumentality has more than one taxable situs, a tax apportioned on the value of the instrumentality will be upheld if it fairly approximates the average physical presence of the instrumentality within the taxing state. [Union Tank Line Co. v. Wright, 249 U.S. 275 (1919)] The *taxpayer has the burden* of proving that an instrumentality has acquired a taxable situs outside his domiciliary state.

      1)   **Proper Apportionment**
      The following methods have been upheld:

         (i)   Using the proportion of *miles traveled* within the taxing state to the total number of miles traveled by the instrumentalities in the entire operation. [Ott v. Mississippi Valley Barge Line Co., 336 U.S. 169 (1949)]

         (ii) Computing the *average number of instrumentalities* (tank cars) *physically present* in the taxing state on any one day during the tax year and taxing that portion at full value—*i.e.*, as if in the state all year. [Johnson Oil Refining Co. v. Oklahoma, 290 U.S. 158 (1933)]

      Note: Because different states may use different apportionment formulas to tax the same property, there may still be some double taxation of the same instrumentalities. However, the double taxation should be minimal if proper apportionment formulas have been used.

E.   **PRIVILEGE, LICENSE, FRANCHISE, OR OCCUPATION TAXES**
   Privilege, license, franchise, and occupation taxes are cumulatively known as "doing business" taxes. States generally can impose such taxes—on companies engaged exclusively in interstate commerce, as well as on interstate companies engaged in local commerce—for the privilege of doing business within the state. Such taxes may be measured by a flat amount or by a proportional rate based on revenue derived from the taxing state. In either case, the tax must meet the basic requirements—the activity taxed must have a *substantial nexus to the taxing state*; and the tax must be *fairly apportioned*, must *not discriminate* against interstate commerce, and must *fairly relate to services provided* by the state. [Complete Auto Transit, Inc. v. Brady, 430 U.S. 274 (1977)—*overruling* Spector Motor Service v. O'Connor, 340 U.S. 602 (1951)]

Examples: 1) A privilege tax for doing business, based on the gross income derived from transporting goods within the state, can be applied to a trucking company that delivers goods coming from outside the state. [Complete Auto Transit, Inc. v. Brady, *supra*]

2) An occupation tax on all businesses, based on gross income derived within the state, can be applied to a stevedoring company operating within the state that loads and unloads ships carrying goods in interstate commerce. [Department of Revenue v. Association of Washington Stevedoring Cos., 435 U.S. 734 (1978)—*overruling* Joseph v. Carter & Weekes Stevedoring Co., 330 U.S. 442 (1947)]

1. Taxpayer Has Burden of Proof

The taxpayer has the burden of showing that the state's apportionment formula is unfair. However, a state tax that discriminates against interstate commerce will be held invalid regardless of whether the taxpayer can show that an actual, unfair multiple burden is imposed on his business.

XI. POWER OF STATES TO TAX FOREIGN COMMERCE

A. IMPORT-EXPORT CLAUSE

Article I, Section 10, Clause 2 provides: "No state shall, without the Consent of the Congress, lay any Imposts or Duties on Imports or Exports, except what may be absolutely necessary for executing its inspection Laws . . . ."

1. State Taxation of "Imports" Prohibited Absent Congressional Consent

The Import-Export Clause prohibits the states from imposing any tax on imported goods as such or on commercial activity connected with imported goods *as such* (*i.e.,* taxes discriminating against imports), except with congressional consent. [Brown v. Maryland, 25 U.S. 419 (1827)]

2. State Taxation of "Exports" Prohibited

The Import-Export Clause prohibits the states from imposing any tax on goods after they have entered the "export stream."

B. COMMERCE CLAUSE

The Commerce Clause gives Congress the exclusive power to regulate foreign commerce and thus inherently limits a state's power to tax that commerce. Therefore, a state tax applied to foreign commerce must meet all of the Commerce Clause tests that apply to state taxation of interstate commerce. (*See* X.A., *supra*.) And even if a state tax meets those tests, the tax is invalid if it would (i) create a substantial risk of international multiple taxation or (ii) prevent the federal government from "speaking with one voice" regarding international trade or foreign affairs issues. [Barclays Bank PLC v. Franchise Tax Board, 512 U.S. 298 (1994)]

PART FOUR: INDIVIDUAL GUARANTEES AGAINST GOVERNMENTAL OR PRIVATE ACTION

XII. LIMITATIONS ON POWER AND STATE ACTION REQUIREMENT

A. CONSTITUTIONAL RESTRICTIONS ON POWER OVER INDIVIDUALS

The Constitution provides individuals with a number of rights that restrict the power of the government (*e.g.,* the right to speak freely). Some rights/restrictions are applicable only to the federal government, some are applicable only to state and local governments, and some are applicable to all governmental bodies. A few even apply to private action. Several constitutional provisions also give Congress the power to adopt legislation to protect individual rights.

Note: The Constitution sets the ***minimum level*** of protection for individuals. States generally are free to grant broader protections than those granted in the United States Constitution.

1. Bill of Rights

The Bill of Rights (first 10 Amendments to the Constitution) is the most important source of limitations on the federal government's power. By its terms, the Bill is not applicable to the states, although most of its safeguards have been held to be applicable to the states through the Fourteenth Amendment Due Process Clause.

a. Rights Applicable to States

The Supreme Court has stated that only those safeguards in the Bill of Rights that are "essential to liberty" are applicable to the states through the Fourteenth Amendment. Included in this concept are: ***all the First Amendment*** guarantees (speech, press, assembly, right to petition, free exercise, and nonestablishment of religion); the ***Second Amendment*** right to bear arms; the ***Fourth Amendment*** (unreasonable search and seizure); some ***elements of the Fifth Amendment*** (privilege against self-incrimination; compensation for taking of private property for public use); the ***Sixth Amendment*** (speedy and public trial by impartial jury, notice and right of confrontation, compulsory process, and right to legal counsel in all serious criminal proceedings); and the ***Eighth Amendment*** (cruel and unusual punishment, excessive bail, and excessive fine provisions are ***assumed*** to be incorporated but there is no precise ruling).

b. Rights Not Applicable to States

There are four provisions of the Bill of Rights that have not yet been incorporated into the Due Process Clause:

(i) The ***Third Amendment*** prohibition against quartering troops in a person's home;

(ii) The ***Fifth Amendment*** right to a grand jury indictment in criminal cases;

(iii) The ***Seventh Amendment*** right to a jury trial in civil cases; and

(iv) The ***Eighth Amendment*** right against excessive fines.

[*See* McDonald v. Chicago, 130 S. Ct. 3020 (2010)] The ***Tenth Amendment***, by its terms, limits the federal government's power over states, and so is inapplicable to the states.

2. Thirteenth Amendment

The Thirteenth Amendment provides that slavery shall not exist in the United States.

a. No Requirement of State Action

The amendment contains no language limiting its effect to governmental action (*e.g.,* "no *state* shall . . . "); thus, it is applicable even to *private action*.

b. Congressional Power

The enabling clause of the Thirteenth Amendment gives Congress the power to adopt appropriate legislation, and the Supreme Court apparently will uphold legislation proscribing almost any private racially discriminatory act that can be characterized as a *"badge or incident of slavery."*

Examples: The Supreme Court has upheld legislation:

1) Prohibiting private parties from refusing to rent or sell housing to a person because of race [Jones v. Alfred H. Mayer Co., 392 U.S. 409 (1968)];

2) Prohibiting private, nonsectarian schools from refusing to admit nonwhite children [Runyon v. McCrary, 427 U.S. 160 (1967)]; and

3) Prohibiting a private employer from discriminating in hiring on the basis of race [Patterson v. McLean Credit Union, 491 U.S. 164 (1989)].

Note: The above are examples of where Congress used its power to adopt statutes prohibiting "badges of slavery"; the proscribed activities would not necessarily be held to violate the Thirteenth Amendment absent the legislation.

3. Fourteenth Amendment

The Fourteenth Amendment *prohibits states* (not the federal government or private persons) from depriving any person of life, liberty, or property without due process and equal protection of the law. As discussed above, this amendment is a most important source of limitations on the states' power over individuals, because, through the Due Process Clause, most of the protections of the Bill of Rights are applicable to the states.

Note: The meaning of due process and equal protection will be discussed later in this outline.

a. Requirement of State Action

The Fourteenth Amendment applies only if there is action by a state or local government, government officer, or private individual whose behavior meets the requirements for state action (*see* B., below).

b. Scope of Congressional Power

Section 5 of the Fourteenth Amendment is an enabling clause giving Congress the power to adopt *appropriate legislation* to enforce the rights and guarantees

provided by the Fourteenth Amendment. Under Section 5, Congress may **not** expand existing constitutional rights or create new ones—it may only enact laws to prevent or remedy violations of rights already recognized by the courts. To adopt a valid law, Congress must point to a history or pattern of state violation of such rights and adopt legislation that is **congruent and proportional** (*i.e.*, narrowly tailored) to solving the identified violation. Note, however, that when Congress is dealing with a type of discrimination that the Supreme Court reviews using heightened scrutiny (*i.e.*, race, national origin, or gender—*see* XVIII.D., E., *infra*), Congress will generally have more power to act.

Examples: 1) The Americans With Disabilities Act ("ADA") includes provisions that, among other things, prohibit states from discriminating against disabled persons in hiring practices and requires states to make reasonable accommodations for disabled employees. Under the Fourteenth Amendment Equal Protection Clause, the Court has recognized a right of disabled people to be free from irrational state discrimination. In adopting the ADA, Congress did not identify a history or pattern of irrational employment practices by the states. Even if there were such a pattern, the provisions here were not congruent and proportional to remedying irrational discrimination; they are overinclusive, because they prohibit states from making employment decisions that are constitutional under the rational basis test. [Board of Trustees of University of Alabama v. Garrett, 531 U.S. 356 (2001)] Under similar reasoning, the Supreme Court has held that Congress has no power under Section 5 to broadly restrict **age discrimination by state employers**. [Kimel v. Florida Board of Regents, 528 U.S. 62 (2000)]

2) The Supreme Court held that there is no violation of the First Amendment, applicable to the states through the Fourteenth Amendment, where a state law incidentally burdens a religious practice. [Employment Division v. Smith, XXII.C.3., *infra*] In response, Congress adopted a statute, purportedly under Section 5, providing that a state may not burden religious practices absent a compelling interest. The statute was held unconstitutional because it sought to expand substantive First Amendment rights beyond those recognized by the Supreme Court. [City of Boerne v. Flores, 521 U.S. 507 (1997)]

Compare: The Court has held that Congress **has** power under Section 5 to provide that state governments may be sued for violating Title II of the ADA (which prohibits state and local government discrimination against people with disabilities in government programs, services, or activities) when the discrimination involves access to the courts. *Rationale:* The right of meaningful access to judicial proceedings is a "fundamental right" under the Due Process Clause, and is thus subject to "heightened judicial scrutiny" much more demanding than "rational basis." This heightened scrutiny makes it "easier for Congress to show a pattern of state constitutional violations." [Tennessee v. Lane, 541 U.S. 509 (2004)]

4. **Fifteenth Amendment**

The Fifteenth Amendment is a limitation on both the ***states and the federal government***. It prohibits them from denying any citizen the right to vote on account of race or color. As indicated above, the Fifteenth Amendment contains an enabling clause that allows Congress to adopt legislation protecting the right to vote from discrimination.

5. **Commerce Clause**

The Supreme Court has allowed Congress to use the Commerce Clause to limit the power of individuals over other individuals—by adopting legislation barring private racial discrimination in activities "connected with" interstate commerce. Recall that under the affectation doctrine, almost any activity can be said to be connected with interstate commerce. (*See* II.A.4.a.1), *supra.*)

    a. **Civil Rights Act**

Provisions of the Civil Rights Act of 1964 ***barring discrimination in places of public accommodation*** are proper and valid exercises of commerce power.

    b. **Extent of Commerce Power**

The reach of the commerce power is broad. Any business that is ***open to interstate travelers*** or that ***uses products shipped in interstate commerce*** is covered. [Daniel v. Paul, 395 U.S. 298 (1969)—private resort held to be a public place of accommodation encompassed within the Act because drinks and entertainment facilities had been purchased and shipped through interstate commerce]

6. **Rights of National Citizenship**

The Supreme Court has also allowed Congress to limit the power of private individuals to infringe upon others' rights of national citizenship (*e.g.,* the right of interstate travel, the right to assemble to petition Congress for redress), without pointing to any specific constitutional source for the power. [Griffin v. Breckenridge, 403 U.S. 88 (1971)]

B. STATE ACTION REQUIREMENT

As indicated above, the Constitution generally prohibits only governmental infringement of constitutional rights. Thus, to find some action unconstitutional, it is generally necessary to attribute the action to the state, which includes government agencies and officials acting under the color of state law. However, this does not mean that the act must be directly by a government actor; "state action" can be found in the actions of seemingly private individuals who (i) perform exclusive public functions, or (ii) have significant state involvement in their activities.

1. **Exclusive Public Functions**

The Supreme Court has found that certain activities are so ***traditionally*** the ***exclusive*** prerogative of the state that they constitute state action even when undertaken by a private individual or organization. To date, only running a town and running an election for public office have been found to be such exclusive public functions.

Examples: 1) The owner of a "company town" with ***all*** of the attributes of a public town (*e.g.,* homes, sidewalks, streets, police and fire protection, etc.) cannot deny a person's First Amendment right to distribute religious literature in the town,

since the company town is equivalent to a town. [Marsh v. Alabama, 326 U.S. 501 (1946)] However, the owner of a shopping mall can deny people their First Amendment right to picket, since a mall does not have all of the attributes of a town. [Hudgens v. NLRB, 424 U.S. 507 (1976)]

2) Running elections is an exclusive public function, so if a private organization runs a preprimary that has a substantial effect on who is ultimately elected, its actions will be state action. [Terry v. Adams, 345 U.S. 461 (1953)—county political group whose candidate almost always runs unopposed in primary and general election cannot discriminate]

a. Must Be Traditional *and* Exclusive Function

To be state action, the activity must be *both* a *traditional* and *exclusive* government function. Thus, the Court has held that a warehouseman authorized by statute to sell goods stored with him for unpaid charges is not exercising state action when he makes the sale, because while resolution of private disputes is a traditional public function, it is not exclusive—the bailor had state law remedies to check abuses by the warehouseman. [Flagg Brothers v. Brooks, 436 U.S. 149 (1978)] State action exists, and due process guarantees apply, *only if* the creditor uses judicial or executive agencies to secure properties in the possession of the debtor.

2. Significant State Involvement—Facilitating Private Action

"State action" also exists whenever a state *affirmatively* facilitates, encourages, or authorizes acts of discrimination by its citizens. Note, however, that there must be some sort of affirmative act by the state approving the private action; it is not enough that the state permits the conduct to occur.

a. Instances of Significant State Involvement

1) Official Encouragement

Purportedly private action will be given state action status if the action is encouraged or sanctioned by the state.

a) Judicial Approval

State court enforcement of *restrictive covenants prohibiting sale or lease of property to blacks* constitutes state action even in civil proceedings between private parties. [Shelley v. Kraemer, 334 U.S. 1 (1948)]

(1) Peremptory Challenges

The use of peremptory challenges, even by a private party, constitutes state action, both because jury selection is a traditional public function and because there is overt, significant participation by the government (the judge) in the jury selection process. Thus, private litigants and defendants are prohibited from using peremptory challenges in a discriminatory manner. [*See* Edmonson v. Leesville Concrete, 500 U.S. 614 (1992); Georgia v. McCollum, 505 U.S. 42 (1992)]

b) Official Acts

State action may be found in the absence of an unconstitutional statute or ordinance if it appears that the state sanctions constitutional violations by its own officers.

(1) Discriminatory Law Enforcement

The Court reversed a conviction of sit-in demonstrators where no statute or ordinance required segregation but the mayor and police had announced publicly that they would invoke trespass and breach of the peace laws to enforce a local custom of racial separation in eating places. [Lombard v. Louisiana, 373 U.S. 267 (1963)]

(2) Apparent Legal Authority

Even if a state forbids officers from acting in a certain way (*e.g.,* depriving persons of their constitutional rights), the forbidden action may still constitute state action if the state puts the actor in a position to commit the unconstitutional act.

Example: A sheriff beat a prisoner to death in an effort to secure a confession. Both the state and the sheriff were held liable. The actions of the sheriff involved "state action" because the sheriff *acted under "the color of state law*—the state in effect cloaked him with the apparent legal authority." [Screws v. United States, 325 U.S. 91 (1945)]

(3) Public Defenders

A public defender *does not act for the state* when he represents an indigent client. Therefore, negligence or malpractice by the public defender is not a denial of due process because the public defender's actions are not "state actions." [Polk County v. Dodson, 454 U.S. 312 (1982)]

2) State Authorization

In *Reitman v. Mulkey,* 387 U.S. 369 (1967), the Court invalidated a state constitutional provision that *repealed* all existing *state laws banning discrimination* in the sale or lease of property and prohibited reenactment of such laws in the future because such laws "authorize" private discrimination.

3) The State as Lessor for a Racially Discriminatory Lessee

In *Burton v. Wilmington Parking Authority,* 365 U.S. 715 (1961), Delaware was held responsible under the Fourteenth Amendment Equal Protection Clause for the exclusion of blacks from a coffee shop which was located in a public building. The shop was constructed by and leased from the state. The *maintenance* of the facility was *paid for with public funds* and Delaware was able to charge a higher rent because it allowed the restaurant owner to cater to the prejudices of its white customers.

4) Administration of Private Discriminatory Trust by Public Officials

State action exists where city personnel maintain a park, "open to all except blacks," under a private trust. [Evans v. Newton, 382 U.S. 296 (1966)]

5) Entwinement of State and Private Entities
The fact that a state entity helps formulate and adopts the rules of a private entity, and chooses to follow the order of the private entity pursuant to those rules, does not convert the private entity's action into state action. However, a state may be so entwined with a private organization that the organization's actions will be considered state action. [Brentwood Academy v. Tennessee Secondary School Athletic Association, 531 U.S. 288 (2001)]

Example: The National Collegiate Athletic Association ("NCAA") is a voluntary association of public and private universities that establishes rules for its members regarding collegiate sports. Pursuant to its rules, the NCAA urged a member college to suspend its coach for recruiting violations. The coach cannot successfully sue the NCAA for violating his constitutional rights because there is no state action. [National Collegiate Athletic Association v. Tarkanian, 488 U.S. 179 (1988)]

Compare: An association that regulates high school sports within a single state: (i) to which most public high schools belong; (ii) whose governing body is made up mostly of public school officials; (iii) whose meetings are held during regular school hours; (iv) whose employees may join the state retirement system; and (v) which is funded by gate receipts from the regulated sports is so entwined with the state that its action can be considered state action. [Brentwood Academy v. Tennessee Secondary School Athletic Association, *supra*]

b. Instances of Insignificant State Involvement

1) Heavily Regulated Businesses and/or Granting of a Monopoly to a Utility

a) Electric Company
State action will not be found merely because the state has granted a monopoly to a business or heavily regulates it.

Example: In *Jackson v. Metropolitan Edison*, 419 U.S. 345 (1974), **no state action** was found where an electric company terminated the user's service without notice and hearing. The state had not directed or ordered the termination and the fact that the company was heavily regulated and the state commission had approved private utility regulations authorizing such termination was not enough.

b) Nursing Home
A nursing home operated by a private corporation did **not exercise state action** when it discharged Medicaid patients, even though its operation was extensively regulated by the government. [Blum v. Yaretsky, 457 U.S. 991 (1982)]

      c)   School
A school operated by a private corporation did ***not*** exercise state action when it discharged teachers (allegedly in violation of their First Amendment rights) even though the school had contracts with the state to educate or care for many of its students and it received almost all of its operating funds from the government. [Rendell-Baker v. Kohn, 457 U.S. 830 (1982)]

2)   Licensing and Provision of Essential Services
Granting a liquor license and providing essential services (police, fire, water, power, etc.) to a ***private club*** that imposes racial restrictions on its members and guests are ***not*** sufficient to constitute state action. [Moose Lodge v. Irvis, 407 U.S. 163 (1972)]

3)   Congressional Grant of Corporate Charter and Exclusive Name
Congressional grant of a corporate charter and exclusive use of a name is not sufficient to constitute state action. [San Francisco Arts & Athletics, Inc. v. United States Olympic Committee, 483 U.S. 522 (1987)—congressional charter and grant of exclusive name "Olympic" does not clothe United States Olympic Committee with state action]

4)   No Government Duty to Protect Individuals from Harm by Private Persons
The mere refusal of government agents to protect a victim from harm by a private person will not result in a finding that the harm was attributable to "state action," at least when state law does not give the victim a right to government protection. [DeShaney v. Winnebago County Department of Social Services, 489 U.S. 189 (1989)—government not responsible for harm inflicted on a child by his father, even though government social worker had reason to believe the child was being abused and did nothing to protect the child] However, if government employees enter into an agreement or conspiracy with private persons to cause harm to a victim, the victim's injuries are the result of state action; the private persons, as well as the government employees with whom they conspired, will have violated the victim's constitutional rights. [Screws v. United States, a.1)b)(2), *supra*; Dennis v. Sparks, 449 U.S. 24 (1980)]

C.   TIPS FOR BAR EXAM

1.   State Must Be "Significantly Involved" in Private Entity
The state must be "significantly involved" in the private entity. Merely granting a license or providing essential services is insufficient.

2.   No Constitutional Mandate to Outlaw Discrimination
States are not constitutionally required to outlaw discrimination. The Constitution forbids only their encouraging or authorizing it.

XIII.   RETROACTIVE LEGISLATION

A.   CONTRACT CLAUSE—IMPAIRMENT OF CONTRACT
The Contract Clause prohibits ***states*** from enacting any law that ***retroactively*** impairs contract rights. It does not affect contracts not yet entered into.

1. **Not Applicable to Federal Government**
There is no comparable clause applicable to the federal government, although a flagrant contract impairment would be forbidden by the Due Process Clause of the Fifth Amendment.

2. **Only Applicable to State Legislation**
The provision applies only to state *legislation*, not court decisions. [*See* Tidal Oil v. Flanagan, 263 U.S. 444 (1924)]

3. **Basic Impairment Rules**

   a. **Private Contracts**
   The Contract Clause prevents only *substantial impairments* of contract (*i.e.,* destruction of most or all of a party's rights under a contract). However, not all substantial impairments are invalid. In determining whether legislation is valid under the Contract Clause, use a three-part test:

   (i) Does the legislation substantially impair a party's rights under an existing contract? If it does not, the legislation is valid under the Contract Clause. If it does, it will be valid *only if* it:

   (ii) Serves an important and legitimate public interest; and

   (iii) Is a reasonable and narrowly tailored means of promoting that interest.

   Examples: 1) A Minnesota statute that imposed a moratorium on mortgage foreclosures during a severe depression did not violate the Contract Clause. [Home Building & Loan Association v. Blaisdell, 290 U.S. 398 (1934)]

   2) A state statute that restricted underground coal mining to protect a variety of public and private uses of surface land (and buildings) and that left the owners of subsurface mining rights with some reasonable value in, or return from, their investment does not violate the Contract Clause. [Keystone Bituminous Coal Association v. DeBenedictis, 480 U.S. 470 (1987)]

   b. **Public Contracts—Stricter Scrutiny**
   Public contracts (*i.e.,* those in which the state or political subdivision is a party) are tested by the same basic test detailed above; however, they will likely receive stricter scrutiny, especially if the legislation reduces the contractual burdens on the state. When applying the three-part test, note the following:

   (i) There is no substantial impairment if the state has reserved the power to *revoke, alter, or amend* either in the contract itself or in a statute or law the terms of which should be considered to be incorporated into the contract [Dartmouth College v. Woodward, 17 U.S. 518 (1819)];

   (ii) In determining whether the law serves as a legitimate public interest, note that the state cannot be obligated by contract to refrain from exercising its police powers necessary to protect the health and safety of its residents; and

(iii) To be narrowly tailored, the law should not constitute an unnecessarily broad repudiation of contract obligations.

Example: In *Allied Structural Steel Co. v. Spannaus,* 438 U.S. 234 (1978), the Court invalidated state pension reform legislation which increased the obligation of companies under preexisting pension plans to employees who previously had terminated their work for the company or who previously had retired from employment with the company. Because the legislation constituted a substantial impairment of contract by changing the compensation for work already completed and because it was not necessary to remedy an important social problem in the nature of an emergency, it was held to be a violation of the Contract Clause.

B. EX POST FACTO LAWS

1. Two Ex Post Facto Clauses

Neither the state nor the federal government may pass an ex post facto law. [Art. I, §9—federal prohibition; Art. I, §10—state prohibition] An ex post facto law is *legislation* that *retroactively* alters the *criminal law* (not civil regulation, such as denial of professional licenses) in a *substantially prejudicial* manner so as to deprive a person of any right previously enjoyed *for the purpose of punishing the person for some past activity.*

a. What Is "Criminal"

If a law's *purpose* is civil rather than punitive, it is not an ex post facto law unless its *effect* is so *clearly* punitive as to negate the legislature's intention.

Example: A law requiring any sex offender within the state to register and provide his name, address, place of employment, vehicle information, etc., to law enforcement authorities and authorizing law enforcement authorities to make some of this information public is not an ex post facto law, even if noncompliance can be punished criminally, and even if some of the law is contained in the state's criminal code. The goal of such a law is not to punish or stigmatize. Rather, legislatures have found that sex offenders pose a high risk of reoffending, and the release of the information required under the act is intended to protect the public from sex offenders. [Smith v. Doe, 538 U.S. 84 (2003)]

b. Retroactive Alterations

A statute retroactively alters a law in a substantially prejudicial manner if it:

(i) Makes criminal an act that *was innocent when done*;

(ii) Prescribes *greater punishment* for an act than was prescribed for the act when it was committed; or

(iii) *Reduces the evidence* required to convict a person of a crime from what was required at the time that the act was allegedly committed.

Example: A statute of limitations reflects a legislative judgment that after a certain time, no quantum of evidence is sufficient to convict. Thus, a law that

revives the possibility of a criminal prosecution after the previously applicable statute of limitations has expired is an unconstitutional ex post facto law. [Stonger v. California, 539 U.S. 607 (2003)]

2. **Distinguish—Procedural Changes**

Mere procedural changes in state law will not necessarily trigger the Ex Post Facto Clause. A modified law can be applied to a crime committed before the law's modification if the defendant had notice of the possible penalty and the modified law does not increase the burden on the defendant.

Example: Florida had a death penalty statute that was invalidated by the Supreme Court because the statute restricted discretion in sentencing. Before a new statute was enacted, D committed a murder. Florida then passed a new death penalty provision that complied with Supreme Court criteria. The new provision was applied at D's trial, and he was sentenced to death. This was not a prohibited ex post facto law, since the earlier statute (although unconstitutional) gave D notice of the possible penalty and the new provision made it *less likely* that the death penalty would be imposed in a given case. [Dobbert v. Florida, 432 U.S. 282 (1977)]

3. **Indirect "Application" to Courts**

Although the Ex Post Facto Clauses prohibit only retroactive *legislation*, the Supreme Court has held that due process prohibits courts from retroactively interpreting criminal law in an unexpected and indefensible way. [Rogers v. Tennessee, 532 U.S. 451 (2001)—state supreme court's abolition of common law "year and a day rule" (which prohibits prosecution for murder if the victim dies more than a year after an attack) was not unexpected and indefensible because medical science has undermined the rule's usefulness and the rule has already been abolished in most jurisdictions]

C. BILLS OF ATTAINDER

A bill of attainder is a legislative act that *inflicts punishment without a judicial trial* upon individuals who are designated either by name or in terms of past conduct. Past conduct acts to define who those particular persons are.

1. **Two Clauses**

Both the *federal and state governments* are prohibited from passing bills of attainder.

2. **Two Requirements Preclude Finding of Bill of Attainder**

These provisions *require both judicial machinery* for trial and punishment of crime and *definition of criminal conduct in such general terms* as not to ensnare within the definition a single individual or small group for punishment because of past behavior.

Example: The Court found a provision in the Landrum-Griffin Act, making it a crime for a member of the Communist Party to act as an officer or employee of a labor union, to be legislative punishment for a party membership, and hence a bill of attainder. [United States v. Brown, 381 U.S. 437 (1965)]

3. ***Nixon* Case**

In *Nixon v. Administrator of General Services,* 433 U.S. 425 (1977), Congress passed legislation to authorize government control of the presidential papers and tape recordings of former President Nixon. The Supreme Court held that this was *not a bill of attainder*. The

circumstances of the Nixon resignation made him a unique "class of one" as to the need to control his papers. The act was held "**nonpunitive**" and in pursuance of **important public policy**.

4. Draft Registration Case

In *Selective Service System v. Minnesota Public Interest Research Group,* 468 U.S. 841 (1984), the Court upheld a federal statute denying financial aid for higher education to male students between the ages of 18 and 26 who had failed to register for the draft. The law required applicants for the aid to file a statement with their institutions of higher learning certifying their compliance. Failure to register within 30 days of one's 18th birthday was a felony, but the regulations allowed men who failed to register in a timely manner to qualify for aid by registering late. The Court found that this was **not a bill of attainder**. The law reasonably **promoted nonpunitive goals** and was **not a legislative punishment** taken on the basis of any irreversible act, since aid was awarded to those who registered late. The Court also found that the statute did not violate the Fifth Amendment privilege against self-incrimination.

D. DUE PROCESS CONSIDERATIONS

Under the Due Process Clauses of the Fifth and Fourteenth Amendments, retroactive legislation or other governmental action may be, but is not necessarily, a violation of the Constitution. The question of whether a retroactive law (that does not violate the Contracts, Ex Post Facto, or Bill of Attainder Clauses) violates due process is a **substantive due process** issue. If the law does not relate to a fundamental civil right, the retroactive law should be upheld if it is rationally related to a legitimate government interest.

Examples: 1) A retroactive tax law will be upheld as long as the retroactive aspects of the law are rationally related to legitimate government interests. [United States v. Carlton, 512 U.S. 26 (1994)—upholding retroactive modification of the estate tax]

2) Retroactive legislation affecting **merely a remedy** does not violate due process (*e.g.,* repealing or extending a statute of limitations), unless it would oust an already vested property interest. [Chase Securities Corp. v. Donaldson, 325 U.S. 304 (1945)—permissible to revive a previously dead cause of action]

XIV.   PROCEDURAL DUE PROCESS

A.   BASIC PRINCIPLE

The Due Process Clauses of the Fifth Amendment (applicable to the federal government) and the Fourteenth Amendment (applicable to the states) provide that the government shall not take a person's life, liberty, or property without due process of law. Due process contemplates fair process/procedure, which requires at least an opportunity to present objections to the proposed action to a fair, neutral decisionmaker (not necessarily a judge).

1.   When Is Individualized Adjudication Required?

There is a right to procedural due process only when the government acts to deprive an **individual** of life, liberty, or property (*see* below). There is no right to individualized adjudication when the government acts generally, even if the action will result in burdening individuals' life, liberty, or property interests.

Example: A state legislature need not provide individuals with an opportunity for a hearing when adopting the general requirements for obtaining a driver's license (*e.g.,* age, residence, ability, etc.), but it must provide individualized process to determine whether a particular person meets the requirements.

2. **Intentional Deprivation vs. Negligent Deprivation**

    Fair process is required for ***intentional*** acts of the government or its employees. If an injury is caused to a person through the mere ***negligence*** of a government employee, there is no violation of the Due Process Clause. [Daniels v. Williams, 474 U.S. 327 (1986); Davidson v. Cannon, 474 U.S. 344 (1986)]

    a. **"Deprivation"**

        A "deprivation" of life, liberty, or property requires more than a mere denial of certain kinds of remedies. Only when the government affords ***no*** remedy or ***inadequate*** remedies may a deprivation of life, liberty, or property result. [Florida Prepaid Postsecondary Education Expense Board v. College Savings Bank, 527 U.S. 627 (1999)]

3. **Fair, Neutral Decisionmaker—Judge Bias**

    The Due Process Clause requires a judge to recuse himself when he has ***actual bias*** (*e.g.,* he has a direct, personal, substantial, pecuniary interest in a case) or when there is merely a ***serious risk of actual bias***. A serious risk of actual bias exists when "under a realistic appraisal of psychological tendencies and human weakness," the judge's interest poses such a risk of actual bias or prejudice that it must be forbidden. [Caperton v. A. T. Massey Coal Co., 129 S. Ct. 2252 (2009)]

    Example: The chairman of a company spent over $3 million to support an attorney's campaign to be elected to the state supreme court after a $50 million verdict was entered against the chairman's company, knowing that the supreme court would eventually hear the appeal of the verdict. The $3 million was more than the total amount spent by all of the other supporters of the attorney, and the attorney won by fewer than 50,000 votes. When the case was appealed, the winner of the verdict asked the newly elected justice to recuse himself. Under these circumstances, recusal was required. [Caperton v. A. T. Massey Coal Co., *supra*]

4. **Protection vs. Creation**

    The due process provisions do not create property or liberty interests; their purpose is to provide ***procedural safeguards against arbitrary deprivation***. Hence, the Fourteenth Amendment Due Process Clause does not, for example, give out-of-state attorneys the right to appear in state courts without meeting a state's bar admission requirements. [Leis v. Flynt, 439 U.S. 438 (1979)]

B. IS LIFE, LIBERTY, OR PROPERTY BEING TAKEN?

Older Supreme Court cases indicated that due process protects "rights," but not "privileges." This approach is no longer followed; rather the Court will determine whether a ***legitimate*** liberty or property interest is being taken.

1. **Liberty**

    The term "liberty" is not specifically defined. It includes more than just freedom from bodily

restraints (*e.g.,* it includes the right to contract and to engage in gainful employment). A deprivation of liberty occurs if a person:

(i)   Loses significant freedom of action; *or*

(ii) Is denied a freedom provided by the Constitution or a statute.

Examples of liberty interests include:

a.   Commitment to Mental Institution

1)   Adults
Adults are entitled to an ***adversary hearing*** before they are indefinitely committed to a mental institution against their will. The state must prove the basis for commitment by "clear and convincing" evidence. However, after a person has been acquitted of criminal charges on the basis of an insanity defense, the acquitted defendant can be committed if a court finds by a "preponderance of the evidence" that the person should be committed to a mental health care facility. [Jones v. United States, 463 U.S. 354 (1983)]

2)   Minor Children
Minor children have a substantial liberty interest in not being confined unnecessarily for medical treatment. Thus, they are entitled to a ***screening by a "neutral factfinder"*** before commitment to a mental institution. Mere parental consent to commitment is not enough. [Parham v. J.R., 442 U.S. 584 (1979)]

b.   Injury to Reputation
Injury to reputation in itself is not a deprivation of liberty or property. [Paul v. Davis, 424 U.S. 693 (1976)] However, if governmental acts (such as a statement of reasons given for termination of public employment) so injure a person's reputation that he will have ***lost significant employment or associational opportunities***, there is a loss of liberty.

c.   Exercise of Fundamental Constitutional Rights
The Due Process Clause protects a person's freedom to engage in activities that involve fundamental constitutional rights, such as the right to speak and associate, the right to travel, and the right to vote.

1)   Application—Government Employee's Freedom of Speech
A public employee may not be discharged for engaging in ***constitutionally protected speech***. (*See* XXI.C.1., *infra.*) If a government employee is discharged for her speech or writing, a hearing must be held to determine whether the speech was protected. If so, the employee cannot be fired. [*See* Givhan v. Western Line Consolidated School District, 439 U.S. 410 (1979)—Court held that teacher could not be fired for privately communicating her grievances about working conditions or opinions concerning public issues to her employer]

2.   Property
"Property" includes more than personal belongings and realty, chattels, or money, but an

abstract need or desire for (or a unilateral expectation of) the benefit is not enough. There must be a *legitimate claim* or *"entitlement"* to the benefit under state or federal law. [Board of Regents v. Roth, 408 U.S. 564 (1972); Leis v. Flynt, *supra*] Examples of property interests include:

a.   **Public Education**
There is a property interest in public education when school attendance is required. Thus, a significant suspension (*e.g.,* 10 days) requires procedural due process. [Goss v. Lopez, 419 U.S. 565 (1975)]

b.   **Welfare Benefits**
One has a property interest in welfare benefits if she has previously been determined to meet the statutory criteria. [Goldberg v. Kelly, 397 U.S. 254 (1970)]

c.   **Continued Public Employment**
If there is a state statute or ordinance that creates a public employment contract, or there is some clear practice or mutual understanding that an employee can be terminated only for "cause," then there is a property interest [Arnett v. Kennedy, 416 U.S. 134 (1974)]; but if the employee holds his position only at the "will" of the employer, there is no property interest in continued employment [Bishop v. Wood, 426 U.S. 341 (1976)].

C.   **WHAT TYPE OF PROCESS IS REQUIRED?**
While all intentional governmental deprivations of life, liberty, or property require fair process, what constitutes fair process in terms of the timing and scope of the hearing varies according to the circumstances of the deprivation. The Court will weigh:

(i)   The importance of the *individual interest* involved;

(ii)   The value of specific *procedural safeguards* to that interest; and

(iii)   The *governmental interest* in fiscal and administrative efficiency.

[Mathews v. Eldridge, 424 U.S. 319 (1976)] In all situations, the Court will probably require *fair procedures* and an *unbiased decisionmaker.* Normally, the person whose interest is being deprived should also receive *notice* of the government's action and have an *opportunity to respond before* termination of the interest. However, the court may allow a post-termination hearing in situations where a pre-termination hearing is highly impracticable. The Court has made the following rulings with regard to specific types of deprivations:

1.   **Welfare Benefits**
Due process requires an *evidentiary hearing prior to termination* of welfare benefits. It need not be a judicial or quasi-judicial trial if there is adequate post-termination review; but the recipient must have timely and adequate *notice* of the reasons for the proposed termination, the right to confront adverse witnesses, and the right to present his own arguments and evidence orally. Counsel need not be provided, but must be permitted. Finally, the decision must be based solely on evidence adduced at the hearing and must be rendered by an impartial decisionmaker (thus disqualifying any participant in the termination proposal under review). [Goldberg v. Kelly, *supra*]

2. **Disability Benefits**
No prior evidentiary hearing is required for termination of disability benefits, as long as there is *prior notice* to the recipient, an opportunity to respond in writing, and a *subsequent evidentiary hearing* (with retroactive payment if the recipient prevails). *Rationale*: Disability benefits (unlike welfare benefits) are not based on financial need and hence are not vital. [Mathews v. Eldridge, *supra*]

3. **Public Employment**
A public employee who is subject to removal only for "cause" (and who, therefore, has a property interest in his job) generally must be given *notice* of charges against him that are to be the basis for his job termination, and a *pre-termination opportunity to respond* to those charges. The employee does not have to be given a full, formal hearing before his termination, as long as there is a fair system of pre-termination notice, an opportunity to respond (to the person making the termination decision), and a *subsequent evidentiary hearing* regarding the termination (with reinstatement if the employee prevails). [Cleveland Board of Education v. Loudermill, 470 U.S. 532 (1985)] *But note:* If there is a *significant reason* for not keeping the employee on the job, he may be suspended without pay and without an opportunity to respond, as long as there is a prompt post-suspension hearing with reinstatement and back pay if the employee prevails. [Gilbert v. Homar, 520 U.S. 924 (1997)—police officer suspended after being arrested and formally charged with a felony]

4. **Public Education—Disciplinary Suspension**
Although no formal evidentiary hearing is required before a student may be temporarily suspended (for 10 days or less), due process usually requires *notice* of the charges and an *opportunity to explain*. However, if the student's presence poses a danger to persons or property, or threatens to disrupt the academic process, such notice and hearing may *follow* removal as soon as practicable. [Goss v. Lopez, *supra*]

   a. **Corporal Punishment in Public School**
   This may involve constitutionally protected "liberty." However, the traditional common law tort remedies for excessive punishment satisfy procedural due process, and a prior hearing is not required. [Ingraham v. Wright, 430 U.S. 651 (1977)]

5. **Public Education—Academic Dismissal**
No prior evidentiary hearing is required when a student is dismissed for "academic" deficiencies rather than for "disciplinary" reasons. Due process is satisfied if the student is adequately informed of the deficiency and given an opportunity to respond. [Board of Curators v. Horowitz, 435 U.S. 78 (1978)]

6. **Creditors' Remedies**
Pretrial remedies, such as attachment of property or garnishment of wages, that are merely designed to provide a plaintiff with some guarantee that there will be assets to satisfy a judgment against the defendant if the plaintiff eventually wins the case *should not be issued by a court without notice* to the defendant and a *hearing prior to the issuance* of the order. A court may issue a temporary order of this type if: (i) there are exigent circumstances that justify the order; and (ii) the defendant is given a hearing after the order is issued but prior to trial. [Sniadach v. Family Finance Corp., 395 U.S. 337 (1969); Connecticut v. Doehr, 501 U.S. 1 (1991)] However, laws authorizing creditors to garnish assets, or a conditional seller to seize or sequester property, will be upheld *without prior notice* to the debtor *if*:

a.   The creditor posts a security bond;

b.   The application is made to a judge, is not conclusory, and documents narrowly confined facts susceptible of summary disposition; *and*

c.   Provision is made for an early hearing at which the creditor must show probable cause.

7. Driver's License

The state generally must afford a *prior hearing* before a driver's license is suspended or terminated. [Bell v. Burson, 402 U.S. 535 (1971)] However, a post-suspension hearing satisfies due process where a statute mandates suspension of a driver's license for refusing to take a breathalyzer test upon arrest for drunk driving. [Mackey v. Montrym, 443 U.S. 1 (1979)]

8. Parental Status Litigation and Hearing

a.   Termination of Parental Status

Due process does *not require the appointment of counsel* for indigent parents in every case in which the state seeks to terminate parental status (*i.e.*, take children from their parents), *but* only when "fundamental fairness" requires the appointment. [Lassiter v. Department of Social Services, 452 U.S. 18 (1981)] To terminate parental rights, the state must prove its allegations of parental neglect or misconduct by "clear and convincing evidence." [Santosky v. Kramer, 455 U.S. 745 (1982)]

b.   Paternity Actions

A state may allow paternity to be established in a support proceeding brought by a mother or child by a *preponderance of evidence*—no greater burden of proof is required by the Due Process Clause. [Rivera v. Minnich, 483 U.S. 574 (1987)] However, due process requires the state to *pay for blood tests* that might exculpate an indigent defendant in a paternity action if the *state is responsible for the lawsuit* (the suit is brought by a state agency or the state requires the mother to bring the civil paternity suit). [Little v. Streater, 452 U.S. 1 (1981)]

c.   Hearings for Men Who Seek to Establish Paternity

1)   Unmarried Father Living with Mother

If the father of an illegitimate child is a part of a "family unit" that includes the child, the relationship between the father and child will be protected by due process. [Stanley v. Illinois, 405 U.S. 645 (1972)—state cannot take child from father after mother dies, unless state has a fair process to determine whether the parental relationship should be severed]

2)   Father Who Never Tried to Establish Paternity

The father of an illegitimate child who has never attempted to establish a legal or personal relationship with the child has no right to notice prior to the adoption of the child by other persons. [Lehr v. Robertson, 463 U.S. 248 (1983)]

3)   Mother Married to Another Man

The Supreme Court has upheld a statute that presumed that a child born during

wedlock was the husband's child where the statute allowed an alleged biological father to have a hearing regarding visitation rights, but the Court did not rule on whether a biological father could be denied visitation under these circumstances without a hearing. [Michael H. v. Gerald D., 491 U.S. 110 (1989)]

9. **Detention of Citizen Enemy Combatants**
Due process requires that a ***citizen held in the United States*** as an "enemy combatant" have a meaningful opportunity to contest the factual basis for his detention before a neutral decisionmaker. However, due process does not forbid some tailoring of the proceedings to alleviate burdens that they may impose on Executive authority during an ongoing military conflict. This may include accepting some use of hearsay, permitting government rebuttable presumptions, and ***perhaps*** use of a properly authorized and constituted military tribunal. [Hamdi v. Rumsfeld, 542 U.S. 507 (2004)—effect of views of five Justices in two separate opinions]

Example: Hamdi, an American citizen, was captured in Afghanistan, classified as an "enemy combatant" for allegedly taking up arms with the Taliban, and transported to a naval brig in Charleston, SC. Hamdi's father brought a habeas corpus petition on his behalf. The appellate court held that because Hamdi was caught in a combat zone, he had no right to refute the government's charges. The Supreme Court reversed, holding that Hamdi was at least entitled to some hearing to contest the factual basis for his detention before a neutral decisionmaker. [Hamdi v. Rumsfeld, *supra*]

10. **Notice of Adversary Proceedings**
When the government seeks to use a judicial or administrative process to take or terminate property interests, it ***must give notice*** to those persons whose property interests may be taken by that process. The form of notice must be reasonably designed to insure that those persons will in fact be notified of the proceedings.

Example: Personal notice or notice by mail must be given to both mortgagor and mortgagee before a "tax sale" of property for unpaid taxes. [Mennonite Board of Missions v. Adams, 462 U.S. 791 (1983)]

11. **Civil Forfeitures**
Procedural due process limits the government's ability to seize property allegedly subject to forfeiture (which most often occurs when the government claims that the property was connected to, or was the product of, criminal activity). Absent exceptional circumstances, the government must provide the owner of ***real property*** notice and an opportunity for some type of hearing ***prior*** to seizing real property. [United States v. James Daniel Good Real Property, 510 U.S. 43 (1993)] However, the government might be able to seize ***personal property prior*** to providing the owner a hearing, since personal property can be hidden or destroyed. [Calero-Toledo v. Pearson Yacht Leasing Co., 416 U.S. 663 (1974)]

D. DUE PROCESS RIGHTS ARE SUBJECT TO WAIVER
Due process rights are subject to waiver. However, the Supreme Court has not clearly defined the standard for determining whether someone has validly waived the right to a hearing before governmental deprivation of liberty or property. Presumably, any such waiver must be ***voluntary***. Additionally, it is possible that a waiver will be valid only if it is made ***knowingly*** (with an understanding of the nature of the rights being waived).

E. ACCESS TO COURTS—INDIGENT PLAINTIFFS

There may often be a fee for government services, including a fee for use of courts (*e.g.*, a filing fee). Whether the government must waive such fees for indigents depends on the nature of the rights involved.

1. Fundamental Rights—Waiver Required

The Supreme Court has required a waiver of government fees when the imposition of a fee would deny a fundamental right to the indigent. (Fundamental rights are examined in the substantive due process and equal protection sections of this outline.)

Examples: 1) The government cannot deny an indigent the right to marry or divorce because of the indigent's inability to pay a marriage license fee or a divorce court filing fee.

2) The government must waive even a reasonable filing fee for candidates for electoral office if it can be shown that the candidate cannot afford to pay the filing fee. The right to be a candidate is connected to the fundamental right of individuals to vote for candidates of their choice.

3) The government may not require an indigent to pay the cost of a transcript in order to appeal from termination of her parental rights. [M.L.B. v. S.L.J., 519 U.S. 102 (1997)]

2. Nonfundamental Rights—Waiver Not Required

When there is no fundamental right regulated by the imposition of a fee, the government can refuse to grant the service to those persons who cannot pay the required fee.

Examples: 1) The federal government can refuse to grant access to bankruptcy courts to persons who cannot pay a filing fee. There is no fundamental right to receive a bankruptcy discharge from debts.

2) A state can limit judicial review of welfare termination hearings to those persons who pay a $25 fee.

XV. THE "TAKING" CLAUSE

A. IN GENERAL

The Fifth Amendment prohibits governmental taking of private property "for public use without just compensation." The prohibition is applicable to the states through the Fourteenth Amendment [Chicago Burlington & Quincy Railroad v. Chicago, 166 U.S. 226 (1897)], and taking questions often arise in connection with states' exercise of their police power (*i.e.*, the power to legislate for the health, welfare, safety, etc., of the people).

1. Not a Grant of Power

The Fifth Amendment is not a grant of power, but rather is a limitation on power (*i.e.*, a taking must be for a public purpose and compensation must be paid). The power for a taking must arise out of some other source (*e.g.*, the police power).

2. Scope of Taking

The concept of a governmental taking probably originally contemplated only physical appropriations of property. Today, however, the term also encompasses some governmental action

that significantly damages property or impairs its use (*e.g.,* frequent flyovers by airplanes near airport [United States v. Causby, 328 U.S. 256 (1946)]). Moreover, even intangibles may be the subject of a taking. [*See* Ruckelshaus v. Monsanto Co., 467 U.S. 986 (1984)—government requirement that trade secret be disclosed may be a taking where government takes and discloses the secret in such a way that it diminishes the secret's economic value and interferes with reasonable, investment-backed expectations of its holders]

B. "PUBLIC USE" LIMITATION LIBERALLY CONSTRUED

The Court will not review underlying policy decisions, such as general desirability for a particular public use or the extent to which property must be taken therefor. A use will be held to be "public" as long as it is rationally related to a legitimate public purpose, *e.g.,* health, welfare, safety, moral, social, economic, political, or aesthetic ends. The government may even authorize a taking by private enterprise, as long as the taking will redound to the public advantage (*e.g.,* railroads and public utilities).

Example: A city adopted an integrated development plan to revitalize its ailing economy by buying up privately held land in its riverfront area, developing some land into parks, and transferring the rest to developers who would open marinas, stores, etc. Pursuant to the plan, the city bought up land from willing sellers and initiated condemnation proceedings against owners who refused to sell. The recalcitrant owners brought suit against the city, claiming that the use for which the city was condemning the land (*i.e.,* to transfer the land to private developers) was not a public use. The Supreme Court held that a taking is for public use so long as the government acts out of a reasonable belief that the taking will benefit the public, and taking private property to promote economic development has long been accepted as a public use. [Kelo v. City of New London, 545 U.S. 469 (2005)]

C. "TAKING" VS. "REGULATION"

While the government must fairly compensate an owner when her property is taken for public use, it need not pay compensation for mere regulation of property. Thus, whether government action amounts to a taking or is merely regulation is a crucial issue. The question is one of degree; there is no clear cut formula for determining whether there has been a taking. The following guidelines have emerged.

1. Actual Appropriation or Physical Invasion

A taking will almost always be found if there is an actual appropriation or destruction of a person's property or a permanent physical invasion by the government or by authorization of law.

Examples: A taking was found in the following situations:

1) Ordinance requiring landlords to allow installation of cable TV in their rental units but limiting to $1 the fee landlords could charge for this access. [Loretto v. Teleprompter Manhattan CATV Corp., 458 U.S. 419 (1982)]

2) Statute ***abolishing*** rights of descent and devise of property (although government has broad authority to regulate this area). [Hodel v. Irving, 481 U.S. 704 (1987)]

3) Requirement that public be given free access to a privately developed waterway. [Kaiser Aetna v. United States, 444 U.S. 164 (1980)]

a.   **Exception—Emergencies**
A taking is less likely to be found in emergency situations, even where there is destruction or actual occupation of private property.

Examples: 1) No compensation was required when the state ordered the destruction of cedar trees that threatened to spread disease to apple orchards. [Miller v. Schoene, 276 U.S. 272 (1928)]

2) No compensation was required when federal troops destroyed oil facilities to prevent them from falling into enemy hands. [United States v. Caltex, Inc., 344 U.S. 149 (1952)]

2.   **Use Restrictions**

a.   **Denial of *All* Economic Value of Land—Taking**
If a government regulation denies a landowner of *all* economic use of his land, the regulation is equivalent to a physical appropriation and is thus a taking unless principles of nuisance or property law that existed when the owner acquired the land make the use prohibitable. [Lucas v. South Carolina Coastal Council, 505 U.S. 1003 (1992)—state's zoning ordinance, adopted after owner purchased lots, amounted to a taking because the ordinance prohibited owner from erecting any permanent structures on his lots]

1)   **Temporary Denials of All Economic Use**
Temporarily denying an owner of all economic use of property does not constitute a per se taking. Instead, the Court will carefully examine and weigh all the relevant circumstances—the planners' good faith, the reasonable expectations of the owners, the length of the delay, the delay's actual effect on the value of the property, etc.—in order to determine whether "fairness and justice" require just compensation. [Tahoe-Sierra Preservation Council, Inc. v. Tahoe Regional Planning Agency, 535 U.S. 302 (2002)—finding no taking where there was a 32-month moratorium on land development in the Lake Tahoe Basin while a comprehensive land-use plan was being developed for the area]

b.   **Decreasing Economic Value**
Regulations that merely decrease the value of property (*e.g.,* prohibit its most beneficial use) do not necessarily result in a taking, *as long as they leave an economically viable use for the property*. The Court considers the economic impact of the regulation on the claimant and whether the regulation substantially interferes with distinct, investment-backed expectations of the claimant. [Penn Central Transportation Co. v. New York, 438 U.S. 255 (1978)]

Example: The Court upheld a "landmark" zoning ordinance that prohibited altering the external appearance of Grand Central Station. It found historic preservation to be an important government interest and that certain rights granted to the landmark owners mitigated their loss. [Penn Central Transportation Co. v. New York, *supra*]

1)   **Building/Development Permits—Transfer of Occupation Rights**
Municipalities often attempt to condition building or development permits on a landowner's (i) conveying title to part, or all, of the property to the government or (ii)

granting the public access to the property (*e.g.*, an easement across the property). Such conditions constitute an uncompensated taking unless (i) the government can show that the condition relates to a legitimate government interest and (ii) the adverse impact of the proposed building/development on the area is roughly proportional to the loss caused to the property owner from the forced transfer of occupation rights. [Nollan v. California Coastal Commission, 483 U.S. 825 (1987); Dolan v. City of Tigard, 512 U.S. 374 (1994)]

Example: City agreed to approve a permit to expand plaintiff's retail store and pave a parking lot on the condition that plaintiff dedicate land for (i) a public greenway and (ii) a bike path. The Supreme Court found that City did not show a sufficient relationship between the dedications and the impact that the expansion would have on the area. [Dolan v. City of Tigard, *supra*]

2) Utility Rate Regulation
There is no taking where the government sets rates that utility companies can charge, as long as the rates are not set so low that they are unjust and confiscatory. [Duquesne Light Co. v. Barash, 488 U.S. 299 (1989)]

3) Zoning Ordinances
The Court has long held that governments may adopt zoning ordinances that regulate the way real property may be used, pursuant to the police power (*e.g.*, limiting development in a particular area to single-family homes, restricting buildings to a particular height, etc.). Such regulations generally do not amount to a taking—even if they deny an owner the highest and best use of her property—unless they: (i) amount to a physical appropriation, as in *Loretto*, (ii) deny an owner of all economic use, as in *Lucas*, or (iii) unreasonably interfere with distinct, investment-backed expectations as set out in *Penn Central*. [*See* Lingle v. Chevron, 544 U.S. 528 (2005)]

3. Remedy
If a property owner challenges a regulation and the court determines that there was a taking, the government will be required to either:

(i) ***Pay the property owner compensation*** for the taking (*see* below); or

(ii) ***Terminate the regulation and pay the owner for damages*** that occurred while the regulation was in effect (*i.e.,* temporary taking damages).

[First English Evangelical Church v. County of Los Angeles, 482 U.S. 304 (1987)]

a. Who May Sue
The right to claim a "taking" is **not** limited to persons who held title to the property at the time a challenged use restriction was imposed. A person who purchases property after a regulation is in place still may bring a taking claim. [Palazzolo v. Rhode Island, 533 U.S. 606 (2001)]

D. "JUST COMPENSATION"
The owner is entitled to the ***reasonable value*** of her property ***at the time of the taking***—fair

market value. The test is ordinarily a *loss to the owner*, not a gain to the taker. Due process guarantees notice and hearing, administrative or judicial, on the amount of compensation, but the hearing need not precede the taking.

1. **"Worthless" Property**
   Because just compensation is measured by the loss to the owner and not by the gain to the taker, property that is "worthless" to the owner can be the subject of a taking, but no compensation need be paid when it is taken.

   Example: A state law required attorneys to keep clients' funds in trust accounts on behalf of their clients and to pay to the client any interest earned on the funds. If a client's funds were too small to earn enough interest to exceed the costs of distributing the interest, the attorneys were required to pay the interest over to a legal aid charity. Although this requirement constitutes a taking, no compensation is due because the clients have not suffered a pecuniary loss. [Brown v. Legal Foundation of Washington, 538 U.S. 216 (2003)]

XVI. INTRODUCTION TO SUBSTANTIVE DUE PROCESS AND EQUAL PROTECTION

A. RELATIONSHIP BETWEEN SUBSTANTIVE DUE PROCESS AND EQUAL PROTECTION

The Due Process Clauses and the Equal Protection Clause guarantee the fairness of laws—substantive due process guarantees that laws will be reasonable and not arbitrary, and equal protection guarantees that similarly situated persons will be treated alike. Both guarantees require the Court to review the *substance of the law* rather than the procedures employed.

1. **Substantive Due Process**
   Generally where a law limits the liberty of *all* persons to engage in some activity, it is a due process question.

2. **Equal Protection**
   Where a law treats a person or class of persons differently from others, it is an equal protection question. [*See* Village of Willowbrook v. Olech, 528 U.S. 562 (2000)—equal protection claims may be brought by a class with as few as one member] However, an at-will government employee who claims to be a victim of arbitrary discrimination cannot use the "class of one" theory to make an equal protection claim. [Engquist v. Department of Agriculture, 533 U.S. 591 (2008)]

3. **Examples**
   If a law prohibits all persons from purchasing contraceptive devices, there is a due process issue; if the law prohibits only purchases by unmarried persons, there is an equal protection issue. A state's refusal to have any publicly funded schools raises a due process issue; a state law that establishes separate schools for children of different races raises an equal protection issue.

4. **Note—Clauses Not Necessarily Mutually Exclusive**
   Since both clauses protect against unfairness, both may be appropriate challenges to the

same governmental act, and a discussion of both may be appropriate in an essay answer. On the MBE, however, the examiners will probably not include both as alternatives in the same question. The above approaches can be used as a rough guideline of when each clause applies.

B. WHAT STANDARD OF REVIEW WILL THE COURT APPLY?

The Court employs one of three tests in reviewing laws under these clauses, depending on the circumstances.

1. Strict Scrutiny (Maximum Scrutiny)

The Court uses the strict scrutiny standard when a suspect classification or fundamental right (these terms will be discussed *infra*) is involved. Under the strict scrutiny standard, a law will be upheld only if it is **necessary** to achieve a **compelling** or **overriding** government purpose. The Court will always consider whether less burdensome means for accomplishing the legislative goal are available. Most governmental action examined under this test fails.

a. Burden of Proof on Government

When the strict scrutiny standard is applied, the **government** will have the burden of proving that the law is necessary. The Court will not allow a loose fitting law (*i.e.,* if a law reaches more people or conduct than is necessary (overinclusive) or does not reach all of the people or conduct sought to be regulated (underinclusive), it will likely be struck down).

2. Intermediate Scrutiny

The Court uses intermediate scrutiny when a classification based on gender or legitimacy is involved. Under the intermediate scrutiny standard, a law will be upheld if it is **substantially** related to an **important** government purpose.

a. Burden of Proof Probably on Government

It is unclear who has the burden of proof when the Court uses the intermediate standard, but in most cases, it appears to be the government.

3. Rational Basis (Minimal Scrutiny)

The rational basis standard is used whenever the other two standards are not applicable (*i.e.,* most legislation). Under the rational basis standard, a law will be upheld if it is **rationally related to a legitimate** interest. It is difficult to fail this test, so most governmental action examined under this standard is upheld unless it is **arbitrary** or **irrational**.

a. Burden of Proof on Challenger

Under the rational basis standard, laws are presumed valid. Therefore, the challenger has the burden of proof. This is a very difficult burden to meet, given the deference the Court gives to legislatures under the rational basis standard. (*See* below.)

b. Deference to Legislature

Under the rational basis standard, the Court will usually defer to a legislature's decision that a law is rational. Loose fitting laws are permissible here: The law need not be the best law that could have been written to achieve the legislative goal. Indeed, it need not go far at all toward a conceivable legislative goal; the Court will uphold a law taking a "first step" toward any legitimate goal, even if the Court thinks the law is unwise.

Example: City decided that advertisements on motor vehicles are traffic hazards, so it banned such advertisements except for those on vehicles advertising the owner's own product. Even though the excepted advertisements were no less distracting than the banned ones, the Court upheld the "first step" law. [Railway Express Agency v. New York, 336 U.S. 106 (1949)]

XVII. SUBSTANTIVE DUE PROCESS

A. CONSTITUTIONAL SOURCE—TWO CLAUSES
There are two separate clauses protecting substantive due process:

(i)   The Due Process Clause of the Fifth Amendment (applies to the federal government); and

(ii) The Due Process Clause of the Fourteenth Amendment (applies to state and local governments).

As indicated above, *the same tests* are employed under each clause.

B. APPLICABLE STANDARDS

1. **Fundamental Right—Strict Scrutiny**
    Where a law limits a fundamental right, strict scrutiny will be applied, and the law (or other governmental action) will be upheld only if it is necessary to promote a *compelling or overriding interest*. Fundamental rights include:

    a.   Right to travel;

    b.   Privacy;

    c.   Voting; and

    d.   All First Amendment rights.

2. **All Other Cases—Mere Rationality**
    In all other cases, the mere rationality test is applied, and the law will be upheld if it is *rationally related to any conceivable legitimate end of government*. Examples include the following:

    a.   **Business and Labor Regulations**
         The Court will sustain all varieties of business regulation; *e.g.,* "blue sky" laws, bank controls, insurance regulation, price and wage controls, unfair competition and trade practice controls, etc.

    b.   **Taxation**
         Taxation is also invariably *sustained*. However, discriminatory taxes might still be invalidated.

c. **Lifestyle**

There is, as yet, *no recognized right* to lead a certain lifestyle. Thus, the Supreme Court will uphold laws: prohibiting drugs ("hard" or "soft"), requiring motorcyclists to wear helmets, or requiring police officers to have short hair. [Kelley v. Johnson, 425 U.S. 238 (1976)]

d. **Zoning**

Regulation of the ownership or use of property has also been liberally tolerated by the Court.

1) **Statutes Forbidding Nuisances or Promoting Community's Preferred Lifestyle**

Statutes forbidding certain uses as nuisances have been sustained, as have all kinds of statutes designed to promote the public's enjoyment of space and safety or to promote a community's preferred lifestyle and character. For example, the Supreme Court held that a Long Island suburb could zone out all groups of three or more persons unrelated by blood, adoption, or marriage. [Village of Belle Terre v. Boraas, 416 U.S. 1 (1974)]

2) **Cannot Prohibit Traditionally Related Families from Living Together**

However, you should know that the Supreme Court held that zoning regulations that prohibit members of traditional families from living together (*i.e.,* zoning excluding cousins or grandchildren) violate due process. [Moore v. City of East Cleveland, 431 U.S. 494 (1977)]

e. **Punitive Damages**

The Supreme Court has held that punitive damages do not necessarily violate due process. However, "grossly excessive" damages—those that are unreasonably high to vindicate the state's interest in punishment—are invalid. [TXO Production Corp. v. Alliance Resources Corp., 509 U.S. 443 (1993)]

1) **Factors Considered**

In assessing whether punitive damages violate due process, the key issue is whether the defendant had *fair notice of the possible magnitude* of the punitive damages. In assessing such notice, the Court will look to:

(i) The *reprehensibility* of the defendant's conduct (*e.g.*, whether the defendant caused physical harm rather than merely economic harm, whether the defendant acted with reckless disregard for harm, whether the conduct was repeated rather than isolated, and whether the harm resulted from intentional malice or deceit rather than from an accident);

(ii) The *disparity between* the actual or potential *harm suffered* by the plaintiff and the *punitive award;* and

(iii) The *difference between the punitive damages award and the criminal or civil penalties* authorized for comparable misconduct.

[BMW of North America, Inc. v. Gore, 517 U.S. 559 (1996)]

2) **Rule of Thumb**
Except for particularly egregious conduct—especially when the conduct resulted in only a small amount of compensatory damages—punitive damages should not exceed *10 times the compensatory damages.* [State Farm Mutual Auto Insurance Co. v. Campbell, 538 U.S. 408 (2003)—punitive damages of 145 times compensatory damages violate due process]

f. **Compare—Vagueness Doctrine**
Under the Due Process Clause of the Fourteenth Amendment, a law can be held unconstitutional if it fails to provide minimal guidelines to govern law enforcement officers so as to discourage arbitrary and discriminatory enforcement. [Kolender v. Lawson, 461 U.S. 352 (1983); City of Chicago v. Morales, 527 U.S. 41 (1999)—holding unconstitutional on vagueness grounds an ordinance that allowed officers to disperse suspected gang members when they were "loitering," which was defined as remaining in any one place with no *apparent purpose*]

C. A FEW IRREBUTTABLE PRESUMPTIONS MAY BE INVALID
If the government "presumes facts" against a person so that she is not qualified for some important benefit or right, the irrebuttable presumption may be unconstitutional. Although the Court often characterizes this as a due process question, it is more accurately an equal protection question because the government is creating an arbitrary classification. In any case, if the presumption affects a fundamental right (*e.g.,* right to travel) or a suspect or quasi-suspect classification (*e.g.,* gender), it will likely be invalid under strict scrutiny or intermediate scrutiny analysis, because the administrative convenience created by the presumption is not an important enough interest to justify the burden on the right or class. If some other classification or right is involved, the presumption will likely be upheld under the rational basis standard.

Examples: 1) A state may not presume a teacher incapable of continuous service in the classroom merely because she is four or five months' pregnant or has a child under age three. [Cleveland Board of Education v. LaFleur, 414 U.S. 632 (1974)]

2) The government may presume that a marriage entered into within nine months of a wage earner's death was simply to secure Social Security benefits. [Weinberger v. Salfi, 422 U.S. 749 (1975)]

XVIII. EQUAL PROTECTION

A. CONSTITUTIONAL SOURCE
The Equal Protection Clause of the Fourteenth Amendment has *no counterpart in the Constitution applicable to the federal government*; it is limited to state action. Nevertheless, it is clear that grossly unreasonable discrimination by the federal government violates the *Due Process Clause of the Fifth Amendment.* [Bolling v. Sharpe, 347 U.S. 497 (1954)—racial discrimination in the public schools of the District of Columbia held a violation of due process] Thus, there are really two equal protection guarantees. The Court applies the same standards under either constitutional provision.

B. APPLICABLE STANDARDS
As indicated above, the Court will apply one of three standards when examining governmental

action involving classifications of persons. If a ***suspect classification or fundamental right*** is involved, the strict scrutiny standard will be applied and the action will be struck down unless the government proves that it is necessary to achieve a compelling interest. If a ***quasi-suspect classification*** is involved, the Court will likely require the government to prove that the action is substantially related to an important government interest. If ***any other classification*** is involved, the action will be upheld unless the challenger proves that the action is not rationally related to a legitimate government interest.

C. PROVING DISCRIMINATORY CLASSIFICATION

The mere fact that legislation or governmental action has a discriminatory effect is not sufficient to trigger strict scrutiny or intermediate scrutiny. There must be ***intent*** to discriminate on the part of the government. Intent can be shown in three ways: (i) facial discrimination; (ii) discriminatory application; or (iii) discriminatory motive.

1. Facial Discrimination

A law may include a classification on its face. This type of law, by its own terms, makes an explicit distinction between classes of persons (perhaps by race or gender; *e.g.,* all white males 21 or older may serve as jurors [*see* Strauder v. West Virginia, 100 U.S. 303 (1880)]). In such cases the courts merely have to apply the appropriate standard of review for that classification. (The standards for racial classifications and gender classifications are described below.)

a. Facial Discrimination Absent Racial Language

In a few cases, the Supreme Court has held that a law used a racial classification "on its face" even though the language of the law did not include racial language. In these cases, the Supreme Court found that the law could not be explained except in racial terms.

Example: The Court found that a state law establishing districts for the election of Representatives to the United States Congress should be deemed to use a racial classification on its face because one bizarrely shaped district could not be explained except in terms of establishing a district where minority race voters would control the outcome of the election. The Court did not rule on the question of whether this racial classification was narrowly tailored to a compelling interest, such as remedying proven past discrimination, because that question had not been addressed in the lower courts. [Shaw v. Reno, 509 U.S. 630 (1993)]

Note: If a legislative districting map could be explained in terms other than race, the Court would not find that the law constituted racial discrimination on its face. In such a case, the persons attacking legislative districts as being based on racial classification would have to show that district lines were drawn for a racially discriminatory purpose. [Hunt v. Cromartie, 532 U.S. 234 (2001)—"Hunt II"]

2. Discriminatory Application

In some instances, a law that appears to be neutral on its face will be applied in a different manner to different classes of persons. If the persons challenging the governmental action can prove that the government officials applying the law had a discriminatory purpose (and used discriminatory standards based on traits such as race or gender), the law will be invalidated.

Examples: 1) A law prohibited operating a laundry in wooden buildings, but gave a government agency discretion to grant exemptions. It was shown that most such laundries were owned by people of Chinese descent, but the agency granted exemptions only to non-Asian applicants. The law was deemed to involve racial or national origin classification and was invalidated as applied. [Yick Wo v. Hopkins, 118 U.S. 356 (1886)]

2) Laws allow attorneys to move to strike potential jurors from a jury either for cause or without cause (a peremptory strike). In either case, there is an equal protection violation when it is proved that an attorney excluded a person from a jury on account of the person's race or sex. [*See* Batson v. Kentucky, 476 U.S. 79 (1986); J.E.B. v. Alabama *ex rel.* T.B., 511 U.S. 127 (1994)] Note that because striking potential jurors from a jury significantly involves the state, even attorneys representing private parties are prohibited from discriminatory strikes. (*See* XII.B.2.a.1)a)(1), *supra.*)

3.   **Discriminatory Motive**

Sometimes a government action will appear to be neutral on its face and in its application, but will have disproportionate impact on a particular class of persons (such as a racial minority or women). Such a law will be found to involve a classification (and be subject to the level of scrutiny appropriate to that classification) only if a court finds that the law-making body enacted or maintained the law for a ***discriminatory purpose***. In such cases, the court should admit into evidence statistical proof that the law has a disproportionate impact on one class of persons. However, mere statistical evidence will rarely be sufficient in itself to prove that the government had a discriminatory purpose in passing a law. Statistical evidence may be combined with other evidence of legislative or administrative intent to show that a law or regulation is the product of a discriminatory purpose.

Examples: 1) A police department used results from a written test as a criterion for hiring police officers. Members of identifiable racial minorities consistently got low scores on the test, although there was no proof that the test was written or otherwise employed for the purpose of disadvantaging minority applicants. Because of the absence of nonstatistical proof of discriminatory purpose, there was no equal protection violation. [Washington v. Davis, 426 U.S. 229 (1976)]

2) A state law gave a preference in the hiring and promotion of civil service employees to persons who were honorably discharged from the United States military. The foreseeable and actual impact of this law was to disadvantage the female population of job applicants, because the majority of veterans are men. Because there was no proof (other than the statistical impact of the law) that the legislature enacted the law for the purpose of hurting women (as opposed to the purpose of aiding veterans), the law was upheld.

3) A statistical study showing that black defendants in capital cases are much more likely to receive the death penalty than are white defendants in a state will not in itself establish that a particular black defendant was denied equal protection by being sentenced to death for murder in that state. The statistical study is insufficient to prove purposeful discrimination. [McCleskey v. Kemp, 481 U.S. 279 (1987)]

D. SUSPECT CLASSIFICATIONS

1. Race and National Origin

If governmental action classifies persons based on exercise of a fundamental right or involves a suspect classification (race, national origin, or alienage), strict scrutiny is applied. The result is invalidation of almost every case where the classification would burden a person because of her status as a member of a racial or national origin minority. The only explicit race discrimination upheld despite strict scrutiny was the wartime incarceration of United States citizens of Japanese ancestry on the West Coast. [Korematsu v. United States, 323 U.S. 214 (1944)—found to be necessary to achieve compelling interest of national security]

Example: A state could not deny custody of a child from a previous marriage to a white mother merely because her new husband was black, where the mother was otherwise found to be an appropriate parent. Racial prejudice against mixed race couples does not justify taking a child from his mother. [Palmore v. Sidoti, 466 U.S. 429 (1984)]

a. School Integration

Recall that only intentional discrimination will be found to create discriminatory classifications calling for strict scrutiny (*see* C., *supra*); thus, only intentional segregation in schools will be invalidated under equal protection.

Example: No equal protection violation was found where a school system established attendance zones in a racially neutral manner, but racial imbalance occurred because of housing patterns. [Keyes v. School District No. 1, 413 U.S. 189 (1973)]

1) Remedying Intentional School Segregation

If it is proven that a school board has engaged in the racial districting of schools, the board must take steps to eliminate the effects of that discrimination (*e.g.,* busing students). If the school board refuses to do so, a court may order the school district to take all appropriate steps to eliminate the discrimination.

a) Order Limited

A court may not impose a remedy that goes beyond the purpose of remedying the vestiges of past segregation. Thus, it is impermissible for a court to impose a remedy whose purpose is to attract nonminority students from outside the school district when there is no evidence of past segregation outside the district. [Missouri v. Jenkins, 515 U.S. 70 (1995)—state not required to fund salary increases and remedial programs to create magnet schools to attract suburban students to urban schools]

b. "Benign" Government Discrimination—Affirmative Action

Government action—whether by federal, state, or local governmental bodies—that *favors* racial or ethnic minorities is subject to strict scrutiny, as is government action discriminating *against* racial or ethnic minorities. [Adarand Constructors, Inc. v. Pena, 515 U.S. 200 (1995)—*overruling* Metro Broadcasting, Inc. v. Federal Communications Commission, 497 U.S. 547 (1990), which applied intermediate standard to federal discrimination]

Note: Prior to its ruling in *Adarand, supra*, the Supreme Court upheld a federal requirement that 10% of federal grants for public works be set aside for minority businesses. [Fullilove v. Klutznick, 448 U.S. 448 (1980)] In *Adarand*, the Court reserved judgment on whether a *Fullilove*-type program would survive strict scrutiny. Some commentators have suggested that it might, because the Court might give Congress more deference than the states based on Congress's power under the Enabling Clause of the Fourteenth Amendment (*see* XII.A.3., *supra*), but the continued validity of *Fullilove* is, at best, uncertain.

1) **Remedying Past Discrimination**

The government has a compelling interest in remedying past discrimination against a racial or ethnic minority. Thus, if a court finds that a governmental agency has engaged in racial discrimination, it may employ a race-conscious remedy tailored to end the discrimination and eliminate its effects. A remedy of this type is permissible under the Equal Protection Clause because it is narrowly tailored to further a compelling interest (the elimination of the illegal or unconstitutional discrimination).

Example: When it has been proven that a public employer engaged in persistent racial discrimination, a court may order relief that establishes a goal for the hiring or promotion of minority persons so as to eliminate the effects of the past discrimination. [United States v. Paradise, 480 U.S. 149 (1987)]

2) **Where There Has Been No Past Discrimination by Government**

Even where a state or local government has not engaged in past discrimination, it may have a compelling interest in affirmative action. However, the governmental action must be ***narrowly tailored*** to that interest. [City of Richmond v. J.A. Croson Co., 488 U.S. 469 (1989)]

a) **Remedial Justifications**

(1) **Local Private Discrimination**

Remedying past private discrimination ***within*** the governmental agency's jurisdiction is a compelling interest, but there is no compelling interest in remedying the general effects of societal discrimination. Thus, for a city to give a preference to minority race applicants for city construction contracts, it must identify the past unconstitutional or illegal discrimination against minority-owned construction businesses that it is now attempting to correct. [City of Richmond v. J.A. Croson Co., *supra*]

Example: In *United Jewish Organizations v. Carey,* 430 U.S. 144 (1977), the Court upheld New York's revised voting district plan, based solely on racial statistics, because the revisions were made to insure that minorities that had previously been discriminated against in New York would be represented in the legislature.

(2) **Diversity in Public Education**

A school board may not assign students to a school on the basis of race unless necessary to achieve a compelling interest, such as remedying past unconstitutional (*i.e.,* intentional) discrimination. A majority of the Court has not found diversity itself to be a sufficiently compelling interest. [*See* Parents Involved in Community Schools v. Seattle School District No. 1, 551 U.S. 701 (2007)] However, the law is different for colleges and universities. Colleges and universities have claimed that they have a compelling interest in having a diverse student body—in its own right—because students with diverse backgrounds enhance classroom discussions and the educational experience both in and outside the classroom, promote cross-racial understanding, and break down racial stereotypes for the workforce. The Court has held that it will defer to a state college or university's good faith judgment that it has such a compelling interest. [Grutter v. Bollinger, 539 U.S. 306 (2003); Gratz v. Bollinger, 539 U.S. 244 (2003)] However, the Court has also held that colleges and universities should consider each applicant as an individual. Although race or ethnicity may be deemed a ***plus,*** as one of a range of factors to consider when making an admissions decision, if race or ethnicity is the defining criterion for admission, the admission policy will not be narrowly tailored to achieving the compelling interest of ensuring a diverse student body.

Example: In its admission process, the University of Michigan's law school required admissions officers to assess an applicant's academic ability and ***all other factors*** about the applicant relevant to whether the student will be an asset to the entering class. The school's policies specifically allowed officers to consider whether an applicant was from a group that has historically been discriminated against, such as African-Americans, Hispanics, and Native Americans. The officers were not told to prescribe any particular weight to this factor, although they were told to include enough applicants from historically underrepresented groups to ensure a "critical mass" of such students—*i.e.,* enough minority students so that they do not feel isolated or become spokespersons for their race. At trial, admissions officers testified that the extent that race factored into an admissions decision varied from applicant to applicant, and statistics showed that, while race was a strong factor in admissions decisions, it was not the predominant factor. The Court held that such a program does not violate the Equal Protection Clause. [Grutter v. Bollinger, *supra*]

Compare: To obtain a critical mass of minority students in its undergraduate admissions process, the University of Michigan allowed admissions officers to give students points for being a member of a historically underrepresented minority group and for a variety of other factors (*e.g.,* academic ability, leadership ability, a good admissions essay, etc.).

Being a member of an underrepresented minority group was worth 20 points, while high school leadership ability, a good admissions essay, etc., were worth less than five points each. Applicants with 100 points or more were guaranteed admission into the school. Under these admissions policies, virtually every academically qualified applicant who was from a group defined as a historically underrepresented minority group was admitted to the school. Such a program violates the Equal Protection Clause because it makes race the predominant factor in making admissions decisions and so is not sufficiently narrowly tailored. [Gratz v. Bollinger, *supra*]

Note: The Court has similarly held that while public schools might have a compelling interest in a racially diverse faculty, a school board may not fire or lay off white teachers with greater seniority than minority race teachers for the sole purpose of maintaining racial balance in a faculty during a period when teacher layoffs are necessary. [Wygant v. Jackson Board of Education, 476 U.S. 267 (1989)]

c. **Discriminatory Legislative Apportionment**
Race can be considered in drawing up new voting districts, but it **cannot be the predominant factor.** If a plaintiff can show that a redistricting plan was drawn up predominantly on the basis of racial considerations (as opposed to the more traditional factors, such as compactness, contiguity, and community interest), the plan will violate the Equal Protection Clause **unless** the government can show that the plan is **narrowly tailored** to serve a **compelling state interest.** [Miller v. Johnson, 515 U.S. 900 (1995)—while eradicating the effects of past discrimination would be a compelling state interest, the redistricting here was driven by the Justice Department's policy of maximizing the number of districts where racial minority members are the majority, which is not a compelling interest]

d. **Private Affirmative Action**
Private employers, of course, are not restricted by the Equal Protection Clause, since the Clause applies only to the government, and private employers lack state action. Nevertheless, Congress has adopted statutes regulating private discrimination by employers pursuant to its power under the enabling provisions of the Thirteenth and Fourteenth Amendments and the Commerce Clause. Thus, if an exam question asks whether private employer discrimination is valid, the answer generally cannot be based on equal protection.

2. **Alienage Classifications**

a. **Federal Classifications**
The standard for review of federal government classifications based on alienage is not clear, but they never seem to be subject to strict scrutiny. Because of Congress's plenary power over aliens, these classifications are valid if they are **not arbitrary and unreasonable.** Thus, federal Medicare regulations could establish a five-year residency requirement for benefits that eliminated many resident aliens. [Mathews v. Diaz, 426 U.S. 67 (1976)]

b. **State and Local Classifications**

State/local laws are *subject to strict scrutiny* if based on alienage. A "compelling state interest" must be shown to justify disparate treatment. For example, a state law requiring United States citizenship for welfare benefits, civil service jobs, or a license to practice law will be struck down because there is no compelling interest justifying the requirement.

1) **Exception—Participation in Self-Government Process**

If a law discriminates against alien participation in the functioning of the state government, the *rational basis* standard is applied.

Examples: 1) A state cannot require a notary public to be a citizen. A notary's responsibilities are essentially clerical and do not fall within the exception for positions related to participation in the governmental process, and there is no compelling government interest justifying such a requirement. [Bernal v. Fainter, 467 U.S. 216 (1984)]

2) A state can validly refuse to hire aliens as police officers and *primary* and *secondary* school teachers (because such teachers influence the attitudes of young minds toward government, the political process, and citizenship, as well as provide an example for civic virtues) and for all other positions that have a direct effect on the functioning of government. [Ambach v. Norwick, 441 U.S. 68 (1979); Cabell v. Chavez-Salido, 454 U.S. 432 (1982)]

c. **Undocumented Aliens**

1) **Punitive Laws Against "Illegal" Alien Adults**

The Supreme Court has *not* held that undocumented ("illegal") aliens are a suspect classification. Thus, a state law that denies benefits to (or imposes burdens on) persons who are in the United States without the permission of the federal government might be upheld under the rational basis test as long as the law was not totally arbitrary.

2) **Education Rights of Alien Children**

In *Plyler v. Doe,* 457 U.S. 202 (1982), the Court held that a state denied equal protection to undocumented alien children when it denied them state-supported primary or secondary education. However, the Supreme Court upheld a state statute that permitted a school district to deny tuition-free education to any child (whether or not he was a United States citizen) who lived apart from his parent or lawful guardian if the child's presence in the school district was for the "primary purpose" of attending school in the district. The state does not have to consider such a child to be a bona fide resident of the school district. [Martinez v. Bynum, 461 U.S. 321 (1983)]

E. **QUASI-SUSPECT CLASSIFICATIONS**

Classifications based on gender or legitimacy are almost always suspect. When analyzing government action based on such classifications, the Court will apply the intermediate standard and strike the action unless it is *substantially related* to an *important* government interest.

1. **Gender**
The Court has expressly held that the ***government*** bears the burden of proof in gender discrimination cases and that an ***"exceedingly persuasive justification"*** is required in order to show that gender discrimination is substantially related to an important government interest. [United States v. Virginia, 518 U.S. 515 (1996)]

   a. **Intentional Discrimination Against Women**
   Gender classifications that ***intentionally*** discriminate against women will generally be invalid under the intermediate standard, because the government is unable to show the "exceedingly persuasive justification" that is required.

   Examples: 1) A statute giving the husband, as head of the household, the right to unilaterally dispose of property jointly owned with his wife violates equal protection. [Kirchberg v. Feenstra, 450 U.S. 455 (1981)]

   2) A statute giving preference to males over females to act as administrator of an estate violates equal protection. [Reed v. Reed, 404 U.S. 71 (1971)—ease in determining who should serve is not an important interest]

   Compare: 1) A state law that excluded from state disability insurance benefits "disabilities" arising from normal pregnancy and childbirth was upheld on a holding that it did not constitute a gender classification and so did not constitute intentional discrimination. [Geduldig v. Aiello, 417 U.S. 484 (1974)]

   2) A state statute granting a hiring preference to veterans was upheld even though the result would disadvantage women since most veterans are men. The Court found that the purpose of the statute was to help veterans, not to discriminate against women. [Personnel Administrator of Massachusetts v. Feeney, 442 U.S. 256 (1979)]

   1) **Government Interest Must Be Genuine**
   The "important government interest" advanced to justify categorization on the basis of gender must be ***genuine***—not hypothesized for the purpose of litigation defense. Neither may the government's justification rely on ***overbroad generalizations*** about males and females that will create or perpetuate the legal, social, and economic inferiority of women. [United States v. Virginia, *supra*]

   Example: When a state military school's policy of admitting only men was challenged, the state justified the policy, claiming that: (i) offering a diversity of educational approaches within the state (*e.g.,* some schools having men only, some having women only, and some having both) yields important educational benefits, and (ii) females ***generally*** would not be able to meet the school's physical requirements and would not do well under the school's adversarial approach to education. The Supreme Court found these arguments unavailing. There was no evidence that the single-sex school in question was established or had been maintained with a view toward fostering a diversity of educational opportunities, and

there was some evidence that *some* women could meet the school's physical requirements and thrive under the school's adversative approach. [United States v. Virginia, *supra*]

b. Affirmative Action Benefiting Women
Classifications benefiting women that are designed to *remedy past discrimination* against women will generally be upheld.

Examples: 1) Social Security and tax exemptions that entitle women to greater benefits to make up for past discrimination in the workplace are valid. [Califano v. Webster, 430 U.S. 313 (1977)]

2) A Navy rule granting female officers longer tenure than males before mandatory discharge for nonproduction is valid to make up for past discrimination against females in the Navy. [Schlesinger v. Ballard, 419 U.S. 498 (1975)]

c. Intentional Discrimination Against Men
Intentional discrimination against men generally is invalid. However, a number of laws have been held valid as being substantially related to an important government interest.

1) Invalid Discrimination
The following have been held invalid under the Equal Protection Clause:

a) *Denial to admit males to a state university or nursing school* [Mississippi University for Women v. Hogan, 458 U.S. 718 (1982)];

b) Law that provides that *only wives are eligible for alimony* [Orr v. Orr, 440 U.S. 268 (1979)];

c) Law that permits *unwed mother, but not unwed father, to stop adoption* of offspring [Caban v. Mohammed, 441 U.S. 380 (1979)]; and

d) Law providing a *higher minimum drinking age for men* than for women [Craig v. Boren, 429 U.S. 190 (1976)].

2) Valid Discrimination
The following have been upheld under the Equal Protection Clause despite their discriminatory intent:

a) Law punishing males but not females for *statutory rape* (sexual intercourse with a minor) [Michael M. v. Superior Court, 450 U.S. 464 (1981)—classification was found to be substantially related to important interest of preventing pregnancy of minors];

b) *Male-only draft registration* [Rostker v. Goldberg, 453 U.S. 57 (1981)—classification was found to be substantially related to important interest of preparing combat troops]; and

    c)   A law granting ***automatic United States citizenship to nonmarital children born abroad to American mothers***, but requiring American fathers of children born abroad to take specific steps to establish paternity in order to make such children United States citizens. [Nguyen v. Immigration and Naturalization Service, 533 U.S. 53 (2001)—promotes the important governmental interest of avoiding proof of paternity problems, which are more difficult to resolve for fathers]

2. Legitimacy Classifications

Distinctions drawn between legitimate and illegitimate children are also reviewed under the intermediate scrutiny standard. Such classifications "must be ***substantially related*** to an ***important*** governmental objective." [Clark v. Jeter, 486 U.S. 456 (1988)]

a. No Punitive Purpose

When the Court examines a classification based on illegitimacy, it gives greater attention to the purpose behind the distinction. It will not uphold discriminatory legislation intended to punish the offspring of illicit relationships.

1) Inheritance from Father

A state statute cannot absolutely exclude illegitimate children from inheriting from their intestate fathers. [Trimble v. Gordon, 430 U.S. 762 (1977)]

Note: However, to promote efficient disposition of property at death (an important government interest), a state can require that the paternity of the father be proved before his death, since the requirement is substantially related to the important interest. [Lalli v. Lalli, 439 U.S. 259 (1978)]

2) Statute of Limitations on Paternity Suits May Be Discriminatory

The Supreme Court struck down a state statute that required illegitimate children to bring paternity suits within six years of their birth while allowing legitimate children to seek support from parents at any time. The Court found that the law was not related to the state interest of preventing stale or fraudulent claims. [Clark v. Jeter, *supra*]

b. Immigration Preference to Legitimate Children—Permissible

Due to the plenary power over immigration, the Court upheld a federal law granting immigration preferences to legitimate children. [Fiallo v. Bell, 430 U.S. 787 (1977)]

F. OTHER CLASSIFICATIONS

All other classifications are reviewed under the rational basis standard and will be upheld unless they bear no rational relationship to any conceivable legitimate government interest. Nevertheless, if the government has no interest in denying a benefit or imposing a burden on a group of persons other than a societal fear or dislike of them, the classification will not meet the standard.

Examples: 1) The Court struck down a zoning ordinance that allowed denial of a special use permit to a group of unrelated, mentally retarded persons who wished to share a residential home or apartment building. Retarded persons are not a suspect or quasi-suspect class and the right to housing is not a fundamental right; thus the Court applied the rational basis standard. It found that the sole reason the permit

was denied was the applicants' mental condition and that the government has no legitimate interest in prohibiting mentally retarded persons from living together. [Cleburne v. Cleburne Living Center, Inc., 473 U.S. 432 (1985)]

2) Several municipalities passed ordinances banning discrimination in housing, employment, etc., based on sexual orientation. In response, the state voters adopted a state constitutional amendment prohibiting any state or local action protecting the status of persons based on their homosexual or bisexual orientation. *Held:* A state constitutional provision that identifies persons by a single trait and then denies them the right to seek *any* specific protections from the law—no matter how local or widespread the injury—is so unprecedented as to imply animosity toward such persons and is thus not related to any legitimate state interest. [Romer v. Evans, 517 U.S. 620 (1996)]

1. Age Not Suspect

Age is not a suspect class. Thus, government action based on age will be upheld if there is a conceivable rational basis for the classification. [*See, e.g.,* Massachusetts Board of Retirement v. Murgia, 427 U.S. 307 (1976)—police officer can be forced to retire at age 50, even though he is as physically fit as a younger officer; Gregory v. Ashcroft, 501 U.S. 452 (1991)—a state constitution that requires state judges to retire at age 70 does not violate the Equal Protection Clause]

2. Wealth Not Suspect

The Court has never held that wealth alone is a "suspect classification." However, the lack of wealth, or the inability to pay a governmentally required fee, cannot be the sole basis upon which a person is deprived of a *fundamental* constitutional right.

Example: The government will be required to waive a marriage license fee or divorce court fee for a person who cannot afford to pay that fee. Marriage and divorce rights are part of the right of privacy.

a. Abortions

The Supreme Court upheld the governmental refusal to pay for abortions. The Court found that a woman did not have a fundamental constitutional right to obtain abortion services, but only a fundamental right to make her decision to have an abortion without government interference.

b. Education

The Supreme Court has not yet held education to be a fundamental right. The Court has not found that children are denied equal protection when the government provides greater educational opportunities for children who can afford to pay for access to the best state-operated schools. In fact, the Court has upheld the use of a property tax to fund local schools where the tax system resulted in children in districts with a high tax base getting a significantly better education than children in tax districts that could not afford significant taxes for education. [San Antonio Independent School District v. Rodriguez, 411 U.S. 1 (1973)] The Court has also upheld a statute that authorizes some school districts in the state to charge user fees for bus transportation to the local public schools. [Kadrmas v. Dickinson Public Schools, 487 U.S. 450 (1988)]

XIX. FUNDAMENTAL RIGHTS

A. INTRODUCTION

Certain fundamental rights are protected under the Constitution. If they are denied to everyone, it is a substantive due process problem. If they are denied to some individuals but not to others, it is an equal protection problem. The applicable standard in either case is strict scrutiny. Thus, to be valid the governmental action must be *necessary* to protect a *compelling interest*.

B. RIGHT OF PRIVACY

Various privacy rights, including marriage, sexual relations, abortion, and childrearing, are fundamental rights. Thus, regulations affecting these rights are reviewed under the *strict scrutiny* standard and will be upheld only if they are *necessary* to a *compelling interest*.

1. Marriage

The right of a male and female to enter into (and, probably, to dissolve) a marriage relationship is a fundamental right. Although not all cases examining marriage regulations clearly use the compelling interest standard, a law prohibiting a class of adults from marrying is likely to be invalidated unless the government can demonstrate that the law is narrowly tailored to promote a compelling or overriding or, at least, important interest.

Note: The Court has indicated that there is a "marital zone of privacy" [*see* Griswold v. Connecticut, 381 U.S. 479 (1965)], so it will likely grant broader protection to private sexual relations between married persons than it does concerning nonmarried persons.

a. Special Test in Prisoners' Rights Cases

A statute or regulation that restricts the constitutional rights of prison inmates will be upheld as long as the statute or regulation "is reasonably related to legitimate penological interests."

Example: Even under this lenient standard, a prison regulation that prohibited an adult prisoner from establishing a legal marriage relationship with another adult unless the prison superintendent approved the marriage was held invalid, because the regulation was not reasonably related to any asserted penological interest. [Turner v. Safley, 482 U.S. 78 (1987)]

2. Use of Contraceptives

A state cannot prohibit distribution of nonmedical contraceptives to adults except through licensed pharmacists, nor prohibit sales of such contraceptives to persons under 16 who do not have approval of a licensed physician. [Carey v. Population Services International, 431 U.S. 678 (1977)]

3. Abortion

The Supreme Court has held that the right of privacy includes the right of a woman to have an abortion under certain circumstances without undue interference from the state. [Roe v. Wade, 410 U.S. 113 (1973)] However, because the Court has held that the states have a compelling interest in protecting the health of both the woman and the fetus that may become a child, it is difficult to apply the normal "strict scrutiny" analysis to abortion regulations (since these two compelling interests may conflict with each other and with the woman's privacy right). Moreover, the Supreme Court has actively been changing the rules

regarding abortions and the Justices have not come to agreement on any applicable standard. In the Court's latest announcement, the plurality opinion adopted two rules: a pre-viability rule and a post-viability rule.

a. Pre-Viability Rule—No Undue Burdens

Before viability (*i.e.,* a realistic possibility of maintaining the fetus's life outside the womb), a state may adopt regulations protecting the mother's health and the life of the fetus only if the regulation does not impose an "undue burden" or substantial obstacle to the woman's right to have an abortion. The Court has not specifically defined what will constitute an undue burden, stating that a state can adopt a statute designed to persuade a woman to choose childbirth over abortion as long as the statute is reasonably related to that purpose and does not put a *substantial* obstacle to abortion in the woman's path. A statute will not impose a substantial obstacle or an undue burden simply because it has the incidental effect of making it more difficult or more expensive to obtain an abortion. [Planned Parenthood of Southeastern Pennsylvania v. Casey, 505 U.S. 833 (1992)]

1) Informed Consent—No Undue Burden

States can require abortions to be performed by licensed physicians, and it is not an "undue burden" to require the *physician* to provide the woman with truthful information about the nature of the abortion procedure, the health risks of abortion and childbirth, and the probable gestational age of the fetus. [Planned Parenthood of Southeastern Pennsylvania v. Casey, *supra*]

2) Waiting Period—No Undue Burden

Requiring a 24-hour waiting period between the time the woman gives her informed consent and the time of the abortion does not amount to an undue burden. [Planned Parenthood of Southeastern Pennsylvania v. Casey, *supra*]

3) Parental Consent—No Undue Burden

A state may require a minor to obtain her parents' (one or both) consent to have an abortion (or give notice to them even if their consent is not required) if there is a "bypass procedure" whereby the minor may obtain the abortion (without notice to or consent of her parents) with the consent of a judge. The judge is required to make a prompt decision as to (i) whether the minor is sufficiently mature to make her own abortion decision, and (ii) if she is not sufficiently mature, whether having an abortion without notice to her parents is in her best interests. [Hodgson v. Minnesota, 497 U.S. 417 (1990); Ohio v. Akron Center for Reproductive Health, 497 U.S. 502 (1990); Planned Parenthood of Southeastern Pennsylvania v. Casey, *supra;* Lambert v. Wicklund, 520 U.S. 292 (1997)]

4) Compare—Spousal Consent Is Undue Burden

It is an undue burden to require a woman to sign a statement that she has notified her spouse that she is about to undergo an abortion. [Planned Parenthood of Southeastern Pennsylvania v. Casey, *supra*]

5) "Physician Only" Requirement—No Undue Burden

A law restricting the performance of abortions to licensed physicians does not impose an undue burden on a woman seeking an abortion. [Mazurek v. Armstrong, 520 U.S. 968 (1997)—*per curiam*]

6) **"Partial-Birth Abortion" Ban—No Undue Burden**
A federal law (the Partial-Birth Abortion Ban Act of 2003) prohibiting "intact D&E" (a type of abortion procedure in which a live fetus is partially delivered, killed, and then fully removed from the woman's body) does not *on its face* impose an undue burden where other abortion procedures are available (*e.g.,* a D&E not involving partial live delivery), the law includes specific anatomical standards and an exception to protect the woman's life, and there is uncertainty within the medical profession whether banning the intact D&E procedure creates a significant health risk for women. Although the Court generally upheld the statute, it also held that the statute could not be applied in situations wherein the woman's health would be endangered. [Gonzales v. Carhart, 550 U.S. 124 (2007)— *distinguishing* Stenberg v. Carhart, 530 U.S. 914 (2000)—which invalidated a state partial-birth abortion ban that did not contain clearly defined anatomical standards nor provide any health exception]

7) **Other Regulations Uncertain**
Prior to *Planned Parenthood of Southeastern Pennsylvania v. Casey, supra,* the Supreme Court upheld a requirement that abortions be performed in a clinic or medical facility with all of the basic medical equipment that would be found in a hospital surgery room. The Court also upheld a requirement that tissue from an aborted fetus be sent to a pathologist. These holdings surely are still valid. But the Court struck down certain other regulations (*e.g.,* requiring early term abortions to be approved by another doctor or hospital committee). Whether these regulations would be found to be undue burdens is uncertain.

b. **Post-Viability Rule—May Prohibit Abortion Unless Woman's Health Threatened**
Once the fetus has become viable, the state's interest in the fetus's life can override the woman's right to choose an abortion, but it does not override the state's interest in the woman's health. Thus, after viability the state can prohibit a woman from obtaining an abortion unless an abortion is necessary to protect the mother's life or health. However, viability is itself a medical question, and a state cannot unduly interfere with the attending physician's judgment as to the reasonable likelihood that the fetus can survive outside the womb. [Colautti v. Franklin, 439 U.S. 379 (1979)]

c. **Remedy**
When a court is faced with a statute restricting access to abortions that may be applied in an unconstitutional manner so as to harm the mother's health, it should *not* invalidate the statute in its entirety if the statute has valid applications. Instead, the court should attempt to fashion narrower declaratory and injunctive relief against the unconstitutional applica- tion. [Ayotte v. Planned Parenthood of Northern New England, 546 U.S. 320 (2006)]
Example: Court should not have invalidated an entire statute requiring minors to give parents notice before obtaining an abortion merely because the statute did not include an exception for cases where the minor's health is at stake; rather, it should be "declared invalid to the extent that it reaches too far, but otherwise left intact." [Ayotte v. Planned Parenthood of Northern New England, *supra*]

d. **Financing Abortions**
Neither federal nor local governments are required to grant medical benefit payments

for abortions to indigent women, even if they grant benefits to indigent women for childbirth services. [Maher v. Roe, 432 U.S. 464 (1977); Harris v. McRae, 448 U.S. 297 (1980)] Moreover, a state may prohibit the public funding of abortions by prohibiting the use of public facilities for abortions and prohibiting any public employee acting within the scope of her public employment from performing or assisting in the performance of abortions. [Webster v. Reproductive Health Services, 492 U.S. 490 (1989)]

4. Obscene Reading Material

The right of privacy encompasses the freedom to read obscene material in your home, except for child pornography. [Stanley v. Georgia, 394 U.S. 557 (1969); Osborne v. Ohio, 495 U.S. 103 (1990)] It does not, however, include the right to sell, purchase, receive, or transport obscene material. [Paris Adult Theatre v. Slayton, 413 U.S. 49 (1973)]

5. Keeping Extended Family Together

The right of privacy includes the right of family members—even extended ones—to live together. Thus, a zoning ordinance cannot prohibit extended families from living in a single household since there is no compelling interest to justify such a rule. [Moore v. City of East Cleveland, 431 U.S. 494 (1977)]

6. Rights of Parents

Parents have a fundamental right to make decisions concerning the care, custody, and control of their children. [Troxel v. Granville, 530 U.S. 57 (2000)]

a. Education

Although the state may prescribe reasonable educational standards, it may ***not*** require that all children be educated in public schools. [Pierce v. Society of Sisters, 268 U.S. 510 (1925)] Neither may the state forbid education in a language other than English. [Meyer v. Nebraska, 262 U.S. 390 (1923)]

b. Visitation

A state law was found to be overbroad and in violation of parents' rights where it (i) authorized the courts to grant "any person" (including grandparents) a right to visit a child upon finding that this would be in the child's best interests, and (ii) did not allow the judge to give significant weight to the parent's offer of meaningful visitation opportunity and the traditional presumption that a fit parent will act in the child's best interests. [Troxel v. Granville, *supra*]

7. Intimate Sexual Conduct

The state has no legitimate interest in making it a crime for ***fully consenting adults*** to engage in ***private*** intimate sexual conduct that is not commercial in nature. [Lawrence v. Texas, 539 U.S. 558 (2003)—a state law making it a crime for members of the same sex to engage in sodomy violates the Due Process Clause]

8. Freedom from Collection and Distribution of Personal Data

The right of privacy does not prevent the state from accumulating and computerizing the names and addresses of patients for whom dangerous drugs are prescribed. [Whalen v. Roe, 429 U.S. 589 (1977)] And the state can republish the recording of an official act, such as an arrest. [Paul v. Davis, 424 U.S. 693 (1976)]

C.   RIGHT TO VOTE

The right of all United States citizens over 18 years of age to vote is mentioned in the Fourteenth, Fifteenth, Nineteenth, Twenty-Fourth, and Twenty-Sixth Amendments. It extends to all national and state government elections, including primaries. The right is fundamental; thus, restrictions on voting, other than on the basis of age, residency, or citizenship, are *invalid* unless they can pass strict scrutiny.

1.   Restrictions on Right to Vote

a.   Residency Requirements

Relatively short residency requirements restricting the right to vote (*e.g.,* 30 days) are valid because there is a compelling interest in ensuring that only bona fide residents vote. However, longer residency requirements will probably be held invalid (*e.g.,* one year) because they discriminate against newer residents without a compelling reason, and thus violate the Equal Protection Clause. Such residency requirements might also violate the right to travel interstate. (*See* D.1.b.1), *infra.*) Note also that Congress may override state residency requirements in *presidential* elections. [Oregon v. Mitchell, 400 U.S. 112 (1970)]

1)   Members of Armed Forces

The right to vote cannot automatically be denied to members of the armed forces stationed at a particular locality. They must be given an opportunity to prove their bona fide residency. [Carrington v. Rash, 380 U.S. 89 (1965)]

2)   Compare—Nonresidents

Laws that prohibit nonresidents from voting are generally valid as long as they have a rational basis. [*See* Holt Civic Club v. City of Tuscaloosa, 439 U.S. 60 (1978)—upholding denial of right to vote in city elections to persons outside of city limits, but within the city's police and licensing jurisdiction]

b.   Property Ownership

Conditioning the right to vote, to be a candidate, or to hold office on property ownership is usually invalid under the Equal Protection Clause, since property ownership is not necessary to any compelling governmental interest related to voting. [*See, e.g.,* Kramer v. Union Free School District, 395 U.S. 621 (1969)—requirement of owning property or having children in schools to vote in school board elections struck] However, certain special purpose elections (*e.g.,* water storage district elections) can be based on property ownership. (*See* below.)

c.   Poll Taxes

Poll taxes are prohibited under the Twenty-Fourth Amendment, and the Supreme Court has held that they also violate equal protection because wealth is not related to the government's interest in having voters vote intelligently. [Harper v. Virginia Board of Elections, 383 U.S. 663 (1966)]

d.   Primary Elections

1)   State Regulation of Party Primaries

States may exercise some control over primary elections, but such regulation is

subject to restrictions under the First Amendment (freedom of political association) and the Fourteenth Amendment (Equal Protection Clause). Thus, to prevent interparty "raiding," the Supreme Court has held that states can require a person to have been registered with a party for a reasonable time before that party's primary election in order to be eligible to vote in the primary. [Rosario v. Rockefeller, 410 U.S. 752 (1973)—11 months' registration upheld; Kusper v. Pontikes, 414 U.S. 51 (1973)—23 months not upheld] However, if a political party wishes to open its primary elections to anyone, whether or not registered with the party, the state cannot prohibit this because the state interest here is overridden by the right of political association. [Tashjian v. Republican Party of Connecticut, 479 U.S. 208 (1986)]

2) States May Subsidize Primaries of Major Parties
States may subsidize the primaries of major parties without similarly defraying the costs of mechanisms through which minor parties qualify candidates for the general election [American Party of Texas v. White, 415 U.S. 767 (1974)— upholding law requiring new or small parties to proceed by petition or convention at their own expense rather than by publicly funded primary], as long as new or small parties are given some effective way to qualify for the general election [Williams v. Rhodes, 393 U.S. 23 (1968)—unduly burdensome petition requirements for new or small parties struck down as not justified].

2. Dilution of Right to Vote

a. One Person, One Vote Principle
The Equal Protection Clause of the Fourteenth Amendment has been interpreted to prohibit state dilution of the right to vote, and Article I has been interpreted to place the same type of restriction on the federal government.

1) Establishing Voting Districts
Whenever a governmental body establishes voting districts for the election of representatives, the number of persons in each district may not vary significantly. This is commonly referred to as the one person, one vote principle.

a) Congressional Elections—Almost Exactly Equal
States establish the districts for congressional elections. However, the Supreme Court requires *almost exact mathematical equality* between the *congressional* districts within a state; thus, deviations of even a few percentage points between the congressional districts within a state may result in the invalidation of the congressional district plan.

(1) Compare—Apportionment Among the States
Congress apportions representatives among the states "according to their respective number." [Art. I, §2] Congress's good faith choice of method in so apportioning the representatives commands far more deference than state districting decisions and is *not* subject to the same precise mathematical standard as state plans. [United States Department of Commerce v. Montana, 503 U.S. 442 (1992)]

b) **State and Local Elections—Variance Not Unjustifiably Large**
The variance in the number of persons included in districts for the purpose of electing representatives to a ***state or local governmental body*** must not be unjustifiably large, but the districts need not be within a few percentage points of each other: If a state can show that the deviation from mathematical equality between districts is reasonable and tailored to promote a legitimate state interest, the law establishing the districts may be upheld. [Mahan v. Howell, 410 U.S. 315 (1973)—16% variance in district populations was upheld in light of state's interest in preserving political subdivisions, although 30% variance would be excessive]

c) **Scope**
The one person, one vote principle applies to almost every election where a person is being elected to perform normal governmental functions. [Hadley v. Junior College District, 397 U.S. 50 (1970)—trustees for junior college district] However, there are a few exceptions to note:

(1) **Exception—Appointed Officials and Officials Elected "At Large"**
The apportionment requirement is inapplicable to appointed officials. Neither is it applicable in at-large systems of election, because in such a system there are no electoral districts to violate the one person, one vote principle. However, if an at-large voting system were established or maintained for the purpose of suppressing the voting power of minority race voters, it would be unconstitutional.

(2) **Exception—Special Purpose Government Units (Water Storage Districts)**
The government can limit the class of persons who are allowed to vote in an election of persons to serve on a special purpose government unit ***if*** the government unit has a special impact on the class of enfranchised voters. To date, the Supreme Court has found only "water storage districts" to be so specialized that their governing boards are not subject to the one person, one vote principle. [Salyer Land Co. v. Tulane Water District, 410 U.S. 719 (1973); Ball v. James, 451 U.S. 355 (1981)—apportionment rules do not apply to water district even if the district is major supplier of electricity in the state]

2) **Standardless Recount**
Counting uncounted ballots in a presidential election without standards to guide ballot examiners in determining the intent of the voter violates the Fourteenth Amendment Equal Protection Clause. [Bush v. Gore, 531 U.S. 98 (2000)]

b. **Gerrymandering**

1) **Racial Gerrymandering**
As indicated above, race (and presumably other suspect classifications) cannot be the predominant factor in drawing the boundaries of a voting district unless the district plan can pass muster under strict scrutiny. [*See* Miller v. Johnson, XVIII.D.1.c., *supra*] Moreover, a district's bizarre shape can be used to show that

race was the predominant factor in drawing the district's boundaries [*see* Shaw v. Reno, XVIII.C.1.a., *supra*], although a bizarre shape is not necessary to such a finding. Note that the person challenging the reapportionment has the burden of proving the race-based motive. [Shaw v. Hunt, 517 U.S. 899 (1996)]

2) Political Gerrymandering

The Court has **never** ruled that a legislative redistricting map should be overturned on the basis of political gerrymandering, and a number of Justices have suggested that political gerrymandering is a nonjusticiable issue. [Vieth v. Jubelirer, 541 U.S. 267 (2004); *and see* League of United Latin American Citizens v. Perry, 548 U.S. 399 (2006)—refusing to find a constitutional violation when there was mid-decade redistricting for partisan political reasons]

c. Multi-Member Districts

A state is generally free to have some multi-member districts together with some single-member districts, as long as the number of members representing a district is proportional to its population. However, single-member or multi-member districts will be held to violate equal protection (even though they meet the one person, one vote principle) if the district lines were drawn on the basis of unconstitutional criteria, such as to suppress the voting power of racial minorities or an identifiable political group.

3. Candidates and Campaigns

a. Candidate Qualifications

1) Fee Must Not Preclude Indigents as Candidates

States may not charge candidates a fee that results in making it impossible for indigents to run for office. An unreasonably high filing fee (which was not tailored to promote a substantial or overriding state interest) might be held totally invalid so that no candidate would have to pay the fee. A reasonable, valid fee would have to be waived for an indigent candidate who could not pay the fee.

2) Restrictions on Ability of Person to Be a Candidate

Restrictions on the ability of persons to be candidates must be examined to see if they violate either the First Amendment right of political association or the Fourteenth Amendment Equal Protection Clause. Such regulations are judged on a sliding scale of scrutiny. (*See* XXI.B., *infra*.)

Example: The Court invalidated a March deadline for filing a nominating petition for independent candidates for a November election where the state allowed the major political parties to name their candidates later in the year. [Anderson v. Celebrezze, 460 U.S. 780 (1983)]

Note: A state may require candidates to show reasonable support (signatures or votes) to qualify to have their names placed on the ballot. [Munro v. Socialist Workers Party, 479 U.S. 189 (1986)—upholding requirement of receipt of at least 1% of the votes cast in the primary election]

3) Required Resignation of Office Is Permissible

A state may require state officials to resign their office if they enter an election for another government office. [Clements v. Fashing, 457 U.S. 957 (1982)]

b. **Campaign Funding, Contributions, and Expenditures**
Government *may* allocate more public funds to the two "major" parties than to "minor" parties for political campaigns, and may withhold public funding from candidates who do not accept reciprocal limits on their total campaign expenses; but such expenses cannot otherwise be limited, unlike campaign contributions to political candidates, which may be limited if government chooses. (XXI.B., *infra*.)

4. **Extraordinary Majorities—Referendum Elections**
The government may require a supermajority vote for voter referendums, even though such a requirement might give a minority disproportionate power. [Gordon v. Lance, 403 U.S. 1 (1971)—upholding 60% requirement for referendum approval; Town of Lockport v. Citizens for Community Action, 430 U.S. 259 (1977)—upholding requirement that new county charter be approved by separate majorities of city and noncity voters]

5. **Replacement of Incumbent Legislators**
A state may validly give to a political party the right to name an interim appointee to the legislature to fill out the unexpired term of a legislator from that political party who left office. No voter is denied equal protection by this system. [Rodriguez v. Popular Democratic Party, 457 U.S. 1 (1982)]

D. RIGHT TO TRAVEL

1. **Interstate Travel**

   a. **Nature of the Right**
   Individuals have a fundamental right to travel from state to state, which encompasses the right: (i) to leave and enter another state, and (ii) to be treated equally if they become permanent residents of that state. [Saenz v. Roe, VII.C.3., *supra*—striking California law that limited welfare benefits for new residents to what they would have received in their prior state of residence]

   b. **Standard of Review**
   When a state uses a durational residency requirement (a waiting period) for dispensing benefits, that requirement normally should be subject to the "strict scrutiny" test. This means that the government must show that the waiting period requirement is tailored to promote a compelling or overriding interest. However, in some right to travel cases, the Court has not been clear as to whether it is using this strict scrutiny, compelling interest standard of review. The important point to note for the bar exam is that state residency requirements should not be upheld merely because they have some theoretical rational relationship to an arguably legitimate end of government.

      1) **Examples**
      Because of the ad hoc nature of these rulings, we will list four examples of Supreme Court decisions in this area:

         a) A one-year waiting period before a person may receive subsistence welfare payments is *invalid*. Similarly, a law providing that persons residing in the state for less than a year may receive welfare benefits no greater than those paid in the state of prior residence is also invalid. [Saenz v. Roe, *supra*]

b) A one-year waiting period for state subsidized medical care is *invalid*.

c) A one-year waiting period to get a divorce is *valid*.

d) A state may require a voter to register to vote in a party primary 10 months before the primary election (to avoid interparty "raiding"). However, a 23-month registration period would be *invalid*.

c. **Distinctions Between Old and New Residents**

Some state laws that have an adverse impact on new residents do not involve a waiting period. For example, a state may attempt to dispense state benefits on the basis of the length of time a person has resided in the state. A state law that distinguishes between residents of the state on the sole basis of their length of residency will serve no legitimate state interest. This type of law should be *stricken* under the rational basis test because it has *no rational relationship* to any legitimate state interest.

Examples: 1) A state statute that dispensed differing amounts of state money to residents of the state based on each resident's length of residence was held invalid.

2) A state statute that grants an annual property tax exemption to a veteran of military service only if he resided in the state before a specific date (May 1976) is invalid.

3) A state law that grants a hiring preference (for civil service employment) to a veteran only if he was a resident of the state prior to joining the armed services is invalid.

2. **International Travel**

The Supreme Court has not yet declared that the right to international travel is fundamental, although the right appears to be *protected from arbitrary federal interference* by the Due Process Clause of the Fifth Amendment. The Court has held that this right is not violated when the federal government refuses to pay Social Security benefits to persons who leave the country. The test here is "mere rationality, not strict scrutiny." [Califano v. Aznavorian, 439 U.S. 170 (1978)] Congress may give the executive branch the power to revoke the passport of a person whose conduct in another country presents a danger to United States foreign policy. [Haig v. Agee, 453 U.S. 280 (1981)] The Treasury Department, with congressional authorization, could restrict travel to and from Cuba without violating the Fifth Amendment. [Regan v. Wald, 468 U.S. 222 (1984)]

E. **RIGHT TO REFUSE MEDICAL TREATMENT**

The Supreme Court had held that the right to refuse medical treatment is a part of an individual's "liberty" that is protected by the Fifth and Fourteenth Amendment Due Process Clauses. However, the Supreme Court has not ruled that this aspect of liberty is a "fundamental right" and *has not* explained which standard of review should be used. Nevertheless, the Court has ruled on the validity of several types of legislation.

1. **Vaccination**

An individual can be made to submit to vaccination against contagious diseases because of the governmental and societal interest in preventing the spread of disease. [Jacobsen v. Massachusetts, 197 U.S. 11 (1905)]

2. **Refusal of Medical Treatment**
   The Supreme Court has assumed (without deciding) that a mentally competent adult has the right to refuse lifesaving medical treatment (including lifesaving nutrition). [Cruzan v. Director, Missouri Department of Health, 497 U.S. 261 (1990)]

   a. **Compare—No Right to Assisted Suicide**
      There is no general right to commit suicide; thus, a state may ban persons from giving individuals assistance in committing suicide. [Washington v. Glucksberg, 521 U.S. 702 (1997)] It is not irrational to permit competent persons to refuse life-sustaining treatment but prohibit physicians to assist in suicide because there is a logical, rational, and well-established distinction between letting someone die and making someone die. [Vacco v. Quill, 521 U.S. 793 (1997)]

   b. **Compare—Criminal Defendants**
      Under the Due Process Clause, the government may *involuntarily* administer antipsychotic drugs to a mentally ill defendant facing serious criminal charges in order to make him competent to stand trial if: (i) the treatment is medically appropriate, (ii) the treatment is substantially unlikely to cause side effects that may undermine the fairness of the trial, and (iii) considering less-intrusive alternatives, the treatment is necessary to further important governmental trial-related interests. [Sell v. United States, 539 U.S. 166 (2003)]

PART FIVE: FIRST AMENDMENT FREEDOMS

The First Amendment prohibits Congress from establishing a religion or interfering with the exercise of religion, abridging the freedom of speech or the press, or interfering with the right of the people to assemble. These prohibitions have been made applicable to the states through the Fourteenth Amendment. The freedoms, however, are not absolute, and exam questions often focus on their boundaries. The following material will outline the scope of each freedom.

XX. FREEDOM OF SPEECH AND ASSEMBLY

A. **GENERAL PRINCIPLES**
   The freedoms of speech and assembly protect the free flow of ideas, a most important function in a democratic society. Thus, whenever the government seeks to regulate these freedoms, the Court will weigh the importance of these rights against the interests or policies sought to be served by the regulation. When analyzing regulations of speech and press, keep the following guidelines in mind:

1. **Government Speech**
   The Free Speech Clause restricts government *regulation of private speech*; it does not require the government to aid private speech nor restrict the government from expressing its views. The government generally is free to voice its opinions and to fund private speech that furthers its views while refusing to fund other private speech, absent some other constitutional

limitation, such as the Establishment Clause or Equal Protection Clause. Because government speech does not implicate the First Amendment, it is not subject to the various levels of scrutiny that apply to government regulation of private speech (*see infra*). [Pleasant Grove City, Utah v. Summum, 129 S. Ct. 1125 (2009)] Generally, government speech and government funding of speech will be upheld if it is ***rationally related to a legitimate state interest.***

Examples: 1) The government may choose to aid a union representing government employees by providing for payroll deductions of general union dues while refusing to allow payroll deductions that will be used by unions to fund political activities. The decision not to collect funds for political activities is rationally related to a legitimate government interest (*i.e.,* avoiding the appearance of favoritism), and thus the refusal to collect such funds is constitutional. [Ysursa v. Pocatello, 129 S. Ct. 1093 (2009)]

2) The government may fund family planning services but except from funding services that provide abortion information. [Rust v. Sullivan, 500 U.S. 173 (1991)]

3) The government may refuse to fund artists whose work it finds offensive. [National Endowment for the Arts v. Finley, 524 U.S. 569 (1998)]

a. Public Monuments

A city's placement of a ***permanent*** monument in a public park is government speech and thus is not subject to Free Speech Clause scrutiny. This is true even if the monument is privately donated. By displaying the monument, the government is disseminating a message, and the message is not necessarily the message of the donor(s). As a corollary, the government cannot be forced to display a permanent monument with a message with which the government disagrees, and the government's refusal to display a proffered monument likewise is not subject to Free Speech Clause scrutiny.

Example: A city with a Ten Commandments monument in its park was not required to display a religious monument of another religion (the "Seven Aphorisms" of the Summum faith). The Ten Commandments monument, although privately donated, was deemed government speech. When the government is the speaker, it may engage in content-based choices. [Pleasant Grove City, Utah v. Summum, *supra*] (*Note:* While an Establishment Clause issue was not raised in *Summum,* a concurring opinion suggested that the Ten Commandments monument did not violate the Establishment Clause because it was one of 15 monuments in the park recognizing the historical roots and morals of the community. [*And see* Van Orden v. Perry, XXII.D.2.a.2), *infra*])

b. Compare—Government Funding of Private Messages

In contrast to government funding of speech for the purpose of promoting its own policies (such as the family planning services involved in *Rust v. Sullivan, supra*), when the government chooses to fund private messages, it generally must do so on a viewpoint neutral basis. [*See* Rosenberger v. Rector and Visitors of the University of Virginia, 515 U.S. 819 (1995)—state university exclusion of religious magazine from program financially supporting many other types of student publications violates the First Amendment]

1) Exception—Funding of the Arts

From a financial standpoint, the government cannot fund all artists, and choosing

among those it will fund and those it will not inevitably must be based on the content of the art. [National Endowment for the Arts v. Finley, *supra*]

2. Content vs. Conduct

A regulation seeking to forbid communication of specific ideas (*i.e.,* a ***content*** regulation) is less likely to be upheld than a regulation of the ***conduct*** incidental to speech.

a. Content

It is presumptively unconstitutional for the government to place burdens on speech because of its content. To justify such content-based regulation of speech, the government must show that the regulation (or tax) is ***necessary*** to serve a ***compelling*** state interest and is narrowly drawn to achieve that end. [Simon & Schuster, Inc. v. Members of the New York State Crime Victims Board, 502 U.S. 105 (1991)—striking a law requiring that proceeds to criminals from books and other productions describing their crimes be placed in escrow for five years to pay claims of victims of the crimes]

1) Exception—Unprotected Categories of Speech

The Supreme Court has previously determined that certain categories of speech (*e.g.,* obscenity, defamation, and "fighting words"; *see* C., *infra*) generally are proscribable despite the First Amendment. Even in these cases, however, the Court is less likely to uphold a prior restraint (*i.e.,* a regulation prohibiting speech before it occurs) than a punishment for speech that has already occurred.

2) Content-Neutral Speech Regulations

While content-based regulation of speech is subject to strict scrutiny, content-neutral speech regulations generally are subject to ***intermediate scrutiny***—they will be upheld if the government can show that: (i) they advance ***important*** interests unrelated to the suppression of speech, and (ii) they ***do not burden substantially more speech than necessary*** to further those interests. [Turner Broadcasting System, Inc. v. FCC, 512 U.S. 622 (1994)]

b. Conduct

The Court has allowed the government more leeway in regulating the conduct related to speech, allowing it to adopt content-neutral, ***time, place,*** and ***manner*** regulations. Regulations involving public forums (*i.e.,* forums historically linked with the exercise of First Amendment freedoms) must be ***narrowly tailored*** to achieve an ***important*** government interest (*e.g.,* a prohibition against holding a demonstration in a hospital zone). Regulations involving nonpublic forums must have a reasonable relationship to a legitimate regulatory purpose (*e.g.,* a law prohibiting billboards for purposes of traffic safety).

3. Reasonableness of Regulation

a. Overbroad Regulation Invalid

Since the purpose of the freedoms of speech and assembly is to encourage the free flow of ideas, a regulation will not be upheld if it is overbroad (*i.e.,* prohibits ***substantially*** more speech than is necessary). If a regulation of speech or speech-related conduct punishes a ***substantial amount of protected speech,*** judged in relation to the regulation's plainly legitimate sweep, the regulation is ***facially invalid*** (*i.e.,* it may not be enforced against anyone—not even a person engaging in activity that is not constitutionally protected) unless a court has limited construction of the regulation so as to remove

the threat to constitutionally protected expression. [Virginia v. Hicks, 539 U.S. 113 (2003)] If a regulation is not substantially overbroad, it can be enforced against persons engaging in activities that are not constitutionally protected.

Examples: 1) The Supreme Court struck down as overbroad an ordinance that prohibited speech that *"in any manner"* interrupts a police officer in the performance of her duties. [Houston v. Hill, 482 U.S. 451 (1987)]

2) An airport authority rule that bans *"all* First Amendment activities" within the "central terminal area" is invalid as being substantially overbroad. [Board of Airport Commissioners v. Jews for Jesus, 482 U.S. 569 (1987)]

3) A law banning *all* door-to-door solicitations will be struck as being overbroad [Martin v. City of Struthers, 319 U.S. 141 (1943)], but a law requiring solicitors to obtain a homeowner's consent to solicit is valid [Breard v. City of Alexandria, 341 U.S. 622 (1951)].

4) An ordinance that prohibited *all* canvassers from going onto private residential property to promote *any* cause without first obtaining a permit was overbroad. While the government may have an interest in preventing fraud from door-to-door solicitation, the permit requirement here went beyond cases where fraud was likely to occur, and applied to religious proselytization, advocacy of political speech, and enlisting support for unpopular causes. [Watchtower Bible and Tract Society of New York, Inc. v. Village of Stratton, 536 U.S. 150 (2002)]

5) A city ordinance that prohibits homeowners from displaying *any sign* on their property except "residence identification" or "for sale" signs is invalid because the ordinance bans virtually all residential signs. [Ladue v. Gilleo, 512 U.S. 43 (1994)]

b.   Void for Vagueness Doctrine

If a criminal law or regulation fails to give persons reasonable notice of what is prohibited, it may violate the Due Process Clause. This principle is applied somewhat strictly when First Amendment activity is involved in order to avoid the chilling effect a vague law might have on speech (*i.e.*, if it is unclear what speech is regulated, people might refrain from speech that is permissible for fear that they will be violating the law). Vagueness issues most often arise in relation to content regulations, but the same principles would apply to time, place, and manner restrictions.

Examples: 1) A municipal ordinance that prohibited vagrants was held void for vagueness when it defined vagrants as "rogues and vagabonds . . . lewd, wanton, and lascivious persons . . . persons wandering or straying around from place to place without any lawful purpose or object . . . ." [Papachristou v. City of Jacksonville, 405 U.S. 156 (1972)]

2) A statute that prohibits attorneys representing clients in a pending case from making statements that would have a substantial likelihood of prejudicing a trial, but that also allows attorneys to make public statements regarding the "general nature of the defense" they will present at trial, is void for vagueness, because it does not give fair notice of the

types of trial-related statements that are punishable. [Gentile v. State Bar, 501 U.S. 1030 (1991)]

1) Burden on Challenger

The person challenging the validity of the regulation has the burden of showing substantial overbreadth. [Virginia v. Hicks, *supra*]

2) Funding Speech Activity

Greater imprecision is allowed when the government acts as a patron in funding speech activity than when enacting criminal statutes or regulatory schemes, because speakers are less likely to steer clear of forbidden areas when only a subsidy is at stake. [National Endowment for the Arts v. Finley, 1., *supra*— requirement that NEA consider standards of "decency" and "respect for values of American people" is not invalid on its face]

c. Cannot Give Officials Unfettered Discretion

A regulation cannot give officials broad discretion over speech issues; there must be *defined standards* for applying the law. The fear, of course, is that the officials will use their discretionary power to prohibit dissemination of ideas that they do not agree with. This issue usually arises under licensing schemes established to regulate the time, place, and manner of speech. To be valid, such licensing schemes must be related to an important government interest, contain procedural safeguards (*see* D.2., *infra*), and not grant officials unbridled discretion.

Example: County required persons desiring to hold a parade, march, or rally to first obtain a permit from the county administrator. The administrator was empowered to charge up to $1,000 for the permit, but could adjust the fee to meet the necessary expenses of administration and police protection. This scheme is invalid because it gives the administrator unbridled discretion despite the $1,000 limit. It also is unconstitutional because it is a content-based restriction (the administrator theoretically would adjust the costs based on the popularity of the subject at issue— an unpopular subject would require greater police protection). [Forsyth County, Georgia v. Nationalist Movement, 505 U.S. 123 (1992)]

1) Unlimited Discretion—Void on Face

If a statute gives licensing officials unbridled discretion, it is *void on its face*, and speakers need not even apply for a permit. They may exercise their First Amendment rights even if they could have been denied a permit under a valid law, and they may not be punished for violating the licensing statute. [Lovell v. City of Griffin, 303 U.S. 444 (1938)]

Examples: 1) An ordinance vesting officials with the power to grant or deny parade permits based on their judgment as to the effect of the parade on community "welfare" or "morals" is unconstitutional on its face. [Shuttlesworth v. Birmingham, 394 U.S. 147 (1969)] Similarly, ordinances giving officials broad discretion as to who may place magazine racks on public property or who may obtain licenses to solicit door to door are invalid. [City of Lakewood v. Plain Dealer Publishing Co., 486 U.S. 750 (1988); Lovell v. City of Griffin, *supra*]

2) A statute prohibiting excessively loud sound trucks is valid [Kovacs v. Cooper, 336 U.S. 77 (1949)], but an ordinance giving officials discretion as to who may use sound trucks is invalid [Saia v. New York, 334 U.S. 558 (1948)].

2) Statutes Valid on Face

If the licensing statute is valid on its face because it contains adequate standards, a speaker may not ignore the statute, but must seek a permit. If he is denied a permit, even if he believes the denial was incorrect, he must then seek reasonably available administrative or judicial relief. Failure to do so precludes later assertion that his actions were protected by the First Amendment. [Poulos v. New Hampshire, 345 U.S. 395 (1953)]

4. Scope of Speech

a. Includes Freedom Not to Speak

The freedom of speech includes not only the right to speak, but also the right to refrain from speaking or endorsing beliefs with which one does not agree—the government may not compel an individual personally to express a message with which he disagrees.

Examples: 1) A state *cannot force school children to salute* or say a pledge to the flag. [West Virginia State Board of Education v. Barnette, 319 U.S. 624 (1943)]

2) A motorist *could not be punished* for blocking out the portion of his automobile license plate bearing the motto "Live Free or Die"; as long as he left the license plate in a condition that served its auto identification purpose, he did not have to display a slogan endorsed by the state. [Wooley v. Maynard, 430 U.S. 705 (1977)]

3) A state may not require private parade organizers to include in their parade groups with messages with which the organizers disagree. [Hurley v. Irish-American Gay, Lesbian & Bisexual Group of Boston, 515 U.S. 557 (1995)]

1) Mandatory Financial Support

Although the government may not compel a person to express a message, the government may tax people and use the revenue to express a message with which people disagree.

a) Government Speech

The Court has held that compelled support of government speech does *not* raise First Amendment concerns. [Johanns v. Livestock Marketing Association, 544 U.S. 550 (2005)—beef producers can be required to pay an assessment to support generic advertising of beef approved by a semi-governmental producers' board and ultimately by the Secretary of Agriculture—even if they think generic advertising is a waste of money—because the advertisements are governmental speech]

b) **Compare—Private Speech**

On the other hand, it appears that people **cannot** be compelled to subsidize **private** messages with which they disagree.

Examples: The Court has held that while teachers may be forced to pay union dues to a private union representing a majority of their fellow teachers, and attorneys may be forced to join a mandatory bar association, people may not be forced to pay sums that will be used to support political views that, or candidates whom, they do not endorse. [Abood v. Detroit Board of Education, 431 U.S. 209 (1977); Keller v. State Bar of California, 496 U.S. 1 (1990)]

(1) **Exception—University Activity Fees**

The government can require public university students to pay a student activity fee even if the fee is used to support political and ideological speech by student groups whose beliefs are offensive to the student, as long as the program is viewpoint neutral (*see* B.2.a., *infra*). [Board of Regents v. Southworth, 529 U.S. 217 (2000)]

2) **State Can Require Shopping Center to Permit Persons to Exercise Speech Rights**

Note that the freedom not to speak does not prohibit a state's requiring a large shopping center (that is open to the public) to permit persons to exercise their speech rights on shopping center property—at least as long as the particular message is not dictated by the state and is not likely to be identified with the owner of the shopping center. [Pruneyard Shopping Center v. Robins, 447 U.S. 74 (1980)]

b. **Includes Symbolic Conduct**

Speech includes not only verbal communication, but also conduct that is undertaken to communicate an idea. Of course, not all regulation of symbolic conduct is prohibited. The Court will uphold a conduct regulation if: (i) the regulation is within the constitutional power of the government; (ii) it furthers an important governmental interest; (iii) the governmental interest is **unrelated to suppression of speech**; and (iv) the incidental burden on speech is no greater than necessary. [United States v. O'Brien, 391 U.S. 367 (1968)—upholding a prohibition against burning draft cards to protect the government's important interest in facilitating the smooth functioning of the draft system] Note, however, that a regulation is **not** invalid simply because there is some imaginable alternative that might be less burdensome on speech. [Rumsfeld v. Forum for Academic and Institutional Rights, 547 U.S. 47 (2006)—statute requiring schools of higher education to grant the military access to recruit on campus is not invalid merely because the military could take out ads in newspapers, on television, etc.]

Example: A state may prohibit public nudity, even as applied to nude dancing at bars and places of adult entertainment. Although nude dancing is marginally within the protections of the First Amendment—because it involves the communication of an erotic message—the government has a "substantial" interest in combating crime and other "secondary effects" caused by the presence of adult entertainment establishments that is unrelated to the suppression of free expression. [Barnes v. Glen

Theatre, Inc., 501 U.S. 560 (1991); City of Erie v. Pap's A.M., 529 U.S. 277 (2000)—city council made findings regarding secondary effects]

Compare: 1) A prohibition against students wearing armbands to protest the war in Vietnam was struck because it had no regulatory interest other than prohibiting the communicative impact of the conduct. [Tinker v. Des Moines Independent Community School District, 393 U.S. 503 (1969)]

2) A prohibition against mutilating a United States flag (except in cases of proper disposal of a soiled flag) was held invalid as an attempt to restrain speech; the Court found that no imminent breach of the peace was likely to result, and the government has no other interest in prohibiting such burnings. [United States v. Eichman, 496 U.S. 310 (1990)]

c.   **Excludes Freedom to Bar Military Recruitment**
Requiring schools of higher education to allow military recruiters to recruit on campus or risk losing federal funding does not implicate free speech rights. This is so even if the schools disagree with the military's ban against homosexuals. School recruitment receptions are not inherently expressive from the schools' standpoint; they are merely a way to help students obtain jobs. Schools are not being asked to say or refrain from saying anything, and neither are they being asked to associate with the military in any significant way. Moreover, there is little chance that a person would attribute the military's positions to the schools. Therefore, there is no First Amendment violation. [Rumsfeld v. Forum for Academic and Institutional Rights, *supra*]

5.   **Prison Speech**
A regulation concerning the activities of prison inmates, including *any* First Amendment speech activities, is governed by a different standard in order to facilitate prison order: The regulation will be upheld if it is *reasonably related to legitimate penological interests.* [Shaw v. Murphy, 532 U.S. 223 (2001)] Thus, a restriction on *incoming* mail will be upheld if it is rational; a restriction on *outgoing* mail must be narrowly tailored because there is less of a penological interest involved. [*See* Thornburgh v. Abbott, 490 U.S. 401 (1989)]

B.   **TIME, PLACE, AND MANNER RESTRICTIONS—REGULATION OF CONDUCT**
All speech is conveyed through physical action (*e.g.,* talking, writing, distributing pamphlets, etc.), and while the freedom of belief is absolute, the freedom to convey beliefs cannot be. The extent to which government may regulate speech-related conduct depends on whether the forum involved is a public forum, a designated public forum, a limited public forum, or a nonpublic forum.

1.   **Public Forums and Designated Public Forums**
Public property that has historically been open to speech-related activities (*e.g.,* **streets, sidewalks,** and **public parks**) is called a public forum. Public property that has not historically been open to speech-related activities, but which the government has thrown open for such activities on a permanent or temporary basis, by practice or policy (*e.g.,* school rooms that are open for after-school use by social, civic, or recreation groups), is called a designated public forum. The government may regulate speech in public forums and designated public forums with reasonable time, place, and manner regulations.

a. **Test**

To be valid, government regulations of speech and assembly in public forums and designated public forums must:

(i) Be *content neutral* (*i.e.,* subject matter neutral and viewpoint neutral);

(ii) Be *narrowly tailored* to serve an *important* government interest; and

(iii) Leave open *alternative channels* of communication.

Remember: Even if a regulation meets the above conditions, it might still be struck down on other grounds (*e.g.,* overbreadth, vagueness, unfettered discretion; *see* A.3., *supra*).

1) **Content Neutral**

The regulation cannot be based on the content of the speech, absent substantial justification (*see* C., *infra*).

Examples: 1) The Court held invalid an ordinance allowing peaceful *labor* picketing near schools, but prohibiting all other picketing, since it was a content-based restriction. [Chicago Police Department v. Mosely, 408 U.S. 92 (1972)]

2) A law may not forbid only those signs within 500 feet of a foreign embassy that are critical of the foreign government. [Boos v. Barry, 485 U.S. 312 (1988)]

2) **Narrowly Tailored**

The regulation must be narrowly tailored (*i.e.,* it may not burden *substantially* more speech than is necessary to further the significant government interest). However, the regulation need not be the least restrictive means of accomplishing the goal.

Example: A law requiring persons performing at a city's theater to use the city's sound equipment is narrowly tailored to the city's interest in preventing excessive noise. [Ward v. Rock Against Racism, 491 U.S. 781 (1989)]

Compare: An ordinance that prohibited *all* canvassers from going onto private residential property to promote *any* cause without first obtaining a permit was not narrowly tailored to the interest of preventing fraud because it included too much speech that was not likely to give rise to fraud (*e.g.,* religious proselytization, advocacy of political speech, and enlisting support for unpopular causes). [Watchtower Bible and Tract Society of New York, Inc. v. Village of Stratton, A.3.a., *supra*]

Note: A regulation that is not narrowly tailored might also fail on overbreadth grounds. (*See* A.3.a., *supra*.)

3) Important Interest

The regulation must further an important government interest. Such interests include: traffic safety, orderly crowd movement, personal privacy, noise control, litter control, aesthetics, etc.

Example: The Court upheld the constitutionality of a state law prohibiting persons within 100 feet of a health care facility from approaching within eight feet of those seeking access to the health care facility for purposes of oral protest, education, or counseling. The Court found that the law was a content-neutral regulation of speech and a reasonable time, place, and manner restriction that served the important interest of preserving access to health care facilities. [Hill v. Colorado, 530 U.S. 703 (2000)—statute upheld against challenge by petitioners who wished to "counsel" women as they enter abortion clinics]

4) Alternative Channels Open

The law must leave open alternative channels of communication; *i.e.,* other reasonable means for communicating the idea must be available.

b. Examples—Residential Areas

1) Targeted Picketing

The Supreme Court upheld a statute that prevented focused residential picketing (*i.e.,* picketing in front of a single residence). The street/sidewalk involved was a public forum, but the ordinance passed the three-part test: (i) it was content neutral because it regulated the location and manner of picketing rather than its message; (ii) it was narrowly tailored to the important interest of protecting a homeowner's privacy (because it applied only to focused picketing); and (iii) alternative means of communications were available because the protesters could march *through* the neighborhood in protest. [Frisby v. Schultz, 487 U.S. 474 (1988)]

2) Charitable Solicitations

Charitable solicitations for funds in residential areas are within the protection of the First Amendment. However, they are subject to reasonable regulation.

Example: A state cannot require professional fundraisers (before making an appeal for funds) to disclose to potential donors the percentage of contributions collected over the previous year that were actually turned over to the charity. The disclosure is not necessary to promote the state interest of protecting the public from fraud. However, the state can require a fundraiser to disclose her professional status. [Riley v. National Federation of the Blind of North Carolina, 487 U.S. 781 (1988)] In *Riley,* the Court also invalidated a restriction on the fees that professional fundraisers could charge a charity, because the particular statute was not narrowly tailored to protect either the public or the charities.

Compare: States have a significant interest in preventing fraudulent charitable solicitations. This interest justifies charging a telemarketing firm

with fraud for telling persons solicited that the firm pays "a significant amount of each donation" to the charity, when in fact the firm keeps 85% of gross receipts. [Illinois *ex rel.* Madigan v. Telemarketing Associates, Inc., 538 U.S. 600 (2003)]

3) Permits
A state may not require persons to obtain permits in order to canvass door-to-door for noncommercial or nonfundraising purposes. [Watchtower Bible and Tract Society of New York, Inc., v. Village of Stratton, *supra*]

c. Example—Designated Public Forum
Schools generally are not public forums. However, if a public school or university allows private organizations and members of the public to use school property for meetings when school programs or classes are not in session, the property is a designated public forum for that time, and the school cannot deny a religious organization permission to use the property for meetings merely because religious topics will be discussed. Such a restriction would be content discrimination. [Widmar v. Vincent, 454 U.S. 263 (1981); Lamb's Chapel v. Center Moriches Union Free School District, 508 U.S. 384 (1993)]

d. Injunctions
Injunctions that restrict First Amendment activity in public forums are treated differently from generally applicable ordinances because injunctions present a greater risk of censorship and discriminatory application. The test to be used to determine whether an injunction that restricts speech or protest is constitutional depends on whether the injunction is content neutral.

1) Content Based—Necessary to a Compelling Interest
If the injunction is content based, it will be upheld only if it is necessary to achieve a compelling government interest.

2) Content Neutral—Burdens No More Speech than Necessary
If the injunction is content neutral, it will be upheld only if it burdens no more speech than is necessary to achieve an *important* government purpose.

Example: Parts of an injunction establishing a 36-foot buffer zone between protesters and abortion clinic entrances were upheld. [Madsen v. Women's Health Center, 512 U.S. 753 (1994)]

Compare: An injunction providing for a "floating buffer zone" of 15 feet between protesters and persons entering and leaving an abortion clinic was held to violate the First Amendment. The floating zone barred all verbal and written communication from a normal conversational distance on public sidewalks, and thus burdened more speech than necessary to ensure ingress and egress from the clinic. [Schenk v. Pro-Choice Network of Western New York, 519 U.S. 357 (1997)]

2. Limited Public Forums and Nonpublic Forums
Other than streets, sidewalks, parks, and designated public forums, most public property is

considered to be a limited public forum or a nonpublic forum. The government can regulate speech in such a forum to *reserve the forum for its intended use*. Regulations will be upheld if they are:

(i) *Viewpoint neutral*; and

(ii) *Reasonably related to a legitimate government purpose*.

a. Viewpoint Neutral

Regulations on speech in nonpublic forums need not be content neutral; *i.e.,* the government may allow speech regarding some subjects but not others. However, such regulations must be *viewpoint* neutral; *i.e.,* if the government allows an issue to be presented in a nonpublic forum, it may not limit the presentation to only one view.

Example: If a high school newspaper is a nonpublic forum, a school board could decide to prohibit articles in the paper regarding nuclear power. However, it may not allow an article in favor of nuclear power and prohibit an article against nuclear power.

Similarly, the government may discriminate based on the identity of the speaker in nonpublic forums (*e.g.,* a school board might limit speakers to licensed teachers).

b. Reasonableness

Regulation of speech and assembly in nonpublic forums need only be rationally related to a legitimate governmental objective.

Example: A city bus is not a public forum. The city, therefore, may constitutionally sell space for signs on the public buses for commercial and public service advertising while refusing to sell space for political or public issue advertising in order to minimize the appearance of favoritism and the risk of imposing on a captive audience. [Lehman v. Shaker Heights, 418 U.S. 298 (1974)]

c. Significant Cases

1) Military Bases

Military bases are not public forums; thus, on-base speech and assembly may be regulated, even during open houses where the public is invited to visit. [*See* United States v. Albertini, 472 U.S. 675 (1985)] However, if the military leaves its streets open as thoroughfares, they will be treated as public forums. [Flower v. United States, 407 U.S. 197 (1972)]

2) Schools

Generally, schools and school-sponsored activities are not public forums. Thus, speech (and association) in schools may be reasonably regulated to serve the school's educational mission.

Examples: 1) Schools can control the content of student speeches or student newspapers for legitimate pedagogical concerns. [*See, e.g.,* Bethel School District No. 403 v. Fraser, 478 U.S. 675 (1986)—student suspended for sexually explicit speech at school assembly] Similarly, a school may prohibit student speech that may be interpreted as advocating or celebrating the use of illegal drugs ("BONG HiTS

4 JESUS") during a school-supervised activity (*e.g.,* a field trip). [Morse v. Frederick, 551 U.S. 393 (2007)]

2) To be given access to the platform of official school recognition and school funding, a public law school may require extracurricular student groups to accept all students regardless of their "status or beliefs." [Christian Legal Society v. Martinez, 130 S. Ct. 2971 (2010)—school could deny funding to group that limited membership to persons who were willing to sign a statement of faith based on Christianity and excluded persons who supported homosexuality and premarital sex; *and see* XXI.D., *infra*]

3) A state association that regulates interscholastic high school sports of schools that ***voluntarily join*** may prohibit certain recruiting statements to middle-school students for athletic programs. Even if the message involves a matter of public concern, the rule is ***necessary*** for managing an effective high school athletic league. [Tennessee Secondary School Athletic Association v. Brentwood Academy, 551 U.S. 291 (2007)]

Compare: A school was forbidden to prohibit the wearing of black armbands in the school (to protest government policies), because that prohibition was designed to suppress communication, *i.e.,* not related to regulatory interest. [Tinker v. Des Moines Independent Community School District, A.4.b., *supra*]

3) Government Workplace or Charity

Neither a government workplace (including a court building and its grounds) nor a government controlled charity drive constitutes a public forum.

Examples: 1) The government may conduct an annual fundraising drive that includes some charities but excludes others on some ideologically neutral basis (*e.g.,* all charities that lobby). However, it cannot exclude a charity merely because it disagrees with the organization's political views. [Cornelius v. NAACP Legal Defense and Education Fund, Inc., 473 U.S. 788 (1985)]

2) A state may develop a system for meeting with and hearing the views of a select group of its employees (*e.g.,* union representatives) while denying the ability to voice opinions at such restricted meetings to other government employees. [Minnesota State Board v. Knight, 465 U.S. 271 (1984)]

Compare: In a public forum, the government cannot restrict the ability to participate in public speech on the basis of union membership. Thus, the Court has held that a teacher cannot be constitutionally prohibited from speaking at a meeting of the school board that was open to the public. [City of Madison Joint School District No. 8 v. Wisconsin Employment Relations Commission, 429 U.S. 167 (1976)]

4) **Postal Service Property**

Although sidewalks generally are public forums, sidewalks on postal service property are not public forums. [United States v. Kokinda, 497 U.S. 720 (1990)]

5) **Signs on Public Property**

The Supreme Court has upheld a city ordinance prohibiting posting signs on public property (including sidewalks, crosswalks, street lamp posts, fire hydrants, and telephone poles), even if the sign is temporary in nature and could be removed without damage to the public property. [Members of City Council v. Taxpayers for Vincent, 466 U.S. 789 (1984)]

6) **Airport Terminals**

Airport terminals operated by a public authority are *not* public forums. Thus, it is reasonable to ban *solicitation* within airport terminals, since it presents a risk of fraud to hurrying passengers. [International Society of Krishna Consciousness v. Lee, 505 U.S. 672 (1992)] However, it is *not* reasonable to ban *leafletting* within multipurpose terminals having qualities similar to a shopping mall [Lee v. International Society of Krishna Consciousness, 505 U.S. 830 (1992)]; although such leafletting can still be subject to reasonable time, place, and manner regulations (*see* B.1., *supra*).

7) **Candidate Debates on Public Television**

A public television station debate for congressional candidates from major parties or who have strong popular support is not a "public forum" because such debates are not open to a class of speakers (*e.g.*, all candidates), but rather to selected members of the class. Exclusion of candidates who are not from a major party and who lack popular support is permissible because these criteria are (i) viewpoint neutral and (ii) reasonable in light of the logistics for an educationally valuable debate. [Arkansas Educational Television Commission v. Forbes, 523 U.S. 666 (1998)]

8) **Mailboxes**

A letter/mailbox at a business or residence is *not* a public forum. Thus, the government may prohibit the placing of unstamped items in post boxes to promote efficient mail service. [United States Postal Service v. Council of Greenburgh Civic Association, 453 U.S. 114 (1981)]

C. **UNPROTECTED SPEECH—REGULATION OR PUNISHMENT BECAUSE OF CONTENT**

Restrictions on the content of speech must be necessary to achieve a compelling government interest. As indicated above, very few restrictions on the content of speech are tolerated. The Court allows them only to prevent grave injury. The following is a list of the only reasons for which the Court has allowed content-based restrictions on speech (*i.e.,* the following are categories of unprotected speech):

(i) It creates a *clear and present danger* of imminent lawless action.

(ii) It constitutes *"fighting words"* as defined by a narrow, precise statute.

(iii) The speech, film, etc., is *obscene*. (This category includes "child pornography.")

(iv) The speech constitutes *defamation*, which may be the subject of a civil "penalty" through a tort action brought by the injured party in conformity with the rules set out *infra*.

(v)   The speech violates regulations against *false or deceptive advertising—commercial speech is protected* by the First Amendment and it cannot be proscribed simply to help certain private interests.

(vi)   The government can demonstrate a *"compelling interest"* in limitation of the First Amendment activity.

Recall that even if a regulation falls within one of the above categories, it will not necessarily be held valid; it might still be held to be void for vagueness or overbreadth. (*See* A.3., *supra*.)

1.   Clear and Present Danger of Imminent Lawlessness
A state cannot forbid advocating the use of force or of law violation unless such advocacy (i) *is directed to producing or inciting imminent lawless action,* and (ii) *is likely to produce or incite such action*. [Brandenberg v. Ohio, 395 U.S. 444 (1969)]

   Example: The "clear and present danger" test has been applied to hold that a state may not punish as contempt out-of-court utterances critical of a judge, absent special circumstances showing an extremely high likelihood of serious interference with the administration of justice. [*See* Wood v. Georgia, 370 U.S. 375 (1962)]

   a.   Allows for Sanctions Against Speech
   The test allows for sanctions against speech causing demonstrable danger to important government interests. Disclosure of United States intelligence operations and personnel is "clearly not protected" speech. [Haig v. Agee, 453 U.S. 280 (1981)]

   b.   Compelling Justification Test
   A similar test—one of "compelling justification"—was employed to hold unconstitutional the Georgia legislature's refusal to seat Julian Bond, an elected black representative, where Bond's speeches, critical of United States policy on Vietnam and the draft, led the legislature to doubt his fitness and his ability to take the oath of office in good faith. [Bond v. Floyd, 385 U.S. 116 (1966)]

2.   Fighting Words

   a.   True Threats
   The First Amendment does not protect "true threats"—statements meant to communicate an intent to place an individual or group in fear of bodily harm. [Virginia v. Black, 538 U.S. 343 (2002)—a state may ban cross burning done with an intent to intimidate; because of cross burning's long history as a signal of impending violence, the state may specially regulate this form of threat, which is likely to inspire fear of bodily harm]

   b.   States May Ban Words Likely to Incite Physical Retaliation
   States are free to ban the use of "fighting words," *i.e.,* those personally abusive epithets that, when addressed to the ordinary citizen, are inherently likely to incite immediate physical retaliation. [Chaplinsky v. New Hampshire, 315 U.S. 568 (1942)] *Chaplinsky* has, however, been narrowly read. Thus, in *Cohen v. California,* 403 U.S. 15 (1971), the Court held that the state may not punish the defendant for wearing a jacket bearing the words "Fuck the Draft," pointing out that "while the four-letter word displayed by Cohen in relation to the draft is commonly employed in a personally provocative fashion, in this instance, it was clearly not directed to the person of the hearer."

c. **Statutes Regulating Fighting Words Tend to Be Overbroad or Vague**
While this classification of punishable speech continues to exist *in theory*, the Court rarely upholds punishments for the use of such words. Statutes that attempt to punish fighting words will tend to be overbroad or vague; the statute will define the punishable speech as "opprobrious words," "annoying conduct," or "abusive language." Such statutes will fail, as their imprecise terms could be applied to protected (nonfighting words) speech. Such a statute could not be used to punish a person for saying to a police officer, "White son of a bitch, I'll kill you." [Gooding v. Wilson, 405 U.S. 518 (1972); Lewis v. City of New Orleans, 415 U.S. 130 (1974)]

d. **Statutes Cannot Be Content-Based—Limits Hate Crime Legislation**
Although the general class of "fighting words" is proscribable under the First Amendment, the Supreme Court generally will not tolerate in fighting words statutes restrictions that are designed to punish only certain viewpoints (*i.e.,* proscribing fighting words only if they convey a particular message). [R.A.V. v. City of St. Paul, 505 U.S. 377 (1992)—ordinance that applies only to those fighting words that insult or provoke violence on the basis of race, religion, or gender is invalid]

1) **Compare—Punishing Racially Motivated Conduct**
The First Amendment does not protect conduct simply because it happens to be motivated by a person's views or beliefs. Thus, a state can increase a convicted defendant's sentence for aggravated battery based on the fact that the defendant selected the victim of his crime because of the victim's race. [Wisconsin v. Mitchell, 508 U.S. 476 (1993)] However, punishment may not be increased merely because of the defendant's abstract beliefs. [Dawson v. Delaware, 503 U.S. 159 (1992)—unconstitutional to increase defendant's sentence merely because it was proved that he belongs to an organization that advocates racism]

3. **Obscenity**
Obscenity is *not protected* speech. [Roth v. United States, 354 U.S. 476 (1957)] The Court has defined "obscenity" as a description or depiction of sexual conduct that, taken *as a whole*, by the *average person*, applying *contemporary community standards*:

(i) Appeals to the *prurient interest* in sex;

(ii) Portrays sex in a *patently offensive* way; and

(iii) *Does not have serious literary, artistic, political, or scientific value*—using a national, reasonable person standard, rather than the contemporary community standard. [Miller v. California, 413 U.S. 15 (1973); Pope v. Illinois, 481 U.S. 497 (1987)]

a. **Elements**

1) **Appeal to Prurient Interest**
The dominant theme of the material considered as a *whole* must appeal to the prurient interest in sex of the average person. The Supreme Court has found this to include that which appeals to *shameful or morbid interests* in sex, but not that which incites *lust* (insofar as lust may include a *normal* interest in sex). [Brockett

v. Spokane Arcades, Inc., 472 U.S. 491 (1985)] For exam purposes, it is probably sufficient merely to know the standard (since its application is a fact determination).

a) Average Person
Both sensitive and insensitive adults may be included in determining contemporary community standards, but children may not be considered part of the relevant audience.

b) Material Designed for Deviant Group
Where the allegedly obscene material is designed for and primarily disseminated to a clearly defined deviant sexual group (*e.g.,* sadists), rather than to the public at large, the prurient appeal requirement is satisfied if the ***dominant theme*** of the material, taken as a whole, ***appeals to the prurient interest of that group.*** [Mishkin v. New York, 383 U.S. 502 (1966)]

2) Patently Offensive

a) Community Standard
The material must be patently offensive in affronting contemporary community standards regarding the description or portrayal of sexual matters.

b) National Standard Not Required
A statewide standard is permissible but not mandatory. A juror may draw on knowledge of the community or vicinity from which he comes, and the court may either direct the jury to apply "community standards" without specifying the "community," or define the standard in more precise geographic terms. [Hamling v. United States, 418 U.S. 87 (1974); Jenkins v. Georgia, 418 U.S. 153 (1974)]

3) Lacking in Serious Social Value
The fact that the material may have some redeeming social value will not necessarily immunize it from a finding of obscenity. It must have serious literary, artistic, political, or scientific value, using a national standard. [Pope v. Illinois, *supra*]

4) Standard May Be Different for Minors
The state can adopt a specific definition of obscenity applying to materials sold to minors, even though the material might not be obscene in terms of an adult audience. [Ginsberg v. New York, 390 U.S. 629 (1968)] However, government may not prohibit the sale or distribution of material to adults merely because it is inappropriate for children.

Example: Because of the present lack of "gateway" technology that would permit speakers on the Internet to block their communications, a federal statute's bar on transmitting "indecent" or "patently offensive" messages to minors effectively amounts to a total ban and thus violates the First Amendment right of adults to receive such materials. [Reno v. American Civil Liberties Union, 521 U.S. 844 (1997)]

Compare: To prevent minors from getting harmful material, the government *may* condition its support of Internet access in public libraries on their installing software to block obscenity and child pornography—at least when the library will unblock filtered material on any adult user's request. [United States v. American Library Association, Inc., 539 U.S. 194 (2003)]

a) Pictures of Minors

To protect minors from exploitation, the government may prohibit the sale or distribution of *visual* depictions of sexual conduct involving minors, even if the material would not be found obscene if it did not involve children. [New York v. Ferber, 458 U.S. 747 (1982)] The government may also prohibit *offers* to provide (and requests to obtain) material depicting children engaged in sexually explicit conduct when the prohibition requires scienter and does not criminalize a substantial amount of protected speech. Such offers of material that is unlawful to possess have no First Amendment protection. [United States v. Williams, 553 U.S. 285 (2008)]

b) Compare—Simulated Pictures of Minors

The government may not bar visual material that only appears to depict minors engaged in sexually explicit conduct, but that in fact uses young-looking adults or computer generated images. [Ashcroft v. Free Speech Coalition, 535 U.S. 234 (2002)] A holding otherwise would bar speech that is not obscene under the *Miller* test and that does not involve the exploitation of children as in *Ferber.*

b. Question of Fact and Law

1) Jury Question

The determination of whether material is obscene is a question of fact for the jury. Of course, the judge can grant a directed verdict if the evidence is such that a reasonable, unprejudiced jury could not find that all parts of the test have been met.

2) Independent Review by Appellate Court

Appellate courts will conduct an independent review of constitutional claims, when necessary, to assure that the proscribed materials "depict or describe patently offensive 'hard core' sexual conduct." [Jenkins v. Georgia, *supra*]

3) Evidence of Pandering

In close cases, evidence of "pandering"—commercial exploitation for the sake of prurient appeal—by the defendant may be probative on whether the material is obscene. Such evidence may be found in the defendant's advertising, his instructions to authors and illustrators of the material, or his intended audience. In effect, this simply accepts the purveyor's own estimation of the material as relevant. [Ginzburg v. United States, 383 U.S. 463 (1966)]

4) Evidence—Similar Published Materials Not Automatically Admissible

The state need not produce expert testimony. Evidence that similar materials are

available on community newsstands, or that the publication has acquired a second-class mailing privilege, does not necessarily show that the material is not obscene and hence is not automatically admissible. Nor is there any automatic right to have other materials held not to be obscene admitted into evidence. [Hamling v. United States, *supra*]

c. **Statutes Must Not Be Vague**

1) **Sweeping Language**
    Attempts to define obscenity broadly have encountered difficulties before the Court.

    Examples: 1) A statute banning publication of news or stories of "bloodshed or lust so massed as to become vehicle for inciting crime" is unconstitutionally vague and uncertain. [Winters v. New York, 333 U.S. 507 (1948)]

    2) The Court held invalid a statute prohibiting the sale of any book "tending to the corruption of the morals of youth." [Butler v. Michigan, 352 U.S. 380 (1957)]

2) **Construction May Save Vague Statute**
    A state statute will be upheld if it meets the tests as construed by the courts of the state. Thus, a seemingly vague obscenity statute may be saved by a state supreme court opinion that limits it to a proscription of depictions of specific types of sexual conduct. [Ward v. Illinois, 431 U.S. 767 (1977)]

d. **Land Use Regulations**
    A land use (or zoning) regulation may limit the location or size of adult entertainment establishments (*i.e.*, businesses that focus on sexual activities) if the regulation is designed to reduce the secondary effects of such businesses (*e.g.*, rise in crime rates, drop in property values and neighborhood quality, etc.). However, regulations may not ban such establishments altogether. [City of Los Angeles v. Alameda Books, Inc., 535 U.S. 425 (2002)]

    Example: A city ordinance limiting adult entertainment establishments to one corner of the city occupying less than 5% of the city's area was deemed constitutional. [City of Renton v. Playtime Theatres, Inc., 475 U.S. 41 (1986)]

e. **Liquor Regulation**
    The Twenty-First Amendment grants states more than the usual regulatory authority with respect to intoxicating beverages. Therefore, regulations prohibiting explicit live sexual entertainment and films in establishments licensed to sell liquor by the drink, even though proscribing some forms of visual presentation that would not be obscene under *Miller,* do not violate the First Amendment as long as they are not "irrational."

f. **Display**
    The Court has suggested that the state *may regulate* the display of certain material, to prevent it from being so obtrusive that an unwilling viewer cannot avoid exposure to it. [Redup v. New York, 386 U.S. 767 (1967)]

g. **Private Possession of Obscenity**

Private possession of obscenity at home cannot be made a crime because of the constitutional right of personal privacy. [Stanley v. Georgia, 394 U.S. 557 (1969)] However, the protection does not extend beyond the home. Thus, importation, distribution, and exhibition of obscene materials can be prohibited.

1) **Exception—Child Pornography**

The state may make private possession of child pornography a crime, even private possession for personal viewing in a residence. [Osborne v. Ohio, 495 U.S. 103 (1990)]

4. **Defamatory Speech**

When a person is sued for making a defamatory statement, the First Amendment places restrictions on the ability of the government (through its tort law and courts) to grant a recovery where the person suing is a *public official or public figure*, or where the defamatory statement involves an issue of *public concern*. In these cases, the plaintiff must prove not only the elements of defamation required by state law, but also that the statement was *false* and that the person making the statement was at *fault* to some degree in not ascertaining the truth of the statement.

a. **Falsity**

At common law, a defamatory statement was presumed to be false; to avoid liability for an otherwise defamatory statement on the ground that it was true, the defendant had to assert truth as an affirmative defense. The Supreme Court has rejected this presumption in all public figure or public concern cases. In these cases, the plaintiff must prove by clear and convincing evidence that the statement was false. [Philadelphia Newspapers, Inc. v. Hepps, 475 U.S. 767 (1986)]

1) **Requirement of Factual Statement**

To be defamatory, the false statement must be viewed by a reasonable person as a statement of fact, rather than as a statement of opinion or a parody. Furthermore, a public figure cannot circumvent the First Amendment restrictions by using a different tort theory to collect damages for a published statement about him that is not a false statement of fact.

Example: Even though a publisher may have intended to cause psychological distress to a public figure by publishing statements about him that were derogatory, the public figure cannot receive a judgment for "emotional distress" damages if a reasonable person who read or viewed the publication would not understand it to contain a statement of fact about that public figure. [Hustler Magazine Inc. v. Falwell, 485 U.S. 46 (1988)]

Note: The fact that a publisher labels a statement as "opinion" will not provide First Amendment protection if the statement would reasonably be understood to be a statement of fact. [Milkovich v. Lorain Journal Co., 497 U.S. 1 (1990)]

b. **Fault**

At common law, a defendant who had no reason to know that the statement he was making was false and defamatory could still be liable for defamation. Now, however,

a plaintiff in a public figure or public concern case must prove fault on the part of the defendant. The degree of fault required is higher when the plaintiff is a public official or public figure than when the plaintiff is a private person suing on a matter of public concern.

1) Public Official or Public Figure—Malice Required

A public official may not recover for defamatory words relating to his official conduct or a matter of public concern without clear and convincing evidence that the statement was made with "malice" (defined below). [New York Times v. Sullivan, 376 U.S. 254 (1964)] This rule has since been extended to public figure plaintiffs. (Note that while the Supreme Court has not specifically held that all statements regarding public officials or public figures necessarily involve matters of public concern, a case to the contrary should be rare.)

a) Malice Defined

Malice was defined by the Supreme Court in *New York Times v. Sullivan* as:

(i) *Knowledge* that the statement was false, *or*

(ii) *Reckless disregard* as to its truth or falsity.

The plaintiff must show that the defendant was subjectively aware that the statement he published was false or that he subjectively *entertained serious doubts* as to its truthfulness.

(1) Malice in False Quotation Cases

Proof that a defamation plaintiff was inaccurately quoted does not, by itself, prove actual malice, even if the quotation was intentionally altered by the defendant. If the published "quotation" is substantially accurate, the plaintiff may not collect damages. To show malice, the public figure plaintiff must prove that the defendant's alteration of the quotation materially changed the meaning of the actual statements made by the plaintiff. [Masson v. New Yorker Magazine, Inc., 501 U.S. 496 (1991)]

(2) Permitted Inquiries by Plaintiff

In attempting to prove knowing or reckless disregard of the truth, the plaintiff may inquire into the state of mind of those who edit, produce, or publish (*i.e.,* conversations with editorial colleagues). [Herbert v. Lando, 441 U.S. 153 (1979)]

(3) Petition Clause Does Not Protect Defamatory Statement Made with Malice

The First Amendment guarantees individuals the right to "petition government for a redress of grievances." However, this right to petition the government does not grant absolute immunity to persons who make defamatory statements about public officials or public figures in their communications with government officials. The defamed individual may

prevail by meeting the *New York Times* requirements. [McDonald v. Smith, 472 U.S. 479 (1985)]

b) Two Ways to Become a Public Figure

(1) General Fame or Notoriety
A person may be a public figure for all purposes and all contexts if he achieves "***general fame or notoriety*** in the community and pervasive involvement in the affairs of society," although "a citizen's participation in community and professional affairs" does not render him a public figure for all purposes.

(2) Involvement in Particular Controversy
A person may "***voluntarily inject*** himself or be drawn into a particular controversy to influence the resolution of the issues involved" and thereby become a public figure for a limited range of issues. [Gertz v. Robert Welch, Inc., 418 U.S. 323 (1974)]

Note that *Gertz* appears to allow for the possibility of a person's being an involuntary public figure for a limited range of issues, although such a case would be "exceedingly rare."

c) Examples of Persons Not Deemed Public Figures

(1) Spouse of Wealthy Person
Marriage to an extremely wealthy person and divorcing such a person does not amount to voluntarily entering the public arena, even though press conferences are held by the plaintiff, because going to court is the only way she could dissolve her marriage. [Time, Inc. v. Firestone, 424 U.S. 448 (1976)]

(2) Person Engaging in Criminal Conduct
A person who engages in ***criminal conduct*** does not automatically become a public figure even when the defamatory statements relate solely to his conviction. [Wolston v. Reader's Digest Association, 443 U.S. 157 (1979)]

(3) Scientist in Federally Funded Program
A behavioral scientist engaged in ***federally funded*** animal research studies is not a public figure because he applies for federal grants and ***publishes*** in professional journals. [Hutchinson v. Proxmire, 443 U.S. 111 (1979)]

2) Private Individual Suing on Matter of Public Concern—At Least Negligence Required
When a private individual is defamed, there is less of a need to protect freedom of speech and press and more of a need to protect private individuals from injury from defamation because they do not have opportunities as effective for rebuttal

as public figures. Accordingly, defamation actions brought by private individuals are subject to constitutional limitations only when the defamatory statement involves a matter of public concern. And even in those cases, the limitations are not as great as those established for public officials and public figures. [Gertz v. Robert Welch, Inc., *supra*] When the defamatory statement involves a matter of public concern, *Gertz* imposes two restrictions on private plaintiffs: (i) it prohibits liability without fault, and (ii) it restricts the recovery of presumed or punitive damages.

a)   **No Liability Without Proof of at Least Negligence**
The plaintiff must show that the defendant was negligent in failing to ascertain the truth of the statement. If the plaintiff establishes negligence but not malice, which is a higher degree of fault, he also has to provide competent evidence of "actual" damages. (This changes the common law rule that damages would be presumed by law for injury to reputation and did not need to be proved by the plaintiff.) Actual damages may be awarded not only for economic losses but also for injury to the plaintiff's reputation in the community and for personal humiliation and distress.

b)   **Presumed or Punitive Damages Allowed Only If Malice Established**
If the plaintiff establishes that the defendant made the statement with malice, the actual damage requirement is extinguished. The plaintiff can recover whatever damages are permitted under state law (usually presumed damages and even punitive damages in appropriate cases). In other words, there is no constitutional protection for statements made with malice, even though a matter of public concern is involved.

c)   **What Is a Matter of Public Concern?**
The courts decide on a case-by-case basis whether the defamatory statement involves a matter of public concern, looking at the content, form, and context of the publication. [Dun & Bradstreet, Inc. v. Greenmoss Builders, Inc., 472 U.S. 749 (1985)]
Example: In *Dun & Bradstreet,* the Court determined that a credit agency's erroneous report of plaintiff's bankruptcy, distributed to five subscribers, was speech solely in the private interest of the speaker and its specific business audience. Therefore, because a matter of public concern was not involved, the First Amendment restrictions did not apply and the state court award of presumed and punitive damages was upheld.

3)   **Private Individual Suing on Matter Not of Public Concern**
The Supreme Court has not imposed constitutional restrictions on defamation actions brought by private individuals that do not involve a matter of public concern. Hence, presumed and punitive damages can be recovered even if malice is not established.

c.   **Procedural Issues**

1) Federal Summary Judgment Standard

When ruling on a motion for summary judgment in a federal court defamation action in a case involving an issue of public concern, a judge must apply the clear and convincing evidence standard (*i.e.,* the judge should grant the motion *unless* it appears that the plaintiff could meet his burdens of proving falsity and actual malice at trial by clear and convincing evidence). However, the Supreme Court has not clearly held that state courts must follow this practice under similar circumstances.

2) Judicial Review

An appellate court must review a defamation case by conducting an independent review of the record to determine if the finder of fact (the jury) could have found that the malice standard was met in the case. [Harte-Hanks Communications, Inc. v. Connaughton, 491 U.S. 657 (1989)]

d. Recovery for Depiction in a False Light

To recover damages for depiction in a false light (as opposed to a defamatory injury to reputation) arising out of comments directed at activities of public interest, an individual must establish *falsity* and *actual malice* whether or not he qualifies as a public figure under *Time, Inc. v. Hill,* 385 U.S. 374 (1967). However, it is *assumed* that the Court would now modify this to mirror the *Gertz* negligence rule for private plaintiffs.

e. True Privacy Actions

1) Publishing True Fact of Public Record

A newspaper or broadcaster cannot be sued for publishing a true fact once it is lawfully obtained from the public record or otherwise released to the public. [Cox Broadcasting Corp. v. Cohn, 420 U.S. 469 (1975)—rape victim's name already in court records open to the public; The Florida Star v. B.J.F., 491 U.S. 524 (1989)— rape victim's name inadvertently given to the press by police]

2) Publishing Name of Juvenile Charged with Crime

A state cannot require judicial approval before the media can print the name of a juvenile charged with murder where the name of the juvenile was obtained through legal means (reporter heard name of defendant over police frequency radio and questioned witnesses to the crime). [Smith v. Daily Mail Publishing Co., 443 U.S. 97 (1979)]

3) Publishing Information on Judge's Competency

A state cannot make it a crime to publish information, released in a confidential proceeding, concerning the competency of members of the state judiciary. [Landmark Communications v. Virginia, 435 U.S. 829 (1978)]

f. Commercial Privacy—Disclosing a Private Performance Can Violate "Right to Publicity"

In *Zacchini v. Scripps-Howard Broadcasting Co.,* 433 U.S. 562 (1977), the Court held that state law could award damages to an entertainer who attempted to restrict the showing of his act to those who paid admission, when a television station broadcast his entire act. Here the "human cannonball" had his entire 15-second act broadcast over his objection.

g. **Copyright Infringement**
The First Amendment does not require an exception to copyright protection for material written by a former President or other public figures. Magazines have no right to publish such copyrighted material beyond the statutory fair use exception. [Harper & Row Publishers v. Nation Enterprises, 471 U.S. 539 (1985)]

5. **Some Commercial Speech**
False advertising is not protected by the First Amendment, although commercial speech in general does have some First Amendment protection. In determining whether a regulation of commercial speech is valid, the Supreme Court asserts that it uses a four-step process. However, it may be easiest to think about this as an initial question followed by a three-step inquiry. *First,* determine whether the commercial speech concerns a lawful activity and is not misleading or fraudulent. Speech proposing an unlawful transaction (*e.g.,* "I will sell you this pound of heroin for X dollars") and fraudulent speech may be outlawed. If the speech regulated concerns a *lawful activity* and is *not misleading or fraudulent*, the regulation will be valid only if it:

(i) Serves a *"substantial"* government interest;

(ii) *"Directly advances"* the asserted interest; and

(iii) Is *narrowly tailored* to serve the substantial interest. This part of the test does *not* require that the "least restrictive means" be used. Rather, there must be a *reasonable fit* between the legislation's end and the means chosen. [Board of Trustees of State University of New York v. Fox, 492 U.S. 469 (1989)]

[Central Hudson Gas v. Public Service Commission, 447 U.S. 557 (1980)]

Examples: A city could not prohibit the use of newsracks on sidewalks for the distribution of commercial publications (such as free publications advertising products or real estate for sale) if the city allowed sidewalk newsracks for the distribution of newspapers. There is no "reasonable fit" between the category of commercial speech and any substantial interest. Commercial newsracks do not cause any physical or aesthetic harm different from that caused by newspaper newsracks. [Cincinnati v. Discovery Network, Inc., 507 U.S. 410 (1993)] Similarly, a law prohibiting beer bottle labels from displaying alcohol content was held invalid because, although the government has a substantial interest in preventing "strength wars," the government did not show that the label prohibition advanced this interest in a material way. [Rubin v. Coors Brewing Co., 514 U.S. 476 (1995)]

a. **Complete Bans**
Complete bans on truthful advertisement of lawful products are very unlikely to be upheld due to a lack of tailoring. Thus, the Court has *struck down* total bans against advertising:

(i) Legal abortions;

(ii) Contraceptives;

(iii) Drug prices;

(iv) Attorneys' services; and

(v) Liquor prices.

Note that the Twenty-First Amendment—giving states the power to regulate liquor commerce within their borders—does not give states power to override First Amendment protections.

1) Commercial Sign Regulation
It is unclear whether billboards may be totally banned from a city. However, they can be regulated for purposes of traffic safety and aesthetics.

a) Blockbusting
A town could not prohibit the use of outdoor "for sale" signs by owners of private homes as a way of reducing the effect of "blockbusting" real estate agents (*i.e.,* encouraging homeowners to sell at reduced prices because of the threat of a sudden influx of minorities). [Linmark Associates v. Willingboro Township, 431 U.S. 85 (1977)]

b. Required Disclosures
Commercial speech is protected largely because of its value to consumers. Thus, the government may require commercial advertisers to make certain disclosures if they are not unduly burdensome and they are reasonably related to the state's interest in preventing deception. [*See, e.g.*, Milavetz, Gallop & Milavetz, P.A. v. United States, 130 S. Ct. 1324 (2010)—advertisements by lawyers (and others) as debt relief agencies may be required to include information about their legal status and the nature of the assistance provided, as well as the possibility of the debtor's filing for bankruptcy]

c. Special Attorney Advertising Rules
The Court has upheld prohibitions against in-person solicitation by attorneys for pecuniary gain [Ohralik v. Ohio State Bar, 436 U.S. 447 (1978)—state interest in protecting lay persons from fraud and overreaching is substantial, and prohibition here is narrowly tailored and directly advances that interest] and sending mail solicitations to accident victims and their relatives within 30 days following an accident [Florida Bar v. Went For It, Inc., 515 U.S. 618 (1995)—state interest in protecting lawyers' reputation is substantial, and ban here is narrowly tailored and directly advances that interest].

D. PRIOR RESTRAINTS
A prior restraint is any governmental action that would prevent a communication from reaching the public (*e.g.,* a licensing system, a prohibition against using mails, an injunction, etc.). Prior restraints are not favored in our political system; the Court would rather allow speech and then punish it if it was unprotected. However, the Court will uphold prior restraints if some special harm would otherwise result. As with other restrictions on speech, a prior restraint must be narrowly tailored to achieve some compelling or, at least, significant governmental interest. The Court has also required that certain procedural safeguards be included in any system of prior restraint.

1. **Sufficiency of Governmental Interest**

   The Supreme Court has not adopted a brightline standard for determining when a prior restraint is justified, but it has said that the government's burden is heavy. For exam purposes, you should ask whether there is some ***special societal harm*** that justifies the restraint.

   a. **National Security**

      National security is certainly a sufficient harm justifying prior restraint. Thus, a newspaper could be prohibited from publishing troop movements in times of war. [Near v. Minnesota, 283 U.S. 697 (1931)] However, the harm must be more than theoretical. Thus, the Court refused to enjoin publication of *The Pentagon Papers* on the basis that publication might possibly have a detrimental effect on the Vietnam War. [New York Times v. United States, 403 U.S. 713 (1971)]

   b. **Preserving Fair Trial**

      Preserving a fair trial for an accused might be a sufficient basis for prior restraint. However, the restraint will be upheld only if it is the only sure way of preserving a fair trial. [Nebraska Press Association v. Stewart, 427 U.S. 539 (1976)]

      1) **Compare—Grand Jury Prior Restraint**

         A state law prohibiting a grand jury witness from ever disclosing the testimony he gave to the grand jury (even after the grand jury term had ended) violates the First Amendment. Such a law is not narrowly tailored to a compelling interest, since any such interest that the government may have in protecting the grand jury process can be protected by a nonpermanent prohibition. [Butterworth v. Smith, 494 U.S. 624 (1990)]

   c. **Contractual Agreements**

      The Supreme Court has held that prior restraint is permissible where the parties have contractually agreed to the restraint. [Snepp v. United States, 444 U.S. 507 (1980)—CIA agent contractually agreed to give agency a prepublication review of any item related to his employment]

   d. **Military Circumstances**

      The Supreme Court has held that the interests of maintaining discipline among troops and efficiency of operations on a military base justify a requirement that persons on a military base obtain the commander's permission before circulating petitions.

   e. **Obscenity**

      The Court has held in a number of cases that the government's interest in preventing the dissemination of obscenity is sufficient to justify a system of prior restraint.

2. **Procedural Safeguards**

   The Supreme Court has held that no system of prior restraint will be upheld unless it provides the persons whose speech is being restrained certain procedural safeguards. The safeguards arose in the context of movie censorship for obscenity, but the court has held that similar safeguards must be provided in all prior restraint cases:

(i) The standards must be "***narrowly drawn, reasonable, and definite,***" so as to include only prohibitable speech (*e.g.,* improper to permanently enjoin witness from disclosing grand jury testimony; government interest can be protected by nonpermanent injunction [Butterworth v. Smith, *supra*]);

(ii) If the restraining body wishes to restrain dissemination of an item, it must ***promptly seek an injunction*** (*e.g.,* improper to allow 50 days before seeking injunction [Teitel Film Corp. v. Cusack, 390 U.S. 139 (1968)]); and

(iii) There must be a ***prompt and final judicial determination*** of the validity of the restraint (*e.g.,* improper to leave an injunction in place pending an appeal that could take up to a year; government must either lift the injunction or expedite the appeal [National Socialist Party v. Village of Skokie, 432 U.S. 43 (1977)]).

A number of other cases, especially in the area of movie censorship, also provide that the ***government bears the burden*** of proving that the speech involved is unprotected. [Freedman v. Maryland, 380 U.S. 51 (1965)]

Example: A federal statute authorized the Postmaster General (i) to deny use of the mails and postal money orders for materials found to be obscene in an administrative hearing, and (ii) to obtain a court order, upon a showing of probable cause, to detain incoming mail pending completion of the administrative hearing. The Court found that this denial of use of the mails violated the First Amendment: The procedures did not require the government to initiate proceedings to obtain a final judicial determination of obscenity, failed to assure prompt judicial review, and failed to limit any restraint in advance of a final judicial determination to preserving the status quo for "the shortest fixed period compatible with sound judicial resolution." [Blount v. Rizzi, 400 U.S. 410 (1971)]

3. Obscenity Cases

Much of the case law in the area of prior restraint has arisen in connection with banning obscenity.

a. Seizure of Books and Films

As with any seizure by the government, seizures of books and films may be made only upon probable cause that they contain obscenity or are otherwise unlawful. (*See* Criminal Procedure outline.)

1) Single Seizures

Seizures of a single book or film (to preserve it as evidence) may be made only with a warrant issued by a neutral and detached magistrate. And even here, a prompt post-seizure determination of obscenity must be available. If other copies of a seized film are not available to the exhibitor, he must be allowed to make a copy so that he may continue showing the film until a final determination has been made. [Heller v. New York, 413 U.S. 483 (1973)] Of course, if the materials are available for sale to the general public, an officer may enter into the establishment and purchase the book or film to use it as evidence in a later prosecution without obtaining a warrant. [Maryland v. Macon, 472 U.S. 463 (1985)]

2) **Large Scale Seizures**

"Large scale" seizures of allegedly obscene books and films—"to destroy them or block their distribution or exhibition"—must be *preceded* by a *full adversary hearing* and a judicial determination of obscenity. [Fort Wayne Books, Inc. v. Indiana, 489 U.S. 46 (1989)]

3) **Forfeiture of Business**

The First Amendment does not prohibit forfeiture of a defendant's adult entertainment business after the defendant has been found guilty of violating the Racketeer Influenced and Corrupt Organizations Act and criminal obscenity laws, even though the business assets included nonobscene books and magazines, where the entire business was found to be part of the defendant's racketeering activity. [Alexander v. United States, 509 U.S. 544 (1993)]

b. **Injunction**

After seizing material, the government may enjoin its further publication only after it is determined to be obscene in a *full judicial hearing*. [Kingsley Books, Inc. v. Brown, 354 U.S. 436 (1957)]

c. **Movie Censorship**

The Court has noted that movies are different from other forms of expression, and that time delays incident to censorship are less burdensome for movies than for other forms of expression. Thus, the Court allows governments to establish censorship boards to screen movies *before* they are released in the community, as long as the procedural safeguards mentioned above are followed. The censor bears the burden of proving that the movie is unprotected speech.

d. **Burden on Government**

When the government adopts a content-based, prior restraint of speech, the government has the burden of proving that the restriction is the least restrictive alternative to accomplish its goal. [Ashcroft v. American Civil Liberties Union, 542 U.S. 656 (2004)— upholding a preliminary injunction against enforcement of a statute requiring age verification for access to Internet websites with sexually explicit material, and criminalizing the failure to obtain age verification, because less restrictive alternatives (*e.g.,* parents installing filters) are available]

E. **FREEDOM OF THE PRESS**

As a general rule, the press has no greater freedom to speak than does the public. However, a number of issues have arisen in the freedom of press context.

1. **Publication of Truthful Information**

Generally, the press has a right to publish information about a matter of public concern, and this right can be restricted only by a sanction that is narrowly tailored to further a state interest of the highest order. The right applies even if the information has been unlawfully obtained in the first instance, as long as (i) the speech relates to a matter of public concern, (ii) the publisher did not obtain it unlawfully or know who did, and (iii) the original speaker's privacy expectations are low. [Bartnicki v. Vopper, 532 U.S. 514 (2001)]

Example: During heated collective bargaining negotiations between a teachers' union and a school board, an unknown person intercepted a cell phone call between

a union negotiator and the union's president. The tape was forwarded to a radio commentator, who played it on the radio. The commentator was sued for damages under civil liability provisions of state and federal wiretap laws that prohibited intentional disclosure of the contents of an electronically transmitted conversation when one has reason to know that the conversation was intercepted unlawfully. The Supreme Court held that the statute violated the First Amendment as applied under these circumstances. [Bartnicki v. Vopper, *supra*]

2. Access to Trials

The First Amendment guarantees the public and press a right to attend criminal trials. But the right may be outweighed by an overriding interest articulated in findings by the trial judge. [Richmond Newspapers v. Virginia, 448 U.S. 555 (1980)—no majority opinion] The right probably applies to civil trials, although the Supreme Court has not conclusively resolved that issue.

a. Access to Voir Dire Examination

The First Amendment guarantee of public and press access to criminal trials also includes access to proceedings involving the voir dire examination of potential jurors. In *Press-Enterprise Co. v. Superior Court,* 464 U.S. 501 (1984), the Court found that a trial court could not constitutionally close voir dire examination of potential jurors without consideration of alternatives to closure even though, in some circumstances, there may be a compelling interest in restricting access to such proceedings to protect the privacy of potential jurors or the fairness of the trial.

b. Access to Other Pretrial Proceedings

Pretrial proceedings are presumptively subject to a First Amendment right of access for the press and public. Thus, a law requiring that all preliminary hearings be closed to the press and public violates the First Amendment. [El Vocero de Puerto Rico (Caribbean International News Corp.) v. Puerto Rico, 508 U.S. 147 (1993)—per curiam] If the prosecution and defense counsel seek to have a judge close pretrial proceedings, the judge would have to make specific findings on the record demonstrating (i) that closure was essential to preserve "higher" or "overriding" values, and (ii) that the closure order was narrowly tailored to serve the higher or overriding value. [Press-Enterprise Co. v. Superior Court, 478 U.S. 1 (1986)]

If the prosecution seeks to have a pretrial hearing or trial closed to the public and the defendant objects to the closure, there will be a Sixth Amendment violation if the judge excludes the public and the press from the hearing or trial without a clear finding that a closure order was necessary to protect an overriding interest.

c. Compelling Interest in Protecting Children

The government has a compelling interest in protecting children who are victims of sex offenses. Portions of trials wherein such children testify may be closed to the public and press, but only if the trial court makes a finding that such closure is necessary to protect the child in the individual case. A state statute, however, violates the First Amendment if it requires closure of the trial during testimony of a child victim of a sex offense without a finding of necessity by the trial judge. [Globe Newspaper Co. v. Superior Court, 457 U.S. 596 (1982)]

d.   **Protective Order in Publishing Information Gained in Pretrial Discovery**
The Supreme Court has upheld a state trial court "protective order" prohibiting a newspaper defendant in a defamation suit from publishing, disseminating, or using information gained through pretrial discovery from the plaintiff in any way except where necessary for preparation for trial. [*See* Seattle Times Co. v. Rhinehart, 467 U.S. 20 (1984)]

3.   **Requiring Members of the Press to Testify Before Grand Juries**
In *Branzburg v. Hayes,* 408 U.S. 665 (1972), the Court held that requiring a journalist to appear and testify before state or federal grand juries *does not abridge freedom of speech or press*, despite the claim that such a requirement would so deter the flow of news from confidential sources as to place an unconstitutionally heavy burden on the First Amendment interest in the free flow of information to the public. The Court's opinion refused to create—and even rejected—a conditional privilege not to reveal confidential sources to a grand jury conducting a good faith inquiry. This position was affirmed in *New York Times v. Jascalevich,* 439 U.S. 1331 (1978).

4.   **Interviewing Prisoners**
Although the First Amendment protects prisoners, and especially those corresponding with them by mail, from a sweeping program of censorship [Procunier v. Martinez, 416 U.S. 396 (1974)], it does not permit journalists to insist upon either interviewing specified prisoners of their choice [Pell v. Procunier, 417 U.S. 817 (1974)] or inspecting prison grounds [Houchins v. KQED, Inc., 438 U.S. 1 (1978)].

5.   **Business Regulations or Taxes**
Press and broadcasting companies can be subject to general business regulations (*e.g.,* antitrust laws) or taxes (*e.g.,* federal or state income taxes). Thus, a tax or regulation applicable to both press and non-press businesses will be upheld, even if it has a special impact on a portion of the press or broadcast media, as long as it is not an attempt to interfere with First Amendment activities. However, no tax or regulation impacting on the press or subpart of the press may be based on the content of the publication absent a compelling justification.

Examples: 1) State tax on publisher's use of more than $100,000 of paper and ink products annually violates the First Amendment. [Minneapolis Star & Tribune v. Minnesota Commissioner of Revenue, 460 U.S. 575 (1983)]

2) State sales tax or "receipts tax" on the sale of general interest magazines that exempts newspapers and religious, professional, trade, and sports journals from the tax violates the First Amendment. [Arkansas Writers' Project, Inc. v. Ragland, 481 U.S. 221 (1987)]

3) A state sales tax that exempted the sales of newspapers and magazines from the tax but did not give a similar exemption to the sale of broadcast services (cable or subscription television) did not violate the First Amendment. The tax was not based on the content of broadcasts and did not target a small category of publishers. The tax was applicable to all cable or satellite television sales. (There is no comparable sale of "free TV" such as network broadcasts.) [Leathers v. Medlock, 499 U.S. 439 (1991)]

6. **Monetary Damages for Failure to Keep Identity Confidential**
   When a reporter or publisher promises a "source person" to keep his identity confidential and then publishes the source person's name, state contract law or promissory estoppel law may allow the source person to recover from the reporter or publisher any damages caused by the publication of his identity. [Cohen v. Cowles Media Co., 501 U.S. 663 (1991)]

7. **Broadcasting Regulations**
   Radio and television broadcasting may be more closely regulated than the press. *Rationale:* Due to the limited number of frequencies available, broadcasters have a special privilege—and, consequently, a special responsibility to give suitable time to matters of public interest and to present a suitable range of programs. The paramount right is the ***right of viewers and listeners*** to receive information of public concern, rather than the right of broadcasters to broadcast what they please.

   a. **Fairness Doctrine**
      Accordingly, the Court has upheld, under a regulatory "fairness doctrine" (which is no longer enforced), FCC orders requiring a radio station to offer free broadcasting time (i) to opponents of political candidates or views endorsed by the station, and (ii) to any person who has been personally attacked in the course of a broadcast, for a reply to the attack. [Red Lion Broadcasting Co. v. FCC, 395 U.S. 367 (1969)]

      1) **Compare—Grant of Equal Newspaper Space**
         A statute granting political candidates a right to equal space to reply to criticism by the newspaper ***violates*** First Amendment freedom of the press. Decisions respecting size and content of newspaper are forbidden to government. [Miami Herald Publishing Co. v. Tornillo, 418 U.S. 241 (1974)]

   b. **Newspaper Ownership of Radio or TV Station**
      Similarly, to promote the diversity of information received by the public, the FCC may forbid ownership of a radio or television station by a daily newspaper located in the same community. [FCC v. National Citizens Committee, 436 U.S. 775 (1978)]

   c. **Prohibiting Indecent Speech**
      Because of a broadcast's ability to invade the privacy of the home, the First Amendment does not forbid imposing civil sanctions on a broadcaster for airing a full monologue (in contrast to isolated use of a few such words) of "patently offensive sexual and excretory speech," even though it is not "obscene"—at least at those times when children are likely to be listening. [FCC v. Pacifica Foundation, 438 U.S. 726 (1978)]

   d. **Political Advertisements**
      The First Amendment does ***not*** require broadcasters to accept political advertisements.

   e. **Elimination of Editorial Speech from Stations Receiving Public Grants**
      Congress violated the First Amendment when it forbade any noncommercial educational station receiving a grant from the Corporation for Public Broadcasting from engaging in "editorializing." [FCC v. League of Women Voters, 468 U.S. 364 (1984)] This was the ***suppression of speech*** because of its content; the elimination of editorial speech from stations receiving public grants of this type was not narrowly tailored to promote

an overriding government purpose regarding the regulation of broadcasting in general or noncommercial broadcasters in particular. Congress could deny persons receiving the federal funds the right to use those funds for editorial activities, but it could not condition the receipt of those funds upon a promise not to engage in any such speech.

8. **Cable Television Regulation**
    While generally regulations of newspapers are subject to strict scrutiny, and regulations of the broadcast media are subject to less critical review, regulations of cable television transmissions are subject to review by a standard somewhere between these two. *Rationale:* The physical connection to a viewer's television set makes the cable subscriber a more captive audience than a newspaper reader and distinguishes cable from newspapers, which cannot prevent access to competing newspapers. On the other hand, unlike broadcast media, which is limited to a small number of frequencies (*see* 7., *supra*), there is no practical limitation on the number of cable channels; thus, the government's interest in protecting viewers' rights is weaker with regard to cable. [Turner Broadcasting System, Inc. v. FCC, A.2.a.2), *supra*]

    Example: A law requiring cable operators to carry local stations is subject to "intermediate scrutiny" since it is content neutral (*see* A.2.a.2), *supra*). Since a "must carry" provision directly serves the important interest of preserving economic viability of local broadcasters and promotes the dissemination of information to noncable viewers, it is constitutional. [Turner Broadcasting System, Inc. v. FCC, *supra*]

    a. **Compare—Content-Based Cable Broadcast Regulations**
        A content-based cable broadcast regulation will be upheld only if it passes muster under the strict scrutiny test. [United States v. Playboy Entertainment Group, Inc., 529 U.S. 803 (2000)—law requiring cable operators to limit "sexually oriented" programs to after 10 p.m. is invalid because of the less restrictive alternative of enabling each household to block undesired channels]

9. **Internet Regulation**
    The strict standard of First Amendment scrutiny, rather than the more relaxed standard applicable to broadcast regulation, applies to regulation of the Internet. *Rationale:* In contrast to broadcasting, there is no scarcity of frequencies (*see* 7., *supra*) on the Internet and little likelihood that the Internet will unexpectedly invade the privacy of the home (*see* 7.c., *supra*). [Reno v. American Civil Liberties Union, C.3.a.4), *supra*]

XXI. FREEDOM OF ASSOCIATION AND BELIEF

A. **NATURE OF THE RIGHT**
    Although the First Amendment does not mention a right of freedom of association, the right to join together with other persons for expressive or political activity is protected by the First Amendment. However, the right to associate for expressive purposes is ***not absolute***. At the very least, the right may be infringed to serve a ***compelling government interest***, unrelated to the suppression of ideas, that cannot be achieved through means significantly less restrictive of associational freedoms. However, in some cases, as noted below, a more lenient standard will apply.

    Examples: 1) A state's interest in ending invidious discrimination justifies prohibiting private clubs that are large and basically unselective in their membership, or that are often

used for business contacts, from discriminating on the basis of race, creed, color, national origin, or sex—at least when it is not shown that this would impede the individual members' ability to engage in First Amendment activity. [New York State Club Association, Inc. v. New York City, 487 U.S. 1 (1988); Board of Directors of Rotary Club International v. Rotary Club of Duarte, 481 U.S. 537 (1987); Roberts v. United States Jaycees, 468 U.S. 609 (1984)]

2) A federal statute making it a crime to provide "material *support* or resources" of any kind to a *foreign terrorist* organization with *knowledge* of its being designated a foreign terrorist organization by the federal government does not violate the freedom of association (or speech). The statute does not forbid mere membership or association with the organization, only material support (which was defined in the statute). Moreover, given the difficulty of obtaining information about terrorist threats, any burden that the statute places on a person's freedom of association is justified. [Holder v. Humanitarian Law Project, 130 S. Ct. 2705 (2010)]

Compare: 1) A state antidiscrimination law may not bar the Boy Scouts from excluding an openly gay assistant scoutmaster from membership. Forced inclusion would *significantly burden* the right of expressive association of the Boy Scouts, since one of the *sincerely held* purposes of the Scouts is to instill certain moral values in young people, including the value that "homosexual conduct is not morally straight." [Boy Scouts of America v. Dale, 530 U.S. 640 (2000)]

2) A city ordinance that restricted admission to certain dance halls to persons between the ages of 14 and 18 was constitutional; it did not have to be justified with a compelling interest because the associational activity of meeting in a dance hall is not an activity within the protection of the First Amendment. [Dallas v. Stanglin, 490 U.S. 19 (1989)]

B. ELECTORAL PROCESS

Laws regulating the electoral process might impact on First Amendment rights of speech, assembly, and association. The Supreme Court uses a *balancing test* in determining whether a regulation of the electoral process is valid: if the restriction on First Amendment activities is severe, it will be upheld only if it is narrowly tailored to achieve a compelling interest, but if the restriction is reasonable and nondiscriminatory, it generally will be upheld on the basis of the states' important regulatory interests. [Burdick v. Takushi, 504 U.S. 428 (1992)—upholding prohibition against write-in candidates]

Example: A state may require in-person voters to show a government-issued voter ID. This is an "evenhanded" protection of the integrity of the electoral process and is justified by "sufficiently weighty" interests of detecting voter fraud and protecting public confidence in elections. Thus, the requirement is plainly legitimate and is not *"facially invalid."* [Crawford v. Marion County Election Board, 553 U.S. 181 (2008)]

1. Ballot Regulation

a. Signature Requirements
The Court has found that the interest of running an efficient election supports a requirement

that candidates obtain a reasonable number of signatures to get on the ballot. [Munro v. Socialist Workers Party, 479 U.S. 189 (1986)—1%] Similarly, a state's interest in promoting transparency and accountability in elections is sufficient to justify public disclosure of the names and addresses of persons who sign ballot petitions. [Doe v. Reed, 130 S. Ct. 2811 (2010)] However, the Court struck down a severe ballot restriction requiring new political parties to collect twice as many signatures to run for county office as for state office. [Norman v. Reed, 502 U.S. 279 (1992)]

b. **Primary Voting Regulations**

A state may enforce a party rule requiring that a person be registered as a member of the party within a reasonable amount of time prior to a primary to be able to vote. [Rosario v. Rockefeller, 410 U.S. 752 (1973)] It may also require that voters in a party's primary be registered either in the party *or as independents*. *Rationale:* The burden on the party's associational rights is *not severe*. Thus, strict scrutiny does not apply and the state's important regulatory interests (*e.g.,* in preserving political parties as viable identifiable groups, preventing party raiding, etc.) are sufficient to justify the restriction. [Clingman v. Beaver, 544 U.S. 581 (2005)] However, a state may not prohibit a party from allowing independent voters to vote in the party's primary if the party wishes to allow independent voters to participate; such a requirement constitutes a severe burden on the associational rights of the party and can be justified only if it is narrowly tailored to serve a compelling interest. [Tashjian v. Republican Party of Connecticut, 479 U.S. 208 (1986)]

c. **Single Party Limitation**

A state law that prohibits an individual from appearing on the ballot as the candidate of more than one party does *not* impose a severe burden on the association rights of political parties. The state's interest in ballot integrity and political stability are "sufficiently weighty" to justify the law. [Timmons v. Twin Cities Area New Party, 520 U.S. 351 (1997)]

d. **"Nonpartisan" Blanket Primary**

A state primary ballot law providing that candidates *self-identify* their party preference and that the two top vote getters advance to the general election does not *on its face* violate the association rights of political parties. *Rationale:* (i) The law does not state that any candidate is a party's nominee, (ii) there was no evidence that voters would be confused by the self-identifications, and (iii) the state may design a ballot that will make this clear. [Washington State Grange v. Washington State Republican Party, 552 U.S. 442 (2008)]

2. **Party Regulation**

The state has less interest in governing party activities than in governing elections in general. Thus, the Court has held invalid a statute prohibiting the governing committee of a political party from endorsing or opposing candidates in primary elections. [Eu v. San Francisco County Democratic Central Committee, 489 U.S. 214 (1989); *and see* California Democratic Party v. Jones, 530 U.S. 567 (2000)—state cannot require political parties to allow nonparty members to vote in the party's primary election] Similarly, it has held invalid state regulations concerning the selection of delegates to a national party convention and the selection of candidates at such elections. [Cousins v. Wigoda, 419 U.S. 477 (1975); Democratic Party v. LaFolette, 450 U.S. 107 (1981)]

a. **Judicial Candidate Selection**

A state law that permits political parties to choose nominees for state judgeships at state conventions does not violate the freedom of association rights of candidates for judgeships simply because the historic domination of party leaders results in strongly favoring those that they support. *Rationale:* This process "has been a traditional means of choosing party nominees." [New York State Board of Elections v. Lopez Torres, 552 U.S. 196 (2008)]

3. **Limits on Contributions**

A statute limiting election campaign contributions is not tested under a strict scrutiny standard; rather, it must be "closely drawn" to match a "sufficiently important interest"—an intermediate scrutiny standard. [McConnell v. Federal Election Commission, 540 U.S. 93 (2003)]

a. **To Political Candidate**

Laws limiting the amount of money that a person or group may contribute to a political candidate are **valid**, since the government has a sufficiently important interest in stopping the fact (or appearance) of corruption that may result from large contributions. Moreover, such laws do not substantially restrict freedom of expression or freedom of association (as long as the contributor may spend his money directly to discuss candidates and issues). [Buckley v. Valeo, 424 U.S. 1 (1976)]

1) **Equalizing Large Expenditures**

A law increasing contribution limits for a candidate whose wealthy opponent achieves an advantage by spending personal funds (exceeding $350,000) violates the First Amendment. *Rationale*: Although Congress may raise contribution limits for both candidates in situations of this kind, "penalizing" a self-financing candidate who robustly expresses the right to advocate his own election cannot be justified by leveling opportunities for candidates of different personal wealth. [Davis v. Federal Election Commission, 128 S. Ct. 2759 (2008)]

b. **To Ballot Referendum Committee**

The government may **not** limit contributions to a political committee that supports or opposes a ballot referendum (as opposed to one that supports a political candidate). Such a limitation on contributions to influence referendum elections violates the freedoms of speech and association. [Citizens Against Rent Control v. Berkeley, 454 U.S. 290 (1982)]

c. **Disclosure of Contributors or Recipients of Money**

The government may require a political party or committee to disclose the names of contributors or recipients of money to or from the party or committee. However, if the party or committee can show a "reasonable probability" that disclosure will cause harm to the party, committee, or private individuals, they have a First Amendment right to refuse to make such disclosures. [Brown v. Socialist Workers '74 Campaign Committee, 454 U.S. 1122 (1982)]

4. **Limits on Expenditures**

As discussed above, the government **may** limit the amount that a person is permitted to **contribute** to another's campaign. However, the government **may not** limit the amount that

a person *expends* on his own campaign. [Buckley v. Valeo, *supra*] Neither may the government limit the amount that a person spends to get a candidate elected, as long as the expenditures are not contributed directly to the candidate nor coordinated with that of the candidate (*i.e.,* as long as the expenditures are independent of the candidate and are not disguised contributions). Thus, corporations, unions, etc., may spend whatever they desire to get a candidate elected. [*See, e.g.,* Citizens United v. Federal Election Commission, 130 S. Ct. 876 (2010)]

5.   **Compare—Regulations of Core Political Speech**
Regulation of "core political speech" must be distinguished from regulation of the process surrounding elections. Regulation of "core political speech" will be upheld only if it passes muster under strict scrutiny. [McIntyre v. Ohio Elections Commission, 514 U.S. 334 (1995)]

a.   **Prohibiting Any Election Day Campaigning**
A state law prohibiting *any* campaigning on election day has been held *invalid* as applied to a newspaper urging people to vote in a certain way. The right to comment on political issues is one of the most essential elements of free speech, and such conduct by newspapers would pose little danger to conducting elections. [Mills v. Alabama, 384 U.S. 214 (1966)]

1)   **Compare—Hundred-Foot Limit**
A law prohibiting campaign activity within 100 feet of a polling place is *valid*. Even though the law is content based and concerns an essential element of free speech, it is *necessary* to serve the *compelling* interest of preventing voter intimidation and election fraud. [Burson v. Freeman, 504 U.S. 191 (1992)]

b.   **Prohibiting Anonymous Campaign Literature**
Laws prohibiting distribution of anonymous campaign literature involve core political speech and have been stricken because they were not narrowly tailored to a compelling state interest. [McIntyre v. Ohio Elections Commission, *supra*; Buckley v. American Constitutional Law Foundation, 525 U.S. 182 (1999)]

c.   **Prohibiting Judge Candidates from Announcing Their Views**
A rule prohibiting candidates for judicial election from announcing their views on disputed legal and political issues violates the First Amendment. This is both a content-based restriction and a restriction on core political speech. In either case, it can be justified only if it is necessary to a compelling state interest. Two state interests were suggested to support the rule here: It is necessary to maintain an impartial judiciary and it is necessary to preserve the appearance of impartiality. The Court found that the rule is "woefully underinclusive" and so is not tailored at all toward achieving these goals. For example, it allows candidates to show bias toward political parties while it prohibits them from stating an opinion about political issues. The Court also found that finding judges without any preconceptions in favor of particular legal views is not a compelling interest because it would be both impossible to find such a person and undesirable. [Republican Party of Minnesota v. White, 536 U.S. 765 (2002)]

d.   **Distinguishing Political Speech from Candidate Advocacy**
An ad concerning a political issue, even if sponsored by a corporation, run during an election campaign will be considered to be core political speech—rather than candidate

advocacy—unless it is susceptible of no reasonable interpretation other than one as an appeal to vote for or against a particular candidate. [Federal Election Commission v. Wisconsin Right to Life, Inc., 551 U.S. 449 (2007)—ad urging voters to contact their senators to encourage them to end a filibuster of federal judicial nominations was core political speech—and could not be banned—even when one of the senators was running for re-election]

C. BAR MEMBERSHIP AND PUBLIC EMPLOYMENT

The government often requires persons who accept government jobs to submit to loyalty oaths and refrain from certain conduct (*e.g.*, campaigning). Such regulations often impact upon the freedom of speech and association.

1. Restraints on Conduct

If a government employer seeks to fire an employee (or to terminate a relationship with an independent contractor) for speech-related conduct, one of two tests will apply, depending on whether the speech involved a matter of public concern. If a matter of public concern is involved, courts must carefully balance the employee's rights as a citizen to comment on a matter of public concern against the government's interest as an employer in the efficient performance of public service. If the speech did not involve a matter of public concern, the courts should give a wide degree of deference to the government employer's judgment concerning whether the speech was disruptive.

Examples: 1) A teacher cannot be fired for writing a letter to a newspaper attacking school board policies. [Pickering v. Board of Education, 391 U.S. 563 (1968)]

2) The Court held invalid the firing of a clerical employee from a constable's office for expressing her disappointment that an assassination attempt on President Reagan did not succeed, because in context the statement could not be understood to be an actual threat or an action that would interfere with the running of the office; rather, the Court viewed it as a commentary on the public issue of the President's policies. [Rankin v. McPherson, 483 U.S. 378 (1987)]

Compare: The Court upheld the firing of an attorney for circulating in the office a petition regarding transfer policies. [Connick v. Myers, 461 U.S. 138 (1983)]

a. Official Duty Exception

A government employer may punish a public employee's speech whenever the speech is made pursuant to the employee's official duties. This is true even if the speech touches on a matter of public concern. [Garcetti v. Ceballos, 547 U.S. 410 (2006)]

Example: P, a district attorney, reviewed a case, concluded that there were irregularities in an underlying search warrant, contacted his supervisors, and suggested dismissing the case. P's supervisors nevertheless proceeded with the prosecution. At a hearing challenging the warrant, P again raised his concerns about the warrant, but the court rejected the challenge. P claims that he was then subjected to retaliatory employment actions because of his testimony and sued his employer for violating his First Amendment rights. P's employer denied undertaking any retaliatory actions, but even if such actions did occur, no First Amendment

violation could occur here because the speech was undertaken as part of P's job—a government employer may evaluate an employee based on any writing or speech that the employee undertakes as part of his official duties. [Garcetti v. Ceballos, *supra*]

b. Participation in Political Campaigns

The federal government *may* prohibit federal executive branch employees from taking an active part in political campaigns. The rationale is twofold: to further nonpartisanship in administration and to protect employees from being coerced to work for the election of their employers. [United Public Workers v. Mitchell, 330 U.S. 75 (1947)]

c. Bans on Receiving Honoraria

A provision of the Ethics in Government Act banning government employees from accepting an honorarium for making speeches, writing articles, or making appearances was held to violate the First Amendment when applied to "rank and file" employees. Such a rule deters speech within a broad category of expression by a massive number of potential speakers and thus can be justified only if the government can show that the employees' and their potential audiences' rights are outweighed by the necessary impact the speech would have on actual operation of the government. The government failed to cite any evidence of misconduct related to honoraria by the rank and file employees, and so failed to meet the burden here. [United States v. National Treasury Employees Union, 513 U.S. 454 (1995)]

d. Patronage

The First Amendment freedoms of political belief and association forbid the hiring, promotion, transfer, firing, or recall of a public employee because of political party affiliation unless the hiring authority demonstrates that party affiliation is an appropriate requirement for the effective performance of the public office involved, *e.g.,* "policy-making" or "confidential" nature of work. [Rutan v. Republican Party of Illinois, 497 U.S. 62 (1990)]

2. Loyalty Oaths

It is permissible for the federal government to require employees and other public officers to take loyalty oaths. However, such oaths will not be upheld if they are overbroad (*i.e.,* prohibit constitutionally protected activities) or are vague so that they have a chilling effect on First Amendment activities.

a. Overbreadth

1) Knowledge of Organization's Aim Required

Public employment cannot be denied to persons who are simply members of the Communist Party because only knowing membership with "specific intent to further unlawful aims" is unprotected by the First Amendment. [Keyishian v. Board of Regents, 385 U.S. 589 (1967)]

2) Advocacy of Doctrine Protected

A political party may not be denied a place on the ballot for refusing to take a loyalty oath that it does not advocate violent overthrow of the government as an

abstract doctrine. The First Amendment forbids "statutes regulating advocacy that are not limited to advocacy of action." [Communist Party v. Whitcomb, 414 U.S. 441 (1974)]

b. Vagueness

1) Oaths Upheld
Compare the following oaths that have been upheld:

a) To Support the Constitution
An oath that required public employees and bar applicants to "support the Constitution of the United States" and the state constitution has been upheld. [Connell v. Higgenbotham, 403 U.S. 207 (1971)]

b) To Oppose the Overthrow of the Government
An oath required of all state employees "to oppose the overthrow of the government . . . by force, violence, or by an illegal or unconstitutional method" has also been upheld. The Court read this oath as akin to those requiring the taker simply to "support" the Constitution, "to commit themselves to live by the constitutional processes of our system." Moreover, the oath provided fair notice, because its violation could be punished only by a prosecution for perjury, which required proof of knowing falsity. [Cole v. Richardson, 405 U.S. 676 (1972)]

2) Oath Not Upheld
A loyalty oath for public employees that they "promote respect for the flag and . . . reverence for law and order" is void for vagueness, since a refusal to salute the flag on religious grounds might be found in breach thereof. [Baggett v. Bullitt, 377 U.S. 360 (1964)]

3. Disclosure of Associations
Forcing disclosure of First Amendment activities as a condition of public employment, bar membership, or other public benefits may have a chilling effect. Thus, the state cannot force every prospective government employee to disclose *every* organizational membership. Such a broad disclosure has *insufficient relation* to loyalty and professional competence, and the state has available *less drastic means* to achieve its purpose. [Shelton v. Tucker, 364 U.S. 479 (1960)] The state may inquire only into those activities that are relevant to the position. If the candidate fails to answer relevant questions, employment may be denied. [Konigsberg v. State Bar of California, 366 U.S. 36 (1961)]

a. Fifth Amendment Limitation
If the job candidate refuses to answer on a claim of the privilege against self-incrimination, denial of the job violates the Fifth and Fourteenth Amendments. [Spevack v. Klein, 385 U.S. 511 (1967)] However, if individuals are ordered by appropriate authorities to answer questions "specifically, directly, and narrowly relating to their official duties," and they refuse to do so by claiming the privilege against self-incrimination, they may be denied the job or discharged without violating the Fifth Amendment, if they were given immunity from the use of their answers or the fruits thereof in a criminal prosecution. [Lefkowitz v. Turley, 414 U.S. 70 (1973); Gardner v. Broderick, 392 U.S. 273 (1968)]

4. **Practice of Law**

Regulation of the legal profession may conflict with the freedom of association rights of certain groups because it may impair their ability to band together to advise each other and utilize counsel in their common interest.

a. **Countervailing State Interest Required**

To overcome a group's right to exercise its First Amendment rights, the state must show a substantial interest, such as evidence of objectionable practices occurring or an actual or clearly threatened conflict of interest between lawyer and client.

Examples: 1) The NAACP encouraged, instructed, and offered to represent parents of black children to litigate against school segregation. This was held to be protected political expression. The state's ban on solicitation of legal business was inapplicable because the NAACP sought no monetary gain. [NAACP v. Button, 371 U.S. 415 (1963)]

2) A railroad labor union recommended a specific lawyer to pursue rights of members injured on the job, and also obtained a fee from a lawyer for performing investigative services. This was held protected. [Brotherhood of Railroad Trainmen v. Virginia, 377 U.S. 1 (1964)]

D. **SCHOOL SPONSORSHIP OF EXTRACURRICULAR CLUBS**

The Supreme Court has held that the compelling interest test does not apply to infringement cases involving public school sponsorship of extracurricular clubs; instead, the test used in limited-public-forum-speech cases applies—sponsorship of associations can be subject to regulation that is *viewpoint neutral* and *reasonably related to a legitimate government interest*. (*See* XX.B.2.c.2), *supra*.)

Example: A public law school officially recognized student groups and gave them funding from mandatory student activity fees only if the groups accepted all students regardless of their "status or beliefs" (*i.e.,* the "all comers" policy). A group that required students to sign a statement of faith based on Christian beliefs and denied membership to persons who supported homosexuality and premarital sex sought an exemption from the "all comers" policy and was denied. The group sued the school, claiming that the policy violated members' associational rights. *Held:* The "all comers" policy is constitutional. It is viewpoint neutral in that it draws no distinctions on point of view. Moreover, it is reasonably related to school purposes such as encouraging tolerance and providing leadership, educational, and social opportunities to all students. [Christian Legal Society v. Martinez, XX.B.2.c.2), *supra*]

XXII.   FREEDOM OF RELIGION

A. **CONSTITUTIONAL PROVISION**

The First Amendment provides "Congress shall make no law respecting an establishment of religion, or prohibiting the free exercise thereof."

B. **APPLICABILITY TO THE STATES**

Both the Establishment and Free Exercise Clauses of the First Amendment apply to the states under the Fourteenth Amendment.

C. FREE EXERCISE CLAUSE

1. No Punishment of Beliefs

The Free Exercise Clause prohibits the government from punishing (denying benefits to, or imposing burdens on) someone on the basis of the person's ***religious beliefs***. It is sometimes said that the government can engage in such activity only if it is necessary to achieve a compelling interest; sometimes the rule is stated as a total prohibition of such government actions. In any case, the Supreme Court has never found an interest that was so "compelling" that it would justify punishing a religious belief.

a. What Constitutes Religious Belief?

The Supreme Court has not defined what constitutes a religious belief. However, it has made clear that religious belief does not require recognition of a supreme being [Torcaso v. Watkins, 367 U.S. 488 (1961)], and need not arise from a traditional, or even an organized, religion [*see* Frazee v. Illinois Department of Employment Security, 489 U.S. 829 (1989)]. One possible definition is that the "belief must occupy a place in the believer's life parallel to that occupied by orthodox religious beliefs." [United States v. Seeger, 380 U.S. 163 (1965)—interpreting statutory, rather than constitutional, provision] In any case, the Court has never held an asserted religious belief to be not religious for First Amendment purposes.

1) Courts May Not Find Religious Beliefs to Be False

The courts may not declare a religious belief to be "false." For example, if a person says he talked to God and that God said the person should solicit money, he cannot be found guilty of fraud on the basis that God never made such a statement. However, the court may determine whether the person is sincerely asserting a belief in the divine statement. [United States v. Ballard, 322 U.S. 78 (1944), *as described in* Employment Division v. Smith, 494 U.S. 872 (1990)]

b. Religious Oaths for Governmental Jobs Prohibited

The *federal* government may not require any federal office holder or employee to take an oath based on a religious belief as a condition for receiving the federal office or job, because such a requirement is prohibited by Article VI of the Constitution. State and local governments are prohibited from requiring such oaths by the Free Exercise Clause. [Torcaso v. Watkins, *supra*]

c. States May Not Exclude Clerics from Public Office

A state may not exclude clerics (persons who hold an office or official position in a religious organization) from being elected to the state legislature, or from other governmental positions, because that exclusion would impose a disability on these persons based upon the nature of their religious views and their religious status. [McDaniel v. Paty, 435 U.S. 618 (1978)]

2. No Punishment of Religious Conduct Solely Because It Is Religious

The Supreme Court has stated that the Free Exercise Clause prohibits the government from punishing conduct merely because it is religious or displays religious belief (*e.g.*, the state cannot ban the use of peyote only when used in religious ceremonies). [Employment Division v. Smith, *supra*—dicta] A law that is designed to suppress actions only because the actions are religiously motivated is not a neutral law of general applicability. Such a law will be invalid unless it is necessary to promote a compelling interest.

Example: A city law that prohibited the precise type of animal slaughter used in the ritual of a particular religious sect violated the Free Exercise Clause because the Court found that the law was designed solely to exclude the religious sect from the city. The law was not a neutral law of general applicability; nor was the law necessary to promote a compelling interest. [Church of the Lukumi Babalu Aye, Inc. v. Hialeah, 508 U.S. 520 (1993)]

Compare: A state law that excluded pursuit of a degree in ***devotional theology*** from a college scholarship program for all students did ***not*** violate the Free Exercise Clause. Although a school ***could*** provide such scholarships without violating the Establishment Clause (*see infra*), the Free Exercise Clause does not require such scholarships. The exclusion from scholarship eligibility does not show animus toward religion, but rather merely reflects a decision not to fund this activity. Moreover, the burden that the exclusion imposes on religion is modest, and there is substantial historical support against using tax funds to support the ministry. [Locke v. Davey, 540 U.S. 712 (2004)]

3.   **States Can Regulate General Conduct—Criminal Laws and Other Regulations**
Of course, states may prohibit or regulate conduct in general, and this is true even if the prohibition or regulation happens to interfere with a person's religious practices. The Free Exercise Clause cannot be used to challenge a law of general applicability unless it can be shown that the law was motivated by a desire to interfere with religion. [Employment Division v. Smith, *supra*]

a.   **Generally No Exemptions Required**
The Free Exercise Clause does not require exemptions from criminal laws or other governmental regulations for a person whose religious beliefs prevent him from conforming his behavior to the requirements of the law. In other words, a law that regulates the conduct of all persons can be applied to prohibit the conduct of a person despite the fact that his religious beliefs prevent him from complying with the law.

b.   **Examples**
The Supreme Court has held that no religious exemption was required from the following religiously neutral regulations, even though certain groups objected because the regulation interfered with conduct inspired by sincerely held religious beliefs:

1)   Prohibition against ***use of peyote*** [Employment Division v. Smith, *supra*— challenged by person whose religious beliefs require use of peyote during religious ceremony];

2)   ***Denial of tax exempt status to schools that discriminate*** on the basis of race [Bob Jones University v. United States, 461 U.S. 574 (1983)—challenged by religious school whose tenets require certain separations of races];

3)   Requirement that employers comply with ***federal minimum wage laws*** [Tony and Susan Alamo Foundation v. Secretary of Labor, 471 U.S. 290 (1985)—challenged by employer that argued minimum wages interfere with members' religious desires to work without compensation];

4) Requirement that employers pay *Social Security taxes* [United States v. Lee, 455 U.S. 252 (1982)—challenged by person whose religious beliefs prohibited payment and receipt of Social Security type payments]; and

5) *Sales and use taxes* [Jimmy Swaggart Ministries v. Board of Equalization of California, 493 U.S. 378 (1990)—challenged as applied to sales of goods and literature by religious group].

4. Unemployment Compensation Cases—Some Exemptions Required

Many state unemployment compensation programs make payments only to persons who are involuntarily unemployed (*i.e.,* were fired or laid off rather than resigned), and who are available for work (*i.e.,* willing to accept offered employment). Here, however, unlike other areas of regulation, the Supreme Court has held that the states must grant religious exemptions. Thus, if a person resigns from a job or refuses to accept a job because it conflicts with her religious beliefs, the state must pay her unemployment compensation if she is otherwise entitled.

Examples: 1) A state cannot deny unemployment compensation merely because the applicant quit a job rather than work on a "holy day" on which religious beliefs forbid work. [Sherbert v. Verner, 374 U.S. 398 (1963)]

2) A state cannot deny unemployment compensation merely because the applicant quit his job rather than work on production of military equipment after his factory converted from nonmilitary to military production. [Thomas v. Review Board, 450 U.S. 707 (1981)]

a. Need Not Belong to Formal Religious Organization

A person does not have to be a member of a formal religious organization to receive the above exemptions from unemployment compensation requirements. All that is required is that the person *sincerely hold* religious beliefs that prevent him from working on a certain day or on military products. [Frazee v. Illinois Department of Employment Security, 1.a., *supra*]

b. Limitation—Criminal Prohibitions

The unemployment compensation cases do not give individuals a right to disregard criminal laws due to their religious beliefs. Thus, unemployment compensation laws may disqualify persons fired for "misconduct" (which includes any violation of criminal law).

Example: A person was fired from his job as a counselor at a private drug abuse clinic when it was discovered that he used peyote (at times when he was not at work) for religious reasons. All use of peyote was illegal in the state (even if the use was part of a religious ceremony). The Supreme Court held that unemployment compensation could properly be denied here. [Employment Division v. Smith, *supra*]

5. Right of Amish Not to Educate Children

The Supreme Court has required an exemption for the Amish from a neutral law that required school attendance until age 16, because a fundamental tenet of Amish religion forbids secondary education. The Court found that the Amish are productive and law-abiding, and ruled that the right to educate one's children (*see* XIX.B.6., *supra*) and the Free Exercise Clause outweighed the state's interest here. [Wisconsin v. Yoder, 406 U.S. 205 (1972)]

D. ESTABLISHMENT CLAUSE
The Establishment Clause prohibits laws respecting the establishment of religion.

1. **Sect Preference**

    If a law or government program includes a preference for some religious sects over others, it will almost certainly be held invalid because the compelling interest test applies: To be valid, the law or program must be *narrowly tailored* to promote a *compelling interest*.

    Example: A state law created a public school district whose boundaries were intentionally set to match the boundaries of a particular Jewish neighborhood (so that several handicapped students would not have to be sent outside their neighborhood to attend special education classes that the state required and which the students' private school could not adequately provide). The Supreme Court found the law unconstitutional. [Board of Education v. Grumet, 512 U.S. 687 (1994)]

2. **No Sect Preference—*Lemon* Test**

    If government action does not involve a sect preference, the compelling interest test is not used; instead, the government action will be valid under the Establishment Clause if it:

    (i)   Has a *secular purpose*;

    (ii) Has a *primary effect* that neither advances nor inhibits religion; *and*

    (iii) Does not produce *excessive government entanglement* with religion.

    [Lemon v. Kurtzman, 403 U.S. 602 (1971)—the *"Lemon"* test] (Note that some recent cases have simply focused on whether the action is neutral as between the religious and nonreligious when there is no endorsement of a particular religion.) The Establishment Clause cases can be grouped into three categories: (i) a limited group of cases unconnected to financial aid or education; (ii) cases involving financial aid to religiously affiliated institutions; and (iii) cases concerning religious activities in public schools. The details regarding the Supreme Court rulings are given below.

    a. **Cases Unconnected to Financial Aid or Education**

        In cases unconnected to financial aid or education, a good rule of thumb is that a law favoring or burdening religion or a specific religious group in particular will be invalid, but a law favoring or burdening a larger segment of society that happens to include religious groups will be upheld.

        Example: The government may not delegate governmental power to religious organizations because such action would involve excessive governmental entanglement. [Larkin v. Grendel's Den, Inc., 459 U.S. 116 (1982)—statute gave church-affiliated schools power to veto nearby liquor licenses]

        Compare: The IRS may deny tax exemptions claimed for religious donations when the sums were paid to the church *in exchange for services* (*e.g.*, classes) since this is a general rule that applies to all charities. [Hernandez v. Commissioner of Internal Revenue, 490 U.S. 680 (1989)]

        1) **State Legislature Can Employ a Chaplain**

            Despite the principle of separation of church and state, the Court has held that a

state legislature could employ a chaplain and begin each legislative day with a prayer. [Marsh v. Chambers, 463 U.S. 783 (1983)] This decision was based on the history of legislative prayer in America; it does not modify the "Religious Activities in Public Schools" rulings examined below.

2) Displays of Ten Commandments on Public Property

If a display of the Ten Commandments is shown to have a *"predominantly religious purpose,"* it violates the Establishment Clause; otherwise, the Ten Commandments may be displayed. [McCreary County v. ACLU, 545 U.S. 844 (2005)]

Example: Two counties posted large copies of the Ten Commandments in their courthouses. After complaints based on the Establishment Clause, each county adopted a resolution calling for a more extensive exhibit showing that the Commandments are Kentucky's "precedent legal code" and noting the state legislature's acknowledgment of Christ as the "Prince of Ethics." The displays were then modified to add smaller copies of other historic texts with religious references (*e.g.,* the "endowed by their creator" clause of the Declaration of Independence). A district court found the displays invalid under the *Lemon* test because they lacked any secular purpose. The counties again modified the displays—without any guiding resolutions—to include eight equally sized items around the Ten Commandments (including the Bill of Rights and a picture of Lady Justice) and the title "Foundations of American Law and Government." The ACLU moved to enjoin these displays, claiming that their purpose was still religious rather than secular. Given the displays' history, the Supreme Court agreed, finding that the taint from the earlier displays had not been dissipated even though, on their faces, the most current displays appeared not to have a religious purpose. [McCreary County v. ACLU, *supra*]

Compare: A monument of the Ten Commandments on a 22-acre State Capitol ground displaying 17 monuments and 21 historical markers commemorating the state's "people, ideals, and events that compose its identity" communicated not only a religious message but also a secular moral message, and its setting suggested that the state intended the secular message to predominate. [Van Orden v. Perry, 545 U.S. 677 (2005)]

3) Some Holiday Displays Are Permissible

If the *government* maintains a holiday-Christmastime display that does not appear to endorse religion, the display will survive review under the three-part Establishment Clause test. If a government's holiday display includes religious symbols (*e.g.,* a nativity scene or a menorah) as well as other holiday decorations (*e.g.,* a Christmas tree or a Santa Claus figure), the courts will hold that the display: (i) has a secular purpose (based on the history of government recognition of holidays); (ii) has a primary nonreligious effect (it does not endorse religion); and (iii) does not create excessive entanglement between government and religion. If the display includes only the religious symbols (*e.g.,* only a nativity scene), it will violate the

Establishment Clause because it has a religious effect (it "endorses" religion). [County of Allegheny v. ACLU, 492 U.S. 573 (1989)]

4) Absolute Right Not to Work on a Sabbath Impermissible

The state may not force employers to grant all employees an absolute right to refrain from working on their sabbath, because the primary effect of such a law is to advance religion. [Estate of Thornton v. Caldor, 472 U.S. 703 (1985)] However, a state may require employers to make reasonable efforts to accommodate employee religious practices.

5) Exemptions from Antidiscrimination Laws

The federal government may exempt religious organizations from the federal statutory prohibition against discrimination in employment on the basis of religion, at least regarding their nonprofit activities. Thus, a janitor can be discharged from his employment at a gymnasium owned by a religious organization (which was open to the public and run as a nonprofit facility) because he was not a member of that religious organization. [Corporation of the Presiding Bishop of the Church of Jesus Christ of Latter-Day Saints v. Amos, 483 U.S. 327 (1987)]

b. Cases Involving Financial Benefits to Church-Related Institutions

A statute authorizing governmental aid to a religiously affiliated institution (hospital, school, etc.) must be tested under the general test detailed above (secular purpose, primary effect, and excessive entanglement). However, the Supreme Court applies these tests with greater strictness when the government aid is going to a religiously affiliated grade school or high school than it does when the aid is going to another type of religiously affiliated institution (such as a college or hospital).

1) Recipient-Based Aid

The government may give aid in the form of financial assistance to a defined class of persons as long as the class is defined without reference to religion or religious criteria. Such a program is valid even if persons who receive the financial assistance are thereby enabled to attend a religiously affiliated school.

Examples: 1) The Supreme Court upheld a state program that made education subsidy payments directly to a blind or disabled student even though a student used his aid to study at a Christian college for the purpose of becoming a pastor or missionary. The class of persons who received the aid was defined without reference to any religious criteria; only an incidental benefit would go to the religiously affiliated college or vocational training institution. The aid program thus passed review under the purpose, effect, and entanglement tests. [Witters v. Washington Department of Services, 474 U.S. 481 (1986)]

2) The Court held that the Establishment Clause would not prevent a public school district from paying for a sign language interpreter for a deaf student at a religious high school under a religiously neutral program of aid to all handicapped school children in both public and private schools. [Zobrest v. Catalina Foothills School District, 509 U.S. 1 (1993)]

(2) Programs reimbursing private schools for *writing achievement tests* (this would have the primary effect of advancing religion since the schools could write tests advancing their religious mission) [Levitt v. Community for Public Education, 413 U.S. 472 (1973)].

4) Tax Exemption for Religious, Charitable, or Educational Property

An exemption from property taxation for "real or personal property used exclusively for religious, educational, or charitable purposes" does not violate the Establishment Clause. Neither the purpose nor the effect of such an exemption is the advancement or the inhibition of religion, and it constitutes neither sponsorship nor hostility, nor excessive government entanglement with religion. The "government does not transfer part of its revenue to churches but simply abstains from demanding that the church support the state . . . ." [Walz v. Tax Commission, 397 U.S. 664 (1970)]

5) Tax Exemption Available Only to Religions

Although religious schools or religious associations may be included in tax exemptions available to a variety of secular and religious organizations, a tax exemption that is available only for religious organizations or religious activities violates the Establishment Clause. [Texas Monthly, Inc. v. Bullock, 489 U.S. 1 (1989)—an exemption from the sales and use tax for religious magazines or books (but no other publications) violates the Establishment Clause]

c. Religious Activities in Public Schools

1) Prayer and Bible Reading

Prayer and Bible reading in school are invalid as establishments of religion. [Engel v. Vitale, 370 U.S. 421 (1962); Abington School District v. Schempp, 374 U.S. 203 (1963)] It does not matter whether participation is voluntary or involuntary, and neither does it matter that the prayer period is designated as a period of silent prayer or meditation. [Wallace v. Jaffree, 472 U.S. 38 (1985)] This rule extends to prohibit public school officials from having clerics give invocation and benediction prayers at graduation ceremonies. [Lee v. Weisman, 505 U.S. 577 (1992)] Similarly, a school policy authorizing students to elect whether to have a student invocation before varsity games, to select a student to deliver it, and to decide its content *violates* the Establishment Clause. Unlike student speeches at an open public forum (*see* 4), below), this policy's purpose is to encourage religious messages. [Santa Fe Independent School District v. Doe, 530 U.S. 290 (2000)]

2) Posting Ten Commandments in Classroom Is Invalid

Posting the Ten Commandments on the walls of public school classrooms plainly serves a religious purpose and is invalid, despite the legislature's statement that it was for a secular purpose. [Stone v. Graham, 449 U.S. 39 (1980)]

3) Released-Time Programs

a) In Public School Building

Programs in which regular classes end an hour early one day a week and

religious instruction is given in public school classrooms to students who request it are invalid. [McCollum v. Board of Education, 333 U.S. 203 (1948)]

b) Nonpublic Building Used

Programs in which participating children go to religious classes conducted at religious centers away from the public school do not violate the Establishment Clause. [Zorach v. Clauson, 343 U.S. 306 (1952)]

4) Accommodation of Religious Students—On-Campus Meetings

As discussed at XX.B.1.c., *supra*, under the Free Speech Clause, if a public school allows members of the public and private organizations to use school property when classes are not in session, it cannot deny a religious organization permission to use the property for meetings merely because religious topics will be discussed. Such an "equal access rule" does not violate the Establishment Clause because the primary purpose of such programs is secular (to accommodate all interests), people are not likely to assume that the government endorses the religious ideas discussed, and there is no excessive government entanglement, at least where the meetings are not run by school personnel. [Good News Club v. Milford Central School, 533 U.S. 98 (2001)]

5) Curriculum Controls

A government statute or regulation that modifies a public school curriculum will violate the Establishment Clause if it fails the secular purpose test, primary effect test, or excessive government entanglement test.

Example: A state statute that prohibited the teaching of human biological evolution in the state's public schools was held to violate the Establishment Clause because the Supreme Court found that the legislature had a religious purpose for enacting the statute. [Epperson v. Arkansas, 393 U.S. 97 (1968)] Similarly, the Court invalidated a state statute that prohibited instruction regarding "evolution science" (the theory of human biological evolution) in the public schools unless that instruction was accompanied by instruction regarding "creation science," because the Court found that the legislature enacted this statute for the purpose of promoting religion. [Edwards v. Aguillard, 482 U.S. 578 (1987)]

ESSAY EXAM QUESTIONS

INTRODUCTORY NOTE

The essay questions that follow have been selected to provide you with an opportunity to experience how the substantive law you have been reviewing may be tested in the hypothetical essay examination question context. These sample essay questions are a valuable self-diagnostic tool designed to enable you to enhance your issue-spotting ability and practice your exam writing skills.

It is suggested that you approach each question as though under actual examination conditions. The time allowed for each question is 60 minutes. You should spend 15 to 20 minutes spotting issues, underlining key facts and phrases, jotting notes in the margins, and outlining your answer. *If* you organize your thoughts well, 40 minutes will be more than adequate for writing them down. Should you prefer to forgo the actual writing involved on these questions, be sure to give yourself no more time for issue-spotting than you would on the actual examination.

The BARBRI technique for writing a well-organized essay answer is to (i) spot the issues in a question and then (ii) analyze and discuss each issue using the "CIRAC" method:

C — State your ***conclusion*** first. (In other words, you must think through your answer ***before*** you start writing.)

I — State the ***issue*** involved.

R — Give the ***rule(s)*** of law involved.

A — ***Apply*** the rule(s) of law to the facts.

C — Finally, restate your ***conclusion***.

After completing (or outlining) your own analysis of each question, compare it with the BARBRI model answer provided herein. A passing answer does ***not*** have to match the model one, but it should cover most of the issues presented and the law discussed and should ***apply the law to the facts*** of the question. Use of the CIRAC method results in the best answer you can write.

EXAM QUESTION NO. 1

Sierra Toxics, Inc. ("Sierra"), is a privately owned company engaged in the business of disposing of toxic waste generated by chemical and pharmaceutical plants. Sierra operates pursuant to a license issued by the Commissioner of Ecological Preservation of the state of Alpha. This license authorizes Sierra to contract with such plants to provide the following services: (i) collection of toxic waste at the plant site; and (ii) transportation of that waste to Sierra's disposal station, which is located in Alpha, three miles from the border with the state of Beta.

Pursuant to the authority granted by its license, for the past 10 years Sierra has contracted to provide services to plants in Alpha, and, a few years ago, expanded its business to serve plants just across the border in Beta. The Beta plants that contract with Sierra dispose of approximately one-half their toxic waste output through that company and the remainder of their waste through disposal companies located in Beta.

Shortly after Sierra extended its services to the Beta plants, the residents of the town in which Sierra's disposal station is situated became alarmed at the amount of toxic waste stored there. These residents were concerned about the proximity of such toxic waste, both to their homes and to the reservoir located in their town which supplies water to households in the immediate surrounding area.

The residents petitioned the Commissioner of Ecological Preservation to close Sierra's disposal station. Sierra objected. The Commissioner held an open hearing on the matter at which numerous witnesses testified. After that hearing, the Commissioner resolved the dispute by issuing an order that, effective immediately, use of Sierra's disposal station would be limited to toxic waste removed from chemical and pharmaceutical plants in Alpha only. The Beta plants were barred from disposing of their toxic waste through Sierra.

Both Sierra and the state of Beta have filed suit against the Alpha Commissioner of Ecological Preservation, seeking to rescind that order. The two lawsuits have been consolidated for trial before the judge whom you serve as law clerk. The judge has asked you to prepare a memorandum identifying the claims raised and the defenses asserted, and analyzing the legal bases for all such claims and defenses.

Prepare the memorandum.

EXAM QUESTION NO. 2

State University has had a nationally prominent football program for many years. A recent investigation by the American Athletic Association ("AAA"), consisting of public and private educational institutions nationwide, including State University, uncovered serious violations of the rules and regulations of the Association. These included recruiting infractions which implicated the head football coach. After a hearing conducted by the Association in which State University participated and in which Coach was a witness, the Association placed State University on probation for two years. It ordered that further sanctions will be imposed unless Coach is suspended for the probationary period. The president of State University has notified Coach of his intent to impose the required suspension.

As part of his fight against the suspension, Coach granted an interview to the sports editor of the student newspaper in which he disputed the Association's charges. The president has directed the paper not to publish the resulting article, and the editorial staff has complied.

Frustrated by his inability to tell his side of the story and threatened by loss of his job, Coach has retained your law firm to institute appropriate action.

Prepare a legal memorandum setting forth Coach's causes of action, the legal basis for each, and the defenses to be anticipated.

EXAM QUESTION NO. 3

A bill has been introduced in the legislature of the state of Uphoria which would limit appointment of members of the state police force to male citizens of the United States who are over the age of 20 years.

Senator Strate is chairman of the committee to which this bill has been referred, and he requires a carefully written summary analyzing the legal principles implicated by this bill. He retains you to prepare this summary in clear and concise language so that it may be used by members of his committee in their consideration of the merits of the bill.

Comply with the senator's request.

EXAM QUESTION NO. 4

Irma LaTouce and Lester DeJacques were employed as dancers at a Fun City cocktail lounge. Both dancers received a weekly salary plus commissions on drinks purchased for them by customers between performances. Police officers observed Irma and Lester socializing with lounge patrons and brought charges against them under a local ordinance which provided:

> Entertainers in business premises where alcoholic beverages are sold are prohibited from mingling with customers.

The stated purpose of the ordinance was to prevent disorderly conduct in premises where liquor is sold, to encourage temperance, and to discourage opportunities for the solicitation of prostitution or engaging in any other immoral activity.

At the trial before the local municipal court, the dancers testified that the commissions were earned for socializing with the clientele, which involved conversation and casual companionship with men and women who patronized the club. They both admitted that the main purpose of this activity was to get the customers to buy more drinks. It was stipulated that there had been no disorderly conduct in the lounge and that neither defendant had solicited any act of prostitution or engaged in any other immoral activity. The court found both dancers guilty as charged and imposed a fine as provided in the ordinance.

Irma and Lester have now consulted you. They desire to appeal their convictions. Prepare a brief in support of Irma and Lester as petitioners.

ANSWERS TO ESSAY EXAM QUESTIONS

ANSWER TO EXAM QUESTION NO. 1

To: Judge
From: Law Clerk
Re: Sierra Toxics

Commerce Clause: The Commissioner of Ecological Preservation's ("CEP's") order violates the Commerce Clause. At issue is whether a state may prohibit hazardous waste disposal facilities within the state from accepting hazardous wastes from outside the state.

The Commerce Clause gives Congress plenary power to regulate commerce among the states. This power is not exclusive; the states may also regulate commerce. However, state regulation that discriminates against interstate commerce usually will be stricken as violating the Commerce Clause unless the regulation is necessary to achieve an important state interest.

Here, the CEP's order clearly discriminates against interstate commerce since it prohibits disposal of out-of-state wastes but allows disposal of wastes generated within the state. The Commission would no doubt argue that the state's interest in the safety of residents around Sierra's disposal facility necessitates the limitation, but this argument will fail. A nondiscriminatory regulation (*e.g.,* limiting the amount of hazardous waste that may be disposed of at Sierra's plant, regardless of where the hazardous waste was generated) could provide the same protection as the prohibition here. Thus, the regulation discriminates against interstate commerce without valid justification and so violates the Commerce Clause.

Contracts Clause: The order of the CEP might also violate the Contracts Clause. At issue is whether a state order that prohibits a waste disposal facility from accepting wastes from certain customers violates the Contracts Clause.

The Contracts Clause generally prohibits states from acting to retroactively and substantially impair existing contracts rights. However, the bar is not absolute; even if a state act substantially impairs existing contract rights it still will be upheld if the impairment serves an important public interest and the law is reasonable and narrowly tailored to promote that interest.

Here, it is not clear whether the CEP's order substantially impairs any existing contract rights, although we are told that the order prohibits Sierra from accepting hazardous wastes from outside the state, and that Sierra has contracted with out-of-state customers in the past, we are not told whether Sierra has any continuing contracts that would be impaired by the CEP's order. Assuming such contracts exist, the order would violate the Contracts Clause. Since the CEP is a state agency, there is action by the state. And while safeguarding the community from toxic wastes is clearly an important interest, as discussed above the order here is not reasonable to deal with the problem because it does nothing to prevent wastes generated within the state from jeopardizing the community's safety. Accordingly, the order violates the Contracts Clause.

Privileges and Immunities Clause of Article IV: The CEP order might violate the Privileges and Immunities Clause of Article IV, at least with respect to the citizens of state Beta. At issue is whether a state may prohibit nonresidents from contracting for commercial services in the state.

The Privileges and Immunities Clause of Article IV prohibits states from discriminating against nonresidents in matters concerning fundamental rights, which include important commercial activities and civil liberties. However, even if a state discriminates against nonresidents, the discrimination can be upheld if the state has a substantial justification for the different treatment and there are no less

restrictive means to accomplish the state's goal. In any case, the Privileges and Immunities Clause is available only to natural persons; corporations cannot take advantage of its protections.

Here, we are not told whether any of Sierra's customers are natural persons; they might all be corporations. If Beta is allowed to represent the interests of natural persons who are being discriminated against by the CEP's order, the order probably violates the Privileges and Immunities Clause. Contracting for commercial waste disposal services probably is an important commercial activity, and the CEP's order discriminates against nonresidents by completely prohibiting them from contracting on an equal basis with residents of Alpha. And while there probably is substantial justification for the order (to protect the community from hazardous wastes), as discussed above, the order is not the least restrictive means of protecting that interest. Thus, the order could violate the Privileges and Immunities Clause of Article IV.

Procedural Due Process: Finally, it could be argued that Sierra was denied its right to procedural due process. At issue is whether Sierra had an adequate opportunity to present its case.

The Due Process Clause of the Fifth Amendment, made applicable to the states through the Fourteenth Amendment, provides that the government shall not take a person's life, liberty, or property without due process of law. Due process contemplates fair procedures, which requires at least an opportunity to present objections to the proposed action and a fair and neutral decisionmaker. The timing and scope of the hearing due depend on the circumstances of the deprivation. In most cases, the person being deprived of life, liberty, or property should receive notice of the government's proposed action and have an opportunity to respond before the deprivation.

Here, the CEP has limited Sierra's right to contract, a liberty interest. The facts state that a public hearing was held, but we are not told whether Sierra was given individual notice of the meeting or was given an opportunity to speak. Presumably, sufficient notice and an opportunity to respond were given, and thus Sierra was afforded adequate procedural due process.

ANSWER TO EXAM QUESTION NO. 2

To: Partner
From: Associate
Re: Coach's Causes of Action

Coach v. AAA: AAA has informed State University that it will be subject to sanctions unless Coach is suspended for two years. The first issue is whether the action of AAA constitutes state action.

To find state action, an actor must perform public functions or have significant state involvement. It appears, under this standard, that AAA is not a state actor; regulating sports at public and private institutions nationwide is not a function traditionally reserved to the states and neither are its activities so involved with the state so as to rise to the level of state action. [*Compare:* Brentwood Academy v. Tennessee Secondary School Athletic Association, 531 U.S. 288 (2001)—state action found where, among other things, "private" regulating body operated in a single state, was made up mostly of public school officials, and met during school hours]

Furthermore, AAA has given State University a choice of what to do, albeit a coercive choice. State University does not have to suspend Coach; it could choose to accept further sanctions and not suspend Coach. Therefore, no causes of action will lie against AAA because it merely made findings and left it to State University to decide what actions to take. [*See* National Collegiate Athletic Association v. Tarkanian, 488 U.S. 179 (1988)]

Coach v. State University: The actions of State University through its president, however, do constitute state action. The university is an institution of the state, as indicated by its name, and the president is a state actor. The question, then, is what constitutional rights Coach has, and whether these rights were infringed by the university.

We must ascertain whether Coach was removable for cause. An employee removable only for cause has a property interest in his job, and thus is entitled to due process before the state deprives him of his job.

Assuming Coach is removable only for cause, due process requires that he be given notice of the charges against him, as well as a pretermination opportunity to respond to the charges. An evidentiary hearing regarding the termination decision must be provided either before or after the termination, with reinstatement if he prevails. If no cause is required for removal, Coach is an employee at will and is not due any process before or after termination.

We should move to secure the above procedural safeguards for Coach. While Coach participated in the AAA hearing, he appeared only as a witness, and not as a party. Coach is entitled to a more substantial opportunity to respond to the charges against him. Coach has received notice of the decision to suspend him. He may respond to the president's notification of suspension and is entitled to an evidentiary hearing regarding his termination.

The university may assert that a two-year suspension is not the same as a termination. However, our position is that a two-year loss of job and salary is an infringement of Coach's property rights serious enough to warrant a hearing.

Should we bring this claim, the university may institute a defense of ripeness. They could claim that no action has been taken against Coach and that his claim is premature. However, an action is ripe for review when there is the immediate threat of harm. Here, the president has notified Coach of its intent to suspend him. Thus, Coach's claim will not fail for lack of ripeness.

Coach's First Amendment claim: Coach feels silenced by the refusal of the school newspaper to print the views he expressed in his interview. However, Coach's constitutional rights probably have not been violated. First, the contents of a school-funded newspaper can be regulated because the Supreme Court has found that such papers are not public forums, but merely are educational devices.

Even if the newspaper were a public forum, it would not give rise to a cause of action by Coach. Generally, a party cannot assert the constitutional rights of others. To have standing, the claimant must have suffered a direct impairment of his own constitutional rights. Here, a prior restraint has been placed on the newspaper. This is a burden on the newspaper's rights. And while Coach is affected, it is not a direct impairment of his rights. Thus, he lacks standing to bring a suit based in the First Amendment.

ANSWER TO EXAM QUESTION NO. 3

The state of Uphoria's bill would be valid as to its age and citizenship requirements, but would be unconstitutional due to its gender classification.

Under the Equal Protection Clause of the Fourteenth Amendment, government may not treat similar people in a dissimilar manner without a sufficient reason. The strength of the reason necessary depends on the basis of the classification. There are three tests:

The first test is the strict scrutiny or compelling state interest test. This test is used if the classification is based on a suspect classification, which includes race, national origin, or alienage. Under this test, the law is considered to be invalid unless the government can prove that it is necessary to achieve a compelling state objective.

The second test involves intermediate scrutiny. Under this test, the court will strike down a law unless the government can show that the law bears a substantial relation to an important government interest. This is the test used in situations such as that here, where there is a classification based on gender. Gender classifications will be struck down absent an exceedingly persuasive justification, and the government may not rely on overbroad generalizations about males and females that will perpetuate the legal, social, and economic inferiority of women. [United States v. Virginia, 518 U.S. 515 (1996)—striking state military school's policy of admitting only men]

The third test is the rational basis test (minimum scrutiny). Under this test, the classification is valid if there is any conceivable basis upon which the classification might relate to a legitimate governmental interest. In other words, the person challenging the classification must prove that it is arbitrary or irrational. This is a very "loose" test and it is very difficult for a law to fail it. This test is used for all classifications relating to matters of economics or social welfare.

The gender designation of Uphoria's bill limiting the appointment of state police officers to males would fall under the intermediate scrutiny test due to its inherent gender classification. Therefore, this component will only be upheld if it is substantially related to an important governmental interest.

This gender classification is not related to an important governmental interest. As in *United States v. Virginia, supra,* the government will not be able to show that all women are incapable of performing the duties of a state trooper. If Uphoria claims that its bill is based on ability to do the work, it can design a test of each individual's (male or female) ability to perform the work required of a state police officer, and not unfairly discriminate against women. Accordingly, under the intermediate scrutiny test, this bill would be found invalid due to the fact that it discriminates against women without an exceedingly persuasive justification.

The bill also limits appointment of police officers to citizens of the United States. Since this component of the bill is based on alienage, it ordinarily falls under the strict scrutiny-compelling interest test. However, there is an exception to this rule which provides that if, as here, the law discriminates against alien participation in the functioning of state government, the mere rationality test is applied. Under the mere rationality test, a state can validly refuse to hire aliens as police officers, or for other positions which have direct effect on the function of government. [Ambach v. Norwick, 441 U.S. 68 (1979)] Accordingly, the bill would be valid as far as its citizenship requirement is concerned.

The bill sets the age for appointment of a police officer to be over 20 years. The Court has held that age is not a suspect classification, so a rational basis analysis can be applied. The 20-year-old minimum age requirement in this statute would be held constitutional under the rational basis test because of the state's interest in having police officers who are physically and emotionally mature enough to handle the stress of police work.

ANSWER TO EXAM QUESTION NO. 4

A. FIRST AMENDMENT ISSUES

Under the First Amendment, "Congress shall make no law abridging the freedom of speech, or of the press . . . ." This guarantee has been held applicable to the states by reason of the "liberty" protected by the Due Process Clause of the Fourteenth Amendment.

1. Freedom of Association and Belief: The First Amendment protects freedom of association. Here, it appears that the ordinance impinges on the rights of the entertainers to talk and mingle with the customers. As such, the ordinance has the effect of chilling this vital First Amendment right. Thus, on this ground, the ordinance is unconstitutional.

2.   **The Ordinance Is Overbroad:** If a regulation of speech or speech related conduct punishes a substantial amount of protected speech, judged in relation to the regulation's plainly legitimate sweep, the regulation is facially invalid (*i.e.,* it cannot be enforced against anyone—not even a person engaging in activity that is not constitutionally protected.). Here, the stated purposes of the ordinance are to (i) prevent disorderly conduct; (ii) encourage temperance; (iii) discourage prostitution; and (iv) prevent any other immoral activity. While these purposes are legitimate government interests, the ordinance, as written, restricts expression and conduct that are in no way connected with prostitution, immoral activity, etc. Accordingly, the ordinance chills speech and conduct that are protected under the First Amendment. Certainly, the ordinance could be worded to restrict only the activities that are the focus of its basic purposes, *i.e.,* preventing prostitution and drunkenness. Prohibiting mingling of customers and entertainers goes beyond these legitimate purposes. Therefore, the ordinance is unconstitutionally overbroad and cannot be enforced against anyone.

3.   **The Ordinance Is Vague:** Laws regulating speech-related activities are unconstitutional if they are too vague to make absolutely clear what they forbid. To the extent their vagueness suggests that they prohibit constitutionally protected speech, they have a "chilling effect" on speech. Here, the ordinance prohibits the entertainers from "mingling" with customers. The word "mingling" is too vague to define what conduct is proscribed by the ordinance. Thus, it appears that the entertainers may be forced to refrain from conduct and expression protected by the First Amendment in order not to be considered "mingling" with the customers. Because this ordinance has, in this manner, the effect of "chilling" activity and expression that is protected by the First Amendment, it is unconstitutional.

4.   **Effect of Twenty-First Amendment on First Amendment Rights:** The Twenty-First Amendment gives the states much control over the sale and use of intoxicating liquor within their borders. Thus, Fun City's attorneys could argue that the ordinance is a valid exercise of the state's constitutionally granted powers with respect to intoxicating liquors. However, this argument fails because, as a general rule, individual rights guaranteed by the Bill of Rights and the Fourteenth Amendment outweigh state liquor control laws. Here, the ordinance, which constitutes a liquor control regulation, chills First Amendment rights made applicable, to states under the Fourteenth Amendment. Accordingly, the ordinance is unconstitutional.

B.   SUBSTANTIVE DUE PROCESS ISSUES

Substantive due process protects certain fundamental rights not articulated within the text of the Constitution. It is a test of the "reasonableness" of a statute in relation to the government's power to enact such legislation. It prohibits arbitrary government action. The Due Process Clause of the Fourteenth Amendment applies to state and local governments.

Under substantive due process principles, where a fundamental right is limited, the law (or other government action) must be necessary to promote a compelling or overriding state interest. Fundamental rights include interstate travel, privacy, voting, and all rights implied under the First Amendment.

Here the ordinance, as discussed above, chills the entertainers' First Amendment rights of association and speech. From the facts, Fun City has shown no compelling or overriding interest to do so. Accordingly, on this ground, the ordinance violates substantive due process.

C.   EQUAL PROTECTION ISSUES

Under the Equal Protection Clause of the Fourteenth Amendment (applicable to the states), and as an implicit guarantee of the Due Process Clause of the Fifth Amendment (applicable to the federal government), governmental acts that classify people improperly may be invalid. It is unconstitutional for the government to treat similar people in a dissimilar manner absent sufficient justification. Under the "strict scrutiny" test, the classification must be necessary to promote a compelling interest. This test is employed when, as here, the classification affects the exercise of a fundamental right.

Here, the ordinance seeks to classify the entertainers as individuals who cannot exercise certain fundamental rights—those granted by the First Amendment. Thus, to sustain the classification, Fun City must show that it has a "compelling interest" to do so. Clearly, Fun City does not have a compelling interest to make such a classification and, therefore, the ordinance violates equal protection.

D. CONCLUSION

For the foregoing reasons, Irma's and Lester's convictions should be reversed. Irma and Lester have been charged with violation of an ordinance which is overbroad and infringes on their guaranteed constitutional rights.

Corporations

CORPORATIONS

TABLE OF CONTENTS

·(RMBCA)

 **borbri**

PART ONE—CHARACTERISTICS AND FORMATION OF CORPORATIONS

I. CORPORATION VS. OTHER BUSINESS ENTITIES

A. INTRODUCTION

The corporation is a form of business ownership that has advantages and disadvantages over other forms of business ownership. There are even a number of forms of corporations, each with its own advantages and disadvantages. Thus, the first issue to be addressed in corporate law is how the corporate form differs from other business entities and how the various corporate forms differ from each other.

B. GENERAL CHARACTERISTICS OF A CORPORATION

A corporation is a legal entity distinct from its owners. Creation of such an entity generally requires filing certain documents with the state, and running a corporation generally requires more formality than is required to run most other types of business entities. Corporations generally have the following characteristics:

1. Limited Liability for Owners, Directors, and Officers

The owners of a corporation (called "shareholders") generally are not personally liable for the obligations of the corporation; neither are the corporation's directors or officers. Generally only the corporation itself can be held liable for corporate obligations. The owners risk only the investment that they make in the business to purchase their ownership interests ("shares"). Thus, if a person wants to set up a business entity that protects his personal assets from the possibility of being seized to satisfy obligations of the business, a corporation would be a good business form to consider.

2. Centralized Management

Generally, the right to manage a corporation is not spread out among the shareholders, but rather is centralized in a board of directors, who usually delegate day-to-day management duties to officers. Thus, if a person wants to avoid conflicts with co-owners of a business regarding management of the business, a corporation may be a good form of business to choose.

Note: Although the general rule is that a corporation is run by managers, shareholders can enter into agreements vesting management power in themselves rather than in a board.

3. Free Transferability of Ownership

Generally, ownership of a corporation is freely transferable; a shareholder can sell his shares to whomever he wants, whenever he wants, at whatever price he wants in most circumstances. Thus, if a person wants to set up a business entity that will enable him to easily bring in new investors in exchange for ownership interests, the corporate form is worth considering.

Note: Transferability of shares can be restricted by agreement of the shareholders. Such restriction is popular in close corporations so that current owners have some control over who may join their business in the future. Restrictions may also be necessary to assure eligibility of S corporation status. (*See* below.)

(RMBCA)

4. Continuity of Life

A corporation may exist perpetually and generally is not affected by changes in ownership (*i.e.*, sale of shares). Thus, if a person wants to create a business entity that can exist apart from and beyond its current owners, the corporate form is worth considering.

5. Taxation

a. C Corporation

Generally, a corporation is taxed as an entity distinct from its owners; *i.e.*, it must pay income taxes on any profits that it makes, and generally shareholders do not have to pay income tax on the corporation's profits until the profits are distributed. (Under the tax laws, such a corporation is known as a "C corporation.") The corporate tax rate generally is lower than the personal tax rate, and so this arrangement can be advantageous to persons who want to delay the realization of income. However, this advantage comes at a price—double taxation—because when the corporation does make distributions to shareholders, the distributions are treated as taxable income to the shareholders even though the corporation has already paid taxes on its profits.

b. S Corporation

The tax laws permit certain corporations to elect to be taxed like partnerships and yet retain the other advantages (above) of the corporate form. Such corporations are called "S corporations" under the tax laws. Partnerships and S corporations are not subject to double taxation—profits and losses flow directly through to the owners. This may be advantageous when losses are expected for the first few years that the business will be operating, since it allows the owners to offset the losses against their current incomes. It also may result in lower overall taxes on profits because there is no double taxation. However, there are a number of restrictions on S corporations (*e.g.*, stock can be held by no more than 100 persons, generally shareholders must be individuals, there can be only one class of stock [*see* 26 U.S.C. §1361]).

C. COMPARISON WITH SOLE PROPRIETORSHIP

A sole proprietorship is a form of business in which one person owns all of the assets of the business. The sole proprietorship generally does not exist as an entity apart from its owner, and thus little formality is required to form it. However, since a sole proprietorship is not an entity distinct from its owner, its owner is personally liable for the business's obligations and the business "entity" cannot continue beyond the life of the owner. Management is centralized (since there is only one owner), and the owner is free to transfer his interest in the sole proprietorship at will. All profits and losses from the business flow through directly to the owner. Thus, if a person is interested in setting up a business with only one owner, desires little formality, is willing to risk personal assets, and wants to avoid double taxation, the sole proprietorship is worth considering as a business form.

D. COMPARISON WITH PARTNERSHIP

A partnership is similar to a sole proprietorship except that there are at least two owners of a partnership. Little formality is required to form a partnership (just an intention to run as co-owners a business for profit). Partnerships may have a few entity characteristics (*e.g.*, property may be held in the name of the partnership, suits can be maintained in the name of the partnership), but generally partnerships are not treated as legal entities. Partners are personally liable for obligations of the partnership; management generally is not centralized, but rather is spread

among the partners; ownership interests of partners cannot be transferred without the consent of the other partners; and a partnership generally does not continue beyond the lives of its owners (although the partners can agree to allow remaining partners to continue the partnership business after a partner leaves). Finally, as indicated above, profits and losses of a partnership flow through directly to the partners. Thus, if a person is interested in forming a business with more than one owner, does not want to bother with a lot of formality, does not mind sharing management rights with co-owners, does not mind putting personal assets at risk, etc., a partnership might be an appropriate entity to form.

E. COMPARISON WITH LIMITED PARTNERSHIP

A limited partnership is a partnership that provides for limited liability of some investors (called "limited partners"), but otherwise is similar to other partnerships. A limited partnership can be formed only by compliance with the limited partnership statute. There must be at least one general partner, who has full personal liability for partnership debts and has most management rights. Thus, this form of business entity offers limited liability to most investors, centralized management (*i.e.*, management by the general partner(s) rather than by all owners), and the flow-through tax advantages of a partnership, without the 100-investor limit of an S corporation.

F. COMPARISON WITH LIMITED LIABILITY PARTNERSHIP

A limited liability partnership ("LLP") is a relatively new form of business entity that provides for the limited liability of all of its members; there is not a general partner who stands liable for the actions of the partnership. Formation requires filing a "statement of qualification" with the secretary of state. Otherwise, the entity is similar to other partnerships.

G. COMPARISON WITH LIMITED LIABILITY COMPANY

The limited liability company ("LLC") is a relatively new form of business entity designed to offer the limited liability of a corporation and the flow-through tax advantages of a partnership. Like a corporation, it may be formed only by filing appropriate documents with the state, but otherwise it is a very flexible business form: owners may choose centralized management or owner management, free transferability of ownership or restricted transferability, etc. (For more detail, *see* XI., *infra*.)

H. CONSTITUTIONAL CHARACTERISTICS OF A CORPORATION

1. "Person"
Corporations are entitled to due process of law and equal protection of the law. A corporation is entitled to raise the attorney-client privilege, but cannot invoke the privilege against self-incrimination. Generally, unless the context of the statute or constitutional provision requires application only to *natural* persons, a corporation is entitled to the protection and rights afforded thereby.

2. "Citizen"

a. Constitutional References to "Citizens"
A corporation is *not* a citizen for purposes of the Privileges and Immunities Clause of the Constitution. Therefore, state-imposed restrictions on a foreign corporation's activities are valid if they are a reasonable exercise of the state's police power. A foreign corporation is one conducting business in a particular state but not incorporated under that state's laws.

b. Federal Diversity Jurisdiction
By federal statute a corporation is deemed to be a citizen of any state by which it has been incorporated *and* of the state where it has its principal place of business. [28 U.S.C. §1332(c)]

1) Principal Place of Business
A corporation's principal place of business is where the corporation's high level officers direct, control, and coordinate the corporation's activities. Usually it is the corporation's headquarters. [*See* Hertz Corp. v. Friend, 130 S. Ct. 1181 (2010)]

2) Multiple Incorporation
If a corporation has incorporated in more than one state, the preferable rule is that it is deemed to be a citizen of every state of incorporation.

3. "Resident"
A corporation may be a resident of the state where it is incorporated, where it is doing business, and perhaps where it is merely qualified to do business.

4. "Domicile"
A corporation's domicile is the state of its incorporation. Like residence, however, a corporation may have multiple domiciles for some purposes, particularly for state taxation if the corporation has its principal place of business outside the state of its incorporation.

II. FORMATION AND STATUS OF THE CORPORATION

A. CREATED UNDER STATUTE
Corporations are created by complying with state corporate law. A majority of states have laws based on the Revised Model Business Corporation Act ("RMBCA"), and therefore this outline is based on that act. However, some states have varied from certain RMBCA provisions, and those variations will be discussed as well.

B. FORMATION TERMINOLOGY
A corporation formed in accordance with all applicable laws is a de jure corporation and its owners generally will not be personally liable for the corporation's obligations. However, if all applicable laws have not been followed, a business may still be treated as a corporation under the de facto corporation doctrine if there was a good faith attempt to incorporate. Even if no attempt to incorporate was made, under some circumstances, a business may be treated as a corporation for the purposes of a particular transaction under an estoppel theory.

C. FORMATION OF A DE JURE CORPORATION
To form a de jure corporation under the RMBCA, incorporators (*i.e.*, the persons who undertake to form a corporation) must file a document called the "articles of incorporation" with the state and must pay whatever fees the state directs.

1. Incorporator Defined
An incorporator is simply a person who signs the articles of incorporation. Under the RMBCA, only one incorporator is necessary, but there may be more than one. [RMBCA §2.01] In

most states, incorporators may be either natural persons or artificial entities, such as a corporation.

2. Contents of Articles

The articles are required to set out certain basic information about the corporation and may contain any other provision that the incorporators deem appropriate.

a. Mandatory Provisions

The articles must set out:

(i) The ***name of the corporation,*** which must include the word "corporation," "incorporated," "company," "limited," or the like (or an abbreviation of such words) and generally may not be similar to the name of another business entity qualified to do business in the state, unless the other business consents;

(ii) The ***number of shares*** the corporation is authorized to issue;

(iii) The street address of the corporation's ***initial registered office*** and the ***name of the corporation's initial registered agent*** at that office upon whom legal process may be served (the office must be within the state of incorporation, and the agent must be a resident of the state); and

(iv) The ***name and address of each incorporator.***

[RMBCA §2.02(a)]

b. Optional Provisions

The articles may set forth any other provision not inconsistent with law regarding managing the business and regulating the affairs of the corporation. However, it should be noted that the RMBCA includes a number of features that a corporation need not adopt, but if they are adopted they must be provided for in the articles. For example, a corporation may choose to limit directors' liability for damages in certain circumstances, but if a corporation wants to so limit liability, it may do so only by including the limitation in the articles. A number of these conditionally mandatory provisions will be discussed later in this outline.

1) Business Purposes

Traditionally, the articles had to include a statement of the business purposes of the corporation, and the corporation was limited to activities pursuing the stated purposes. Over time, statutes became more lenient and allowed a broad purpose statement, such as "to conduct any lawful business." The RMBCA has gone even further and ***presumes*** that a corporation is formed for ***any lawful business*** unless the articles provide a more restricted business purpose.

a) Ultra Vires Acts

Generally, a corporation is allowed to undertake any action necessary or convenient to carry out its business or affairs. If a corporation includes a narrow purpose statement in its articles of incorporation, it may ***not*** undertake activities unrelated to achieving the stated business purpose (*e.g.,* if the articles state that the corporation's purpose is to operate restaurants, the

corporation may not undertake to run a mink farm). If a corporation undertakes activities beyond the scope of its stated purpose, it is said to be acting "ultra vires."

(1) Effect

At common law, if a corporation acted ultra vires, the action was void; no one could enforce the action. Modern laws and the RMBCA have changed this dramatically. Typically, an ultra vires act is enforceable, and the ultra vires nature of an act may be raised in only three circumstances:

(i) A *shareholder* may sue the corporation to enjoin a proposed ultra vires act;

(ii) The *corporation* may sue an officer or director for damages arising from the commission of an ultra vires act authorized by the officer or director; and

(iii) The *state* may bring an action against the corporation to have it dissolved for committing an ultra vires act.

[RMBCA §3.04(b)] Note that if an officer or director is found liable for committing an ultra vires act, the officer or director may be held *personally* liable for damages. Note also that an ultra vires act will be enjoined only if it is equitable to do so. This generally means that an act involving an innocent third party (*i.e.*, one who did not know that the action was ultra vires) will not be enjoined.

Example: Mary Ann and Ginger incorporate a business called Castaway Foods, Inc. ("CF"). CF's articles include a purpose clause stating that the corporation was formed for the purpose of baking and selling coconut cream pies. The business is successful, and a few years later, in an attempt to expand business, Mary Ann enters into a contract with "Skipper" Jonas Grumby to purchase his tour boat. When Mary Ann tells Ginger about the deal, Ginger is furious and brings an action to enjoin the purchase. The court will grant the injunction only if Skipper knew that the transaction was beyond CF's purpose clause.

(2) Charitable Donations

At one time, charitable donations were thought to be outside the scope of any business purpose, but most states and the RMBCA now allow corporations to make charitable donations. [RMBCA §3.02(13)]

(3) Loans

Formerly, some courts held that corporations did not have the power to make loans to employees, officers, or directors. Today, most states and the RMBCA allow such loans. [RMBCA §3.02(11)]

    2) Initial Directors

The articles may provide the names and addresses of the persons who will serve as the corporation's initial directors until new directors are elected. [RMBCA §2.02(b)]

3. Corporate Existence Begins on Filing by the State

The articles must be submitted to the state (in most states, to the secretary of state or the corporation commission) along with any required filing fees. If the state finds that the articles comply with the requirements of law and that all required fees have been paid, it will file the articles. [RMBCA §2.03] This filing of the articles by the state is conclusive proof of the beginning of the corporate existence.

4. Additional Procedures to Make De Jure Corporation Operative

After the articles are filed, the initial directors will hold an organizational meeting to adopt bylaws, elect officers, and transact other business. If the articles do not name the initial directors, the incorporators call the organizational meeting.

    a. Bylaws

Bylaws may contain any provision for managing the corporation that is not inconsistent with law or the articles of incorporation. [RMBCA §2.06(b)] Bylaws are adopted by the directors, but can usually be modified or repealed by *either* the directors *or* the shareholders. However, the articles of incorporation may reserve this power exclusively to the shareholders. Even without such a reservation, the shareholders may provide that a particular bylaw adopted or amended by them may not be repealed or amended by the directors. [RMBCA §10.20]

        1) Compare—Articles

As will be discussed at IX.B., *infra*, amendment of the articles usually requires a vote of *both* the directors *and* the shareholders. Thus it is less difficult to change a corporate rule contained in the bylaws than it is to change a rule contained in the articles. This is an important planning tool. If future flexibility is desired with regard to a particular aspect of corporate management, the aspect should be addressed in the bylaws rather than the articles.

D. RECOGNITION OF CORPORATENESS WHEN CORPORATION IS DEFECTIVE

As discussed above, one of the main reasons to incorporate is to avoid personal liability for obligations of a business enterprise. This veil of protection generally is available when a de jure corporation is formed (*i.e.*, when all the steps required by statute for incorporation have been followed). The veil of protection may also be available in some circumstances even when all of the steps necessary under the incorporation statute have not been followed—under the de facto corporation or corporation by estoppel doctrines.

1. De Facto Corporation

A de facto corporation has all the rights and powers of a de jure corporation at common law, but it remains subject to direct attack in a *quo warranto* proceeding by the state.

    a. Common Law Requirements

Traditionally, the requirements for establishing a de facto corporation are:

1) **Statute for Valid Incorporation Available**

There must be a corporate law under which the organization could have been legally incorporated, such as the RMBCA.

2) **Colorable Compliance and Good Faith**

There must be colorable compliance with the incorporation laws. "Colorable" compliance means a *good faith attempt to comply* with the state law.

3) **Exercise of Corporate Privileges**

Finally, the corporation must act like a corporation, *i.e.,* conduct the business in its corporate name and exercise corporate privileges.

b. **Limitation on De Facto Doctrine**

Under prior law, the de facto doctrine was thought to be eliminated, but the RMBCA seems to recognize the doctrine in some circumstances. The Act provides that persons who purport to act as or on behalf of a corporation *knowing* that there was no incorporation are liable for all liabilities created in so acting. [RMBCA §2.04] It follows under the common law maxim *expressio unius est exclusio alterius* (expression of one thing is the exclusion of another), that persons who do not know that there was no incorporation will not be liable (*i.e.,* the de facto corporation doctrine probably is available for such persons).

Examples: 1) Andrea and Bart agree to form AbbeyCorp. They properly draw up the necessary papers and Bart tells Andrea that he will file them the next day. Bart forgets to file the papers and forgets to tell Andrea of his failure. The following week, Andrea enters into a contract with a supplier on behalf of AbbeyCorp. Andrea probably can avoid personal liability on the contract under the de facto corporation doctrine.

2) Same facts as above, but the day after Andrea and Bart draw up the articles, Bart mails them to the secretary of state, and a few days after Andrea entered into the contract with the supplier, Andrea and Bart receive a letter from the secretary of state indicating that the articles were not filed because they were missing the incorporators' signatures. Andrea probably can avoid personal liability on the contract under the de facto corporation doctrine.

2. **Corporation by Estoppel**

A business might also be treated as a corporation despite the lack of de jure status under the corporation by estoppel doctrine. Under the doctrine, persons who treat an entity as a corporation will be estopped from later claiming that the entity was not a corporation. The doctrine can be applied either to an outsider seeking to avoid liability on a contract with the purported corporation, or to a purported corporation seeking to avoid liability on a contract with an outsider.

Examples: 1) Suppose X, an outsider, deals with the entity as though it were a valid corporation. Upon discovering a defect in formation, X seeks to hold the shareholders personally liable. A shareholder without prior knowledge of the defect may successfully assert that X is estopped to deny the corporation's existence, since X always treated the corporation as though it were properly formed.

2) Z, an improperly formed corporation, contracts to buy supplies from W. If Z tries to avoid the contract on the basis of its formation defects so that the "shareholders" can purchase goods elsewhere, Z would be treated as a corporation by estoppel.

3. Application of De Facto and Estoppel Doctrines

When an organization is considered to be a de facto corporation, it is treated as if it were de jure, except in a direct attack by the state. That is, its shareholders enjoy limited liability and it has perpetual life, ability to buy and sell property, etc. Estoppel, on the other hand, is applied on a case-by-case basis between two parties to equitably resolve a dispute.

a. Contracts

In contract cases, both doctrines are easily applied. When the parties have previously dealt on a corporate basis, or have assumed there to be a valid corporation, corporate status is generally upheld.

b. Torts

The de facto doctrine has been applied in tort cases [*see* Kardo Co. v. Adams, 231 F. 950 (6th Cir. 1916)], but normally there is little room for an estoppel argument when a tort claim is involved, because recognition of corporateness has no relevance to the commission of the tort (*i.e.,* the plaintiff did not allow herself to be injured in reliance on the fact that the defendant was acting as a corporation). Thus, parties with tort claims are generally free to sue the shareholders of an improperly formed corporation.

c. Liability of Associates

Generally, when the court finds no corporate status, the associates will be held liable as partners. However, courts are prone to hold "*active*" associates (those participating in the particular transaction involved) personally liable, and absolve inactive associates from personal liability. The RMBCA imposes *joint and several liability* for all liabilities created by persons who purport to act as or on behalf of a corporation *with knowledge that no corporation exists*. [RMBCA §2.04]

4. Limitation of Doctrines

Because the incorporation process is very simple, a number of states refuse to recognize either or both the de facto corporation doctrine and/or the doctrine of incorporation by estoppel.

E. DISREGARD OF CORPORATE ENTITY (PIERCING THE CORPORATE VEIL)

In some circumstances, even though a corporation has been validly formed, the courts will hold the shareholders, officers, or directors *personally liable* for corporate obligations because the corporation is abusing the legislative privilege of conducting business in the corporate form. This is frequently called "piercing the corporate veil." This doctrine counterbalances the de facto corporation and corporation by estoppel doctrines, for here a *valid corporate existence is ignored* in equity to serve the ends of justice.

1. Elements Justifying Piercing the Corporate Veil

As a general rule, a de jure corporation will be treated as a legal entity until sufficient reason to the contrary appears. Each case is different, but there are three recurring situations in which the veil is often pierced: (i) when corporate formalities are ignored; (ii) when the corporation is inadequately capitalized at the outset; and (iii) to prevent fraud.

a. Alter Ego (Ignoring Corporate Formalities)

If a corporation is the "alter ego," "agent," or "instrumentality" of a sole proprietor or of another corporation, its separate identity may be disregarded.

1) Individual Shareholders

If the shareholders treat the assets of the corporation as their own, use corporate funds to pay their private debts, fail to keep separate corporate books, and fail to observe corporate formalities (such as holding meetings, issuing stock, and conducting business by resolution), courts often find that the corporate entity is a mere "alter ego" of the shareholders. However, sloppy administration alone may not be sufficient to warrant piercing the corporate veil. The operation of the corporation must result in some ***basic injustice*** so that equity would require that the individual shareholders respond to the damage they have caused.

Note: As will be discussed later, the RMBCA allows the shareholders to vest power to run the corporation in themselves, rather than in a board of directors. Their doing so is ***not*** a ground for disregarding the corporate veil, even if it results in a failure to keep corporate records. [RMBCA §7.32; *and see* V.C.3., *infra*]

2) Parent-Subsidiary Corporations

A subsidiary or affiliated corporation will not be deemed to be a separate corporate entity if the formalities of separate corporate procedures for each corporation are not observed. For example, both corporations must be held out to the public as separate entities; separate meetings of directors and officers should be held; identical or substantially overlapping directors and officers should be avoided; and corporate policies should be significantly different.

3) Affiliated Corporations

If one person owns most or all of the stock in several corporations, a question may arise as to whether one of the corporations, although not formally related to the other, should be held responsible for the other's liabilities. Dominating stock ownership alone is not enough in such a case, unless the majority shareholder dominates finances, policies, and practices of both corporations so that both are a business conduit for the principal shareholder.

b. Inadequate Capitalization

It is generally accepted that shareholders will be personally liable for their corporation's obligations if ***at incorporation*** they fail to provide adequate capitalization. The shareholders must "put at the risk of the business ***unencumbered capital reasonably adequate for its prospective liabilities.***" Undercapitalization cannot be proved merely by showing that the corporation is now insolvent. However, if insolvency occurs soon after incorporation, it may be a primary indicator of undercapitalization.

1) One-Person or Close Corporation

No absolute test for adequate capitalization has been formed. In any case, the corporation should have enough capital "to pay debts when they become due." The scope of the contemplated operations of the corporation, and the potential liability foreseeable from the operations, are factors to consider.

    2)   **Parent-Subsidiary Corporations**

A parent corporation's inadequate capitalization of a subsidiary corporation may constitute constructive fraud on all persons who deal with that subsidiary. One additional test should be applied in the parent-subsidiary situation: whether the subsidiary may reasonably expect to achieve independent financial stability from its operation.

  c. **Avoidance of Existing Obligations, Fraud, or Evasion of Statutory Provisions**

The corporate entity will be disregarded any time it is necessary to prevent fraud or to prevent an individual shareholder from using the corporate entity to avoid his *existing* personal obligations.

    1)   **Avoiding Liability**

The mere fact that an individual chooses to adopt the corporate form of business to avoid personal liability is not, of itself, a reason to pierce the corporate veil.

    2)   **Fraud**

The corporate veil will be pierced whenever the avoidance of personal liability through the formation of a corporation operates as a fraud on creditors or other outsiders.

Example: If A is bound by a covenant not to compete with B, he cannot avoid the covenant by forming a corporation and having it compete with B.

2. **Who Is Liable?**

When the corporate entity is ignored and the shield of limited liability is pierced, the persons composing the corporate entity may be held personally liable.

  a. **Active-Inactive Tests**

Normally, only the persons who were active in the management or operation of the business will be held personally liable. In other words, passive investors who acted in good faith will not be held liable for corporate obligations.

  b. **Theories of Liability**

    1)   **Joint and Several**

When shareholders are held liable, they will be held liable for the entire amount of the claim (even if it exceeds the amount that would have been considered "adequate capitalization"). Liability for obligations of the corporation is extended to the shareholders as joint and several liability.

    2)   **Property Cases**

If a corporation has conveyed its assets to a shareholder in fraud of creditors, upon piercing the corporate veil the assets may be reached on principles of fraudulent conveyance.

3. **Types of Liability**

  a. **Tort**

A tort victim is often a successful plaintiff under the theory of piercing the corporate

veil, since he usually has not been involved with the corporation in a transactional sense, and should not be forced to sue an insolvent corporate shell for his damages.

b. Contract

Courts are reluctant to pierce the corporate veil in contract cases, since the contracting party has an opportunity to investigate the financial condition of the corporation and, in the absence of misrepresentation or fraud, has a less equitable claim for relief. When the creditor deals at arm's length with the corporation, the court will most likely effect the reasonable expectation of the parties and force the creditor to look only to the corporation for satisfaction of the contract.

c. Bankruptcy and Subordination of Claims

When the corporation is insolvent and some of the shareholders have claims as "creditors," the shareholders' claims may be subordinated to those of the other creditors *if equity so requires* (*e.g.,* because of fraud). This is an application of "piercing the corporate veil" by refusing to recognize the shareholders as creditors of a separate legal entity—the corporation.

In the subordination situation, called the "Deep Rock" doctrine from the case that first applied it, a court has discretion to subordinate the shareholder's claim to any class of creditors, including subordinating the claim even as to unsecured creditors.

4. Who May "Pierce"?

a. Creditors

The creditors of a corporation are the most likely persons to pierce the corporate veil, and the cases involving disregard of corporateness primarily involve creditors.

b. Shareholders

Generally, those who choose to conduct business in the corporate form may not disregard the corporate entity at their will to serve their own purposes. Courts virtually never pierce the corporate veil at the request of the shareholder.

III. CAPITAL STRUCTURE

A. TYPES OF CORPORATE SECURITIES

Corporate capital comes from the issuance of many types of "securities." The word "security" is used generically to describe many obligations, including equity obligations (*e.g.,* shares of stock) and debt obligations (*e.g.,* bonds).

1. Debt Securities

A debt security represents a creditor-debtor relationship with the corporation, whereby the corporation has borrowed funds from an "outside creditor" and promises to repay the creditor. A debt security holder has *no ownership interest* in the corporation.

2. Equity Securities

An equity security is an instrument representing an investment in the corporation whereby its

holder becomes a part *owner of the business*. Equity securities are shares of the corporation, and the investor is called a shareholder.

B. DEBT SECURITIES

A debt obligation usually has a stated maturity date and a provision for interest. Debt obligations may be secured (a "mortgage bond") or unsecured (a "debenture"), and may be payable either to the holder of the bond (a "coupon" or "bearer" bond) or to the owner registered in the corporation's records (a "registered bond"). A debt obligation may also have special features; *e.g.*, it may provide that it is convertible into equity securities at the option of the holder, or it might provide that the corporation may redeem the obligation at a specified price before maturity of the obligation.

C. EQUITY SECURITIES (SHARES)

1. Terminology

The shares that are described in a corporation's articles are called the "*authorized shares*." The corporation may not sell more shares than are authorized. Shares that have been sold to investors are "*issued and outstanding*." Shares that are reacquired by the corporation are no longer issued and outstanding, and so revert to being "authorized shares" (formerly reacquired shares became "treasury shares"). [*See* RMBCA §6.03] Shares may be "certificated" (*i.e.*, represented by share certificates) or "uncertificated" (*i.e.*, not represented by certificates, but described in a written statement of information). [RMBCA §§6.25, 6.26]

2. Classification of Shares

As stated above, equity securities represent an ownership interest in the corporation. A corporation may choose to issue only one type of shares, giving each shareholder an equal ownership right (in which case the shares are generally called "*common shares*"), or it may divide shares into *classes*, or *series within a class*, having varying rights, as long as one or more classes together have unlimited voting rights and one or more classes together have a right to receive the corporation's net assets on dissolution. [RMBCA §6.01] The RMBCA allows rights to be varied even among shares of the *same class*, as long as the variations are set forth in the articles. [RMBCA §6.01(e)]

a. Classes and Series Must Be Described in Articles

If shares are to be divided into classes, the articles must (i) prescribe the number of shares of each class, (ii) prescribe a distinguishing designation for each class (*e.g.*, "Class A preferred," "Class B preferred," etc.), and (iii) either describe the rights, preferences, and limitations of each class or provide that the rights, preferences, and limitations of any class or series within a class shall be determined by the board of directors prior to issuance. [RMBCA §§6.01, 6.02]

1) Authorized Rights, Preferences, and Limitations

The RMBCA specifies the types of rights, preferences, and limitations that may be used to vary classes and series. The articles may authorize shares that:

(i)   Have special, conditional, or limited *voting rights*, or no right to vote;

(ii) Can be *redeemed or converted* for cash, indebtedness, securities, or other property (the redemption or conversion can take place at the option of the corporation or the shareholder, or on the occurrence of a specified event);

      (iii) Entitle the holders to *distributions, including dividends*; or

      (iv) Have *preference over any other class of shares with respect to distributions*, including on dissolution of the corporation.

[RMBCA §6.01(c)]

3. Fractional Shares

A corporation may: (i) issue certificates representing fractions of a share or pay in money the fair value of fractions of a share as determined by the board; (ii) arrange for the disposition of fractional shares by those entitled to the fractional shares; or (iii) issue scrip that entitles the holder to a full share on surrendering enough scrip to equal a full share. [RMBCA §6.04(a)]

a. Rights of Holders of Fractional Shares and Scrip

A certificate representing fractions of a share entitles the holder to exercise the rights of a shareholder. In contrast, the holder of scrip may not exercise any rights of a shareholder unless otherwise provided in the scrip. [RMBCA §6.04(c)]

4. Subscription Agreements

A subscription is an offer to purchase shares from a corporation. Subscriptions can be made to existing corporations or to corporations to be formed.

a. Acceptance and Revocation

A subscription does not become a contract until it is accepted by the corporation. Nevertheless, under the RMBCA, a *preincorporation* subscription is irrevocable by the subscriber for *six months* from the date of the subscription unless otherwise provided in the terms of the subscription, or unless all subscribers consent to revocation. [RMBCA §6.20(a)]

b. Payment

Unless otherwise provided in the subscription agreement, subscriptions for shares are payable on demand by the board of directors.

1) Discrimination Not Allowed

The board of directors may not discriminate among subscribers in calling for payment of subscriptions. Any demand for payment must be uniform as to all shares of the same class or as to all shares of the same series. [RMBCA §6.20(b)]

2) Penalties for Failure to Pay

If a subscriber fails to pay under a subscription agreement, the corporation may collect the amount owed as it would any other debt. Alternatively, the subscription agreement may set forth other penalties for failure to pay. However, the corporation may not effect a rescission or forfeiture unless the subscriber fails to cure the default within 20 days after the corporation sends *written notice* of default to the subscriber. Note that rescission is the corporation's (not the subscriber's) option. A subscriber may not escape her liability by voluntarily rescinding. Also, the board of directors may release, settle, or compromise any subscription or dispute arising from a subscription, unless otherwise provided in the subscription agreement. [RMBCA §6.20(d)]

5. **Consideration for Shares**

The RMBCA prescribes rules regarding the types and amount of consideration that may be received in exchange for stock issued by the corporation.

a. **Forms of Consideration**

Traditionally, states limited the type of consideration that could be received by a corporation issuing stock (stock could be issued only in exchange for cash, property, or services already rendered). The RMBCA has virtually abandoned such limitations and allows stock to be issued in exchange for *any tangible or intangible property or benefit to the corporation.* [RMBCA §6.21(b)] However, a number of states have not gone as far as the RMBCA and still prohibit corporations from issuing stock in exchange for promissory notes or future services. The best approach for the exam is to recite the RMBCA rule but then mention the possible limitation.

b. **Amount of Consideration**

1) **Traditional Par Value Approach**

Traditionally, the articles of incorporation would indicate whether the corporation's shares were to be issued with a stated par value or with no par value. Stock with a par value could not be issued by the corporation for less than the par value (although this rule did not apply to stock repurchased by the corporation and held as treasury shares). Furthermore, the money received from the issuance of par value stock had to go into a special account—called stated capital. The stated capital account could not be reduced below the aggregate par value of all the stock that had been issued. The idea was to guarantee creditors that the corporation would be capitalized at a certain level.

2) **RMBCA Approach**

The RMBCA generally does not follow the traditional par value approach and instead allows corporate directors to issue stock for whatever consideration they deem adequate. The RMBCA also provides that the board of directors' *good faith determination* as to the adequacy of the consideration received is *conclusive* as to whether the stock exchanged for the consideration is validly issued, fully paid, and nonassessable. [RMBCA §6.21] However, the articles of incorporation may set forth a par value for shares, and if they do, presumably shares cannot be sold for less than par, as under the traditional rule. [RMBCA §2.02(b)(2)(iv)]

Example: Roger and Tony form Genie Carpets, Inc. ("Genie") to manufacture faux Persian rugs. Genie's articles authorize the issuance of 1,000 shares of stock. The corporation issued its first 500 shares at a price of $1,000 each. Bellows approached Roger and Tony and offered to sell to the corporation his carpet manufacturing facility in exchange for 500 shares of Genie stock. Although a six-month-old appraisal found the property to be worth $400,000, other factors made Roger and Tony believe the property to be worth more, so they agreed to the transaction. One of Genie's shareholders thinks the facility was not sufficient consideration and brings suit to have the issuance to Bellows declared invalid. The suit will fail. The board's good faith determination of value is

conclusive as to whether the stock exchanged for the consideration is validly issued, fully paid, and nonassessable.

a) Watered Stock

Historically, if par value stock was issued for less than its par value, the original purchaser and the directors who authorized the sale would be liable for the difference (known as "water") between the par value and the amount received. Since the RMBCA provides that stock is validly issued, fully paid, and nonassessable when the corporation receives the consideration for which the board authorized the issuance, there can be no watered stock problem under the RMBCA. However, the RMBCA does not clearly address how to approach this issue if a corporation's articles provide for a par value. If this issue should come up in an exam question, recite the RMBCA rule, but note that a court might hold that directors may not sell stock for less than any par value stated in the articles and are personally liable for damages caused to the corporation if they issue stock for less than the stated par value.

c. Unpaid Stock

A shareholder is liable to pay the corporation the full consideration for which her shares were authorized to be issued. [RMBCA §6.22] If the shareholder fails to pay the full consideration, the shares are referred to as "unpaid stock." If the corporation is insolvent, a trustee in bankruptcy can enforce the corporation's claim for unpaid stock.

6. Federal Law

Certain aspects regarding the issuance of corporate securities are governed by the federal Securities Act of 1933 ("SA"). [15 U.S.C. §§77a *et seq.*] Although the Act appears to be outside the scope of most bar exams, a brief discussion of it follows.

a. Registration and Prospectus Requirements

In general, the 1933 Act requires issuers of stock to register the issuance with the Securities Exchange Commission ("SEC"). [15 U.S.C. §77f] The registration statement must include all information that a reasonable investor would consider important in deciding whether to invest (*e.g.*, balance sheet, profit and loss statement, director compensation, plans for expansion, etc.). The Act also requires the issuer to provide each investor with a prospectus summarizing the information in the registration statement. [15 U.S.C. §77j]

b. Exemptions

Registration is expensive and time-consuming, but there are a number of exemptions from the registration requirement. For example, securities issued by banks, governments, or charitable organizations are generally exempt. Similarly, issuances of securities offered and sold only to persons residing in a single state are exempt. Issuances of less than $1 million are exempt, as are issuances made to sophisticated investors and no more than 35 "unaccredited" (*i.e.,* inexperienced) investors. [*See* 15 U.S.C. §§77c, 77d(2)]; SA Rules 504, 505, 506]

c. Civil Liability

Under Securities Act section 11 [15 U.S.C. §77k], *anyone* who signs a registration statement (including lawyers, accountants, and corporate officers) is liable for any damages

caused by a false statement in the registration statement unless the person can prove that he reasonably believed the statement to be true after making a ***reasonable investigation*** or that the plaintiff knew of the false statement. Somewhat similar liability attaches under Securities Act section 12 when a security is sold without registering or providing a prospectus as required. [15 U.S.C. §77l]

PART TWO—INTRACORPORATE PARTIES

IV. PROMOTERS

A. PROMOTERS PROCURE CAPITAL AND OTHER COMMITMENTS
The first step in forming a corporation is the procurement of commitments for capital and other instrumentalities that will be used by the corporation after formation. This is done by promoters. Generally, promoters enter into contracts with third parties who are interested in becoming shareholders of the corporation once it is formed (*i.e.*, "stock subscriptions"). Promoters might also enter into contracts with others for goods or services to be provided to the corporation once it is formed. Usually, the promoters will go on to serve as incorporators, but this is not necessary.

B. PROMOTERS' RELATIONSHIP WITH EACH OTHER
Absent an agreement indicating a contrary relationship, promoters are considered to be joint venturers, and they occupy a ***fiduciary relationship to each other***. As fiduciaries, promoters are prohibited from secretly pursuing personal gain at the expense of their fellow promoters or the corporation to be formed.

Example: Arnie and Barb have agreed to form a corporation to engage in a real estate business. Arnie tells Barb that he can acquire a piece of land suitable for subdividing for $100,000. Arnie acquires the land for $70,000 and pockets the difference. Arnie is liable to Barb for breach of a fiduciary duty, since the promotion began when Arnie and Barb agreed to form the corporation.

C. PROMOTERS' RELATIONSHIP WITH CORPORATION
Upon incorporation, the promoters owe fiduciary duties to the corporation and to those persons investing in it. The promoters' duty in this respect is one of fair disclosure and good faith. Promoters are not permitted to retain a secret profit resulting from transactions with, or on behalf of, the corporation. Promoters' liabilities will arise under one of three theories: (i) breach of fiduciary duty; (ii) fraud or misrepresentation; or (iii) obtaining unpaid stock.

1. Breach of Fiduciary Duty Arising from Sale to Corporation
A promoter who profits on the sale of property to the corporation may be liable to the corporation for the profit, or may be forced to rescind the sale, unless the promoter has disclosed all of the material facts of the transaction.

a. Independent Board of Directors
If the transaction is disclosed to an independent board of directors (not under the control of the promoter) and approved, there is no breach of a fiduciary duty.

b. Disclosure to Subscribers or Shareholders
If the board of directors is not completely independent, the promoter's transaction must

be approved by the shareholders or subscribers to the stock of the corporation. The promoter is insulated from a breach of fiduciary duty if the subscribers knew of the transaction at the time they subscribed or, after full disclosure, unanimously ratified the transaction. Disclosure must be to all shareholders, not merely to the controlling share-holders. In addition, disclosure must include those ***persons contemplated as part of the initial financing scheme***. [Old Dominion Copper Mining & Smelting Co. v. Bigelow, 203 Mass. 159 (1909)]

Example: Alex, Becky, and Chloe decide to form a corporation with 200,000 shares of authorized common stock. They plan to sell 50,000 shares to the public. Prior to formation they obtain subscriptions to 20,000 shares. Alex, Becky, and Chloe contribute property in exchange for 150,000 shares and they "profit" on the transaction. They obtain approval of the transaction from the subscribers for the 20,000 shares. The remaining 30,000 shares are sold within three weeks after formation of the corporation, but the promoters do not disclose their profit to the new shareholders. Under the *Bigelow* rule, the promoters are liable to the corporation because the transaction was not approved by all shareholders who were contemplated as part of the original promotion plan.

c. Promoters' Purchase of All the Stock

If the promoters purchase all the stock of the corporation themselves, with no inten-tion to resell the stock to outsiders, but subsequently do sell their individual shares to outsiders, they ***cannot be liable*** for breach of a fiduciary duty with respect to their promoter transactions, since at the time they purchased the stock there was no one from whom the profit was kept secret.

2. Fraud

Promoters may always be held liable if plaintiffs can show that they were defrauded by the promoters' fraudulent misrepresentations or fraudulent failure to disclose all material facts. The basis of this liability can be either common law fraud or the state and federal securities acts.

3. Federal Securities Law

The failure to disclose material facts or any material misrepresentations of a fact in connec-tion with the purchase or sale of securities may violate rule 10b-5 of the Securities Exchange Act. (*See* XIV.A., *infra.*)

D. PROMOTERS' RELATIONSHIP WITH THIRD PARTIES—PREINCORPORATION AGREEMENTS

1. Promoter's Liability

The RMBCA provides that if a person acts on behalf of a corporation, knowing that there has been no incorporation, the person is jointly and severally liable for any obligations incurred. [RMBCA §2.04] Thus, as a general rule, if a promoter enters into an agreement with a third party to benefit a planned, but as of yet unformed, corporation, the promoter is personally liable on the agreement.

Example: Fred and Barney agree to pool their money to form a corporation ("Dyno, Inc.") to run a rock quarry. Fred approaches Mr. Slate, explains his

plans, and enters into a contract to purchase a small quarry from Slate for $100,000—$50,000 to be paid at closing and an additional $50,000 to be paid six months later. The contract provides that the closing will not be held for 45 days so that Fred and Barney will have time to incorporate Dyno, Inc. before the closing. Fred signs the contract, "Fred, on behalf of Dyno Inc." Subsequently, Fred and Barney have a falling out, and Dyno, Inc. is never formed. Fred probably will be found to be personally liable on the contract with Mr. Slate since he entered the contract knowing that Dyno, Inc. had not yet been formed.

a. Liability Continues After Formation Absent Novation

A promoter's liability on preincorporation agreements continues after the corporation is formed, even if the corporation adopts the contract and benefits from it. The promoter's liability can be ***extinguished only if there is a novation***—an agreement among the parties releasing the promoter and substituting the corporation. To clearly establish a novation, the third party should expressly release the promoter after the corporation has adopted the contract, although some cases have implied a novation from the conduct of the third party and the corporation.

Example: Same facts as in the example in 1., above, but Fred and Barney do not have a falling out, Dyno, Inc. is formed, and a few days later the parties close on the quarry. At the closing, title to the quarry is transferred to Dyno, Inc. Despite Dyno, Inc.'s adoption of the purchase contract, Fred remains personally liable for the remainder of the purchase price unless the parties agreed to a novation at the closing.

b. Exception—Agreement Expressly Relieves Promoter of Liability

If the agreement between the parties expressly indicates that the promoter is not to be bound, there is no contract. Such an arrangement may be construed as a revocable offer to the proposed corporation. The promoter has no rights or liabilities under such an arrangement.

c. Promoter Indemnification

When a promoter is liable on a preincorporation contract and the corporation thereafter adopts the contract but no novation is agreed upon, the promoter may have the right of indemnification from the corporation if he is subsequently held liable on the contract.

2. Corporation's Liability

a. General Rule—No Liability Prior to Incorporation

Since the corporate entity does not exist prior to incorporation, it is not bound on contracts entered into by the promoter in the corporate name. A promoter cannot act as an agent of the corporation prior to incorporation, since an agent cannot bind a nonexistent principal.

b. Adoption

The corporation may become bound on promoter contracts by adopting them. The effect of an adoption is to make the corporation a party to the contract at the time it adopts, although adoption of the contract by the corporation does not of itself relieve the

promoter of his liability. The liability of the corporation runs from the date of adoption, not from the making of the original contract. Adoption may be express (*e.g.,* by board of directors' resolution) or implied (*e.g.,* by acquiescence or conduct normally constituting estoppel).

V. SHAREHOLDERS

A. SHAREHOLDER CONTROL OVER MANAGEMENT

1. Direct Control
At common law, shareholders have no right to directly control the day-to-day management of their corporation. Instead, the right to manage is vested in the board of directors, who usually delegate their day-to-day management duties to officers. This is still the general rule under the RMBCA. However, the RMBCA also allows a departure from the general rule: Shareholders may enter into agreements concerning management of the corporation, including an agreement to vest the powers that the board would ordinarily have in one or more shareholders. The requirements for such agreements are discussed at C.3., *infra*.

2. Indirect Control
Even absent a shareholder agreement vesting direct control of the corporation in shareholders, shareholders have indirect control over their corporation through their power to elect directors, amend the bylaws, and approve fundamental changes to the corporation.

a. Shareholders Elect and May Remove Directors
Shareholders have the right to elect directors. [RMBCA §8.03(c)] The shareholders may also remove a director, ***with or without cause***, at any time. [RMBCA §8.08]

b. Shareholders May Modify Bylaws
As discussed above (II.C.4.a., *supra*), shareholders have the power to adopt, amend, or repeal bylaws.

c. Shareholders Must Approve Fundamental Corporate Changes
Changes to the fundamental structure of a corporation cannot be made without the approval of the shareholders. Shareholder approval is required in cases of merger, sale of corporate assets outside the ordinary course of business, dissolution, and for other extraordinary corporate matters. Similarly, amendments to the articles of incorporation may require shareholder approval. (*See* IX., *infra*.)

B. SHAREHOLDERS' MEETINGS AND VOTING POWER

1. Convening Meetings

a. Annual Meetings
Corporations must hold annual meetings, the primary purpose of which is the election of directors. [RMBCA §7.01] If a meeting is not held within the earlier of six months after the end of the corporation's fiscal year or 15 months after the last annual meeting, the court in the county where the corporation's principal office is located may order an

annual meeting to be held on the application of any shareholder entitled to participate in an annual meeting. [RMBCA §7.03(a)]

b. Special Meeting

The board of directors, or those persons authorized to do so by the articles or bylaws, may call special meetings during the year to conduct business that requires shareholder approval. A special meeting may also be called by the holders of at least 10% of all the votes entitled to be cast at the meeting. [RMBCA §7.02]

2. Place of the Meeting

Shareholders' meetings may be held *anywhere* within or outside the state, at the place stated in or fixed in accordance with the bylaws. If no place is so stated or fixed, annual meetings are held at the corporation's principal office. [RMBCA §§7.01(b), 7.02(c)]

3. Notice

Generally, written notice of the shareholders' meetings—special or annual—must be sent to the shareholders entitled to vote at the meeting. [RMBCA §7.05]

a. Time Within Which Notice Must Be Sent

Under the RMBCA, the notice must be delivered not less than 10 days or more than 60 days before the meeting. [RMBCA §7.05(a)]

b. Contents of Notice

The notice must state the place, day, and hour of the meeting. For special meetings, the purpose(s) for which the meeting is called must also be stated in the notice. [RMBCA §7.05(a)]

c. Notice May Be Waived

Action taken at a meeting can be set aside if notice was improper. However, a shareholder will be held to have waived any defects in notice if the shareholder (i) waives notice in a *signed writing* either before or after the meeting or (ii) *attends the meeting* and does not object to notice at the beginning of the meeting (or, if the defect is that the notice did not identify a special purpose, when the purpose is first brought up). [RMBCA §7.06]

4. Eligibility to Vote

a. Record Date

A corporation's bylaws may fix, or provide the manner of fixing, a *record date* to determine which shareholders are entitled to notice of a meeting, to vote, or to take any other action. If the bylaws do not so provide, the board may specify a date as the record date. The record date may not be more than *70 days* before the meeting or action requiring a determination of shareholders. [RMBCA §7.07]

1) If Record Date Not Set

If there is no fixed record date, the record date will be the day before the first notice of the meeting is delivered to the shareholders. [RMBCA §7.05(d)]

b. **Shareholders' List for Meeting**

After a record date for a meeting has been fixed, the corporation must prepare an alphabetical list of all shareholders entitled to notice of a shareholders' meeting. The list must show each shareholder's address and the number of shares held by each shareholder. [RMBCA §7.20(a)]

1) **List Available for Inspection**

Beginning two business days after notice of the meeting for which the list was prepared is given, and continuing through the meeting, the shareholders' list must be made available for inspection by any shareholder or her agent at the corporation's principal office or at another place identified in the notice. The shareholder may, by written demand, inspect and copy the list during regular business hours. [RMBCA §7.20(b)]

a) **Refusal to Allow Inspection**

If the corporation refuses to allow inspection of the list, the court in the county where the corporation's principal office (or if none, its registered office) is located may, on application by the shareholder, order the inspection or copying at the corporation's expense. The court may postpone the meeting for which the list was prepared until completion of the inspection or copying, but a refusal or failure to prepare or make available the shareholders' list otherwise does *not* affect the validity of actions taken at the meeting. [RMBCA §7.20(d), (e)]

c. **Voting Entitlement of Shares**

Unless otherwise provided in the articles, each outstanding share, regardless of class, is entitled to one vote on a matter to be voted on at a shareholders' meeting. Shares held by one corporation in a second corporation generally may be voted like any other outstanding shares, unless the second corporation owns a majority of shares entitled to vote for directors of the first corporation (*e.g.*, a subsidiary holding shares of its parent usually cannot vote those shares). [RMBCA §7.21(a), (b)] Note that shares held by the corporation in a fiduciary capacity (*e.g.*, under an employee stock ownership plan) can be voted by the corporation. [RMBCA §7.21(c)]

d. **Corporation's Acceptance of Votes**

If the name signed on a vote, consent, waiver, or proxy appointment corresponds to that of a shareholder, the corporation is entitled to accept the vote, consent, etc., if the corporation is acting in good faith. The corporation may also accept signatures from representatives (*e.g.,* an executor, an officer of an entity that holds the shares, a guardian of the owner of the shares, etc.). However, if the corporate officer authorized to tabulate votes has a good faith, reasonable doubt about the validity of a signature or about the signatory's authority to sign for the shareholder, the corporation may reject the vote, consent, waiver, or proxy appointment. [RMBCA §7.24]

5. **Proxies**

A shareholder may vote his shares either in person or by proxy executed in writing by the shareholder or his attorney-in-fact. [RMBCA §7.22]

a. **Duration of Proxy**
A proxy is valid for only 11 months unless it provides otherwise.

b. **Revocability of Proxy**
An appointment of a proxy generally is revocable by a shareholder and may be revoked in a number of ways (*e.g.,* in writing, by the shareholder's showing up to vote himself, or by the later appointment of another proxy). A proxy will be irrevocable only if the appointment form ***conspicuously states that it is irrevocable*** and the appointment is ***coupled with an interest***. Appointments coupled with an interest include the appointment of any of the following:

(i) A *pledgee*;

(ii) A ***person who purchased*** or agreed to purchase the shares;

(iii) A ***creditor*** of the corporation who extended credit to the corporation under terms requiring the appointment;

(iv) An ***employee*** of the corporation whose employment contract requires the appointment; or

(v) A ***party to a voting agreement***.

[RMBCA §7.22(d)]

1) **Death or Incapacity of Shareholder**
Death or incapacity of a shareholder appointing a proxy does ***not*** affect the right of the corporation to accept the authority of the proxy unless the corporate officer authorized to tabulate votes receives ***written notice*** of the death or incapacity prior to the time the proxy exercises her authority under the appointment. [RMBCA §7.22(e)]

c. **Statutory Proxy Control**
Proxies are subject to federal control under the Securities Exchange Act of 1934. Section 14 of the Act regulates the shareholder voting machinery for corporations subject to the registration requirements of section 12 and the reporting requirements of section 13. Generally, these rules require a proxy statement describing the matter being submitted to a vote of the security holders together with the proper form of proxy on which the holders can vote for or against each matter being submitted.

1) **Basic Requirements**
The rules governing proxy solicitation basically require that:

(i) There must be full and fair disclosure of all ***material*** facts with regard to any management-submitted proposal upon which the shareholders are to vote;

(ii) Material misstatements, omissions, and fraud in connection with the solicitation of proxies are prohibited; and

(iii) Management must include certain shareholder proposals on issues other than the election of directors and allow proponents to explain their position.

[15 U.S.C. §78n]

2) Key Issue—Materiality

In determining whether the proxy rules have been violated, courts will focus on whether the statement of fact or omission was material. Whether a statement of fact or omission is material depends on the likelihood that a reasonable shareholder would consider it important in deciding how to vote.

3) Shareholder Proposals

The federal proxy rules generally provide that a shareholder proposal that is proper for consideration under state law must be included in the management's proxy statement along with a brief statement explaining the shareholder's reason for supporting the proposal's adoption if the proposal is submitted to the corporation in a timely fashion. To preclude exclusion from management's proxy materials, the shareholder submitting the proposal must be a beneficial owner of the security that would be entitled to vote on the proposal at a shareholders' meeting and must have continuously held, for at least one year prior to the date the proposal is submitted, the lesser of 1% or $2,000 in market value of the security. The proponent must continue to hold such securities through the date of the meeting.

Example: Making a recommendation to the board of directors that they increase the number of directors would be a proper action for shareholders; but a proposal to require an increase in the dividends would not be a proper action, since that decision is a matter entirely within the board's discretion.

6. Mechanics of Voting

a. Quorum

A quorum must attend a meeting before a vote may validly be taken. A *majority of the votes entitled to be cast* on the matter by a particular voting group (*see* below) will constitute a quorum unless the articles provide *greater* quorum requirements. Once a share is represented at a meeting, it is deemed present for quorum purposes for the remainder of the meeting; thus, a shareholder cannot prevent a vote by leaving before the vote is taken. [RMBCA §§7.25, 7.27]

1) Voting by Group

The articles may, and the RMBCA does, require approval by certain groups of shares separately under some circumstances. For example, an amendment to the articles must be approved by a share group when the share group will be significantly affected if the amendment is approved. (*See* IX.B.2.a., *infra*.)

b. Voting—In General

Generally, each outstanding share is entitled to one vote unless the articles provide otherwise. [RMBCA §7.21] (The articles may provide that a certain class or classes shall have more than one vote—weighted voting—or no vote. [RMBCA §§6.01, 6.02]) If a quorum exists, an action will be deemed approved by the shareholders (or appropriate shareholder group) if the *votes cast in favor of the action exceed the votes*

cast against the action, unless the articles provide for a greater voting requirement. [RMBCA §§7.25, 7.27]

c. **Director Elections**

Unless the articles provide otherwise, directors are elected by a ***plurality*** of the votes cast at a meeting at which there is a quorum. In other words, as long as a quorum is present, the candidates receiving the most votes—even if not a majority—win.

1) **Cumulative Voting Optional**

Instead of the normal one share, one vote paradigm, the articles may provide for ***cumulative voting*** in the election of directors. [RMBCA §7.28] Cumulative voting is a device that gives minority shareholders a better chance to elect a director to the board than the shareholders would have using the ordinary voting procedure described above. In cumulative voting, each share may cast as many votes as there are board vacancies to be filled. Thus, if three directors are to be elected, each voting share is entitled to cast three votes. The votes may be cast for a single candidate, or they may be divided among the candidates in any manner that the shareholder desires.

Example: Tammy owns 300 voting shares of Circle X stock. Nine directors are to be elected at the next annual meeting. Tammy is entitled to cast 2,700 votes (300 shares x 9 vacancies). She may cast all 2,700 votes for one candidate or divide her 2,700 votes in any manner she desires.

a) **Notice Required for Cumulative Voting**

Even if the articles provide for cumulative voting, shares may not be cumulatively voted unless the notice for the meeting in question conspicuously states that cumulative voting is authorized or at least one shareholder in the class possessing the right to vote cumulatively notifies the corporation of her intent to vote cumulatively at least 48 hours before the meeting. [RMBCA §7.28(d)]

b) **Devices to Avoid Cumulative Voting**

To protect minority shareholders, cumulative voting was and still is required in a number of states. When cumulative voting was largely mandatory, a number of devices were developed to avoid its effects (*e.g.*, reducing the size of the board, staggering the election of directors, giving certain classes of shares the sole right to elect certain directors, electing directors on separate ballots, etc.). If the devices were employed for proper corporate purposes, they were upheld, but if no proper purpose was found, the devices were held to have been improperly imposed.

Example: A corporation may decide to stagger the election of directors (*see* VI.C.3.a., *infra*) in order to ensure continuity on the board, even though reducing the number of directors to be elected each year makes it more difficult for minority shareholders to elect a director.

Compare: A corporation with cumulative voting probably would be prohibited from electing directors on separate ballots, since a

simple majority would then be able to elect each director, thus negating the effect of cumulative voting.

2) Classification of the Board
The articles may grant certain classes of shares the right to elect a certain director or number of directors. Only shareholders of that class may vote to fill the specified position(s). [RMBCA §8.04]

d. Class Voting on Article Amendments
Whenever an amendment to the articles of incorporation affects only one class of shares (Class A common, preferred, etc.), that class generally has the right to vote on the amendment *even if the class would not otherwise be permitted to vote* at a shareholders' meeting. Typical situations where class voting may occur include:

(i) A *change in the designation, preferences, rights* (including preemptive and dividend rights), *or aggregate number of shares of a class;*

(ii) An *exchange, reclassification, or cancellation of some of the shares* of the class or a change of the shares of the class into a different class; and

(iii) The *creation of a new class having superior rights* to the shares of this particular class.

[RMBCA §10.04] Generally, it may be said that class voting should be used if a proposed amendment has any effect—adverse or advantageous—on holders of the class.

7. Shareholders May Act Without Meeting by Unanimous Written Consent
Shareholders may take action without a meeting by the unanimous written consent of all shareholders entitled to vote on the action. [RMBCA §7.04]

C. SHAREHOLDER AGREEMENTS
Shareholders may enter into several types of agreements in an effort to protect their voting power, proportionate stock ownership, or other special interests in the corporation. Although most shareholder agreements are encountered in the close corporation (where stock is held by a few individuals and is not actively traded), most of these agreements can be used in any corporation.

1. Voting Trusts
To ensure that a group of shares will be voted a particular way in the future, one or more shareholders may create a voting trust by (i) entering into a signed agreement setting forth the trust's terms and (ii) transferring legal ownership of their shares to the trustee. The trust may contain any lawful provision not inconsistent with the trust purposes, and the trustee must vote the shares in accordance with the trust. A copy of the trust agreement and the names and addresses of the beneficial owners of the trust must be given to the corporation. The trust is not valid for more than 10 years unless it is extended by agreement of the parties. [RMBCA §7.30]

2. Voting Agreements
Rather than creating a trust, shareholders may enter into a written and signed agreement that

provides for the manner in which they will vote their shares. Unless the voting agreement provides otherwise, it will be *specifically enforceable*. Unlike a voting trust, such an agreement need not be filed with the corporation and is not subject to any time limit. [RMBCA §7.31]

3. **Shareholder Management Agreements**

The shareholders may enter into an agreement among themselves regarding almost *any aspect of the exercise of corporate powers or management*. For example, an agreement may:

(i) *Eliminate* the board of directors or *restrict* the discretion or powers of the board;

(ii) *Govern the authorization or making of distributions*;

(iii) *Establish who shall be directors or officers*, as well as their terms and conditions of office, or the manner of selection or removal; or

(iv) *Transfer* to one or more shareholders or other persons the *authority to exercise the corporate powers* or to manage the business and affairs of the corporation.

[RMBCA §7.32(a)]

a. **Statutory Requirements**

To be valid, the agreement must either (i) be set forth in the *articles or bylaws*, and be approved by all persons who are shareholders at the time of the agreement or (ii) be set forth in a *written agreement signed by all persons who are shareholders* at the time of the agreement, and be filed with the corporation. Unless otherwise provided, the agreement is valid for 10 years. The agreement is subject to amendment or termination only by *all* persons who are shareholders at the time of the amendment, unless the agreement provides otherwise. [RMBCA §7.32(b)]

b. **Enforceability**

Any party to the agreement may enforce it against any other party. One who purchases shares without knowledge of the agreement is entitled to rescind the purchase. [RMBCA §7.32(c)]

c. **Termination of Agreement's Effectiveness**

The agreement ceases to be effective when shares of the corporation are listed on a national securities exchange or are regularly traded in a market maintained by a member of a national or affiliated securities association. [RMBCA §7.32(d)]

d. **Agreement Does Not Impose Personal Liability on Shareholders**

Even if the agreement treats the corporation as a partnership or results in failure to observe corporate formalities, the agreement does not constitute a ground for imposing personal liability on any shareholder for the acts or debts of the corporation. [RMBCA §7.32(f)]

4. **Restrictions on Transfer of Shares**

Another way shareholders may control the destiny of their corporation is by imposing

restrictions on transfers of outstanding shares. The articles, the bylaws, an agreement among shareholders, or an agreement between shareholders and the corporation may impose restrictions on the transfer of the corporation's shares for *any reasonable purpose* (*e.g.*, to preserve the corporation's eligibility for S corporation status or for a securities law exemption). [RMBCA §6.27]

a. Permissible Restrictions
The RMBCA permits restrictions that:

(i) Obligate the shareholder to *first offer* the corporation or other persons an opportunity to acquire the restricted shares;

(ii) Obligate *the corporation or other persons to acquire* the restricted shares;

(iii) Require the corporation, the holders of any class of its shares, or another person to *approve the transfer* of the restricted shares, if the requirement is not manifestly unreasonable; or

(iv) *Prohibit transfer* of the restricted shares to designated persons or classes, if the prohibition is not manifestly unreasonable.

[RMBCA §6.27(d)]

b. Enforceability
A permitted stock transfer restriction is enforceable against the holder of the stock or a transferee of the holder only if (i) the restriction's existence is *noted conspicuously on the certificate* (or is contained in the information statement, if the shares are uncertificated) or (ii) the holder or transferee *had knowledge* of the restriction. [RMBCA §6.27(b)]

5. Agreements Affecting Action by Directors
The board has the authority to exercise corporate powers and to manage the business and affairs of the corporation. However, limitations may be imposed on this authority by the articles or by a shareholders' agreement, as discussed above. [RMBCA §8.01]

D. SHAREHOLDERS' INSPECTION RIGHTS
At common law, shareholders had a qualified right to inspect corporate books and records: They could inspect upon request if they had a *proper purpose* for the inspection. Proper purposes are those purposes reasonably related to the person's interest as a shareholder, such as waging a proxy battle, investigating possible director or management misconduct, seeking support for a shareholder initiative, etc. Improper purposes are purposes aimed primarily at personally benefiting the inspecting shareholder, such as to obtain the names and addresses of the shareholders in order to create a commercial mailing list to sell to third parties.

1. RMBCA Approach—In General
The RMBCA generally continues the common law approach. Under the RMBCA, a shareholder may inspect the corporation's books, papers, accounting records, shareholder records, etc. To exercise this right, the shareholder must give *five days' written notice* of his request, stating a *proper purpose* for the inspection. The shareholder need not personally conduct the inspection; he may send an attorney, accountant, or other agent. [RMBCA

§16.02] Some states limit inspection to shareholders who: (i) hold at least 5% of the corporation's outstanding shares, or (ii) have held any lesser number of shares for at least six months.

a. Unqualified Right
The RMBCA also includes an exception to the general rule. It provides that any shareholder may inspect the following records *regardless of purpose*: (i) the corporation's articles and bylaws, (ii) board resolutions regarding classification of shares, (iii) minutes of shareholders' meetings from the past three years, (iv) communications sent by the corporation to shareholders over the past three years, (v) a list of the names and business addresses of the corporation's current directors and officers, and (vi) a copy of the corporation's most recent annual report.

b. Right May Not Be Limited
The right of inspection may not be abolished or limited by the articles or bylaws. [RMBCA §16.02(d)]

c. Inspection by Court Order
If a corporation does not allow a required inspection, a court may order that the inspection and copying take place. Where a court so orders, it must also order the corporation to pay the shareholder's costs incurred in obtaining the order, unless the corporation proves that its refusal to allow inspection was in good faith. [RMBCA §16.04]

E. PREEMPTIVE RIGHTS
When the corporation proposes to issue additional shares of stock, the current shareholders often want to purchase some of the new shares in order to maintain their proportional voting strength. The common law granted shareholders such a right, known as the "preemptive right." Under the RMBCA, a shareholder *does not have any preemptive rights unless* the articles of incorporation so provide. [RMBCA §6.30(a)]

1. Waiver
A shareholder may waive her preemptive right. A waiver evidenced by a writing is irrevocable *even if it is not supported by consideration*. [RMBCA §6.30(b)(2)]

2. Limitations
Even if the articles provide for preemptive rights, the rights *do not* apply to:

(i) Shares *issued as compensation* to directors, officers, agents, or employees of the corporation;

(ii) Shares *authorized in the articles that are issued within six months* after incorporation;

(iii) Shares *issued for consideration other than money* (*i.e.,* shares issued in exchange for property or services); or

(iv) Shares *without general voting rights but having a distribution preference*.

[RMBCA §6.30(b)(3), (4)] Moreover, holders of nonpreferential voting shares have no preemptive rights in any class of preferred shares unless the preferred shares are convertible into shares without preferential rights. [RMBCA §6.30(b)(5)]

3. Sales to Outsiders

Shares subject to preemptive rights that are not acquired by shareholders can be issued to anyone else for up to one year following their offer to the shareholders, as long as they are sold for no less than the price at which they were offered to the shareholders. Sales for less than the price offered to the shareholders or after one year are subject to the shareholders' preemptive rights. [RMBCA §6.30(b)(6)]

F. SHAREHOLDER SUITS

Shareholders enjoy a dual personality. They are entitled to enforce their own claims against the corporation, officers, directors, or majority shareholders by *direct* action. Shareholders are also the guardians of the corporation's causes of action, provided no one else in the corporation will assert them. In this sense, shareholders may sue *derivatively* to enforce the corporate cause of action, as long as they meet the requirements specified by law and they have made necessary demands on the corporation or the directors to enforce the cause of action. In either capacity, direct or derivative action, the shareholder may sue for herself and for others similarly situated.

1. Direct Actions

a. Nature of Action

A breach of a fiduciary duty *owed to the shareholder* by an officer or director of a corporation is a proper subject for a shareholder's direct action against that officer or that director. However, be careful to distinguish breaches of duty owed to a shareholder from duties owed to the corporation. If the duty is owed to the corporation rather than to an individual shareholder, the cause of action is derivative rather than direct. The basic tests are: (i) who suffers the most immediate and direct damage? and (ii) to whom did the defendant's duty run?

b. Recovery

In a shareholder direct action, any recovery is for the benefit of the individual shareholder, or, if the action was a class action, for the benefit of the class.

2. Derivative Actions

a. Nature of Action

The derivative action is often described as a "representative" action, since the shareholders are enforcing the rights of another—*i.e.,* the corporation. Recovery in a derivative action generally goes to the corporation rather than to the shareholder bringing the action.

b. Standing—Ownership at Time of Wrong

To commence or maintain a derivative proceeding, a shareholder must have been a shareholder of the corporation *at the time of the act or omission* complained of, or must have become a shareholder through *transfer by operation of law* from one who was a shareholder at that time. Also, the shareholder must fairly and adequately represent the interests of the corporation. [RMBCA §7.41]

c. Demand Requirements

The shareholder must make a *written demand* on the corporation to take suitable

action. A derivative proceeding may not be commenced until 90 days after the date of demand, unless: (i) the shareholder has earlier been notified that the corporation has rejected the demand; or (ii) irreparable injury to the corporation would result by waiting for the 90 days to pass. [RMBCA §7.42]

1) If Demand Futile

Under older law, demand was excused if it would be futile (*e.g.*, where a shareholder is seeking damages from the entire board for breach of duty, they are unlikely to approve the action). However, it has been argued that this exception does not apply under the RMBCA for two reasons: (i) the RMBCA does not provide for the exception; and (ii) even though it may seem futile to ask the directors to sue themselves, the demand gives the directors an opportunity to resolve the issue through means other than litigation

d. Corporation Named as Defendant

In a derivative action, the corporation is named as a party defendant. Although the cause of action asserted belongs to the corporation (so the corporation is the real plaintiff in interest), the failure of the corporation to assert its own claim justifies aligning it as a defendant.

e. Dismissal If Not in Corporation's Best Interests

If a majority of the directors (but at least two) who have no personal interest in the controversy found *in good faith after reasonable inquiry* that the suit is not in the corporation's best interests, but the shareholder brings the suit anyway, the suit may be dismissed on the corporation's motion. [RMBCA §7.44] Good business reasons for the directors' refusal might be the fact that there is no likelihood of prevailing, or that the damage to the corporation from litigating would outweigh any possible recovery.

1) Burden of Proof

To avoid dismissal, in most cases the *shareholder* bringing the suit has the burden of proving to the court that the decision was *not* made in good faith after reasonable inquiry. However, if a majority of the directors had a personal interest in the controversy, the *corporation* will have the burden of showing that the decision was made in good faith after reasonable inquiry. [RMBCA §7.44(e)]

f. Discontinuance or Settlement Requires Court Approval

A derivative proceeding may be discontinued or settled only with court approval. [RMBCA §7.45]

g. Court May Order Payment of Expenses

Upon termination of a derivative action, the court may order the corporation to pay the plaintiff's reasonable expenses (including attorneys' fees) incurred in the proceeding if it finds that the action has resulted in a substantial benefit to the corporation. If the court finds that the action was commenced or maintained without reasonable cause or for an improper purpose, it may order the plaintiff to pay reasonable expenses of the defendant. [RMBCA §7.46]

G. DISTRIBUTIONS

1. Types of Distributions

Distributions of the corporation's assets to shareholders may take a number of forms: Dividends can be paid to shareholders in the form of cash or indebtedness while the corporation is operating. Shares can be redeemed from shareholders where there is a redemption right (*i.e.,* a built-in right of the corporation to repurchase the shares in a forced sale at a particular price) or repurchased (a voluntary sale by a current shareholder and purchase by the corporation). Finally, liquidating distributions can be paid to the shareholders when the corporation is dissolved. [RMBCA §1.40(6)]

2. Rights to Distributions

At least one class of stock must have a right to receive the corporation's net assets on dissolution. [RMBCA §6.01(b)] Beyond this rule, the articles may provide for distributions in any manner.

a. Declaration Generally Solely Within Board's Discretion

Even if the articles authorize distributions, the decision whether or not to declare distributions generally is *solely within the directors' discretion* (recall, however, that a shareholder agreement can change this rule; *see* C.3., *supra*), subject to any limitations in the articles and statutory solvency requirements (*see* below). The shareholders have no general right to compel a distribution; it would take a very strong case in equity to induce a court to interfere with the directors' discretion.

1) Limitations

a) Solvency Requirements

A distribution is not permitted if, after giving it effect, either:

(i) The corporation would *not be able to pay its debts as they become due* in the usual course of business (*i.e.,* the corporation is insolvent in the bankruptcy sense); or

(ii) The corporation's *total assets would be less than the sum of its total liabilities plus* (unless the articles permit otherwise) the amount that would be needed, if the corporation were to be dissolved at the time of the distribution, *to satisfy the preferential rights* on dissolution of shareholders whose preferential rights are superior to those receiving the distribution (*i.e.,* the corporation is insolvent in the balance sheet sense).

[RMBCA §6.40(c)]

b) Restrictions in the Articles

The articles may restrict the board's right to declare dividends. For example, to assure repayment, a creditor might be able to have the corporation include in its articles a provision prohibiting payment of any distributions unless the corporation earns a certain amount of profits.

c) **Share Dividends**

Distributions of a corporation's own shares (*i.e.,* "share dividends" or "stock dividends") to its shareholders are excluded from the definition of "distribution" under the RMBCA. [RMBCA §1.40(6)] Therefore, the above solvency rules are inapplicable to share dividends. However, shares of one class or series may not be issued as a share dividend with respect to shares of another class or series unless one of the following occurs: (i) the articles so authorize; (ii) a majority of the votes entitled to be cast by the class or series to be issued approves the issuance; or (iii) there are no outstanding shares of the class or series to be issued. [RMBCA §6.23]

2) **Historical Note—Par Value and Capital Accounts**

Under traditional corporate laws, distributions were also prohibited unless there was sufficient money in a particular account or accounts. Generally, dividends could be paid only from accounts containing "surplus," such as an account containing retained earnings; dividends could not be paid out of the "stated capital account," which had to contain at least the aggregate par value of all outstanding par value shares. These limitations no longer apply in most states.

b. **Contractual Rights with Regard to Distributions**

1) **Limitations and Preferences**

As discussed previously, a corporation need not give each shareholder an equal right to receive distributions. Shares may be divided into classes with varying rights (*e.g.,* some classes may be redeemable, others not; some may have no right to receive distributions, others could have preferences; etc.). The following are common preference terms with which you should be familiar:

a) **(Noncumulative) Preferred Shares**

Shares that have a preference usually are entitled to a fixed amount of money (*e.g.,* $5 each year if the preference is a dividend preference, $5 on dissolution if the preference is a liquidation preference) before distributions can be made with respect to nonpreferred shares. Note that the right is not absolute; the directors must still declare a dividend before the preferred shareholder has any right to receive it. Unless the dividend is cumulative (*see infra*), the right to a dividend preference for a particular year is extinguished if a dividend is not declared for that year.

b) **Cumulative Preferred Shares**

Cumulative preferred shares are like noncumulative preferred shares, but if a dividend is not declared in a particular year, the right to receive the preference accumulates and must be paid before nonpreferred shares may be paid any dividend.

Example: NavaCorp has 1,000 shares of $5 cumulative preferred stock outstanding. The directors did not declare a dividend in 2006 or 2007. If the directors want to declare a dividend in 2008, they will have to pay the cumulative preferred shareholders $15,000 (1,000 shares x $5 x 3 years) before any payment can be made to shares without a preference.

c) **Cumulative If Earned Shares**

If shares are "cumulative if earned," dividends for any one year cumulate only if the corporation's total earnings for that year exceed the total amount of the preferred dividends that would have to be paid out for that year.

d) **Participating Shares**

Generally, preferred shares are entitled only to their stated preference. However, preferred shares may be designated as "participating," in which case they have a right to receive whatever the nonpreferred shares receive in addition to the preference.

2) **Rights After Declaration—Same as a General Creditor**

As established above, shareholders have no general right to receive distributions. However, once a distribution is lawfully declared, the shareholders generally are treated as creditors of the corporation, and their claim to the distribution is equal in priority to claims of other unsecured creditors. [RMBCA §6.40(f)] Note, however, that a distribution can be enjoined or revoked if it was declared in violation of the solvency limitations, the articles, or a superior preference right.

c. **Who May Receive—Shareholder of Record on Record Date**

Once declared, dividends are payable to the persons named as shareholders in the corporate records on a particular date—known as the record date. If shares have been sold prior to the record date but have not been transferred on the corporation's books, the corporation pays the record owner (*i.e.,* the seller), and the beneficial owner (*i.e.,* the purchaser) must look to the seller for payment.

3. **Liability for Unlawful Distributions**

A director who votes for or assents to a distribution that violates the above rules is personally liable to the corporation for the amount of the distribution that *exceeds what could have been properly distributed*. A director will be deemed to have assented to the declaration of a distribution if she was present at the meeting at which the declaration was made and failed to dissent either during the meeting or by 5 p.m. on the business day next following the meeting. [RMBCA §8.33]

a. **Good Faith Defense**

A director is not liable for distributions approved in good faith (i) based on financial statements prepared according to reasonable accounting practices, or on a fair valuation or other method that is reasonable under the circumstances [RMBCA §6.40(d)]; or (ii) by relying on information from officers, employees, legal counsel, accountants, etc., or a committee of the board of which the director is not a member [RMBCA §8.30(b)].

b. **Contribution**

A director who is held liable for an unlawful distribution is entitled to contribution from (i) *every other director* who could be held liable for the distribution; and (ii) *each shareholder*, for the amount she accepted knowing that the distribution was improper. [RMBCA §8.33(b)]

H. SHAREHOLDERS' LIABILITIES

1. **General Rule—No Fiduciary Duty**
   Generally, shareholders may act in their own personal interests and owe no fiduciary duty to the corporation or their fellow shareholders except as outlined above concerning shareholder liability for:

   1) Unpaid stock;

   2) A pierced corporate veil; and

   3) Absence of de facto corporation when the shareholder knew that there was no incorporation.

2. **Liability Pursuant to Shareholder Agreement**
   As discussed above, shareholders may enter into agreements that vest some or all of the right to manage the corporation in one or more shareholders. When such agreements exist, the shareholder(s) in whom the management power is vested have the liabilities that a director ordinarily would have with respect to that power. [RMBCA §7.32(e)]

3. **Close Corporations**
   Shareholders in a close corporation (*i.e.*, a corporation owned by a few persons) owe each other the same duty of loyalty and utmost good faith that is owed by partners to each other. [Donahue v. Rodd Electrotype Co., 328 N.E.2d 505 (Mass. 1975)]

4. **Limitations on Controlling Shareholders**
   Certain common law limitations have emerged with regard to the sale by controlling shareholders (an individual or group) of a controlling interest. A controlling shareholder must refrain from using his control to obtain a special advantage or to cause the corporation to take action that unfairly prejudices the minority shareholders. [Pepper v. Litton, 308 U.S. 295 (1939)]

   Examples: 1) Controlling shareholders who sell the controlling interest to individuals who subsequently loot the company to the detriment of the minority shareholders will be liable for damages, unless reasonable measures were taken to investigate the character and reputation of the buyer.

   2) Majority shareholders were held liable to minority shareholders where the 85% majority shareholders transferred their shares to a holding company and then made a public offering of the holding company shares, because the result was that the minority shareholders were left holding shares that had no appreciable market value. [Jones v. H.F. Ahmanson & Co., 1 Cal. 3d 93 (1969)]

   a. **Sale at a Premium**
      No case has specifically held that controlling shareholders were liable simply for selling a controlling interest at a price unavailable to the other shareholders—*i.e.*, a price that includes a premium attributable solely to the right to control the corporation. However, in *Perlman v. Feldman*, 219 F.2d 173 (2d Cir. 1955), the controlling shareholders were held liable for the sale of their shares at a premium, where the court found that the premium really was paid for the right to allocate scarce materials during wartime. This

wartime right of allocation was considered a corporate asset, and the rule has always been that shareholders who *illegally* sell corporate assets for their own benefit will be forced to disgorge their profit.

b. Controlling Shareholder Under Securities Laws

Controlling shareholders generally are treated as "insiders" under the Securities Exchange Act and may be liable under the securities laws for trading on inside information. (*See* XIV.A., *infra*.) Shareholders owning more than 10% of a class of a corporation's stock may be liable for making short swing profits. (*See* XIV.B., *infra*.)

VI. DIRECTORS

A. GENERAL POWERS

Unless the articles or a shareholder agreement provides otherwise, the board of directors of the corporation has general responsibility for the management of the business and the affairs of the corporation. [RMBCA §8.01]

B. QUALIFICATIONS

The articles of incorporation or bylaws may prescribe qualifications for directors. A director need not be a resident of the state or a shareholder of the corporation unless so required by the articles or bylaws. [RMBCA §8.02]

C. NUMBER, ELECTION, AND TERMS OF OFFICE

1. Number of Directors—One or More as Set in Articles or Bylaws

The board of directors may consist of one or more individuals, as the articles or bylaws provide. In lieu of a set number of directors, the articles or bylaws may provide a variable range for the size of the board by fixing a minimum and maximum number of directors. If a variable range is established, the number may be fixed or changed from time to time, within the specified minimum and maximum, by the shareholders or the board. [RMBCA §8.03]

2. Election of Directors

The directors are elected at the first annual meeting of the shareholders, and at each annual meeting thereafter unless the directors' terms are staggered. [RMBCA §8.03(d)]

3. Terms of Directors

Directors' terms expire at the annual shareholders' meeting following their election, except for directors with staggered terms. [RMBCA §8.05(a), (b)] Even if a director's term expires, she remains in office until her successor is elected and qualifies. [RMBCA §8.05(e)]

a. Staggering Director Terms

If there are at least nine directors, the articles may divide the directors into two or three groups (as close to equal in size as is possible) to serve staggered two- or three-year terms. Thus, only one-half or one-third of the board is elected each year. [RMBCA §8.06] Such staggering of terms ensures some continuity in the board, but it also lessens the effect of cumulative voting since fewer directors are elected at each annual meeting.

4. **Resignation of Director**

A director may resign at any time by delivering written notice to the board, its chairperson, or the corporation. The resignation takes effect when notice is delivered, unless the notice specifies a later effective date or event. [RMBCA §8.07]

5. **Vacancies May Be Filled by Directors or Shareholders**

Absent a contrary provision in the articles, a vacancy on the board may be filled by either the shareholders or the board. If the directors remaining in office constitute fewer than a quorum, they may fill the vacancy by the affirmative vote of a majority of all the directors remaining in office. [RMBCA §8.10(a)]

a. **Where Director Elected by Voting Group**

If the vacant office was held by a director elected by a voting group of shareholders, only holders of shares of that voting group may vote to fill the vacancy if it is filled by shareholders. [RMBCA §8.10(b)]

D. REMOVAL OF DIRECTORS

Directors may be removed *with or without cause* by the shareholders, unless the articles provide that removal may be only for cause. [RMBCA §8.08]

1. **Cumulative Voting Limitation**

If less than the entire board is to be removed, a director elected by cumulative voting may not be removed if the votes cast against her removal would have been sufficient to elect her if cumulatively voted at an election of the board.

2. **Where Director Elected by Voting Group**

If a director is elected by a voting group of shareholders, only shareholders of that group may vote to remove the director.

E. DIRECTORS' MEETING

The board may hold regular or special meetings either within or outside the state. Unless otherwise provided in the articles or bylaws, the board may permit any or all directors to participate in a regular or special meeting by, or conduct the meeting through, the use of any means of communication by which *all directors participating may simultaneously hear each other* (*e.g.,* a conference call). [RMBCA §8.20]

1. **Initial Meeting**

After incorporation, the board must hold an organizational meeting, called by a majority of directors. The directors complete the organization of the corporation at this meeting by appointing officers, adopting bylaws, and carrying on any other business brought up at the meeting. [RMBCA §2.05]

2. **Notice of Meetings**

Regular board meetings may be held *without notice*. Special meetings require at least *two days' notice* of the date, time, and place of the meeting, but a purpose need not be included in the notice. [RMBCA §8.22]

a. **Notice May Be Waived**

A director may waive notice by a signed writing, filed with the minutes or corporate

records. Attendance at or participation in a meeting waives notice unless the director, at the beginning of the meeting or promptly on her arrival, objects to holding the meeting or transacting business at the meeting, and does not thereafter vote for or assent to action taken at the meeting. [RMBCA §8.23]

3. Quorum

A majority of the board of directors constitutes a quorum for the meeting unless a higher or lower number is required by the articles of incorporation or the bylaws, but a quorum may be *no fewer than one-third* of the board members. [RMBCA §8.24]

a. Breaking Quorum

A quorum must be present *at the time the vote is taken* for the vote to constitute valid action. Thus, even if a quorum is present at the beginning of a meeting, a group of minority directors may break quorum by leaving a meeting before a vote is taken. This is not true of shareholders at shareholders' meetings. Once a shareholder is present for a shareholders' meeting, he is deemed present even if he leaves.

4. Approval of Action

If a quorum is present, resolutions will be deemed approved if approved by a *majority of directors present* unless the articles or bylaws require the vote of a greater number. [RMBCA §8.24(c)]

a. Right to Dissent

A director who is present at a board meeting when corporate action is taken is deemed to have assented to the action taken unless:

(i) *The director objects at the beginning of the meeting*, or promptly on her arrival, to holding it or transacting business at the meeting;

(ii) *The director's dissent or abstention* from the action taken is *entered in the minutes* of the meeting; *or*

(iii) *The director delivers written notice* of her dissent or abstention to the presiding officer of the meeting before its adjournment.

[RMBCA §8.24(d)]

b. Action May Be Taken Without Meeting by Unanimous Written Consent

Action required or permitted to be taken at a directors' meeting may be taken without a meeting if the action is taken by *all directors*. Each director must sign a *written consent* that describes the action taken and is included in the minutes or filed with the corporate records. [RMBCA §8.21]

F. MAY DELEGATE AUTHORITY TO COMMITTEES OR OFFICERS

The board of directors is not expected to participate in the daily business affairs of the corporation. Rather, they usually delegate management functions for daily business affairs to executive committees or to officers.

1. **Executive Committees**
    The board may create one or more committees, each made up of *two or more members* of the board. [RMBCA §8.25]

    a. **Selection**
        Creation of a committee and appointment of its members must be approved by the greater of (i) a majority of all directors in office when the action is taken or (ii) the number of directors required to take action under statutory voting requirements. [RMBCA §8.25(b)]

    b. **Powers**
        Subject to the following limitations, each committee may exercise the authority granted to it by the board. However, a committee may *not* do any of the following:

        (i)   Authorize *distributions*;

        (ii) Approve or *submit to shareholders* any action that requires shareholder approval;

        (iii) *Fill vacancies* on the board or a committee;

        (iv) *Amend articles* of incorporation;

        (v)   *Adopt, amend, or repeal bylaws*;

        (vi) *Approve a plan of merger* not requiring shareholder approval;

        (vii) *Authorize reacquisition of shares*, except according to a formula or method prescribed by the board; or

        (viii) *Authorize the issuance, sale, or contract for sale of shares,* or determine the relative rights and preferences of a class or series (however, the board may authorize a committee or an executive officer of the corporation to do so within limits set forth by the board).

        [RMBCA §8.25(d), (e)]

2. **Officers**
    The officers have whatever duties the board prescribes. The board remains responsible for supervision of the officers despite the delegation of duty.

G. **DIRECTORS' RIGHT TO INSPECT**
    Directors have a right to inspect corporate books. [RMBCA §16.05]

H. **DE FACTO DIRECTORS**
    Directors who have not been properly elected, either by a failure to call a proper shareholders' meeting, an error in the balloting, or a failure to satisfy bylaw qualifications, are de facto directors. De facto directors bind the corporation in their performance of normal director activities.

I. **DIRECTORS' DUTIES AND LIABILITIES**
    The directors' management duties are typical fiduciary duties, including the duty of due care, the duty of loyalty, and the duty to protect the interests of the other intracorporate parties.

1. **Personal Liability of Directors May Be Limited**

   The articles of incorporation can limit or eliminate directors' personal liability for money damages to the corporation or shareholders for action taken, or failure to take action, as a director. However, no provision can limit or eliminate liability for (i) the amount of a financial benefit received by the director to which she is not entitled, (ii) an intentionally inflicted harm on the corporation or its shareholders, (iii) unlawful corporate distributions, or (iv) an intentional violation of criminal law. [RMBCA §2.02(b)(5)]

2. **Duty of Care**

   Directors are vested with the duty to manage the corporation to the best of their ability; they are not insurers of corporate success, but rather are merely required to discharge their duties:

   (i)   In *good faith*;

   (ii) *With the care that an ordinarily prudent person in a like position* would exercise under similar circumstances; and

   (iii) In a manner the directors *reasonably believe to be in the best interests of the corporation*.

   [RMBCA §8.30(a)] Directors who meet this standard of conduct will not be liable for corporate decisions that, in hindsight, turn out to be poor or erroneous. At common law, this was known as the *"business judgment rule."*

   a. **Burden on Challenger**

      The person challenging the directors' action has the burden of proving that the statutory standard was not met. [RMBCA §8.30(d)]

   b. **Director May Rely on Reports or Other Information**

      In discharging her duties, a director is entitled to rely on information, opinions, reports, or statements (including financial statements), if prepared or presented by any of the following:

      (i)   *Corporate officers or employees* whom the director reasonably believes to be reliable and competent;

      (ii) *Legal counsel, accountants, or other persons* as to matters the director reasonably believes are within such person's professional competence; or

      (iii) A *committee* of the board of which the director is not a member, if the director reasonably believes the committee merits confidence.

      [RMBCA §8.30(b)]

   c. **Doctrine of Waste**

      As part of their duty of care, directors have a duty not to waste corporate assets by overpaying for property or employment services (*e.g.,* by paying someone an amount substantially above market value for services or property).

3. **Duty to Disclose**

The directors also have a duty to disclose material corporate information to other members of the board (*e.g.*, information material to a decision by the board to approve a financial statement). [RMBCA §8.30(c)]

4. **Duty of Loyalty (Common Law)**

A director owes a duty of loyalty to her corporation and will not be permitted to profit at the expense of the corporation. The problems in this area involve the director's dealings with the corporation and her potential conflict of interest; her dealings with third parties and her usurpation of a corporate opportunity; and her dealings with shareholders, which may raise insider trading issues.

a. **Conflicting Interest Transactions**

If a director has a personal interest in a transaction in which her corporation is a party, a conflict of interest arises.

1) **What Constitutes a Conflicting Interest Transaction?**

A director has a conflicting interest with respect to a transaction or proposed transaction if the director knows that she or a related person (*e.g.*, a spouse, parent, child, grandchild, etc.):

(i) *Is a party* to the transaction;

(ii) *Has a beneficial financial interest* in, or is so closely linked to, the transaction that the interest would reasonably be expected to influence the director's judgment if she were to vote on the transaction; or

(iii) Is a *director, general partner, agent, or employee* of another entity with whom the corporation is transacting business and the transaction is of such importance to the corporation that it would in the normal course of business be brought before the board (the so-called interlocking directorate problem).

[RMBCA §8.60]

2) **Standards for Upholding Conflicting Interest Transaction**

A conflicting interest transaction will not be enjoined or give rise to an award of damages due to the director's interest in the transaction if:

(i) The transaction was approved by a *majority of the directors* (but at least two) *without a conflicting interest* after all material facts have been disclosed to the board;

(ii) The transaction was approved by *a majority of the votes entitled to be cast by shareholders without a conflicting interest* in the transaction after all material facts have been disclosed to the shareholders (notice of the meeting must describe the conflicting interest transaction); or

(iii) The transaction, judged according to circumstances at the time of commitment, was *fair to the corporation*.

[RMBCA §§8.61 - 8.63]

a) **Interested Director's Presence at Meeting Irrelevant**
The presence of the interested director(s) at the meeting at which the directors or shareholders voted to approve the conflicting interest transaction does not affect the action. [RMBCA §§8.62(c), 8.63(c)]

b) **Special Quorum Requirements**
Because the director with a conflicting interest has no right to vote whether to approve the transaction, quorum requirements are changed for purposes of the vote on the transaction. *For purposes of a directors' meeting*, a majority of the directors without a conflicting interest, but not less than two, constitutes a quorum for purposes of the vote on the transaction. [RMBCA §8.62(c)] *For purposes of a shareholders' meeting*, a quorum consists of a majority of the votes entitled to be cast, not including shares owned or controlled directly or beneficially by the director with the conflicting interest. [RMBCA §8.63(c)]

c) **Factors to Be Considered in Determining Fairness**
In determining whether a transaction is fair, courts traditionally look to factors such as adequacy of the consideration, corporate need to enter into the transaction, financial position of the corporation, and available alternatives.

d) **Statutory Interpretation**
It has been argued that the RMBCA's conflicting interest statute is not quite as absolute as it seems. For example, a transaction approved by the board or shareholders might still be set aside if the party challenging the transaction can prove that it constitutes a waste of corporate assets. On the other hand, a transaction approved by *all* of the shareholders probably cannot be set aside, because the shareholders would be estopped from complaining.

e) **Remedies**
Possible remedies for an improper conflicting interest transaction include enjoining the transaction, setting aside the transaction, damages, and similar remedies. [*See* RMBCA §8.61(b)]

3) **Directors May Set Own Compensation**
Despite the apparent conflict of interest, unless the articles or bylaws provide otherwise, the board may set director compensation. [RMBCA §8.11] Of course, setting an unreasonable compensation will breach the directors' fiduciary duties.

b. **Corporate Opportunity Doctrine**
The directors' fiduciary duties prohibit them from diverting a business opportunity from their corporation to themselves without first giving their corporation an opportunity to act. This is sometimes known as a "usurpation of a corporate opportunity" problem.

1) **Corporation Must Have Interest or Expectancy**
A usurpation problem will not arise from every business opportunity that comes

to the directors. Directors are prohibited from taking advantage of business opportunities only if their corporation would have an *interest or expectancy* in the business opportunity.

Example: Saguaro Corp. packages cactus seeds to sell to tourists. Business is good, and the corporation needs to expand its packaging facility. Rick, a Saguaro director, learns that the owner of a lot adjacent to Saguaro's factory might be interested in selling the lot. Rick approaches the owner, who agrees to sell the lot to Rick. Because Saguaro Corp. has an interest in expanding, the lot is a corporate opportunity, and Rick must give the corporation a chance to purchase the lot before he may do so.

a)   Scope of Interest
A corporation's interest does not extend to every conceivable business opportunity, but neither does the opportunity have to be necessary to the corporation's current business. The closer the opportunity is to the corporation's *line of business*, the more likely a court will find it to be a corporate opportunity.

b)   Lack of Financial Ability Probably Not a Defense
The corporation's lack of financial ability to take advantage of the opportunity probably is not a defense. The director should still present the opportunity to the corporation and allow the corporation to decide whether it can take advantage of the opportunity.

2)   Board Generally Decides
Because the board generally makes decisions concerning management of the corporation, it is the board that must decide whether to accept an opportunity or to reject it; generally, shareholders need not be consulted.

3)   Remedies
If a director does not give the corporation an opportunity to act, but rather usurps the opportunity, the corporation can recover the profits that the director made from the transaction or may force the director to convey the opportunity to the corporation, under a constructive trust theory, for whatever consideration the director purchased the opportunity.

c.   Competing Business
Directors are permitted to engage in unrelated businesses, but a clear conflict of interest may arise if the director's personal business is in direct competition with the corporation.

d.   Common Law Insider Trading—Special Circumstances Rule
Federal statutes control most insider trading litigation. However, the statutes do not destroy common law actions for insider trading, and common law concepts appear occasionally in bar exam questions. Traditionally at common law, a director owes fiduciary duties only to the corporation and not to individual shareholders. Therefore, a director was free to buy and sell corporate shares without disclosing to the prospective seller or buyer any inside knowledge that the director had. However, this rule gave

insiders an unfair advantage, and eventually state courts developed the ***special circumstances rule***. Under the rule, if special circumstances exist which may have a significant impact on the value of the stock being traded (*e.g.,* the director knows of an upcoming extraordinary dividend or a planned merger), those circumstances may give rise to a fiduciary duty to disclose them to the person with whom the director is dealing, and a failure to completely disclose will result in the breach of that duty.

VII. OFFICERS

A. IN GENERAL

The RMBCA does not require a corporation to have any specific officers, but rather provides that a corporation shall have the officers described in its bylaws or appointed by the board pursuant to the bylaws. An officer may appoint other officers or assistant officers if so authorized by the bylaws or the board. One person may simultaneously hold more than one office. [RMBCA §8.40]

B. DUTIES

Officers' duties are determined by the bylaws or, to the extent consistent with the bylaws, by the board or an officer so authorized by the board. [RMBCA §8.41]

C. POWERS

The officers are agents of the corporation and receive their power to manage from the directors. The ordinary rules of agency determine the authority and powers of the officers and agents. Authority may be actual or apparent. If authority exists, actions taken by an officer or agent (such as entering into contracts) bind the corporation.

1. Actual Authority

An officer's actual authority includes not only the authority expressly granted to the officer by the directors, the bylaws, the articles, and statutes, but also any authority that may be implied by the express grant. Appointment to the following offices implies the following powers absent an express provision otherwise:

a. President

There is a presumption that the president has implied authority to enter into contracts and otherwise act on behalf of the corporation in the ordinary course of corporate affairs. The president also is deemed to have any actual authority that the corporation's secretary certifies that the board has given to the president.

b. Vice President

The vice president has implied authority to act when the president is unavailable because of death, illness, or other incapacity.

c. Secretary

The secretary has implied authority to keep and certify the corporate records.

d. Treasurer

The treasurer has implied authority to receive and keep corporate funds.

2. Apparent Authority

When the corporation "holds out" an officer as possessing certain authority, thereby inducing others reasonably to believe that the authority exists, the officer has apparent authority to act and to bind the corporation even though actual authority to do so has not been granted.

D. STANDARD OF CONDUCT

The officers' standard of conduct is similar to the standard for directors: If an officer has any discretionary authority with respect to any duties, the officer must carry out her duties *in good faith*, *with the care an ordinarily prudent person in a like position* would exercise under similar circumstances, and in a manner she *reasonably believes to be in the best interests of the corporation*. [RMBCA §8.42(a)]

E. RESIGNATION AND REMOVAL

Despite any contractual term to the contrary, an officer has the power to resign at any time by delivering notice to the corporation, and the corporation has the power to remove an officer at any time, *with or without cause*. If the resignation or removal constitutes a breach of contract, the nonbreaching party's rights to damages are not affected by the resignation or removal, but note that mere appointment to office itself does not create any contractual right to remain in office. [RMBCA §§8.43, 8.44]

VIII. INDEMNIFICATION OF DIRECTORS, OFFICERS, AND EMPLOYEES

A. IN GENERAL

If a person is made a party to a legal proceeding because of his status as a director, officer, employee, or agent of the corporation, depending on the circumstances, the corporation may be required to indemnify the person, may have discretion to indemnify the person, or may be prohibited from indemnifying the person.

B. MANDATORY INDEMNIFICATION

Unless limited by the articles, a corporation *must* indemnify a director or officer who *prevailed* in defending the proceeding against the officer or director for reasonable expenses, including attorneys' fees incurred in connection with the proceeding. [RMBCA §§8.52, 8.56(c)]

C. DISCRETIONARY INDEMNIFICATION

A corporation *may* indemnify a director for reasonable expenses incurred in *unsuccessfully defending* a suit brought against the director on account of the director's position if:

(i) The director acted in *good faith*; and

(ii) Believed that her conduct was:

    i. In the *best interests of the corporation* (when the conduct at issue was within the director's official capacity);

    ii. *Not opposed to the best interests of the corporation* (when the conduct at issue was not within the director's official capacity); or

iii. *Not **unlawful*** (in criminal proceedings).

[RMBCA §8.51]

1. Exceptions

A corporation does not have discretion to indemnify a director who is unsuccessful in defending (i) a direct or derivative action when the ***director is found liable to the corporation*** or (ii) an action charging that the director received an ***improper benefit***. [RMBCA §8.51(d)]

2. Who Makes Determination?

Generally, the determination whether to indemnify is to be made by a disinterested majority of the board, or if there is not a disinterested quorum, by majority of a disinterested committee or by legal counsel. The shareholders may also make the determination (the shares of the director seeking indemnification are not counted). [RMBCA §8.55(b)]

3. Officers

Officers generally may be indemnified to the same extent as a director. [RMBCA §8.56]

D. COURT-ORDERED INDEMNIFICATION

A court may order indemnification whenever it is appropriate. [RMBCA §8.54]

E. ADVANCES

A corporation may advance expenses to a director defending an action as long as the director furnishes the corporation with a statement that she believes she met the appropriate standard of conduct and that she will repay the advance if she is later found to have not met the appropriate standard. [RMBCA §8.53]

F. LIABILITY INSURANCE

A corporation may purchase liability insurance to indemnify directors for actions against them even if the directors would not have been entitled to indemnification under the above standards. [RMBCA §8.55]

G. AGENTS AND EMPLOYEES

The RMBCA does not limit a corporation's power to indemnify, advance expenses to, or maintain insurance on an agent or employee. [RMBCA §8.58(e)]

PART THREE—CHANGES IN STRUCTURE

IX. FUNDAMENTAL CHANGES IN CORPORATE STRUCTURE

A. INTRODUCTION

The RMBCA permits corporations to undertake fundamental changes to their structure, but because it would be unfair to force a person to remain an owner of a fundamentally changed corporation, the Act provides special procedures that allow shareholders to vote whether to adopt a fundamental change, and in some cases provides dissenting shareholders a right to have the corporation purchase their shares after a fundamental change has been approved.

1. **Types of Fundamental Corporate Changes**
    The RMBCA provides special procedures for the following corporate changes: most amendments of the articles, mergers, share exchanges, dispositions of substantially all property outside the usual and regular course of business, and dissolution.

2. **General Procedure for Fundamental Change**
    The basic procedure for adopting a fundamental corporate change is the same for all fundamental changes:

    a. ***A majority of the board of directors adopts a resolution*** recommending the fundamental change;

    b. ***Notice*** of the proposed change is sent to ***all shareholders*** (whether or not entitled to vote). The notice must (i) describe the change and inform the shareholders that a vote will be taken on the matter at a shareholders' meeting, and (ii) be given not less than 10 or more than 60 days before the meeting;

    c. The change is ***approved by a majority of all votes entitled to be cast and by a majority of any voting group entitled to vote as a group***; and

    d. The change is formalized in ***articles*** (*e.g.*, articles of amendment, articles of merger, etc.), which are ***filed*** with the state.

B. AMENDMENTS OF THE ARTICLES OF INCORPORATION

A corporation may amend its articles at any time to add or change a provision that is required or permitted, or to delete a provision that is not required. [RMBCA §10.01] Certain "housekeeping" amendments can be made without shareholder approval, but most require approval by the shareholders.

1. **Amendments that Board Can Make Without Shareholder Approval**
    The board of directors may make any amendment to the articles before any shares are issued. [RMBCA §10.05] Once shares have been issued, the board may make the following amendments without approval by the shareholders:

    (i)   To ***extend the corporation's duration*** if the corporation was formed when the law required a limited duration;

    (ii) To ***delete the names and/or addresses of the initial directors*** or registered agent or office;

    (iii) To ***change the authorized number of shares*** to implement a share split, as long as there is ***only one class*** of shares outstanding;

    (iv) To ***change the company name*** by substituting a ***different word or abbreviation*** than the one currently ***indicating the corporation's corporate status*** (*e.g.*, "Co." in place of "Inc.") or changing a geographical attribute (*e.g.*, "X Corp. of Arizona" in place of "X Corp."); and

    (v)   Any other change ***permitted by the RMBCA without shareholder approval***.

    [RMBCA §10.02]

2. Amendments by Board and Shareholders

Any amendment to the articles other than those listed above requires implementation of the general fundamental change procedure as discussed *supra* (*i.e.*, resolution of the board, notice to the shareholders, approval by the shareholders, and filing articles of amendment with the state). [RMBCA §10.03(a)]

a. Vote Required

In addition to the shareholder vote that is ordinarily required to pass fundamental corporate changes, an amendment must also be approved by a majority of the votes of any voting group that would have dissenters' rights with respect to the amendment. [RMBCA §10.03(e)(1)] Dissenters' rights arise if the amendment will do one of the following:

(i) *Change the aggregate number of authorized shares* of the class;

(ii) *Change shares of the class into a different number* of shares (*e.g.,* a stock split);

(iii) *Exchange or reclassify shares of the class* into shares of another class or of another class into shares of this class;

(iv) *Change the rights or preferences* of the shares of the class, including limiting or denying existing preemptive rights;

(v) *Change the rights of another class, or create another class*, so that the changed or new class has *rights or preferences equal or superior* to rights and preferences of this class; or

(vi) *Cancel rights to distributions* that have accumulated, but have not yet been declared for, the shares of the class.

[RMBCA §10.04]

C. MERGER, SHARE EXCHANGE, AND CONVERSION

The RMBCA provides that the basic procedure for fundamental corporate changes must be followed to approve a merger, share exchange, or conversion. A merger involves the blending of one or more corporations into another corporation, and the latter corporation survives while the merging corporations cease to exist following the merger. A share exchange involves one corporation purchasing all of the outstanding shares of one or more classes or series of another corporation. A conversion involves one business entity changing its form into another business entity, such as a corporation changing into an LLC or a partnership.

1. Not All Shareholders Need Approve

Mergers, share exchanges, and conversions vary a little from the basic fundamental change procedure in that not all shareholders have a right to approve these procedures under all circumstances.

a. Merger

1) No Significant Change to Surviving Corporation

Approval by shareholders of the *surviving* corporation on a plan of merger is *not* required if *all* the following conditions exist:

(i) The articles of incorporation of the surviving corporation will *not differ* from the articles before the merger;

(ii) Each shareholder of the survivor whose shares were outstanding immediately prior to the effective date of the merger will hold the *same number of shares*, with identical preferences, limitations, and rights; and

(iii) The *voting power* of the shares issued as a result of the merger will comprise no more than *20%* of the voting power of the shares of the surviving corporation that were outstanding immediately prior to the merger.

[RMBCA §§11.04(g); 6.21(f)]

2) Short Form Merger of Subsidiary

A parent corporation owning at least 90% of the outstanding shares of each class of a subsidiary corporation may merge the subsidiary into itself *without the approval of the shareholders or directors of the subsidiary*. [RMBCA §11.05] This is known as a "short form merger." The parent must mail a copy of the plan of merger to each shareholder of the subsidiary who does not waive the mailing requirement in writing. Articles of merger may not be delivered to the state for filing until at least 30 days after the plan was mailed to the shareholders.

b. Share Exchange

In a share exchange, only the shareholders of the corporation whose shares will be *acquired* in the share exchange need approve; a share exchange is *not* a fundamental corporate change for the acquiring corporation. [RMBCA §11.03(a)] Notice requirements are the same as for amendment of the articles.

c. Conversion

The procedure for effecting a conversion generally is the same as the procedure for approving a merger in which the converting corporation is not the survivor (*see* A.2., *supra*).

2. Effect

a. Merger

Where there is a merger, every other corporation that is a party to the merger merges into the surviving corporation, and the separate existence of every corporation except the survivor ends. All property owned by the separate entities, and all obligations of the separate entities, become the property and obligations of the surviving corporation. A proceeding pending against a party to the merger may continue as if the merger did not occur, or the surviving corporation may be substituted.

b. Share Exchange

When a share exchange takes effect, the shares of each acquired corporation are exchanged as provided in the plan, and the former holders of the shares are entitled only to the exchange rights provided in the plan. The corporations remain separate.

D. DISPOSITION OF PROPERTY OUTSIDE THE USUAL AND REGULAR COURSE OF BUSINESS

A sale, lease, exchange, or other disposition of *all or substantially all* of a corporation's property outside of the usual and regular course of business is a fundamental corporate change *for the corporation disposing of the property*. Thus, the corporation disposing of the property must follow the fundamental change procedure. [RMBCA §12.02(a)] Note that the corporation *purchasing* the property is not undergoing a fundamental corporate change, and so approval from that corporation's shareholders is not required.

1. What Constitutes "Substantially All"?

A sale will be considered to be of substantially all assets if it leaves the corporation *without* significant continuing business activities. Generally, this means a sale of more than 75% of the corporation's assets which also account for at least 75% of the corporation's revenues. [*See* RMBCA §12.02(a)]

2. Compare—Dispositions Within Usual and Regular Course of Business

A disposition of a corporation's property within the usual and regular course of business is not a fundamental change and need not be approved by the shareholders. [RMBCA §12.01(a)(1)]

3. Compare—Mortgages, Pledges, Etc.

The fundamental change procedure need not be followed to approve the grant of a mortgage, pledge, or similar security interest, even if the security interest is in all or substantially all of a corporation's assets, and even if the grant is not within the usual and regular course of the corporation's business. [RMBCA §12.01(a)(2)]

4. Effect on Purchaser

Generally, the purchaser of another corporation's property does not become liable for the seller's obligations; the seller remains solely liable. However, if the disposition of property is really a disguised merger, a court might treat it as a merger under the de facto merger doctrine and hold the purchaser liable for the seller's obligations just as if a merger had occurred.

a. Factors Contributing to De Facto Merger

Courts adopting the de facto merger doctrine have stressed a number of factors that can cause an ostensible sale of assets or stock to be recharacterized as a merger:

1) The fact that the acquiring corporation *used its own stock as consideration* rather than cash or promissory notes;

2) The fact that the *acquired corporation was required to dissolve*;

3) In the case of an acquisition of stock, the fact that the *acquired corporation was merged* into the acquiring corporation after its stock had been acquired; and

4) The fact that the *smaller corporation was buying the assets of the larger* corporation (rather than the converse).

E. PROTECTION AGAINST AND LIMITATIONS ON FUNDAMENTAL CHANGES

1. **Dissenting Shareholders' Appraisal Remedy**
   Shareholders who are dissatisfied with the terms of a fundamental corporate change usually are permitted to compel the corporation to buy their shares at a fair value by following a special statutory procedure. In most cases, absent fraud, misrepresentation, or improper procedure, a shareholder entitled to appraisal rights may not challenge a completed corporate action for which appraisal rights are available (*i.e.*, the appraisal right generally is a shareholder's exclusive remedy for completed corporate action). [RMBCA §13.02]

   a. **Who May Dissent?**

      1) **Merger**
         Any shareholder *entitled to vote* on a plan of merger and *shareholders of the subsidiary* in a short form merger have the right to dissent. [RMBCA §13.02(a)(1)]

      2) **Share Exchange**
         Shareholders of the corporation whose shares are being *acquired* in a share exchange have the right to dissent. [RMBCA §13.02(a)(2)]

      3) **Disposition of Property**
         A shareholder who is *entitled to vote* on a disposition of all or substantially all of the corporation's property outside the usual and regular course of business is entitled to dissent. This does not include a sale pursuant to court order, or a cash sale pursuant to a plan by which the net sale proceeds will be distributed to the shareholders within one year of the date of sale. [RMBCA §13.02(a)(3)]

      4) **Amendment of Articles**
         A shareholder has a right to dissent from an amendment of the articles that *materially and adversely affects the shareholder's rights* (*e.g.*, changes preferential redemption or preemptive rights, limits voting rights, or reduces the shareholder's shares to fractional shares to be purchased by the corporation), unless there is a court order for reorganization. [RMBCA §13.02(a)(4)]

   b. **Procedure**

      1) **Corporation Must Give Shareholders Notice**
         If a proposed corporate action will create dissenters' rights, the notice of the shareholders' meeting at which a vote on the action will be taken must state that the shareholders will be entitled to exercise their dissenting rights. [RMBCA §13.20(a)] If the action may be taken without a vote of the shareholders (*e.g.*, in a short form merger), they must be given notice that the action was taken and of their right to dissent. [RMBCA §13.20(b)]

      2) **Shareholder Must Give Notice of Intent to Demand Payment**
         If the shareholder will be entitled to vote and wishes to exercise her dissenting rights, she must, *before a vote is taken*, deliver *written notice of her intent to demand payment* for her shares if the proposed action is taken. Also, she cannot vote in favor of the proposed action. Failure to satisfy these requirements means that the shareholder is not entitled to payment for her shares. [RMBCA §13.21(a)]

3)   Corporation Must Give Dissenters Notice

If the proposed action is approved at the shareholders' meeting, the corporation *must notify, within 10 days* after the vote, all shareholders who filed an intent to demand payment. The notice must tell the shareholders when and where they must submit their shares and state the other terms of the repurchase. The corporation cannot set the time for receiving the payment demands less than 40 or more than 60 days after the date the corporation's notice is delivered. [RMBCA §13.22]

4)   Shareholders Must Demand Payment

A shareholder who is sent a dissenter's notice must then *demand payment* in accordance with the notice given by the corporation. [RMBCA §13.23]

5)   Corporation Must Pay

When the proposed action is taken, the corporation must pay the dissenters the *amount the corporation estimates as the fair value* of the shares, plus accrued interest. Along with the payment, the corporation must send the corporation's balance sheet and income statement, and an explanation of how fair value and interest were determined. [RMBCA §13.25]

6)   Notice of Dissatisfaction

If the shareholder is dissatisfied with the corporation's determination of value, the shareholder has 30 days in which to send the corporation her *own estimate of value* and demand payment of that amount (or the difference between her estimate and the amount sent by the corporation). [RMBCA §13.26]

7)   Court Action

If the corporation does not want to pay what the shareholder demanded, *the corporation* must file an action in court within 60 days after receiving the shareholder's demand, requesting the court to determine the fair value of the shares. If the corporation fails to file suit within 60 days, it will be required to pay the shareholder the amount the shareholder demanded. [RMBCA §13.30]

2.   Tender Offers and Corporate Control Transactions

It is common for one corporation to try to take over another corporation. The federal Williams Act and state control share acquisition statutes have been devised to help protect shareholders of the company being acquired.

a.   Federal Regulation of Tender Offers—The Williams Act

A tender offer is an offer to shareholders (the offerees) of a corporation (the target) asking them to tender their shares in exchange for either cash or securities. The tender offer is usually made by another corporation (the bidder), but the bidder may also be an individual or a group. Tender offers have replaced proxy fights as the primary method of gaining control over a target corporation. Tender offers are regulated in a number of respects by the Williams Act, which added sections 13(d), 14(d), and 14(e) to the Securities Exchange Act of 1934.

1)   Regulation of the Bidder

What constitutes a tender offer within the meaning of the Williams Act is not settled. For bar exam purposes, a tender offer will usually include most of the following elements:

(i) A *widespread solicitation of public shareholders*;

(ii) For a *substantial percentage* of the target's stock;

(iii) At a *premium price* (above the prevailing market price);

(iv) *Contingent* on the tender of a fixed number of shares.

Open market purchases made anonymously generally are not considered to be tender offers within the meaning of the Act.

a) **Disclosure Required**
Section 14(d) requires any person who makes a tender offer for a class of registered securities which would result in the person owning more than **5%** of a class of securities of the target to file a schedule 14D containing extensive disclosure of the identity of the bidder, past dealings between the bidder and the target, the bidder's source of funds, the bidder's plans concerning the target, the bidder's financial statements (if the bidder is not an individual), and the arrangements, if any, made between the bidder and those holding important positions with the target. [15 U.S.C. §78n(d)]

Note: Anyone who *obtains* more than 5% of any class of registered equity securities must file a somewhat similar (schedule 13D) disclosure.

b) **Regulation of Terms of Tender Offer**
Under section 14(d) and rules 14d and 14e:

(1) A tender offer *must be held open for at least 20 days*;

(2) A tender offer *must be open to all security holders of the class* of securities subject to the tender offer;

(3) Shareholders *must be permitted to withdraw tendered shares* while the offer remains open;

(4) If the offer is oversubscribed, the bidder *must purchase on a pro rata basis* from among the shares deposited during the first 10 days or such other period as the bidder designates; and

(5) If the tender offer price is increased, the *higher price must be paid to all tendering shareholders.*

2) **Regulation of the Target**
Rule 14e-2 requires the management of the target corporation, within 10 business days from the date the tender offer is first published, to give its shareholders a statement disclosing that the target either: (i) recommends acceptance or rejection of the tender; (ii) expresses no opinion and is remaining neutral toward the tender offer; or (iii) is unable to take a position with respect to the tender offer. In any case, the statement must also include the reasons for the position taken.

3) General Antifraud Provisions

The Williams Act also contains a broad antifraud provision prohibiting any false or misleading statements or omissions in connection with a tender offer, by either the offeror, the target (*i.e.,* the incumbent management in attempting to oppose the tender offer), or any other person.

a) Shareholders of Target Have Standing for Civil Damage Action

The shareholders of the target corporation, as the primary beneficiaries of the Williams Act, have standing under the Act to bring a civil action for *damages* or an injunction for violation of the Act. An unsuccessful bidder does *not* have standing to assert a claim for damages against a successful competing bidder or the target for violation of the Act [Piper v. Chris-Craft Industries, Inc., 430 U.S. 1 (1977)], although the bidder might have standing to seek an injunction against any false statements.

b) SEC May Seek Injunction

The SEC clearly has standing to seek to enjoin false or misleading statements under the Williams Act.

b. State Regulation—Control Share Acquisition Statutes

A number of states have also sought to protect shareholders from takeovers, particularly hostile takeovers. Although state regulations vary, of states adopting such legislation, control share acquisition statutes are the most popular. Under a control share acquisition statute, if a designated stock ownership threshold (*e.g.,* 20% of the shares in a class) is crossed by an acquiring shareholder, he loses the right to vote the acquired shares until the right to vote is restored by a vote of a majority of the shares held by disinterested shareholders. Since this could leave a takeover bidder powerless to control the management of the target corporation, it can prevent hostile takeovers.

Example: A state statute has three thresholds: 20%, 33%, and 50%. If a purchase of shares takes the purchaser across one of these lines, voting power in the control shares can be restored only with approval of the target's disinterested shareholders.

1) Limitation on Scope

The first generation of control share acquisition statutes were very broad, attempting to reach all tender offers made to target shareholders who were residents of the state and all target corporations doing business in the state. The Supreme Court held that such broad statutes were unconstitutional, both because they imposed an undue burden on interstate commerce and because they conflicted with the Williams Act and so violated the Supremacy Clause. [*See, e.g.,* Edgar v. MITE Corp., 457 U.S. 624 (1982)] However, the Court has upheld narrow statutes. To be valid, the statute should be applicable only to *corporations or transactions significantly connected to the state*, such as a corporation whose principal place of business is in the regulating state and which has a significant number of shareholders (*e.g.,* 1,000 shareholders, 10% of the target class, etc.) in the regulating state.

X. DISSOLUTION AND LIQUIDATION

A. INTRODUCTION

Dissolution is the termination of the corporate existence. To dissolve the corporation, some act must be taken, which may be voluntary by the corporation or its aggregate members, or may be involuntary through judicial proceedings.

B. VOLUNTARY DISSOLUTION

Dissolution by corporate action without judicial proceedings is termed voluntary dissolution and may be accomplished in the following ways:

1. Dissolution by Incorporators or Initial Directors

A majority of the incorporators or initial directors may dissolve the corporation if *shares have not yet been issued or business has not yet been commenced* by delivering articles of dissolution to the state. All corporate debts must be paid before dissolution, and if shares have been issued, any assets remaining after winding up must be distributed to the shareholders. [RMBCA §14.01]

2. Dissolution by Corporate Act

The corporation may dissolve voluntarily by an act of the corporation, involving both board of directors and shareholder approval. The standard procedure for *fundamental corporate change* is followed. [RMBCA §14.02]

3. Effect of Dissolution

A corporation that has been dissolved continues its corporate existence, but is not allowed to carry on any business except that which is appropriate to *wind up and liquidate its affairs*. Permissible activities include collection of assets, disposal of property that will not be distributed in kind to shareholders, discharging liabilities, and distributing remaining property among shareholders according to their interests. Dissolution does not transfer title to the corporation's property, change quorum or voting requirements, suspend proceedings pending against or by the corporation, or prevent commencement of a proceeding by or against the corporation. [RMBCA §14.05]

a. Barring Claims Against the Corporation

A claim can be asserted against a dissolved corporation—even if the claim does not arise until after dissolution—to the extent of the corporation's undistributed assets. If the assets have been distributed to the shareholders, a claim can be asserted against each shareholder for his pro rata share of the claim, to the extent of the assets distributed to him. To provide some finality for liquidating distributions, the RMBCA provides special procedures that a corporation may follow in order to bar claims against the corporation sooner than they might be barred under the statute of limitations for the claims.

1) Known Claims Against Dissolved Corporation—120 Days

To bar known claims against the corporation, the corporation must notify its known claimants in writing of the dissolution. The notice must describe the procedure for asserting a claim and set a deadline not less than 120 days from the effective date of notice by which the claim must be received. A claim is barred

if a claimant who receives notice fails to deliver the claim by the deadline, or if a claimant whose claim has been rejected does not commence a proceeding to enforce the claim within 90 days from the effective date of the rejection. [RMBCA §14.06]

2) Unknown Claims Against Dissolved Corporation—Five Years

To bar claims not known to the corporation, the corporation must publish notice of its dissolution in a newspaper in the county where the corporation's principal place of business is located. The notice must describe the procedure for asserting a claim and state that a claim will be barred unless a proceeding to enforce it is commenced within five years after notice is published. [RMBCA §14.07]

4. Revocation of Voluntary Dissolution

A corporation may revoke a voluntary dissolution by using the same procedure that was used to approve the dissolution. The revocation relates back to and takes effect as of the effective date of the dissolution, so that the corporation may resume carrying on its business as if there had never been a dissolution. [RMBCA §14.04]

C. ADMINISTRATIVE DISSOLUTION

1. Grounds for Administrative Dissolution

The state may bring an action to administratively dissolve a corporation for any of the following reasons:

(i) *Failure to pay any fees or penalties* imposed by law within 60 days after their due date;

(ii) *Failure to deliver the annual report* to the state within 60 days after it is due;

(iii) *Failure to maintain a registered agent in the state* for 60 days or more;

(iv) *Failure to notify the state of a change in registered agent* within 60 days; or

(v) *Expiration of the period of corporate duration* set forth in the articles of incorporation.

[RMBCA §14.20]

2. Procedure and Effect

If grounds for dissolution exist as set forth above, the state must serve the corporation with written notice. If the corporation does not correct the grounds for dissolution or show that the grounds do not exist within *60* days after service of notice, the state effectuates the dissolution by signing a certificate of dissolution. [RMBCA §14.21]

3. Reinstatement May Be Retroactive for up to Two Years

A corporation that is administratively dissolved may apply for reinstatement within two years after the effective date of dissolution. The application must state that the grounds for dissolution did not exist or that they have been eliminated. *Reinstatement relates back* to the date of dissolution and the corporation may resume carrying on business as if the dissolution had never occurred. [RMBCA §14.22]

D. JUDICIAL DISSOLUTION

1. Action by Attorney General
The attorney general may seek judicial dissolution of a corporation on the ground that the corporation *fraudulently obtained its articles* of incorporation or that the corporation is *exceeding or abusing its authority*. [RMBCA §14.30(a)(1)]

2. Action by Shareholders
Shareholders may seek judicial dissolution on any of the following grounds:

(i)   The *directors are deadlocked* in the management of corporate affairs, the shareholders are unable to break the deadlock, and *irreparable injury* to the corporation is threatened, or corporate affairs cannot be conducted to the advantage of the shareholders because of the deadlock;

(ii) The directors have acted or will act in a manner that is *illegal, oppressive, or fraudulent*;

(iii) The *shareholders are deadlocked* in voting power and have *failed to elect one or more directors* for a period that includes at least two consecutive annual meeting dates; or

(iv) *Corporate assets are being wasted or misapplied to noncorporate purposes*.

[RMBCA §14.30(a)(2)]

a. Election to Purchase in Lieu of Dissolution
If the proceeding to dissolve is by the shareholders and the corporation has no shares listed on a national securities exchange or regularly traded in a market maintained by one or more members of a national or affiliated securities association, the corporation (or one or more shareholders) may elect to purchase the shares owned by the petitioning shareholder at their fair value. The petitioning shareholder may not dispose of her shares without court permission until the repurchase is completed. [RMBCA §14.34]

3. Action by Creditors
Creditors may seek judicial dissolution if: (i) the creditor's claim has been reduced to judgment, execution of the judgment has been returned unsatisfied, and *the corporation is insolvent*; or (ii) the corporation has admitted in writing that the creditor's claim is due and owing and *the corporation is insolvent*. [RMBCA §14.30(a)(3)]

4. Action by Corporation—Court Supervision of Voluntary Dissolution
A court may dissolve a corporation in an action by the corporation to have its voluntary dissolution continued under court supervision. [RMBCA §14.30(a)(4)]

PART FOUR—LIMITED LIABILITY COMPANIES, PROFESSIONAL CORPORATIONS, AND FOREIGN CORPORATIONS

XI. LIMITED LIABILITY COMPANIES

A. INTRODUCTION

A majority of states have adopted statutes providing for the creation of Limited Liability Companies ("LLCs").

B. PURPOSE

An LLC is an entity eligible to be taxed like a partnership while offering its owners (called "members") the limited liability that shareholders of a corporation enjoy. Under current tax laws, unless an LLC requests to be taxed as a corporation, it will receive partnership tax treatment (*i.e.*, the LLC will not be treated as a taxable entity; profits and losses flow through the LLC to its owners).

1. Compare—S Corporations and Limited Partnerships

If a person is seeking a business format that offers limited personal liability and an opportunity to control the business, an LLC may be better than a Subchapter S corporation (a corporation that elects to be taxed as a partnership under the Tax Code) in that an LLC is not subject to the limitations of Subchapter S (*e.g.*, S corporations are limited to 100 or fewer shareholders). Similarly, an LLC may be better than a limited partnership because limited partnership acts require that there be at least one general partner, who is personally liable for the partnership's obligations; the LLC statutes do not require that a member (*i.e.*, shareholder) of the LLC be personally liable.

2. Controlling Law—Statute vs. Operating Agreement

Although LLCs are governed by statute, the statute provides that LLC members may adopt *operating agreements* to control most aspects of the LLC's business and management. These agreements will control unless contrary to law.

3. Distinct Entity

An LLC is treated as an entity distinct from its members. It may hold property in its own name, sue or be sued, etc.

C. FORMATION

An LLC is formed by filing articles of organization with the secretary of state.

1. Contents of Articles

The articles of an LLC must include the following:

a. A statement that the entity is an LLC;

b. The name of the LLC, which must include an indication that it is an LLC;

c. The street address of the LLC's registered office and name of its registered agent; and

d. The names of all of the members.

2. Management

Management of the LLC is presumed to be by all members. Other management arrangements can be made (*e.g.*, management by only some of the members or by outside managers), but they must be specified in the articles. If management is by the members: (i) a majority vote is required to approve most decisions and (ii) each member is an agent of the LLC (*i.e.*, the LLC may be bound by the acts of any member).

    a.   **Fiduciary Duties of Managers**

Managers of an LLC owe the LLC duties of care and loyalty similar to those duties owed by a director of a corporation. (*See* VI.I., *supra*.) Thus, because of the duty of loyalty, managers may not divert business opportunities of the LLC to themselves, nor may they profit secretly at the expense of the corporation. The duty of care varies from state to state. Some apply a rule similar to the standard for directors of a corporation—managers must act in good faith, with the care of a reasonably prudent person acting under similar conditions, in a manner reasonably believed to be in the best interests of the LLC. In such states, managers also would have the benefit of the business judgment rule—if they meet the above standard, they cannot be held personally liable for business decisions that turn out poorly. (*See* VI.I.2., *supra*.) Other states are even more lenient and require only that the manager(s) refrain from acting with gross negligence, recklessly, with intent to harm the LLC, or in knowing violation of the law.

D.   LIABILITY OF MEMBERS

As indicated above, members generally are ***not*** personally liable for the LLC's obligations. Courts may pierce the LLC veil of limited liability to reach the personal assets of members to satisfy LLC obligations under circumstances similar to those under which the courts would pierce the veil of a corporation; *e.g.,* where the LLC is the alter ego of the manager(s), for inadequate capitalization at the inception of the LLC, or if the LLC was formed to perpetrate a fraud (*see* II.E., *supra*). However, because by statute LLCs can be run with fewer formalities than a corporation (*e.g.,* no meetings or elections are required), lack of formalities generally will not be a ground for piercing an LLC.

E.   SHARING OF PROFITS AND LOSSES

Profits and losses of an LLC are allocated ***on the basis of contributions***.

F.   MEMBERS' ACTIONS AGAINST THE LLC

A member who has been injured personally by his LLC (*e.g.,* through breach of contract) can bring a direct action against the LLC to recover. A member may also bring a derivative action on behalf of his LLC under circumstances similar to those in which a shareholder may bring a derivative action against his corporation. (*See* V.F.2., *supra*.) As in a derivative action in a corporation, a member may be required to make a demand on the LLC's manager(s) before bringing a derivative action unless it would be futile to do so.

G.   TRANSFERS OF INTEREST

An assignment of a member's interest in an LLC transfers only the member's right to receive profits and losses. Management rights are not transferred. One can become a member (*i.e.,* management rights can be transferred) only with the consent of ***all*** members.

H.   DISSOLUTION

Disassociation (*e.g.,* death, retirement, resignation, bankruptcy, incompetence, etc.) of an LLC member generally causes dissolution of the LLC.

XII.   PROFESSIONAL CORPORATIONS

A.   INTRODUCTION

The RMBCA and most states prohibit professionals from forming general corporations for the

purpose of practicing their professions. This rule was based on the idea that professionals should not be able to avoid personal liability for their own malpractice by hiding behind the corporate veil. Eventually, however, states began to adopt special statutes permitting professionals to incorporate so that they could take advantage of certain federal tax provisions that were available only to corporations. The statutes generally treat professional corporations like any other corporation but limit share ownership to licensed professionals and make it clear that a professional practicing in the corporation will still be personally liable for his own malpractice despite the corporate form.

1. Governing Law
Except where the state professional corporation statute provides otherwise, a professional corporation operates in the same manner as a regular business corporation and is governed by the general corporations law.

B. FORMATION

1. Election and Filing
A person or group of persons licensed to practice a profession may elect to practice as a professional corporation. The articles of incorporation are basically the same as in a regular business corporation and are filed in the same manner. However, the articles must state that the corporation is a professional corporation and that its purpose is to render professional services. [Model Business Corporation Act Professional Corporation Supplement ("P.C. Supp.") §10] A corporation organized under the general corporation laws may elect professional corporation status by amending its articles to reflect the change. [P.C. Supp. §10]

2. Corporate Name
The name of a professional corporation must contain one of the following: "professional corporation," "professional association," "service corporation," or the abbreviation "P.C.," "P.A.," or "S.C." The name also must conform with any rule of the licensing authority that has jurisdiction over the corporation's profession. [P.C. Supp. §15]

C. PROFESSIONS TO WHICH APPLICABLE
Professional corporations may be formed by any person licensed in a profession that is not allowed to incorporate under the state's general corporations law. The list of licensed professions varies from state to state, but generally includes: architects; attorneys; certified public accountants; engineers; medical professionals such as dentists, doctors, and pharmacists; and psychologists. [P.C. Supp. §3(7)]

D. OPERATION OF PROFESSIONAL CORPORATION

1. Generally Only One Profession
Generally, a professional corporation may practice only one profession unless and to the extent that other state law allows a professional to practice a combination of professions. [P.C. Supp. §11]

2. Practice Limited to Licensed Personnel
A professional corporation may engage in the practice of a profession only through persons who are licensed to practice the profession in the state. However, the professional corporation

may employ unlicensed persons in capacities in which they are not rendering professional services to the public (*e.g.*, secretaries, receptionists). [P.C. Supp. §13]

3. Director and Officer Qualifications
Under the P.C. Supplement, at least half of the board and all of the officers of a professional corporation (except the secretary and treasurer) must be licensed to practice the profession for which the corporation is organized. [P.C. Supp. §30]

4. Shareholders and Proxies Must Be Licensed Professionals
Shares in a professional corporation may be issued to and held by only licensed professionals, partnerships, and other professional corporations practicing the profession for which the corporation is organized. [P.C. Supp. §20] Moreover, proxies to vote shares may be issued only to licensed professionals. [P.C. Supp. §31] If a shareholder dies or becomes disqualified to practice, the corporation must acquire the shareholder's shares or cause the shares to be acquired by another qualified professional. [P.C. Supp. §23]

5. Shares
Shares of a professional corporation must conspicuously note that they are shares of a professional corporation and that their transferability is restricted. Such shares may be transferred only to licensed professionals, partnerships, and other professional corporations practicing the profession for which the professional corporation is organized. [P.C. Supp. §§21 - 22]

E. LIABILITY ISSUES
Although the professional practice is "incorporated," the professional remains personally liable, along with the corporation, for his own malpractice or misconduct in rendering professional services. However, shareholders generally are not liable for the malpractice of their fellow shareholders and employees except to the extent that they were supervising or cooperating with the fellow shareholder or employee. [P.C. Supp. §34]

XIII. FOREIGN CORPORATIONS

A. POWER TO EXCLUDE
"A state has unlimited power to exclude or regulate foreign corporations other than those engaged in interstate commerce, since corporations are not citizens within the meaning of the Privileges and Immunities Clause." [Paul v. Virginia, 75 U.S. 168 (1869)]

B. ADMISSION
Usually, a foreign corporation may not transact business within a state until it has obtained a "certificate of authority" from the secretary of state.

1. Contents of Application for Certificate of Authority
The application must include the same basic information as is contained in the articles of a domestic corporation.

2. Issuance of Certificate
On finding compliance with law and payment of fees, the secretary will issue a certificate of authority.

C. STATE POWER OVER INTERNAL AFFAIRS OF FOREIGN CORPORATIONS

A foreign corporation may not be denied a certificate of authority because the laws of its state of incorporation governing its organization and internal affairs differ from the host jurisdiction.

D. EFFECT OF TRANSACTING BUSINESS WITHOUT CERTIFICATE

1. Cannot Bring Suit

Until a foreign corporation has obtained a certificate of authority to do business, a common penalty is refusal to allow access to state courts. The corporation may defend suits. However, it usually may obtain the certificate at any time, even after suit has been commenced.

2. No Effect on Contracts

Failure to obtain a certificate does not usually impair the validity of any contract or corporate act, although a minority of jurisdictions render contracts of an unauthorized foreign corporation void or voidable.

PART FIVE—SECURITIES REGULATION

XIV. RULE 10b-5, SECTION 16(b), AND SARBANES-OXLEY

A. RULE 10b-5

Under rule 10b-5 [17 C.F.R. §240.10b-5], it is unlawful for any person, directly or indirectly, by the use of any means or instrumentality of interstate commerce or the mails, or of any facility of any national securities exchange, to:

(i) Employ any device, scheme, or artifice *to defraud*;

(ii) *Make any untrue statement of a material fact or omit to state a material fact* necessary in order to make the statements made, in light of the circumstances under which they were made, not misleading; or

(iii) Engage in any act, practice, or course of business that *operates or would operate as a fraud or a deceit* upon any person, in connection with the purchase or sale of any security.

A violation of the rule can result in a private suit for damages, an SEC suit for injunctive relief, or criminal prosecution.

1. General Elements of Cause of Action

A private plaintiff must show the following elements to recover damages under rule 10b-5:

a. Fraudulent Conduct

The plaintiff must show that the defendant engaged in some fraudulent conduct. This can take a number of forms, *e.g.*, making a material misstatement or making a material omission.

1) Materiality

A statement or omission will be considered material if there is a *substantial*

likelihood that a reasonable investor would consider it important in making her investment decision.

Example: Several insiders bought stock in their mining company on the basis of inside information regarding a substantial mineral find. When the information was publicly released, the price of the stock soared. The mineral find was a material fact. [SEC v. Texas Gulf Sulphur Co., 401 F.2d 833 (2d Cir. 1968)]

2) Scienter

To be fraudulent and actionable under rule 10b-5, the conduct complained of must have been undertaken with an *intent to deceive, manipulate, or defraud*. The Supreme Court has held that this standard includes cases where a misstatement was made knowingly, but has reserved the issue whether misstatements that are made recklessly are proscribed (the circuit courts have uniformly held recklessness to be sufficient).

b. In Connection with the Purchase or Sale of a Security by Plaintiff

If the plaintiff is a private person, the fraudulent conduct must be in connection with the purchase or sale of a security by the plaintiff. The term "in connection with" is interpreted broadly. [SEC v. Zandford, 535 U.S. 813 (2002)—broker's sale of client's securities with intent to misappropriate the proceeds constituted fraud in connection with a sale of a security by plaintiff] The term includes transactions such as exchanges of stock for assets, mergers, contracts to sell, etc. It excludes potential purchasers who did not buy (because of the fraud) and people who already own shares and refrain from selling (because of the fraud). [*See* Blue Chip Stamps v. Manor Drug Stores, 421 U.S. 723 (1975)]

1) Nontrading Defendants Can Be Held Liable

Note that the focus here is on a sale or purchase *by the plaintiff*; the defendant need not have purchased or sold any securities. Thus, a nontrading defendant, such as a company that intentionally publishes a misleading press release, can be held liable to a person who purchased or sold securities on the market on the basis of the press release.

2) Private Plaintiff May Not Maintain Suit Based on Aiding and Abetting

An action brought by a *private plaintiff* pursuant to section 10(b) of the 1934 Act may not be based on a defendant's status as an "aider and abettor" of other defendants' fraud [Central Bank of Denver, N.A. v. First Interstate Bank of Denver, N.A., 511 U.S. 164 (1994)]; but the *government* may base an action on aiding and abetting [1934 Act §20(f)].

c. In Interstate Commerce

The fraudulent conduct must involve the use of some means of interstate commerce; something as simple as use of the telephone or the mail will suffice.

d. Reliance

Generally, it is said that reliance is an element of a rule 10b-5 cause of action. However, in a nondisclosure case reliance is presumed; *i.e.,* the plaintiff need not prove reliance on the undisclosed information. Similarly, in a misrepresentation action on securities

sold in a well-defined market (*e.g.*, national stock exchange), reliance on any public misrepresentations may be presumed based on the *fraud on the market theory*: An investor who buys or sells stock at the price set by the market does so in reliance on the integrity of that stock, which in turn is based on publicly available information. [Basic, Inc. v. Levinson, 485 U.S. 224 (1988)] Thus, it appears that only in the case of face-to-face misrepresentation (*i.e.*, stock not sold on an exchange) will the plaintiff have to prove reliance.

1) Rebuttal of Presumption

The presumption of reliance may be rebutted (*e.g.*, by showing that the plaintiff would have acted the same way even with full disclosure, that the price was not affected by the misrepresentation, or that the plaintiff did not trade in reliance on the integrity of the market).

e. Damages

A private plaintiff must show that the defendant's fraud caused the plaintiff damages.

2. Insider Trading

While it may not be obvious, rule 10b-5's greatest impact is to prohibit most instances of trading securities on the basis of inside information (*i.e.*, information not disclosed to the public that an investor would think is important when deciding whether or not to invest in a security). Early insider trading cases focused on the duty of the trader to *disclose or abstain* from trading. Now, it is clear that a person violates rule 10b-5 if he breaches a *duty of trust and confidence* owed to: (i) the issuer, (ii) shareholders of the issuer, or (iii) in the case of misappropriators (*see* below), another person who is the source of the material nonpublic information. [*See* Rule 10b5-1(a)]

a. Who May Be Liable?

1) "Insiders"

Anyone who breaches a duty not to use inside information for personal benefit can be held liable under rule 10b-5. Typical securities insiders, such as directors, officers, controlling shareholders, and employees of the issuer are deemed to owe a duty of trust and confidence to their corporation which is breached by trading on inside information. Constructive insiders, such as a securities issuer's CPAs, attorneys, and bankers performing services for the issuer, also owe such a duty.

Example: On Monday, Dee, the president of a publicly held mining company, is told by company geologists that they just discovered a huge cache of gold on company property. Dee contacts the company's outside attorney, Alex, to discuss how she should go about disclosing the information. Dee and Alex decide that it would be best to announce the information to the public on Friday. The announcement will probably cause the price of the company's stock to skyrocket. Neither the geologists, Dee, nor Alex may purchase company stock before the information is made public, unless they disclose the information to the seller.

2) Tippers and Tippees

Where an insider gives a tip of inside information to someone else who trades

on the basis of the inside information, the tipper can be liable under rule 10b-5 if the tip was made for *any improper purpose* (*e.g.*, in exchange for money or a kickback, as a gift, for a family member's benefit, for reputational benefit, etc.). The tippee can be held liable derivatively if the tipper breached a duty *and* the tippee knew that the tipper was breaching the duty.

Example: Same facts as in a., above. If Dee meets her brother Bob in a restaurant and tells him about the gold find, and Bob purchases company stock before the announcement, Dee can be held liable as a tipper and Bob can be held liable as a tippee. But if a stranger, Steve, overhears Dee explain that the company has just discovered gold and purchases stock before the public announcement is made, Steve would not be liable under rule 10b-5.

3) **Misappropriators**

Under the misappropriation doctrine, *the government* can prosecute a person under rule 10b-5 for trading on market information (*i.e.*, information about the supply of or demand for stock of a particular company) in breach of a duty of trust and confidence *owed to the source of the information*; the duty need not be owed to the issuer or shareholders of the issuer. [United States v. O'Hagan, 521 U.S. 642 (1997)] Rule 10b5-2 provides a nonexclusive list of circumstances under which a person will be deemed to owe a duty of trust and confidence in a misappropriation case:

(i) When the person *agrees to maintain information in confidence*;

(ii) When the person communicating the information and the person with whom it is communicated have a *history of sharing confidences* so that the recipient of the information should know that the person communicating the information expects the recipient to maintain confidentiality; or

(iii) When the person *receives the information from a spouse, child, parent, or sibling* (unless the recipient can prove that he had no reason to know that the information was confidential).

[Rule 10b5-2]

Example: Alex works as an attorney at a law firm. BigCorp retains Alex's firm in connection with a tender offer it is planning to make. Alex does not work on the tender offer in any way, but he comes across information about it while in the firm's photocopy room. If Alex trades in securities related to the tender offer, he can be held liable under rule 10b-5 in an action by the government, because by trading on the information, he breaches a duty of trust and confidence that he owes to the firm. [*See* United States v. O'Hagan, *supra*]

3. **Remedies**

a. **In General**

The federal courts have exclusive jurisdiction over claims arising under rule 10b-5.

To remedy a rule 10b-5 violation, *individual* plaintiffs can sue for damages or rescission. *Damages* are based on the difference between the price paid (or received) by the plaintiff, and the average share price in the 90-day period after corrective information is disseminated. [1934 Act §21D(e)] *Rescission* is available in lieu of damages. Note that *punitive damages* are *not* available under rule 10b-5, but might be under appropriate state-law claims for fraud.

b. **Insider Trading Sanctions Act and Insider Trading and Securities Fraud Enforcement Act**

The Insider Trading Sanctions Act [1934 Act §21A] provides an important weapon against insider trading. It authorizes the SEC to sue persons who illegally trade on the securities exchanges while in possession of material, nonpublic information (and their tippees), as well as persons who violate the Act by communicating such information, for a *civil penalty* equal to three times the profit gained or loss avoided by the defendant's unlawful purchase, sale, or communication. This treble-damages penalty is important, because it means a defendant may lose more than his ill-gotten profits, thereby creating a powerful disincentive to insider trading.

1) **Private Right of Action—Insider Trading and Securities Fraud Enforcement Act**

The Act creates a private remedy against one who illegally trades while in possession of material, nonpublic information on behalf of any person who contemporaneously traded the same class of securities. Damages are limited, however, to the *profit gained or loss avoided* by the defendant in the subject transactions. [1934 Act §20A(1), (2)]

2) **Criminal Penalties**

The penalties above are in addition to all other existing sanctions, including jail terms of up to 10 years, and criminal fines of up to $1 million for individuals and $2.5 million for corporations.

B. SECTION 16(b)

Section 16(b) of the Securities Exchange Act of 1934 [15 U.S.C. §78p] provides that any profit realized by a director, officer, or shareholder owning more than 10% of the outstanding shares of the corporation from any purchase and sale, or sale and purchase, of any equity security of his corporation within a period of *less than six months* must be returned to the corporation. The section applies to publicly held corporations whose shares are *traded on a national exchange or* that have *at least 500 shareholders* in any outstanding class and *more than $10 million in assets*.

1. Strict Liability Imposed

The purpose of section 16(b) is to prevent unfair use of inside information and internal manipulation of price. This is accomplished by imposing strict liability for covered transactions whether or not there is any material fact that should or could have been disclosed—no proof of use of inside information is required.

2. Elements of Cause of Action

a. **Purchase and Sale or Sale and Purchase Within Six Months**

Section 16(b) applies only to profits from purchases and sales made within a six-month

period. In most instances, it is easy to define a purchase or sale. However, there are some areas of corporate stock transactions—such as reclassification, conversion, and exercise of stock options—where the time and event of purchase or sale is uncertain. The test normally applied to determine whether there is a purchase or sale is whether "this is the kind of transaction in which abuse of inside information is likely to occur."

b. Equity Security
Section 16(b) applies only to purchases and sales of equity securities. An equity security is any security other than a pure debt instrument, including options, warrants, preferred stock, common stock, etc.

c. Officer, Director, or More than Ten Percent Shareholder
Section 16(b) applies only to purchases and sales made by officers, directors, or more than 10% shareholders.

1) Deputization of Director
Ordinarily, it is easy to identify the officers, directors, and 10% shareholders of a corporation. In some instances, however, a person may "deputize" another person to act as his representative on the board. In these cases, securities transactions of the principal will come within section 16(b).

2) Timing Issues

a) Officers or Directors
Purchases or sales made by persons **before** becoming an officer or director generally are excluded from the scope of section 16(b), because a person generally does not have access to the inside information sought to be protected from abuse under section 16(b) before becoming an officer or director. On the other hand, purchases and sales made within six months after ceasing to be an officer or director can come within section 16(b).

b) More than Ten Percent Shareholder
A person is a more than 10% shareholder if he directly or indirectly owns more than 10% of any class of equity security of the corporation at the time immediately before **both** the purchase and the sale. Thus, the purchase that brings a shareholder over the 10% threshold is not within the scope of section 16(b).

3. Profit Realized
The profit recoverable under section 16(b), known as "short swing profits," includes not only traditional profits, but also losses avoided. "Profit" is determined by matching the *highest sales price against the lowest purchase price* during any six-month period. Remember that use of inside information is not material to this recovery.

Example: Don Director purchases 100 shares of his company's stock at $9 on February 1. He sells 100 shares on August 1 at $7 per share. He then buys 100 shares at $1 per share on November 15. Despite the fact that the stock he purchased in February was sold at a loss of $2 per share in August, and he now holds shares with a basis of $1, he will be liable for a profit under section 16(b).

The August sale will be matched with the November purchase, resulting in a "profit" of $6 per share, and causing him to be liable in the amount of $600.

C. THE SARBANES-OXLEY ACT OF 2002

1. Introduction

The Sarbanes-Oxley Act ("SOA") was enacted in 2002 in response to corporate financial scandals (*e.g.*, at the Enron and Worldcom companies). The SOA primarily affects companies registered under the 1934 Act (*i.e.*, those whose shares are traded on a national securities exchange or that have at least 500 record shareholders and more than $10 million in assets).

2. Public Company Accounting Oversight Board

The SOA provides for the creation of a Public Company Accounting Oversight Board to register public accounting firms that prepare audit reports for companies reporting under the 1934 Act. The Board establishes rules for auditing, quality control, ethics, and independence relating to preparation of audit reports. Only a public accounting firm registered with the Oversight Board may prepare or issue audit reports with respect to a registered company. [15 U.S.C. §7212(a)]

3. Corporate Responsibility

a. Public Company Audit Committees

The SOA requires the board of directors of each 1934 Act company to establish an audit committee comprised of board members. The audit committee is responsible for overseeing the appointment, compensation, and work performed by the registered public accounting firm. [15 U.S.C. §78j-1]

b. Corporate Responsibility for Financial Reports

Under the SOA, companies filing reports under the 1934 Act must have their chief executive officer ("CEO"), chief financial officer ("CFO"), or similar person certify in each report, among other things, that:

(i) The officer has *reviewed the report*;

(ii) Based on the officer's knowledge, the *report is true and does not contain any material omissions*;

(iii) The report *fairly presents the financial position* of the company; and

(iv) The *signing officer is responsible* for establishing internal controls, has designed such controls to ensure that material information is made known to the officer, and has *evaluated the controls within 90 days* prior to the report.

[15 U.S.C. §7241] The SOA provides for criminal fines of up to $5 million and imprisonment for up to 20 years for willfully certifying an untrue report.

c. **Forfeiture of Bonuses and Profits**
If a company is required to restate financial reports because of misconduct with respect to the reports, the company's CEO *and* CFO must reimburse the company for any bonus or other incentive-based compensation received by them during the 12-month period after the inaccurate reports were filed with the SEC or made public (whichever is earlier). The officers must also turn over to the company any profit that they made from the sale of the company's securities during the same 12-month period. [15 U.S.C. §7243]

d. **Prohibition Against Insider Trades During Pension Blackout Periods**
Directors and executive officers of 1934 Act companies may not purchase or sell the company's stock during a blackout period if the stock was acquired in connection with the officer's or director's services for the company. A blackout period is a period of at least three consecutive days when at least 50% of the company's employees who participate in the company's retirement plan are prohibited from transferring their interests in the company's securities in the plan. However, blackout periods that are regularly scheduled and described in the plan and disclosed to the employees before they join the plan are excluded. [15 U.S.C. §7244(a)(1)]

   1) **Remedies**
If a director or officer violates this rule, the company can force the turnover of any profits, regardless of fault or intent. Any shareholder can file a derivative suit to recover the profit if the company fails to take action against the officer or director within 60 days after the shareholder requests the company to take action to recover the profits. [15 U.S.C. §7244(a)(2)]

e. **Prohibition Against Personal Loans to Executives**
A company generally may not make any new personal loans to any director or executive officer of the company except to the extent that the loans are made in the ordinary course of the company's consumer credit business and on terms no more favorable than the company offers to the general public. [15 U.S.C. §78m(k)(1)]

4. **Corporate and Criminal Fraud**

a. **Criminal Penalties for Destruction, Alteration, Etc.**
The SOA makes it a crime punishable by fine and imprisonment for up to 20 years for anyone to knowingly alter, destroy, mutilate, falsify, etc., a document or record with intent to impede a federal investigation. [18 U.S.C. §1519]

b. **Criminal Penalty for Destruction of Corporate Audit Records**
The SOA makes it a crime for an accountant who conducts an audit of a 1934 Act company, punishable by fine and up to 10 years' imprisonment, to willfully fail to keep all workpapers related to the audit for at least five years. [18 U.S.C. §1520]

c. **Statute of Limitations for Fraud**
The SOA provides that the statute of limitations for private cases for securities fraud is the later of two years after discovery of the facts giving rise to the cause of action or five years after the action accrued. [28 U.S.C. §1658(b)]

d. **Whistleblower Protection**

The SOA creates a statutory cause of action for persons who are discharged because they lawfully provided information to their supervisors or the federal government regarding any conduct that they reasonably believed to be a violation of the securities laws. [18 U.S.C. §1514A] The SOA also protects employees who testify in, participate in, or file securities or antifraud proceedings. Remedies include reinstatement, back pay, attorneys' fees, and litigation costs. These protections also extend to contractors, subcontractors, and agents of the issuer.

e. **Criminal Penalties for Defrauding Shareholders and the Public**

The SOA makes securities fraud crimes punishable by a fine and imprisonment of up to 25 years. [18 U.S.C. §1348]

ESSAY EXAM QUESTIONS

INTRODUCTORY NOTE

The essay questions that follow have been selected to provide you with an opportunity to experience how the substantive law you have been reviewing may be tested in the hypothetical essay examination question context. These sample essay questions are a valuable self-diagnostic tool designed to enable you to enhance your issue-spotting ability and practice your exam writing skills.

It is suggested that you approach each question as though under actual examination conditions. The time allowed for each question is 30 minutes. You should spend 10 minutes spotting issues, underlining key facts and phrases, jotting notes in the margins, and outlining your answer. *If* you organize your thoughts well, 20 minutes will be more than adequate for writing them down. Should you prefer to forgo the actual writing involved on these questions, be sure to give yourself no more time for issue-spotting than you would on the actual examination.

The BARBRI technique for writing a well-organized essay answer is to (i) spot the issues in a question and then (ii) analyze and discuss each issue using the "CIRAC" method:

C — State your *conclusion* first. (In other words, you must think through your answer *before* you start writing.)

I — State the *issue* involved.

R — Give the *rule(s)* of law involved.

A — *Apply* the rule(s) of law to the facts.

C — Finally, restate your *conclusion*.

After completing (or outlining) your own analysis of each question, compare it with the BARBRI model answer provided herein. A passing answer does *not* have to match the model one, but it should cover most of the issues presented and the law discussed and should *apply the law to the facts* of the question. Use of the CIRAC method results in the best answer you can write.

EXAM QUESTION NO. 1

Dodds was interested in organizing a corporation to manufacture space equipment. He sought out Henry, who formerly worked for NASA, and offered him the position of general manager of the corporation when formed. Dodds entered into a contract with Henry, signing it, "Dodds, Promoter for Ace Tech, Inc., a corporation to be formed." When the business was incorporated two months later, the five-person board of directors rejected Henry as general manager.

Charlotte, who had subscribed to 100 shares of stock prior to incorporation, notified the board that she was rescinding her subscription. The board issued 100 shares of stock to Gibson in consideration of his obtaining a loan for the corporation in the amount of $100,000, which was due in three years. The board created a five-person executive committee of three directors, the general counsel, and the chief financial officer. At the request of the president, the board voted a contribution of $1,000 to Siwash University Medical School.

Assume that Ace Tech, Inc., was incorporated in a state following the Revised Model Business Corporation Act.

Discuss:

(1) What are Henry's rights against the corporation and Dodds?
(2) Can Charlotte rescind her subscription?
(3) Was the stock issuance to Gibson valid?
(4) Was the creation of the executive committee valid?
(5) Was the contribution valid?

Explain.

EXAM QUESTION NO. 2

A, B, and C formed Manhurt Corporation, and each purchased 5,000 shares, duly paying for such shares in cash. One year later, the corporation issued 500 shares to Biltmore in consideration of his promise to perform accounting and bookkeeping services for the corporation for one year in the future. The corporation also issued 5,000 shares to Grunt in consideration for his promised conveyance of a five-acre tract of land to the corporation on which the corporation proposed to build its corporate head-quarters. The land was never conveyed to the corporation. Two years ago, the corporation issued 5,000 shares of preferred stock to R, S, and T at par value.

The corporation operated for four years and then filed bankruptcy proceedings. The facts indicate that on organization of the corporation, it had liabilities of $64,000 and assets of only $33,000. How-ever, it had set up an asset on its balance sheet in the amount of $32,000 for goodwill. As a result of this entry, it had a surplus at the end of each of its fiscal years. The preferred shareholders had received a dividend of $5,000 two years ago. At that time, the corporation was current on the payment of all its debts.

The trustee in the bankruptcy proceedings brought an action against the shareholders to recover the dividend, alleging they had been paid when the corporation was insolvent or when its capital was impaired.

Discuss the following:

(1) Were the shares issued to Grunt valid?

(2) Were the shares issued to Biltmore valid?

(3) Is the trustee in bankruptcy entitled to recover the amount of the dividends from the pre-ferred shareholders?

Give reasons.

EXAM QUESTION NO. 3

Several years ago, Able, Baker, and Campbell properly incorporated Transport, Inc., a highway freight hauling business. Able and Baker each own 45% of Transport stock, and Campbell owns 10%. Since its incorporation, Transport has been quite profitable. However, most of its earnings have been retained to help the business grow, and only small dividends have been paid to the three shareholders.

Able, the president of Transport, is in charge of finance and sales for the business. Baker, the vice president, is in charge of operations. Able and Baker make all major decisions by consensus. Campbell is an artist and does not participate in the business operations. No shareholder or director meetings have ever been called or held. Able, who has expensive tastes and lives beyond his means, often uses corporate funds of Transport to pay his personal bills, telling Baker that once he gets his personal finances in order he will repay the company.

Last year, Able and Baker decided to expand Transport's hauling business to start hauling hazardous waste from local factories to a newly constructed hazardous waste disposal facility. Recognizing that hauling hazardous waste would be a risky business, Able and Baker wanted to keep the hazardous waste hauling activities separate from the rest of Transport's business. They formed a new corporation called HotTrucks, Inc., which was properly incorporated as a wholly owned subsidiary of Transport. Transport contributed the use (but not ownership) of a fleet of 10 trucks to HotTrucks. HotTrucks's only asset was its right to use the trucks. In order to save money, Able and Baker did not obtain general business liability insurance for HotTrucks.

Able and Baker thought it wise not to be directors or officers of HotTrucks, so they asked Campbell to serve as the sole director and officer of HotTrucks. Campbell did not want to spend time on business matters when he could be working on his paintings. However, he agreed to serve as director and officer on the understanding that Able and Baker would handle all day-to-day management and operation of the business and that Campbell would not have to attend any directors' meetings or make business decisions.

A month ago, one of the trucks operated by HotTrucks crashed through the front of a video store. Baker, who was the driver of the truck, had negligently fallen asleep at the wheel. The regularly scheduled driver had called in sick, and Baker had taken his place, not having slept for 20 hours. The accident seriously injured five people.

(1) On what basis, if any, can the injured persons hold Transport liable for tort claims resulting from the HotTrucks accident? Explain.

(2) On what basis, if any, can the injured persons hold Able, Baker, and Campbell personally liable for such claims? Explain.

EXAM QUESTION NO. 4

The articles of incorporation of Ergo, Inc. authorize the issuance of 400,000 Class A Common Shares and 1,000,000 Class B Common Shares, all of which are issued and outstanding. Dart owns all of the Class A shares and none of the Class B shares. Ergo's articles provide that Ergo has seven directors elected by straight voting, with Class A shares to elect four directors and Class B shares to elect three directors.

Several months ago, Ergo's board of directors properly approved an expansion plan for the business that would require $5 million of additional capital. At their regular February 1 meeting, the directors discussed possible sources to fund the expansion plan. One Class B director suggested that Ergo borrow the funds from a bank.

Dart, who had elected herself as one of the Class A directors, suggested that Ergo issue a new class of shares that Dart would purchase for $5 million. The new class of shares (Class C Preferred) would be entitled to a cumulative preferred dividend. In support of this alternative, Dart presented an opinion from an independent investment bank that stated:

(1) $5 million would be a fair value for the Class C Preferred; and

(2)   In the long run, payment of the proposed preferred dividend would be less costly to Ergo than interest payments on a loan.

After one hour of spirited discussion of these alternatives, all seven directors voted to recommend to the shareholders that Ergo's articles be amended to authorize the issuance of the Class C Preferred as proposed by Dart. A special meeting of the shareholders was properly called for the purpose of voting on the proposed amendment to the articles.

Prior to that meeting, a proxy statement was issued to all shareholders disclosing all relevant information about the plan to issue the Class C Preferred to Dart. However, the proxy statement did not disclose the alternative funding method the Class B director initially proposed. At the shareholders' meeting a quorum was present, and the amendment to the articles was adopted by the following vote:

	In Favor	Opposed
Class A Shares	400,000	0
Class B Shares	720,000	100,000

Following shareholder approval, the Ergo board of directors met to consider the issuance of the newly authorized Class C Preferred. All seven directors voted to issue the Class C Preferred to Dart for $5 million in cash.

A Class B shareholder filed a derivative action against the directors to enjoin the issuance of the Class C Preferred to Dart. The Class B shareholder alleged (1) that the directors erred in deciding to issue the Class C Preferred rather than borrow the money from the bank; (2) that the directors had breached their duty of care to Ergo; and (3) that Dart had breached her duty of loyalty to Ergo. Considering the Class B shareholder's allegations and all possible defenses, who is likely to prevail? Explain.

ANSWERS TO ESSAY EXAM QUESTIONS

ANSWER TO QUESTION 1

(1) ***Henry's rights:*** Henry has no rights against the corporation but can hold Dodds personally liable. At issue is liability on a preincorporation contract.

Dodds acted as a promoter. A promoter is a person who undertakes to procure capital and other instrumentalities to be used by a corporation after it is formed. As a general rule, a promoter is liable on a preincorporation contract unless the contract clearly states that the parties do not intend the promoter to be liable, in which case the "contract" will be treated as a continuing offer to the corporation to be formed. A corporation, however, is not liable on a preincorporation contract until it adopts the contract. A corporation generally is considered to be formed upon filing of its articles of organization.

Here, Dodds entered into the contract with Henry two months before the corporation was formed. The contract provided that Henry was to be the corporation's general manager. Thus, Henry was acting as a promoter. The contract does not clearly indicate that the parties did not intend Dodds to be personally liable; it merely states that Dodds was signing as a promoter for a corporation to be formed. Thus, Dodds is liable on the contract. The corporation, on the other hand, is not liable to Henry because the corporation never adopted the contract. Indeed, the board affirmatively rejected Henry as general manager. Thus, the board is not liable on the contract, and only Henry can be held liable.

(2) ***Charlotte's rescission:*** Charlotte cannot rescind her subscription. At issue is whether a preincorporation subscription can be rescinded.

At common law, a preincorporation subscription is rescindable until it is accepted, and this is the rule that still applies to post incorporation subscription agreements. However under the Revised Model Business Corporation Act ("RMBCA"), a preincorporation subscription agreement is irrevocable for six months unless the other subscribers consent to the revocation. Thus, assuming that six months have not passed since Charlotte entered into her subscription agreement, she cannot rescind.

(3) ***Gibson's stock:*** The issuance of stock to Gibson was valid. At issue is whether Gibson gave proper consideration.

Under the traditional approach, stock could not be issued in exchange for services to be performed. However, under the RMBCA, stock may be issued in exchange for any benefit to the corporation, including promises to perform work in the future. The board's good faith valuation of the work performed is conclusive. Thus, the issuance of the stock in exchange for Gibson's procuring a loan for the corporation is valid.

(4) ***Executive committee:*** The creation of the executive committee was improper. At issue is whether an executive committee can include persons other than directors.

The RMBCA provides that unless the articles or bylaws provide otherwise, the board of directors can create one or more executive committees to which board authority may be delegated. However, the RMBCA provides only for appointment of board members to committees. Here, the board attempted to create an executive committee comprised of three directors, the corporation's general counsel and the corporation's chief financial officer. Because the general counsel and chief executive officer are not board members, the creation of the committee was invalid.

(5) ***Contribution to medical school:*** The contribution to the medical school was valid. At issue is whether a corporation can make charitable contributions.

At common law, a corporation generally has the power to do anything in furtherance of its business purposes. Charitable contributions often were seen as serving no valid business purpose and so, sometimes, were prohibited. However, a number of states allowed charitable contributions because they aid the corporation's good standing in the community. The RMBCA specifically allows charitable donations. Thus, the donation here was proper.

ANSWER TO EXAM QUESTION NO. 2

(1)   The shares issued to Grunt are valid in states following the Revised Model Business Corporation Act ("RMBCA") rules for the issuance of stock, but they are unpaid. At issue is whether the consideration received for the stock was proper.

Although states following the traditional view limit valid forms of consideration for issuance of stock to money paid, labor done, or property actually conveyed, states following the RMBCA have expanded this view. They allow shares to be issued for any tangible or intangible property or benefit to the corporation. Thus, Grunt's promise to convey real property was valid consideration, but because he never in fact conveyed the property, his stock is considered to be unpaid. Because the stock is unpaid, the corporation or its creditors can hold Grunt liable for the agreed upon price. Therefore, the trustee in bankruptcy can hold Grunt liable for the value of the property as the corporation's or the creditors' representative.

(2)   The shares issued to Biltmore are valid. Here, again, the issue is whether the consideration received for the shares was valid. And again, traditionally, states did not allow shares to be issued in exchange for promises of future performance; only services already performed were valid consideration for the issuance of stock. However, as discussed above, in states following the modern RMBCA approach, a corporation may issue shares in exchange for any benefit to the corporation, and a promise to perform future services certainly qualifies as a benefit.

(3)   The trustee in bankruptcy may be able to recover the dividends paid to the preferred shareholders. At issue is whether the corporation was insolvent when the dividends were paid.

Dividends cannot be paid if: (i) the corporation is insolvent (unable to pay its debts as they come due) or will be rendered insolvent by the payment (equity test); or (ii) the corporation has net assets less than zero, including the amount payable at the time of distribution to shareholders having preferential rights in liquidation (balance sheet test). The valuation of the corporation's assets must be in good faith and the financial statements must have been prepared in accordance with accounting procedures and principles reasonable under the circumstances.

Here, the corporation was always solvent in the equity sense because it was able to pay its debts as they came due. However, it would have been insolvent in the balance sheet sense in every year that it paid the dividends if the corporation's relatively large allocation to "goodwill" was improper. Whether the goodwill allocation was improper depends on facts not given in the question (*e.g.,* was this a service corporation where assets are almost all goodwill; was the corporation well-established; etc.). If the allocation to goodwill was proper, the dividends would have been valid, and the trustee cannot now recover them. On the other hand, if the allocation was improper, the corporation would have been insolvent when it paid the dividends. If dividends are distributed when a corporation is insolvent, its creditors can recover the improperly paid dividends from the shareholders to whom they were paid, if they knew the dividends were improper.

ANSWER TO EXAM QUESTION NO. 3

(1)   The injured people may be able to hold Transport liable either because HotTrucks is merely an alter ego of Transport or because Transport did not adequately capitalize HotTrucks. At issue is whether there are grounds to pierce the corporate veil in order to hold the parent corporation liable for its subsidiary corporation's obligations.

Generally, a shareholder is not liable for corporate obligations; only the corporation is liable. This general rule applies even when the shareholder is a corporation: A parent corporation generally is not

liable for the obligations for its subsidiaries. However, in certain circumstances, the corporate veil will be pierced and a shareholder will be held liable for corporate obligations. Two possible grounds for piercing are present here: First, a court will pierce the corporate veil if the parent corporation does not adequately fund its subsidiary, *i.e.,* contribute enough money at formation to enable the subsidiary to pay prospective liabilities. The court might also look to whether the subsidiary can expect to achieve independent financial stability. Second, a court also will pierce the corporate veil if the subsidiary is merely an alter ego of the parent (*e.g.*, the officers and directors are the same, assets are shared, separate books are not kept, etc.).

Here, it could be argued that HotTrucks was both undercapitalized and a mere alter ego of Transport. HotTrucks's only asset was the right to use Transport's trucks. Given that the nature of HotTrucks's business (hauling hazardous wastes) involved great risks, it could be argued that to adequately capitalize HotTrucks, Transport had to contribute at least enough money to purchase liability insurance. Having failed to do so, Transport should now be held liable for liabilities arising from HotTrucks's operations. The fact that the tort claims here do not arise from the hazardous nature of HotTrucks's loads is inconsequential; it is foreseeable that any kind of trucking company will have liabilities arising from accidents in which its vehicles are involved.

The corporate veil can also be pierced on alter ego grounds. Although the two corporations technically had separate boards and officers, in fact, that was a sham. Able and Baker operated both corporations. Moreover, the two corporations shared assets. We are not told whether separate books were kept, whether profits were siphoned off to Transport, etc. But the facts we do know probably are a sufficient basis for piercing.

(2) If the tort victims are allowed to reach Transport's assets, as discussed above, and Transport does not have sufficient funds to cover HotTrucks's liabilities, the victims may be able to pierce the corporate veil to reach Able's assets under an alter ego theory. A court will allow a tort victim to reach a shareholder's personal assets if the shareholder has ignored the separateness of the corporation and some injustice results. Able did not recognize the separateness of Transport since he used corporate funds to pay personal debts. Because this may be the very reason that Transport does not have enough money to pay the tort victims, it would be a sufficient ground on which to pierce.

The tort victims could hold Baker liable for his own negligence. While generally a shareholder, officer, and/or director is not personally liable for his corporation's obligations, a person is always liable for his own torts. Here, Baker was negligent in that he was driving the truck having not slept in 20 hours, fell asleep, and drove into the video store.

The victims probably could not reach Campbell's personal assets. Although he was a director of both corporations, as discussed above, shareholders, directors, and officers generally are not liable for the obligations of their corporation. No grounds for piercing apply to Campbell: His failure to hold or attend directors' and shareholders' meetings constitute sloppy corporate administration, but sloppy administration alone is not a ground for piercing; it must be coupled with some other injustice. Since Campbell's nonfeasance did not really contribute to the tort victim's losses, the court will probably not pierce on these grounds.

ANSWER TO EXAM QUESTION NO. 4

The corporation is likely to prevail in the derivative action on all counts. At issue is the approval of a director's conflicting interest transaction.

As a preliminary matter, the first issue to consider is whether the shareholder may bring a derivative action at all. Generally, to bring a derivative action, a shareholder must have been a shareholder at

the time of the act or omission complained of or must have become a shareholder through operation of law (*e.g.*, through inheritance). The shareholder must also fairly and adequately represent the interests of the corporation and must make written demand on the corporation that it take suitable action. If the corporation finds, after making a good faith, reasonable inquiry, that an action would not be in the corporation's best interests, its decision generally will be upheld.

Here, the shareholder presumably was a shareholder at the time of the act complained of, and nothing indicates that the shareholder would not fairly and adequately represent the corporation's interests. However, neither does anything indicate that the shareholder made a demand on the corporation that it take suitable action. Some courts will excuse demand if it would be futile, but others will not. The shareholder might claim that demand would be futile here because all of the directors are charged with wrongdoing, and a court might be inclined to agree. Nevertheless, in many states, that would not be a sufficient excuse.

(1)   The Class B shareholder cannot prevail on a claim that the directors erred in deciding to issue Class C preferred rather than borrow funds from a bank. At issue is the business judgment rule.

Directors generally are vested with the power to manage the business and affairs of the corporation. They may act on this power by a majority vote at a meeting at which a quorum of directors are present. If they manage the corporation to the best of their ability in good faith, with the care that an ordinarily prudent person in a like position would exercise, and in a manner that they reasonably believe is in the best interests of the corporation, a court will not second-guess their decisions. A person challenging director action has the burden of proving that the above standard was not met.

Here, all of the directors voted to issue preferred stock rather than to borrow funds from a bank. This decision will be upheld unless the Class B shareholder can show that the directors breached their duty of care. As will be discussed in (2), below, the shareholder will probably be unable to make such a showing. Therefore, the shareholder will be unable to prevail on this claim.

(2)   The Class B shareholder will also be unable to show that the directors breached their duty of care. The standard of care that the directors must meet is discussed in part (1), above. In discharging his duties, a director is allowed to rely on reports from (i) corporate officers whom the director reasonably believes to be reliable and competent, and (ii) corporate outsiders as to matters that the director reasonably believes to be within the outsider's professional competence.

Here, the Class B shareholder will argue that it was unreasonable to rely on Dart's opinion as to what was best for the corporation because Dart had a conflicting personal interest in the transaction (she was to buy the Class C stock). Such an argument probably would prevail. However, it is a closer question whether the other directors breached a duty in relying on the independent banker's opinion. On the one hand, the opinion was provided by Dart; on the other hand, the opinion was of an independent investment bank. Given the independence of the opinion, the fact that the directors had a one-hour "spirited discussion" regarding the issue, and that the decision did not involve a major change to the corporation (it was about how to fund a change rather than about the change itself), a court would probably determine that the directors met their burden and that the Class B shareholder's claim that the directors breached their duty of care is without merit.

(3)   Finally, the shareholder's claim that Dart breached her duty of loyalty is without merit. While directors owe their corporation a duty of loyalty that prohibits the directors from profiting at the expense of the corporation, not every deal between a director and the corporation is prohibited. Indeed, a transaction in which a director has a conflicting personal interest will not be set aside because of that interest if the director discloses all of the material facts of the transaction and the deal is approved by a disinterested majority of the directors or the shareholders or the deal is fair. Here, it appears that all of the material facts of the transaction were disclosed to the directors, who voted to approve the transaction. While Dart's personal interest in the transaction prevents her vote from counting and might also invalidate the votes of the directors she controls (because if they voted against her, she could replace

them), every other director in the corporation voted in favor of the transaction. Thus, the transaction was approved by a disinterested majority of the directors.

The transaction was also approved by a majority of the shareholders. The shareholder bringing the derivative suit would probably argue that not all of the material facts were disclosed to the shareholders and therefore their vote should not count; the directors did not disclose the possibility of obtaining bank financing. However, because the directors had not approved that option, it does not seem relevant to the decision whether to approve issuance of the new Class C shares.

Finally, it also appears that the deal was fair, at least according to the independent investment bank (*see* discussion above). Therefore, the court should probably find against the shareholder on this count as well.

Criminal Procedure

CRIMINAL PROCEDURE

TABLE OF CONTENTS

I. CONSTITUTIONAL RESTRAINTS ON CRIMINAL PROCEDURE

A. INTRODUCTION

The development of numerous constitutional limitations upon the manner in which a criminal suspect may be arrested, convicted, and punished has rendered much of criminal procedure an inquiry into constitutional law.

B. INCORPORATION OF BILL OF RIGHTS INTO DUE PROCESS

The first eight amendments to the United States Constitution apply by their terms only to the federal government. However, the Supreme Court has incorporated many of these rights into the due process requirement binding on the states by virtue of the Fourteenth Amendment. Those portions of the Bill of Rights "fundamental to our concept of ordered liberty" have been so incorporated. [Duncan v. Louisiana, 391 U.S. 145 (1968)]

C. CONSTITUTIONAL REQUIREMENTS BINDING ON STATES

The following rights have been held binding on the states under the due process provisions of the Fourteenth Amendment:

(i) The Fourth Amendment *prohibition against unreasonable searches and seizures* [Wolf v. Colorado, 338 U.S. 25 (1949)], and the *exclusionary rule* requiring that the result of a violation of this prohibition not be used as evidence against the defendant [Mapp v. Ohio, 367 U.S. 643 (1961)];

(ii) The Fifth Amendment *privilege against compulsory self-incrimination* [Malloy v. Hogan, 378 U.S. 1 (1964)];

(iii) The Fifth Amendment *prohibition against double jeopardy* [Benton v. Maryland, 395 U.S. 784 (1969)];

(iv) The Sixth Amendment right to a *speedy trial* [Klopfer v. North Carolina, 386 U.S. 213 (1967)];

(v) The Sixth Amendment right to a *public trial* [*In re* Oliver, 333 U.S. 257 (1948)];

(vi) The Sixth Amendment right to *trial by jury* [Duncan v. Louisiana, 391 U.S. 145 (1968)];

(vii) The Sixth Amendment right to *confront witnesses* [Pointer v. Texas, 380 U.S. 400 (1965)];

(viii) The Sixth Amendment right to *compulsory process* for obtaining witnesses [Washington v. Texas, 388 U.S. 14 (1967)];

(ix) The Sixth Amendment right to *assistance of counsel* in felony cases [Gideon v. Wainwright, 372 U.S. 335 (1963)], and in misdemeanor cases in which imprisonment is imposed [Argersinger v. Hamlin, 407 U.S. 25 (1972)]; and

(x) The Eighth Amendment *prohibition against cruel and unusual punishment* [Robinson v. California, 370 U.S. 660 (1962)].

Note: The Constitution provides the floor of protection for criminal defendants. States are free to grant greater protection, and many do.

D. CONSTITUTIONAL RIGHTS NOT BINDING ON STATES

Two provisions of the Bill of Rights have not been held binding on the states.

1.   Right to Indictment

The right to indictment by a grand jury for capital and infamous crimes has been held not to be binding on the states. [Hurtado v. California, 110 U.S. 516 (1884)]

2.   Prohibition Against Excessive Bail

It has not yet been determined whether the Eighth Amendment prohibition against excessive bail creates a right to bail (or whether it simply prohibits excessive bail where the right to bail exists) and whether it is binding on the states. However, most state constitutions create a right to bail and prohibit excessive bail.

II.   EXCLUSIONARY RULE

A.   IN GENERAL

The exclusionary rule is a judge-made doctrine that prohibits the introduction, at a criminal trial, of evidence obtained in violation of a defendant's Fourth, Fifth, or Sixth Amendment rights.

1.   Rationale

The main purpose of the exclusionary rule is to deter the government (primarily the police) from violating a person's constitutional rights: If the government cannot use evidence obtained in violation of a person's rights, it will be less likely to act in contravention of those rights. The rule also serves as one remedy for deprivation of constitutional rights (other remedies include civil suits, injunctions, etc.).

2.   Scope of the Rule

a.   Fruit of the Poisonous Tree

Generally, not only must ***illegally obtained evidence*** be excluded, but also ***all evidence obtained or derived*** from exploitation of that evidence. The courts deem such evidence the tainted fruit of the poisonous tree. [Nardone v. United States, 308 U.S. 338 (1939); Wong Sun v. United States, 371 U.S. 471 (1963)]

Example: D was arrested ***without probable cause*** and brought to the police station. The police read D his *Miranda* warnings three times and permitted D to see two friends. After being at the station for six hours, D confessed. The confession must be excluded because it is the direct result of the unlawful arrest—if D had not been arrested illegally, he would not have been in custody and would not have confessed. [Taylor v. Alabama, 457 U.S. 687 (1982)]

Compare: Police ***have probable cause*** to arrest D. They go to D's home and improperly arrest him without a warrant, in violation of the Fourth Amendment (*see* III.B.2.b.3), *infra*). D confesses at home, and the police then take him to the station. D confesses again at the station. The home confession must be excluded from evidence because it is the fruit of the illegal arrest, but the station house confession is admissible because it is not a fruit of the unlawful arrest. Because the police had probable cause to arrest D, they did not gain anything from the unlawful arrest—they could have lawfully arrested D the moment he stepped outside of his

home and then brought him to the station for his confession. Thus, the station house confession was not an exploitation of the police misconduct; *i.e.,* it was not a fruit of the fact that D was arrested at home as opposed to somewhere else. [New York v. Harris, 495 U.S. 14 (1990)]

1) Limitation—Fruits Derived from *Miranda* Violations
The fruits derived from statements obtained in violation of *Miranda* (*see* IV.D.1., *infra*) may be admissible despite the exclusionary rule. (*See* IV.D.4.b., *infra*.)

b. Exception—Breaking the Causal Chain
Under the fruit of the poisonous tree doctrine, the exclusionary rule can be very broadly applied. Recently, however, the Court has begun to narrow the scope of the rule by balancing its purpose (deterrence of government misconduct) against its costs (exclusion of probative evidence). The Court generally will not apply the rule when it will not likely deter government misconduct. Thus, if there is a weak link between the government misconduct and the evidence (*i.e.,* it is not likely that the misconduct caused the evidence to be obtained), the Court will probably not exclude the evidence.

1) Independent Source
Evidence is admissible if the prosecution can show that it was obtained from a source independent of the original illegality.

Example: Police illegally search a warehouse and discover marijuana, but do not seize it. The police later return to the warehouse with a valid warrant based on information totally unrelated to the illegal search. If police seize the marijuana pursuant to the warrant, the marijuana is admissible. [Murray v. United States, 487 U.S. 533 (1988)]

2) Intervening Act of Free Will
An intervening act of free will by the defendant will break the causal chain between the evidence and the original illegality and thus remove the taint. [Wong Sun v. United States, 371 U.S. 471 (1963)]

Example: The defendant was released on his own recognizance after an illegal arrest but later returned to the station to confess. This voluntary act of free will removed any taint from the confession. [Wong Sun v. United States, *supra*]

Compare: The reading of *Miranda* warnings, even when coupled with the passage of six hours and consultation with friends, was not sufficient to break the causal chain under the facts of *Taylor v. Alabama* (*see* 2.a., above).

3) Inevitable Discovery
If the prosecution can show that the police would have discovered the evidence whether or not they had acted unconstitutionally, the evidence will be admissible. [Nix v. Williams, 467 U.S. 431 (1984)]

4) Live Witness Testimony
It is difficult for a defendant to have live witness testimony excluded as the fruit

of illegal police conduct, because a more direct link between the unconstitutional police conduct and the testimony is required than for exclusion of other evidence. The factors a court must consider in determining whether a sufficiently direct link exists include the extent to which the witness is freely willing to testify and the extent to which excluding the witness's testimony would deter future illegal conduct. [United States v. Ceccolini, 435 U.S. 268 (1978)]

5) In-Court Identification
The defendant *may not exclude* the witness's in-court identification on the ground that it is the fruit of an unlawful detention. [United States v. Crews, 445 U.S. 463 (1980)]

B. LIMITATIONS ON THE RULE

1. Inapplicable to Grand Juries
A grand jury witness may not refuse to answer questions on the ground that they are based on evidence obtained from an unlawful search and seizure [United States v. Calandra, 414 U.S. 338 (1974)], unless the evidence was obtained in violation of the federal wiretapping statute [Gelbard v. United States, 408 U.S. 41 (1972)].

2. Inapplicable to Civil Proceedings
The exclusionary rule does not forbid one sovereign from using in civil proceedings evidence that was illegally seized by the agent of another sovereign. [United States v. Janis, 428 U.S. 433 (1976)] Moreover, the Supreme Court would probably allow the sovereign that illegally obtained evidence to use it in a civil proceeding. The exclusionary rule does apply, however, to a proceeding for forfeiture of an article used in violation of the criminal law, when forfeiture is clearly a penalty for the criminal offense. [One 1958 Plymouth Sedan v. Pennsylvania, 380 U.S. 693 (1965)]

Example: Evidence that is inadmissible in a state criminal trial because it was illegally seized by the police may be used by the IRS. [United States v. Janis, *supra*]

3. Inapplicable to Violations of State Law
The exclusionary rule does not apply to mere violations of state law. [*See* Virginia v. Moore, 533 U.S. 164 (2008)]

Example: Police arrested D for driving on a suspended license, searched him, and found cocaine on his person. Under state law, arrest was not authorized for driving on a suspended license, and D moved to suppress the evidence found during the search. *Held:* Because it is constitutionally reasonable for the police to arrest a person if the police have probable cause to believe that the person has committed even a misdemeanor in their presence (*see* III.B.2.b.2), *infra*), and the police here had probable cause to believe that D committed the offense of driving on a suspended license, D's arrest was constitutionally reasonable and, thus, did not violate the Fourth Amendment, the state law notwithstanding. [*See* Virginia v. Moore, *supra*]

4. Inapplicable to Internal Agency Rules
The exclusionary rule applies only if there is a violation of the Constitution or federal law; it does not apply to a violation of only internal agency rules. [United States v. Caceres, 440 U.S. 741 (1979)]

5. **Inapplicable in Parole Revocation Proceedings**
The exclusionary rule does not apply in parole revocation proceedings. [Pennsylvania v. Scott, 524 U.S. 357 (1998)]

6. **Good Faith Exception**
The exclusionary rule does not apply when the police arrest or search someone erroneously but in good faith, thinking that they are acting pursuant to a valid arrest warrant, search warrant, or law. [United States v. Leon, 468 U.S. 897 (1984); Herring v. United States, 129 S. Ct. 695 (2009)] *Rationale:* One of the main purposes of the exclusionary rule is to deter improper police conduct, and this purpose cannot be served where police are acting in good faith.

   a. **Exceptions to Good Faith Reliance on Search Warrant**
   The Supreme Court has suggested four exceptions to the good faith defense for reliance on a defective search warrant. A police officer cannot rely on a defective search warrant in good faith if:

      1) The affidavit underlying the warrant is so lacking in probable cause that no reasonable police officer would have relied on it;

      2) The warrant is defective on its face (*e.g.,* it fails to state with particularity the place to be searched or the things to be seized);

      3) The police officer or government official obtaining the warrant lied to or misled the magistrate; or

      4) The magistrate has "wholly abandoned his judicial role."

7. **Use of Excluded Evidence for Impeachment Purposes**
Some illegally obtained evidence that is inadmissible in the state's case in chief may nevertheless be used to impeach the defendant's credibility if he takes the stand at trial.

   a. **Voluntary Confessions in Violation of *Miranda***
   An otherwise voluntary confession taken in violation of the *Miranda v. Arizona* requirements is admissible at trial for impeachment purposes. [Harris v. New York, 401 U.S. 222 (1971); Oregon v. Hass, 420 U.S. 714 (1975)] However, a truly involuntary confession is not admissible for any purpose. [Mincey v. Arizona, 437 U.S. 385 (1978)]

   b. **Fruit of Illegal Searches**
   The prosecution may use evidence obtained from an illegal search that is inadmissible in its direct case to impeach the defendant's statements made in response to proper cross-examination reasonably suggested by the defendant's direct examination [United States v. Havens, 446 U.S. 620 (1980)], but such illegally obtained evidence cannot be used to impeach the trial testimony of witnesses other than the defendant [James v. Illinois, 493 U.S. 307 (1990)].

8. **Knock and Announce Rule Violations**
Exclusion is not an available remedy for violations of the knock and announce rule pertaining to the execution of a warrant. [Hudson v. Michigan, 547 U.S. 586 (2006)]

> *Example:* Where officers violate the knock and announce rule (*see* III.C.4.f.3), *infra*), the exclusionary rule will not be applied to exclude evidence resulting from the search. *Rationale:* The exclusionary remedy is too attenuated from the purposes of the knock and announce rule of protecting human life and limb, property, privacy, and dignity. Moreover, the cost of excluding relevant evidence because of claims that the knock and announce rule was violated is too high when compared to the deterrence benefit that will be gained. Finally, there are other deterrents to prevent officers from violating the rule, such as civil suits and internal police disciplinary sanctions. [Hudson v. Michigan, *supra*]

C. HARMLESS ERROR TEST

A conviction will not necessarily be overturned merely because improperly obtained evidence was admitted at trial; the harmless error test applies, so a conviction can be upheld if the conviction would have resulted despite the improper evidence. On appeal, the government bears the burden of showing **beyond a reasonable doubt** that the admission was harmless. [Chapman v. California, 386 U.S. 18 (1967); Milton v. Wainwright, 407 U.S. 371 (1972)] In a habeas corpus proceeding, if a petitioner claims a constitutional error, the petitioner must be released if the error had **substantial and injurious effect or influence** in determining the jury's verdict. [Brecht v. Abrahamson, 507 U.S. 619 (1993)] If the judge is in "grave doubt" as to the harm (*e.g.*, where the record is evenly balanced as to harmlessness), the petition must be granted. [O'Neal v. McAninch, 513 U.S. 432 (1995)]

D. ENFORCING THE EXCLUSIONARY RULE

1. Right to Hearing on Motion to Suppress
The defendant is entitled to have the admissibility of evidence or a confession decided as a matter of law by a judge out of the hearing of the jury. [Jackson v. Denno, 378 U.S. 368 (1964)] It is permissible to let the jury reconsider the "admissibility" of the evidence if the judge finds it admissible, but there is no constitutional right to such a dual evaluation. [Lego v. Twomey, 404 U.S. 477 (1972)] And the defendant is not constitutionally entitled to have a specific finding of fact on each factual question. [LaVallee v. Delle Rose, 410 U.S. 690 (1973)]

2. Burden of Proof
The government bears the burden of establishing admissibility by a preponderance of the evidence. [Lego v. Twomey, *supra*]

3. Defendant's Right to Testify
The defendant has the right to testify at the suppression hearing without his testimony being admitted against him at trial on the issue of guilt. [Simmons v. United States, 390 U.S. 377 (1968)]

III. FOURTH AMENDMENT

A. IN GENERAL
The Fourth Amendment provides that people should be free in their persons from **unreasonable** searches and seizures.

1. **Search**
    A search can be defined as a governmental intrusion into an area where a person has a reasonable and justifiable expectation of privacy.

2. **Seizure**
    A seizure can be defined as the exercise of control by the government over a person or thing.

3. **Reasonableness**
    What is reasonable under the Fourth Amendment depends on the circumstances. For example, certain searches and seizures are considered to be reasonable only if the government has first obtained a warrant authorizing the action, while other searches and seizures are reasonable without a warrant. The material that follows specifically outlines the requirements for searches and seizures under the Fourth Amendment.

B. **ARRESTS AND OTHER DETENTIONS**
    Governmental detentions of persons, including arrests, certainly constitute seizures of the person, so they must be reasonable to comply with the Fourth Amendment. Whether a seizure of the person is reasonable depends on the scope of the seizure (*e.g.,* is it an arrest or merely an investigatory stop?) and the strength of the suspicion prompting the seizure (*e.g.,* an arrest requires probable cause, while an investigatory detention can be based on reasonable suspicion).

1. **What Constitutes a Seizure of the Person?**
    Generally, it is obvious when police arrest or seize a person. When it is not readily apparent, the Supreme Court has indicated that a seizure occurs only when a reasonable person would believe that she is not free to leave. [Michigan v. Chesternut, 486 U.S. 567 (1988)—police pursuit of suspect generally not a seizure] This requires a *physical application of force* by the officer or a *submission* to the officer's show of force. It is not enough that the officer merely ordered the person to stop. [California v. Hodari D., 499 U.S. 621 (1991)]

    Example: Officers boarded a bus shortly before its departure and asked individuals for identification and consent to search their luggage. The mere fact that people felt they were not free to leave because they feared that the bus would depart does not make this a seizure of the person. The test is whether, under the totality of the circumstances, a reasonable person would feel that he was not free to decline the officers' requests or otherwise terminate the encounter. [Florida v. Bostick, 501 U.S. 429 (1991)]

    Compare: Without a warrant or probable cause, at around 3 a.m. in January, six police officers went to Kaupp's home. At least three officers entered his room, awoke him, and told him that they wanted him to "go and talk" about a murder. Kaupp replied, "Okay" and was handcuffed and taken out of his house, shoeless and dressed only in his underwear. Kaupp was taken to the murder scene and then to the police station, where he confessed to playing a minor role in the crime. Kaupp's attorney sought to have Kaupp's confession suppressed as the fruit of an illegal arrest, but the court ruled that Kaupp was not arrested until after his confession—he consented to going to the police station by saying, "Okay" and was handcuffed only pursuant to a policy adopted to protect officers when transporting persons in their squad cars. Kaupp was convicted and sentenced to 55 years' imprisonment. The Supreme Court overturned the conviction on appeal, finding that Kaupp's,

"Okay" was merely an assent to the exercise of police authority, that a reasonable person would not know that the handcuffs were merely for the protection of the officers, and that it cannot seriously be suggested that under the circumstances a reasonable person would feel free to tell the officers when questioning started that he wanted to go home and go back to bed. [Kaupp v. Texas, 538 U.S. 626 (2003)]

2. Arrests

An arrest occurs when the police take a person into custody against her will for purposes of criminal prosecution or interrogation.

a. Probable Cause Requirement

An arrest must be based on probable cause. Probable cause to arrest is present when, at the time of arrest, the officer has within her knowledge reasonably trustworthy facts and circumstances sufficient to warrant a reasonably prudent person to believe that the suspect has committed or is committing a crime. [Beck v. Ohio, 379 U.S. 89 (1964)]

Example: D was in the front passenger seat of a car that the police stopped for speeding late at night. The driver consented to a search of the car. The police found almost $800 in the car's glove compartment and bags of cocaine hidden in the back seat. None of the men admitted ownership of these items. Under the circumstances, the police had probable cause to believe that D, alone or with the other occupants, committed the crime of possession of cocaine. [Maryland v. Pringle, 540 U.S. 366 (2004)]

1) Mistaken Offense

An arrest is not invalid merely because the grounds stated for the arrest at the time it was made are erroneous, as long as the officers had other grounds on which there was probable cause for the arrest. [Devenpeck v. Alford, 543 U.S. 146 (2005)]

Example: Police officers pulled Defendant over on suspicion that he was impersonating an officer because his car had police-type lights. They found his answers to their questioning evasive. Upon discovering that Defendant was taping their conversation, they arrested him, erroneously thinking that the taping violated a state privacy law. *Held:* If the officers had probable cause to arrest Defendant for impersonating an officer, the arrest was valid; it does not matter that they lacked probable cause for the "offense" they stated at the time of the arrest. [Devenpeck v. Alford, *supra*]

b. Warrant Generally Not Required

In contrast to the rule for searches, police generally need not obtain a warrant before arresting a person in a ***public place***, even if they have time to get a warrant. [United States v. Watson, 423 U.S. 411 (1976)]

1) Felony

A police officer may arrest a person without a warrant when she has ***reasonable grounds to believe*** that a felony has been committed and that the person before her committed it.

2) Misdemeanor

An officer may make a warrantless arrest for a misdemeanor ***committed in her***

presence. A crime is committed in the officer's "presence" if she is aware of it through any of her senses.

Note: The police may make a warrantless misdemeanor arrest even if the crime for which the arrest is made cannot be punished by incarceration. [Atwater v. Lago Vista, 532 U.S. 318 (2001)]

3) Exception—Home Arrests Require Warrant
The police must have an arrest warrant to effect a nonemergency arrest of an individual in her own home. [Payton v. New York, 445 U.S. 573 (1980)] All warrantless searches of homes are presumed unreasonable. The burden is on the government to demonstrate sufficient exigent circumstances to overcome this presumption. [Welsh v. Wisconsin, 466 U.S. 740 (1984)]

a) Homes of Third Parties
Absent exigent circumstances, the police executing an arrest warrant may not search for the subject of the warrant in the home of a third party without first obtaining a separate search warrant for the home. [Steagald v. United States, 451 U.S. 204 (1981)]

c. Effect of Invalid Arrest
An unlawful arrest, *by itself*, has no impact on a subsequent criminal prosecution. Thus, if the police improperly arrest a person (*e.g.,* at his home without a warrant), they may detain him if they have probable cause to do so [*see* New York v. Harris, 495 U.S. 14 (1990)], and the invalid arrest is not a defense to the offense charged [Frisbie v. Collins, 342 U.S. 519 (1952)]. Of course, evidence that is a fruit of the unlawful arrest may not be used against the defendant at trial because of the exclusionary rule.

3. Other Detentions

a. Investigatory Detentions (Stop and Frisk)
Police have the authority to briefly detain a person for investigative purposes even if they lack probable cause to arrest. To make such a stop, police must have a *reasonable suspicion* supported by *articulable facts* of criminal activity or involvement in a completed crime. [Terry v. Ohio, 392 U.S. 1 (1968)] *Note:* If the police also have reasonable suspicion to believe that the detainee is armed and dangerous, they may also conduct a frisk (a limited search) to ensure that the detainee has no weapons (*see* C.5.e., *infra*).

1) Reasonable Suspicion Defined
The Court has not specifically defined "reasonable suspicion." It requires something more than a vague suspicion (*e.g.,* it is not enough that the detainee was in a crime-filled area [Brown v. Texas, 443 U.S. 47 (1979)]), but full probable cause is not required. Whether the standard is met is judged under the totality of the circumstances. [United States v. Sokolow, 490 U.S. 1 (1989)]

Examples: 1) Reasonable suspicion justifying a stop is present when: (i) a suspect who is standing on a corner in a high crime area (ii) flees after noticing the presence of the police. Neither factor standing alone is enough to justify a stop, but together they are sufficiently suspicious. [Illinois v. Wardlow, 528 U.S. 119 (2000)]

2) Police had reasonable suspicion—and therefore there was no Fourth Amendment violation—where they detained Defendant at an airport while dogs sniffed his bags for drugs based on the following facts known by the police: (i) Defendant paid for airline tickets in cash with small bills; (ii) Defendant traveled under a name that did not match the name for the phone number he gave; (iii) Defendant traveled to a drug source city (Miami) and stayed for only 48 hours, while his flight time was 20 hours; (iv) Defendant appeared nervous; and (v) Defendant refused to check his bags. [United States v. Sokolow, *supra*] *Note:* The fact that these suspicious circumstances are part of a drug courier profile used by the police neither helps nor hurts the totality of the circumstances inquiry.

2) Source of Suspicion

Like probable cause, reasonable suspicion need not arise from a police officer's personal knowledge. The suspicion can be based on a flyer, a police bulletin, or a report from an informant. [United States v. Hensley, 469 U.S. 221 (1985)]

a) Informant's Tips

Where the source of suspicion of criminal activity is an informant's tip, the tip must be accompanied by indicia of reliability sufficient to make the officer's suspicion reasonable.

Example: Police received an anonymous tip asserting that a woman was carrying cocaine and predicting that she would leave a specified apartment at a specified time, get into a specified car, and drive to a specified motel. After observing that the informant had accurately predicted the suspect's movements, it was reasonable for the police to think that the informant had inside knowledge that the suspect indeed had cocaine, thus justifying a *Terry* stop. [Alabama v. White, 496 U.S. 325 (1990)]

Compare: Police received an anonymous tip that a young black man in a plaid shirt standing at a particular bus stop was carrying a gun. When police arrived at the bus stop, they found a young black man there wearing a plaid shirt. They searched the man and found an illegal gun. Here there was not sufficient indicia of reliability in the tip to provide reasonable suspicion. The fact that the informant knows a person is standing at a bus stop does not show knowledge of any inside information; any passerby could observe the suspect's presence. Unlike the tip in *White,* the tip here did not provide predictive information and left police with no way to test the informant's knowledge and credibility. [Florida v. J.L., 529 U.S. 266 (2000)]

3) Duration and Scope

To be valid under *Terry,* the investigatory stop must be relatively brief and in any event no longer than is necessary to conduct a limited investigation to verify the officer's suspicions.

a) **Identification May Be Required**

As long as the police have the reasonable suspicion required to make a *Terry* stop, they may require the detained person to identify himself (*i.e.,* state his name), and the detainee may be arrested for failure to comply with such a requirement. [Hiibel v. Sixth Judicial District Court, 542 U.S. 177 (2004)] In dicta, the Court suggested that it would recognize an exception to this rule under the Fifth Amendment right against self-incrimination (*see* XIV., *infra*) if by merely giving his name, the detainee may incriminate himself, but noted that such a case would be rare.

4) **Development of Probable Cause**

If during an investigatory detention, the officer develops probable cause, the detention becomes an arrest, and the officer can proceed on that basis. He can, for example, conduct a full search incident to that arrest.

5) **What Constitutes a Stop?**

If an officer merely approaches a person but does not detain her, no arrest or investigatory detention occurs. Not even reasonable suspicion is necessary in such cases. A seizure or stop occurs only if a reasonable person would believe she is not free to leave. (*See* B.1., *supra*.)

6) **Property Seizures on Reasonable Suspicion**

Police may briefly seize items upon reasonable suspicion that they are or contain contraband or evidence, but such seizures must be limited. [United States v. Place, 462 U.S. 696 (1983)—90-minute detention of luggage reasonably suspected to contain drugs unconstitutional]

b. **Automobile Stops**

Stopping a car is a seizure for Fourth Amendment purposes. Thus, generally, police may not stop a car unless they have at least reasonable suspicion to believe that a law has been violated. However, in certain cases where special law enforcement needs are involved, the Court allows police to set up roadblocks to stop cars without individualized suspicion that the driver has violated some law. To be valid, it appears that such roadblocks must: (i) stop cars on the basis of some neutral, articulable standard (*e.g.,* every car or every third car); and (ii) be designed to serve purposes closely related to a particular problem pertaining to automobiles and their mobility. [*See* Delaware v. Prouse, 440 U.S. 648 (1979); *and see* Indianapolis v. Edmond, 531 U.S. 32 (2000)]

Examples: 1) Because of the gravity of the drunk driving problem and the magnitude of the states' interest in getting drunk drivers off the roads, police may set up roadblocks to check the sobriety of all drivers passing by. [Michigan Department of State Police v. Sitz, 496 U.S. 444 (1990)]

2) Because of the difficulty of discerning whether an automobile is transporting illegal aliens, police may set up roadblocks near the border to stop every car to check the citizenship of its occupants. [United States v. Martinez-Fuerte, 428 U.S. 543 (1976); *and see* United States v. Villamonte-Marquez, 462 U.S. 579 (1983)—suspicionless boarding of boat in channel leading to open sea justified on similar grounds]

Compare: The police may not set up roadblocks to check cars for illegal drugs. The nature of such a checkpoint is to detect evidence of ordinary criminal wrongdoing unrelated to use of cars or highway safety. If suspicionless stops were allowed under these circumstances, all suspicionless seizures would be justified. [Indianapolis v. Edmond, *supra*]

1) Seizure of Occupants

An automobile stop constitutes a seizure not only of the automobile's driver, but also any passengers as well. *Rationale:* Such a stop curtails the travel of the passengers as well the driver, and a reasonable passenger in a stopped vehicle would not feel free to leave the scene without police permission. [Brendlin v. California, 551 U.S. 249 (2007)]

Example: Officer pulled Driver's car over for, admittedly, no valid reason. Upon approaching Driver's car and asking Driver for her license, Officer noticed that Passenger resembled a person wanted for parole violation. Officer confirmed his suspicion via radio and arrested Passenger. Upon searching Passenger, Officer discovered drug paraphernalia. *Held:* Passenger has standing to challenge the admissibility of the drug paraphernalia as the fruit of an unlawful seizure.

2) Distinguish—Informational Roadblocks

If the police set up a roadblock for purposes other than to seek incriminating information about the drivers stopped, the roadblock likely will be constitutional.

Example: The police set up a roadblock to ask drivers if they had any information about a deadly hit and run that occurred a week earlier, approximately where the roadblock was set up. D was arrested at the roadblock for driving under the influence of alcohol after he nearly ran over one of the officers stationed at the roadblock. The Court held that the roadblock and arrest were constitutional. [Illinois v. Lidster, 540 U.S. 419 (2004)]

3) Police May Order Occupants Out

Provided that a police officer has lawfully stopped a vehicle, in the interest of officer safety, the officer may order the occupants (*i.e.*, the vehicle's driver *and* passengers) to get out. Moreover, if the officer reasonably believes that the detainee is armed and dangerous, she may conduct a frisk of the detainee. She may also search the passenger compartment of the vehicle to look for weapons, even after the driver and other occupants have been ordered out of the vehicle. [Pennsylvania v. Mimms, 434 U.S. 106 (1977); Maryland v. Wilson, 519 U.S. 408 (1997); Thornton v. United States, 541 U.S. 615 (2004)]

4) Pretextual Stops

If an officer has probable cause to believe that a traffic law has been violated, the officer may stop the suspect's car, even if the officer's ulterior motive is to investigate whether some *other law*—for which the officer lacks reasonable suspicion—is being violated. [Whren v. United States, 517 U.S. 806 (1996)—police in a high drug area stopped D's car after observing D wait a long time at an intersection, abruptly turn without signaling, and speed off at an unreasonable speed; *and see*

Arkansas v. Sullivan, 532 U.S. 769 (2001)] Furthermore, as long as the police do not extend the valid stop beyond the time necessary to issue a ticket and conduct ordinary inquiries incident to such a stop, it does not violate the Fourth Amendment to allow a narcotics detection dog to sniff the car. [Illinois v. Caballes, 543 U.S. 405 (2005); *and see* C.3.b.1)b), *infra*]

c. **Detention to Obtain a Warrant**
If the police have probable cause to believe that a suspect has hidden drugs in his house, they may, for a reasonable time, prohibit him from going into the house unaccompanied so that they can prevent him from destroying the drugs while they obtain a search warrant. [Illinois v. McArthur, 531 U.S. 326 (2001)—police kept suspect from reentering his trailer alone for two hours while an officer obtained a warrant]

d. **Occupants of Premises Being Searched May Be Detained**
Pursuant to the execution of a *valid warrant* to search for contraband, the police may detain occupants of the premises while a proper search is conducted. [Michigan v. Summers, 452 U.S. 692 (1981)]

e. **Station House Detention**
Police officers must have *full probable cause* for arrest to bring a suspect to the station for questioning [Dunaway v. New York, 442 U.S. 200 (1969)] or for fingerprinting [Hayes v. Florida, 470 U.S. 811 (1985)]. The Supreme Court has suggested that under some limited circumstances it might be permissible to require a person to go to the police station for investigatory purposes without probable cause for arrest [Davis v. Mississippi, 394 U.S. 721 (1969)], but the Court has never found such circumstances to exist.

4. **Grand Jury Appearance**
For all practical purposes, seizure of a person (by subpoena) for a grand jury appearance is *not within the Fourth Amendment's protection*. Even if, in addition to testifying, the person is to be asked to give handwriting or voice exemplars, there is no need for the subpoena to be based on probable cause or even objective suspicion. In other words, a person compelled to appear cannot assert that it was unreasonable to compel the appearance. However, the Supreme Court has suggested that it is conceivable that such a subpoena could be unreasonable if it was extremely broad and sweeping or if it was being used for harassment purposes. [United States v. Dionisio, 410 U.S. 1 (1973); United States v. Mara, 410 U.S. 19 (1973)]

5. **Deadly Force**
There is a Fourth Amendment "seizure" when a police officer uses deadly force to apprehend a suspect. An officer may not use deadly force unless it is *reasonable* to do so under the circumstances. [Scott v. Harris, 550 U.S. 372 (2007)]
Example: It was reasonable for an officer to end a chase by bumping a suspect's car (which ultimately resulted in the suspect's becoming a paraplegic) where the suspect was driving at high speeds and weaving in and out of traffic. Under such circumstances, the suspect's conduct posed an immediate threat to his own life and the lives of innocent bystanders. [Scott v. Harris, *supra*]

Compare: It was unreasonable to shoot a fleeing burglar who refused to stop when ordered to do so where there was no evidence that the suspect was armed or posed any threat to the police or others. [Tennessee v. Garner, 471 U.S. 1 (1985)]

C. EVIDENTIARY SEARCH AND SEIZURE

Like arrests, evidentiary searches and seizures must be reasonable to be valid under the Fourth Amendment. Reasonableness here usually means that the police must have obtained a warrant before conducting the search, but there are six circumstances where a warrant is not required (*see* 5., *infra*).

1. General Approach

A useful analytical model of the law of search and seizure requires answers to the following questions:

a. Does the defendant have a *Fourth Amendment right*?

1) Was there *governmental conduct*?

2) Did the defendant have a *reasonable expectation of privacy*?

b. If so, did the police have a *valid warrant*?

c. If the police did not have a valid warrant, did they make a *valid warrantless search* and seizure?

2. Governmental Conduct Required

The Fourth Amendment generally protects only against governmental conduct and not against searches by private persons. Government agents here include only the *publicly paid police* and those *citizens acting at their direction* or behest; private security guards are not government agents unless deputized as officers of the public police.

Example: A private freight carrier opened a package and resealed it; police later reopened the package. The Supreme Court found that this was not a "search" under the Fourth Amendment because the police found nothing more than the private carrier had found. Moreover, the warrantless field test of a substance found in the package to determine whether it was cocaine was not a Fourth Amendment "seizure," even though the testing went beyond the scope of the original private search. [United States v. Jacobsen, 466 U.S. 109 (1984)]

3. Reasonable Expectation of Privacy

To have a Fourth Amendment right, a person must have a reasonable expectation of privacy with respect to the place searched or the item seized.

a. Standing

It is not enough merely that *someone* has an expectation of privacy in the place searched or the item seized. The Supreme Court has imposed a standing requirement so that a person can complain about an evidentiary search or seizure only if it violates his *own* reasonable expectations of privacy. [Rakas v. Illinois, 439 U.S. 128 (1978)] Whether a person has a legitimate expectation of privacy generally is based on the *totality of*

the circumstances, considering factors such as ownership of the place searched and location of the item seized. [Rawlings v. Kentucky, 448 U.S. 98 (1980)] The Court has held that a person has a legitimate expectation of privacy any time:

(i) She *owned or had a right to possession* of the place searched;

(ii) The *place searched was in fact her home*, whether or not she owned or had a right to possession of it; or

(iii) She was an *overnight guest* of the owner of the place searched [Minnesota v. Olson, 495 U.S. 91 (1990)].

1) Search of Third-Party Premises
Standing does not exist merely because a person will be harmed by introduction of evidence seized during an illegal search of a third person's property.

Example: A police officer peered through the closed window blind of Lessee's apartment and observed Lessee and defendants bagging cocaine. When defendants left the apartment, the officer followed them to their car and arrested them. The car and apartment were searched, and cocaine and a weapon were found. At trial, defendants moved to suppress all evidence, claiming that the officer's peeking through the window blind constituted an illegal search. It was determined that defendants had spent little time in Lessee's apartment and had come there solely to conduct a business transaction (*i.e.*, bagging the cocaine). *Held:* The defendants did not have a sufficient expectation of privacy in the apartment. They were there only for a few hours and were not overnight guests. Moreover, they were there for business purposes rather than social purposes, and there is a lesser expectation of privacy in commercial settings. Therefore, the defendants had no Fourth Amendment protections in the apartment and cannot challenge the search. [Minnesota v. Carter, 525 U.S. 83 (1999)]

2) No Automatic Standing to Object to Seizure of Evidence in Possessory Offense
Formerly, a defendant had automatic standing to object to the legality of a search and seizure anytime the evidence obtained was introduced against her in a possessory offense. (This allowed a defendant to challenge the search without specifically admitting possession of the items.) Because a defendant at a suppression hearing may now assert a legitimate expectation of privacy in the items without his testimony being used against him at trial [*see* Simmons v. United States, *supra*, II.D.3.], the automatic standing rule has been abolished as unnecessary [United States v. Salvucci, 448 U.S. 83 (1980)].

3) No Automatic Standing for Co-Conspirator
That a co-conspirator may be aggrieved by the introduction of damaging evidence does not give the co-conspirator automatic standing to challenge the seizure of the evidence; the co-conspirator must show that her own expectation of privacy was violated. [United States v. Padilla, 508 U.S. 77 (1993)]

b. Things Held Out to the Public

1) **Generally—No Expectation of Privacy**
A person does not have a reasonable expectation of privacy in objects held out to the public, such as *the sound of one's voice* [United States v. Dionisio, *supra*, B.4.]; one's *handwriting* [United States v. Mara, *supra*, B.4.]; *paint on the outside of a car* [Cardwell v. Lewis, 417 U.S. 583 (1974)]; *the smell of one's luggage or car* (*e.g.,* drug sniffs by narcotics dogs) [United States v. Place, 462 U.S. 696 (1983); Illinois v. Caballes, B.3.b.4), *supra*]; *account records held by the bank* [United States v. Miller, 425 U.S. 435 (1976)]; *an automobile's movement* on public roads and arrival at a private residence, even if detection of such movement requires the use of an electronic beeper placed on the automobile by the police [United States v. Knotts, 460 U.S. 276 (1983)]; *or magazines offered for sale* [Maryland v. Macon, 472 U.S. 463 (1985)].

   a) **Compare—Squeezing Luggage**
   Although the Supreme Court has held that one does not have a reasonable expectation of privacy in the smell of one's luggage, one does have a reasonable expectation of privacy in luggage against physically invasive inspections. Squeezing luggage to discern its contents constitutes a search. [Bond v. United States, 529 U.S. 334 (2000)]
   Example: After completing an immigration status check of passengers on a bus, Officer began walking toward the front of the bus and squeezing soft-sided luggage in the overhead compartment. Upon feeling what felt like a brick in Defendant's bag, Officer searched the bag and found a "brick" of methamphetamine. The Court held that while travelers might expect their luggage to be lightly touched or moved from time to time, they do not expect their luggage to be subjected to an exploratory squeeze. Therefore, Officer's conduct constitutes a search under the Fourth Amendment. [Bond v. United States, *supra*]

   b) **Dog Sniffs at Traffic Stops**
   As long as the police have lawfully stopped a car and do not extend the stop beyond the time necessary to issue a ticket and conduct ordinary inquiries incident to such a stop, a dog sniff of the car does not implicate the Fourth Amendment. [Illinois v. Caballes, 1), *supra*—Fourth Amendment was not violated when, during a routine traffic stop, a police officer walked a narcotics detection dog around defendant's car and the dog alerted to the presence of drugs, even though before the dog alerted, the officer did not have a reasonable and articulable suspicion that would justify a search; the sniff is not a search]

2) **"Open Fields" Doctrine**
Furthermore, under the "open fields" doctrine, areas outside the "curtilage" (dwelling house and outbuildings) are subject to police entry and search—these areas are "held out to the public" and are unprotected by the Fourth Amendment. (The Court will consider the building's proximity to the dwelling, whether it is within the same enclosure—such as a fence—that surrounds the house, whether the building is used for activities of the home, and the steps taken by the resident to

protect the building from the view of passersby.) [Oliver v. United States, 466 U.S. 170 (1984)] Even a building such as a barn may be considered to be outside the curtilage and therefore outside the protection of the Fourth Amendment. [United States v. Dunn, 480 U.S. 294 (1987)] In addition, the Fourth Amendment does not prohibit the warrantless search and seizure of garbage left for collection outside the curtilage of a home. [California v. Greenwood, 486 U.S. 35 (1988)]

3) Fly-Overs

The police may, within the Fourth Amendment, fly over a field or yard to observe with the naked eye things therein. [California v. Ciraolo, 476 U.S. 207 (1986)] Even a low (400 feet) fly-over by a helicopter to view inside a partially covered greenhouse is permissible. [Florida v. Riley, 488 U.S. 445 (1989)—plurality decision based on flight being permissible under FAA regulations] The police may also take aerial photographs of a particular site. [Dow Chemical Co. v. United States, 476 U.S. 227 (1986)]

a) Compare—Technologically Enhanced Searches of Homes

The Supreme Court has held that because of the strong expectation of privacy within one's home, obtaining by sense enhancing technology any information regarding the interior of a home that could not otherwise have been obtained without physical intrusion constitutes a search, at least where the technology in question is not in general public use. [Kyllo v. United States, 533 U.S. 27 (2001)—use of thermal imager on defendant's home from outside the curtilage to detect the presence of high intensity lamps commonly used to grow marijuana constitutes a search]

4) Vehicle Identification Numbers

A police officer may constitutionally reach into an automobile to move papers to observe the auto's vehicle identification number. [New York v. Class, 475 U.S. 106 (1986)]

4. Searches Conducted Pursuant to a Warrant

To be reasonable under the Fourth Amendment, most searches must be pursuant to a warrant. The warrant requirement serves as a check against unfettered police discretion by requiring police to apply to a neutral magistrate for permission to conduct a search. A search conducted without a warrant will be invalid (and evidence discovered during the search must be excluded from evidence) unless it is within one of the six categories of permissible warrantless searches (*see* 5., *infra*).

a. Requirements of a Warrant

To be valid, a warrant must:

1) Be issued by a ***neutral and detached magistrate***;

2) Be ***based on probable cause*** established from facts submitted to the magistrate by a government agent upon oath or affirmation; and

3) ***Particularly describe*** the place to be searched and the items to be seized.

b. Showing of Probable Cause

A warrant will be issued only if there is probable cause to believe that seizable evidence will be found on the premises or person to be searched. [Carroll v. United States, 267 U.S. 132 (1925)] The officers requesting the warrant must submit to the magistrate an affidavit containing sufficient facts and circumstances to enable the magistrate to make an independent evaluation of probable cause (*i.e.,* the officers cannot merely present their conclusion that probable cause exists). [United States v. Ventresca, 380 U.S. 102 (1965)]

1) May Be Anticipatory

It is sufficient that there is reason to believe that seizable evidence will be found on the premises to be searched at a future date when the warrant will be executed; there need not be reason to believe that there is seizable material on the premises at the time the warrant is issued. [United States v. Grubbs, 547 U.S. 90 (2006)— warrant was properly issued when it "predicted" that seizable material would be found in defendant's home after police delivered to the home pornographic material that the defendant had ordered]

2) Use of Informers—Totality of Circumstances Test

If the officers' affidavit of probable cause is based on information obtained from informers, its sufficiency is determined by the *totality of the circumstances*. [Illinois v. Gates, 462 U.S. 213 (1983)] The affidavit need not contain any particular fact about the informer, as long as it includes enough information to allow the magistrate to make a common sense evaluation of probable cause (*i.e.,* that the information is trustworthy).

a) Reliability, Credibility, and Basis of Knowledge

Formerly, the affidavit had to include information regarding the reliability and credibility of the informer (*e.g.,* she has given information five times in the past and it has been accurate) and her basis for the knowledge (*e.g.,* she purchased cocaine from the house to be searched). These are still relevant factors, but are no longer prerequisites.

b) Informer's Identity

Generally, the informer's identity need *not* be revealed to obtain a search warrant [McCray v. Illinois, 386 U.S. 300 (1967)] (although if the informer is a material witness to the crime, her identity may have to be revealed at or before trial).

c) Going "Behind the Face" of the Affidavit

When a defendant attacks the validity of a search warrant, the Fourth Amendment permits her to contest the validity of some of the assertions in the affidavit upon which the warrant was issued. The defendant may go "behind the face" of the affidavit.

(1) Three Requirements to Invalidate Search Warrant

A search warrant issued on the basis of an affidavit that, on its face, is sufficient to establish probable cause will be invalid if the defendant establishes *all three* of the following:

(i)   A *false statement* was included in the affidavit by the affiant (*i.e.,* the police officer applying for the warrant);

(ii) The affiant ***intentionally or recklessly*** included that false statement (*i.e.,* the officer either knew it was false or included it knowing that there was a substantial risk that it was false); and

(iii) The false statement was ***material*** to the finding of probable cause (*i.e.,* without the false statement, the remainder of the affidavit could not support a finding of probable cause). Thus, the mere fact that an affiant intentionally included a false statement in the affidavit apparently will not automatically render the warrant invalid under Fourth Amendment standards.

[Franks v. Delaware, 438 U.S. 154 (1978)]

(2)   Evidence May Be Admissible Even Though Warrant Not Supported by Probable Cause

A finding that the warrant was invalid because it was not supported by probable cause will not entitle a defendant to exclude the evidence obtained under the warrant. Evidence obtained by police in ***reasonable reliance*** on a facially valid warrant may be used by the prosecution, despite an ultimate finding that the warrant was not supported by probable cause. [United States v. Leon, 468 U.S. 897 (1984); *and see* Massachusetts v. Sheppard, 468 U.S. 981 (1984)—technical defect in warrant insufficient basis for overturning murder conviction]

c.   Warrant Must Be Precise on Its Face

The warrant must describe with reasonable precision the place to be searched and the items to be seized. If it does not, the warrant is unconstitutional, even if the underlying affidavit gives such detail. [Groh v. Ramirez, 540 U.S. 551 (2004)]

Examples: 1) A warrant authorizes the search of premises at 416 Oak Street for heroin. The structure at 416 Oak Street is a duplex. Is the warrant sufficiently precise? No. In a multi-unit dwelling, the warrant must specify which unit is to be searched. *But note:* If police reasonably believe there is only one apartment on the floor of a building, the warrant is not invalid if they discover, during the course of their search, that there are in fact two apartments on the floor. Indeed, any evidence police seize from the wrong apartment prior to the discovery of the error will be admissible. [Maryland v. Garrison, 480 U.S. 79 (1987)]

2) A was believed to have committed criminal fraud in regard to certain complex land transactions. A search warrant was issued authorizing the search for and seizure of numerous described documents and "other fruit, instrumentalities and evidence of the crime at this time unknown." Was the warrant sufficiently precise? Yes, given the complex nature of the crime and the difficulty of predicting precisely what form evidence of guilt would take. [Andresen v. Maryland, 427 U.S. 463 (1976)]

d. Search of Third-Party Premises Permissible

The Fourth Amendment does not bar searches of premises belonging to persons not suspected of crime, as long as there is ***probable cause*** to believe evidence of someone's guilt (or something else subject to seizure) will be found. Thus, a warrant can issue for the search of the offices of a newspaper if there is probable cause to believe evidence of someone's guilt of an offense will be found. [Zurcher v. Stanford Daily, 436 U.S. 547 (1978)]

e. Neutral and Detached Magistrate Requirement

The magistrate who issues the warrant must be neutral and detached from the often competitive business of law enforcement.

Examples: 1) The state attorney general is not neutral and detached. [Coolidge v. New Hampshire, 403 U.S. 443 (1971)]

2) A clerk of court may issue warrants for violations of city ordinances. [Shadwick v. City of Tampa, 407 U.S. 345 (1972)]

3) A magistrate who receives no salary other than compensation for each warrant issued is not neutral and detached. [Connally v. Georgia, 429 U.S. 245 (1977)]

4) A magistrate who participates in the search to determine its scope is not neutral and detached. [Lo-Ji Sales, Inc. v. New York, 442 U.S. 319 (1979)]

f. Execution of a Warrant

1) Must Be Executed by the Police

Only the police (and not private citizens) may execute a warrant. Moreover, when executing a warrant ***in a home***, the police may not be accompanied by a member of the media or any other third party unless the third party is there to aid in executing the warrant (*e.g.*, to identify stolen property that might be found in the home). [Wilson v. Layne, 526 U.S. 603 (1999)—unreasonable to allow newspaper reporter and photographer to accompany police during execution of an arrest warrant in plaintiff's home] *Rationale:* To be reasonable, police action pursuant to a warrant must be related to the objectives of the warrant. The presence of reporters or other third parties not aiding in the execution of the warrant renders the search unreasonable. Note that while the First Amendment prohibition against abridging freedom of the press is an important right, it does not supersede the very important Fourth Amendment right of persons to be free of unreasonable searches.

2) Execution Without Unreasonable Delay

The warrant should be executed without unreasonable delay because probable cause may disappear.

3) Announcement Requirement

Generally, an officer executing a search warrant must knock and announce her authority and purpose and await admittance for a reasonable time or be refused admittance before using force to enter the place to be searched.

a) **Sufficiency of Delay**
If the officers executing a warrant have a reasonable fear that evidence, such as cocaine, will be destroyed after they announce themselves, a limited 15-20 second delay before using force to enter the house is reasonable. [United States v. Banks, 540 U.S. 31 (2004)]

b) **"No Knock" Entry Possible**
No announcement need be made if the officer has reasonable suspicion, based on facts, that knocking and announcing would be *dangerous or futile* or that it would *inhibit the investigation*, e.g., because it would lead to the destruction of evidence. [Richards v. Wisconsin, 520 U.S. 385 (1997)] Whether a "no knock" entry is justified must be made on a case-by-case basis; a blanket exception for warrants involving drug investigations is impermissible. [Richards v. Wisconsin, *supra*] *Note:* The fact that property damage will result from a "no knock" entry does not require a different standard—reasonable suspicion is sufficient. [United States v. Ramirez, 523 U.S. 65 (1998)]

c) **Remedy**
Recall that the Supreme Court has held that the exclusionary rule will not be applied to cases where officers violate the knock and announce rule. (*See* II.B.8., *supra*.)

4) **Seizure of Unspecified Property**
When executing a warrant, the police generally may seize any contraband or fruits or instrumentalities of crime that they discover, whether or not specified in the warrant.

5) **Search of Persons Found on the Premises**
A search warrant does not authorize the police to search persons found on the premises who are not named in the warrant. [Ybarra v. Illinois, 444 U.S. 85 (1979)] If the police have probable cause to arrest a person discovered on the premises to be searched, however, they may search her *incident to the arrest*.

6) **Detention of the Occupants**
A warrant to search for contraband founded on probable cause implicitly carries with it the limited authority to detain occupants of the premises while a proper search is conducted. [Michigan v. Summers, *supra*, B.3.d.]

5. **Exceptions to Warrant Requirement**
There are *six exceptions* to the warrant requirement; *i.e.,* six circumstances where a warrantless search is reasonable and therefore is valid under the Fourth Amendment. To be valid, a warrantless search must meet all the requirements of at least one exception.

a. **Search Incident to a Lawful Arrest**
The police may conduct a warrantless search incident to an arrest as long as it was made on probable cause. [*See* Virginia v. Moore, II.B.3., *supra*]

1) **Constitutional Arrest Requirement**
If an arrest violates the Constitution, then any search incident to that arrest also will violate the Constitution.

2) Any Arrest Sufficient

The police may conduct a search incident to arrest whenever they arrest a person, and this is true even if the arrest is invalid under state law, as long as the arrest was constitutionally valid (*e.g.,* reasonable and based on probable cause). Although the rationale for the search is to protect the arresting officer and to preserve evidence, the police need not actually fear for their safety or believe that they will find evidence of a crime as long as the suspect is placed under arrest. [United States v. Robinson, 414 U.S. 218 (1973)]

a) Issuance of Traffic Citation—Insufficient Basis

For traffic violations, if the suspect is not arrested, there can be no search incident to arrest, even if state law gives the officer the option of arresting a suspect or issuing a citation. [Knowles v. Iowa, 525 U.S. 113 (1999)—a nonconsensual automobile search conducted after the suspect was issued a citation for driving 43 m.p.h. in a 25 m.p.h. zone was illegal, and contraband found during the search was excluded from evidence] *Rationale:* When a citation is issued, there is less of a threat to the officer's safety than there is during an arrest, and the only evidence that needs to be preserved in such a case (*e.g.,* evidence of the suspect's speeding or other illegal conduct) has already been found.

3) Geographic Scope

Incident to a constitutional arrest, the police may search the person and areas into which he might reach to obtain weapons or destroy evidence (his *"wingspan"*). [Chimel v. California, 395 U.S. 752 (1969)] The arrestee's wingspan follows him as he moves. Thus, if the arrestee is allowed to enter his home, police may follow and search areas within the arrestee's wingspan in the home. [Washington v. Chrisman, 455 U.S. 1 (1982)] The police may also make a *protective sweep* of the area beyond the defendant's wingspan if they believe accomplices may be present. [Maryland v. Buie, 494 U.S. 325 (1990)]

a) Automobiles

After arresting the occupant of an automobile, the police may search the interior of the auto incident to the arrest *if* at the time of the search:

(i) The *arrestee is unsecured and still may gain access* to the interior of the vehicle; or

(ii) The police reasonably believe that *evidence of the offense for which the person was arrested* may be found in the vehicle.

[Arizona v. Gant, 129 S. Ct. 1710 (2009)] *Gant* overturned a practice permitting a search incident to arrest of the entire interior of an auto whenever the person arrested had recently been in the auto. This practice was based on a broad interpretation of an earlier case, *New York v. Belton,* 453 U.S. 454 (1981).

Example: A police officer stopped a vehicle for speeding. Upon approaching the vehicle, he smelled burnt marijuana and saw an envelope on the floor marked with the street name

of a certain type of marijuana. He ordered the car's four occupants out of the vehicle and arrested them for unlawful possession of marijuana. Having only one pair of handcuffs and no assistance, he could not secure the arrestees. He had them stand apart from each other and proceeded to search the vehicle. During the search, the officer discovered cocaine in a jacket in the vehicle. The search was a valid search incident to arrest either because an "unsecured" arrestee easily could have gained access to the vehicle, or because the officer could reasonably believe that the vehicle contained evidence of the drug charge on which he arrested the occupants. [New York v. Belton, *supra*]

Compare: The police arrested defendant for driving on a suspended license shortly after he stepped out of his car. Defendant was then handcuffed and placed in a squad car. The police then searched the passenger compartment of defendant's car and found cocaine in a jacket in the car. The search here was an *invalid* search incident to arrest. Because defendant was handcuffed and locked in a squad car, he could not likely gain access to the interior of his car in order to destroy evidence or procure a weapon. Nor did the police have any reason to believe that the car contained any evidence relevant to the charge of driving on a suspended license. [Arizona v. Gant, *supra*]

4) Must Be Contemporaneous with Arrest
A search incident to an arrest must be contemporaneous in time and place with the arrest. [Preston v. United States, 376 U.S. 364 (1964); United States v. Chadwick, 433 U.S. 1 (1977)]

a) Automobiles
At least with regard to searches of automobiles, the term "contemporaneous" does not necessarily mean "simultaneous." Thus, for example, if the police have reason to believe that an automobile from which a person was arrested contains *evidence of the crime for which the arrest was made*, they may search the interior of the automobile incident to arrest after the arrestee has been removed from the automobile and placed in a squad car; and this is so even if the arrestee was already outside of the automobile at the time he was arrested, as long as he was a recent occupant of the automobile. [*See* Thornton v. United States, 541 U.S. 615 (2004)]

5) Search Incident to Incarceration or Impoundment
The police may search an arrestee's personal belongings before incarcerating him after a valid arrest. [Illinois v. Lafayette, 459 U.S. 986 (1983)] Similarly, the police may search an entire vehicle—including closed containers within the vehicle—that has been impounded. [Colorado v. Bertine, 479 U.S. 367 (1987)]

b. "Automobile" Exception
If the police have probable cause to believe that a vehicle such as an automobile contains

contraband or fruits, instrumentalities, or evidence of a crime, they may search the vehicle without a warrant. [Carroll v. United States, 267 U.S. 132 (1925)] *Rationale:* Automobiles and similar vehicles are mobile and so will not likely be available for search by the time an officer returns with a warrant. Moreover, the Supreme Court has declared that people have a lesser expectation of privacy in their vehicles than in their homes.

Note: Similarly, if the police have probable cause to believe that the car itself is contraband, it may be seized from a public place without a warrant. [Florida v. White, 526 U.S. 559 (1999)]

Example: On three occasions, the police observed Defendant selling cocaine from his car, giving the police probable cause to believe that Defendant's car was used to transport cocaine. Under state law, a car used to transport cocaine is considered to be contraband subject to forfeiture. Several months later, the police arrested Defendant on unrelated drug charges while he was at work and seized his car from the parking lot without a warrant, based on their prior observations. While inventorying the contents of the car, the police found cocaine and brought the present drug charges against Defendant. The cocaine was admissible into evidence. Even though the police did not have probable cause to believe that the car contained cocaine when it was seized, they did have probable cause to believe that it was contraband and therefore seizable, and inventory searches of seized items are proper (*see* 6.b., *infra*). [Florida v. White, *supra*]

1)   **Scope of Search**

If the police have full probable cause to search a vehicle, they can search the ***entire vehicle*** (including the trunk) and all containers within the vehicle that ***might contain the object*** for which they are searching. [United States v. Ross, 456 U.S. 798 (1982)] Thus, if the police have probable cause to believe that drugs are within the vehicle, they can search almost any container, but if they have probable cause to believe that an illegal alien is hiding inside the vehicle, they must limit their search to areas where a person could hide.

a)   **Passenger's Belongings**

The search is not limited to the driver's belongings and may extend to packages belonging to a passenger. [Wyoming v. Houghten, 526 U.S. 295 (1999)—search of passenger's purse upheld where officer noticed driver had syringe in his pocket] *Rationale:* Like a driver, a passenger has a reduced expectation of privacy in a car.

b)   **Limited Probable Cause—Containers Placed in Vehicle**

If the police only have probable cause to search a container (recently) placed in a vehicle, they may search that container, but the search may not extend to other parts of the car. [California v. Acevedo, 500 U.S. 565 (1991)]

Example: Assume police have probable cause to believe that a briefcase that D is carrying contains illegal drugs. Unless they arrest D, they may not make a warrantless search of the briefcase

because no exception to the warrant requirement applies. They follow D, and he places the briefcase in a car. They may then approach D and search the briefcase, even though they could not search it before it was placed in the car. They may not search the rest of the car, however, because D has not had an opportunity to move the drugs elsewhere in the car. Presumably, if some time passes and D has an opportunity to move the drugs, the police will have probable cause to search the entire car.

2)   Motor Homes
The automobile exception extends to any vehicle that has the attributes of mobility and a lesser expectation of privacy similar to a car. For example, the Supreme Court has held that it extends to motor homes if they are not at a fixed site. [California v. Carney, 471 U.S. 386 (1985)]

3)   Contemporaneousness Not Required
If the police are justified in making a warrantless search of a vehicle under this exception at the time of stopping, they may tow the vehicle to the station and search it later. [Chambers v. Maroney, 399 U.S. 42 (1970)]

Example: A vehicle search, based on probable cause, conducted three days after the vehicle was impounded is permissible. [United States v. Johns, 469 U.S. 478 (1985)]

c.   Plain View
The police may make a warrantless seizure when they:

(i)   Are *legitimately on the premises*;

(ii)   Discover *evidence, fruits or instrumentalities* of crime, or *contraband*;

(iii)   See such evidence *in plain view*; and

(iv)   *Have probable cause* to believe (*i.e.*, it must be immediately apparent) that the item *is* evidence, contraband, or a fruit or instrumentality of crime.

[Coolidge v. New Hampshire, *supra*, 4.e.; Arizona v. Hicks, 480 U.S. 321 (1987)]

Examples: 1) Police may seize *unspecified property* while executing a search warrant.

2) Police may seize from a lawfully stopped automobile an opaque balloon that, based on knowledge and experience, the police have probable cause to believe contains narcotics, even though the connection with the contraband would not be obvious to the average person. [Texas v. Brown, 460 U.S. 730 (1983)]

Compare: While investigating a shooting in an apartment, Officer spotted two sets of expensive stereo equipment which he had reasonable suspicion (but not probable cause) to believe were stolen. Officer moved some of the

components to check their serial numbers. Such movement constituted an invalid search because of the lack of probable cause. [Arizona v. Hicks, *supra*]

1) Inadvertence Not Required

Formerly, the plain view exception applied only if the evidence was inadvertently discovered, but inadvertence is no longer a requirement. [Horton v. California, 496 U.S. 128 (1990)]

Example: Police have probable cause to believe that the weapons and proceeds from an armed robbery are at D's home. If they obtain a warrant only to search for the proceeds, they still may seize the weapons if they are found in plain view during the search.

d. Consent

The police may conduct a valid warrantless search if they have a ***voluntary and intelligent*** consent to do so. Knowledge of the right to withhold consent, while a factor to be considered, is not a prerequisite to establishing a voluntary and intelligent consent. [Schneckloth v. Bustamonte, 412 U.S. 218 (1973)]

Example: After Deputy stopped Defendant for speeding, gave him a verbal warning, and returned his license, Deputy asked Defendant if he was carrying any drugs in the car. Defendant answered "no" and consented to a search of his car, which uncovered drugs. Defendant argued that his consent was invalid because he had not been told that he was free to go after his license was returned. The Supreme Court, applying the principles of *Schneckloth*, found that no such warning was necessary. Voluntariness is to be determined from all of the circumstances, and knowledge of the right to refuse consent is just one factor to be considered in determining voluntariness. [Ohio v. Robinette, 519 U.S. 33 (1996)]

Note: An officer's false announcement that she has a warrant negates the possibility of consent. [Bumper v. North Carolina, 391 U.S. 543 (1968)]

1) Authority to Consent

Any person with an ***apparent equal right to use or occupy*** the property may consent to a search, and any evidence found may be used against the other owners or occupants. [Frazier v. Cupp, 394 U.S. 731 (1969); United States v. Matlock, 415 U.S. 164 (1973)] The search is valid even if it turns out that the person consenting to the search did not actually have such right, as long as the police reasonably believed that the person had authority to consent. [Illinois v. Rodriguez, 497 U.S. 177 (1990)]

a) Limitation—Where Party Is Present and Objects

The police may not act on consent from an occupant if a co-occupant is present and objects to the search and the search is directed against the co-occupant. [Georgia v. Randolph, 547 U.S. 103 (2006)]

b) Parents and Children

A parent generally has authority to consent to a search of a child's room (even

an adult child), as long as the parent has access to the room, but, depending on the child's age, might not have authority to consent to a search of locked containers within the child's room. [*See, e.g.,* United States v. Block, 590 F.2d 535 (4th Cir. 1978)—mother had authority to consent to search of 23-year-old son's room but not a locked footlocker in the room] Whether a child has authority to consent to a search of a parent's house or hotel room is a question of whether it is reasonable to believe that the child had such authority. [*See* United States v. Gutierrez-Hermosillo, 142 F.3d 1225 (10th Cir. 1998)—14-year-old had authority to allow police into father's hotel room while father was present] Even a relatively young child probably has authority to consent to a search of the common areas of a home or her own room. [*See, e.g.,* Lenz v. Winburn, 51 F.3d 1540 (11th Cir. 1995)—nine-year-old had authority to consent to entry into her home]

2) Scope of Search

The scope of the search is limited by the *scope of the consent*. However, consent extends to all areas to which a reasonable person under the circumstances would believe it extends.

Example: Police stopped D for a traffic violation, told him that they suspected him of carrying drugs, and asked for permission to search the car. D consented. The officers found a bag containing cocaine. At trial, D argued that his consent did not extend to any closed container (the bag). The Supreme Court held that because D knew the police were searching for drugs and did not place any restriction on his consent, it was reasonable for the police to believe that the consent extended to all areas where drugs might be found. [Florida v. Jimeno, 500 U.S. 248 (1991)]

e. Stop and Frisk

1) Standards

As noted above (*see* B.3.a., *supra*), a police officer may *stop* a person without probable cause for arrest if she has an articulable and *reasonable suspicion* of criminal activity. In such circumstances, if the officer also *reasonably believes* that the person may be *armed and presently dangerous*, she may conduct a protective *frisk*. [Terry v. Ohio, *supra*, B.3.a.; United States v. Cortez, 449 U.S. 411 (1981)]

2) Scope of the Intrusion

a) Patdown of Outer Clothing

The scope of the frisk is generally limited to a patdown of the outer clothing for concealed instruments of assault. [Terry v. Ohio, *supra*] However, an officer may reach directly into an area of the suspect's clothing, such as his belt, without a preliminary frisk, when she has specific information that a weapon is hidden there, even if the information comes from an informant's tip lacking sufficient reliability to support a warrant. [Adams v. Williams, 407 U.S. 143 (1972)]

b) Automobiles

If a vehicle has been properly stopped for a traffic violation, a police officer may order the driver out of the vehicle even without a suspicion of criminal activity. If the officer then reasonably believes that the driver or any passenger may be armed and dangerous, she may conduct a frisk of the suspected person. [Pennsylvania v. Mimms, 434 U.S. 106 (1978); Arizona v. Johnson, 129 S. Ct. 781 (2009)] Moreover, the officer may search the vehicle, even if the officer has *not arrested* the occupant and has ordered the occupant out of the vehicle, provided the search is *limited to those areas in which a weapon may be placed* or hidden and the officer possesses a reasonable belief that the occupant is dangerous. [Michigan v. Long, 463 U.S. 1032 (1983)]

c) Identification May Be Required

As long as the police have the reasonable suspicion required to make a *Terry* stop, they may require the detained person to identify himself (*i.e.,* state his name), and the detainee may be arrested for failure to comply with such a requirement except, perhaps, where the detainee may make a self-incrimination claim. [*See* Hiibel v. Sixth Judicial District Court, *supra*, B.3.a.3)a)]

d) Time Limit

There is no rigid time limit for the length of an investigative stop. The Court will consider the purpose of the stop, the reasonableness of the time in effectuating the purpose, and the reasonableness of the means of investigation to determine whether a stop was too long. [United States v. Sharpe, 470 U.S. 675 (1985)]

3) Admissibility of Evidence

If a police officer conducts a patdown within the bounds of *Terry*, the officer may reach into the suspect's clothing and seize any item that the officer reasonably believes, based on its *"plain feel,"* is a *weapon or contraband*. [Terry v. Ohio, *supra*; Minnesota v. Dickerson, 508 U.S. 366 (1993)—excluding from evidence cocaine that officer found during valid patdown because officer had to manipulate package to discern that it likely was drugs] Properly seized items are admissible as evidence against the suspect.

f. Hot Pursuit, Evanescent Evidence, and Other Emergencies

1) Hot Pursuit Exception

Police officers in hot pursuit of a *fleeing felon* may make a warrantless search and seizure. The scope of the search may be as broad as may reasonably be necessary to prevent the suspect from resisting or escaping. [Warden v. Hayden, 387 U.S. 294 (1967)] When the police have probable cause and attempt to make a warrantless arrest in a "public place," they may pursue the suspect into private dwellings. [United States v. Santana, 427 U.S. 38 (1976)]

2) Evanescent Evidence Exception

The police may seize without a warrant evidence likely to disappear before a warrant can be obtained, such as a blood sample containing alcohol [Schmerber v. California, 384 U.S. 757 (1966)] or fingernail scrapings [Cupp v. Murphy, 412 U.S. 291 (1973)].

3) Emergencies

Emergencies that threaten health or safety if not immediately acted upon will justify a warrantless search. This includes situations where the police see someone injured or threatened with injury. [*See, e.g.,* Brigham City v. Stuart, 547 U.S. 389 (2006)] Whether an emergency exists is determined objectively, from the officer's point of view. [Michigan v. Fisher, 130 S. Ct. 546 (2010)] Some states refer to this as the *community caretaker exception.*

Examples: 1) Police responded to a domestic disturbance call at a home. Upon arriving, they found blood on the hood of a pickup truck and windows broken out of the home. They saw defendant through an open window, screaming and with a cut on his hand. An officer asked if medical attention was needed, and defendant told the officer to get a warrant. The officer then opened the house door part way, and defendant pointed a gun at the officer. Evidence of the gun need not be suppressed as the fruit of an unlawful entry. The officer could have objectively believed that the defendant could have attacked a spouse or child who needed aid or that defendant was in danger himself. [Michigan v. Fisher, *supra*]

                  2) A warrantless search may be justified to find contaminated food or drugs [*see, e.g.,* North American Cold Storage v. City of Chicago, 211 U.S. 306 (1908)] or to discover the source of a fire while it is burning (but not after it is extinguished) [Michigan v. Tyler, 436 U.S. 499 (1978)].

Compare: The need to search a murder scene, without more, does not justify a warrantless search. [Mincey v. Arizona, *supra*, II.B.7.a.]

6. Administrative Inspections and Searches

a. Warrant Required for Searches of Private Residences and Businesses

Inspectors must have a warrant for searches of private residences and commercial buildings. [Camara v. Municipal Court, 387 U.S. 523 (1967); Michigan v. Clifford, 464 U.S. 287 (1984)—warrantless administrative search of fire-damaged residence by officials seeking to determine origin of fire violated owners' Fourth Amendment rights; owners retained reasonable expectation of privacy in the damaged structure, and the warrantless search was unconstitutional] However, the same standard of probable cause as is required for other searches is not required for a valid administrative inspection warrant. A showing of a general and *neutral enforcement plan* will justify issuance of the warrant, which is designed to guard against selective enforcement. [Marshall v. Barlow's, Inc., 436 U.S. 307 (1978)]

1) Exceptions Permitting Warrantless Searches

a) Contaminated Food

A warrant is not required for the seizure of spoiled or contaminated food. [North American Cold Storage v. City of Chicago, *supra*]

b) Highly Regulated Industries

A warrant is not required for searches of businesses in highly regulated

indutries, because of the urgent public interest and the theory that the business has impliedly consented to warrantless searches by entering into a highly regulated industry. Such industries include liquor [Colonnade Catering Corp. v. United States, 397 U.S. 72 (1970)], guns [United States v. Biswell, 406 U.S. 311 (1972)], strip mining [Donovan v. Dewey, 452 U.S. 594 (1981)], and automobile junkyards [New York v. Burger, 479 U.S. 812 (1987)], but not car leasing [G.M. Leasing Corp. v. United States, 429 U.S. 338 (1977)] or general manufacturing [Marshall v. Barlow's, Inc., *supra*].

b.   Inventory Searches

The police may search an arrestee's personal belongings in order to inventory them before incarcerating the arrestee. [Illinois v. Lafayette, *supra*, 5.a.5)] Similarly, the police may search an entire vehicle—including closed containers within the vehicle—that has been impounded, as long as the search is part of an established department routine. [Colorado v. Bertine, *supra*, 5.a.5)]

c.   Search of Airline Passengers

Courts have generally upheld searches of airline passengers prior to boarding. This seems to be regarded as somewhat akin to a consent or administrative search. One court, however, has held that a passenger must be permitted to avoid such a search by agreeing not to board the aircraft.

d.   Public School Searches

A warrant or probable cause is not required for searches conducted by public school officials; only ***reasonable grounds*** for the search are necessary. This exception is justified due to the nature of the school environment. [New Jersey v. T.L.O., 469 U.S. 325 (1985)] The Court has also upheld a school district rule that required students participating in ***any extracurricular activity*** to submit to random urinalysis drug testing monitored by an adult of the same sex. [Board of Education v. Earls, 536 U.S. 822 (2002)]

1)   Reasonableness Standard

A school search will be held to be reasonable only if:

(i)   It offers a ***moderate chance of finding evidence*** of wrongdoing;

(ii)   The measures adopted to carry out the search are ***reasonably related to the objectives of the search;*** and

(iii)   The search is ***not excessively intrusive*** in light of the age and sex of the student and nature of the infraction.

[New Jersey v. T.L.O., *supra;* Safford Unified School District #1 v. Redding, 129 S. Ct. 2633 (2009)]

Example: A 13-year-old student was brought before her school's principal. The principal had found in the students's day planner several knives and lighters and a cigarette. The student admitted that the planner was hers but said that she had loaned it to her friend and that the items must be her friend's. The principal then showed the student a number of pain killers that were banned from the school absent advance permission and said he had a report that the student had distributed such pills to others. The student said she did not know

anything about the pills, but allowed the principal's assistant to search her outer clothing and backpack. No contraband was found. The principal then sent the student to the school nurse, who had her remove her outer clothing and pull her underwear away from her body so if any drugs were hidden in them, they would fall out. No drugs were found, and the student brought an action, claiming that the search violated her constitutional rights. *Held:* The number of pills involved (five), their nondangerous nature, and the lack of any specific reason to believe that the student might have been hiding pills in her underwear makes the strip search here excessively intrusive. [Safford Unified School District #1 v. Redding, *supra*]

e. Parolees
The Supreme Court has upheld warrantless searches of a parolee and his home—even without reasonable suspicion—where a state statute provided that as a condition of parole, a parolee agreed that he would submit to searches by a parole officer or police officer at any time, with or without a search warrant or probable cause. The Court held that such warrantless searches are reasonable under the Fourth Amendment because a parolee has a diminished expectation of privacy under such a statute and the government has a heightened need to search parolees because they are less likely than the general population to be law abiding. [*See* Samson v. California, 547 U.S. 843 (2006)]

f. Government Employees' Desks and Files
A warrantless search of a government employee's desk and file cabinets is permissible under the Fourth Amendment if it is reasonable in scope and if it is justified at its inception by a noninvestigatory, work-related need or a reasonable suspicion of work-related misconduct. [O'Connor v. Ortega, 480 U.S. 709 (1987)]

g. Drug Testing
Although government-required drug testing constitutes a search, the Supreme Court has upheld such testing without a warrant, probable cause, or even individualized suspicion when justified by *"special needs"* beyond the general interest of law enforcement.

Examples: 1) The government can require railroad employees who are involved in accidents to be tested for drugs after the accidents. [Skinner v. Railway Labor Executives' Association, 489 U.S. 602 (1989)]

2) The government can require persons seeking Customs positions connected to drug interdiction to be tested for drugs. There is a special need for such testing because persons so employed will have ready access to large quantities of drugs. [National Treasury Employees Union v. Von Raab, 489 U.S. 656 (1989)]

3) The government can require public school students who participate in *any extracurricular activities* to submit to random drug tests because of the special interest schools have in the safety of their students. [Board of Education v. Earls, *supra*]

Compare: 1) Special needs do not justify a warrantless and nonconsensual urinalysis test to determine whether a pregnant woman has been using cocaine, where the main purpose of the testing is to generate evidence

that may be used by law enforcement personnel to coerce women into drug programs. [Ferguson v. Charleston, 532 U.S. 67 (2001)]

2) The government may not require candidates for state offices to certify that they have taken a drug test within 30 days prior to qualifying for nomination or election—there is no special need for such testing. [Chandler v. Miller, 520 U.S. 305 (1997)]

7.   Searches in Foreign Countries and at the Border

a.   Searches in Foreign Countries
The Fourth Amendment does *not* apply to searches and seizures by United States officials in foreign countries and involving an alien, at least where the alien does not have a substantial connection to the United States. Thus, for example, the Fourth Amendment was held not to bar the use of evidence obtained in a warrantless search of an alien's home in Mexico. [United States v. Verdugo-Urquidez, 494 U.S. 259 (1990)]

b.   Searches at the Border or Its Functional Equivalent
Neither citizens nor noncitizens have any Fourth Amendment rights at the border or its functional equivalent as part of the concept of national sovereignty. A functional equivalent of the border might be a point near the border where several routes all leading to the border merge.

c.   Roving Patrols

1)   Stops
Roving patrols inside the United States border may stop an automobile for questioning of the occupants if the officer *reasonably suspects* that the automobile may contain illegal aliens, but the apparent Mexican ancestry of the occupants alone cannot create a reasonable suspicion. [United States v. Brignoni-Ponce, 422 U.S. 873 (1975)]

2)   Searches
A roving patrol inside the border may not conduct a warrantless search unless the requirements of one of the *exceptions* to the warrant requirement, such as the "automobile" exception (probable cause) or consent, are met. [Almeida-Sanchez v. United States, 413 U.S. 266 (1973)]

d.   Fixed Checkpoints
Border officials may stop an automobile at a fixed checkpoint inside the border for questioning of the occupants even *without a reasonable suspicion* that the automobile contains illegal aliens. [United States v. Martinez-Fuerte, *supra*, B.3.b.] Officials may disassemble stopped vehicles at such checkpoints, even without reasonable suspicion. [United States v. Flores-Montano, 541 U.S. 149 (2004)] However, the Supreme Court has suggested that nonroutine, personal searches at the border (*e.g.,* strip searches or body cavity searches) may require probable cause.

e.   Opening International Mail
Permissible border searches include the opening of international mail, which postal

regulations authorize when postal authorities have **reasonable cause** to suspect that the mail contains **contraband**, although the regulations prohibit the authorities from reading any correspondence inside. [United States v. Ramsey, 431 U.S. 606 (1977)]

1) Reopening

Once customs agents lawfully open a container and identify its contents as illegal, their **subsequent reopening** of the container after it has been resealed and delivered to defendant is not a search within the meaning of the Fourth Amendment, unless there is a substantial likelihood that the container's contents have been changed during any gap in surveillance. [Illinois v. Andreas, 463 U.S. 765 (1983)]

f. Immigration Enforcement Actions

The Supreme Court held that the I.N.S., which has been replaced by the Citizenship and Immigration Services Division of the Department of Homeland Security, may do a "factory survey" of the entire work force in a factory, to determine citizenship of each employee, without raising Fourth Amendment issues. The "factory survey" is not "detention" or a "seizure" under the Fourth Amendment. [Immigration & Naturalization Service v. Delgado, 466 U.S. 210 (1984)] Furthermore, evidence illegally obtained, in violation of the Fourth Amendment, may be used in a civil deportation hearing. [Immigration & Naturalization Service v. Lopez-Mendoza, 468 U.S. 1032 (1984)]

g. Detentions

If the officials have a "reasonable suspicion" that a traveler is smuggling contraband in her stomach, they may detain her for a time reasonable under the circumstances. *Rationale:* Stopping such smuggling is important, yet very difficult; stomach smuggling gives no external signs that would enable officials to meet a "probable cause" standard in order to conduct a search. [United States v. Montoya de Hernandez, 473 U.S. 531 (1985)—16-hour detention upheld until traveler, who refused an X-ray, had a bowel movement]

8. Wiretapping and Eavesdropping

a. Fourth Amendment Requirements

Wiretapping and any other form of electronic surveillance that violates a reasonable expectation of privacy constitute a search under the Fourth Amendment. [Katz v. United States, 389 U.S. 347 (1967)] In *Berger v. New York*, 388 U.S. 41 (1967), the Supreme Court indicated that for a valid **warrant** authorizing a wiretap to be issued, the following **requirements** must be met:

1) A showing of **probable cause** to believe that a **specific crime** has been or is being committed must be made;

2) The **suspected persons** whose conversations are to be overheard must be **named**;

3) The warrant must **describe with particularity** the conversations that can be overheard;

4) The wiretap must be limited to a **short period of time** (although extensions may be obtained upon an adequate showing);

5) *Provisions* must be made for the *termination* of the wiretap when the desired information has been obtained; and

6) A *return* must be made to the court, showing what conversations have been intercepted.

b. Exceptions

1) "Unreliable Ear"
A speaker assumes the risk that the person to whom she is talking is unreliable. If the person turns out to be an informer wired for sound or taping the conversation, the speaker has no basis in the Fourth Amendment to object to the transmitting or recording of the conversation as a warrantless search. [United States v. White, 401 U.S. 745 (1971)]

2) "Uninvited Ear"
A speaker has no Fourth Amendment claim if she makes no attempt to keep the conversation private. [Katz v. United States, *supra*]

c. Judicial Approval Required for Domestic Security Surveillance
A neutral and detached magistrate must make the determination that a warrant should issue authorizing electronic surveillance, including internal security surveillance of domestic organizations. The President may not authorize such surveillance without prior judicial approval. [United States v. United States District Court, 407 U.S. 297 (1972)]

d. Federal Statute
Title III of the Omnibus Crime Control and Safe Streets Act regulates interception of private "wire, oral or electronic communications." [18 U.S.C. §§2510-2520] All electronic communication surveillance (*e.g.,* phone taps, bugs, etc.) must comply with the requirements of this federal statute, which exhibits a legislative decision to require more than the constitutional minimum in this especially sensitive area.

e. Pen Registers
A pen register records only the numbers dialed from a certain phone. The Fourth Amendment does not require prior judicial approval for installation and use of pen registers. [Smith v. Maryland, 442 U.S. 735 (1979)] Neither does Title III govern pen registers, because Title III applies only when the *contents* of electronic communications are intercepted. However, by statute [18 U.S.C. §§3121 *et seq.*], police must obtain a court order finding pen register information to be relevant to an ongoing criminal investigation before utilizing a pen register. Note, however, that information obtained in violation of the statute would not necessarily be excluded from evidence in a criminal trial; the statute merely provides a criminal penalty.

f. Covert Entry to Install a Bug Permissible
Law enforcement officers do not need prior express judicial authorization for a covert entry to install equipment for electronic surveillance, which has been approved in compliance with Title III. [Dalia v. United States, 441 U.S. 238 (1979)]

D. METHODS OF OBTAINING EVIDENCE THAT SHOCK THE CONSCIENCE
Due process of law requires that state criminal prosecutions be conducted in a manner that does not offend the "sense of justice" inherent in due process. Evidence obtained in a manner offending that sense is *inadmissible*, even if it does not run afoul of one of the specific prohibitions against particular types of misconduct.

1. Searches of the Body
Intrusions into the human body implicate a person's most deep-rooted expectations of privacy. Thus, Fourth Amendment requirements apply. Ultimately, the "reasonableness" of searches into the body depends on weighing society's need for the evidence against the magnitude of the intrusion on the individual (including the threat to health, safety, and dignity issues). [Winston v. Lee, 470 U.S. 753 (1985)]

   a. Blood Tests
   Taking a blood sample (*e.g.,* from a person suspected of drunk driving) by common-place medical procedures "involves virtually no risk, trauma, or pain" and is thus a *reasonable* intrusion. [Schmerber v. California, *supra*, C.5.f.2)]

   b. Compare—Surgery
   But a surgical procedure under a general anesthetic (to remove a bullet needed as evidence) involves significant risks to health and a severe intrusion on privacy, and thus is *unreasonable*—at least when there is substantial other evidence. [Winston v. Lee, *supra*]

2. Shocking Inducement
If a crime is induced by official actions that themselves shock the conscience, any conviction therefrom offends due process.
Example: D appears before a state legislative commission. Members of the commission clearly indicate that the privilege against self-incrimination is available to D, although in fact D could be convicted for failure to answer. Can D's conviction for refusal to answer be upheld? No, because the crime was induced by methods that shock the conscience. [Raley v. Ohio, 360 U.S. 423 (1959)]

IV. CONFESSIONS

A. INTRODUCTION
The admissibility of a defendant's confession or incriminating admission involves analysis under the Fourth, Fifth, Sixth, and Fourteenth Amendments. We have already discussed Fourth Amendment search and seizure limitations. The Fifth Amendment gives defendants rights against testimonial self-incrimination. The Sixth Amendment gives defendants rights regarding the assistance of counsel. The Fourteenth Amendment protects against involuntary confessions.

B. FOURTEENTH AMENDMENT—VOLUNTARINESS
For confessions to be admissible, the Due Process Clause of the Fourteenth Amendment requires that they be voluntary. Voluntariness is assessed by looking at the totality of the circumstances, including the suspect's age, education, and mental and physical condition, along with the setting, duration, and manner of police interrogation. [Spano v. New York, 360 U.S. 315 (1959)]

Examples: 1) A confession will be involuntary where it was obtained by physically beating the defendant. [Brown v. Mississippi, 297 U.S. 278 (1936)]

2) D was being held for questioning. O, a young officer who was a friend of D, told D that if he did not obtain a confession, he would lose his job, which would be disastrous for his wife and children. D confessed, but the Court found the confession involuntary. [Leyra v. Denno, 347 U.S. 556 (1954)]

1. Must Be Official Compulsion
Only official compulsion will render a confession involuntary for purposes of the Fourteenth Amendment. A confession is not involuntary merely because it is the product of mental disease that prevents the confession from being of the defendant's free will. [Colorado v. Connelly, 479 U.S. 157 (1986)]

2. Harmless Error Test Applies
A conviction will not necessarily be overturned if an involuntary confession was erroneously admitted into evidence. The harmless error test applies, and the conviction will not be overturned if the government can show that there was other overwhelming evidence of guilt. [Arizona v. Fulminante, 499 U.S. 279 (1991)]

3. Can "Appeal" to Jury
A finding of voluntariness by the trial court does not preclude the defendant from introducing evidence to the jury of the circumstances of the confession in order to cast doubt on its credibility. [Crane v. Kentucky, 476 U.S. 683 (1986)]

C. SIXTH AMENDMENT RIGHT TO COUNSEL APPROACH
The Sixth Amendment provides that in all criminal prosecutions, the defendant has a right to the assistance of counsel. The right protects defendants from having to face a complicated legal system without competent help. It applies at all ***critical stages*** of a criminal prosecution after formal proceedings have begun. [Rothgery v. Gillespie, 554 U.S. 191 (2008)] The right is violated when the police deliberately elicit an incriminating statement from a defendant without first obtaining a waiver of the defendant's right to have counsel present. [*See* Fellers v. United States, 540 U.S. 519 (2004)] Since *Miranda,* below, the Sixth Amendment right has been limited to cases where ***adversary judicial proceedings*** have begun (*e.g.,* ***formal charges have been filed***). [Massiah v. United States, 377 U.S. 201 (1964)] Thus, the right does not apply in precharge custodial interrogations.

Examples: 1) The Sixth Amendment right to counsel is violated when an undisclosed, paid government informant is placed in the defendant's cell, after defendant has been indicted, and deliberately elicits statements from the defendant regarding the crime for which the defendant was indicted. [United States v. Henry, 447 U.S. 264 (1980)] However, it is not a violation merely to place an informant in a defendant's cell—the informant must take some action, beyond mere listening, designed deliberately to elicit incriminating remarks. [Kuhlman v. Wilson, 477 U.S. 436 (1986)]

2) The right to counsel is violated when police arrange to record conversations between an indicted defendant and his co-defendant. [Maine v. Moulton, 474 U.S. 159 (1985)]

1. **Stages at Which Applicable**
    The defendant has the right to be represented by privately retained counsel, or to have counsel appointed for him by the state if he is indigent, at the following stages:

    (i)   Custodial police interrogation [Miranda v. Arizona, *infra*, D.1.];

    (ii)   Post-indictment interrogation whether custodial or not [Massiah v. United States, *supra*];

    (iii)   Preliminary hearings to determine probable cause to prosecute [Coleman v. Alabama, *infra*, VI.C.];

    (iv)   Arraignment [Hamilton v. Alabama, 368 U.S. 52 (1961)];

    (v)   Post-charge lineups [Moore v. Illinois, *infra*, V.B.1.a.];

    (vi)   Guilty plea and sentencing [Mempa v. Rhay, 389 U.S. 128 (1967); Moore v. Michigan, 355 U.S. 155 (1957); Townsend v. Burke, 334 U.S. 736 (1948)];

    (vii)   Felony trials [Gideon v. Wainwright, 372 U.S. 335 (1963)];

    (viii) Misdemeanor trials when imprisonment is actually imposed or a suspended jail sentence is imposed [Scott v. Illinois, 440 U.S. 367 (1979); Alabama v. Shelton, 535 U.S. 654 (2002)];

    (ix)   Overnight recesses during trial [Geders v. United States, 425 U.S. 80 (1976)];

    (x)   Appeals as a matter of right [Douglas v. California, 372 U.S. 353 (1963)]; and

    (xi)   Appeals of guilty pleas and pleas of nolo contendere [Halbert v. Michigan, 545 U.S. 605 (2005); *and see* X.B.1.a., *infra*].

    Note: The Fifth Amendment right to counsel is involved at (i) and (ii), above; the Sixth Amendment right is also involved at (ii) and at all the remaining stages.

2. **Stages at Which Not Applicable**
    The defendant does not have a constitutional right to be represented by counsel at the following stages:

    a.   Blood sampling [Schmerber v. California, *supra,* III.D.1.a.];

    b.   Taking of handwriting or voice exemplars [Gilbert v. California, 388 U.S. 263 (1967)];

    c.   Pre-charge or investigative lineups [Kirby v. Illinois, 406 U.S. 682 (1972)];

    d.   Photo identifications [United States v. Ash, *infra*, V.B.1.c.];

    e.   Preliminary hearings to determine probable cause to detain [Gerstein v. Pugh, 420 U.S. 103 (1975)];

f.   Brief recesses during the defendant's testimony at trial [Perry v. Leeke, 488 U.S. 272 (1989)];

g.   Discretionary appeals [Ross v. Moffitt, 417 U.S. 600 (1974)];

h.   Parole and probation revocation proceedings [Gagnon v. Scarpelli, 411 U.S. 778 (1973)]; and

i.   Post-conviction proceeding (*e.g.,* habeas corpus) [Pennsylvania v. Finley, 481 U.S. 551 (1987)] including petitions by death-row inmates [Murray v. Giarratano, 492 U.S. 1 (1989)].

3.   Offense Specific

The Sixth Amendment right to counsel is "offense specific." Thus, if a defendant makes a Sixth Amendment request for counsel for one charge, he must make another request if he is subsequently charged with a separate, unrelated crime if he desires counsel for the second charge. Similarly, even though a defendant's Sixth Amendment right to counsel has attached regarding one charge, he may be questioned without counsel concerning an unrelated charge. [Illinois v. Perkins, 496 U.S. 292 (1990)]

Example: D was in jail on a battery charge. Because the police suspected D of an unrelated murder, they placed an undercover officer in D's cell. The officer elicited damaging confessions from D regarding the murder. The interrogation did not violate the Sixth Amendment because D had not been charged with the murder. [Illinois v. Perkins, *supra*] Neither did the interrogation violate D's Fifth Amendment right to counsel under *Miranda.* (*See* D.2.a., *infra.*)

a.   Test for "Different Offenses"

The test for determining whether offenses are different under the Sixth Amendment is the *Blockburger* test (*see* XIII.C.1., *infra*). Under the test, two crimes are considered different offenses if each requires proof of an additional element that the other crime does not require. [Texas v. Cobb, 532 U.S. 162 (2001)]

4.   Waiver

The Sixth Amendment right to counsel may be waived. The waiver must be knowing, voluntary, and intelligent. Moreover, the waiver does not necessarily require the presence of counsel, at least if counsel has not actually been requested by the defendant but rather was appointed by the court. [Montejo v. Louisiana, 129 S. Ct. 2079 (2009)]

Example: Defendant was arrested, was given *Miranda* warnings (*see* D.1., *infra*), and confessed to a murder. He was then brought before a judge, who appointed counsel to represent Defendant. Later that day, police officers went to Defendant's cell and asked him to help them find the weapon he used to commit the murder. The police gave Defendant a fresh set of *Miranda* warnings and convinced him to write a letter apologizing to his victim's widow. Later, the appointed attorney met with Defendant. At trial, the attorney argued that the letter was taken in violation of Defendant's Sixth Amendment right to counsel. *Held:* Because Defendant had not requested the appointment of an attorney, his right to an attorney was not violated. [Montejo v. Louisiana, *supra*]

5. **Remedy**

If the defendant was entitled to a lawyer at trial, the failure to provide counsel results in **automatic reversal of the conviction**, even without any showing of specific unfairness in the proceedings. [Gideon v. Wainwright, I.C., *supra*] Similarly, erroneous disqualification of privately retained counsel results in automatic reversal. [United States v. Gonzalez-Lopez, 548 U.S. 140 (2006)] However, at **nontrial proceedings** (such as a post-indictment lineup), the harmless error rule applies to deprivations of counsel. [United States v. Wade, 388 U.S. 218 (1967)]

6. **Impeachment**

A statement obtained in violation of a defendant's Sixth Amendment right to counsel, while not admissible in the prosecution's case-in-chief, may be used to impeach the defendant's contrary trial testimony. [Kansas v. Ventris, 129 S. Ct. 1841 (2009)] This rule is similar to the rule that applies to *Miranda* violations. (*See* D.4.a., *infra.*)

Example: After Defendant was charged with murder and arrested for aggravated robbery, police placed an informant in his cell, telling the informant to keep his ears open. The informant told Defendant that he looked like he had something serious on his mind (which probably was sufficient to violate Defendant's Sixth Amendment right to counsel). Defendant responded that he had just shot a man in the head and taken his money. At trial, after Defendant testified that an accomplice had shot and robbed the victim, the informant then testified as to what he heard. *Held:* The informant's testimony was admissible for impeachment purposes. [Kansas v. Ventris, *supra*]

D. **FIFTH AMENDMENT PRIVILEGE AGAINST COMPELLED SELF-INCRIMINATION—*MIRANDA***

The Fifth Amendment, applicable to the states through the Fourteenth Amendment, provides that no person "shall be compelled to be a witness against himself . . . ." This has been interpreted to mean that a person shall not be compelled to give self-incriminating testimony. The scope of what is considered to be "testimony" under the amendment will be discussed later (*see* XIV., *infra*). This section explains the applicability of the amendment to confessions.

1. **The Warnings**

In *Miranda v. Arizona*, 384 U.S. 436 (1966), the Fifth Amendment privilege against compelled self-incrimination became the basis for ruling upon the admissibility of a confession. The *Miranda* warnings and a valid waiver are **prerequisites to the admissibility** of any statement made by the accused during custodial interrogation. A person in custody must, prior to interrogation, be clearly informed that:

(i)   He has the right to remain silent;

(ii) Anything he says can be used against him in court;

(iii) He has the right to the presence of an attorney; and

(iv) If he cannot afford an attorney, one will be appointed for him if he so desires.

Note: The Supreme Court has held that the holding of *Miranda* was based on the **requirements** of the Fifth Amendment as made applicable to the states through the Fourteenth

Amendment, and therefore Congress cannot eliminate the *Miranda* requirements by statute. [Dickerson v. United States, 530 U.S. 428 (2000)—invalidating a statute that purportedly eliminated *Miranda*'s requirements that persons in custody and being interrogated be informed of the right to remain silent and the right to counsel]

a. Need Not Be Verbatim

Miranda requires that all suspects be informed of their rights without considering any prior awareness of those rights. The warnings need not be given verbatim, as long as the substance of the warning is there. [Duckworth v. Eagan, 492 U.S. 195 (1989)—upholding warning that included statement, "We [the police] have no way of giving you a lawyer, but one will be appointed for you, if you wish, if and when you go to court"] The failure to advise a suspect of his right to appointed counsel may be found to be harmless error. [Michigan v. Tucker, 417 U.S. 433 (1974); California v. Prysock, 453 U.S. 355 (1981)]

b. Rewarning Not Needed After Break

There is generally no need to repeat the warnings merely because of a break in the interrogation, *unless* the time lapse has been so long that a failure to do so would seem like an attempt to take advantage of the suspect's ignorance of his rights.

2. When Required

Anyone in police custody and accused of a crime, no matter how minor a crime, must be given *Miranda* warnings *prior to interrogation* by the police. [Berkemer v. McCarty, 468 U.S. 420 (1984)]

a. Governmental Conduct

Miranda generally applies only to interrogation by the publicly paid police. It does not apply where interrogation is by an informant who the defendant does not know is working for the police. [Illinois v. Perkins, *supra*—*Miranda* warnings need not be given before questioning by a cellmate covertly working for the police] *Rationale:* The warnings are intended to offset the coercive nature of police-dominated interrogation, and if the defendant does not know that he is being interrogated by the police, there is no coercive atmosphere to offset.

1) State-Ordered Psychiatric Examination

The Fifth Amendment privilege against self-incrimination forbids admission of evidence based on a psychiatric interview of defendant who was not warned of his right to remain silent. [Estelle v. Smith, 451 U.S. 454 (1981)] The admission of such evidence may, however, constitute harmless error. [Satterwhite v. Texas, 486 U.S. 249 (1988)]

2) Limits on *Miranda*

Miranda suggested that every encounter between police and citizen was inherently coercive. Hence, interrogation would result in compelled testimony for Fifth Amendment purposes. However, the Supreme Court has been narrowing the scope of *Miranda's* application.

a) Meeting with Probation Officer

Admission of rape and murder by a probationer to his probation officer was

not compelled or involuntary, despite the probationer's obligation to periodically report and be "truthful in all matters." [Minnesota v. Murphy, 465 U.S. 420 (1984)]

b) Uncharged Witness at Grand Jury Hearing

The *Miranda* requirements **do not apply** to a witness testifying before a grand jury, even if the witness is under the compulsion of a subpoena. Such a witness who has not been charged or indicted does not have the right to have counsel present during the questioning, but he may consult with an attorney outside the grand jury room. A witness who gives false testimony before a grand jury may be convicted of perjury even though he was not given the *Miranda* warnings. [United States v. Mandujano, 425 U.S. 564 (1976); United States v. Wong, 431 U.S. 174 (1977)]

b. Custody Requirement

Whether a person is in custody depends on whether the person's freedom of action is denied in a significant way. The more a setting resembles a traditional arrest (*i.e.,* the more constrained the suspect feels), the more likely the Court will consider it to be custody. If the detention is voluntary, it does not constitute custody. [*See* Berkemer v. McCarty, *supra*; Oregon v. Mathiason, 429 U.S. 492 (1977)] If the detention is long and is involuntary (*e.g.,* the detainee is in jail on another charge), it will likely be held to constitute custody. [*See* Mathas v. United States, 391 U.S. 1 (1968)]

Example: D is in custody when he is awakened in his own room in the middle of the night by four officers surrounding his bed, who then begin to question him. [Orozco v. Texas, 394 U.S. 324 (1969)]

1) Test Is Objective

The initial determination of whether a person is in custody depends on the ***objective*** circumstances of the interrogation, not on the subjective views harbored by either the interrogating officers or the person being interrogated. Thus, for example, an officer's belief that the person being questioned is not a suspect cannot bear on the custody issue unless that view is somehow manifested. [Stansbury v. California, 511 U.S. 318 (1994)] Similarly, consideration of a suspect's age and inexperience is inappropriate, because these are subjective factors. [Yarborough v. Alvarado, 541 U.S. 652 (2004)]

2) Traffic Stops Generally Not Custodial

Although a routine traffic stop curtails a motorist's freedom of movement, such a stop is presumptively temporary and brief, and the motorist knows that he typically will soon be on his way; therefore, the motorist should not feel unduly coerced. Thus, *Miranda* warnings normally need not be given during a traffic stop.

Example: Officer stopped Defendant for weaving in and out of traffic. When Officer noticed Defendant had trouble standing, he performed a field sobriety test, which Defendant failed. Without giving *Miranda* warnings, Officer then asked Defendant if he had been drinking, and Defendant admitted to recent drinking and drug use. The admission is admissible. [Berkemer v. McCarty, *supra*]

c. **Interrogation Requirement**

"Interrogation" refers not only to express questioning, but also to any words or actions on the part of the police that the police should know are reasonably likely to elicit an incriminating response from the suspect. [Rhode Island v. Innis, 446 U.S. 291 (1980)] However, *Miranda* does not apply to **spontaneous statements** not made in response to interrogation, although officers must give the warnings before any follow-up questioning. Neither does *Miranda* apply to routine booking questions (*e.g.,* name, address, age, etc.), even when the booking process is being taped and may be used as evidence. [Pennsylvania v. Muniz, 496 U.S. 582 (1990)—defendant failed sobriety test and had trouble answering booking questions]

Examples: 1) Police comments about the danger a gun would present to handicapped children, which resulted in a robbery suspect's leading them to a weapon, did not constitute interrogation when the officers were not aware that the suspect was peculiarly susceptible to an appeal to his conscience. [Rhode Island v. Innis, *supra*]

2) Allowing a suspect's wife to talk to the suspect in the presence of an officer who is taping the conversation with the spouses' knowledge does not constitute interrogation. [Arizona v. Mauro, 481 U.S. 520 (1987)]

1) **Break in Interrogation—Questioning by Different Police Agencies**

When a second police agency continues to question a suspect at a point when the first police department terminates its questioning, the impact of an earlier denial of rights by the first department carries over into the questioning by the second agency. [Westover v. United States, 384 U.S. 436 (1966)]

3. **Right to Waive Rights or Terminate Interrogation**

After receiving *Miranda* warnings, a detainee has several options: do nothing, waive his *Miranda* rights, assert the right to remain silent, or assert the right to consult with an attorney.

a. **Do Nothing**

If the detainee does not respond at all to *Miranda* warnings, the Court will not presume a waiver [*see* Fare v. Michael, 442 U.S. 707 (1979)], but neither will the Court presume that the detainee has asserted a right to remain silent or to consult with an attorney. Therefore, the police may continue to question the detainee. [*See* Berghuis v. Thompkins, 130 S. Ct. 2250 (2010)]

b. **Waive Rights**

The detainee may waive his rights under *Miranda*. To be valid, the government must show by a preponderance of the evidence that the waiver was ***knowing, voluntary, and intelligent***. The Court will look to the totality of the circumstances in determining whether this standard was met. But it appears that if the government can show that the detainee received *Miranda* warnings and then chose to answer questions, that is probably sufficient. [*See* Berghuis v. Thompkins, *supra*—suspect scarcely said anything after receiving *Miranda* warnings, but was held to have voluntarily waived his right to remain silent when he responded "yes" to an incriminating question posed three hours into his interrogation]

1) **Police Deception of Detainee's Lawyer**
If the *Miranda* warnings are given, a voluntary confession will be admissible even if the police lie to the detainee's lawyer about their intent to question the detainee or fail to inform the detainee that his lawyer is attempting to see him, as long as adversary judicial proceedings have not commenced. [Moran v. Burbine, 475 U.S. 412 (1986)]

c. **Right to Remain Silent**
At any time prior to or during interrogation, the detainee may indicate that he wishes to remain silent. Such an indication must be explicit, unambiguous, and unequivocal (*e.g.,* the detainee's failure to answer does not constitute an invocation of the right to remain silent). [Berghuis v. Thompkins, *supra*] If the detainee so indicates, all *questioning related to the particular crime must stop.*

1) **Police May Resume Questioning If They "Scrupulously Honor" Request**
The police may reinitiate questioning after the detainee has invoked the right to remain silent, as long as they "scrupulously honor" the detainee's request. This means, at the very least, that the police may not badger the detainee into talking and must wait a significant time before reinitiating questioning.
Example: In the Supreme Court's only opinion directly on point, it allowed police to reinitiate questioning where: (i) the police *immediately ceased questioning* upon the detainee's request and did not resume questioning for several hours; (ii) the detainee was *rewarned* of his rights; and (iii) questioning was *limited to a crime that was not the subject of the earlier questioning.* [Michigan v. Mosely, 423 U.S. 96 (1975)]

d. **Right to Counsel**
At any time prior to or during interrogation, the detainee may also invoke a *Miranda* (*i.e.,* Fifth Amendment) right to counsel. If the detainee invokes this right, *all questioning must cease* until the detainee is provided with an attorney or initiates further questioning himself. [Edwards v. Arizona, 451 U.S. 477 (1981)]

1) **Police May Not Resume Questioning About Any Crime**
Once the detainee invokes his right to counsel under *Miranda,* all questioning must cease; the police may not even question the detainee about a totally unrelated crime, as they can where the detainee merely invokes the right to remain silent. [*See* Arizona v. Roberson, 486 U.S. 675 (1988)] *Rationale:* The right to counsel under *Miranda* is a prophylactic right designed by the Court to prevent the police from badgering a detainee into talking without the aid of counsel, and this purpose can be accomplished only if *all* questioning ceases. [*See* McNeil v. Wisconsin, 501 U.S. 171 (1991)]

a) **Compare—Detainee May Initiate Resumption of Questioning**
The detainee may waive his right to counsel after invoking the right, and thus initiate resumption of questioning.
Example: The detainee cut off interrogation by asking for an attorney, but then asked the interrogating officer, "What is going to happen to me now?" The officer explained that the detainee

did not have to talk, and the detainee said he understood. The officer then described the charge against the detainee and gave him fresh *Miranda* warnings. The detainee then confessed after taking a polygraph test. The Court upheld admission of the confession into evidence, finding that the detainee had validly waived his rights. [Oregon v. Bradshaw, 462 U.S. 1039 (1983)]

b) Scope of Right—Custodial Interrogation
The Fifth Amendment right to counsel under *Miranda* applies whenever there is custodial interrogation.

c) Compare—Sixth Amendment Right "Offense Specific"
Recall that the Sixth Amendment right to counsel (*see* C., *supra*) attaches only after formal proceedings have begun. Moreover, whereas invocation of the Fifth Amendment right prevents all questioning, the Sixth Amendment right is "offense specific." (*See* C.3., *supra*.)

2) Request Must Be Unambiguous and Specific
A Fifth Amendment request for counsel can be invoked only by an ***unambiguous*** request for counsel ***in dealing with the custodial interrogation***. [McNeil v. Wisconsin, *supra*; Davis v. United States, 512 U.S. 452 (1994)] The request must be sufficiently clear that a reasonable police officer in the same situation would understand the statement to be a request for counsel.

Examples: 1) The statement by the suspect being interrogated, "Maybe I should talk to a lawyer," is not an unambiguous request for counsel under the Fifth Amendment, and so does not prevent further questioning.

2) D was arrested and charged with robbery. At his initial appearance, he requested the aid of counsel. After D's appearance, the police came to D's cell, gave him *Miranda* warnings, and questioned D about a crime unrelated to the robbery. D made incriminating statements. D's Fifth Amendment right to counsel was not violated because D did not request counsel in dealing with the interrogation. His post-charge request for counsel at his initial appearance was a ***Sixth Amendment*** request for counsel, which is offense specific (*see* C.3., *supra*).

3) Ambiguities Relevant Only If Part of Request
Once the detainee has expressed an unequivocal desire to receive counsel, no subsequent questions or responses may be used to cast doubt on the request and all questioning of the detainee must cease. Where the request is ambiguous, police may ask clarifying questions, but are not required to do so; rather, they may continue to interrogate the detainee until an unambiguous request is received. [Davis v. United States, *supra*] Note that if the detainee agrees to answer questions orally, but requests the presence of counsel before making any written statements, the detainee's oral statements are admissible. The detainee's agreement to talk constitutes a voluntary and knowing waiver of the right to counsel. [Connecticut v. Barrett, 479 U.S. 523 (1987)]

4)   Counsel Must Be Present at Interrogation

Mere consultation with counsel prior to questioning does not satisfy the right to counsel—the police cannot resume questioning the detainee in the absence of counsel. [Minnick v. Mississippi, 498 U.S. 146 (1991)] Of course, counsel need not be present if the detainee waives the right to counsel by initiating the exchange. (*See* 1)a), *supra.*)

Example: The detainee answered a few questions during interrogation, but then requested an attorney. He was allowed to meet with his attorney three times. Subsequently, in the absence of counsel, police resumed interrogating the detainee, and he made incriminating statements. The Court held that the statements must be excluded from evidence. [Minnick v. Mississippi, *supra*]

5)   Duration of Prohibition

The prohibition against questioning a detainee after he requests an attorney lasts the entire time that the detainee is in custody for interrogation purposes, plus 14 more days after the detainee returns to his normal life. After that point, the detainee can be questioned regarding the same matter upon receiving a fresh set of *Miranda* warnings. [Maryland v. Shatzer, 130 S. Ct. 1213 (2010)—while in prison, detainee was questioned about alleged sexual abuse, invoked his right to counsel, and was released back into the general prison population (his normal life); police could reinitiate questioning after 14 days without first providing counsel]

6)   Statements Obtained in Violation May Be Used to Impeach

As indicated above, if the detainee requests counsel, all questioning must cease unless counsel is present or the detainee initiates a resumption of questioning. If *the police* initiate further questioning, the detainee's statements cannot be used by the prosecution in its case in chief, but they can be used to *impeach the detainee's* trial testimony, as long as the court finds that the detainee voluntarily and intelligently waived his right to counsel. [Michigan v. Harvey, 494 U.S. 344 (1990)] Note, however, that such illegally obtained evidence cannot be used to impeach trial testimony of witnesses other than the detainee. [James v. Illinois, 493 U.S. 307 (1990)]

4.   Effect of Violation

Generally, evidence obtained in violation of *Miranda* is inadmissible at trial.

a.   Use of Confession for Impeachment

A confession obtained in violation of the defendant's *Miranda* rights, but otherwise voluntary, may be used to *impeach the defendant's testimony* if he takes the stand at trial, even though such a confession is inadmissible in the state's case in chief as evidence of guilt. [Harris v. New York, 401 U.S. 222 (1971); Oregon v. Hass, 420 U.S. 714 (1975)] However, a truly involuntary confession is *inadmissible* for any purpose. [Mincey v. Arizona, *supra,* II.B.7.a.]

1)   Silence

The prosecutor may not use the defendant's silence after receiving *Miranda* warnings to counter the defendant's insanity defense. [Wainwright v. Greenfield, 474 U.S. 284 (1986)]

2) May Be Harmless Error
A single question by the prosecutor about the defendant's silence may constitute harmless error when followed by an objection sustained by the judge and an instruction to jurors to disregard the question. [Greer v. Miller, 483 U.S. 756 (1987)]

b. Warnings After Questioning and Confession
If the police obtain a confession from a detainee without giving him *Miranda* warnings and then give the detainee *Miranda* warnings and obtain a subsequent confession, the subsequent confession will be inadmissible if the "question first, warn later" nature of the questioning was intentional (*i.e.*, the facts make it seem like the police used this as a scheme to get around the *Miranda* requirements). [Missouri v. Seibert, 542 U.S. 600 (2004)] However, a subsequent valid confession may be admissible if the original unwarned questioning seemed unplanned and the failure to give *Miranda* warnings seemed inadvertent. [*See* Oregon v. Elstad, 470 U.S. 298 (1985)]

c. Nontestimonial Fruits of an Unwarned Confession
If the police fail to give *Miranda* warnings and during interrogation a detainee gives the police information that leads to nontestimonial evidence, the evidence will be suppressed if the failure was purposeful, but if the failure was not purposeful, the evidence probably will not be suppressed. [*See* United States v. Patane, 542 U.S. 630 (2004)]

5. Public Safety Exception to *Miranda*
If *police interrogation* is reasonably prompted by *concern for public safety*, responses to the questions may be used in court, even though the suspect is in custody and *Miranda* warnings are not given. [New York v. Quarles, 467 U.S. 649 (1984)—suspect was handcuffed and asked where he had hidden his gun; the arrest and questioning were virtually contemporaneous, and the police were reasonably concerned that the gun might be found and cause injury to an innocent person]

V. PRETRIAL IDENTIFICATION

A. IN GENERAL
The purpose of all the rules concerning pretrial identification is to ensure that when the witness identifies the person at trial, she is identifying the person who committed the crime and not merely the person whom she has previously seen at the police station.

B. SUBSTANTIVE BASES FOR ATTACK

1. Sixth Amendment Right to Counsel

a. When Right Exists
A suspect has a right to the presence of an attorney at any *post-charge lineup or showup*. [Moore v. Illinois, 434 U.S. 220 (1977); United States v. Wade, 388 U.S. 218 (1967)] At a lineup, the witness is asked to pick the perpetrator of the crime from a group of persons, while a showup is a one-to-one confrontation between the witness and the suspect for the purpose of identification.

b. Role of Counsel at a Lineup
The right is simply to have an attorney present during the lineup so that the lawyer can

observe any suggestive aspects of the lineup and bring them out on cross-examination of the witness. There is no right to have the lawyer help set up the lineup, to demand changes in the way it is conducted, etc.

c. Photo Identification
The accused does *not* have the right to counsel at photo identifications. [United States v. Ash, 413 U.S. 300 (1973)] However, as in the case of lineups, the accused may have a due process claim regarding the photo identification. (*See 2., infra.*)

d. Physical Evidence
The accused does *not* have the right to counsel when the police take physical evidence such as handwriting exemplars or fingerprints from her.

2. Due Process Standard
A defendant can attack an identification as denying due process when the identification is *unnecessarily suggestive* and there is a *substantial likelihood of misidentification*. It is clear that both parts of this standard must be met for the defendant to win, and that to meet this difficult test, the identification must be shown to have been extremely suggestive.

Examples: 1) A showup at a hospital did not deny the defendant due process when such a procedure was necessary due to the need of an immediate identification, the inability of the identifying victim to come to the police station, and the possibility that the victim might die. [Stovall v. Denno, 388 U.S. 293 (1967)]

2) A photo identification with only six snapshots did not violate due process where the procedure was necessary because perpetrators of a serious felony (robbery) were at large, and the police had to determine if they were on the right track, and the Court found little danger of misidentification. [Simmons v. United States, 390 U.S. 377 (1968)]

3) No substantial likelihood of misidentification was found in the showing of a single photograph to a police officer two days after the crime. [Manson v. Brathwaite, 432 U.S. 98 (1977)]

4) A fundamentally unfair procedure, such as when the perpetrator of the crime is known to be black and the suspect is the only black person in the lineup, would violate the due process standard.

C. THE REMEDY
The remedy for an unconstitutional identification is *exclusion* of the in-court identification (unless it has an independent source).

1. Independent Source
A witness may make an in-court identification despite the existence of an unconstitutional pretrial identification if the in-court identification has an independent source. The factors a court will weigh in determining an independent source include the opportunity to observe the defendant at the time of the crime, the ease with which the witness can identify the defendant, and the existence or absence of prior misidentifications.

2. Hearing
The admissibility of identification evidence should be determined at a suppression hearing in

the absence of the jury, but exclusion of the jury is not constitutionally required. [Watkins v. Sowders, 449 U.S. 341 (1981)] The government bears the burden of proof as to the presence of counsel or a waiver by the accused, or as to an independent source for the in-court identification, while the defendant must prove an alleged due process violation.

D. NO RIGHT TO LINEUP
The defendant is not entitled to any particular kind of identification procedure. The defendant may not demand a lineup.

E. NO SELF-INCRIMINATION ISSUE
Because a lineup does not involve compulsion to give evidence *"testimonial"* in nature, a suspect has no basis in the Fifth Amendment privilege against compelled self-incrimination to refuse to participate in one. [United States v. Wade, *supra,* B.1.a.]

VI. PRETRIAL PROCEDURES

A. PRELIMINARY HEARING TO DETERMINE PROBABLE CAUSE TO DETAIN (*"GERSTEIN* HEARINGS")
A defendant has a Fourth Amendment right to be released from detention if there is no probable cause to hold him. Thus, a defendant has a right to a determination of probable cause. A preliminary hearing is a hearing held after arrest but before trial to determine whether probable cause for detention exists. The hearing is an informal, ex parte, nonadversarial proceeding.

1. When Right Applies
If probable cause has already been determined (*e.g.,* the arrest is pursuant to a grand jury indictment or an arrest warrant), a preliminary hearing need not be held. If no probable cause determination has been made, a defendant has a right to a preliminary hearing to determine probable cause if *"significant pretrial constraints on the defendant's liberty"* exist. Thus, the right applies if the defendant is released only upon the posting of bail or if he is held in jail in lieu of bail. It does not apply if the defendant is released merely upon the condition that he appear for trial.

Note: The fact that the defendant has been released does not preclude a finding of a significant constraint on liberty, because many conditions can be attached to liberty.

2. Timing
The hearing must be held within a reasonable time, and the Court has determined that 48 hours is presumptively reasonable. [Riverside County v. McLaughlin, 500 U.S. 44 (1991)]

3. Remedy
There is *no real remedy* for the defendant for the mere denial of this hearing, because an unlawful detention, without more, has no effect on the subsequent prosecution. However, if evidence is discovered as a result of the unlawful detention, it will be suppressed under the exclusionary rule.

B. PRETRIAL DETENTION

1. Initial Appearance
Soon after the defendant is arrested, she must be brought before a magistrate who will advise her of her rights, set bail, and appoint counsel if necessary. The initial appearance may be

combined with the *Gerstein* hearing, but will be held whether or not a *Gerstein* hearing is necessary. For misdemeanors, this appearance will be the trial.

2. **Bail**
Most state constitutions or statutes create a right to be released on appropriate bail (either on personal recognizance or on a cash bond).

   a. **Due Process Concerns**
   Because denial of release on bail deprives a person of liberty, such denials must comply with the Due Process Clause. In upholding the Federal Bail Reform Act (which permits a court to detain an arrestee if the judge determines that no condition of release would ensure the arrestee's appearance or the safety of any person or the community), the Court held that denial of bail does not violate substantive due process (by imposing punishment before a defendant is found guilty), because the denial of bail is not punishment but a regulatory solution to the problem of persons committing crimes while out on bail. The Court also held that the federal act does not violate procedural due process because it provides detainees with a right to a hearing on the issue, expedited review, etc. [United States v. Salerno, 479 U.S. 1026 (1987)] Similar state statutes would likely be upheld, but a state statute that arbitrarily denies bail (*e.g.,* by not allowing the detainee to present evidence or denying release to a whole class of detainees) would probably violate the Due Process Clause.

   b. **Right to Be Free from Excessive Bail**
   Where the right to release exists, state constitutions and state statutes—and perhaps the Eighth Amendment as well—prohibit "excessive" bail. This has traditionally been interpreted to require that bail be set no higher than is necessary to ensure the defendant's appearance at trial.

   c. **Bail Issues Are Immediately Appealable**
   In most jurisdictions and under federal law, a refusal to grant bail or the setting of excessive bail may be appealed immediately, as an exception to the final judgment rule for appeals. If not immediately appealable, the denial of bail can be reached by an immediate petition for a writ of habeas corpus. Once the defendant is convicted, an appeal of a pretrial bail decision is moot. [Murphy v. Hunt, 455 U.S. 478 (1982)]

   d. **Defendant Incompetent to Stand Trial**
   As to deprivation of pretrial liberty by commitment of one who is not competent to stand trial, the standards for commitment and subsequent release must be essentially identical with those for the commitment of persons not charged with crime; otherwise, there is a denial of equal protection. [Jackson v. Indiana, 406 U.S. 715 (1972)]

3. **Pretrial Detention Practices**
Pretrial detention practices that are reasonably related to the interest of maintaining jail security, such as double-bunking, prohibiting inmates from receiving from the outside food and personal items or books not mailed directly from the publisher, routine inspections while the detainees remain outside their rooms, and body cavity searches following contact visits, do not violate due process or the Fourth Amendment and without more do not constitute punishment. [Bell v. Wolfish, 441 U.S. 520 (1979)]

C. **PRELIMINARY HEARING TO DETERMINE PROBABLE CAUSE TO PROSECUTE**
A later preliminary hearing may be held to determine whether probable cause to prosecute exists.

The accused has the *right to counsel* at this hearing [Coleman v. Alabama, 399 U.S. 1 (1970)], and both the prosecutor and the accused may present evidence for the record. The accused may waive the hearing. Either side may use this hearing to preserve testimony of a witness unavailable at trial (*e.g.,* the witness testifies at the preliminary hearing and dies before trial) provided there was some opportunity to cross-examine the witness at the preliminary hearing. [Ohio v. Roberts, 448 U.S. 56 (1980)]

D. GRAND JURIES

The Fifth Amendment right to indictment by grand jury has not been incorporated into the Fourteenth Amendment, but some state constitutions require grand jury indictment.

1. Charging Grand Juries

Most states east of the Mississippi and the federal system use the grand jury as a regular part of the charging process. The charging grand jury *determines probable cause to prosecute* by returning the bill of indictment submitted by the prosecutor as a "true bill." Western states generally charge by filing an information, a written accusation of crime prepared and presented by the prosecutor. Informations also are used when the defendant waives her right to grand jury indictment.

2. Special or Investigative Grand Juries

Special or investigative grand juries are used almost everywhere. This type of grand jury investigates, on its own motion, crime in the particular jurisdiction, and can initiate a criminal case by bringing an indictment.

3. Grand Jury Proceedings

a. Secrecy and Defendant's Lack of Access

Grand jury proceedings are conducted in secret. In most jurisdictions, a defendant has no right to notice that a grand jury is considering an indictment against her, to be present and confront witnesses at the proceeding, or to introduce evidence before the grand jury.

b. Particularized Need Required for Prosecutor's Access to Grand Jury Materials

The "particularized need" standard generally required under Rule 6(e) of the Federal Rules of Criminal Procedure in order to obtain access to grand jury materials must be shown by state attorneys general [Illinois v. Abbott, 460 U.S. 557 (1983)], as well as Justice Department attorneys [United States v. Sells Engineering, Inc., 463 U.S. 418 (1983)]. The disclosure of such materials to the Internal Revenue Service for the purpose of assessing tax liability, rather than for litigation, is not permitted. [United States v. Baggot, 463 U.S. 476 (1983)]

c. Subpoena Powers of Grand Jury

The grand jury may use its subpoena power to investigate the matters before it or to initiate criminal investigations of its own. Rather than returning an indictment, grand juries sometimes issue a report.

1) Government Need Not Prove Relevance

A grand jury subpoena may be quashed only if the opposing party can prove that there is no reasonable possibility that the material sought will be relevant to the grand jury investigation. The government has no initial burden of proving that the material is relevant. [United States v. R. Enterprises, Inc., 498 U.S. 292 (1991)]

2) Defamatory Reports

If the defendant or any other person believes that she has been defamed by a grand jury report, she may make a motion to seal the report.

d. No Right to Counsel or *Miranda* Warnings

A witness subpoenaed to testify before a grand jury does not have the right to receive the *Miranda* warnings, and the witness may be convicted of perjury despite the lack of warnings if she testifies falsely. A grand jury witness does not have the right to have an attorney present, but she may consult with an attorney outside the grand jury room. [United States v. Mandujano, *supra*, IV.D.2.a.2)b); United States v. Wong, *supra*, IV.D.2.a.2)b)]

e. No Right to "Potential Defendant" Warnings

A witness who is under investigation and may well become a defendant is not entitled to a warning that she is a "potential defendant" when called to testify before the grand jury. [United States v. Washington, 431 U.S. 181 (1977)]

f. No Right to Have Evidence Excluded

A grand jury may base its indictment on evidence that would not be admissible at trial [Costello v. United States, 350 U.S. 359 (1956)], and a grand jury witness may not refuse to answer questions on the grounds that they are based upon unconstitutionally obtained evidence [United States v. Calandra, 414 U.S. 338 (1974)]. Nor may an indicted defendant have the indictment quashed on the grounds that it is based upon illegally obtained evidence.

g. No Right to Challenge Subpoena on Fourth Amendment Grounds

A suspect-witness (or any witness, for that matter) subpoenaed before a grand jury cannot attack the subpoena on the ground that the grand jury lacked "probable cause"— or any reason at all—to call her for questioning. No such attack can be made even if the subpoena also requires the witness to provide a handwriting exemplar, a voice sample, or otherwise cooperate with law enforcement officials in a manner not violating the self-incrimination privilege.

h. Exclusion of Minorities

Minorities may not be excluded from grand jury service. A conviction resulting from an indictment issued by a grand jury from which members of a minority group have been excluded will be reversed without regard to the harmlessness of the error. [Vasquez v. Hillery, 474 U.S. 254 (1986)] Note that the defendant and the excluded members need not be of the same race. [Campbell v. Louisiana, 523 U.S. 392 (1998)]

i. Dismissal Seldom Required for Procedural Defect

An indicted defendant is seldom entitled to dismissal of an indictment upon a showing that procedural error occurred during the grand jury proceedings. Generally, she is entitled to dismissal only upon a showing that the error substantially influenced the grand jury's decision to indict. [Bank of Nova Scotia v. United States, 487 U.S. 250 (1988)—defendant failed to show that prosecutorial misconduct before grand jury substantially influenced its decision to indict]

j. Exculpatory Evidence

An indictment may not be dismissed by a federal court for a prosecutor's failure to

present exculpatory evidence to the grand jury unless the prosecutor's conduct violates a preexisting constitutional, legislative, or procedural rule. [United States v. Williams, 504 U.S. 36 (1992)]

E. SPEEDY TRIAL

1. Societal Interest
The Sixth Amendment right to a speedy trial is an unusual one in that the interests of society and the defendant coincide.

2. Constitutional Standard
A determination of whether the defendant's right to a speedy trial has been violated will be made by an evaluation of the totality of the circumstances. The following factors should be considered:

(i)   Length of the delay;

(ii) Reason for the delay;

(iii) Whether the defendant asserted his right; and

(iv) Prejudice to the defendant.

[Barker v. Wingo, 407 U.S. 514 (1972)]

Example: A defendant who was arrested 8½ years after his federal indictment due solely to the government's neglect and who promptly asserted his right to a speedy trial claim was ***presumptively prejudiced*** so that an actual showing of prejudice was not necessary. [Doggett v. United States, 505 U.S. 647 (1992)]

a. Delays Caused by Assigned Counsel
Delays caused by counsel assigned by the court to the defendant should ordinarily be attributed to the defendant and not to the state. [Vermont v. Brillon, 129 S. Ct. 1283 (2009)]

3. Remedy—Dismissal
The remedy for a violation of the constitutional right to a speedy trial is dismissal with prejudice. [Strunk v. United States, 412 U.S. 434 (1973)]

4. When Right Attaches
The right to a speedy trial does not attach until the defendant has been ***arrested or charged***. It is very difficult to get relief for a pre-arrest delay under this standard, because the defendant must show prejudice from a delay, and good faith investigative delays do not violate due process. [United States v. Lovasco, 431 U.S. 783 (1977)]

A defendant is not entitled to speedy trial relief for the period between the dismissal of charges and later refiling. [United States v. MacDonald, 456 U.S. 1 (1982)] The only limitation on pre-arrest delay (other than general due process requirements) seems to be the statute of limitations for the particular crime.

a. **Knowledge of Charges Unnecessary**
The Speedy Trial Clause attaches even if the defendant does not know about the charges against him and is thus not restrained in any way. [Doggett v. United States, *supra*]

5. **Special Problems**
Two situations create special speedy trial problems:

a. **Detainees**
A defendant incarcerated in one jurisdiction who has a charge pending in another jurisdiction has a right to have the second jurisdiction exert reasonable efforts to obtain his presence for trial of these pending charges. Failure to exert such efforts violates his right to speedy trial. [Smith v. Hooey, 393 U.S. 374 (1969)]

b. **Indefinite Suspension of Charges**
It is a violation of the right to speedy trial to permit the prosecution to indefinitely suspend charges, such as permitting the government to dismiss "without prejudice," which permits reinstatement of the prosecution *at any time*. [Klopfer v. North Carolina, 386 U.S. 213 (1967)—nolle prosequi that indefinitely suspended the statute of limitations violated speedy trial requirements]

F. **PROSECUTORIAL DUTY TO DISCLOSE EXCULPATORY INFORMATION AND NOTICE OF DEFENSES**

1. **Prosecutor's Duty to Disclose Exculpatory Evidence**
The government has a duty to disclose material, exculpatory evidence to the defendant. [Brady v. Maryland, 373 U.S. 83 (1963)] Failure to disclose such evidence—whether willful *or inadvertent*—violates the Due Process Clause and is grounds for reversing a conviction if the defendant can prove that:

(i) The evidence at issue is *favorable to the defendant* because it impeaches or is exculpatory; and

(ii) *Prejudice has resulted* (*i.e.*, there is a *reasonable probability* that the result of the case would have been different if the undisclosed evidence had been presented at trial).

[Strickler v. Green, 527 U.S. 263 (1999); United States v. Bagley, 473 U.S. 667 (1985)] *Note:* If the prosecution can show that the verdict is strongly supported by other evidence, sufficient prejudice will not be found.

a. **Exception—Reports on Sexually Abused Minors**
A defendant may not automatically obtain investigative reports made by a state agency in charge of investigating sexually abused minors because of the confidentiality of the minors' records. Such reports can be obtained only if they are *favorable* to the defendant and are *material* to guilt or punishment. [Pennsylvania v. Ritchie, 480 U.S. 39 (1987)]

b. **Probably Must Be Relevant to Merits**
The duty to disclose appears to extend only to evidence relevant to the prosecution's case in chief. Material going to a defense not on the merits probably need not be disclosed. [*See* United States v. Armstrong, 517 U.S. 456 (1996)—material relevant to

defendant's claim that he was selected for prosecution because of his race need not be disclosed]

c. Duty Does Not Apply at Post-Conviction Proceedings

A prosecutor's obligation to disclose material, exculpatory evidence under *Brady* does not apply at post-conviction proceedings. [District Attorney's Office for the Third Judicial District v. Osborne, 129 S. Ct. 2308 (2009)—a convicted offender has no federal due process right to obtain post-conviction access to a state's evidence for DNA testing in the absence of any indication that available state post-conviction relief procedures are fundamentally unfair]

2. Notice of Alibi and Intent to Present Insanity Defense

a. Reciprocity Required

The prosecution may demand to know whether the defendant is going to plead insanity or raise an alibi as a defense. If the defendant is going to raise an alibi, he must list his witnesses. In return, the prosecution is required to list the witnesses it will call to rebut the defendant's defense. [Williams v. Florida, 399 U.S. 78 (1970); Wardius v. Oregon, 412 U.S. 470 (1973)]

b. Commenting on Failure to Present the Alibi

The prosecutor may not comment at trial on the defendant's failure to produce a witness named as supporting the alibi or on the failure to present the alibi itself. But the prosecutor may use the notice of an alibi to *impeach* a defendant who takes the stand and testifies to a different alibi.

G. COMPETENCY TO STAND TRIAL

1. Competency and Insanity Distinguished

Competency to stand trial must be carefully distinguished from the insanity defense, although both rest on a defendant's abnormality. Insanity is a defense to the criminal charge; a defendant acquitted by reason of insanity may not be retried and convicted, although she may be hospitalized under some circumstances. *Incompetency* to stand trial depends on a defendant's mental condition at the *time of trial*, unlike *insanity*, which turns upon a defendant's mental condition at the *time of the crime*. Incompetency is not a defense but rather a bar to trial. A defendant who is incompetent to stand trial cannot be tried. But if she later regains her competency, she can then be tried and—unless she has a defense—convicted. Note that a defendant who is competent to stand trial is competent to plead guilty.

2. Due Process Standard

Due process of law, as well as the state law of most jurisdictions, prohibits the trial of a defendant who is incompetent to stand trial. A defendant is incompetent to stand trial under the due process standard if, because of her present mental condition, she either:

(i) Lacks a rational as well as a factual *understanding of the charges and proceedings*; or

(ii) Lacks sufficient present *ability to consult with her lawyer* with a reasonable degree of understanding.

[Dusky v. United States, 362 U.S. 402 (1960)]

a.   **Forced "Cure"**
Under the Due Process Clause, the government may *involuntarily* administer antipsy-chotic drugs to a mentally ill defendant facing serious criminal charges in order to make him competent to stand trial if: (i) the treatment is medically appropriate, (ii) the treatment is substantially unlikely to cause side effects that may undermine the fairness of the trial, and (iii) considering less-intrusive alternatives, the treatment is necessary to further important governmental trial-related interests. [Sell v. United States, 539 U.S. 166 (2003)]

3.   **Trial Judge's Duty to Raise Competency Issue**
If evidence of a defendant's incompetency appears to the trial judge, the judge has a consti-tutional obligation to conduct further inquiry and determine whether in fact the defendant is incompetent. If a defendant is tried and convicted but it later appears she was incompetent to stand trial, the judge's failure to raise the issue or to request a determination of competency does not constitute a "waiver." [Pate v. Robinson, 383 U.S. 375 (1966)]

Example: During preliminary proceedings at X's trial for robbery, X, while in open court, speaks irrationally and repeatedly interrupts the proceedings by shouting to a nonexistent dog in the courtroom. What, if anything, must the trial judge do before proceeding to trial? The facts here clearly require the trial judge to investigate and determine X's competency to stand trial. The judge must hold a hearing and determine whether X is mentally ill and, if so, whether she can consult with her lawyer and understand the charges and proceedings. This must be done even if neither X nor her lawyer raises the issue.

4.   **Burden Can Be Placed on Defendant**
A state can require a criminal defendant to prove that he is not competent to stand trial by a preponderance of the evidence; this does not violate due process. [Medina v. California, 505 U.S. 437 (1992)] However, requiring a defendant to prove incompetence by *clear and convincing evidence* violates due process. [Cooper v. Oklahoma, 517 U.S. 348 (1996)]

5.   **Detention of Defendant**

a.   **Based on Incompetency**
A defendant who has been found incompetent may be detained in a mental hospital for a brief period of time for evaluation and treatment. But she cannot be hospitalized indefinitely or for a long period of time simply because she has been found incompetent. This can be done only if independent "civil commitment" proceedings are begun and result in her commitment. [Jackson v. Indiana, 406 U.S. 715 (1972)]

b.   **Based on Insanity**
A defendant who has made a successful insanity defense can be confined in a mental hospital for a term longer than the maximum period of incarceration for the offense. The insanity acquittee is not entitled to any separate civil commitment hearing at the expiration of the maximum sentence. [Jones v. United States, 463 U.S. 354 (1983)] However, a defendant acquitted by reason of insanity who is determined to have recov-ered sanity cannot be indefinitely committed in a mental facility merely because he is unable to prove himself not dangerous to others. [Foucha v. Louisiana, 504 U.S. 71 (1992)]

H. PRETRIAL PUBLICITY AND THE RIGHT TO A FAIR TRIAL

Excessive pretrial publicity prejudicial to the defendant may require change of venue or retrial.

Examples: 1) Defendant sought and was improperly denied a change of venue on the ground of local prejudice. His trial by a jury that was familiar with the material facts and had formed an opinion as to his guilt before the trial began (on the basis of unfavorable newspaper publicity) denied him due process. [Irvin v. Dowd, 366 U.S. 717 (1961)] However, due process will be satisfied if the judge asks the venirepersons whether they were exposed to pretrial publicity, and if so, whether it would affect their impartiality and ability to hear the case with an open mind. The judge does not have to ask about the specific source or content of the pretrial information. [Mu'Min v. Virginia, 500 U.S. 415 (1991)]

2) A new trial is required where defendant sought and was denied a change of venue after a televised interview in which defendant admitted that he had perpetrated the crimes with which he was charged, and the jury was drawn from the people who had seen the interview. [Rideau v. Louisiana, 373 U.S. 723 (1963)—jurors' claims that they could be neutral were inherently implausible]

3) Defendant's request for a change of venue because of pretrial publicity was denied because state law did not permit a change of venue in misdemeanor cases. *Held:* The law violates the right to trial by an impartial jury; a defendant must be given the opportunity to show that a change of venue is required in his case. [Groppi v. Wisconsin, 400 U.S. 505 (1971)]

VII. TRIAL

A. BASIC RIGHT TO A FAIR TRIAL

1. Right to Public Trial

The Sixth and Fourteenth Amendments guarantee the right to a public trial. [*In re* Oliver, 333 U.S. 257 (1948); Herring v. New York, 422 U.S. 853 (1975)] However, the extent of this right varies according to the stage of the proceeding involved.

a. Preliminary Probable Cause Hearing

Preliminary hearings to determine whether there is probable cause on which to prosecute are presumptively open to the public and the press. [Press Enterprise Co. v. Superior Court, 478 U.S. 1 (1986)]

b. Suppression Hearings

The Sixth Amendment right to a public trial extends to *pretrial suppression hearings*. Such hearings may not be closed to the public unless:

(i) The party seeking closure shows an *overriding interest* likely to be prejudiced by a public hearing;

(ii) The closure is *no broader than necessary* to protect such an interest;

(iii) *Reasonable alternatives* to closure have been considered; and

(iv) *Adequate findings* to support closure are entered by the trial court.

[Waller v. Georgia, 467 U.S. 39 (1984)]

c. **Voir Dire of Prospective Jurors**
The right to a public trial includes voir dire of prospective jurors. Trial courts must make every reasonable effort to accommodate public attendance. [Presley v. Georgia, 130 S. Ct. 721 (2010)—Sixth Amendment violated when judge did not allow defendant's uncle to remain in courtroom during voir dire, stating that prospective jurors could not mingle with the uncle and needed all of the rows of seats in the courtroom]

d. **Trial**
The press and the public have a right under the First Amendment to attend the trial itself, even when the defense and prosecution agree to close it. A judge may not exclude the press and the public from a criminal trial without first finding that closure is necessary for a fair trial. [Richmond Newspapers, Inc. v. Virginia, 448 U.S. 555 (1980)]

1) **Televising Permissible**
The state may constitutionally permit televising criminal proceedings over the defendant's objection. [Chandler v. Florida, 449 U.S. 560 (1981)]

2. **Right to an Unbiased Judge**
Due process is violated if the judge is shown to have *actual malice* against the defendant or to have had a *financial interest* in having the trial result in a verdict of guilty.
Example: D is tried before a "mayor's court" presided over by a judge who is also the mayor of the town. Half of the town's income comes from fines imposed in the court after convictions. Is the trial permissible? No. The judge has too great a financial interest in the outcome to meet due process standards. [Ward v. City of Monrocville, 409 U.S. 57 (1972)]

3. **Must Judge Be a Lawyer?**
A defendant in a minor misdemeanor prosecution has no right to have the trial judge be a lawyer, if upon conviction he has a right to trial de novo in a court with a lawyer-judge. [North v. Russell, 427 U.S. 328 (1976)] It is likely, however, that in serious crime cases the Supreme Court will require that the judge be law-trained.

4. **Right to Be Free of Trial Disruption**
Due process is violated if the trial is conducted in a manner or atmosphere making it unlikely that the jury gave the evidence reasonable consideration. Televising and broadcasting parts of a trial, for example, may interfere with courtroom proceedings and influence the jury by emphasizing the notoriety of the trial to such an extent that it infringes the defendant's right to a fair trial. [Estes v. Texas, 381 U.S. 532 (1965)]

5. **Trial in Prison Clothing**
It is unconstitutional for the state to *compel* the defendant to stand trial in prison clothing. If the defendant does not wish to be tried in prison clothing, he must make a timely objection. [Estelle v. Williams, 425 U.S. 501 (1976)] Similarly, the Due Process Clause prohibits the use of visible shackles during the trial and penalty phase of a capital proceeding unless the court makes a specific finding that their use is justified by concerns about courtroom security or risk of escape. [Deck v. Missouri, 544 U.S. 622 (2005)]

6. Right to Have Jury Free from Unfair Influences

If the jury is exposed to influences favorable to the prosecution, due process is violated.

Example: During X's trial, two sheriffs, who were also prosecution witnesses, were in constant and intimate association with the jurors, eating with them, running errands for them, etc. Did the trial violate due process standards? Yes, since this association must have influenced the jurors' assessment of the credibility of the witnesses. [Turner v. Louisiana, 379 U.S. 466 (1965)]

7. No Right to Preservation of Potentially Exculpatory Evidence

Defendants have no right to have the police preserve all evidence for trial, at least where it is not certain that the evidence would have been exculpatory. Due process is violated, however, if the police *in bad faith* destroy evidence potentially useful to the defense at trial. [Arizona v. Youngblood, 488 U.S. 51 (1988)—no due process violation where police failed to preserve seminal fluid on sodomy victim's clothing; California v. Trombetta, 467 U.S. 479 (1984)— same result where police failed to preserve samples of defendant's breath]

B. RIGHT TO TRIAL BY JURY

The Sixth Amendment right to trial by jury applies to the states. [Duncan v. Louisiana, 391 U.S. 145 (1968)] The cases after *Duncan,* while zealously guarding the jury trial right, have permitted the states great latitude in the details of jury use and conduct because of (i) the view that many of the details of the jury were historical accidents, (ii) the belief that the jury will act rationally, and (iii) the cost.

1. Right to Jury Trial Only for "Serious" Offenses

There is no constitutional right to jury trial for petty offenses, but only for serious offenses. Also, there is no right to jury trial in juvenile delinquency proceedings. [McKeiver v. Pennsylvania, 403 U.S. 528 (1971)]

a. What Constitutes a Serious Offense?

For purposes of the right to jury trial, an offense is serious if *imprisonment for more than six months* is authorized. If imprisonment of six months or less is authorized, the offense is presumptively petty, and there is no right to a jury trial. [Blanton v. City of North Las Vegas, 489 U.S. 538 (1989)] The presumption may be overcome by showing additional penalties, but a possibility of a $5,000 fine and five years' probation is not sufficient to overcome the presumption that the crime is petty. [United States v. Nachtigal, 507 U.S. 1 (1993)]

1) Aggregation of Petty Offenses

The right to a jury trial does not arise when in a single proceeding, sentences for multiple petty offenses are imposed which result in an aggregate prison sentence of more than six months. [Lewis v. United States, 518 U.S. 322 (1996)]

b. Contempt

1) Civil Contempt—No Jury Trial Right

If a penalty is imposed for purposes of compelling future compliance with a court order and the witness can avoid further penalty by complying with the order (*e.g.,* judge sentences witness to prison until she is willing to testify), the proceeding is one of "civil" contempt and no jury trial is required.

2) **Criminal Contempt—"Six Months" Rule**
When there is no statutorily authorized penalty for a crime, such as criminal contempt, the actual sentence governs the right to jury trial. Cumulative penalties totaling more than six months cannot be imposed in a ***post-verdict contempt adjudication*** without affording the defendant the right to a jury trial. [Codispoti v. Pennsylvania, 418 U.S. 506 (1974)]

3) **Summary Contempt Punishment During Trial**
If the judge summarily imposes punishment for contempt during trial, the penalties may aggregate more than six months without a jury trial. [Codispoti v. Pennsylvania, *supra*]

4) **Appellate Modification Sufficient**
An appellate court may reduce the sentence imposed for contempt to six months or less and thereby protect the conviction and sentence imposed without a jury from constitutional attack. [Taylor v. Hayes, 418 U.S. 488 (1974)]

5) **Probation**
A judge may place a contemnor on probation for a term of up to five years without affording him the right to jury trial as long as revocation of probation would not result in imprisonment for more than six months. [Frank v. United States, 395 U.S. 147 (1969)]

2. **Number and Unanimity of Jurors**

a. **No Right to Jury of Twelve**
There is no constitutional right to a jury of 12, but there must be *at least six* jurors to satisfy the right to jury trial under the Sixth and Fourteenth Amendments. [Ballew v. Georgia, 435 U.S. 223 (1978)]

b. **No Absolute Right to Unanimity**
There is no right to a unanimous verdict. The Supreme Court has upheld convictions based upon 11-1, 10-2, and 9-3 votes [Apodaca v. Oregon, 406 U.S. 404 (1972); Johnson v. Louisiana, 406 U.S. 356 (1972)], but probably would not approve an 8-4 vote for conviction. Six-person juries must be unanimous. [Burch v. Louisiana, 441 U.S. 130 (1979); Brown v. Louisiana, 447 U.S. 323 (1980)]

3. **Right to Venire Selected from Representative Cross-Section of Community**
A defendant has a right to have the venire from which the jury is selected be from a representative cross-section of the community. A defendant can complain of an exclusion of a significant segment of the community from the venire, even if he is not a member of that excluded segment. [Taylor v. Louisiana, 419 U.S. 522 (1975); Holland v. Illinois, 493 U.S. 474 (1990)]

a. **Showing of Exclusion of Significant Group Sufficient**
To make out a case for exclusion, the defendant need only show the underrepresentation of a distinct and numerically significant group. [Taylor v. Louisiana, *supra*]

b. **No Right to Proportional Representation on Particular Jury**
The cross-sectional requirement applies only to the venire from which the jury is

selected. A defendant does not have the right to proportional representation of all groups on his particular jury. [Holland v. Illinois, *supra*]

c. **Use of Peremptory Challenges for Racial and Gender-Based Discrimination**
In contrast to striking potential jurors for cause, a prosecutor generally may exercise peremptory challenges for any rational *or irrational* reason. However, the Equal Protection Clause forbids the use of peremptory challenges to exclude potential jurors solely on account of their race or gender. [Batson v. Kentucky, 476 U.S. 79 (1989); J.E.B. v. Alabama, 511 U.S. 127 (1994)]

1) **Proving Strike Improper**
An equal protection-based attack on peremptory strikes involves three steps: (i) The defendant must show *facts or circumstances that raise an inference* that the exclusion of potential jurors was based on race or gender. (ii) If such a showing is made, the prosecutor must then come forward with a *race-neutral explanation* for the strike. The reason for the strike need not be reasonable, as long as it is race-neutral. [Purkett v. Elem, 514 U.S. 765 (1995)—explanation that potential jurors were struck because of their long hair and beards was sufficient] (iii) The judge then determines whether the prosecutor's explanation was the genuine reason for striking the juror, or merely a pretext for purposeful discrimination. If the judge believes that the *prosecutor was sincere*, the strike may be upheld. [Purkett v. Elem, *supra*]

Example:	That a stricken juror was young, had no ties to the community, and was disrespectful were sufficient grounds to support a peremptory strike. [Rice v. Collins, 546 U.S. 333 (2006)]
Compare:	During voir dire in a murder case, an African-American college student voiced concern that the trial might interfere with his student teaching, which he needed to fulfill to graduate college. The student's dean was called and agreed to work with him on rescheduling. The prosecutor asked no further questions about the matter. Nevertheless, the prosecutor used a peremptory challenge to exclude the student. When the peremptory strike was challenged, the prosecutor explained that he was concerned that, because of the student's pressing educational needs, he would find the defendant guilty of a lesser charge to avoid a lengthy capital sentencing hearing. As a result of peremptory challenges and challenges for cause, no African-Americans were included in the final jury. *Held:* Because white jurors also stated that they had pressing needs but were not excluded, and because it is unlikely that one juror could shorten the trial (he would have to convince the other jurors to follow his lead), the prosecutor's rationale for the strike was just a pretext and should not have been upheld. [Snyder v. Louisiana, 552 U.S. 472 (2008)]

Note: The defendant need not be a member of the group excluded. [Powers v. Ohio, 499 U.S. 400 (1991)]

2) **Defendants**
It is also unconstitutional for a criminal *defendant* or the defendant's attorney to use peremptory challenges in a racially discriminatory manner. [Georgia v.

McCollum, 505 U.S. 42 (1992)] The same rule probably applies to a defendant's peremptory strike based on gender.

d.   Distinct and Significant Groups
A fair cross-section of the community must include minorities and women, and possibly other distinct and significant groups. A state may neither exclude women from jury duty nor automatically exempt them upon request. [Duren v. Missouri, 439 U.S. 357 (1979)]

4.   Right to Impartial Jury

a.   Right to Questioning on Racial Bias
A defendant is entitled to questioning on voir dire specifically directed to racial preju- dice whenever race is inextricably bound up in the case. [Ham v. South Carolina, 409 U.S. 524 (1973)] In *noncapital* cases, the mere fact that the victim is white and the defendant is black is not enough to permit such questioning. [Ristaino v. Ross, 424 U.S. 589 (1976); Rosales-Lopez v. United States, 451 U.S. 182 (1982)] However, a *capital* defendant accused of an interracial crime is entitled to have prospective jurors informed of the victim's race and is entitled to voir dire questioning regarding the issue of racial prejudice. [Turner v. Murray, 476 U.S. 28 (1986)]

b.   Juror Opposition to Death Penalty
In cases involving capital punishment, a state may not automatically exclude for cause all prospective jurors who express a doubt or scruple about the death penalty. [Wither- spoon v. Illinois, 391 U.S. 510 (1968); Adams v. Texas, 448 U.S. 38 (1980)]

1)   Standard—Impair or Prevent Performance
The standard for determining when a prospective juror should be excluded for cause is whether the juror's views would *prevent or substantially impair* the performance of his duties in accordance with his instructions and oath. [Wainwright v. Witt, 469 U.S. 412 (1985)] Thus, if a juror's doubts or scruples about the death penalty prevent or substantially impair the performance of his duties, he may be excluded from the jury, and the fact that this may result in a "death qualified" jury does not infringe on a defendant's constitutional rights. [Lockhart v. McCree, 476 U.S. 162 (1986)] However, if a juror has scruples about the death penalty, but could perform her duties and follow instructions, it is error to exclude the juror.

2)   Improper Exclusion May Result in Reversal
A death sentence imposed by a jury from which a juror was improperly excluded is subject to automatic reversal. [Gray v. Mississippi, 481 U.S. 648 (1987)]

c.   Juror Favoring Death Penalty
If a jury is to decide whether a defendant in a capital case is to be sentenced to death, the defendant must be allowed to ask potential jurors at voir dire if they would automati- cally give the death penalty upon a guilty verdict. A juror who answers affirmatively should be excluded for cause because such a juror has indicated the same type of inability to follow jury instructions (as to mitigating circumstances) as a juror who has indicated an inability to impose the death penalty under any circumstances (*see supra*). [Morgan v. Illinois, 504 U.S. 719 (1992)]

d. Use of Peremptory Challenge to Maintain Impartial Jury

Peremptory challenges are not constitutionally required. Therefore, if a trial court refuses to exclude a juror for cause whom the court should have excluded, and the defendant uses a peremptory challenge to remove the juror, there is no constitutional violation. [Ross v. Oklahoma, 487 U.S. 81 (1988); United States v. Martinez-Salazar, 528 U.S. 304 (2000)]

5. Inconsistent Verdicts

Inconsistent jury verdicts (*e.g.,* finding defendant guilty of some counts but not guilty on related counts or one defendant guilty and a co-defendant not guilty on the same evidence) are not reviewable. A challenge to an inconsistent verdict would be based upon pure speculation because it is impossible to tell on which decision the jury erred. [United States v. Powell, 469 U.S. 57 (1984)]

6. Sentence Enhancement

If substantive law provides that a sentence may be increased beyond the statutory maximum for a crime if additional facts (other than prior conviction) are proved, proof of the facts must be submitted to the jury and proved beyond reasonable doubt; the defendant's right to jury trial is violated if the judge makes the determination. [Apprendi v. New Jersey, 530 U.S. 466 (2000)]

Examples: 1) The right to jury trial was violated where a statute allowed a defendant's sentence to be increased by 10 years if the sentencing judge found by a preponderance of the evidence that the crime was motivated by hate. [Apprendi v. New Jersey, *supra*]

2) Following a jury adjudication of a defendant's guilt of first degree murder, a trial judge is prohibited by the Sixth Amendment from determining whether aggravating factors justify imposition of the death penalty. The jury must make such a determination. [Ring v. Arizona, 536 U.S. 584 (2002)]

a. Guilty Pleas

The same general rule applies to sentencing enhancements after guilty pleas.

Example: Defendant pleaded guilty to kidnapping. Based on the facts admitted, under state law Defendant's maximum penalty was 53 months' imprisonment, but the judge found that Defendant acted with deliberate cruelty—an additional factor that allowed adding time to the standard sentence range—and imposed a 90-month sentence. Because the facts supporting Defendant's exceptional sentence were neither admitted by him nor found by a jury, his sentence violated the Sixth Amendment right to a trial by jury. [Blakely v. Washington, 542 U.S. 296 (2004)]

b. Harmless Error Test Applies

In deciding whether to overturn a sentence for failure to submit a sentencing factor to the jury, the harmless error test is applied. [Washington v. Recuenco, 548 U.S. 212 (2006)]

c. Distinguish—Judge May Decide Whether Sentences Run Consecutively

The Supreme Court has refused to extend the *Apprendi/Blakely* doctrine to the decision of whether sentences for multiple crimes are to run consecutively or concurrently. A state legislature may give to its judges (rather than the jury) the power to make such a

decision even though it is based on the facts of the case. *Rationale:* Historically, judges have been entrusted with such decisions. The framers of the Constitution probably did not intend the Sixth Amendment's right to a jury trial to supplant this practice. [Oregon v. Ice, 129 S. Ct. 711 (2009)]

C. RIGHT TO COUNSEL

A defendant has a right to counsel under the Fifth and Sixth Amendments. The Fifth Amendment right applies at all custodial interrogations (*see* IV.D., *supra*). The Sixth Amendment right applies at all *critical stages* of a prosecution after formal proceedings have begun (*see* IV.C., *supra*), including trial.

1. Remedy

Recall that if the defendant was entitled to a lawyer at trial, the failure to provide counsel results in *automatic reversal of the conviction*, even without any showing of specific unfairness in the proceedings. Similarly, erroneous disqualification of privately retained counsel results in automatic reversal. However, at *nontrial proceedings* (such as a post-indictment lineup), the harmless error rule applies to deprivations of counsel. (*See* IV.C.5., *supra*.)

2. Waiver of Right to Counsel at Trial and Right to Defend Oneself

A defendant has a right to represent himself *at trial* as long as his waiver is *knowing and intelligent* [Faretta v. California, 422 U.S. 806 (1975); Godinez v. Moran, 509 U.S. 389 (1993)] and he is *competent* to proceed pro se [Indiana v. Edwards, 554 U.S. 135 (2008)]. The Court has held that a waiver will be held to be voluntary and intelligent if the trial court finds—after carefully scrutinizing the waiver—that the defendant has a rational and factual understanding of the proceeding against him. The Court has not established the standard for determining whether the defendant is mentally competent. It has noted that a defendant may be mentally competent to stand trial and yet incompetent to represent himself, based on the trial judge's consideration of the defendant's emotional and psychological state.

Note: On appeal, a defendant has no right to represent himself. [Martinez v. Court of Appeal, 528 U.S. 152 (2000)]

3. Indigence and Recoupment of Cost

As indicated above, if the defendant is indigent, the state will provide an attorney. Indigence involves the present financial inability to hire counsel, but none of the right to counsel cases defines indigence precisely. In any case, judges generally are reluctant to refuse to appoint counsel because of the risk of reversal should the defendant be determined indigent. The state generally provides counsel in close cases of indigence, but it may then seek reimbursement from those convicted defendants who later become able to pay. [Fuller v. Oregon, 417 U.S. 40 (1974)]

4. Effective Assistance of Counsel

The Sixth Amendment right to counsel includes the right to effective counsel. The ineffective assistance claim is the most commonly raised constitutional claim. With this claim, the defendant seeks to secure not malpractice damages, but rather a reversal of his conviction and a new trial.

a. Effective Assistance Presumed

Effective assistance of counsel is *presumed* unless the adversarial process is so undermined

by counsel's conduct that the trial cannot be relied upon to have produced a just result. [Strickland v. Washington, 466 U.S. 668 (1984)]

b.   Right Extends to First Appeal
Effective assistance of counsel is also guaranteed on a first appeal as of right. [Evitts v. Lucey, 469 U.S. 387 (1985)]

c.   Circumstances Constituting Ineffective Assistance
An ineffective assistance claimant must show:

(i)   *Deficient performance* by counsel; and that

(ii)   But for such deficiency, the ***result of the proceeding would have been different*** (*e.g.,* defendant would not have been convicted or his sentence would have been shorter).

[Strickland v. Washington, *supra*] Typically, such a claim can be made out only by specifying particular errors of trial counsel, and cannot be based on mere inexperience, lack of time to prepare, gravity of the charges, complexity of defenses, or accessibility of witnesses to counsel. [United States v. Cronic, 466 U.S. 648 (1984)]

Examples: The Sixth Amendment right to counsel was violated when an attorney failed to timely file a motion to suppress evidence [Kimmelman v. Morrison, 477 U.S. 365 (1986)]; or failed to file a timely notice of appeal [Evitts v. Lucey, 469 U.S. 387 (1985)]. Sixth Amendment rights were also violated in a death penalty case when trial counsel failed to fully investigate the defendant's life history and had reason to believe that the investigation would turn up mitigating circumstances [Wiggins v. Smith, 539 U.S. 510 (2003)], and when defense counsel failed to look at the case file of defendant's prior crime that the prosecution had indicated would be central to proving aggravating circumstances justifying imposition of the death penalty, even when family members and the defendant himself have suggested that no mitigating evidence is available [Rompilla v. Beard, 545 U.S. 374 (2005)].

d.   Circumstances Not Constituting Ineffective Assistance
Circumstances not constituting ineffective assistance include:

1)   Trial Tactics
Courts will not grant relief for any acts or omissions by counsel that they view as trial tactics.

Examples: 1) It was not ineffective assistance in a capital murder trial to fail to obtain a client's affirmative consent to the strategy of going to trial and not challenging guilt (rather than pleading guilty) in hopes of having more credibility at sentencing. [Florida v. Nixon, 543 U.S. 175 (2005)]

2) It was not ineffective assistance when appointed counsel for an indigent defendant refused to argue nonfrivolous issues that the attorney had decided, in the exercise of her judgment, not to present. [Jones v. Barnes, 463 U.S. 745 (1983)]

3) It was not ineffective assistance when an attorney failed to present mitigating evidence or make a closing argument at a capital sentencing proceeding when counsel asserted that mitigating evidence had just been presented at trial, the defendant's mother and other character witnesses would not have been effective and might have revealed harmful information, and a closing argument would have allowed rebuttal by a very persuasive lead prosecutor. [Bell v. Cone, 535 U.S. 685 (2002)]

2) Failure to Raise Constitutional Claim that Is Later Invalidated
The failure of a defendant's counsel to raise a federal constitutional claim that was the law at the time of the proceeding but that was later overruled does not prejudice the defendant within the meaning of the Sixth Amendment and does not constitute ineffective assistance of counsel. [Lockhart v. Fretwell, 506 U.S. 364 (1993)]

5. Conflicts of Interest
Joint representation (*i.e.,* a single attorney representing co-defendants) is not per se invalid. However, if an attorney advises the trial court of a resulting conflict of interest at or before trial, and the court refuses to appoint separate counsel, the defendant is entitled to *automatic reversal*. [Holloway v. Arkansas, 435 U.S. 475 (1978); Cuyler v. Sullivan, 446 U.S. 335 (1980)] If the defendant does not object to joint representation in a timely manner, to obtain reversal the defendant must show that the attorney *actively* represented conflicting interests and thereby prejudiced the defendant. [Burger v. Kemp, 483 U.S. 776 (1987)]

a. Conflict with Attorney Is Rarely Ground for Relief
A defendant can rarely obtain relief by claiming a conflict of interest between himself and counsel. Conflicts between a defendant and his attorney are best analyzed as claims of ineffective assistance of counsel. To be successful, the defendant must demonstrate that the conflict with his attorney was so severe that the attorney could not effectively investigate or present the defendant's claims.

b. No Right to Joint Representation
While a defendant ordinarily has the right to counsel of her own choosing, a defendant has no right to be jointly represented with her co-defendants. Trial courts have the authority to limit joint representation to avoid potential and actual conflicts of interest. Even when all of the defendants waive any claim to conflicts of interest, the trial court can still prohibit the joint representation. [Wheat v. United States, 486 U.S. 153 (1988)]

6. Right to Support Services for Defense
Where a defendant has made a preliminary showing that he is likely to be able to use the insanity defense, the state must provide a psychiatrist for the preparation of the defense. Where a state presents evidence that the defendant is likely to be dangerous in the future, the defendant is entitled to psychiatric examination and testimony in the sentencing proceeding. [Ake v. Oklahoma, 470 U.S. 68 (1985)]

7. Seizure of Funds Constitutional
The right to counsel does not forbid the seizure—under the federal drug forfeiture statute [21 U.S.C. §853]—of drug money and property obtained with drug money, even when such

money and property were going to be used by the defendant to pay his attorney of choice. [Caplin & Drysdale, Chartered v. United States, 491 U.S. 617 (1989)]

8. Right Limited While Testifying

A defendant has a general right to consult with his attorney during the course of trial; however, he has no right to consult with his attorney while he is testifying. Whether a defendant has a right to consult with his attorney during breaks in his testimony depends on the character of the break. Generally, the longer the break, the more likely the Court will find the right. [*Compare* Geders v. United States, *supra*, IV.C.1.—defendant must be allowed to talk with attorney during overnight break in defendant's testimony because ordinary trial tactics can be, and usually are, discussed during such breaks—*with* Perry v. Leeke, 488 U.S. 272 (1989)—sequestration during 15-minute break between defendant's direct testimony and cross-examination permissible because cross-examination of uncounseled witness more likely to lead to truth]

D. RIGHT TO CONFRONT WITNESSES

The Sixth Amendment grants to the defendant in a criminal prosecution the right to confront adverse witnesses. This right, held applicable to the states in *Pointer v. Texas*, 380 U.S. 400 (1965), seeks to ensure that:

(i) The fact finder and the defendant ***observe the demeanor*** of the testifying witness; and

(ii) The defendant has the opportunity to ***cross-examine*** any witness testifying against him.

The defendant is entitled to a face-to-face encounter with the witness, but absence of face-to-face confrontation between the defendant and the accuser does not violate the Sixth Amendment when preventing such confrontation serves an important public purpose (such as insulating a child witness from trauma) and the reliability of the witness's testimony is otherwise assured. [Maryland v. Craig, 497 U.S. 836 (1990)]

1. Right Not Absolute

a. Disruptive Defendant

A defendant has no absolute right to confront witnesses, as a judge may remove a disruptive defendant. [Illinois v. Allen, 397 U.S. 337 (1970)]

b. Voluntarily Leaving Courtroom

A defendant has not been deprived of his right of confrontation if he voluntarily leaves the courtroom during the trial, and the trial continues in his absence. [Taylor v. United States, 414 U.S. 17 (1974)]

c. Government May Discourage Attendance

Government action that has an effect of discouraging a defendant's attendance at trial will not necessarily violate the right to attend and confront witnesses.

Example: Defendant attended his trial and testified in his own defense as the last witness. On summation, the prosecutor commented to the jury that they should consider that by choosing to testify last, defendant had an opportunity to listen to all of the other witnesses and adjust his testimony

accordingly. After he was convicted, defendant claimed that the prosecutor's summation was unconstitutional because it used defendant's constitutionally protected right to attend trial as a tool to impeach his credibility and so would have the effect of discouraging attendance. The Supreme Court held that the right to attend may be burdened and upheld the conviction. [Portuondo v. Agard, 529 U.S. 61 (2000)]

2. Introduction of Co-Defendant's Confession

A right of confrontation problem develops with the introduction of a co-defendant's confession because of the inability of the nonconfessing defendant to compel the confessing co-defendant to take the stand for cross-examination at their joint trial.

a. General Rule—Confession Implicating Co-Defendant Prohibited

If two persons are tried together and one has given a confession that implicates the other, the right of confrontation prohibits the use of that statement, even with instructions to the jury to consider it only as going to the guilt of the "confessing" defendant. [Bruton v. United States, 391 U.S. 123 (1968)] A co-defendant's confession is inadmissible even when it interlocks with the defendant's own confession, which is admitted. [Cruz v. New York, 481 U.S. 186 (1987)]

b. Exceptions

Such a statement may be admitted if:

1) All portions referring to the other defendant can be eliminated. *Note:* It is not sufficient merely to insert a blank or some other substitution for the name of the other defendant; the redaction must not indicate the defendant's involvement. [*Compare* Richardson v. Marsh, 481 U.S. 200 (1987)—after redaction, confession indicated that defendant and a third party (who was not a co-defendant) participated in the crime and contained no indication of co-defendant's involvement, *with* Gray v. Maryland, 523 U.S. 185 (1998)—redaction "me, deleted, deleted, and a few other guys killed" the victim held to clearly refer to co-defendant];

2) The confessing defendant takes the stand and subjects himself to cross-examination with respect to the truth or falsity of what the statement asserts. This rule applies even if he denies having ever made the confession. [Nelson v. O'Neil, 402 U.S. 622 (1973)] In effect, an opportunity at trial to cross-examine the hearsay declarant with respect to the underlying facts makes the declaration nonhearsay for purposes of the Confrontation Clause; or

3) The confession of the nontestifying co-defendant is being used to rebut the defendant's claim that his confession was obtained coercively. The jury must be instructed as to the purpose of the admission. [Tennessee v. Street, 471 U.S. 409 (1985)]

3. Prior Testimonial Statement of Unavailable Witness

Under the Confrontation Clause, prior testimonial evidence (*e.g.,* statements made at prior judicial proceedings) may *not* be admitted unless:

(i) The declarant is *unavailable*; and

(ii) The defendant had an ***opportunity to cross-examine*** the declarant at the time the statement was made.

[Crawford v. Washington, 541 U.S. 36 (2004)]

Example: Crawford and his wife, Sylvia, confronted Lee at his apartment after Lee allegedly attempted to rape Sylvia. A fight ensued and Crawford stabbed Lee. Crawford was charged with assault and attempted murder. At trial, Crawford testified that he thought that Lee had reached for something in his pocket before Crawford stabbed him and that the stabbing was in self-defense. To negate this claim, the prosecution introduced a recording of Sylvia's statement to the police indicating that Lee's hands may have been out and open while he was being stabbed. Under state law, Crawford has a privilege that prevents Sylvia from testifying at trial. Crawford objects to introduction of the recording. Although Sylvia's statement would be admissible under the hearsay exception for statements made against penal interest—because she led Crawford to Lee's apartment and facilitated the assault—it is inadmissible under the Confrontation Clause because there was no opportunity for cross-examination here (*i.e.*, Crawford was not present and able to examine Sylvia when the police were questioning her). [Crawford v. Washington, *supra*]

a. What Is "Testimonial"?

In *Crawford* the Supreme Court did not provide a comprehensive definition of the term "testimonial," raising many questions for both state and federal judges as to the reach of the Court's ruling. However, the Court held that, at a minimum, the term includes testimony from a preliminary hearing, grand jury hearing, former trial, or police interrogation.

1) Police Interrogation

Statements made in response to police interrogation are nontestimonial when made under circumstances indicating that the primary purpose of the interrogation is to enable the police to respond to an ongoing emergency, but statements are testimonial when there is no ongoing emergency and the primary purpose of the interrogation is to establish or prove past acts.

Example: A domestic battery victim called 911 to report that she was being beaten. The operator asked whether the victim knew the name of her assailant, and the victim provided defendant's name. Defendant was apprehended and charged. The victim did not appear at defendant's trial, but the prosecutor sought to introduce the 911 tape. Defendant objected, claiming a Confrontation Clause violation. The Supreme Court held that the response to the question about the assailant's name was nontestimonial because it was given to enable the police to respond to an ongoing emergency. [Davis v. Washington, 547 U.S. 813 (2006)]

Compare: In a companion case to *Davis*, the police had responded to a domestic battery complaint. When they arrived at defendant's home, his wife—the complainant—met them at the door and told them that everything was fine. She nevertheless invited the officers

into the home. While one officer kept defendant busy in the kitchen, the other officer questioned the wife and got her to fill out and sign a battery affidavit. Defendant was then arrested. The wife did not appear at defendant's trial but the prosecutor offered her affidavit of battery into evidence over defendant's Confrontation Clause objection. *Held:* The wife's statements were testimonial, as the affidavit was made as part of an investigation into past criminal conduct and no emergency was in progress when the police arrived. [Hammon v. Indiana, 547 U.S. 813 (2006)]

2) Results of Forensic Lab Testing

The results of forensic laboratory testing are testimonial in nature. Therefore, a lab report is not admissible into evidence at trial under the Confrontation Clause unless the technician who produced the test report is unavailable and the defendant had an opportunity to cross-examine him. [Melendez-Diaz v. Massachusetts, 129 S. Ct. 2527 (2009)—prohibiting introduction of lab report specifying that powder recovered from defendant was cocaine of a certain weight]

b. Forfeiture by Wrongdoing

A defendant can be held to have forfeited a Confrontation Clause claim by wrongdoing. However, the Court will not find a forfeiture by wrongdoing unless the wrongdoing was intended to keep the witness from testifying. [Giles v. California, 128 S. Ct. 2678 (2008)]

Example: Defendant shot Victim, his ex-girlfriend, six times, and she died as a result. At Defendant's murder trial, he claimed that Victim threatened him first and was coming toward him to mount an attack. To rebut this claim, the prosecution offered testimony that Victim had made in a complaint to the police three weeks before her death, alleging that Defendant beat her and choked her. Defendant objected to introduction of Victim's statements to the police, claiming that their admission would violate his confrontation rights. *Held:* Absent a finding that Defendant killed Victim with the intent to keep her from testifying, the forfeiture by wrongdoing exception to the Confrontation Clause's requirements does not apply and it would, therefore, be improper to admit Victim's statements into evidence. [Giles v. California, *supra*]

E. BURDEN OF PROOF AND SUFFICIENCY OF EVIDENCE

1. Burden of Proof

a. Proof Beyond a Reasonable Doubt

The Due Process Clause requires in all criminal cases that the state prove guilt beyond a reasonable doubt. [*In re* Winship, 397 U.S. 358 (1970)] The prosecution must have the burden of proving the elements of the crime charged. Thus, the Supreme Court has held that if "malice aforethought" is an element of murder, the state may not require the defendant to prove that he committed the homicide in the heat of passion, on the rationale that this would require the defendant to disprove the element of malice aforethought. [Mullaney v. Wilbur, 421 U.S. 684 (1975)] However, a state may impose the burden of proof upon the defendant in regard to an ***affirmative defense*** such as insanity [Leland v. Oregon, 343 U.S. 790 (1952)] or self-defense [Martin v. Ohio, 480 U.S. 228 (1987)].

Example: Under state law, in a prosecution for second degree murder, the state must prove intentional causing of death. A defendant is entitled to acquittal of second degree murder and conviction of manslaughter if he proves by a preponderance of the evidence that he acted under the influence of "an extreme emotional disturbance." May the burden of proving that be placed on the defendant? Yes, because it does not affect the state's obligation to prove all elements of the crime of second degree murder. [Patterson v. New York, 432 U.S. 197 (1977)]

b. **Presumption of Innocence**

Although not mentioned in the Constitution, the presumption of innocence is a basic component of a fair trial. A defendant does not have an absolute right to a jury instruction on the presumption of innocence, but the trial judge should evaluate the totality of the circumstances, including (i) the other jury instructions, (ii) the arguments of counsel, and (iii) whether the weight of the evidence was overwhelming, to determine whether such an instruction is necessary for a fair trial. [Kentucky v. Whorton, 441 U.S. 786 (1979)]

2. **Presumptions**

A permissive presumption allows, but does not require, the jury to infer an element of an offense from proof by the prosecutor of the basic fact, while the jury must accept a mandatory presumption even if it is the sole evidence of the elemental fact.

a. **Permissive Presumptions—Rational Relation Standard**

A permissive presumption must comport with the standard that there be a rational connection between the basic facts that the prosecution proved and the ultimate fact presumed, and that the latter is more likely than not to flow from the former. [Ulster County Court v. Allen, 442 U.S. 140 (1979)]

b. **Mandatory Presumptions Unconstitutional**

A mandatory presumption or a presumption that shifts the burden of proof to the defendant violates the Fourteenth Amendment's requirement that the state prove every element of a crime beyond a reasonable doubt. [Sandstrom v. Montana, 442 U.S. 510 (1979)]

Examples: 1) A mandatory presumption was created by jury instructions in a "malice murder" trial which stated that the "acts of a person of sound mind and discretion are presumed to be the product of a person's will, but the presumption may be rebutted," and a "person of sound mind and discretion is presumed to intend the natural and probable consequences of his acts, but the presumption may be rebutted." These instructions are unconstitutional because they would lead a reasonable juror to conclude that the state's burden of proof on intent to kill may be inferred from proof of the defendant's acts unless the defendant proves otherwise. [Francis v. Franklin, 471 U.S. 307 (1985)]

2) In a criminal contempt proceeding for failure to pay child support, the state may not presume that the defendant was able to pay the amount due. One of the elements of contempt is the ability to comply with the

court's order. Thus, the state may not presume ability to pay, but rather ability to pay must be proved beyond a reasonable doubt. [Hicks v. Feiock, 485 U.S. 624 (1988)]

3. Sufficiency of Evidence

The requirement of proof beyond a reasonable doubt in the Due Process Clause means that the sufficiency of the evidence supporting a criminal conviction in state court is, to some extent, a federal constitutional issue. Due process is violated if, viewing all the evidence in the light most favorable to the prosecution, no rational judge or jury would have found the defendant guilty of the crime of which he was convicted. [Jackson v. Virginia, 443 U.S. 307 (1979)]

a. Confessions Must Be Corroborated

A criminal conviction cannot rest entirely on an uncorroborated extrajudicial confession. If the defendant does not admit guilt in court, the prosecution must introduce extrinsic evidence that, at the least, tends to establish the trustworthiness of the admission. [Wong Sun v. United States, II.A.2.b.2), *supra;* Opper v. United States, 384 U.S. 84 (1954)]

4. Prior Act Evidence

Under the Due Process Clause, as a general constitutional rule, prior act evidence is admissible for various purposes if it is probative and relevant. Thus in a criminal trial evidence of prior bodily injury was admissible to show that a child victim had sustained repeated and/ or serious injuries by nonaccidental means (the "battered child syndrome") to infer that the victim's death was not accidental, even though there was no direct evidence linking the prior injuries to the defendant. [Estelle v. McGuire, 502 U.S. 62 (1991)]

5. Right to Present Defensive Evidence

Due process requires an opportunity to establish innocence.

Example: The arbitrary exclusion of a class of defense witnesses violates both due process and the right to compel the production of witnesses on one's own behalf.

a. Application—Barring Claim that Third Party Committed Crime

A state cannot impose a rule prohibiting a defendant from suggesting that a third party committed the crime whenever there is strong forensic evidence of the defendant's guilt. [Holmes v. South Carolina, 547 U.S. 319 (2006)] Proffered evidence can be excluded if it is shown to be flawed, but not merely because of the perceived strength of the prosecutor's case.

b. Application—Exclusionary Rules of Evidence

Even exclusionary rules of evidence that are valid on their face may combine to deprive a defendant of a fair opportunity to rebut the prosecution's case.

Examples: 1) Given the right to an acquittal if there is reasonable doubt on any element of a criminal charge, a defendant is denied a fair trial when the state's hearsay rule prevents him from showing that another person has confessed to the crime for which he is being tried, and where the state's rule against impeaching one's own witness prevents the defendant from even using the prior confession to cast doubt on the credibility of the confessor's unexpectedly damning testimony. [Chambers v. Mississippi, 410 U.S. 284 (1973)]

2) A state's per se rule excluding hypnotically refreshed testimony unconstitutionally infringes on a defendant's right to present testimony on his own behalf. A per se rule excludes even testimony that may be reliable. [Rock v. Arkansas, 479 U.S. 1079 (1987)]

c. Exclusion as Sanction
A trial court may, however, exclude defense evidence as a sanction for the defendant's violation of discovery rules or procedures. For example, if the defendant's attorney fails to give advance notice that a witness will testify, the trial court may prohibit that witness from testifying. [Taylor v. Illinois, 484 U.S. 400 (1988)]

VIII. GUILTY PLEAS AND PLEA BARGAINING

A. GUILTY PLEA WAIVES RIGHT TO JURY TRIAL
A guilty plea is a waiver of the Sixth Amendment right to jury trial. Between 70% and 95% of all criminal cases are settled by guilty pleas.

B. BASIC TRENDS

1. Intelligent Choice Among Alternatives
The Court from 1970 to the present has indicated an unwillingness to disturb a guilty plea it views as an intelligent choice among the defendant's alternatives on the advice of counsel.

2. Contract View
There is a trend toward the contract view of plea negotiation and bargaining. In this view, the plea agreement should be revealed in the record of the taking of the plea and its terms enforced against both the prosecutor and the defendant. [Ricketts v. Adamson, 483 U.S. 1 (1987)]

C. TAKING THE PLEA

1. Advising Defendant of the Charge, the Potential Penalty, and His Rights
The judge must determine that the plea is *voluntary and intelligent.* This must be done by addressing the defendant personally in open court *on the record.* [McCarthy v. United States, 394 U.S. 459 (1969); Boykin v. Alabama, 395 U.S. 238 (1969)] Specifically, the judge must be sure that the defendant knows and understands things like:

(i) *The nature of the charge* to which the plea is offered and the *crucial elements* of the crime charged [Henderson v. Morgan, 426 U.S. 637 (1976)—plea involuntary if defendant not informed that intent is an element of the murder charge against him];

(ii) The *maximum possible penalty* and any *mandatory minimum* (but the failure to explain special parole terms is not fatal [United States v. Timmreck, 441 U.S. 780 (1979)]); and

(iii) That he has a *right not to plead guilty* and that, if he does, he *waives the right to trial.*

a. Attorney May Inform Defendant
The judge need not personally explain the elements of each charge to the defendant on the record. Rather, the constitutional prerequisites of a valid plea may be satisfied where the

record accurately reflects that the nature of the charge and the elements of the crime were explained to the defendant by his own counsel. [Bradshaw v. Stumpf, 545 U.S. 175 (2005)]

b. Unfairly Informed Defendant Not Bound
If counsel makes unfair representations to the defendant concerning the result of the defendant's pleading guilty, and the defendant can prove this, the defendant is not bound by her record answer, obtained at the plea taking, that her counsel made no such representations. [Blackledge v. Allison, 431 U.S. 63 (1977)]

2. Remedy
The remedy for a failure to meet the standards for taking a plea is withdrawal of the plea and *pleading anew.*

3. Factual Basis for Plea Not Constitutionally Required
There is no general requirement that the record contain evidence of the defendant's guilt or other factual basis for the plea. (*But see* D.1., below.)

D. COLLATERAL ATTACKS ON GUILTY PLEAS AFTER SENTENCE
Those pleas that are seen as an intelligent choice among the defendant's alternatives are immune from collateral attack.

Examples: 1) A plea is not involuntary merely because it was induced by a fear of the death penalty, which could be imposed only after a jury trial. Fear of the death penalty is like fear of any other penalty, which is the reason defendants plead guilty. [Brady v. United States, 397 U.S. 742 (1970)]

2) Fear of a coerced confession in the hands of the state will not support a collateral attack, and the defendant will be bound to his choice to plead guilty. If the defendant thought the confession was coerced, he should have made a motion to suppress; if he did not, the court will think it was because he believed he could not win. [McMann v. Richardson, 397 U.S. 759 (1970)]

3) Unconstitutional, systematic, racial exclusion in the indicting grand jury will not entitle the defendant to collateral relief. Here also, the Court views the choice not to object and to plead guilty as the result of the defendant's informed decision as to what course would be in his best interest. [Tollett v. Henderson, 411 U.S. 258 (1973)]

1. Plea Offered by Defendant Who Denies Guilt
When a defendant pleads guilty despite protesting his innocence, the plea will be seen as an intelligent choice by the defendant, and withdrawal of the plea will not be permitted when there is other strong evidence of guilt in the record. Admission of guilt is not a constitutional requisite to imposition of criminal penalty. [North Carolina v. Alford, 400 U.S. 25 (1970)]

2. Bases for an Attack on a Guilty Plea After Sentence

a. Plea Involuntary
Failure to meet the constitutional standards for taking a guilty plea will support a post-sentence attack on the plea.

b. Lack of Jurisdiction
The defendant may withdraw his plea if the court lacked jurisdiction to take the plea,

or if prosecution for the offense for which the plea was offered is barred by double jeopardy. [Menna v. New York, 423 U.S. 61 (1975)]

c. Ineffective Assistance of Counsel

Ineffective assistance of counsel undercuts the assumption of an intelligent choice among the defendant's alternatives on the advice of counsel. Therefore, a defendant may successfully attack a guilty plea on the ground that he received ineffective assistance of counsel if, **but for counsel's errors, the defendant probably would not have pleaded guilty** and instead would have insisted on going to trial. [Hill v. Lockhart, 474 U.S. 52 (1985)]

d. Failure to Keep the Plea Bargain

See E.1., below.

E. PLEA BARGAINING

1. Enforcement of the Bargain

A defendant who enters into a plea bargain has a right to have that bargain kept. The plea bargain will be **enforced against the prosecutor and the defendant, but not against the judge**, who does not have to accept the plea.

a. Prosecution

If the prosecution does not keep the bargain, the court should decide whether the circumstances require specific performance of the plea agreement or whether the defendant should be granted an opportunity to withdraw her guilty plea. [Santobello v. New York, 404 U.S. 257 (1971)] However, if the prosecutor withdraws a proposed plea bargain and the accused subsequently pleads guilty on other terms, the original offer cannot be specifically enforced despite the accused's attempt to "accept" the offer. [Mabry v. Johnson, 467 U.S. 504 (1984)]

b. Defendant

If the defendant does not live up to the plea agreement, his plea and sentence can be vacated.

Example: D agrees to testify against a co-defendant in exchange for a reduction in charges from first to second degree murder. If D fails to testify, the prosecution can have D's plea and sentence vacated and reinstate the first degree murder charge. [Ricketts v. Adamson, B.2., *supra*]

2. Power of the State to Threaten More Serious Charge

Consistent with the contract theory of plea negotiation, the state has the power to drive a hard bargain. A guilty plea is not involuntary merely because it was entered in response to the prosecution's threat to charge the defendant with a more serious crime if she does not plead guilty. [Bordenkircher v. Hayes, 434 U.S. 357 (1978)]

3. Power to Charge More Serious Offense

The Supreme Court has held that there is no prosecutorial vindictiveness in charging a more serious offense when defendant demands a jury trial. [United States v. Goodwin, 457 U.S. 368 (1982)]

4. Admission of Statements Made in Connection with Plea Bargaining

Under the Federal Rules of Evidence and of Criminal Procedure, statements made by a

defendant in the course of unsuccessful plea negotiations are inadmissible at trial. However, such statements can be admitted *if* the defendant has knowingly and voluntarily waived the Federal Rules' exclusionary provisions. [United States v. Mezzanatto, 513 U.S. 196 (1995)]

5. No Right to Impeachment or Affirmative Defense Evidence
Defendants are *not* entitled either to impeachment evidence or to evidence relevant to affirmative defenses prior to entering a plea agreement. Failure to provide such evidence does not make a plea involuntary. [United States v. Ruiz, 536 U.S. 622 (2002)]

F. COLLATERAL EFFECTS OF GUILTY PLEAS

1. Conviction May Be Used in Other Proceedings
The Supreme Court has held that evidence of a defendant's conviction, based on a guilty plea in one state, may be introduced at trial in a second state for the purpose of proving a "specification" allowing imposition of the death penalty [Marshall v. Lonberger, 459 U.S. 422 (1983)], and a defendant is "convicted" within the meaning of the firearms disabilities provisions of the 1968 Gun Control Act when the defendant pleads guilty to a state charge punishable by more than one year, even if no formal judgment is entered and the record has been expunged. [Dickerson v. New Banner Institute, 460 U.S. 103 (1983)]

2. Does Not Admit Legality of Search
The Court has decided that a defendant's guilty plea neither admits the legality of the incriminating search nor waives Fourth Amendment claims in a subsequent civil damages action challenging the constitutionality of the incriminating search. [Haring v. Prosise, 462 U.S. 306 (1983)]

IX. CONSTITUTIONAL RIGHTS IN RELATION TO SENTENCING AND PUNISHMENT

A. PROCEDURAL RIGHTS IN SENTENCING

1. Right to Counsel
Sentencing is usually a "critical stage" of a criminal proceeding, thus requiring the assistance of counsel, as substantial rights of the defendant may be affected.
Examples: 1) The absence of counsel during sentencing after a plea of guilty, coupled with the judge's materially untrue assumptions concerning a defendant's criminal record, deprived the defendant of due process. [Townsend v. Burke, 334 U.S. 736 (1984)]

2) The absence of counsel at the time of sentencing where no sentence of imprisonment was imposed, but the defendant was put on probation, deprived the defendant of due process because certain legal rights (*i.e.,* the right to appeal) might be lost by failing to assert them at this time. [Mempa v. Rhay, *supra*, IV.C.1.]

2. Right to Confrontation and Cross-Examination
The *usual* sentence may be based on hearsay and uncross-examined reports. [Williams v. New York, 337 U.S. 241 (1949)]

a. **"New" Proceeding**

Where a magnified sentence is based on a statute (*e.g.,* one permitting indeterminate sentence) that requires new findings of fact to be made (*e.g.,* that defendant is a habitual criminal, mentally ill, or deficient, etc.), those facts must be found in a context that grants the right to confrontation and cross-examination. [Specht v. Patterson, 386 U.S. 605 (1966)]

b. **Capital Sentencing Procedures**

It is clear that a defendant in a death penalty case must have more opportunity for confrontation than need be given a defendant in other sentencing proceedings. [Gardner v. Florida, 430 U.S. 349 (1977)—sentence of death based in part upon report not disclosed to defendant invalid]

B. RESENTENCING AFTER SUCCESSFUL APPEAL AND RECONVICTION

1. **General Rule—Record Must Show Reasons for Harsher Sentence**

If a judge imposes a greater punishment than at the first trial after the defendant has successfully appealed and then is reconvicted, she must set forth in the record the reasons for the harsher sentence based on "objective information concerning identifiable conduct on the part of the defendant occurring after the time of the original sentencing proceedings." [North Carolina v. Pearce, 395 U.S. 711 (1969)] The purpose of this requirement is to ensure that the defendant is not vindictively penalized for exercising his right to appeal.

Note: When a defendant successfully appeals, an exception to the Double Jeopardy Clause permits retrial. (*See* XIII.B.3., *infra.*)

2. **Exceptions**

a. **Reconviction upon Trial De Novo**

Some jurisdictions grant the defendant the right to a trial de novo as a matter of course after a trial in an inferior court. A trial de novo involves a fresh determination of guilt or innocence without reference to the lower conviction or fact of appeal. The rationale of *Pearce* does not apply when the defendant receives a greater sentence upon a trial de novo, because the new judge reduces the likelihood of vindictiveness. [Colten v. Kentucky, 407 U.S. 104 (1972)]

b. **Jury Sentencing**

Pearce does not apply to states that use jury sentencing, unless the second jury was told of the first jury's sentence. [Chaffin v. Stynchcombe, 412 U.S. 17 (1973)]

3. **Recharging in a Trial De Novo**

The prosecutor may not obtain an indictment for a more serious charge in a trial de novo, because of the possibility of prosecutorial vindictiveness and retaliation for exercising the statutory right to a trial de novo. [Blackledge v. Perry, 417 U.S. 21 (1974)]

C. SUBSTANTIVE RIGHTS IN REGARD TO PUNISHMENT

1. **Criminal Penalties Constituting "Cruel and Unusual Punishment"**

The Eighth Amendment prohibition against cruel and unusual punishment places several limitations upon criminal punishments.

a. Punishment Grossly Disproportionate to Offense

A penalty that is grossly disproportionate to the seriousness of the offense committed is cruel and unusual.

Examples: 1) D, convicted of falsifying a public record, received a sentence of 20 years' imprisonment at hard labor. Did this violate the Eighth Amendment? Yes, because the penalty was so disproportionate to the offense. [Weems v. United States, 217 U.S. 349 (1910)]

2) A sentence of life imprisonment without the possibility of parole imposed upon a recidivist following conviction of his seventh nonviolent felony, the uttering of a bad check, is significantly disproportionate to the crime and is thus a violation of the Eighth Amendment. The unconstitutional taint is not eliminated by the possibility of commutation which, unlike parole, is granted on an ad hoc, standardless basis. [Solem v. Helm, 463 U.S. 277 (1983)]

Compare: 1) A mandatory life sentence for possession of a certain quantity of cocaine (650 grams—indicating that the defendant was a dealer) is ***not*** cruel and unusual, even though the statute did not allow consideration of mitigating factors (*compare* death penalty cases, below). [Harmelin v. Michigan, 501 U.S. 957 (1991)]

2) A California "three strikes" law requires imposition of an indeterminate life sentence after a person is found guilty of a felony if the person has previously been convicted of two or more serious or violent felonies. Defendant was convicted of stealing three golf clubs worth $399 each. Although the trial judge had discretion to treat the crime as either felony grand theft or a misdemeanor, she treated the theft as a felony and sentenced Defendant to 25 years to life because he had four previous serious felony convictions. *Held:* The sentence does not constitute cruel and unusual punishment. [Ewing v. California, 538 U.S. 11 (2003)]

b. Proportionality—No Right to Comparison of Penalties in Similar Cases

The Eighth Amendment does not require state appellate courts to compare the death sentence imposed in a case under appeal with other penalties imposed in similar cases. [Pulley v. Harris, 465 U.S. 37 (1984)]

c. Death Penalty

1) For Murder

The death penalty is not inherently cruel and unusual punishment, but the Eighth Amendment requires that it be imposed only under a ***statutory scheme*** that gives the judge or jury reasonable ***discretion,*** full ***information*** concerning defendants, and ***guidance*** in making the decision. [Furman v. Georgia, 408 U.S. 238 (1972); Gregg v. Georgia, 428 U.S. 153 (1976)]

a) Discretion

A jury must be allowed discretion to consider mitigating circumstances in death penalty cases. Thus, a statute cannot make the death penalty mandatory upon conviction of first degree murder [Woodson v. North Carolina, 428

U.S. 280 (1976)], or for the killing of a police officer or firefighter [Roberts v. Louisiana, 431 U.S. 633 (1977)], or for a killing by an inmate who is serving a life sentence [Sumner v. Shuman, 483 U.S. 66 (1987)]. Moreover, it is not sufficient to allow the jury to consider only some mitigating circumstances; they must be allowed to consider any aspect of the defendant's character or any circumstance of his crime as a factor in mitigation. [Penry v. Lynaugh, 492 U.S. 302 (1989)—death sentence reversed because jury was not allowed to consider defendant's mental retardation and abused childhood in mitigation] In addition, a death sentence must be reversed if the jurors may have been confused by jury instructions regarding their right to consider mitigating circumstances. [Mills v. Maryland, 486 U.S. 367 (1988)]

Examples: 1) A statute requires the jury to impose the death penalty if a defendant is convicted of specific crimes with aggravation, but also requires the trial judge to hear evidence of aggravating and mitigating circumstances before sentencing the defendant. The statute is constitutional. [Baldwin v. Alabama, 472 U.S. 372 (1985)]

2) A statute that instructs jurors to impose the death penalty if they find it probable that the defendant would commit criminal acts in the future, considering all aggravating or mitigating evidence presented at trial, was upheld against an argument that the instruction foreclosed consideration of the defendant's youth. The court found that consideration of future dangerousness leaves open ample room for considering youth as a mitigating factor because "the signature qualities of youth are transient." [Johnson v. Texas, 509 U.S. 350 (1993)]

(1) Evidence Required for Mitigation Instruction
Nothing in the Constitution requires state courts to give mitigating circumstance instructions where the jury has heard no evidence on mitigating circumstances. [Delo v. Lashley, 507 U.S. 272 (1993)]

b) Information

(1) Instructions on Lesser Included Offenses
A defendant is not entitled to a jury instruction on every possible lesser included offense supported by the facts in a capital case [Schad v. Arizona, 501 U.S. 624 (1991)], but a statute cannot prohibit instructions on *all* lesser included offenses [Beck v. Alabama, 447 U.S. 625 (1980)]. *Rationale:* If the jurors are not instructed on any lesser included offense and believe that the defendant is guilty of a crime other than murder, they might impose the death penalty rather than let the defendant go unpunished. But if the jury is given instructions on a lesser included offense (*e.g.*, second degree murder), they will not have to make an all or nothing choice, and so a resulting death penalty will stand.

(2) Victim Impact Statements
A "victim impact statement" (*i.e.*, an assessment of how the crime

affected the victim's family) may be considered during the sentencing phase of a capital case. *Rationale:* The defendant has long been allowed to present mitigating factors, so the jury must be allowed to counterbalance the impact on the victim's family in order to "assess meaningfully the defendant's moral culpability and blameworthiness." [Payne v. Tennessee, 501 U.S. 808 (1991)]

c) **Guidance**

A statute providing for the death penalty may not be vague.

Example: A statute that permits imposition of the death penalty when a murder is "outrageously or wantonly vile, horrible, or inhuman in that it involved torture, depravity of mind, or an aggravated battery to the victim" is unconstitutionally vague. [Godfrey v. Georgia, 446 U.S. 420 (1980); Maynard v. Cartwright, 486 U.S. 356 (1988)]

Compare: A statute that imposes the death penalty where the murderer displayed "utter disregard for human life" provides sufficiently clear and objective standards for imposition of the death penalty where the state supreme court had construed the statute to apply only where the killing was committed by a "cold-blooded, pitiless slayer." [Arave v. Creech, 507 U.S. 463 (1993)]

d) **Prior Crimes**

Most states provide that prior crimes by the defendant, particularly those involving force or violence, are aggravating factors that either make the defendant eligible for the death penalty or are weighed by the jurors in reaching their decision on whether to impose the death penalty. If a death sentence is based in any part on a defendant's prior conviction, the sentence must be reversed if the prior conviction is invalidated. [Johnson v. Mississippi, 486 U.S. 578 (1988)]

e) **Standard of Review**

Where a death sentence has been affected by a vague or otherwise unconstitutional factor, the death sentence can still be upheld, but only if all aggravating and mitigating factors involved are reweighed by all of the judges to whom the sentence is appealed and death is still found to be appropriate. [Richmond v. Lewis, 506 U.S. 40 (1993)]

2) **For Rape**

The Eighth Amendment prohibits imposition of the death penalty for the crime of raping an adult woman, because the penalty is disproportionate to the offense. [Coker v. Georgia, 433 U.S. 584 (1977)] Nor may a death sentence be imposed for the rape of a child that was neither intended to result in, nor did result in, death. [Kennedy v. Louisiana, 128 S. Ct. 2641 (2008)]

3) **For Felony Murder**

The death penalty may not be imposed for felony murder where the defendant, as

an accomplice, "did not take or attempt or intend to take life, or intend that lethal force be employed." [Enmund v. Florida, 458 U.S. 782 (1982)] However, the death penalty may be imposed on a felony murderer who neither killed nor intended to kill where he participated in a major way in a felony that resulted in murder, and acted with **reckless indifference to the value of human life**. [Tison v. Arizona, 481 U.S. 137 (1987)—defendants helped prisoner escape and provided him with weapons]

4) Jury Responsibility for Verdict

It is unconstitutional to diminish the jury's sense of responsibility for its role in determining a death sentence. [Caldwell v. Mississippi, 472 U.S. 320 (1985)—prosecutor's comment to the jury that its verdict is reviewable and that the verdict is not the final decision is sufficient to diminish the jury's sense of responsibility; Ring v. Arizona, VII.B.6., *supra*—unconstitutional for judge to determine after jury verdict of guilt whether aggravating factors justify imposition of the death penalty]

a) Compare—Instruction Regarding Failure to Agree

Even at the defendant's request, the court need not instruct the jury of the consequences of its failure to agree on a verdict. [Jones v. United States, 527 U.S. 373 (1999)—Eighth Amendment was not violated where court denied defendant's request that jury be instructed that judge would impose sentence if jury could not unanimously agree]

5) Racial Discrimination

Statistical evidence that black defendants who kill white victims are more likely to receive the death penalty does not establish that the penalty was imposed as a result of unconstitutional discrimination. [McCleskey v. Kemp, 481 U.S. 279 (1987)]

6) Sanity Requirement

The Eighth Amendment prohibits states from inflicting the death penalty upon a prisoner who is insane (*i.e.*, one who was sane at the time the crime was committed and was properly sentenced to death, but is insane at the time of execution). [Ford v. Wainwright, 477 U.S. 399 (1986)]

7) Mental Retardation

It is cruel and unusual punishment to impose the death penalty on a person who is mentally retarded. [Atkins v. Virginia, 536 U.S. 304 (2002)] The state determines, under its own standards, whether an individual is mentally retarded.

8) For Minors

Execution of persons who were under 18 years old at the time they committed their offense (including murder) violates the Eighth Amendment. [Roper v. Simmons, 543 U.S. 551 (2005)]

9) Lethal Injection

The mere possibility that the three-drug lethal injection protocol used by many states to carry out executions **might** be administered improperly and thus cause the condemned unnecessary pain does not make the procedure cruel and unusual punishment. It would be cruel and unusual only if the condemned can prove that there is a serious risk of inflicting unnecessary pain or that an alternative procedure is feasible, may be readily implemented, and in fact significantly reduces substantial risk of severe pain. [Baze v. Rees, 553 U.S. 35 (2008)]

d. "Status" Crimes

A statute that makes it a crime to have a given "status" violates the Eighth Amendment because it punishes a mere propensity to engage in dangerous behavior. But it is no violation of the amendment to make specific activity related to a certain status criminal.

Example: A statute makes it criminal to "be a common drunkard" and to appear in public in an intoxicated condition. May a chronic alcoholic be convicted of both of these? No. He may not be convicted of being a common drunkard, because this is a prohibited status crime. But he may be convicted of appearing in public while intoxicated, because this crime prohibits the act of "appearing." [Powell v. Texas, 392 U.S. 514 (1968)]

2. Recidivist Statutes

A mandatory life sentence imposed pursuant to a recidivist statute does ***not*** constitute cruel and unusual punishment, even though the three felonies that formed the predicate for the sentence were nonviolent, property-related offenses. [Rummel v. Estelle, 445 U.S. 263 (1980)] (There is an apparent conflict with *Solem v. Helm, supra,* C.1.a. While *Solem* is inconsistent with *Rummel,* the Supreme Court declined to distinguish *Rummel* in reaching its holding in *Solem.*)

3. Punishing the Exercise of Constitutional Rights

A punishment of greater length or severity cannot constitutionally be reserved by statute for those who assert their right to plead innocent and to demand trial by jury. [United States v. Jackson, 390 U.S. 570 (1968)—death penalty available only for federal kidnapping defendants who insist on jury trial; penalty of death in such circumstances cannot be carried out, but guilty pleas induced by such a scheme are not automatically involuntary]

4. Consideration of Defendant's Perjury at Trial

In determining sentence, a trial judge may take into account a belief that the defendant, while testifying at trial on his own behalf, committed perjury. This is important in evaluating the defendant's prospects for rehabilitation and does not impose an improper burden upon a defendant's right to testify. [United States v. Grayson, 438 U.S. 41 (1978)]

5. Imprisonment of Indigents for Nonpayment of Fines Violates Equal Protection Clause

Where the aggregate imprisonment exceeds the maximum period fixed by statute and results directly from an involuntary nonpayment of a fine or court costs, there is an impermissible discrimination and a violation of the Equal Protection Clause. [Williams v. Illinois, 399 U.S. 235 (1970)] It is also a violation of equal protection to limit punishment to payment of a fine for those who are able to pay it, but to convert the fine to imprisonment for those who are unable to pay it. [Tate v. Short, 401 U.S. 395 (1971)—30 days or $30]

a. Imprisonment of Parolee for Nonpayment of Fine

A trial court may not revoke a defendant's probation and imprison him for the remainder of the probation term for failure to pay a fine and make restitution without showing that

the defendant actually was capable of payment or that there were no alternative forms of punishment available to meet the state's interest in punishment and deterrence. [Bearden v. Georgia, 461 U.S. 660 (1983)]

X. CONSTITUTIONAL PROBLEMS ON APPEAL

A. NO RIGHT TO APPEAL

There is apparently no federal constitutional right to an appeal. Several Supreme Court opinions suggest that all appeals could constitutionally be abolished.

B. EQUAL PROTECTION AND RIGHT TO COUNSEL ON APPEAL

1. First Appeal

If an avenue of post-conviction review (appellate or collateral) is provided, conditions that make the review less accessible to the poor than to the rich violate equal protection. [Griffin v. Illinois, 351 U.S. 12 (1956)—indigent entitled to free transcript on appeal]

Examples: 1) The Equal Protection Clause was violated where a statute requiring the payment of fees for a transcript of a preliminary hearing was applied to deny a free transcript to an indigent. [Roberts v. LaValle, 389 U.S. 40 (1968)]

2) Requiring reimbursement for costs of a trial transcription only of those incarcerated (not from those fined, given suspended sentence, or placed on probation) violates equal protection. [Rinaldi v. Yaeger, 384 U.S. 305 (1966)] But a state can distinguish between convicted and acquitted defendants in this context and require reimbursement only from those convicted. [Fuller v. Oregon, 417 U.S. 40 (1974)]

3) Illinois rule providing for trial transcript on appeal only in felony cases is an unreasonable distinction in violation of equal protection. Even in misdemeanor cases punishable by fine only, a defendant must be afforded as effective an appeal as a defendant who can pay, and where the grounds of the appeal make out a colorable need for a complete transcript, the burden is on the state to show that something less will suffice. [Mayer v. City of Chicago, 404 U.S. 189 (1971)]

a. Right to Appointed Counsel

Indigents must be given counsel at state expense during a first appeal granted to all as a matter of right. [Douglas v. California, *supra*, IV.C.1.] This rule also extends to appeals by defendants who plead guilty or nolo contendere and who must (under state law) seek leave of the court before bringing an appeal. [Halbert v. Michigan, IV.C.1., *supra*] *Rationale:* Although such appeals are discretionary, they present the first (and likely only) chance for review on the merits that such defendants have. Mere failure to request appointment of counsel does not constitute waiver of the right to assistance of counsel on appeal.

b. Attorney May Withdraw If Appeal Frivolous

An appellate court can permit withdrawal of counsel who concludes that appeal would

be frivolous. However, before doing so, the state must take steps to *ensure that the defendant's right to counsel is not being denied.*

Examples: 1) It is sufficient to (i) require counsel to file a brief referring to anything in the record that might arguably support an appeal (an *Anders* brief) and (ii) require the appellate court to determine that counsel has correctly concluded that appeal is frivolous. [Anders v. California, 386 U.S. 738 (1967)—striking California procedure that allowed counsel to withdraw upon filing a conclusory letter that simply stated the appeal had no merit]

2) It is sufficient to require counsel to (i) summarize the procedural and factual history of the case but (ii) remain silent on the merits of the case unless the appellate court directs otherwise. [Smith v. Robbins, 528 U.S. 259 (2000)—reasoning that this procedure ensures that a "trained legal eye" will search the record and provide some assistance to the reviewing court]

2. Discretionary Appeals

In a jurisdiction using a two-tier system of appellate courts with discretionary review by the highest court, an indigent defendant need not be provided with counsel during the second, discretionary appeal. Representation also need not be provided for an indigent seeking to invoke the United States Supreme Court's discretionary authority to review criminal convictions. [Ross v. Moffit, 417 U.S. 600 (1974)]

C. NO RIGHT TO SELF-REPRESENTATION

On appeal, a defendant has no right to represent himself. [Martinez v. Court of Appeal, 528 U.S. 152 (2000)]

D. RETROACTIVITY

If the Court announces a new rule of criminal procedure (*i.e.*, one not dictated by precedent) in a case on direct review, the rule must be applied to *all other cases on direct review*. [Griffith v. Kentucky, 479 U.S. 314 (1987)] *Rationale:* It would be unfair to allow the one defendant whose case the Supreme Court happened to choose to hear to benefit from the new rule, while denying the benefit to other similarly situated defendants simply because they were not lucky enough to have their case chosen.

XI. COLLATERAL ATTACK UPON CONVICTIONS

A. AVAILABILITY OF COLLATERAL ATTACK

After appeal is no longer available or has proven unsuccessful, defendants may generally still attack their convictions collaterally, usually by beginning a new and separate civil proceeding involving an application for a writ of habeas corpus. This proceeding focuses on the lawfulness of a detention, naming the person having custody as the respondent.

B. HABEAS CORPUS PROCEEDING

1. No Right to Appointed Counsel

An indigent does not have the right to appointed counsel to perfect her petition for a writ of habeas corpus.

2. Burden of Proof

Because the proceeding for a writ of habeas corpus is civil in nature, the petitioner has the burden of proof by a ***preponderance of the evidence*** to show an unlawful detention.

3. State May Appeal

The state may appeal the granting of a writ of habeas corpus, and double jeopardy bars neither the appeal nor retrial after the granting of the writ.

4. Requirement of Custody

The state defendant must be "in custody," but it is sufficient if he is out on bail, probation, or parole. [Hensley v. Municipal Court, 411 U.S. 345 (1973)] Generally, the "in custody" requirement is ***not*** met by a petitioner whose sentence has expired, even if his prior conviction is used to enhance a later one [Maleng v. Cook, 490 U.S. 488 (1989)], but a petitioner who remains in jail on a ***consecutive sentence*** is in custody, even if the jail time for the crime being challenged has expired [Garlotte v. Fordice, 515 U.S. 39 (1995)].

XII. RIGHTS DURING PUNISHMENT—PROBATION, IMPRISONMENT, PAROLE

A. RIGHT TO COUNSEL AT PAROLE AND PROBATION REVOCATIONS

1. Probation Revocation Involving Resentencing

If revocation of probation also involves the imposition of a new sentence, the defendant is entitled to representation by counsel in all cases in which she is entitled to counsel at trial. [Mempa v. Rhay, *supra*, IX.A.1.]

2. Other Situations

If, after probation revocation, an already imposed sentence of imprisonment springs into application, ***or*** the case involves parole revocation, the right to counsel is much more limited.

There is a right to be represented by counsel only if, on the facts of the case, such representation is ***necessary to a fair hearing***. Generally, it will be necessary if the defendant denies commission of the acts alleged or asserts an argument as to why revocation should not occur that is "complex or otherwise difficult to develop or present." In addition, each defendant must be told of her right to request appointment of counsel, and if a request is refused, the record must contain a succinct statement of the basis for the refusal. [Gagnon v. Scarpelli, 411 U.S. 778 (1973)]

B. PRISONERS' RIGHTS

1. Due Process Rights

Prison regulations and operations may create liberty interests protected by the Due Process Clause, but due process is violated only where the regulations and operations ***impose "atypical and significant hardship"*** in relation to the ordinary incidents of prison life. [Sandin v. Conner, 515 U.S. 472 (1995)]

Example: Assignment for an indefinite period to a "supermax" prison (*i.e.,* a maximum

security prison with highly restrictive conditions, designed to segregate the most dangerous prisoners from the general prison population), in which prisoners rarely have visitors, are deprived of almost any environmental or human contact, and from which there is no eligibility for parole, *is* "atypical and extreme hardship." [Wilkinson v. Austin, 545 U.S. 209 (2005)]

Compare: Disciplinary segregation for 30 days does not implicate a liberty interest that triggers due process protections. [Sandin v. Conner, *supra*]

2. **No Fourth Amendment Protections in Search of Cells**
    Prisoners have no reasonable expectation of privacy in their cells, or in personal property in their cells, and hence no Fourth Amendment protection therein. [Hudson v. Palmer, 468 U.S. 517 (1984)] Additionally, prisoners have no right to be present when prison officials search their cells. [Block v. Rutherford, 468 U.S. 576 (1984)]

3. **Right of Access to Courts**
    Prison inmates must have reasonable access to courts, and no unreasonable limitations may be put upon their ability to develop and present arguments. Inmates may not be prevented from consulting with other inmates, unless a reasonable substitute (such as a law library) is provided. [Bounds v. Smith, 430 U.S. 817 (1977); Johnson v. Avery, 393 U.S. 483 (1969)] No absolute bar against law students and other paraprofessionals interviewing inmates for lawyers may be imposed. [Procunier v. Martinez, 416 U.S. 396 (1974)]

    Note: A prisoner's *Bounds* claim of inadequate prison legal resources must include a showing that the alleged deficiencies in the legal resources have resulted in a hindrance of access to court. [Lewis v. Casey, 518 U.S. 343 (1996)]

4. **First Amendment Rights**
    Prison officials need some discretion to limit prisoners' First Amendment activities (*e.g.,* speech and assembly) in order to run a safe and secure prison. Therefore, generally prison regulations *reasonably related to penological interests* will be upheld even though they burden First Amendment rights. [Turner v. Safley, 482 U.S. 78 (1987)] For example, prison officials have broad discretion to regulate incoming mail to prevent contraband and even sexually explicit materials from entering the prison. Officials may even open letters from a prisoner's attorney, as long as they do so in the prisoner's presence and the letters are not read. [*See* Thornburgh v. Abbott, 490 U.S. 401 (1989); Wolff v. McDonnell, 418 U.S. 539 (1974)] However, prison officials have less discretion to regulate outgoing mail, because it usually does not have an effect on prison safety. [Procunier v. Martinez, *supra*]

    Example: Pennsylvania housed its most dangerous and recalcitrant inmates in a special unit in which inmates start at level 2 but can graduate to level 1 with good behavior. Level 2 prisoners are very restricted and are prohibited from receiving any newspapers, magazines, or photographs. A prisoner sued, claiming that these prohibitions deprived him of his First Amendment rights. The prison justified the ban as a tool to encourage better behavior and argued that it was limited in the privileges that it could take away, because these prisoners had already lost most of their privileges. Under these conditions, the prohibition serves a legitimate penological interest and is reasonably related to that interest. [Beard v. Banks, 548 U.S. 521 (2006)]

Note: As a matter of federal **statutory** law (the Religious Land Use and Institutionalized Persons Act of 2000), no state that accepts federal funding for its prisons (and all states do) may place a burden on the **religious exercise** of prisoners unless the burden furthers a **compelling government interest** (*e.g.*, a restriction that is necessary to ensure safety or discipline) and does so by the least restrictive means. [Cutter v. Wilkinson, 544 U.S. 709 (2005)] However, this standard should **not be applied on the MBE**, as that exam focuses on Constitutional Criminal Procedure (*i.e.*, the constitutional standard) rather than on federal statutory standards.

5. **Right to Adequate Medical Care**
"Deliberate indifference to serious medical needs of prisoners" constitutes cruel and unusual punishment in violation of the Eighth Amendment. However, simple negligent failure to provide care—"medical malpractice"—does not violate the amendment. [Estelle v. Gamble, 429 U.S. 97 (1976)] And while prisoners have a liberty interest in refusing medication, they can be forced to take antipsychotic drugs if an unbiased and qualified decisionmaker finds it necessary to protect the prisoner or others. [Washington v. Harper, 494 U.S. 210 (1990)]

C. **NO RIGHT TO BE FREE FROM DISABILITIES UPON COMPLETION OF SENTENCE**
There is no right to be free from state disenfranchisement upon conviction of a felony, even if this continues after completion of the sentence imposed. [Richardson v. Ramirez, 418 U.S. 24 (1974)]

XIII. DOUBLE JEOPARDY

A. **WHEN JEOPARDY ATTACHES**
The Fifth Amendment right to be free of double jeopardy for the same offense has been incorporated into the Fourteenth Amendment. [Benton v. Maryland, 395 U.S. 784 (1969)] The general rule is that once jeopardy attaches, the defendant may not be retried for the same offense.

1. **Jury Trials**
Jeopardy attaches in a jury trial at the **empaneling and swearing** of the jury. [Crist v. Bretz, 437 U.S. 28 (1978)]

2. **Bench Trials**
In bench trials, jeopardy attaches when the **first witness is sworn**.

3. **Juvenile Proceedings**
The **commencement** of an adjudicatory juvenile proceeding (*i.e.*, a hearing at which the court begins to hear evidence regarding the charged act) bars a subsequent criminal trial for the same offense. [Breed v. Jones, 421 U.S. 519 (1975)]

4. **Not in Civil Proceedings**
Jeopardy generally does not attach in civil proceedings other than juvenile proceedings. [One Lot Emerald Cut Stones & One Ring v. United States, 409 U.S. 232 (1972)]
Example: After the defendant is acquitted of criminal charges of smuggling, the government may still seek forfeiture of the items that the defendant allegedly smuggled into the country. [One Lot Emerald Cut Stones & One Ring v. United States, *supra*]

B. EXCEPTIONS PERMITTING RETRIAL
Certain exceptions permit retrial of a defendant even if jeopardy has attached.

1. Hung Jury
The state may retry a defendant whose first trial ends in a hung jury.

2. Mistrial for Manifest Necessity
A trial may be discontinued and the defendant reprosecuted for the same offense when there is a manifest necessity to abort the original trial [United States v. Perez, 22 U.S. 579 (1824); Illinois v. Somerville, 410 U.S. 458 (1973)] or when the termination occurs at the behest of the defendant on any grounds not constituting an acquittal on the merits [United States v. Scott, 437 U.S. 82 (1978)]. Thus, double jeopardy is not an absolute bar to two trials.

3. Retrial After Successful Appeal
The state may retry a defendant who has successfully appealed a conviction, unless the ground for the reversal was insufficient evidence to support the guilty verdict. [Burks v. United States, 437 U.S. 1 (1978)] On the other hand, retrial is permitted when reversal is based on the *weight*, rather than *sufficiency*, of the evidence [Tibbs v. Florida, 457 U.S. 31 (1982)], or where a case is reversed because of erroneously admitted evidence [Lockhart v. Nelson, 488 U.S. 33 (1988)].

Example: If, after weighing the evidence in the record, an appellate court reversed a conviction on appeal, holding that the record did not support a finding of guilt beyond a reasonable doubt, a retrial would be permitted. However, if the appellate court reversed, holding that even if all of the evidence is taken as true, it was not sufficient to prove all of the elements of the crime charged, a retrial would not be permitted.

a. Charges on Retrial
The Double Jeopardy Clause prohibits retrying a defendant whose conviction has been reversed on appeal for any offense more serious than that for which she was convicted at the first trial. This right is violated by *retrial for the more serious offense*, even if at the second trial the defendant is convicted only of an offense no more than that for which she was convicted at the first trial. [Price v. Georgia, 398 U.S. 323 (1970)]

Example: X is charged with murder. She is convicted of manslaughter and her conviction is reversed on appeal. She is again tried for murder and again convicted of manslaughter. May this conviction stand? No, because she could not be retried for anything more serious than manslaughter. This is not harmless error, because the charge of murder in the second trial may have influenced the jury toward conviction of manslaughter.

b. Sentencing on Retrial
The Double Jeopardy Clause generally does *not* prohibit imposition of a *harsher sentence* on conviction after retrial, and such a sentence is valid provided it does not run afoul of the vindictiveness concerns discussed at IX.B.1., *supra*.

1) Death Penalty Cases
When there is a formalized, separate process for imposing the death penalty (*e.g.*, when guilt is first determined and then the jury is presented with evidence on whether to impose death), if at the first trial the jury finds that a death sentence is

not appropriate, a death sentence cannot be imposed at a second trial. [Bullington v. Missouri, 451 U.S. 430 (1981)] However, if the jury makes no such finding (*e.g.*, when a judge imposes a life sentence pursuant to a statute providing for such a sentence when the jury is deadlocked on sentencing), a death sentence can be imposed at a second trial. [Sattazahn v. Pennsylvania, 537 U.S. 101 (2003)—"the relevant inquiry . . . is not whether the defendant received a life sentence the first time around, but whether a first life sentence was an 'acquittal' based on findings sufficient to establish legal entitlement to the life sentence—*i.e.,* findings that the government failed to prove one or more aggravating circumstances beyond a reasonable doubt"] In any case, note that these special rules apply only to capital sentencing proceedings. [Monge v. California, 524 U.S. 721 (1998)]

4. Breach of Plea Bargaining

When a defendant breaches a plea bargain agreement, his plea and sentence can be vacated and the original charges can be reinstated. [Ricketts v. Adamson, VIII.E.1.b., *supra*]

C. SAME OFFENSE

1. General Rule—When Two Crimes Do Not Constitute Same Offense

Two crimes do not constitute the same offense if *each crime requires proof of an additional element* that the other crime does not require, even though some of the same facts may be necessary to prove both crimes. [Blockburger v. United States, 284 U.S. 299 (1932)]

Example: D is arrested after the car he is driving strikes and kills a pedestrian. D is tried on the charges of reckless homicide and driving while intoxicated. D can receive separate punishments for both of the offenses because each crime requires proof of an additional element not required by the other: the homicide charge requires proof of a death but not proof of intoxication, while the driving while intoxicated charge requires proof of intoxication but not proof of a death.

a. Application of *Blockburger*

Under *Blockburger*, the following do *not* constitute the same offenses:

1) Manslaughter with an automobile and hit-and-run;

2) Reckless driving and drunk driving;

3) Reckless driving and failure to yield the right of way; and

4) Uttering a forged check and obtaining money by false pretenses by using the forged check.

2. Cumulative Punishments for Offenses Constituting Same Crime

Imposition of cumulative punishments for two or more statutorily defined offenses, *specifically intended by the legislature to carry separate punishments*, even though constituting the "same" crime under the *Blockburger* test, *supra*, does not violate the prohibition of multiple punishments for the same offense of the Double Jeopardy Clause, when the punishments are *imposed at a single trial*. [Missouri v. Hunter, 459 U.S. 359 (1983)]

Example: D robs a store at gunpoint. D can be sentenced to cumulative punishments for both the robbery and for violating a "Use a gun, go to jail" statute.

Note: Absent a clear intention, it will be presumed that multiple punishments are not intended for offenses constituting the same crime under *Blockburger.* Also, imposition of multiple punishments is prohibited even if the sentences for the two crimes run concurrently. [Rutledge v. United States, 517 U.S. 292 (1996)]

3. **Lesser Included Offenses**

   a. **Retrial for Lesser Included Offense Barred**
      Attachment of jeopardy for the greater offense bars retrial for lesser included offenses. [Harris v. Oklahoma, 433 U.S. 682 (1977)]
      Example: D is convicted of felony murder based on proof that he and an accomplice shot and killed a store clerk during an armed robbery. D cannot then be tried for the armed robbery because it is a lesser included offense of the felony murder. [Harris v. Oklahoma, *supra*]

   b. **Retrial for Greater Offense**
      Attachment of jeopardy for a lesser included offense bars retrial for the greater offense [Brown v. Ohio, 432 U.S. 161 (1977)], except that retrial for murder is permitted if the victim dies after attachment of jeopardy for battery [Diaz v. United States, 223 U.S. 442 (1912)]. However, a state may continue to prosecute a charged offense, despite the defendant's guilty plea to lesser included or "allied" offenses stemming from the same incident. [Ohio v. Johnson, 467 U.S. 493 (1984)—defendant charged with murder and manslaughter, and robbery and theft, arising from the same incident, can be prosecuted for murder and robbery after pleading guilty to manslaughter and theft over state's objection]

      1) **Exception—New Evidence**
         An exception to the double jeopardy bar exists if unlawful conduct that is subsequently used to prove the greater offense (i) has not occurred at the time of the prosecution for the lesser offense, or (ii) has not been discovered despite due diligence. [Garrett v. United States, 471 U.S. 773 (1985)]

4. **Conspiracy and Substantive Offense**
   A prosecution for *conspiracy* is not barred merely because some of the alleged *overt acts* of that conspiracy have already been prosecuted. [United States v. Felix, 503 U.S. 378 (1992)]

5. **Prior Act Evidence**
   The introduction of evidence of a substantive offense as prior act evidence is not equivalent to *prosecution* for that substantive offense, and therefore subsequent prosecution for that conduct is not barred. [United States v. Felix, *supra*]

6. **Conduct Used as a Sentence Enhancer**
   The Double Jeopardy Clause is not violated when a person is indicted for a crime the conduct of which was already used to enhance the defendant's sentence for another crime. [Witte v. United States, 515 U.S. 389 (1995)—defendant indicted for conspiring to import cocaine after the conduct of the conspiracy was used to enhance his earlier sentence when he pleaded guilty to possession of marijuana]

7. **Civil Actions**
   The Double Jeopardy Clause prohibits only repetitive *criminal* prosecutions. Thus, a

state generally is free to bring a civil action against a defendant even if the defendant has already been criminally tried for the conduct out of which the civil action arises. Similarly, the government may bring a criminal action even though the defendant has already faced civil trial for the same conduct. However, if there is clear proof from the face of the statutory scheme that its purpose or effect is to impose a criminal penalty, the Double Jeopardy Clause applies. [Hudson v. United States, 522 U.S. 93 (1998)—finding no clear proof of such purpose or effect where a civil statute allowed a government agency to impose a fine and bar defendants from working in banking industry for improperly approving loans]

D. SEPARATE SOVEREIGNS

The constitutional prohibition against double jeopardy ***does not apply*** to trials by separate sovereigns. Thus, a person may be tried for the same conduct by both a state and the federal government [United States v. Lanza, 260 U.S. 377 (1922)] or by two states [Heath v. Alabama, 474 U.S. 82 (1986)], but not by a state and its municipalities [Waller v. Florida, 397 U.S. 387 (1970)].

E. APPEALS BY PROSECUTION

Even after jeopardy has attached, the prosecution ***may appeal any dismissal*** on the defendant's motion ***not constituting an acquittal on the merits***. [United States v. Scott, 437 U.S. 82 (1978)] Also, the Double Jeopardy Clause does not bar appeals by the prosecution if a ***successful appeal would not require a retrial***, such as when the trial judge granted a motion to set aside the jury verdict. [United States v. Wilson, 420 U.S. 332 (1975)]

1. Appeal of Sentence

Government appeal of a sentence, ***pursuant*** to a congressionally enacted ***statute*** permitting such review, does not constitute multiple punishment in violation of the Double Jeopardy Clause. [United States v. DiFrancesco, 449 U.S. 117 (1980)]

F. ISSUE PRECLUSION (COLLATERAL ESTOPPEL)

The notion of collateral estoppel is embodied in the guarantee against double jeopardy. A defendant may not be tried or convicted of a crime if a prior prosecution by that sovereignty resulted in a ***factual determination inconsistent with one required for conviction***. However, this doctrine has limited utility because of the general verdict in criminal trials.

Examples: 1) Where three or four armed men robbed six poker players in the home of one of the victims and the defendant was charged in separate counts with robbery of each of the six players and was tried on one count and was acquitted for insufficient evidence in a prosecution in which identity was the single rationally conceivable issue in dispute, he may not thereafter be prosecuted for robbery of a different player. [Ashe v. Swenson, 397 U.S. 436 (1970)] A second trial would not have been barred if there had been dispute at the first trial regarding whether the alleged victim was robbed. The court did not adopt the "same transaction" test proposed by some justices, under which a defendant could not be more than once put in jeopardy for offenses arising out of the "same transactions."

2) Where the ultimate issue of identity of the person who mailed a package with a bomb that killed two persons was decided at the first trial at which defendant was acquitted, the defendant may not thereafter be convicted of the second murder, even if the jury in the first trial (for the first murder) did not have all the relevant evidence before it and the state acted in good faith. [Harris v. Washington, 404 U.S. 55 (1971)]

1. **Inconsistent Verdicts**

   If the defendant has been charged with multiple counts and there is an inconsistency in the verdicts among the counts (*e.g.*, the jury acquitted the defendant on some and deadlocked on others), the focus should be on what was decided rather than on what was not decided. That is, the issues necessarily decided in the acquittal will have preclusive effect even if the same issues were involved in the counts on which the jury deadlocked. [Yeager v. United States, 129 S. Ct. 2360 (2009)]

   Example: Defendant was charged with several counts of fraud and insider trading. A necessary element in each count was that Defendant possessed material, nonpublic information and used it unlawfully. He was acquitted of the fraud charges but the jury failed to reach a verdict on the insider trading charges. Retrial is barred on the insider trading counts under the issue preclusion component of the Double Jeopardy Clause. The jury's failure to decide the insider trading counts does not affect the preclusive force of the acquittals on the fraud counts, even though both relied on the same factual elements. [Yeager v. United States, *supra*]

XIV. PRIVILEGE AGAINST COMPELLED SELF-INCRIMINATION

A. APPLICABLE TO THE STATES

As discussed above (*see* IV.D., *supra*), the Fifth Amendment prohibits the government from compelling self-incriminating testimony. The Fifth Amendment prohibition against compelled self-incrimination was made applicable to the states through the Fourteenth Amendment in *Malloy v. Hogan*, 378 U.S. 1 (1964).

B. WHO MAY ASSERT THE PRIVILEGE

Only ***natural persons*** may assert the privilege, not corporations or partnerships. [Bellis v. United States, 417 U.S. 85 (1974)] The privilege is personal, and so may be asserted by a defendant, witness, or party only if the answer to the question might tend to incriminate him.

C. WHEN PRIVILEGE MAY BE ASSERTED

A person may refuse to answer a question whenever his response might furnish a link in the chain of evidence needed to prosecute him.

1. **Proceedings Where Potentially Incriminating Testimony Sought**

   A person may assert the privilege in *any* proceeding in which testimony that could tend to incriminate is sought. The privilege must be claimed in civil proceedings to prevent the privilege from being waived for a later criminal prosecution. If the individual responds to the questions instead of claiming the privilege during a civil proceeding, he cannot later bar that evidence from a criminal prosecution on compelled self-incrimination grounds. [United States v. Kordel, 397 U.S. 1 (1970)]

2. **Privilege Not a Defense to Civil Records Requirements**

   The government may require that certain records be kept and reported on where the records are relevant to an ***administrative purpose***, unrelated to enforcement of criminal laws. Such records acquire a public aspect and are not protected by the Fifth Amendment.

Examples: 1) The government may require people to keep tax records and to report their income on tax forms, because this serves a legitimate administrative purpose. Thus, a person may be prosecuted for failure to file a tax form. However, there is a Fifth Amendment privilege to refuse to answer specific questions on such forms that might be incriminating (*e.g.*, source of income). [United States v. Sullivan, 274 U.S. 259 (1927)] Therefore, if a person chooses to answer incriminating questions on such forms, the answers may be used against him in court, because they were not compelled. [Garner v. United States, 424 U.S. 648 (1976)]

2) A person charged with being an unfit parent in a proceeding to determine whether she should maintain custody of her child may be compelled to produce the child in court. Even though the production might be testimonial in nature (admits control), the state's interest here is civil (protecting the child) rather than punitive in nature. [Baltimore City Department of Social Services v. Bouknight, 493 U.S. 549 (1990)] Note, however, that the state might have to grant immunity to the parent for the production. (*See* H.1., *infra.*)

3) A person may not claim the privilege and fail to comply with a law requiring motorists to stop at the scene of an accident and leave their name and address. [California v. Byers, 402 U.S. 424 (1971)]

a. Limitation—Criminal Law Enforcement Purpose

If the registration requirement is directed not at the general public but at a *select group inherently suspect of criminal activities* and the inquiry is in an area permeated with criminal statutes, the person may assert the privilege to avoid prosecution for failure to comply with the requirement. [Albertson v. Subversive Activities Control Board, 382 U.S. 70 (1965)]

Example: The government may not require registration of a sawed-off shotgun [Haynes v. United States, 390 U.S. 85 (1968)], payment of a wagering excise tax [Grosso v. United States, 390 U.S. 62 (1968)], payment of an occupational tax for engaging in the business of accepting wagers [Marchetti v. United States, 390 U.S. 39 (1968)], individual registration as a member of the Communist Party [Albertson v. Subversive Activities Control Board, *supra*], or the registration of transfer of marijuana [Leary v. United States, 395 U.S. 6 (1969)] if compliance would require self-incrimination.

Note: Such cases as *Marchetti* and *Grosso* do not bar conviction for making false statements on the registration form; to avoid incriminating himself, the individual must instead claim the privilege. [United States v. Knox, 396 U.S. 77 (1969)]

3. Privilege Not Applicable to Identification Request After *Terry* Stop

Merely being required to furnish one's name after a *Terry* stop (*see* III.B.3.a., *supra*) generally does not violate the Fifth Amendment because disclosure of one's name generally poses no danger of incrimination. [*See* Hiibel v. Sixth Judicial District Court, *supra*, III.B.3.a.3)a)]

D. METHOD FOR INVOKING THE PRIVILEGE

How the privilege may be invoked depends upon whether the person seeking to invoke it is a criminal defendant or simply a witness.

1. **Privilege of a Defendant**
    A criminal defendant has a right not to take the witness stand at trial and not to be asked to do so. It is even impermissible to call the jury's attention to the fact that he has chosen not to testify. (*See* G.1., *infra*.)

2. **Privilege of a Witness**
    In any other situation, the privilege does not permit a person to avoid being sworn as a witness or being asked questions. Rather, the person must listen to the questions and specifically invoke the privilege rather than answer the questions.

E.   SCOPE OF PROTECTION

1. **Testimonial but Not Physical Evidence**
    The Fifth Amendment privilege protects only testimonial or communicative evidence and not real or physical evidence. Thus, the state may require a person to produce *blood samples* [Schmerber v. California, *supra*, IV.C.2.], *handwriting exemplars* [Gilbert v. California, *supra*, IV.C.2.], or *voice samples* [United States v. Wade, *supra*, V.E.] without violating the Fifth Amendment, even though such evidence may be incriminating. In addition, a court may order a suspect to authorize foreign banks to disclose records of any accounts he may possess. Merely signing an authorization form is not testimonial if it does not require the suspect to acknowledge the existence of any account. For a suspect's communication to be considered testimonial, it must explicitly or implicitly relate a factual assertion or disclose information. [Doe v. United States, 487 U.S. 201 (1988)]

    Likewise, admission into evidence of a defendant's *refusal to submit to a blood-alcohol test* does not offend the right against self-incrimination even though he was not warned that his refusal might be introduced against him. [South Dakota v. Neville, 459 U.S. 553 (1983)]

2. **Compulsory Production of Documents**
    A person served with a subpoena requiring the production of documents tending to incriminate him generally has no basis in the privilege to refuse to comply, because the act of producing the documents *does not involve testimonial self-incrimination*. Note, however, that if the document *is* within the privilege but in the hands of an attorney, the attorney-client privilege would permit the attorney to refuse to comply with the subpoena. [Fisher v. United States, 425 U.S. 391 (1976)]

    a. **Corporate Records**
        A custodian of corporate records may not resist a subpoena for such records on the ground that the production would incriminate him in violation of the Fifth Amendment. The production of the records by the custodian is not considered a personal act, but rather an act of the corporation, which possesses no Fifth Amendment privilege. [Braswell v. United States, 487 U.S. 99 (1988)]

3. **Seizure and Use of Incriminating Documents**
    The Fifth Amendment does not prohibit law enforcement officers from searching for and seizing documents tending to incriminate a person. The privilege protects only against being compelled to communicate information, not against disclosure of communications made in the past. [Andresen v. Maryland, *supra*, III.C.4.c.]

4. When Does Violation Occur?

A violation of the Self-Incrimination Clause does not occur until a person's compelled statements are used against him in a criminal case. [Chavez v. Martinez, 538 U.S. 760 (2003)]

Example: While Martinez was being treated for a gunshot wound that he received in an altercation with the police, he was interrogated by an officer without having been given *Miranda* warnings. Although Martinez admitted to using heroin and that he had taken an officer's gun during the incident in which he was shot, he was never charged with a crime. Nevertheless, Martinez sued police officers for violating his Fifth Amendment right against compelled self-incrimination. *Held:* Because Martinez had not been charged with a crime, there was no Fifth Amendment violation because his statements were not used against him in a criminal case. [Chavez v. Martinez, *supra*]

F. RIGHT TO ADVICE CONCERNING PRIVILEGE

A lawyer may not be held in contempt of court for her good faith advice to her client to invoke the privilege and refuse to produce materials demanded by a court order. Because a witness may require the advice of counsel in deciding how to respond to a demand for testimony or evidence, subjecting the lawyer to potential contempt citation for her advice would infringe upon the protection accorded the witness by the Fifth Amendment. [Maness v. Meyers, 419 U.S. 449 (1975)]

G. PROHIBITION AGAINST BURDENS ON ASSERTION OF THE PRIVILEGE

1. Comments on Defendant's Silence

A prosecutor may not comment on a defendant's silence after being arrested and receiving *Miranda* warnings. The warnings carry an implicit assurance that silence will carry no penalty. [Greer v. Miller, 483 U.S. 756 (1987)] Neither may the prosecutor ordinarily comment on the defendant's failure to testify at trial. [Griffin v. California, 380 U.S. 609 (1965)] However, where the defendant does not testify at trial, upon timely motion she is constitutionally entitled to have the trial judge instruct the jury that they are to draw no adverse inference from the defendant's failure to testify. [Carter v. Kentucky, 450 U.S. 288 (1981)] Moreover, a judge may warn the jury not to draw an adverse inference from the defendant's failure to testify, without violating the Fifth Amendment privilege, even where the defendant objects to such an instruction. [Lakeside v. Oregon, 435 U.S. 333 (1978)]

a. Exception

The prosecutor can comment on the defendant's failure to take the stand when the comment is in response to defense counsel's assertion that the defendant was not allowed to explain his side of the story. [United States v. Robinson, 485 U.S. 25 (1988)]

b. Harmless Error Test Applies

When a prosecutor impermissibly comments on a defendant's silence, the harmless error test applies. Thus, the error is not fatal where the judge instructs the jury to disregard a question on the defendant's post-arrest silence. [Greer v. Miller, *supra*] Similarly, the error is not fatal where there is overwhelming evidence against the defendant and the prosecutor comments on the defendant's failure to proffer evidence rebutting the victim's testimony. [United States v. Hasting, 461 U.S. 499 (1987)]

2.   **Penalties for Failure to Testify Prohibited**
The state may not chill the exercise of the Fifth Amendment privilege against compelled self-incrimination by imposing penalties for the failure to testify or cooperate with authorities.

Example: The state may not fire a police officer [Garrity v. New Jersey, 385 U.S. 493 (1967)], take away state contracts [Lefkowitz v. Turley, 414 U.S. 70 (1973)], or prohibit a person from holding party office [Lefkowitz v. Cunningham, 431 U.S. 801 (1977)] for failure to cooperate with investigating authorities.

Compare: There was no Fifth Amendment violation where a prisoner was required to disclose all prior sexual activities, including activities that constitute uncharged criminal offenses, in order to gain entry into a sexual abuse treatment program, even though refusal resulted in transfer from a medium security facility to a maximum security facility and curtailment of visitation rights, prison work and earnings opportunities, and other prison privileges. [McKune v. Lile, 536 U.S. 24 (2002)]

H.   ELIMINATION OF THE PRIVILEGE

1.   **Grant of Immunity**
A witness may be compelled to answer questions if granted adequate immunity from prosecution.

   a.   **"Use and Derivative Use" Immunity Sufficient**
The Supreme Court has held that a grant of "use and derivative use" immunity is sufficient to extinguish the privilege. [Kastigar v. United States, 406 U.S. 441 (1972)] This type of immunity guarantees that the testimony obtained and evidence located by means of the testimony will not be used against the witness. This type of immunity is not as broad as "transactional" immunity, which guarantees immunity from prosecution for any crimes related to the transaction about which the witness testifies, because the witness may still be prosecuted if the prosecutor can show that her evidence was derived from a *source independent* of the immunized testimony.

   b.   **Immunized Testimony Involuntary**
Testimony obtained by a *promise of immunity* is, by definition, coerced and therefore involuntary. Thus, immunized testimony may not be used for impeachment of the defendant's testimony at trial. [New Jersey v. Portash, 440 U.S. 450 (1979)] Immunized testimony may be introduced to supply the context for a perjury prosecution. Any immunized statements, whether true or untrue, can be used in a trial for making false statements. [United States v. Apfelbaum, 445 U.S. 115 (1980)]

   c.   **Use of Testimony by Another Sovereign Prohibited**
The privilege against self-incrimination prohibits a state from compelling incriminating testimony under a grant of immunity unless the testimony and its fruits cannot be used by the prosecution in a federal prosecution. Therefore, federal prosecutors may not use evidence obtained as a result of a state grant of immunity, and vice versa. [Murphy v. Waterfront Commission, 378 U.S. 52 (1964)]

2.   **No Possibility of Incrimination**
A person has no privilege against compelled self-incrimination if there is no possibility of incrimination, as, for example, when the statute of limitations has run.

3. Scope of Immunity

Immunity extends only to the offenses to which the question relates and does not protect against perjury committed during the immunized testimony. [United States v. Apfelbaum, *supra*]

I. WAIVER OF PRIVILEGE

The nature and scope of a waiver depends upon the situation.

1. Waiver by Criminal Defendant

A criminal defendant, by taking the witness stand, waives the privilege to the extent necessary to subject her to any cross-examination proper under the rules of evidence.

2. Waiver by Witness

A witness waives the privilege only if she discloses incriminating information. Once such disclosure has been made, she can be compelled to disclose any additional information as long as such further disclosure does not increase the risk of conviction or create a risk of conviction on a different offense.

XV. JUVENILE COURT PROCEEDINGS

A. IN GENERAL

Some—but not all—of the rights developed for defendants in criminal prosecutions have also been held applicable to children who are the subjects of proceedings to have them declared "delinquents" and possibly institutionalized.

B. RIGHTS THAT MUST BE AFFORDED

The following rights must be given to a child during the trial of a delinquency proceeding:

(i) Written *notice* of the charges with sufficient time to prepare a defense;

(ii) The *assistance of counsel* (court-appointed if the child is indigent);

(iii) The *opportunity to confront* and cross-examine witnesses;

(iv) The *right not to testify* (and other aspects of the privilege against self-incrimination); and

(v) The right to have *"guilt"* (the commission of acts making the child delinquent) established by proof *beyond a reasonable doubt*.

[*In re* Gault, 387 U.S. 1 (1967); *In re* Winship, 397 U.S. 358 (1970)]

C. RIGHTS NOT APPLICABLE

1. Jury Trial

The Supreme Court has held inapplicable to delinquency proceedings the right to trial by jury. In the juvenile court context, jury trial is not necessary to assure "fundamental fairness." [McKeiver v. Pennsylvania, 403 U.S. 528 (1971)]

2. **Pretrial Detention Allowable**

A finding that a juvenile is a "serious risk" to society and likely to commit a crime before trial is adequate to support pretrial detention of the juvenile, and does not violate the Due Process Clause as long as the detention is for a strictly limited time before trial may be held. [Schall v. Martin, 467 U.S. 253 (1984)]

D. **DOUBLE JEOPARDY AND "TRANSFER" OF JUVENILE TO ADULT COURT**

In many jurisdictions, a juvenile court may, after inquiry, determine that a juvenile is not an appropriate subject for juvenile court processing and "transfer" the juvenile to adult court for trial as an adult on criminal charges. If the juvenile court begins to hear evidence on the alleged delinquent act, however, jeopardy has attached and the prohibition against double jeopardy prevents the juvenile from being tried as an adult for the same behavior. [Breed v. Jones, XIII.A.3., *supra*]

XVI. FORFEITURE ACTIONS

A. **INTRODUCTION**

State and federal statutes often provide for the forfeiture of property such as automobiles used in the commission of a crime. Actions for forfeiture are brought directly against the property and are generally regarded as quasi-criminal in nature. Certain constitutional rights may exist for those persons whose interest in the property would be lost by forfeiture.

B. **RIGHT TO PRE-SEIZURE NOTICE AND HEARING**

The owner of *personal* property (and others with interests in it) is not constitutionally entitled to notice and hearing before the property is seized for purposes of a forfeiture proceeding. [Calero-Toledo v. Pearson Yacht Leasing Co., 416 U.S. 663 (1974)] A hearing is, however, required before final forfeiture of the property. Where *real property* is seized, notice and an opportunity to be heard is required before the seizure unless the government can prove that exigent circumstances justify immediate seizure. [United States v. James Daniel Good Real Property, 510 U.S. 43 (1994)]

C. **FORFEITURES MAY BE SUBJECT TO EIGHTH AMENDMENT**

The Eighth Amendment provides that excessive fines shall not be imposed. The Supreme Court has held that this Excessive Fines Clause applies only to fines imposed as punishment, *i.e.*, penal fines. The Clause does not apply to civil fines. Thus forfeitures that are penal are subject to the Clause, but forfeitures that are civil are not.

1. **Penal Forfeitures**

Generally, a forfeiture will be considered penal only if it is provided for in a criminal statute. If it is penal and the Clause applies, a forfeiture will be found to be excessive only if it is *grossly disproportionate to the gravity of the offense.* [United States v. Bajakajian, 524 U.S. 321 (1998)]

Example: The Court held that forfeiture of $357,144 for the crime of merely failing to report that that sum was being transported out of the country was grossly disproportionate, because the crime caused little harm (it would have been legal to take the money out of the country; the only harm was that the government was deprived of a piece of information). [United States v. Bajakajian, *supra*]

2. Compare—Nonpenal Forfeitures

a. Civil In Rem Forfeitures
Civil in rem forfeitures treat the property forfeited as a "wrongdoer" under a legal fiction; the action is against the property and not against an individual, and therefore this type of forfeiture is **not** subject to the Excessive Fines Clause.

b. Monetary Forfeitures
Monetary forfeitures (*e.g.*, forfeiture of twice the value of illegally imported goods) have also been found to be remedial in nature where they are brought in civil actions. They are seen as a form of liquidated damages to reimburse the government for losses resulting from the offense. Therefore, they are not subject to the Eighth Amendment. [*See* United States v. Bajakajian, *supra*]

D. PROTECTION FOR "INNOCENT OWNER" NOT REQUIRED
The Due Process Clause does **not** require forfeiture statutes to provide an "innocent owner" defense, *e.g.*, a defense that the owner took all reasonable steps to avoid having the property used by another for illegal purposes, at least where the innocent owner **voluntarily entrusted** the property to the wrongdoer. [Bennis v. Michigan, 517 U.S. 292 (1996)—due process not violated by forfeiture of wife's car that husband used while engaging in sexual acts with a prostitute even though wife did not know of use] In justifying its holding in Bennis, the Court also noted that the statute was not absolute, because the trial judge had discretion to prevent inequitable application of the statute.

ESSAY EXAM QUESTIONS

INTRODUCTORY NOTE

The essay questions that follow have been selected to provide you with an opportunity to experience how the substantive law you have been reviewing may be tested in the hypothetical essay examination question context. These sample essay questions are a valuable self-diagnostic tool designed to enable you to enhance your issue-spotting ability and practice your exam writing skills.

It is suggested that you approach each question as though under actual examination conditions. The time allowed for each question is 30 minutes. You should spend 10 minutes spotting issues, underlining key facts and phrases, jotting notes in the margins, and outlining your answer. *If* you organize your thoughts well, 20 minutes will be more than adequate for writing them down. Should you prefer to forgo the actual writing involved on these questions, be sure to give yourself no more time for issue-spotting than you would on the actual examination.

The BARBRI technique for writing a well-organized essay answer is to (i) spot the issues in a question and then (ii) analyze and discuss each issue using the "CIRAC" method:

C — State your *conclusion* first. (In other words, you must think through your answer *before* you start writing.)

I — State the *issue* involved.

R — Give the *rule(s)* of law involved.

A — *Apply* the rule(s) of law to the facts.

C — Finally, restate your *conclusion*.

After completing (or outlining) your own analysis of each question, compare it with the BARBRI model answer provided herein. A passing answer does *not* have to match the model one, but it should cover most of the issues presented and the law discussed and should *apply the law to the facts* of the question. Use of the CIRAC method results in the best answer you can write.

EXAM QUESTION NO. 1

On April 10, a convenience store was robbed by someone carrying a gun. The store's video camera caught the robbery on tape. The tape was shown on the evening news.

On April 11, an anonymous caller contacted the police saying, "I saw that tape of the robbery. The robber kind of looks like Student. He's an 18-year-old student at the high school."

On April 12, two police officers took the tape to the high school and showed it to the principal, who said, "It could be Student. It's hard to tell because the tape is not clear." The tape was also shown to Student's homeroom teacher, who said, "It might be him, but I couldn't say for sure."

Later that day, the police officers went to the store where Student works after school. They asked the manager if they could talk with Student, who was called to the manager's office. The police introduced themselves to Student and said, "We'd like to talk to you." They walked with Student into the manager's office and shut the door. One police officer sat behind the manager's desk; the other, in full uniform with his revolver visible, sat near the door. Student sat between them. The manager's office measures eight feet by ten feet.

The police officers told Student they wanted to ask him some questions about the convenience store robbery on April 10. Student said he knew nothing about a robbery. He continued to deny that he had any knowledge of the robbery for about 20 minutes. Student did not ask to leave, and neither police officer told Student he was free to leave.

After about 20 minutes, the police officers told Student that they had a videotape of the robbery and that they had shown it to three people, all of whom positively identified Student as the robber.

Student said nothing for a few minutes. One of the police officers then said, "You know, if we can tell the prosecutor that you cooperated, she might go a lot easier on you. I'd hate to see you end up doing a long stretch in prison. Let's just say it's not a nice place." Student then blurted out, "I did the robbery. I used a little air gun."

Immediately after Student made that statement, the police officers informed Student that he was under arrest for the robbery of the convenience store. They read him his *Miranda* rights. Student stated he understood his *Miranda* rights and told the police officers that he was not going to say anything more to them. The police officers placed Student in handcuffs and took him to the police station where he was booked for armed robbery.

Student had had two earlier brushes with the law. When he was 16, he had been found delinquent in juvenile court for auto theft and had been placed on supervision for one year. When he was 17, he had received a ticket for underage drinking and had paid a fine of $150. He is a "C" student, but his teachers believe he is an "underachiever."

Student's defense attorney has filed a motion to suppress Student's statements on three grounds:
(1)   Student's statements were obtained in violation of Student's Fourth Amendment rights.
(2)   Student's statements were obtained in violation of his *Miranda* rights.
(3)   Student's confession was not voluntary.
How should the trial court rule on each of the grounds in the motion to suppress? Explain.

EXAM QUESTION NO. 2

On Memorial Day, the county sheriff's department received an anonymous telephone call advising that Ryan Catwood was involved in the drowning death of Marissa Hooper, whose body had been found two weeks earlier floating in Pickwick Lake. The caller claimed that Ryan had drugged Marissa, carried her onto his bass boat, motored to a remote area of the lake, and dumped her into the water.

Deputies began looking for Ryan, and a radio dispatcher for the sheriff's department issued a BOLO (Be On the Lookout) for a green Explorer SUV registered to Ryan. Later that same day, Deputy Kenny Brisco spotted Ryan's SUV. Deputy Brisco stopped the vehicle and asked Ryan to follow him to the sheriff's department. Ryan did so. He was escorted to a small conference room and introduced to investigator Van Buren. Investigator Van Buren began by telling Ryan that he was not under arrest and could leave at any time.

When Van Buren broached the subject of Marissa's drowning, Ryan denied knowing her. Van Buren left the room and returned with a file. Without speaking, Van Buren began reading. After 10 minutes of silence, Van Buren commented aloud that, any minute, he was expecting to meet an eyewitness who had seen Ryan disposing of a body in Pickwick Lake. Ryan stood up, and Van Buren interjected, "Kid, this is your last chance to talk to me. I'm having the paperwork prepared to charge you with murder." Ryan started hyperventilating and pleading, "Please, don't do that. I'm sorry." Then addressing Van Buren, Ryan said, "I'm having a panic attack. I have got to get out of here!" Van Buren blocked Ryan's exit and told him, "Stay put; I'll call a doctor." Ryan sat down and began muttering that Marissa had threatened to leave him and that no other man was "good enough for her."

Van Buren left and returned with a corrections officer from the jail infirmary. Van Buren told Ryan that the corrections officer would escort him to the infirmary for a medical evaluation, but first, Van Buren advised Ryan of his *Miranda* rights. Ryan signed a rights acknowledgment and waiver form and asked to see a doctor. Without responding, Van Buren began questioning Ryan about when he last saw Marissa. Ryan asked, "Do I need a lawyer just so I can see a doctor?" He added, "Get me a cell phone." Van Buren asked why Ryan needed a cell phone, and Ryan looked at the corrections officer and said, "I'm through talking to that jerk. I want to see a doctor."

The corrections officer announced that he was leaving and would return promptly with a physician. Van Buren stared at Ryan and asked, "What can I do to get you to change your mind?" Ryan asked if Van Buren would "put in a good word" for him with the judge. When Van Buren responded that he would, Ryan broke down and gave a detailed confession of how he murdered Marissa.

Ryan was charged with premeditated, first degree murder, and you are the trial judge assigned to handle the case. Ryan's attorney has filed a motion to suppress any and all statements that Ryan made in Van Buren's presence.

Based upon the facts recited, answer the following questions:

(1)   Should Ryan's statement "Please, don't do that. I'm sorry" and his remarks about Marissa threatening to leave him and no other man "being good enough for her" be suppressed? Why or why not? Explain your answer in detail.

(2)   What effect, if any, do Ryan's question about needing a lawyer and demand for a cell phone have on the admissibility of his subsequent, detailed confession? Explain your answer in detail.

(3)   What effect, if any, do Ryan's statements to the corrections officer that he was through talking with the jerk, Van Buren, and wanted to see a doctor have on the admissibility of his subsequent, detailed confession? Explain your answer in detail.

EXAM QUESTION NO. 3

At approximately 2:00 p.m. on July 2, Jean Hodes, a dispatcher with the Emergency 911 Communications Center in Erehwon, received a call from an unidentified male who sounded panic stricken. The caller reported that Nancy Sotwin was driving erratically on Milkweed Lane at a high rate of speed and had struck a young child riding a bicycle. The caller also related that Sotwin did not stop but drove to a house at the end of the lane, pulled into the attached garage, and closed the garage door.

Erehwon police officers responded to the call. They summoned medical assistance for the child, and several officers approached the residence at the end of the lane and knocked on the front door. When Nancy's adult brother, Andy, answered the door, the officers explained that a vehicular assault had occurred, and the officers asked Andy for permission to search the garage. Andy responded, "Whatever," stepped aside, and pointed to the door leading into the garage. Nancy walked out of the guest bathroom just as one of the officers reached the door, and she shouted to the officers to leave her house. The officer at the door ignored Nancy's protest; he opened the door and walked into the garage where he discovered a Saturn VUE with blood spattered over the right corner of the front bumper. Officers applied for a search warrant to seize the vehicle, and later forensic analysis identified the blood as that of the injured child.

The day following the hit and run, officers canvassed the neighborhood for witnesses. Officers interviewed Doug Wilson, who told them that he was having a late lunch the previous day at the Erehwon Grill and Bar, where he saw Nancy drink five martinis over a 30-minute period. Doug reported that when Nancy left the bar at approximately 1:45 p.m., she was very unsteady on her feet. Soon after the interview, Doug was called to active duty in Iraq for 48 months.

A grand jury indicted Nancy for vehicular assault by intoxication. Pretrial, the defense has moved to suppress the results of the blood analysis as the fruit of an illegal warrantless search of Nancy's garage. Also, anticipating that the prosecution would offer a tape recording of the 911 call and Doug's hearsay statements, the defense challenged admissibility as violating Nancy's constitutional confrontation rights. The state has responded that Nancy's brother, who lived at the residence, provided effective consent to a search of the garage and that the hearsay evidence is nontestimonial and, therefore, not subject to Confrontation Clause scrutiny.

Based on the foregoing, determine:

(1) Whether the warrantless search of the Sotwin garage violated the Fourth Amendment to the United States Constitution.

(2) Whether the federal Confrontation Clause bars admission of the 911 tape recording.

(3) Whether the federal Confrontation Clause bars admission of Doug's statements to the officers.

EXAM QUESTION NO. 4

James Kirk was hunting in a rural area in the state of Pennsyltuckey. He shot at what he thought was a deer. Unfortunately, it was a man in a deerskin coat, and the man died some days later from the wound Kirk caused. Kirk was prosecuted for negligent homicide and was convicted at trial. On appeal, the Pennsyltuckey Court of Appeals reversed, holding that, as a matter of law, the shooting was a "mere misadventure" and could not be the basis for a homicide prosecution.

The local prosecutor drove by the scene of the crime a few days after the court of appeals's decision was handed down. He noticed that Kirk had been hunting from a position only 50 feet from a farmhouse owned by someone other than the victim of the shooting. Accordingly, he has decided to prosecute Kirk for hunting within 400 feet of a dwelling house, a misdemeanor under Pennsyltuckey law. The maximum penalty for hunting within 400 feet of a dwelling house is 10 months' imprisonment and a $500 fine, and a person so convicted may not obtain a hunting license for the next five years. The case has been assigned to Judge Spock, the same judge who tried the first negligent homicide case. Kirk has demanded a jury trial, and he has asked for court-appointed counsel. Judge Spock has ruled that Kirk will have neither. He stated that he would impose no more than six months' imprisonment (in addition to a possible fine, and the five-year loss of hunting privileges). Kirk also asked the court to dismiss the case altogether on the claim that it is barred by the "federal double jeopardy provision."

Assume that Kirk is otherwise qualified to have court-appointed counsel. If Kirk is convicted and receives the stated sentence, what are his chances for a reversal in the court of appeals based on the following arguments: (1) that he should have been given court-appointed counsel; (2) that he should have been given a jury trial or (3) at least, that the same judge who had previously tried him should not have been allowed to try his second case; and (4) that the second prosecution for the same hunting incident is barred by double jeopardy? Explain your answer.

ANSWERS TO ESSAY EXAM QUESTIONS

ANSWER TO EXAM QUESTION NO. 1

(1)   The trial court should deny the motion to suppress based on the Fourth Amendment. At issue is whether Student was unreasonably seized.

As a general rule, evidence obtained in violation of a person's Fourth Amendment rights must be suppressed. The Fourth Amendment, which is applicable to the states through the Due Process Clause of the Fourteenth Amendment, prohibits unreasonable searches and seizures. A person is seized if a reasonable person under the circumstances would not feel free to leave. Whether a seizure is reasonable under the Fourth Amendment depends on the scope of the seizure (*e.g.,* an arrest vs. an investigatory detention) and the strength of the suspicion prompting the seizure (*e.g.,* an arrest requires probable cause while an investigatory detention can be based on reasonable suspicion).

Here, a court probably would find that Student was seized. On the one hand, the officers *asked* Student to go into his manager's office to talk with them and he complied, which makes this seem more like a voluntary questioning situation. On the other hand, an officer stood near the door, in uniform, wearing a gun—a position that would probably send a message to the average person that leaving was out of the question, the questioning went on for 25 minutes, and the officers did not indicate that Student was free to leave. On balance, a court would probably find a seizure here.

Assuming that Student was seized, a court would probably find that the seizure was reasonable. It is unlikely that the police would find that the police had probable cause to make an arrest before Student confessed. Without a warrant, police may arrest a person for a felony, such as the robbery here, only if they have information sufficient to make a reasonable person believe that a felony was committed and the person before them committed it (*i.e.,* probable cause). Here, while the police had sufficient information to reasonably believe that a robbery was committed, the photo identifications of Student all were too uncertain to make a reasonable person believe that Student committed the robbery. However, the police had reasonable suspicion for an investigatory detention.

Under *Terry v. Ohio*, if the police have reasonable suspicion of criminal activity based on articulable facts, they may stop a person without a warrant to conduct a brief investigation. Here, three people said that the person seen committing the robbery on videotape could be Student. These identifications were sufficient to give rise to reasonable suspicion to investigate. Moreover, given that two of the witnesses were familiar with Student and their assertions that Student "could be" and "might be" the robber on the videotape, questioning Student for 25 minutes would probably be considered a reasonable investigation. Thus, the seizure was valid under the Fourth Amendment and Student's statements should not be suppressed on this ground.

(2)   The motion to suppress based on *Miranda* presents a very close question, with no certain result. At issue is whether Student was in custody when he was being interrogated.

To offset the coercive effects of police interrogation, the Supreme Court requires police to give detainees *Miranda* warnings (*e.g.,* that they have a right to remain silent and to an attorney) before conducting any custodial interrogation. Here, the police did not give Student *Miranda* warnings before they began questioning him. That the questioning constituted an interrogation is not in doubt. Interrogation is any police conduct designed to elicit an incriminating response. Here, the officers asked Student questions about the robbery—clearly an interrogation.

The real question here is whether Student was in custody. Whether a person is in custody depends on whether the person's freedom of action is denied in a significant way. The more the situation resembles a formal arrest, the more likely a court will find the person to have been in custody. Here, the facts go both ways: On the one hand, the officers brought Student into a small office, and a uniformed officer with a gun was stationed between Student and the door. Moreover, the officers did not tell Student

that he was free to go at any time. On the other hand, the officers did not place Student under arrest; they merely told him that they wanted to talk to him. They did not restrain Student with handcuffs or take him to the police station. Thus, the result here remains very much an open question with there being no clear result.

(3)   The motion to suppress Student's confession based on voluntariness should be denied. An involuntary confession will be suppressed as a violation of the Due Process Clause of the Fourteenth Amendment. Whether a confession is involuntary is determined under the totality of the circumstances. Here, two police officers questioned Student in a small room, and an armed officer was between Student and the door. Moreover, the officers lied to Student about the strength of their evidence (telling him that three people had positively identified him when in fact no one was sure if it was Student). They also told him that prison would not be good for him.

On the other hand, Student seems to have possessed at least average intelligence (he was a C student), he had experience with the criminal justice system (he was found delinquent for auto theft), he is an adult (18 years old), and the interview was relatively brief (about 25 minutes). Given the latter facts, a court would probably find the confession voluntary. Thus, the motion should be denied.

ANSWER TO EXAM QUESTION NO. 2

(1)   Ryan's "I'm sorry" statement probably will be held admissible, but not his other two initial statements. At issue is whether Ryan was in custody when he made the statements.

Under *Miranda v. Arizona*, law enforcement officers must give specific warnings regarding a person's right to an attorney and right to remain silent prior to any ***custodial interrogation***. Failure to give the required warnings may result in suppression of statements obtained during the interrogation. Because no *Miranda* warnings were given prior to Ryan's statements at issue, if the court concludes that Ryan was in custody and interrogated, the statements will be suppressed. If not, the statements may be used against him.

In this case, therefore, we must determine whether Ryan was (i) interrogated, and (ii) in custody when he made the statement "Please don't do that, I'm sorry" and talked about Marissa leaving him. Although Ryan was not questioned in a traditional sense, an interrogation occurs when officers use words or actions that are likely to produce an incriminating response. Here, Van Buren's 10 minutes of silence followed by the comment that he was going to meet an eyewitness who saw Ryan dispose of the body likely meets the standard, and therefore constitutes an interrogation.

With regard to whether Ryan was in custody, the test is whether a reasonable person in Ryan's circumstances would have concluded that he was not free to leave. Although Van Buren initially told Ryan that he was free to leave, the circumstances were remarkably similar to a custodial interrogation. He traveled to the station, was taken to a small room, and was kept there for a period of time. It is, however, a close call with regard to the "I'm sorry" statement in light of Van Buren's remark that Ryan was not under arrest and could leave anytime. However, when Van Buren blocked Ryan's exit and said "stay put" during Ryan's panic attack, a finding of "custody" becomes more likely. As a result, Ryan's subsequent statements about Marissa leaving him and that "no other man was good enough for her" are more likely to be suppressed.

(2)   Ryan's question about needing a lawyer and request for a cell phone probably will have no effect on the admissibility of his subsequent confession. At issue is whether Ryan properly invoked his right to counsel under *Miranda*.

After the initial statements discussed above, Van Buren advised Ryan of his *Miranda* rights and Ryan signed an acknowledgment and waiver form. A waiver, however, must be voluntary, knowing, and intelligent. Ryan had just suffered a panic attack and had been promised medical attention, but before

receiving it was read his *Miranda* rights and given a rights waiver form. Ryan could argue, therefore, that his waiver was not voluntary, knowing, or intelligent. However, courts applying a totality of the circumstances rarely find a waiver to be involuntary. In this case, therefore, the argument is likely to fail.

Ryan could also argue that the statement "Do I need a lawyer just so I can see a doctor?" followed by a subsequent request for a cell phone constituted an assertion of his right to counsel. If Ryan did assert his right to counsel, all questioning had to cease and any statements taken in violation of the right would likely be suppressed. However, courts have consistently held that an assertion of a right to counsel must be unambiguous. It is very likely, therefore, that a court will hold that Ryan's ambiguous statement was not an effective assertion of his right to counsel and, therefore, the confession will not be suppressed on that basis.

(3) Ryan's pronouncement "I'm through talking to that jerk" probably also will not have any effect on the admissibility of his confession. At issue is whether it constitutes a valid invocation of the right to remain silent.

Under *Miranda*, if a defendant invokes the right to remain silent, questioning must stop and the request must be scrupulously honored. Such an assertion, however, must be clear and unambiguous. Arguably, it is not clear here. Ryan could argue, however, that at least Van Buren understood that Ryan had asserted his right against self-incrimination as demonstrated by Van Buren's question "what can I do to get you to change your mind?" If a court finds that Ryan had validly asserted his right, Van Buren violated that right by continuing the interrogation and trying to get Ryan to change his mind. In that case, the confession may be suppressed as taken in violation of Ryan's right against self-incrimination under the Fifth Amendment. However, it seems more likely that the court would find Ryan's statement ambiguous. In that event, there would be no *Miranda* violation and his subsequent confession would be admissible.

ANSWER TO EXAM QUESTION NO. 3

(1) The warrantless search of the Sotwin garage violated the Fourth Amendment to the United States Constitution. At issue is whether any exception to the warrant requirement is applicable.

Under the Fourth Amendment, which is applicable to the states through the Due Process Clause of the Fourteenth Amendment, searches must be reasonable. Generally, to be reasonable, a search must be pursuant to a warrant. However, the Supreme Court has carved out a number of exceptions to the warrant requirement, including an exception based on consent. A warrant is not needed to conduct a search if the police have valid consent to conduct the search. Consent generally can be granted by anyone with apparent access to the place searched. However, the United States Supreme Court has held that where two occupants are reasonably believed to share authority over the premises, one occupant's consent to search can be vetoed by the other occupant's express refusal. Here, Andy had apparent authority to consent to a search of the home because when the police knocked at the door, Andy, an adult, answered it, and he gave them permission to search. However, when Nancy walked out of the bathroom and shouted at the police to leave, she effectively revoked Andy's consent. Therefore, the search of the garage was unconstitutional and any evidence derived from the search must be suppressed under the exclusionary rule (all evidence obtained in an unconstitutional manner or that is the fruit of an unconstitutional search or seizure must be suppressed from evidence).

It should be noted that the above does not necessarily mean that the blood from the Saturn will be suppressed. If the state can show that the police would have discovered the evidence anyway or that it was obtained from an independent source, the evidence may be admitted. The state might be able to make such a showing here. The facts indicate that after seeing the blood on the Saturn, the police

applied for a search warrant and then tested the vehicle. The facts do not indicate what was included in the warrant. A search warrant will be issued if it shows probable cause to believe that seizable evidence will be found at the place to be searched. Whether probable cause is present is based on the totality of the circumstances. Here, the police probably could have met the probable cause standard even without seeing the blood on the Saturn, because an eyewitness told them that he saw Nancy driving erratically, strike the child, and pull into her garage. Thus, the inevitable discovery or independent source exceptions to the exclusionary rule may apply here.

(2)   The federal Confrontation Clause would not bar admission of the 911 tape recording. At issue is whether the call would be considered testimonial under the Confrontation Clause.

The Confrontation Clause prohibits introduction of prior testimonial evidence unless the declarant is unavailable and the defendant had an opportunity to cross-examine the declarant at the time the statement was admitted. Here, clearly Nancy did not have an opportunity to cross-examine the 911 caller and we do not know if the caller was unavailable for trial. Nevertheless the 911 tape is admissible. The Supreme Court has held that generally, responses to police questioning are testimonial in nature. However, the Court has found that 911 tapes are nontestimonial—even if they include statements made in response to police questions—if the statements are made to enable the police to respond to an ongoing emergency. That was the case here. The call appears to have been made shortly after Nancy hit the young child. Thus, the Confrontation Clause would not bar admission of the tape recording of the call.

(3)   The Confrontation Clause bars admission of Doug's statement to officers. The rules set out in (2), above, apply here. Doug is now unavailable, given that he has been deployed to Iraq. However, unlike the 911 call, Doug's statements were testimonial. They were made in response to police questioning and were not made to enable police to respond to an ongoing emergency. The police interviewed Doug the day after the hit and run took place. Thus, admission of Doug's testimony would violate the Confrontation Clause because Nancy did not have an opportunity to cross-examine Doug when his statements were made.

ANSWER TO EXAM QUESTION NO. 4

(1)   ***Right to Court-Appointed Counsel:*** Kirk should be successful in having his conviction overturned for the court's failure to appoint counsel. At issue is whether Kirk's Sixth Amendment right to counsel has been violated.

The Sixth Amendment guarantees the right to be represented by counsel in all criminal cases. This right turns on whether the sentence that is ***actually*** imposed includes any imprisonment, however short. Thus, it does not matter that the judge said he would not impose a sentence of more than six months. Because Kirk received a sentence that included imprisonment, Kirk was entitled to a court-appointed attorney (the facts state that he was otherwise qualified; the courts have never clarified how inability to afford counsel is to be determined under the Sixth Amendment). Thus, the court should overturn Kirk's conviction on this ground.

(2)   ***Right to Jury Trial:*** Kirk would also be successful in arguing that his conviction should be overturned for the judge's denial of Kirk's request for a jury. At issue is whether Kirk's Sixth Amendment right to a jury trial was violated. The Supreme Court has held the Sixth Amendment jury trial right applicable to the states via the Fourteenth Amendment, but the right applies only to serious, not petty, offenses. A serious offense is one for which more than six months' imprisonment is ***authorized***. Here, although only six months was given, and although this was stated in advance, the crime is serious enough to carry a 10-month possible sentence, so the right to a jury trial attaches. Also, the court may consider the total combination of penalties—the fine and the loss of hunting rights for five years—

in deciding whether the offense is serious. [Blanton v. City of North Las Vegas (1989)] A comparison to the facts of *Blanton* suggests, however, that the additional penalties imposed here would not make much difference.

(3) ***The Same Judge in the Second Case:*** Kirk would not be successful in having his conviction overturned merely because the second prosecution is before the same judge who presided over the first prosecution. At issue is whether Kirk's right to Due Process was violated.

The Due Process Clause of the Fourteenth Amendment includes a guarantee of the fairness of criminal prosecutions. This includes a right to an unbiased decisionmaker. However, the fact that the judge already knows some of the facts in his case because of a prior case is not considered "prejudice" within the meaning of the due process requirement. Moreover, the facts do not show that Kirk preserved the issue for appeal at trial. Thus, Kirk would not be successful in arguing this ground for reversal.

(4) ***Double Jeopardy:*** Kirk would not be successful in arguing that his conviction should be overturned because of double jeopardy. At issue is whether the second prosecution would be considered the same offense as was prosecuted at the first trial.

The Double Jeopardy Clause of the Fifth Amendment provides that people shall not twice be prosecuted for the same offense. The clause is applicable to the states through the Due Process Clause of the Fourteenth Amendment. Whether two offenses constitute the same offense for purposes of the Double Jeopardy Clause depends on whether each crime requires proof of an additional element that the other does not require, even though some of the same facts may be necessary to prove both crimes.

Here, the negligent homicide charge of the first proceeding requires proof of a killing, which is not required in the second prosecution for hunting within 400 feet of a dwelling. And the second prosecution requires proof of hunting within 400 feet of a dwelling, which is not an element of a negligent homicide case. Thus, Kirk would not be successful in arguing that his conviction should be overturned on double jeopardy grounds.

Evidence

EVIDENCE

TABLE OF CONTENTS

I. GENERAL CONSIDERATIONS

A. DEFINING EVIDENCE LAW

The law of evidence is a system of rules and standards by which the admission of proof at the trial of a lawsuit is regulated. The material facts in the controversy are determined by proof that is filtered through the applicable rules of evidence. This proof includes testimony, writings, physical objects, and anything else presented to the senses of the jury.

B. SOURCES OF EVIDENCE LAW

In some states, evidence law is derived from a blend of common law rules and miscellaneous statutes. However, today, most jurisdictions have enacted modern evidence codes, which form a comprehensive set of statutes or rules covering all major areas of evidence law. The most important codification is the Federal Rules of Evidence, which became effective July 1, 1975. The Federal Rules govern on the Multistate Bar Examination.

C. FEDERAL RULES OF EVIDENCE

The Federal Rules of Evidence are applicable in all *civil and criminal* cases in the United States courts of appeal, district courts, Court of Claims, and in proceedings before United States magistrates. [Fed. R. Evid. 101 and 1101] For the most part, the Federal Rules have codified well-established principles of evidence law. Where the Federal Rules depart from the traditional rules of evidence, the adopted Federal Rule is likely to represent an important modern trend, which the states are likely to follow as they revise and codify existing law.

D. THRESHOLD ADMISSIBILITY ISSUES

A shorthand summary of evidence law might be stated in one sentence: *Material* and *relevant* evidence is admissible if *competent*.

1. Materiality: The Proposition to Be Proved

Materiality exists when the proffered evidence relates to one of the substantive legal issues in the case. The key questions to ask regarding materiality are: What issue is the evidence offered to prove? Is that legal issue material to the substantive cause of action or defense in the case? The answer to these questions and the determination of materiality depend upon the substantive legal issues framed by the pleadings. Thus, evidence is immaterial if the proposition for which it is offered as proof is not a legal issue in the case.

Example: In a workers' compensation proceeding, evidence of the claimant's contributory negligence would be immaterial since the workers' compensation statute abrogates it as a defense.

2. Relevance: Probativeness—The Link Between Proof and Proposition

Probativeness embraces the test of materiality and something more. Probative evidence *contributes to proving or disproving* a material issue. Assuming that the issue the evidence is offered to prove is a material one, is the evidence logically probative of that issue? Does the evidence tend to prove that issue? Does the evidence tend to make the material proposition (issue) more probably true or untrue than it would be without the evidence?

Example: Evidence that the defendant drove recklessly on a prior occasion is material because it speaks to the question of his negligence. However, it is not sufficiently probative of the issue of negligence on this particular occasion, and is therefore not relevant.

3. **Federal Rules—Materiality and Probativeness Combined**
   In the Federal Rules of Evidence, as in most modern codes, the requirements of materiality and probativeness are combined into a single definition of relevance. Thus, Federal Rule 401 provides that "relevant evidence" means evidence tending to make the existence of any fact of consequence to the determination of the action (materiality) more or less probable than it would be without the evidence (probativeness). You should watch for both aspects of the relevance problem. Ask yourself (i) whether the fact sought to be proved is itself in issue under the pleadings and the substantive law, and also (ii) whether the evidence helps to prove the fact for which it is offered.

4. **Competence**
   As mentioned above, material and relevant evidence is admissible if competent. Evidence is competent if it *does not violate an exclusionary rule*. Basically, then, if evidence is material and relevant, the only reason such evidence would not be admitted is if it is prohibited by a special exclusionary rule of evidence. Exclusionary rules that prevent admissibility of relevant and material evidence are founded upon one or more of the following:

   a. **Policies Related to Truth-Seeking**
      The need to ensure the reliability and authenticity of evidence is a truth-seeking policy. Examples of exclusionary rules that perform this truth-seeking function are the hearsay rule, the best evidence rule, and Dead Man statutes.

   b. **Policies External to Litigation**
      The need to protect extrajudicial interests of society is an external policy goal. Rules granting testimonial privileges, for example, admittedly hamper the in-court search for truth.

E. **EVIDENCE CLASSIFICATIONS**

1. **Direct or Circumstantial**

   a. **Direct Evidence Relies on Actual Knowledge**
      Direct evidence goes directly to a material issue without intervention of an inferential process. Evidence is direct when the very facts in dispute are communicated by those who have actual knowledge by means of their senses.
      Example: On the issue of whether anyone had recently crossed a snow-covered bridge, the testimony of a witness that he saw a man crossing would be direct evidence.

   b. **Circumstantial Evidence Relies on Inference**
      Circumstantial evidence is indirect and relies on inference. It is evidence of a subsidiary or collateral fact from which, alone or in conjunction with a cluster of other facts, the existence of the material issue can be inferred.
      Example: On the issue of whether anyone had recently crossed a snow-covered bridge, the testimony of a witness that he saw human footprints in the snow on the bridge would be circumstantial evidence.

2. **Testimonial, Documentary, or Real**

a.   ***Testimonial*** evidence is oral evidence given under oath. The witness responds to the questions of the attorneys.

b.   ***Documentary*** evidence is evidence in the form of a writing, such as a contract or a confession.

c.   ***Real*** evidence is the term applied to evidence consisting of things as distinguished from assertions of witnesses about things. Real evidence includes anything conveying a firsthand sense impression to the trier of fact, such as knives, jewelry, maps, or tape recordings.

F.   LIMITED ADMISSIBILITY

1.   Admissible for One Purpose But Not Another
The use of admissible evidence is a frequently encountered problem. It often happens that evidence is admissible for one purpose but is not admissible for another purpose.

Example: At the trial of the accused for assault, defendant's prior conviction for robbery may be shown by the prosecution to impeach the credibility of testimony given by the accused as a witness. The prior conviction is not admissible on the issue of defendant's guilt on the assault charge.

2.   Admissible Against One Party But Not Another
It is also possible that the evidence is admissible against one party but is not admissible against another party.

Example: A post-accident admission of a negligent employee truck driver may be admissible against the truck driver in an action for negligence. However, under certain circumstances it may not be admissible against a defendant employer who owned the truck.

3.   Jury Must Be Properly Instructed
As a general rule, if evidence is admissible for one purpose, it is not excluded merely because of the danger that the jury may also consider it for another incompetent purpose. When evidence that is admissible as to one party or for one purpose but is not admissible as to another party or for another purpose is admitted, the court must, upon request, restrict the evidence to its proper scope and instruct the jury accordingly. [Fed. R. Evid. 105]

II.   RELEVANCE

A.   INTRODUCTION
Relevance, in the sense of probativeness, has to do with the tendency of evidence to ***prove or disprove a material issue***, to render it more probably true, or untrue, than it would have been without the particular evidence. Relevance is concerned with the ***substance or content*** of the evidence, not with the form or manner in which it is offered (*e.g.*, hearsay rule, best evidence rule). It can be stated, as a general proposition, that all relevant evidence is admissible if it is offered in an unobjectionable form and manner. (As usual, there are some exceptions to this generalization, since some perfectly relevant evidence that is in the proper form is excluded for policy reasons.)

B.   DETERMINING RELEVANCE
Relevant evidence is evidence having any tendency to make the existence of any fact that is

of consequence to the determination of an action more probable than it would be without the evidence. [Fed. R. Evid. 401] Note that this definition of relevance includes materiality, since it requires that the disputed fact be of consequence to the determination of the action. The basic questions to ask regarding relevancy are: "What proposition is the evidence being used to prove? Is this a material issue in the case? Is the evidence probative of that proposition?" This type of relevance is sometimes called "logical relevance."

1. **General Rule—Must Relate to Time, Event, or Person in Controversy**

Whenever testimony or exhibit evidence that relates to a time, event, or person other than the time, event, or person directly involved in the controversy being litigated is offered, the relevance of that evidence is suspect and should be examined more carefully. In most cases, a previous similar occurrence proves little or nothing about the one in issue. In addition, the risk of confusion and unfair prejudice usually outweighs the helpfulness of this type of evidence (*see* C., *infra*). Note that when considering the relevance of such evidence, one of the important factors to consider is its proximity in time to the current events. A circumstance that would be relevant had it occurred in close time proximity to the event in question is irrelevant if, instead, it was very remote.

Examples: 1) Defendant is alleged to have run a red light and hit a pedestrian in the crosswalk. Proof that defendant ran other red lights in the past has little probative value in proving the occurrence in question. The probative value of such proof is outweighed by the confusion and unfair prejudice that would result from its admission.

2) On the issue of the fair market value of property in a condemnation action, the relevance of the sale price of other property depends on how comparable the other property is to the property being condemned, how close it is geographically, and how recent that sale was. Sale of a neighbor's comparable property six months ago is probably relevant, but the sale of the same property five years ago probably is not relevant.

3) In a murder prosecution, evidence that the accused had threatened the alleged victim the day before the killing may be very relevant. But compare a threat a week before; a month before; a year before; 10 years before.

2. **Exceptions—Certain Similar Occurrences Are Relevant**

Despite the above rule, previous similar happenings and transactions of the parties and others similarly situated may be relevant if they are probative of the material issue involved, and if that probative value outweighs the risk that the evidence will confuse the jury or result in unfair prejudice. Of course, whenever a similar occurrence is offered to establish an inference about the subject occurrence, the quality of the inference depends on the similarity between the other happening and the one in issue. The following are examples of relevant similar occurrences.

a. **Causation**

Complicated issues of causation may often be established by evidence that concerns other times, events, or persons. For example, evidence that other homes in the same area were damaged by defendant's blasting operations is some evidence that the damage to plaintiff's home was caused by defendant's activities.

b. **Prior False Claims or Same Bodily Injury**
Evidence that a person has previously filed similar *tort claims* or has been involved in *prior accidents* is *generally inadmissible* to show the invalidity of the present claim. At best, such evidence indicates plaintiff's tendency toward litigation or accident-proneness. In either case, the probative value is outweighed by the risk of confusion of issues and undue prejudice.

But if evidence is introduced that the party has made previous similar *false* claims, such evidence is usually relevant, under a common scheme or plan theory, to prove that the present claim is likely to be false. Likewise, where the prior claim was for an injury to the *same portion of plaintiff's body* that she claims was injured in the present case, evidence of the prior claim or injury may be relevant to prove that her present claim is false or exaggerated.

c. **Similar Accidents or Injuries Caused by Same Event or Condition**
Where similar accidents or injuries were caused by the same event or condition, evidence of those prior accidents or injuries is *admissible to prove*:

(i) That a defect or dangerous *condition existed*;

(ii) That the defendant had *knowledge* of the defect or dangerous condition; and

(iii) That the defect or dangerous condition was the *cause* of the present injury.

Example: In an action for dust damage from a mill, it may be proper to introduce evidence that plaintiff's neighbors have previously suffered similar dust damage, in order to prove that the mill created dust, that the mill owners knew of the dust, and that the dust caused plaintiff's damage.

1) **Absence of Similar Accidents**
Many courts are reluctant to admit evidence of the absence of similar accidents to show absence of negligence or lack of a defect. However, where a structural condition is involved and that condition is unchanged, the court has discretion to admit evidence of absence of other complaints to show lack of a defect. Evidence of prior safety history and absence of complaints is admissible to show *defendant's lack of knowledge* of any danger.

d. **Previous Similar Acts Admissible to Prove Intent**
Similar conduct previously committed by a party may be introduced to prove the party's present motive or intent when such elements are relevant.
Example: In an action against a school board for excluding a black child from school, similar exclusions of black children will be admissible into evidence to show intent.

e. **Rebutting Claim of Impossibility**
The requirement that prior occurrences be similar to the litigated act may be relaxed when used to rebut a claim or defense of impossibility. For example, if defendant denies negligent speeding on the ground that his automobile could never go above 50 m.p.h., plaintiff may rebut by showing that on other occasions, even under different circumstances, the vehicle was traveling at 75 m.p.h.

f. Sales of Similar Property

Evidence of sales of similar personal or real property that are not too remote in time is ***admissible to prove value***. However, unlike commonly sold items of personal property, each parcel of real property is considered unique. Thus, the problem of producing evidence of other transactions requires a preliminary finding that the character, usage, proximity, date of sale, etc., are sufficiently similar to the property in issue. Evidence of prices quoted in mere ***offers*** is ***not admissible*** because to determine the sincerity of these offers would lead to collateral disputes. However, offers by a party to the present action to buy or sell the property may be admissible as admissions.

g. Habit

Habit describes one's regular response to a specific set of circumstances (*e.g.,* "she always takes a staircase two steps at a time"). In contrast, character describes one's disposition in respect to general traits (*e.g.,* "she's always in a hurry"). Since habits are more specific and particularized, evidence of habit is relevant and can be introduced in circumstances when it is not permissible to introduce evidence of character. Thus, under Federal Rule 406, "evidence of the habit of a person . . . is relevant to prove that the conduct of the person . . . on a particular occasion was in conformity with the habit . . . ."

Example: Evidence could be introduced to show that a driver habitually failed to stop at a certain stop sign as circumstantial evidence that she failed to stop at the time in question. In contrast, evidence cannot be introduced to show that a person is a careless driver since that is closer to character than habit.

Many states either do not admit evidence of habit to show that a particular act occurred, or else limit admissibility to those cases where there are no eyewitnesses. Federal Rule 406 admits habit evidence freely and abandons the "no eyewitness" requirement. Even where admissible, however, the habit must be shown to be a regular response to a repeated specific situation.

h. Industrial or Business Routine

Just as evidence of personal habit is relevant to show conduct, evidence that a business or firm had an established business routine is relevant as tending to show that a particular event occurred.

Example: Evidence of a regular mailing procedure, such as a custom of picking up letters from a certain table and mailing them, would be relevant as evidence to show that a particular letter left on the table was duly mailed.

i. Industrial Custom as Evidence of Standard of Care

1) Industrial Custom Distinguished from Business Routine

Custom of the industry should be distinguished from business routine. In the latter case, the particular conduct and habit of a party are being offered to show that the party acted in the same manner on the occasion in question. Custom of the industry is offered to prove the actions of other persons in the same industry in an attempt to show adherence to or deviance from an industry-wide standard of care.

2) Relevant to Standard of Care But Not Conclusive
When one of the issues in dispute is negligence arising out of inadequate safety devices or precautions, evidence of general custom or usage in the same kind of business under the same circumstances may be introduced by either party as tending to establish a standard by which reasonable or ordinary care may be judged. Although custom of the trade or business is admissible on the standard of care to be exercised, it is not conclusive.

C. DISCRETIONARY EXCLUSION OF RELEVANT EVIDENCE (PRAGMATIC RELEVANCE)

A trial judge has broad discretion to exclude relevant evidence if its probative value is *substantially* outweighed by the danger of *unfair prejudice*, *confusion of the issues*, or *misleading the jury*, or by considerations of *undue delay*, waste of time, or needless presentation of cumulative evidence. [Fed. R. Evid. 403] *"Unfair surprise"* is listed as an additional basis for exclusion under some state rules, but it was omitted under the Federal Rules on the theory that surprise can be prevented by discovery and pretrial conference or mitigated by granting a continuance.

Certain items of evidence may be directed to a material issue in the case and may be very probative of that issue, but they are excluded because of predictable policies designed to ensure an orderly and efficient proceeding and to encourage certain public policy solutions to legal problems. For example, inflammatory matter, which may be very probative of the issues, will not be admitted because of the potential prejudicial effect on the jury.

D. EXCLUSION OF RELEVANT EVIDENCE FOR PUBLIC POLICY REASONS (POLICY-BASED RELEVANCE)

Certain evidence of questionable relevance is excluded by the Federal Rules because public policy favors the behavior involved. For example, the law encourages the repair of defective premises that cause injury, and consequently, evidence of the subsequent repair may not be admitted to prove antecedent negligence, even though it may be probative of the issue. Evidence excluded for public policy reasons is set forth below.

1. Liability Insurance

a. Inadmissible to Show Negligence or Ability to Pay
Evidence that a person was or was not insured against liability is *not admissible* upon the issue of whether she *acted negligently* or otherwise wrongfully. Nor is it admissible to show *ability to pay* a substantial judgment. [Fed. R. Evid. 411]

b. When Admissible
Proof that a person carried liability insurance may be admissible and relevant for other purposes. Issue identification is important in these cases, since proof of the fact that the defendant maintained insurance *may be used*:

1) To Prove Ownership or Control
Evidence that the defendant maintained insurance may be admitted for the limited purpose of proving the defendant's ownership or control when ownership or control is disputed.
Example: P sues D and alleges that D owned the building in which P fell on a defective staircase, further alleging a cause of action for negligence.

D denies all allegations, and thereby puts in issue the question of ownership of the premises. P may show that D had insured the premises as evidence of ownership, but the evidence will only be used for the limited purpose of proving that issue.

2) For Purposes of Impeachment
Evidence that the defendant is insured may be used for the limited purpose of impeaching a witness.
Example: An investigator testifies on behalf of defendant. Plaintiff may demonstrate the bias or interest of this witness by showing that she is employed by defendant's liability insurance company.

3) As Part of Admission
An admission of liability may be so coupled with a reference to insurance coverage that the reference to insurance cannot be severed without lessening its value as an admission of liability.
Example: "Don't worry; my insurance company will pay off."

2. Subsequent Remedial Measures

a. Inadmissible to Prove Negligence or Culpable Conduct
Evidence of repairs or other precautionary measures made following an injury is inadmissible to prove negligence, culpable conduct, a defect in a product or its design, or a need for a warning or instruction. [Fed. R. Evid. 407] The purpose of the rule is to encourage people to make such repairs.

b. When Admissible
Although evidence of subsequent repairs is not admissible to prove negligence, etc., this evidence may still be admissible for other purposes. Some of these purposes are:

1) To Prove Ownership or Control
Evidence of subsequent repairs performed by the defendant may be introduced to prove ownership or control, since a stranger would hardly make repairs.

2) To Rebut Claim that Precaution Was Not Feasible
Evidence of repairs or other precautionary measures made following an accident is admissible to establish the feasibility of precautionary measures when such feasibility is controverted.

3) To Prove Destruction of Evidence
Evidence of subsequent remedial measures may be admitted to prove that the opposing party has destroyed evidence; *e.g.,* repainting a fender to cover up evidence of a collision (spoliation).

3. Settlement Offers—Negotiations Not Admissible
Evidence of compromises or offers to compromise is inadmissible to prove liability for or invalidity of a claim that is disputed as to validity or amount. Such evidence is also inadmissible to impeach through a prior inconsistent statement. [Fed. R. Evid. 408] *Rationale:* Public policy favors the settlement of disputes without litigation, and settlement would be

discouraged if either side were deterred from making offers by the fear that they would be admitted in evidence.

The Federal Rules also exclude "conduct or statements" made in the course of negotiating a compromise, as well as the offer to compromise itself; therefore, admissions of fact made during compromise negotiations are inadmissible. This position encourages settlements by allowing complete candor between the parties in negotiations. However, "conduct or statements" made during compromise negotiations regarding a civil dispute with a governmental regulatory, investigative, or enforcement authority are not excluded when offered *in a criminal case*. [Fed. R. Evid. 408] Note that Rule 408 does not protect preexisting information simply because it is presented to one's opponent during compromise negotiations; *e.g.,* one may not immunize otherwise admissible information under the guise of disclosing it during compromise negotiations.

a. Must Be a Claim
Although the filing of a suit is not a prerequisite for this exclusionary rule, there must be some indication, express or implied, that a party is going to make some kind of claim. Thus, a party's volunteered admission of fact accompanying an offer to settle immediately following the incident is usually admissible because there has not been time for the other party to indicate an intent to make a claim.

b. Claim Must Be Disputed as to Liability or Amount
To trigger the exclusionary feature of Rule 408, the claim must be disputed as to liability or amount. Thus, if a party admits liability and the amount of liability but offers to settle (rather than litigate) for a lesser amount, every statement made in connection with that offer is admissible.

4. Withdrawn Guilty Pleas and Offers to Plead Guilty Not Admissible
Under the Federal Rules neither withdrawn guilty pleas, pleas of nolo contendere, offers to plead guilty, nor evidence of statements made in negotiating such pleas are admissible in any proceeding. [Fed. R. Evid. 410] Most jurisdictions concur. The *evidentiary value* of a withdrawn plea of guilty as an admission is deemed *offset by the prejudicial effect* of the evidence. Moreover, it is felt that the judge who permitted the withdrawal of the guilty plea must have decided that there was a good reason to withdraw it and, under these circumstances, the significance of the initial plea is minimal. Most courts exclude offers to plead guilty on reasoning similar to that advanced for not admitting offers to compromise as proof of liability in civil cases.

a. Waiver
The protection of Rule 410 for plea negotiations may be validly waived unless there is an affirmative indication that the defendant entered the waiver agreement unknowingly or involuntarily. [United States v. Mezzanatto, 513 U.S. 196 (1995)]

Example: Defendant, who was charged with a drug offense, wished to arrange a deal with the government in exchange for his cooperation. As a prerequisite to this discussion, Prosecutor required that Defendant (i) be completely truthful and (ii) agree that any statements made by him in the course of the plea negotiations could be used to impeach him if he testified in a contrary fashion at trial. Defendant agreed. If at some point thereafter the discussion breaks off and Defendant is tried on the charges,

Prosecutor may use statements made in the plea negotiations to impeach Defendant. [United States v. Mezzanatto, *supra*]

5. Payment of Medical Expenses Not Admissible
Similarly, evidence that a party paid (or offered to pay) the injured party's medical expenses is *not admissible to prove liability* for the injury. [Fed. R. Evid. 409] This rule is based upon the concern that such payment might be prompted solely by "humanitarian motives." However, unlike the situation with compromise negotiation (3., *supra*), *admissions of fact* accompanying offers to pay medical expenses *are admissible.*

E. CHARACTER EVIDENCE—A SPECIAL RELEVANCE PROBLEM
The rules regarding use of character evidence are affected by three major concerns. These are: (i) the purpose for which evidence of character is offered; (ii) the method to be used to prove character; and (iii) the kind of case, civil or criminal.

1. Purposes for Offer of Character Evidence

a. To Prove Character When Character Itself Is Ultimate Issue in Case
When a person's character itself is the ultimate issue in the case, character evidence must be admitted. Cases where character is itself one of the material propositions in issue are confined mostly to civil litigation and are rare even among civil actions.

b. To Serve as Circumstantial Evidence of How a Person Probably Acted
It is the use of character as circumstantial evidence of how a person probably acted that raises the most difficult problems of relevance, especially in criminal cases.

c. To Impeach Credibility of Witness
The discussion of the use of character evidence to impeach the credibility of a witness is postponed for later discussion under the heading of "Credibility—Impeachment." (*See* VI.E., *infra.*)

2. Means of Proving Character
Depending upon the jurisdiction, the purpose of the offer, and the nature of the case, the following types of evidence may be used to prove character:

a. Evidence of Specific Acts as Demonstrating Character
Evidence of specific acts of the person in question as demonstrating that person's character is permitted only in a few instances, such as where character is itself one of the ultimate issues in the case.

b. Opinion Testimony
Witnesses who know the person may testify regarding their opinions about the person's character.

c. Testimony as to Person's General Reputation in Community
Testimony by witnesses as to a person's general reputation in the community is in some sense hearsay, since reputation is really what people say about a person. On the other hand, because reputation is a general indication of character, and because it involves fewer side issues than either of the above methods, it is the most common means of showing character.

3.   Generally Not Admissible in Civil Cases
Evidence of character to prove the conduct of a person in the litigated event is generally not admissible in a civil case. The reasons given are that the slight probative value of character is outweighed by the danger of prejudice, the possible distraction of the jury from the main question in issue, and the possible waste of time required by examination of collateral issues.

Examples: 1) Defendant may not introduce evidence that she is generally a cautious driver to prove that she was not negligent on the day in question.

2) Plaintiff may not introduce evidence that the defendant is usually a reckless driver to prove that she was negligent on the day in question.

Such circumstantial use of prior behavior patterns for the purpose of drawing the inference that, at the time and place in question, the actor probably acted in accord with her prior behavior pattern is not permitted. A person's ***general behavior patterns*** (as distinguished from her habits and business routines) are ***irrelevant*** and inadmissible in evidence.

a.   Exception—When Character Is Directly in Issue
When a person's character itself is one of the issues in the case, character evidence is not only admissible, but indeed is the best method of proving the issue.

Examples: 1) In a defamation action, when D is being sued for calling P a thief and pleads as an affirmative defense that she spoke the truth (*i.e.*, that P is indeed a thief), P's character is clearly in issue.

2) When an employer is charged with negligently retaining an employee "of unstable and violent disposition," the character of the employee is also in issue.

When character is directly in issue, almost all courts will admit evidence of specific acts that show this character (*e.g.*, in Example 1) above, D may offer evidence that on different occasions P has stolen things to show that he is a thief). Under the Federal Rules, any of the types of evidence (***reputation, opinion, or specific acts***) may be used to prove character when character is directly in issue. [Fed. R. Evid. 405(b)]

4.   Accused in a Criminal Case—Prosecution Cannot Initiate, But Accused Can
The general rule is that the prosecution cannot initiate evidence of the bad character of the defendant merely to show that she is more likely to have committed the crime of which she is accused. However, the accused may introduce evidence of her good character to show her innocence of the alleged crime.

The rationale is that even though the evidence is of some relevance, the prosecution should not be permitted to show that the defendant is a bad person, since the jury might then decide to convict her regardless of her guilt of the crime charged. However, since the life or liberty of the defendant is at stake, she should be allowed to introduce evidence of her good character since it may have a tendency to show that she did not commit the crime charged.

a.   How Defendant Proves Character

1)   Reputation and Personal Opinion Testimony
A defendant puts her character in issue by calling a qualified witness to testify

to the defendant's good reputation (or that he has heard nothing bad) *for the trait involved* in the case. Under Federal Rule 405, the witness may also give his personal opinion concerning that trait of the defendant. However, the witness may *not* testify to *specific acts of conduct* of the defendant to prove the trait in issue.

2) Testifying Places Defendant's Credibility—Not Character—in Issue
A defendant does not put her character in issue merely by taking the stand and giving testimony on the facts of the controversy. However, if the defendant takes the stand, she puts her credibility in issue and is subject to impeachment. (*See* "Credibility—Impeachment," VI.E., *infra*.)

b. How Prosecution Rebuts Defendant's Character Evidence
If the defendant puts her character in issue by having a character witness testify as to his opinion of the defendant or the defendant's reputation, the prosecution may rebut in the following manner:

1) Cross-Examination
The prosecution may test the character witness by cross-examination regarding the basis for his opinion or knowledge of the reputation that he has testified about. In most jurisdictions, one is allowed to inquire on cross-examination whether the reputation witness has *heard* of particular instances of the defendant's misconduct pertinent to the trait in question. The rationale is that since the reputation witness relates what he has heard, the inquiry tests the accuracy of his hearing and reporting. Since the character witness may now testify in the form of opinion as well as by reputation, it follows that the basis of the opinion can be exposed. Thus, under Federal Rule 405(a), cross-examination inquiry is allowable as to whether the opinion witness *knows* of, as well as whether he has *heard* of, specific instances of misconduct. The distinction in form between "Have you heard" and "Do you know" is eliminated by the statement in Rule 405(a), which provides that "on cross-examination, inquiry is allowable into relevant specific instances of conduct." Note that if the witness denies knowledge of these specific instances of conduct, the prosecutor *may not* prove them by extrinsic evidence; he is limited to inquiry on cross-examination.

2) Testimony of Other Witnesses as to Defendant's Bad Reputation
The prosecution may rebut the defendant's character evidence by calling qualified witnesses to testify to the defendant's bad reputation or their opinion of the defendant's character for the particular trait involved.

5. Victim in Criminal Case

a. Defendant's Initiative
The defendant may introduce reputation or opinion evidence of a bad character trait of the alleged crime victim when it is relevant to show the defendant's innocence. However, by specific exception, this rule does not extend to showing the bad character of rape victims.

Example: In an assault or murder prosecution where the defendant claims self-defense, she may introduce evidence of the victim's violent character as tending to show that the victim was the aggressor.

b. Prosecution Rebuttal

Once the defendant has introduced evidence of a bad character trait of the alleged victim, the prosecution may counter with reputation or opinion evidence of (i) the *victim's good character*, or (ii) the *defendant's bad character* for the *same trait*. [Fed. R. Evid. 404(a)]

Example: Defendant is charged with the murder of Victim. Defendant pleads self-defense and offers evidence that Victim was a violent person. Prosecutor can rebut such evidence with evidence that Victim was a nonviolent person and/or with evidence that Defendant is a violent person.

c. Rape Cases—Victim's Past Behavior Inadmissible

In any civil or criminal proceeding involving alleged sexual misconduct, evidence offered to prove the sexual behavior or sexual disposition of the alleged victim is generally inadmissible. [Fed. R. Evid. 412(a)]

1) Exceptions in Criminal Cases

In a criminal case, evidence of sexual behavior by the victim offered to prove that a person other than the accused was the *source of semen, injury, or other physical evidence* is admissible. Also, specific instances of sexual behavior between the victim and the accused are admissible by the prosecution, or by the defense to prove *consent*. Evidence of a victim's sexual behavior is also admissible when its exclusion would violate the defendant's constitutional rights. [Fed. R. Evid. 412(b)(1)]

2) Exceptions in Civil Cases

In civil cases, evidence offered to prove the sexual disposition or behavior of the alleged victim is admissible if it is otherwise admissible under the Federal Rules and its probative value substantially outweighs the danger of harm to the victim and of unfair prejudice to any party. Evidence of an alleged victim's reputation is admissible only if it has been placed in controversy by the victim. [Fed. R. Evid. 412(b)(2)]

3) Procedure

To offer evidence under the above exceptions, the party must file a motion 14 days before trial describing the evidence and its purpose, and must serve the motion on all parties and notify the victim. Before admitting the evidence, the court must conduct an in camera hearing and afford the victim and the parties a right to be heard. [Fed. R. Evid. 412(c)]

6. Specific Acts of Misconduct Generally Inadmissible

The basic rule is that when a person is charged with one crime, extrinsic evidence of her other crimes or misconduct is inadmissible if such evidence is offered solely to establish a criminal disposition. Thus, this statement of Federal Rule 404(b) is merely another way of saying that the prosecution may not show the accused's bad character to imply criminal disposition. The danger again is that the jury may convict the defendant because of past crimes rather than because of her guilt of the offense charged.

a. Admissible If Independently Relevant

Evidence of other crimes or misconduct is admissible if these acts are relevant to some

issue other than the defendant's character or disposition to commit the crime charged. While acknowledging that prior acts or crimes are not admissible to show conformity or to imply bad character, Federal Rule 404(b) goes on to say that such prior acts or crimes may be admissible for other purposes (*e.g.*, to show motive, opportunity, intent, preparation, plan, knowledge, identity, or absence of mistake) whenever these issues are relevant in either a ***criminal or a civil case***. Upon request by the accused, the prosecution in a criminal case must provide reasonable notice prior to trial (or during trial if pretrial notice is excused for good cause shown) of the general nature of any of this type of evidence the prosecution intends to introduce at trial.

Example: Husband is on trial for the alleged shooting murder of Wife. Husband claims an accident occurred as he was cleaning the gun. Prosecution may prove that six months ago Husband tried to stab Wife. This evidence is not offered to show that the defendant is the kind of violent man likely to have murdered his wife (*i.e.*, general bad character or violent disposition); rather, it is offered to show absence of mistake, that the killing was probably not an accident.

1)   Examples of Relevant Misconduct

a)   Motive
The commission of a prior crime may be evidence of a motive to commit the crime for which the defendant is accused.

b)   Intent
In many crimes, such as forgery, passing counterfeit money, larceny by trick, and receiving stolen property, intent is the gravamen of the crime. Evidence that defendant committed prior, similar wrongful acts is admissible to establish guilty knowledge and to negate good faith.

c)   Absence of Mistake or Accident
There are cases in which the defense of accident or mistake may be anticipated. In these situations prosecution evidence of similar misconduct by the defendant is admissible to negate the possibility of mistake or accident. (*See* example above.)

d)   Identity
Evidence, including misconduct, that connects this defendant to the crime (*e.g.,* theft of gun used in later crime) is admissible. Similarly, evidence that the accused committed prior criminal acts that are so distinctive as to operate as a "signature" may be introduced to prove that the accused committed the act in question (modus operandi).

e)   Common Plan or Scheme—Preparation
Evidence that the defendant recently stole some burglar tools is probative of the fact that she committed the burglary for which she is accused.

f)   Other
Similar acts or related misconduct may be used to prove opportunity, knowledge,

or any relevant fact other than the accused's general bad character or criminal disposition.

2) Quantum of Proof for Independently Relevant Acts of Misconduct
Under Federal Rule 404(b), independently relevant uncharged misconduct by the defendant will be admissible, without a preliminary ruling, as long as (i) there is *sufficient evidence to support a jury finding* that the defendant committed the prior act (*i.e.,* the standard of Federal Rule 104); and (ii) its probative value on the issue of motive, intent, identity, or other independently relevant proposition is not substantially outweighed by the danger of unfair prejudice (*i.e.,* the test of Federal Rule 403). [Huddleston v. United States, 485 U.S. 681 (1988)]

b. Prior Acts of Sexual Assault or Child Molestation
Evidence of a defendant's prior acts of sexual assault or child molestation is admissible in a civil or criminal case where the defendant is accused of committing an act of sexual assault or child molestation. The party who intends to offer this evidence must disclose the evidence to the defendant 15 days before trial (or later with good cause). [Fed. R. Evid. 413 - 415]

III. JUDICIAL NOTICE

A. JUDICIAL NOTICE OF FACT
Judicial notice is the *recognition of a fact as true without formal presentation of evidence*. In most instances the costly, time-consuming, and cumbersome process of formal proof is required to ensure fact-finding accuracy. However, self-evident propositions need not be subjected to this process, but instead may be judicially noticed. Judicial notice, like the presumption, is a judicial shortcut, a substitute for proof. The underlying policy considerations include expediting the trial and avoiding judicial disrepute where the lack of evidence might result in a conclusion contrary to well-known facts. For example, requiring proof that Washington, D.C., is the capital of the United States would require unnecessary time in a situation where a contrary conclusion would be ridiculous.

1. Facts Appropriate for Judicial Notice
The Federal Rule conforms to the existing state rules governing judicial notice. Federal Rule 201(b) defines a fact that may be noticed as "one not subject to reasonable dispute in that it is either (i) generally known within the territorial jurisdiction of the trial court" (notorious facts), or (ii) "capable of accurate and ready determination by resort to sources whose accuracy cannot reasonably be questioned" (manifest facts). Judicial notice may be taken of such facts *at any time*, whether or not requested, and such notice is mandatory if a party requests and supplies the court with the necessary information. A party is entitled to be heard on the propriety of taking judicial notice and the tenor of the matter noted.

a. Matters of Common Knowledge in the Community—Notorious Facts
Judicial notice will be taken of the body of facts that well-informed persons generally know and accept. Though usually facts of common knowledge are known everywhere, it is sufficient for judicial notice if they are known in the community where the court is sitting.

Examples: A court sitting in New York City will take judicial notice that:

> 1) The streets in Manhattan are numbered east and west from Fifth Avenue and that the odd numbers are on the north side of the street.

> 2) Many people are subject to low blood pressure and poor circulation.

> 3) The ordinary period of human gestation is 280 days.

b.   Facts Capable of Certain Verification—Manifest Facts
Some facts, while not generally known and accepted, are easily verified by resorting to easily accessible, well-established sources.
Examples: 1) Judicial notice will be taken of the time of the rising or setting of the sun and moon on a particular day since this fact, although not commonly known, can be estimated quickly and accurately by reference to an almanac.

2) The court will accept without proof that February 14, 1999, was a Sunday by reference to a calendar.

c.   Judicial Notice of Scientific Principles

1)   Judicial Notice of Scientific Basis of Test Results
Trial courts have increasingly taken judicial notice of scientific principles as a type of manifest fact. Once a particular scientific test or principle has become sufficiently well-established (*i.e.*, generally accepted among the scientific community), courts no longer require proof (expert testimony) of the underlying basis of the test. The results of such a test are therefore admissible into evidence.
Example: A trial court will take judicial notice of the reliability of radar speed tests, ballistics tests, and paternity blood tests, and will admit the results of these tests into evidence upon a showing that the tests were properly conducted.

2)   Conclusiveness of Test Results
Some scientific tests have achieved such universal acceptance that not only are the test results admissible into evidence, but the results are binding on the finder of fact in civil cases.
Example: Where a blood test indicates that the accused father could not have been the parent of the child, that result is conclusive on the issue of paternity, and other evidence on that issue will be excluded.

d.   Judge's Personal Knowledge
What a judge knows personally is not the same as what he may judicially notice. A judge may have to ignore facts that he knows as a private person if those facts are neither commonly known in the community nor capable of certain verification by resort to easily accessible sources of indisputable accuracy.

2.   Procedural Aspects of Judicial Notice

a. **Requirement of a Request**

In instances where the court does not take judicial notice of a fact on its own accord, the general rule is that a party must formally request (*e.g.*, through pleadings or an oral motion) that notice be taken.

b. **Judicial Notice by Appellate Court**

Judicial notice may be taken for the first time on appeal. A reviewing court is required to take judicial notice of any matter that the trial court properly noticed or was obliged to notice.

c. **Conclusiveness of Judicial Notice**

Federal Rule 201(g) provides that a judicially noticed fact is conclusive in a civil case but not in a criminal case. The Federal Rule states that in a civil case, the court shall instruct the jury to accept as conclusive any fact judicially noticed; in a criminal case, on the other hand, the jury is instructed that it may, but is not required to, accept as conclusive any fact judicially noticed.

3. **"Adjudicative" and "Legislative" Facts**

The Federal Rules govern *only judicial notice of "adjudicative" facts* (*i.e.*, facts that relate to the parties in a particular case), not "legislative" facts (*i.e.*, policy facts that relate to legal reasoning and the lawmaking process). The drafters of Federal Rule 201 reasoned that "legislative" facts are a necessary part of the judicial reasoning process, so that a rule imposing a requirement of indisputability and a formal procedure for taking judicial notice of these matters would destroy the concept of judge-made law. [Advisory Committee Note to Rule 201] Therefore, "legislative" facts need not meet the requirements of Rule 201 that facts must be either of common knowledge or capable of indisputable verification to be judicially noticed.

B. **JUDICIAL NOTICE OF LAW—MANDATORY OR PERMISSIVE**

The judge's task of finding applicable law is accomplished by informal investigation of legal source materials. This process, unmentioned in the Federal Rules of Evidence, has been traditionally described in terms of the judge taking judicial notice of the law applicable to the case.

1. **Classification Depends on Accessibility of Source Materials**

Judicial notice of law is mandatory in some instances and permissive in others. This mandatory-permissive classification is explainable in terms of the likely accessibility of source materials for different types of laws. State public law is easily available in reported volumes and, therefore, it is reasonable to require the court to be aware of and to notice it. Descriptions of foreign law or private acts are usually less available and, therefore, the court is permitted—but not required—to judicially notice such laws. In some cases, the contents of such laws may have to be established by proof to the satisfaction of the judge.

2. **Mandatory Judicial Notice**

Most courts must take judicial notice without request of:

a. *Federal public law*—the United States Constitution, federal treaties, public acts of Congress, and federal case law.

b. *State public law*—the constitution, public statutes, and common law of the states.

    c.   ***Official regulations***—the official compilation of codes and rules and regulations of the forum state and the federal government, except those relating to internal organization or management of a state agency.

3. Permissive Judicial Notice

Most courts may, upon being supplied with sufficient information, take judicial notice of municipal ordinances and private acts or resolutions of Congress and of the local state legislature. Similarly, the laws of foreign countries may be judicially noticed.

IV. REAL EVIDENCE

A. IN GENERAL

1. Addressed Directly to Trier of Fact

Real or demonstrative evidence is addressed directly to the trier of fact. The object in issue is presented for ***inspection by the trier of fact***. Ordinarily the evidence is addressed to the sense of sight (*e.g.*, exhibition of injured arm to jury to demonstrate extent of injury), but it may be directed to other senses as well (*e.g.*, sound recording of factory noise played during a nuisance trial).

2. Special Problems

This form of proof, which allows the triers of fact to reach conclusions based upon their own perceptions rather than relying upon those of witnesses, frequently involves special problems. Often there is concern regarding ***proper authentication*** of the "object." Additionally, the possibility exists that physical production of the thing may be too ***burdensome*** or may inspire ***prejudicial emotions*** outweighing its probative value to the litigation.

B. TYPES OF REAL EVIDENCE

1. Direct

Real evidence may be direct evidence; *i.e.*, it may be offered to prove the facts about the object as an end in itself. For example, in a personal injury case, evidence of a permanent injury could be introduced by an exhibition of the injury itself to the trier of fact.

2. Circumstantial

Real evidence may also be circumstantial; *i.e.*, facts about the object are proved as a basis for an inference that other facts are true. For example, in a paternity case, the trier of fact may be shown the child for the purpose of showing that she is of the same race as the alleged father. In this case, the trier of fact is being asked to draw an inference that, since the child and alleged father are of the same race, the paternal relationship exists.

3. Original

Real evidence may be original; *i.e.*, it may have had some connection with the transaction that is in question at the trial. An example of this kind of evidence would be an alleged murder weapon.

4. Prepared

Real evidence may also be prepared; *e.g.*, sketches or models may be made to be shown to the trier of fact. This category of real evidence is called "***demonstrative evidence.***"

C. GENERAL CONDITIONS OF ADMISSIBILITY

Real evidence, like all other forms of evidence, must be *relevant* to the proposition in issue. The admissibility of real proof also depends on additional legal requirements, such as those that follow.

1. Authentication

The object must first be identified as being what the proponent claims it to be. Real evidence is commonly authenticated by recognition testimony or by establishing a chain of custody.

a. Recognition Testimony

If the object has significant features that make it identifiable upon inspection, a witness may authenticate the object by testifying that the object is what the proponent claims it is.

Examples: 1) If a prosecutor offers a knife into evidence and claims that the knife is the very weapon used in the murder, the object may be authenticated by a witness who testifies that he can identify the knife as the one found next to the deceased.

2) If a prosecutor offers a knife into evidence and claims that it is *similar* to the knife used in the murder, it may be authenticated by a witness who testifies that the offered knife is indeed similar to the one found next to the deceased.

3) A witness can testify that a photograph is a fair and accurate representation of that which it is purported to depict.

b. Chain of Custody

If the evidence is of a type that is likely to be confused or can be easily tampered with, the proponent of the object must present evidence of chain of custody. The proponent of the evidence must show that the object has been held in a substantially *unbroken chain of possession.* The proponent need not negate all possibilities of substitution or tampering, but must show adherence to some system of identification and custody.

Example: A custodial chain—from the taking, to the testing, to the exhibiting of the sample—must be established before evidence of a blood alcohol test will be admitted.

2. Condition of Object; Useful Probativeness

If the condition of the object is significant, it must be shown to be in substantially the *same condition at the trial.* Moreover, the object must be logically helpful or reliable in tending to prove the proposition in issue.

Example: Would it be helpful in a paternity proceeding to present the baby so that the trier of fact can ascertain physical resemblance to the alleged father?

3. Legal Relevance

Assuming the object has been properly identified and is probative, the discretion of the trial judge is called upon to decide whether some auxiliary policy or principle outweighs the need to admit the real evidence. Such policies limiting the use of real evidence frequently concern:

a. *Physical inconvenience* of bringing the object into the courtroom;

b. *Indecency or impropriety*; or

c. *Undue prejudice* where the probative value of the object or exhibit is outweighed by the danger of unfair prejudice.

D. PARTICULAR TYPES OF REAL PROOF

1. Reproductions and Explanatory Real Evidence
When properly authenticated, relevant photographs, movies, diagrams, maps, sketches, or other *reproductions are admissible* if their value is not outweighed by the danger of unfair prejudice. On the other hand, items used entirely for *explanatory purposes* (such as skeletons, anatomy charts, etc.) are permitted at a trial, but are usually *not admitted into evidence* and are not given to the jury during its deliberations. These items are not represented to be reproductions of the real thing, but are merely used as aids to testimony.

Example: A doctor may use a model of an average male skeleton to explain his testimony. The skeleton may be marked for identification in order to preserve the record, but it is not admitted into evidence.

Compare: If the skeleton was offered as a reproduction of the bone structure of the deceased, assuming there is no undue prejudice, it may be admitted into evidence on a showing that it accurately represents the bone structure of the deceased.

2. Maps, Charts, Models, Etc.
Maps, charts, models, etc., are usually admissible for the purpose of illustrating testimony. Since these are all reproductions, they must be authenticated by testimonial evidence showing that they are *faithful reproductions* of the object or thing depicted. As with other real evidence, introduction of these items is within the discretion of the court, and they may be excluded where they would be wasteful of time or where they would unduly impress the trier of fact with the importance of the material.

3. Exhibition of Child in Paternity Suits
Almost all courts permit exhibition of the child for the purpose of showing whether she is of the race of the putative father. The courts are divided with respect to the propriety of exhibiting the child in order to prove physical resemblance to the putative father, but a growing majority of courts refuse to permit exhibition of the child.

4. Exhibition of Injuries
The exhibition of injuries in a personal injury or criminal case is generally permitted, but the court has discretion to exclude this evidence if the exhibition would result in unfair prejudice.

5. Jury View of the Scene
Closely related to real and demonstrative evidence is the matter of jury views of premises and places at issue in the case. In the trial court's discretion, they are permitted, sparingly, in both civil and criminal cases. The importance of information that could be obtained by a view, and the ease with which photographs, diagrams, or maps could be substituted for such

a view, will be pivotal considerations to the trial judge. Any significant changes of condition in the premises that are to be viewed will also affect the decision. The trial judge usually need not be present during a jury view. The parties and their attorneys are usually permitted to attend, but the view will be conducted by a disinterested court attaché and neither counsel nor the parties will be permitted to engage in any commentary.

6. Demonstrations

The court, in its discretion, may permit experiments or demonstrations to be performed in the courtroom.

a. Demonstrations Showing Effect of Bodily Injury

Demonstrations to show the effect of bodily injury are usually excluded where the exhibition would reveal hideous wounds, elicit cries of pain, or otherwise unduly dramatize the injury and inflame the minds of the jurors.

b. Demonstrations Under Sole Control of Witness Are Excluded

Demonstrations may also be excluded where they are under the sole control of the witness and thus not subject to effective cross-examination. For example, an injured plaintiff might attempt to demonstrate lack of locomotion by showing that he cannot move a limb. The demonstration itself cannot be effectively cross-examined. However, if testimony is given to the same effect, it may be impeached by contradictory evidence.

c. Scientific Experiments

The judge may permit scientific experiments to be performed in the courtroom provided:

1) The conditions are ***substantially similar*** to those that attended the original event, and

2) The experiment will ***not result in undue waste of time or confusion*** of the issues.

V. DOCUMENTARY EVIDENCE

A. IN GENERAL

Documentary evidence, like other kinds of evidence, ***must be relevant*** in order to be admissible. In the case of writings, the authenticity of the document is one aspect of its relevancy. Of course, documentary evidence, even if fully authenticated and relevant, ***may be excluded if it violates a rule of competency*** such as the best evidence or hearsay rule. Whenever any problem or question concerns a document, you should consider three separate and distinct possible barriers to admissibility (authentication, best evidence, and hearsay).

B. AUTHENTICATION

Before a writing or any secondary evidence of its content may be received in evidence, the writing must be authenticated by proof showing that the writing is what the proponent claims it is. The writing is usually not self-authenticating. It needs a testimonial sponsor or shepherding angel to prove that the writing was made, signed, or adopted by the particular relevant person. [Fed. R. Evid. 901 - 903]

1.   **Quantum of Proof of Authenticity**
Authentication of documentary or, for that matter, real evidence requires only enough evidence to support a finding that the matter is what its proponent claims it is. It is not required that the proponent establish its genuineness by a preponderance of the evidence as a condition to admissibility. All that is necessary under Federal Rules 104(b) and 901 is proof *sufficient to support a jury finding* of genuineness.

2.   **Authentication by Pleadings or Stipulation**
The genuineness of a document may be admitted through the discovery process, through stipulation at pretrial conference, or by a failure to deny an allegation in a pleading.

3.   **Evidence of Authenticity**
In general, a writing may be authenticated by any evidence that serves to establish its authenticity. The Federal Rules do not limit the methods of authentication, but rather list several examples of proper authentication. [Fed. R. Evid. 901]

   a.   **Admissions**
A writing may be authenticated by evidence that the party against whom the writing is offered has either ***admitted*** its authenticity or ***acted upon*** the writing as authentic.

   b.   **Testimony of Eyewitness**
A writing may be authenticated by testimony of one who ***sees it executed*** or ***hears it acknowledged***. Modern statutes eliminate the common law necessity of producing a subscribing witness, unless specifically required by statute. [Fed. R. Evid. 903] If testimony of a subscribing witness is required (*e.g.*, in authenticating a will), his denial or failure to recollect the execution of the writing does not preclude authentication by other evidence.

   c.   **Handwriting Verifications**
A writing may also be authenticated by evidence of the genuineness of the handwriting of the maker.

      1)   **Nonexpert Opinion**
A lay witness who has personal knowledge of the handwriting of the supposed writer may state his opinion as to whether the document is in that person's handwriting. (This is an exception to the opinion rule, *see* VI.C.1., *infra*.) Note, however, that a nonexpert cannot become familiar with the handwriting merely for the purpose of testifying.

      2)   **Comparison of Writings**
An expert witness or the trier of fact (*e.g.*, jury) can determine the genuineness of a writing by comparing the questioned writing with another writing proved to be genuine. (Note that authentication by comparison is not limited to handwriting. Fingerprints, blood, hair, clothing fibers, and numerous other things can be authenticated by comparison with authenticated specimens.)

   d.   **Ancient Documents**
Under the Federal Rules, a document may be authenticated by evidence that it:

(i) Is at least *20 years old*;

(ii) Is in such condition as to be *free from suspicion* concerning its authenticity; and

(iii) Was *found in a place* where such writing, if authentic, would likely be kept.

[Fed. R. Evid. 901(b)(8)]

1) Federal Rules Distinguished from Majority of Jurisdictions

The Federal Rules apply to *all writings*. However, most jurisdictions limit the ancient documents rule to *dispositive instruments* (*e.g.*, deeds, wills, etc.). In addition, most courts require that such documents be over *30 years old*.

e. Reply Letter Doctrine

A writing may be authenticated by evidence that it was written in response to a communication sent to the claimed author. The content of the letter must make it unlikely that it was written by anyone other than the claimed author of the writing.

f. Circumstantial Evidence in General

The rules for ancient documents and reply letters, above, involve authentication by circumstantial evidence. A complete list of ways to authenticate by circumstantial evidence would be impossible. Any proof tending in reason to *establish genuineness* is sufficient. For example, authentication may be established by the content of the writing and a showing that it contains information known only to the purported author. Alternatively it may be demonstrated that the author had the disputed writing in his custody at a prior time under circumstances evidencing his belief in its genuineness.

g. Photographs

As a general rule, photographs are admissible only if identified by a witness as a portrayal of certain facts relevant to the issue and verified by the witness as a correct representation of those facts. It suffices if the witness who identifies the photograph is familiar with the scene or object that is depicted. In general, it is *not necessary to call the photographer* to authenticate the photograph.

1) Unattended Camera—Proper Operation of Camera

In some situations, a photograph will portray an event that was observed *only* by the camera (*i.e.,* there is no witness who can testify to the relevant scene to authenticate the photograph). For example, an unmanned surveillance camera may produce a photograph of a burglar taken at a time when no other person was on the premises. Such a photograph may be admitted upon a showing that the camera was properly operating at the relevant time and that the photograph was developed from film obtained from that camera.

h. X-Ray Pictures, Electrocardiograms, Etc.

Unlike photographs, an X-ray picture cannot be authenticated by testimony of a witness that it is a correct representation of the facts. Therefore, a different procedure of authentication is necessary. First, it must be shown that the *process used is accurate* (as to X-rays, the court will usually take judicial notice of this). Then it must be shown that the *machine itself was in working order* and the *operator was qualified* to operate it.

Finally, a *custodial chain* must be established to forestall the danger that the evidence has been substituted or tampered with.

4. Compare—Authentication of Oral Statements

Oral statements often require authentication as to the *identity of the speaker*. Although this is technically a "relevance" topic, the rules are the same as those that apply to the authenticity of documents.

a. When Necessary

Not all oral statements need to be authenticated; only where the identity of the speaker is important (*e.g.,* admission by a party) is authentication required.

b. Methods of Authentication

1) Voice Identification

A voice, whether heard firsthand or through a device (*e.g.,* a tape recording) may be identified by the opinion of anyone who has heard the voice at *any time*. Thus, in contrast to the rule for handwriting verification, a person can become familiar with a voice after litigation has begun and for the sole purpose of testifying.

2) Telephone Conversations

Statements made during a telephone conversation may be authenticated by one of the parties to the call who testifies to one of the following:

a) He recognized the other party's voice.

b) The speaker has knowledge of certain facts that only a particular person would have.

c) He called, for example, Mr. A's telephone number, and a voice answered, "This is Mr. A" or "This is the A residence." This authenticates the conversation as being with Mr. A or his agent.

d) He called the person's business establishment and talked with the person answering the phone about matters relevant to the business. This is sufficient to show that the person answering the phone held a position in the business.

5. Self-Authenticating Documents

Contrary to the general rule, which requires testimonial sponsorship, there are certain writings that are said to "prove themselves" or to be "self-identifying" on their face. Federal Rule 902 specifically provides that extrinsic evidence of authenticity as a condition to admissibility is not required as to the following:

a. Certified copies of *public records*;

b. *Official publications* (*i.e.,* books, pamphlets, or other publications purporting to be issued by a public authority);

c. Printed materials purporting to be *newspapers or periodicals*;

d. ***Trade inscriptions,*** signs, tags, or labels purporting to have been affixed in the course of business and indicating ownership, control, or origin;

e. ***Documents accompanied by a certificate of acknowledgment*** executed in the manner provided by law by a notary public or other officer authorized by law to take acknowledgments;

f. ***Commercial paper,*** signatures thereon, and documents relating thereto, to the extent provided by general commercial law; and

g. ***Business records*** certified as such by a custodian or other qualified person.

C. BEST EVIDENCE RULE

The best evidence rule is more accurately called the *"original document rule."* It may be stated as follows: In proving the terms of a writing (recording, photograph, or X-ray), where the terms are material, the original writing must be produced. Secondary evidence of the writing, such as oral testimony regarding the writing's contents, is permitted only after it has been shown that the original is unavailable for some reason other than the serious misconduct of the proponent. [Fed. R. Evid. 1002]

1. Rule Expresses Preference for Originals

Simply stated, the rule applies to writings and expresses a preference for originals. It reflects the belief that the exact words of a writing, particularly in the case of operative or dispositive instruments such as contracts, deeds, or wills, should be presented to the court; that there is a hazard of inaccuracy in common methods of approximating the contents of a writing; and that oral testimony based on memory of the terms of the writing presents greater risk of error than oral testimony concerning other situations.

2. Applicability of the Rule

For the most part, the rule applies to two classes of situations: (i) where the writing is a ***legally operative or dispositive instrument*** such as a contract, deed, will, or divorce decree; or (ii) where the ***knowledge of a witness*** concerning a fact results from having ***read*** it in the document.

Examples: 1) Witness may not testify about the content of a written deed unless sufficient reason is given for not producing the original deed.

2) Witness who memorized mileage recorded on car sticker for a certain date, and who had no other source of knowledge on this significant litigated issue, may not testify as to the mileage without establishing a reason for the unavailability of the writing.

3. Nonapplicability of the Rule

a. Fact to Be Proved Exists Independently of Any Writing

Where the fact to be proved has an existence independent of any writing, the best evidence rule does not apply. Therefore, the rule does not apply to all events that happen to have been memorialized by documents. There are many writings that the substantive law does not regard as essential repositories of the facts recorded. These writings happen to record details of essentially nonwritten transactions. As to these, oral

testimony may be given without production of, or explanation for the absence of, the original writings.

Examples: 1) Witness may testify orally that he paid for goods received without producing the receipt that was given.

2) Facts such as birth, marriage, age, and death may be proved orally, although certificates evidencing these facts are in existence. However, since a divorce is effective only by a judicial decree, the best evidence rule requires that the fact of divorce be proved by the decree itself.

3) Testimony heard at a prior trial may be testified to in another case without production of the stenographic transcript of the prior testimony. One who heard the prior testimony can repeat it.

4) Admissions or confessions of a party may be testified to orally by anyone who heard them, even though the admissions or confessions were later reduced to writing.

The above examples are in contrast to those writings that are considered as essential repositories of the facts recorded. Written contracts, deeds, wills, and judgments are viewed as such repositories—they are considered written transactions—and as such are within the rule.

b.   Writing Is Collateral to Litigated Issue
Any narration by a witness is likely to include references to transactions consisting partly of written communications. The best evidence rule does not apply to writings of minor importance (*i.e.*, ones that are collateral) to the matter in controversy. [Fed. R. Evid. 1004(4)] For example, an expert witness testifying on the value of a car is allowed to establish his status as a car dealer without production of his dealer's license. The test of "collateralness" is likely to take into account:

1)   *Centrality* of the writing to the major issues of a litigation;

2)   *Complexity* of the relevant features of the writing; and

3)   Existence of a *genuine dispute* as to the contents of the writing.

c.   Summaries of Voluminous Records
When it would be inconvenient to examine a voluminous collection of writings, recordings, or photographs in court, the proponent may present their contents in the form of a chart, summary, or calculation. [Fed. R. Evid. 1006] However, the originals or duplicates (*see* 4.c., *infra*) must be made available for examination and copying, and the judge may order them to be produced in court.

d.   Public Records
The best evidence rule is modified so that a proponent may offer into evidence a copy of an official record or a copy of a document that has been recorded and filed. Such a copy must be *certified as correct* by the custodian of the document or other person authorized to do so, or *testified to be correct* by a person who compared it to the original.

[Fed. R. Evid. 1005] The purpose of this exception is to prevent the loss or absence of public documents due to litigation.

4. Definitions of "Writings," "Original," and "Duplicate"

a. Writings, Recordings, and Photographs
The Federal Rules govern writings, recordings, and photographs. Writings and recordings are defined broadly as "letters, words, or numbers, or their equivalent; set down by handwriting, typewriting, printing, photostating, photographing, magnetic impulse, mechanical or electronic recording, or other form of data compilation." Photographs are more narrowly defined as "still photographs, X-ray films, and motion pictures." [Fed. R. Evid. 1001]

b. "Original"
An original is the writing or recording itself or any duplicate intended by the person executing it to have the same effect as an original.

Example: D types a letter to P that is defamatory of P. D sends the letter to P himself and a photocopy of the letter to the newspaper. In P's defamation action, the document legally operative to create tort liability is the "published" photocopy, not the letter sent to P.

c. Admissibility of Duplicates
The Federal Rules define a duplicate as "a counterpart produced by the same impression as the original, or from the same matrix, or by means of photography . . . or by mechanical or electronic re-recording, or by chemical reproduction, or by other equivalent techniques which accurately reproduce the original." [Fed. R. Evid. 1001(4)] A duplicate is thus an ***exact copy of an original***, *e.g.,* a carbon copy or photocopy. Duplicates are ***admissible*** the same as originals in federal courts, ***unless*** (i) the authenticity of the original is challenged, or (ii) under the circumstances, it would be unfair to admit the duplicate in place of the original. [Fed. R. Evid. 1003] The rationale for admitting duplicates under such a relaxed standard is that by definition these documents are exact copies of the original, and therefore their introduction into evidence would be objectionable only if some question existed as to the genuineness of the original.

5. Admissibility of Secondary Evidence of Contents
If the proponent cannot produce the original writing or recording in court, he may offer secondary evidence of its contents in the form of copies (*e.g.,* handwritten copies, which would not be considered duplicates because they are not exact copies), notes, or oral testimony about the contents of the original if a satisfactory explanation is given for the nonproduction of the original.

a. Satisfactory Foundation
A valid excuse justifying the admissibility of secondary evidence would include:

1) Loss or Destruction of Original
A proper foundation for the admissibility of secondary evidence is laid by a showing that the original has been lost and cannot be found despite diligent search, or was destroyed in good faith.

2) Original Outside Jurisdiction and Unobtainable

If the document is within the jurisdiction, it must be subpoenaed. If not, some reasonable effort or request to the third party for production must be shown before secondary evidence will be admitted. A proper foundation is laid, however, if it is shown that the original is (i) in the possession of a third party, (ii) outside the jurisdiction, and (iii) unobtainable.

3) Original in Possession of Adversary Who, After Notice, Fails to Produce

If the opponent has custody of the original, a showing of his custody, service of a timely notice to produce, and his failure to produce it in court will justify the admissibility of secondary evidence. Where the pleadings give notice to the opposite party that he will be charged with possession of the writing, service of the notice to produce is unnecessary.

b. No Degrees of Secondary Evidence

The Federal Rules recognize no degrees of secondary evidence. Once a satisfactory explanation for nonproduction of the original is established, the party seeking to prove the contents of a writing, photograph, or recording may do so by any kind of secondary evidence ranging from handwritten copies to oral testimony. This abolition of degrees of secondary evidence is a departure from the rule existing in most American jurisdictions. [Fed. R. Evid. 1004]

c. Testimony or Written Admission of Party

A proponent may prove the contents of a writing, recording, or photograph through the testimony, deposition, or written admission of the party against whom it is offered, and need not account for the nonproduction of the original. [Fed. R. Evid. 1007] However, it is also generally held that the ***contents*** of a writing, photograph, etc., ***cannot be proved simply by out-of-court oral admissions*** of the party against whom such evidence is offered (unless of course the original is otherwise accounted for).

Example: Witness testifies, "I heard D say that the telegram he received stated . . . ." D's oral admissions outside court are inadmissible to prove the contents of the telegram. [Fed. R. Evid. 1007]

6. Functions of Court and Jury

Ordinarily, it is for the court to make the determinations of fact that determine the admissibility of duplicates, other copies, and oral testimony as to the contents of an original. However, the Federal Rules specifically reserve three questions of ***preliminary fact for the jury***:

(i) Whether the original ever existed;

(ii) Whether a writing, recording, or photograph produced at trial is an original; and

(iii) Whether the evidence offered correctly reflects the contents of the original.

[Fed. R. Evid. 1008]

D. PAROL EVIDENCE RULE

The essence of the parol evidence rule is as follows: If an agreement is reduced to writing, that writing is the agreement and hence constitutes the only evidence of it. All ***prior or contemporaneous***

negotiations or agreements *are merged* into the written agreement. Parol (extrinsic) evidence is not admissible to add to, detract from, or alter the agreement as written.

1. Substantive and Evidentiary Aspects

This rule, although actually a part of the substantive law of contracts, is also important as an evidentiary principle because of its *impact on materiality*. Prior and contemporary oral agreements are not material when offered to vary the terms of an apparently complete written contract.

2. Nonapplicability of Parol Evidence Rule

From an evidentiary standpoint, counsel invoking the rule is saying, "Here is the agreement. Its terms, having been reduced to writing by the parties, are indisputable; they cannot be put in issue. It follows that no evidence can be received in respect to those terms." This approach helps to explain why the parol evidence rule does not apply to exclude evidence of prior or contemporaneous agreements on the following issues:

a. Completion of Incomplete or Ambiguous Contract

In some situations, the written instrument may be valid but still incomplete or ambiguous. In these cases, parol evidence is admitted not to contradict or vary the writing but to complete the entire agreement of which the writing was only part. In these situations, parol evidence will be admitted if the contract does not appear on its face to be the entire agreement between the parties and the parol evidence is consistent with, and not contradictory of, the written instrument. If there is uncertainty, ambiguity, or reasonable dispute as to the meaning of contract terms, parol evidence is admissible to explain the ambiguity.

b. Reformation of Contract

Where a party alleges facts, such as mistake, entitling him to reformation of the written agreement, the parol evidence rule is inapplicable. This is so because the party is asserting that, despite the apparently unambiguous contract, its terms do not in fact constitute the agreement intended.

c. Challenge to Validity of Contract

The parol evidence rule does not bar admission of parol evidence to show that what appears to be a contractual obligation is, in fact, no obligation at all. Thus, evidence is admissible to show that the *contract was void or voidable* and has been avoided, or was made subject to a valid *condition precedent* that has not been satisfied. Specifically, parol evidence is admissible to establish or disprove a contract attacked on grounds of:

1) Fraud, duress, or undue influence inducing consent;

2) Lack of consideration;

3) Illegality of subject matter;

4) Material alteration;

5) Nondelivery, if the agreement required delivery for the instrument to be effective; or

6) Execution or delivery upon a condition precedent, as long as the parol condition does not contradict the writing. However, proof of an oral condition subsequent allegedly made at or before the time of the written contract would be barred by the rule.

3. Subsequent Modifications of Written Contract

The rule applies only to negotiations or agreements made ***prior to, or at the time of,*** the execution of the written contract. Parol evidence is admissible to show subsequent modification or discharge of the written contract.

VI. TESTIMONIAL EVIDENCE

A. COMPETENCY OF WITNESSES

Witnesses are not "authenticated" in the same sense as real or documentary evidence. However, they too must pass tests of basic reliability to establish their competence to give testimony. Unlike the authentication situation pertaining to real or documentary proof, witnesses are generally ***presumed to be competent*** until the contrary is demonstrated.

1. Basic Testimonial Qualifications

There are four basic testimonial attributes that every witness must have to some degree. These are the capacity to observe, to recollect, to communicate, and to appreciate the obligation to speak truthfully. These, along with sincerity, are the qualities at which the cross-examiner directs his skill.

A diminution of any of these capacities usually goes only to the weight of the testimony and serves to make the witness less persuasive. However, a witness can be so deficient in one or more of these basic qualifications that she will be deemed incompetent to testify at all. The problem of infancy is a good example for all aspects of the basic qualifications. A witness may be too young ***at the time of the event*** to be able to accurately perceive what happened or to be able to remember at the time of the trial. The witness may also be too young ***at the time of the trial*** to effectively relate or communicate or appreciate the obligation to tell the truth.

a. Ability to Observe—Perception

The issue of a witness's ability to observe may arise in the following manner: W testifies on direct to details of how an intersection automobile collision occurred. On cross-examination, W admits that her attention was directed to the intersection by the sound of the crash. The direct testimony regarding details of the accident occurring before the collision will be stricken.

b. Ability to Remember—Memory

An example of a witness incompetent for this reason would be one who is suffering from senility or amnesia.

c. Ability to Relate—Communication

The ability to relate concerns the ability of the witness to communicate effectively with the trier of fact.

d. **Appreciation of Oath Obligation**
The witness must have sufficient intelligence and character to know and desire to tell the truth. The witness may be sworn by oath or affirmation. However, unsworn testimony may be permissible if the witness (*e.g.*, a child) appreciates the obligation to tell the truth.

2. **Federal Rules of Competency**

a. **Personal Knowledge and Oath Required**
Federal Rule 601 provides that "Every person is competent to be a witness except as otherwise provided in these rules." The rules do not specify any mental or moral qualifications for witness testimony beyond these two limitations:

1) *The witness must have personal knowledge* of the matter he is to testify about. The requirement of "personal knowledge" means that the witness must have observed the matter and must have a present recollection of his observation. [Fed. R. Evid. 602]

2) *The witness must declare he will testify truthfully*, by oath or affirmation. [Fed. R. Evid. 603]

b. **Use of Interpreter**
If a witness requires an interpreter, the interpreter must be qualified and take an oath to make a true translation. [Fed. R. Evid. 604]

c. **Applicability of State Rules in Diversity Cases**
Federal Rule 601 provides that the competency of a witness shall be determined by state law in civil actions "with respect to an element of a claim or defense as to which state law supplies the rule of decision."

3. **Modern Modifications of Common Law Disqualifications**
At common law there were several grounds upon which a person could be disqualified from giving testimony. Persons were incompetent to testify if they had a financial interest in the suit, if they were the spouse of a party, if they lacked religious belief, if they had been convicted of a crime, or if they lacked mental capacity. These common law disqualifications have been almost entirely removed under the Federal Rules and in the vast majority of American jurisdictions.

a. **Lack of Religious Belief**
Lack of religious belief is no longer a basis for excluding a witness. Not only are a person's religious convictions irrelevant in determining the competence of a witness, but they may also not be shown or commented upon for the purpose of affecting the credibility of a witness.

b. **Infancy**
There is *no precise age* at which an infant is deemed competent or incompetent to testify under oath. The competence of an infant depends on the capacity and intelligence of the particular child. This test is an individual one, to be determined by the trial judge upon preliminary examination.

c. **Insanity**

An insane person, even one who has been adjudicated incompetent, *may testify*, provided he understands the obligation to speak truthfully and possesses the capacity to give a correct account of what he has perceived in reference to the issue in dispute.

d. **Conviction of Crime**

The common law disqualification of felons has been removed by statute in most states. However, conviction of a crime may be shown to *affect the credibility* of the competent witness.

e. **Interest**

The common law disqualification of parties or interested persons has been abolished in most states. The only remaining vestiges of this disqualification are the so-called Dead Man Acts, discussed later.

f. **Judge as Witness**

Federal Rule 605 provides that the presiding judge *may not testify as a witness*, and that no objection need be made to preserve the point. The basis for this disqualification is that when the judge is called as a witness, her role as a witness is inconsistent with her role as presiding judge, which requires her to maintain impartiality.

g. **Juror as Witness**

Under Federal Rule 606, jurors are *incompetent to testify* before the jury in which they are sitting. The rationale is that a juror-witness cannot impartially weigh his own testimony and cannot be thoroughly cross-examined for fear of creating antagonism.

The Federal Rule also prevents a juror from testifying in post-verdict proceedings as to matters or statements occurring during the course of jury deliberations, except that a juror may testify as to whether "extraneous prejudicial information" or any "outside influence" was brought to bear on any juror. Also, a juror may testify as to whether there was a mistake in entering the verdict onto the verdict form; *e.g.*, where the verdict form contains a damage amount different from that agreed upon by the jury, or where the form mistakenly states that a criminal defendant is guilty when the jury had agreed that he was not guilty.

4. **Dead Man Acts**

The last remaining vestige of true incompetency of a witness appears in the Dead Man Acts. These statutes exist in most jurisdictions and their provisions vary from state to state. Although there is *no Dead Man Act in the Federal Rules of Evidence*, state Dead Man Acts operate to disqualify witnesses in federal cases where state law provides the rule of decision (most diversity cases). For bar examination purposes, only generalized comments are appropriate, and there are common provisions to most Dead Man Acts that could appear in a multistate bar exam question.

a. **Rationale**

The Dead Man Acts generally provide that a party or person interested in the event, or his predecessor in interest, is incompetent to testify to a *personal transaction or communication with a deceased*, when such testimony is offered against the representative or successors in interest of the deceased. The rationale of the statute is to *protect*

estates from perjured claims. The assumption is that the survivor claimant may lie, since the deceased cannot talk back. Because death has silenced one party, the statute closes the mouth of the living person who, being interested in the litigation's outcome, wishes to testify on her own behalf against someone who is suing or defending in a representative capacity (*e.g.*, executor, administrator, heir, legatee, devisee).

b.   Common Elements
Most Dead Man Acts have the following common elements and applications:

1)   Applicable to Civil Cases Only
The bar to competency created by a Dead Man Act applies only to civil cases and has no application in criminal cases.

2)   Protected Parties
The statute is designed to protect those who claim directly under the decedent. They usually include an executor, administrator, heir, legatee, and devisee. If a protected party is on either side of the lawsuit (suing or defending), the statute applies to prevent an interested person from testifying on his own behalf.
Examples: 1) Plaintiff sues the executor of the estate for a debt owed by the decedent. The executor is a protected party and the act applies.

2) Executor sues defendant for negligence in causing the death of the decedent. Executor is a protected party and the act applies.

3) Heir sues executor, legatees, and devisees in a will contest. Heir is a protected party, as are the adverse parties. The act applies.

3)   Interested Person
A person is "interested in the event" if he stands to gain or lose by the direct and immediate operation of the judgment, or if the judgment may be used for or against him in a subsequent action. Thus, in states where a spouse has an inchoate right in the other spouse's property, both spouses may be interested and incompetent to testify. Similarly, a shareholder of a corporation and the co-maker of a note may be disqualified under the rule.

a)   Predecessor in Interest
Most Dead Man Acts disqualify not only the person interested, but also the predecessor in interest.
Example: If A assigns to B a claim against Decedent, and B sues the estate, both A and B are incompetent. B is interested in the event; A is the person from, through, or under whom B derived his interest.

b)   Party Adverse to Protected Party
As a short rule of thumb, a party adverse to the protected party is always an interested person who will be rendered incompetent by the Dead Man Act. For other nonparty witnesses, ask whether the witness has a *pecuniary interest in the outcome of the case* or is a predecessor in interest with the adverse party.

4) Exceptions and Waiver of the Act

There are numerous situations where the Dead Man Act either will not apply against an interested person or the protected party may waive its effect. Of course, if an exception applies or the statute is waived, the interested person is competent to testify. The following are common to most jurisdictions:

a) Facts Occurring After Death

An interested person may always testify to facts that occurred *after* the death of the deceased, since the protection of the rule is not needed.

b) "Door Openers"

The estate representatives and those claiming under the decedent may *waive the protection* of the statute. Common provisions for waiver include:

(1) If the protected party calls the interested person to testify about the transaction, the interested person may explain all matters about which he is examined.

(2) Where the testimony of the deceased given at a former trial or at a deposition is read in evidence, the interested person may explain all matters about which he is examined.

(3) Where there is a failure to make timely and proper objection. Objection is to the incompetency of the witness, not to the incompetency of the testimony.

(4) If the protected party or an agent of the deceased testifies to a transaction with an interested person, the interested person may testify about the same transaction.

B. FORM OF EXAMINATION OF WITNESS

The judge may exercise reasonable control over the examination of witnesses in order to aid the effective ascertainment of truth, to avoid wasting time, and to protect witnesses from harassment or undue embarrassment. Questions that frequently arise concerning the form of examination of witnesses are: when may leading questions be used, what other types of questions are objectionable, and when and how may a witness use memoranda.

1. Leading Questions

a. Generally Objectionable

A question is leading and generally objectionable on direct examination when it suggests to the witness the fact that the examiner expects and wants to have confirmed. Questions calling for "yes" or "no" answers and questions *framed to suggest the answer desired* are usually leading.

Example: On direct examination plaintiff is asked, "Is it true or not that at the time in question, you were driving well within the speed limit?" The question is leading.

b. When Permitted

Leading questions are permitted on *cross-examination*. Trial judges will usually allow leading questions on *direct examination* in noncrucial areas *if no objection is made:*

     (i)   If used to elicit *preliminary or introductory matter*;

     (ii)   When the witness *needs aid to respond* because of loss of memory, immaturity, or physical or mental weakness; or

     (iii) When the witness is *hostile* and improperly uncooperative, an *adverse* party, or a person *identified with an adverse party*.

     [Fed. R. Evid. 611(c)]

2.   Improper Questions and Answers

The following types of questions are improper and are not permitted:

a. Misleading

A question is misleading and thus is not permitted if it is one that cannot be answered without making an unintended admission.

Example: "Do you still beat your wife?"

b. Compound

Questions that require a single answer to more than one question are not permitted.

Example: "Did you see and hear the intruder?"

c. Argumentative

Argumentative questions, which are leading questions that reflect the examiner's interpretation of the facts, are improper.

Example: "Why were you driving so recklessly?"

d. Conclusionary

A question that calls for an opinion or conclusion that the witness is not qualified or permitted to make is improper.

Example: "What did your friend think about that?" The witness could not know his friend's thoughts, and is not permitted to give his opinion as to his friend's thoughts.

e. Assuming Facts Not in Evidence

An attorney is not allowed to ask a question that assumes a disputed fact is true when it has not been established in the case.

Example: In a case where there is no evidence that Defendant had been drinking, the following question is improper: "After Defendant finished his fifth beer, he got up and went to his car, didn't he?"

f. Cumulative

An attorney is generally not permitted to ask a question that has already been asked and answered. More repetition is allowed on cross-examination than on direct, but if it is apparent that the cross-examiner is not moving forward, the judge may disallow the question.

g. Harassing or Embarrassing

The trial judge, in her discretion, may disallow cross-examination that is unduly harassing or embarrassing.

h. Calls for a Narrative Answer

Some courts generally prohibit questions calling for a narrative answer, *i.e.,* a question allowing a witness to answer by recounting relevant facts, rather than a series of specific questions requiring specific answers.

Example: Tell me what you did on the evening of September 22.

i. Calls for Speculation

An examining attorney may not ask a witness to speculate, *i.e.,* theorize, as to a fact, because such testimony is not based on the witness's personal knowledge.

Example: Where decedent expressed a desire to become an engineer but did not do so, it was speculation for a witness to testify regarding decedent's lost income based on an engineer's salary.

j. Lack of Foundation

A witness must have personal knowledge as to the facts of his testimony. Insufficient personal knowledge may subject testimony to an objection for lack of foundation. Additionally, a party may object on the basis of lack of foundation for real evidence if the proponent has not shown that the evidence is what he purports it to be. (*See* IV.C.1., *supra.*)

k. Nonresponsive Answer

A witness's response must address only the specific question asked by the examining attorney; otherwise the testimony is subject to being stricken for nonresponsiveness.

Example: Q. Did you leave your house on September 22?
A. I went to the dentist and then to the grocery store.
This answer is nonresponsive, as the question calls for a "yes" or "no" response.

3. Use of Memoranda by Witness

A witness cannot read her testimony from a prepared memorandum. However, a memorandum may be used in certain circumstances to refresh the recollection of the witness, to substitute for the witness's forgotten testimony upon authentication of the memorandum, or in cross-examination of the witness.

a. Present Recollection Revived—Refreshing Recollection

A witness may use any writing or thing for the purpose of refreshing her present recollection. She usually may not read from the writing while she actually testifies, since the writing is **not authenticated**, is **not in evidence**, and may be used solely to refresh her recollection. The writing is intended to help her to recall by jogging her memory. The sworn testimony must demonstrate a **present** recollection.

b. Past Recollection Recorded—Recorded Recollection

Where a witness states that she has insufficient recollection of an event to enable her to testify fully and accurately, even after she has consulted a writing given to her on the stand, the **writing itself may be read into evidence** if a proper foundation is laid for its admissibility. This use of a memorandum as evidence of a past recollection is frequently classified as an **exception to the hearsay rule**. The foundation for receipt of the writing into evidence must include proof that:

(i)   The witness at one time had **_personal knowledge_** of the facts recited in the writing;

(ii) The writing was **_made by the witness_** or made **_under her direction_** or that it was **_adopted by the witness_**;

(iii) The writing was **_timely made_** when the matter was fresh in the mind of the witness;

(iv) The writing is **_accurate_** (*i.e.,* witness must vouch for the accuracy of the writing); and

(v)   The witness has **_insufficient recollection_** to testify fully and accurately.

Remember that, under the Federal Rule, if admitted, the writing may be read into evidence and heard by the jury, but **_the document itself is not received_** as an exhibit unless offered by the adverse party. [Fed. R. Evid. 803(5)]

c. **Inspection and Use in Cross-Examination**
Under Federal Rule 612, whenever a witness has used a writing to refresh her memory on the stand, an adverse party is entitled to have the writing produced at trial, to inspect it, to cross-examine the witness thereon, and to introduce into evidence those portions that relate to the witness's testimony. If the witness has refreshed her memory before trial by looking at the writing, it is within the court's discretion to require production of the document and to permit inspection, cross-examination, and introduction of pertinent excerpts.

As noted above, under Federal Rule 803(5), an adverse party may introduce into evidence a writing that the proponent has read into evidence as past recollection recorded.

C. OPINION TESTIMONY
The word "opinion" used in this context includes all opinions, inferences, conclusions, and other subjective statements made by a witness. A basic premise of our legal system is that, in general, witnesses should testify as to facts within their personal knowledge and that the trier of fact should draw any conclusions therefrom. Therefore, the general policy of the law is to restrict the admissibility of opinion evidence, except in cases where the courts are sure that it will be necessary, or at least helpful. Of course, the difference between "fact" and "opinion" is a matter of degree. Therefore, there cannot be any clear-cut opinion rule.

1. Opinion Testimony by Lay Witnesses

a. **General Rule of Inadmissibility**
Opinions by lay witnesses are generally inadmissible. However, there are many cases where, from the nature of the subject matter, no better evidence can be obtained. In these cases, where the event is likely to be perceived as a whole impression (*e.g.*, intoxication, speed) rather than as more specific components, opinions by lay witnesses are generally admitted.

b. **When Admissible**
In most jurisdictions and under the Federal Rules, opinion testimony by lay witnesses is admissible when:

(i) It is rationally ***based on the perception of the witness;***

(ii) It is ***helpful to a clear understanding*** of her testimony or to the determination of a fact in issue; and

(iii) It is ***not based on scientific, technical, or other specialized knowledge*** (if so based, the witness's testimony would need to meet the requirements for expert testimony stated in Rule 702, *see* 2.a., *infra*).

[Fed. R. Evid. 701]

Example: Think how much easier and clearer it is for a witness to say someone looked "drunk" than it is to describe her gait, speech, eyes, diction, breath, and manner. All these things can also be brought out, but the term "drunk" may be more meaningful than any of them.

Some jurisdictions are stricter and allow lay opinion testimony only in cases of "necessity" when it is difficult for the witness to express her perception in any form other than opinion.

c.   **Procedure**

Unless waived by a failure to object, a proper foundation must be laid by showing that the witness had the opportunity to observe the event that forms the basis of her opinion. Additionally, the court in its discretion may require a witness to state the facts observed before stating her opinion.

d.   **Situations Where Opinions of Lay Witnesses Are Admissible**

1)   **General Appearance or Condition of a Person**

Testimony that a person was "elderly," "about 60 years old," "strong," "weak," or "ill" would be admissible, but testimony that a person is suffering from specific diseases or specific injuries—usually requiring knowledge of an expert—would not.

2)   **State of Emotion**

A witness would be permitted to testify that a person appeared "angry," "was joking," or that two persons were "in love" or appeared to have a strong affection for each other.

3)   **Matters Involving Sense Recognition**

A witness would be permitted to testify that an object was "heavy," "red," "bulky," or that a certain beverage tasted like whiskey.

4)   **Voice or Handwriting Identification**

Lay opinion is permissible and often essential to identify telephone voices and handwriting. In these instances a foundation must first be laid to show familiarity with the voice or handwriting.

5)   **Speed of Moving Object**

A witness may estimate in miles per hour the speed of a moving object but must

first show some experience in observing the rate of speed of moving objects. Characterization that a vehicle was going "fast" or "very fast" has been permitted.

6) Value of Own Services
A witness may give her opinion as to the value of her own services.

7) Rational or Irrational Nature of Another's Conduct (Sanity)
In many jurisdictions, a witness is permitted to state her opinion as to the sanity of another person. Some states limit these opinions to testimony describing the acts of a person whose sanity is in question and allow the witness to state only whether those acts impressed her at the time as rational or irrational (*e.g.*, "She acted like a madwoman").

8) Intoxication
A witness who has seen a person and is able to describe that person's actions, words, or conduct, may express an opinion as to whether that person was or was not intoxicated. In many states, the details of the person's appearance must be given as a foundation for the opinion.

Example: In Defendant's trial on a charge of driving while intoxicated, Witness testifies for the prosecution that Defendant "smelled of alcohol, his speech was incoherent, his eyes glassy and bloodshot, he could not stand or walk without assistance, he was slumped over the wheel of his vehicle," and, finally, that he "was intoxicated."

e. Situations Where Opinions of Lay Witnesses Are Not Admissible

1) Agency or Authorization
When agency or authorization is in issue, the witness generally may not state a conclusion as to her authorization. Rather, she must be asked by whom she was employed and the nature, terms, and surrounding circumstances of her employment.

2) Contract or Agreement
When the existence of an express contract is in issue, a witness generally may not state her opinion that an agreement was made. Rather, she must be asked about the facts, the existence or nonexistence of which establish whether a contract existed.

2. Opinion Testimony by Expert Witnesses

a. Requirements of Expert Testimony
The expert may state an opinion or conclusion, provided the following conditions are satisfied:

1) Subject Matter Must Be Appropriate for Expert Testimony
Under Federal Rule 702, expert opinion testimony is admissible if the subject matter is one where scientific, technical, or other specialized knowledge would assist the trier of fact in understanding the evidence or determining a fact in issue.

This test of assistance to the trier of fact subdivides into two requirements:

(i)   The opinion must be *relevant* (*i.e.*, it must "fit" the facts of the case); and

(ii) The methodology underlying the opinion must be *reliable* (*i.e.*, the proponent of the expert testimony must satisfy the trial judge by a preponderance of the evidence that (a) the opinion is based on sufficient facts or data; (b) the opinion is the product of reliable principles and methods; and (c) the expert has reliably applied the principles and methods to the facts of the case).

[Fed. R. Evid. 702; *and see* Kumho Tire Co. v. Carmichael, 526 U.S. 137 (1999); Daubert v. Merrell Dow Pharmaceuticals, Inc., 509 U.S. 579 (1993)]

2)   Witness Must Be Qualified as an Expert
To testify as an expert, a person must have special knowledge, skill, experience, training, or education sufficient to qualify him as an expert on the subject to which his testimony relates. [Fed. R. Evid. 702]

3)   Expert Must Possess Reasonable Probability Regarding His Opinion
The expert must possess reasonable certainty or probability regarding his opinion. If the opinion of the expert is a mere guess or speculation, it is inadmissible.
Example: It would be error to permit plaintiff's medical expert to testify that plaintiff's symptoms "suggested" diabetes and "indicated" that the disease was caused by the accident.

4)   Opinion Must Be Supported by Proper Factual Basis
The expert's opinion may be based upon one or more of these three possible sources of information: (i) facts that the expert knows from his own observation; (ii) facts presented in evidence at the trial and submitted to the expert, usually by hypothetical question; or (iii) facts not in evidence that were supplied to the expert out of court, and which are of a type reasonably relied upon by experts in the particular field in forming opinions on the subject. Note that the expert may give opinion testimony on direct examination without disclosing the basis of the opinion, unless the court orders otherwise. However, the expert may be required to disclose such information on cross-examination. [Fed. R. Evid. 705]

a)   Personal Observation
If the expert has examined the person or thing about which he is testifying, he may relate those facts observed by him and upon which he bases his opinion. [Fed. R. Evid. 703]
Example: An expert may testify that he examined plaintiff's leg following the accident, and in his opinion the plaintiff sustained a compound fracture.

b)   Facts Made Known to Expert at Trial
The expert's opinion may be based upon the evidence introduced at the trial and related to the expert by counsel in the form of a *hypothetical question*. The hypothetical question may be based on facts derived from any of the three sources of information noted above. Federal Rule 705 adopts the modern trend in providing that the hypothetical question need not be asked.

c) **Facts Made Known to Expert Outside Court**

Under Federal Rule 703, the expert may base an opinion upon facts not known personally but supplied to him outside the courtroom (*e.g.*, reports of nurses, technicians, or consultants). The Federal Rule further provides that such facts ***need not be in evidence or even of a type admissible*** in evidence, as long as the facts are of a kind ***reasonably relied upon*** by experts in the particular field. However, if the facts are of a type inadmissible in evidence, the proponent of the expert opinion must ***not*** disclose those facts to the jury unless the court determines that their probative value in assisting the jury to evaluate the expert's opinion ***substantially*** outweighs their prejudicial effect.

Example: A physician bases his expert opinion upon (i) a personal examination of the patient, (ii) statements by the patient as to her medical history, and (iii) medically germane statements by the patient's relatives. The results of the personal examination are admissible and may therefore be relied upon by the physician because they are relevant, material, based on personal knowledge, and not subject to any exclusionary rule. The statements of the patient are admissible through an exception to the hearsay rule. The statements by the relatives, though inadmissible hearsay, may properly form a basis for a physician's expert opinion testimony because they are the facts reasonably relied upon by physicians in making a diagnosis; however, these statements should not be disclosed to the jury without the court first finding that their probative value substantially outweighs prejudice.

b. **Opinion May Embrace Ultimate Issue**

Federal Rule 704(a) and the modern trend repudiate the traditional prohibition on opinions embracing the ultimate issue in the case. The rule provides: "Testimony in the form of an opinion or inference otherwise admissible is not objectionable because it embraces an ultimate issue to be decided by the trier of fact." Note, however, that to be admissible under the Federal Rules, the expert opinion must "assist the trier of fact" to understand the evidence or determine a fact in issue. Thus, an expert's conclusion that "X had testamentary capacity" is still inadmissible because it is not helpful to the jury.

1) **Exception—Criminal Defendant's Mental State**

The Federal Rules ***prohibit*** ultimate issue testimony in one situation: In a criminal case in which the defendant's mental state constitutes an element of the crime or defense, an expert may not state an opinion as to whether the accused did or did not have the mental state in issue. [Fed. R. Evid. 704(b)]

c. **Authoritative Texts and Treatises**

An expert may be cross-examined concerning statements contained in any scientific publication, as long as the publication is established as reliable authority. For example, the witness may be asked, "Doesn't Dr. Killum, in his book on diseases of the pancreas, disagree with your conclusion here?" A publication may be established as reliable by: (i) the direct testimony or cross-examination admission of the expert, (ii) the testimony of another expert, or (iii) judicial notice. Thus, even if the expert refuses to recognize the

text as authoritative, it can be used on cross-examination if its reliability is established by one of the other methods.

The Federal Rules have expanded the admissibility of learned texts and treatises beyond impeachment of experts. Statements from an established treatise may be read into the record as substantive evidence, and may even be introduced on direct examination of a party's own expert. [Fed. R. Evid. 803(18)—exception to hearsay rule] There are two important limitations: (i) an expert must be on the stand when a statement from a treatise is read into evidence; and (ii) the relevant portion is read into evidence but is not received as an exhibit (*i.e.,* the jury never sees it).

D. CROSS-EXAMINATION

1. Necessity for Cross-Examination
Cross-examination of adverse witnesses is a matter of right in every trial of a disputed issue of fact. It is recognized as the ***most efficacious truth-discovering device***. The principal basis for excluding hearsay is that the declarant whose testimony is offered cannot be subjected to the test of cross-examination. If adequate cross-examination is prevented by the death, illness, or refusal of a witness to testify on cross-examination, the direct examination is rendered incompetent and will be stricken.

2. Scope of Cross-Examination
Although a party is entitled as of right to some cross-examination, the extent or scope of cross-examination, like the order of calling witnesses, is frequently a matter of judicial discretion. Cross-examination is hedged about by far fewer rules than is direct examination. On cross-examination, leading questions are permissible, as are, obviously, efforts at impeachment. The most significant restriction is that the scope of cross-examination cannot range beyond the subject matter of the direct examination. This restriction does not apply to inquiries directed toward impeachment of the witness.

a. Restrictions on Scope
Under Federal Rule 611(b) and in the majority of American jurisdictions, ***cross-examination is limited to***: (i) matters brought out on ***direct examination*** and the inferences naturally drawn from those matters, and (ii) matters affecting the ***credibility of the witness***.

b. Significance of Restrictions
The question of the proper scope of cross-examination is important since it affects the ***right to use leading questions***. And, in jurisdictions that do not allow a party to impeach his own witness, going beyond the scope of direct examination means that you have made the witness "your own witness" and therefore cannot impeach his testimony. Further, if the party placing a witness on the stand is the holder of a privilege, the court may hold it waived to the extent that the other party may engage in cross-examination; therefore, the scope of cross-examination permitted may determine to what extent the cross-examining party may inquire into privileged material.

c. Collateral Matters
The general rule is that the cross-examiner is ***bound by the answers of the witness*** to questions concerning collateral matters. Thus, the cross-examiner cannot refute the response of the witness by producing extrinsic evidence. Indeed, some federal courts

resolve the matter under Rule 403 by treating the evidence on the collateral matter as being substantially outweighed by time considerations and the danger of confusion of the issues. Certain matters of impeachment, however, are recognized as sufficiently important to merit development by extrinsic evidence (*e.g.*, bias or interest of the witness may be shown by other evidence, even if denied by the witness on cross-examination). Other matters of impeachment are limited solely to inquiry on cross-examination (*e.g.*, prior misconduct of the witness not resulting in conviction but affecting the witness's credibility). Once beyond recognized impeachment techniques, the test as to what is "collateral" is sufficiently vague to permit a wide exercise of discretion by the trial judge.

E. CREDIBILITY—IMPEACHMENT

Impeachment means the casting of an adverse reflection on the veracity of the witness. The primary method of impeachment is by cross-examination of the witness under attack, although witnesses are often impeached by extrinsic proof that casts doubt on credibility. In terms of relevance, any matter that tends to prove or disprove the credibility of the witness should be admitted here.

1. Accrediting or Bolstering

a. General Rule—No Bolstering Until Witness Impeached

A party may not bolster or accredit the testimony of his witness until the witness has been impeached.

Example: A prior statement made by W at the time of the event that is consistent with W's in-court testimony would not be admissible to show that W's memory of the event is excellent or that he told the same story twice and therefore is especially worthy of belief.

b. Exceptions

The rule against accrediting is subject to exception where timeliness may raise an inference on the substantive issues of the case.

1) Timely Complaint

In certain cases a party may prove that the witness made a timely complaint, in order to bolster the party's credibility.

Examples: 1) Evidence of a prompt complaint of a rape victim is admissible to bolster the complainant's credibility in a subsequent criminal prosecution.

2) Where a defendant in a criminal trial claims that a confession offered against him was obtained by coercion, he may show that he complained of mistreatment at the first suitable opportunity.

2) Prior Identification

Evidence of any prior statement of identification made by a witness is admissible not only to bolster the witness's testimony, but also as substantive evidence that the identification was correct. [Fed. R. Evid. 801(d)(1)(C); *and see* VII.B.1., *infra*]

2. Any Party May Impeach

Contrary to the traditional rule, under which a party could not impeach his own witness, the Federal Rules provide that the credibility of a witness may be attacked by any party, *including the party calling him*. [Fed. R. Evid. 607] Even under the traditional rule, however, a party could impeach his own witness if the witness: (i) was an adverse party, (ii) was hostile, (iii) was one required to be called by law, or (iv) gave damaging surprise testimony.

3. Impeachment Methods—Cross-Examination and Extrinsic Evidence

A witness may be impeached either by cross-examination (by eliciting facts from the witness that discredit his own testimony) or by extrinsic evidence (by putting other witnesses on the stand who will introduce facts discrediting his testimony).

There are certain well-recognized, often-used impeachment methods. These traditional impeachment devices include: the use of prior inconsistent statements; a showing of bias or interest in the litigation; an attack on the character of the witness by showing convictions of crime, prior acts of misconduct, or poor reputation for veracity; and a showing of sensory deficiencies. The basic questions for each of these methods are: Is the examiner limited to impeachment by cross-examination alone, or may he produce extrinsic evidence? If extrinsic evidence is permissible, must a foundation first be laid by inquiry on cross-examination?

a. Prior Inconsistent Statements

For the purpose of impeaching the credibility of a witness, a party may show that the witness has, on another occasion, made statements that are inconsistent with some material part of his present testimony. Under the Federal Rules, an inconsistent statement may be proved by either cross-examination or extrinsic evidence. To prove the statement by extrinsic evidence, certain requirements must first be met: (i) a *proper foundation* must be laid; and (ii) the statement must be *relevant* to some issue in the case, *i.e.*, it cannot be a "collateral matter."

1) Laying a Foundation

Extrinsic evidence of the witness's prior inconsistent statement is admissible only if the witness is, at some point, given an *opportunity to explain or deny* the allegedly inconsistent statement. (The opportunity need not come before introduction of the statement under the Federal Rules.) This foundation requirement may be dispensed with, however, where "the interests of justice otherwise require" (as where the witness has left the stand and is not available when his prior inconsistent statement is discovered). [Fed. R. Evid. 613(b)] The courts generally agree that inconsistent statements by a hearsay declarant may be used to impeach the declarant despite the lack of a foundation (obviously, where the declarant is not a witness no foundation could be laid anyway). [Fed. R. Evid. 806]

2) Evidentiary Effect of Prior Inconsistent Statements

In most cases, prior inconsistent statements are hearsay, admissible only to impeach the witness. However, where the statement was made *under oath at a prior trial, hearing, or other proceeding, or in a deposition, it is admissible nonhearsay* (*i.e.*, it may be considered as substantive proof of the facts stated!). (*See* VII.B.1., *infra*.)

b. Bias or Interest

Evidence that a witness is biased or has an interest in the outcome of a suit tends to

show that the witness has a ***motive to lie***. A witness may always be impeached by extrinsic evidence of bias or interest, provided a proper foundation is laid. Note that evidence that is substantively inadmissible may be admitted for impeachment purposes if relevant to show bias or interest.

Examples: 1) It may be shown that a witness is being paid to testify, that a witness is financing the case, or that he otherwise has a financial interest in the outcome of the litigation.

2) Inferences of bias may be shown by evidence of family or other relationship, business relationship, or by conduct or expressions of the witness demonstrating a friendship toward a party.

3) In a criminal case, it is proper for the defense to ask a prosecution witness whether he has been promised immunity from punishment for testifying, whether an indictment is pending against him, or whether he is on parole. This evidence may show a motive for the witness to curry the favor of the state.

4) Hostility toward a party may be shown by adverse statements against the party, or by the fact that the witness had a fight or quarrel with him or has a lawsuit pending against him.

1) Foundation

Most courts require that before a witness can be impeached by extrinsic evidence of bias or interest, he must first be asked about the facts that show bias or interest on cross-examination. If the witness on cross-examination admits the facts claimed to show bias or interest, it is within the trial judge's discretion to decide whether extrinsic evidence may be introduced as further proof of bias or interest.

2) Justification for Bias

Even though it is shown that a witness is biased, no evidence may be admitted to show that he was justified in his bias. This might make him look more reasonable, but is not very relevant to whether his bias might make him less credible.

c. Conviction of Crime

Under certain circumstances, a witness may be impeached by proof of conviction of a crime. [Fed. R. Evid. 609] The fact that the witness (including a defendant who testifies in a criminal case) has been convicted of a crime may usually be proved by either eliciting an admission on direct or cross-examination or by the record of conviction.

1) Actual Conviction Required

This type of impeachment requires an actual conviction of a crime. The fact that the witness has been arrested or indicted may not be elicited here.

2) Type of Crime

a) Crime Involving Dishonesty

Under the Federal Rules, a witness's character for truthfulness may be attacked (or impeached) by ***any crime*** (felony or misdemeanor) if it can be readily

determined that conviction of the crime required proof or admission of an act of *dishonesty* or *false statement*. In most cases, the statutory elements will indicate whether such an act was required. An indictment, statement of admitted facts, or jury instructions may also be used to show that the crime required proof of dishonesty or false statement. The trial court has no discretion—not even under Federal Rule 403—to disallow impeachment by such crimes.

b) Felony Not Involving Dishonesty
A witness's character for truthfulness may also be attacked, under the Federal Rules, by *any felony* whether or not it involves dishonesty or a false statement. However, if the felony is one that does not involve dishonesty or false statement, the trial court may exercise discretion to exclude it under one of the following standards.

(1) Accused in Criminal Case
If, in a criminal case, the witness being impeached is the accused, the felony conviction will be admitted only if the government shows that its probative value as impeachment evidence outweighs its prejudicial effect.

(2) Witness Other than Accused in Criminal Case
In the case of any witness other than the accused in a criminal case, any felony conviction is admissible, but the court retains discretion under Rule 403 to exclude it if its probative value as impeachment evidence is *substantially outweighed* by the danger of unfair prejudice.

(3) Compare the Balancing Tests
Note that under Federal Rule 609, different balancing tests apply for the exercise of discretion. If the felony conviction is offered to impeach the accused in a criminal case, the discretionary standard (*supra*) favors exclusion, since the probative value of the felony (not involving dishonesty or false statement) must outweigh prejudice. In the case of *all* other witnesses, the balancing test favors admission, since the conviction will be excluded only if the danger of prejudice substantially outweighs its probative value.

3) Must Not Be Too Remote
Under the *Federal Rules*, a conviction is usually too remote and inadmissible if *more than 10 years* have elapsed since the date of *conviction* or the date of *release* from the confinement imposed for the conviction, whichever is the later date. In extraordinary circumstances, such convictions can be admitted, but only if the trial judge determines that the probative value of the conviction substantially outweighs its prejudicial effect, and the adverse party is given notice that the conviction is to be used as impeachment. [Fed. R. Evid. 609(b)]

4) Juvenile Adjudication Generally Not Admissible
Juvenile offenses are generally not admissible for impeachment purposes. However, under the Federal Rules, a judge has the discretion in a criminal case to admit evidence of a juvenile offense committed by a witness other than the accused

if the evidence would be admissible to attack the credibility of an adult and if the evidence is necessary to a determination of the accused's guilt or innocence. [Fed. R. Evid. 609(d); Davis v. Alaska, 415 U.S. 308 (1974)]

5) Effect of Pardon Depends on Basis

In most states, a conviction may be shown even though the witness has subsequently been pardoned. Under the Federal Rules, however, the conviction may not be shown if the pardon was based on innocence or if the person pardoned has not been convicted of a subsequent crime punishable by death or imprisonment in excess of one year. [Fed. R. Evid. 609(c)]

6) Pending Appeal Does Not Affect Admissibility

In most jurisdictions and under the Federal Rules, a conviction may be used to impeach even though an appeal is pending, though the pendency of the appeal may also be shown. [Fed. R. Evid. 609(e)]

7) Constitutionally Defective Conviction Invalid for All Purposes

Where the prior felony conviction was obtained in violation of the defendant's Sixth Amendment rights (*e.g.*, to have counsel, to confront witness, etc.), the conviction is generally invalid for all purposes—including impeachment.

8) Means of Proof—Extrinsic Evidence Permitted

A prior conviction may usually be shown by either an admission on *direct or cross-examination* of the witness or by *introducing a record* of the judgment. *No foundation need be laid*. Note, however, that when a witness is being cross-examined about previous convictions, the questions must be asked in good faith (*i.e.*, with a reasonable belief as to the existence of the conviction). Improper questioning may be grounds for a mistrial.

d. Specific Instances of Misconduct—Bad Acts

1) General Rule—Interrogation Permitted

The traditional majority view is that, subject to discretionary control of the trial judge, a witness may be interrogated upon cross-examination with respect to any immoral, vicious, or criminal act of his life that may *affect his character* and show him to be *unworthy of belief.* Inquiry into "bad acts" is permitted even though the witness was never convicted. Federal Rule 608 permits such inquiry, in the discretion of the court, only if the act of misconduct is *probative of truthfulness* (*i.e.,* is an act of deceit or lying).

2) Counsel Must Inquire in Good Faith

The cross-examiner must act in good faith with some reasonable basis for believing that the witness may have committed the "bad act" inquired about.

Example: It would be error for the prosecution to inquire about an act when the prosecutor knows that the witness has been tried for the act and acquitted.

3) Extrinsic Evidence Not Permitted

Extrinsic evidence of "bad acts" is not permitted. A specific act of misconduct, offered to attack the witness's character for truthfulness, can be elicited *only on*

cross-examination of the witness. If the witness denies the act, the cross-examiner cannot refute the answer by calling other witnesses or producing other evidence. It is not usually improper for the cross-examiner, acting in good faith, to continue the cross-examination after a denial in the hope that the witness will change his answer.

e. Opinion or Reputation Evidence for Truthfulness

1) By Proof of Reputation
A witness may be impeached by showing that she has a poor reputation for truthfulness. The usual method of impeachment is to ask other witnesses about her general reputation for truth and veracity in the community in which she lives. The modern view is to allow evidence of reputation in business circles as well as in the community in which the witness resides.

2) By Opinion Evidence
Most states do not allow the impeaching witness to state her opinion as to the character of a witness for truth and veracity. However, the *Federal Rules allow* an impeaching witness to state her personal opinions, based upon acquaintance, as to the truthfulness of the witness sought to be impeached. [Fed. R. Evid. 608(a)]

f. Sensory Deficiencies
A witness may be impeached by showing that he had no knowledge of the facts to which he testified, or that his faculties of perception and recollection were so impaired as to make it doubtful that he could have perceived those facts. Such a showing can be made either *on cross-examination or by the use of extrinsic evidence*.

1) Defects of Capacity

a) Perceptive Disabilities
It is, of course, proper to show deficiencies of the senses, such as deafness or color blindness, that would have substantially impaired the witness's ability to perceive the facts to which he testifies. It may also be shown that at the time the witness observed the events his perception was temporarily diminished (*e.g.*, that he was sleepy or under the influence of alcohol or drugs).

b) Lack of Memory
A witness can be impeached by showing that he has a poor memory of the events about which he testifies. This is usually done on cross-examination by asking the witness about other related matters to suggest the inference that if his memory of related matters is poor, his recollection of the events to which he is testifying is doubtful.

c) Mental Disorders
Psychiatric evidence of a mental disorder that would affect a witness's credibility has been admitted by some courts (particularly in sex offense cases).

2) Lack of Knowledge

a) Expert Witnesses

The credibility of an expert witness may be attacked by cross-examining him as to (i) his general knowledge of the field in which he is claiming to be an expert, and (ii) his particular knowledge of the facts upon which his opinion is based.

b) Opinion Witnesses

The credibility of an opinion witness may be attacked by showing lack of knowledge. For example, a witness who gives opinion evidence on the value of land may be cross-examined regarding her knowledge of land values and may be asked about sales of other land.

c) Character Witnesses

As discussed earlier, when a character witness testifies to the good character of another (*e.g.*, a defendant), the witness may be cross-examined regarding the basis of his statement that the defendant's character is good. In other words, the testimony of the character witness may be discredited by asking him about specific criminal or immoral acts committed by the defendant, on the theory that if the witness has no knowledge of these acts, he does not really know the defendant's character. [Fed. R. Evid. 405(a)]

In most courts, a character witness may testify only as to *reputation*. Therefore, on cross-examination, the only acceptable form of question is: "Have you *heard* that the defendant . . . ?" However, under the Federal Rules and in modern jurisdictions that permit character witnesses to testify as to their *opinions* of character, questions in the form, "Do you *know* . . . ?" would be proper.

4. Impeachment on Collateral Matter

Where a witness makes a statement not directly relevant to the issues in the case, the rule against impeachment (other than by cross-examination) on a collateral matter applies to bar the opponent from proving the statement untrue either by extrinsic contradictory facts or by a prior inconsistent statement. The purpose of the rule is to avoid the possibility of unfair surprise, confusion of issues, and undue consumption of time resulting from the attempt to prove and disprove facts that are not directly relevant.

Example: Plaintiff's witness testifies, "I saw the accident on the way home from church." If it is conceded that the witness saw the accident, it would be a collateral matter for the defendant to show that the witness was on his way home from a pool hall rather than church. It would not be "collateral" to show that the witness was on his way home from a dinner at the plaintiff's house, because that suggests *bias*, which is a separate basis for impeachment (*see* 3.b., *supra*).

5. Impeachment of Hearsay Declarant

There are many occasions in which out-of-court statements are admitted into evidence by means of exceptions and limitations to the general rule excluding hearsay. These statements are frequently admitted into evidence, even though the person who made the statement (the declarant) does not testify at the trial. The party against whom the statement has been admitted may wish to impeach the credibility of the declarant so that the jury will discount or assign less probative value to the statement. Under Federal Rule 806, the credibility of a

declarant may be attacked (and if attacked, may be supported) by evidence that would be admissible if the declarant had testified as a witness. Of course, the declarant need not be given the opportunity to explain or deny prior inconsistent statements. In addition, the party against whom the out-of-court statement was offered may call the declarant as a witness and cross-examine him about the statement.

6. Rehabilitation

A witness who has been impeached may be rehabilitated on redirect examination or by extrinsic evidence.

a. Explanation on Redirect

For purposes of rehabilitation, the witness on redirect examination may explain or clarify facts brought out on cross-examination.

Example: A witness testifying for the prosecution in an organized crime murder trial admitted to making a prior inconsistent statement. On redirect, the witness is permitted to explain that he gave a prior untruthful statement favoring the defendant out of fear of being killed by the defendant's gang.

b. Good Reputation for Truthfulness

When the witness's general character for truthfulness and veracity has been attacked, the party for whom the impeached witness has testified may call other witnesses to testify to the good reputation for truthfulness of the impeached witness or to give their opinion as to the truthfulness of the impeached witness.

c. Prior Consistent Statement

1) Generally Not Permitted

A party may not ordinarily rehabilitate a witness by showing a prior consistent statement. As a general rule this is true even when the witness has been impeached by showing a prior inconsistent statement. The inconsistency is not removed by the fact that the witness made more than one consistent statement.

2) Exceptions

Where the opposing counsel has impeached the credibility of a witness by making an express or an implied charge that the witness is lying or exaggerating because of some motive, counsel may introduce into evidence a prior consistent statement made by the witness before the time of the alleged motive to lie or exaggerate. Under Federal Rule 801(d)(1)(B), this statement not only is used to bolster the witness's testimony, but also is substantive evidence of the truth of its contents, whether or not made under oath. (*See* VII.B.1., *infra.*)

Example: Defense attorney intimated on cross-examination that the prosecution witness was biased against his client because of a fight they recently had. The prosecutor may introduce evidence of a statement the witness made, consistent with his testimony, before the fight occurred.

F. OBJECTIONS, EXCEPTIONS, OFFERS OF PROOF

1. **Objections**

Unless an objection is made by opposing counsel, almost any kind of evidence will be admitted. Failure to object is deemed a *waiver* of any ground for objection. The trial judge need not raise grounds for objection on her own, but may take notice of plain errors affecting substantial rights (*e.g.,* admission of coerced confession not objected to by defense).

a. **Objections to Trial Testimony**

Objections should be made after the question, but before the answer, if it is apparent that the question calls for inadmissible matter (*e.g.,* hearsay) or that the question is in improper form (*e.g.,* leading). Otherwise, a motion to strike must be made as soon as the witness's answer emerges as inadmissible (*e.g.,* "Q: What color was the automobile? A: My sister told me it was gray.").

b. **Objections to Deposition Testimony**

Objections to the *form* of a question (*e.g.,* leading) are waived unless made during the deposition, thereby affording counsel an opportunity to correct the form of his question. An objection based on a *testimonial privilege* should also be made then, lest it be deemed waived. However, objections going to the substance of a question or answer (*e.g.,* relevance, hearsay) can be postponed until the deposition is offered in evidence.

c. **Specificity of Objections**

An objection may be either *general* ("I object") or *specific* ("Object, hearsay"). The importance of whether an objection is general or specific lies in the extent to which each type preserves the evidentiary issue on appeal. The following rules apply:

1) **General Objection Sustained**

If a general objection is sustained and the evidence excluded, the ruling will be upheld on appeal if there was *any ground* for the objection. In the absence of specificity in the trial court, it will be assumed that the ruling was placed upon the right ground.

2) **General Objection Overruled**

If a general objection is overruled and the evidence admitted, the objection is not available on appeal unless the evidence was *not admissible under any circumstances* for any purpose.

3) **Specific Objection Sustained**

If a specific objection is sustained and the evidence is excluded, the ruling will be upheld on appeal only if the ground stated was the correct one, unless the evidence excluded was not competent and could not be made so.

d. **"Opening the Door"**

One who introduces evidence on a particular subject thereby asserts its relevance and cannot complain, except on grounds other than relevance, if his adversary thereafter offers evidence on the same subject. And counsel need not "stand" on his overruled relevance objection; he can offer counterevidence without thereby abandoning his relevance objection.

e. **Effect of Introducing Part of Transaction**

Where part of a conversation, act, or writing, etc., is introduced into evidence, the

adverse party may require the proponent of the evidence to introduce any other part that ought, in fairness, to be considered contemporaneously with it. [Fed. R. Evid. 106] The party who introduced the original part of the transaction cannot object to the introduction of other parts on the ground of lack of competency or hearsay, etc. The theory is that the party has *waived any objections by introducing the part.*

f.   Motion to Strike—Unresponsive Answers
Unresponsive answers are subject to a motion to strike by examining counsel, but not by opposing counsel. Examining counsel, in other words, can "adopt" an unresponsive answer if it is not objectionable on some other ground.

2.   Exceptions
The common law rule requiring a party to "except" from an adverse trial court ruling in order to preserve the issue for appeal has been abolished in most jurisdictions. In some states, however, a written motion for a new trial, specifying the grounds, may be required.

3.   Offers of Proof
On some occasions, error cannot be based on exclusion of evidence unless there has been an "offer of proof" that discloses the nature, purpose, and admissibility of the rejected evidence. There are three types of "offers of proof."

a.   Witness Offer
Subsequent to a sustained objection by opposing counsel, the examining counsel proceeds with his examination of a witness on the stand, out of the jury's hearing, thus making his record by the question-and-answer method.

b.   Lawyer Offer
Counsel himself states, in narrative form, what the witness would have testified had he been permitted to do so. The "witness offer" is generally preferred to the "lawyer offer" and can be required by the trial court, especially if opposing counsel denies that the witness would testify as narrated.

c.   Tangible Offer
A marked, authenticated, and offered item of tangible evidence is its own offer of proof.

G.   TESTIMONIAL PRIVILEGES
Testimonial privileges, which permit one to refuse to disclose and prohibit others from disclosing certain sorts of confidential information in judicial proceedings, have two basic reasons for their existence: (i) *practicality*, and (ii) society's desire to *encourage certain relationships* by ensuring their confidentiality, even at the high price of losing valuable information.

Some of the testimonial privileges are frankly grounded on hardheaded practicality. The particular kind of disclosure could not be obtained, as a practical matter, even if there were no privilege. No priest, even when confronted by a contempt of court citation, would breach the priest-penitent relationship. Society values some relationships sufficiently that it is willing to protect their confidential nature even at the expense of the loss of information relevant to the issues of a lawsuit. These relationships will be encouraged if confidentiality, when desired, is assured. To put it more concretely, persons might forgo needed medical attention or be less than candid with legal counsel

were there no guarantee that communications made during the physician-patient and attorney-client relationships would be accorded confidential status in legal proceedings.

1. **Federal Rules—No Specific Privilege Provisions**

   The Federal Rules have no specific privilege provisions. Federal Rule 501 provides that the privilege of a witness or person shall be governed by the principles of the common law as they may be interpreted by the courts of the United States in the light of reason and experience. The federal courts currently recognize the attorney-client privilege, the privilege for spousal communications, and the psychotherapist/social worker-client privilege. In civil actions when state law supplies the rule of decision as to an element of a claim or defense, the state law applies with respect to testimonial privileges as well. Thus, in *diversity* cases, the state law of privilege applies.

2. **General Considerations**

   a. **Persons Who May Assert a Privilege**

      A privilege is personal, and may be asserted only by the party whose interest is sought to be protected or by someone authorized to assert it on the holder's behalf (*e.g.,* guardian of incompetent holder). If the privilege is held by more than one person, each of them can claim the privilege. In certain cases, the person with whom the confidence was shared may claim it on the holder's behalf.

   b. **Confidentiality**

      To be privileged, a communication must be shown to have been made in confidence. Many states, however, recognize a presumption that any disclosures made in the course of a relationship for which a privilege exists were made in confidence.

   c. **Comment on Privilege Forbidden**

      No inference should be drawn from the fact that a witness has claimed a privilege. Thus, counsel for the parties and the judge are not permitted to make any comment or argument based on a claim of privilege.

   d. **Waiver**

      All types of privileges are waived by the following:

      (i) *Failure to claim the privilege* by the holder herself or failure to object when privileged testimony is offered;

      (ii) *Voluntary disclosure* of the privileged matter by the holder (or someone else with the holder's consent) unless the disclosure is also privileged; or

      (iii) A *contractual provision* waiving in advance the right to claim a privilege.

      A privilege is not waived where someone wrongfully disclosed information without the holder's consent. Similarly, a waiver of the privilege by one joint holder does not affect the right of another joint holder to claim the privilege.

   e. **Eavesdroppers**

      A privilege based on confidential communications is not abrogated because the communication is overheard by someone whose presence is unknown to the parties; *i.e.,* the

privilege still applies to the parties to the confidential communication. There is some question, however, as to whether the eavesdropper may testify. The traditional view is that the eavesdropper may testify to what he has overheard. But a significant number of modern cases and statutes assert that as long as the holder of the privilege was not negligent, there is no waiver of the privilege, and the eavesdropper is also prohibited from testifying.

3. Attorney-Client Privilege

The first testimonial privilege ever established was the attorney-client privilege. It is a common law privilege, although in some jurisdictions it has now been codified by statute. It carries with it fewer exceptions than any other privilege.

Essentially, communications between an attorney and client, made during professional consultation, are privileged from disclosure. In other words, a client has a privilege to refuse to disclose, and to prevent others from disclosing, confidential communications between herself (or her representative) and her attorney (or her attorney's representative). Objects and preexisting documents are not protected.

a. Attorney-Client Relationship

The attorney-client privilege requires that the attorney-client relationship exist at the time of the communications. The client, or her representative, must be seeking the professional services of the attorney at the crucial time. But note that retainer negotiations, involving disclosures made before the attorney has decided to accept or decline the case, are covered if the other requirements of the privilege are present.

1) Client

A "client," in the context of the typical formulation of the attorney-client privilege, can be an individual private citizen, a public officer, a corporation, or any other organization or entity, public or private, seeking professional legal services.

2) Representative of Client

A "representative of a client" is one having the *authority to obtain legal services or to act on advice* rendered by an attorney, on behalf of the client.

3) Attorney

An "attorney" is any person who is authorized or, in many jurisdictions, who is *reasonably believed* by the client to be authorized, to practice law in any state or nation.

4) Representative of Attorney

A "representative of an attorney" is one employed by the attorney to assist in the rendition of professional services, *e.g.*, a clerk or secretary.

5) Corporation as Client

A corporation, as indicated above, can be a "client" within the meaning of the attorney-client privilege. The statements of *any corporate officials or employees* made to the attorney are protected if they were authorized or directed by the corporation to make such statements.

b. Confidential Communication

A communication is "confidential" if it was not intended to be disclosed to third persons, other than those to whom disclosure would be in furtherance of the rendition of legal services to the client or those who are necessary for the transmission of the communication. Communications made in the known presence and hearing of a stranger are not privileged.

1) Communications Through Agents

Communications made to third persons are confidential, and thus covered by the attorney-client privilege, if necessary to transmit information between the attorney and client. Examples include: communications by the client to the attorney's secretary or messenger; information (not documents) given to the attorney by the client's accountant; communications between the client's liability insurer and the attorney; and communications through an interpreter.

a) Examination by Doctor

When a client is examined by a doctor at the attorney's request, the communications involved between the client and doctor (and the doctor and attorney) are not covered by the physician-patient privilege because no treatment is contemplated. These communications are, however, covered by the attorney-client privilege because the examination is necessary to help the client communicate her condition to the attorney. Note that this privilege would be waived if the doctor were later called as an expert witness by the same client.

Example: P, a pedestrian, was struck by a car driven by D. P employs Attorney to bring a negligence suit against D to recover for the physical injuries P suffered in the accident. Attorney sends P to Dr. Z for an evaluation of the extent and permanence of P's injuries. Attorney does not intend to call Dr. Z as an expert witness at trial. At trial, D's attorney, believing that P may have admitted to some negligence of his own when describing his injury, calls Dr. Z to testify to his examination of P. If P objects, claiming attorney-client privilege, he may prevent Dr. Z from testifying.

2) No Privilege Where Attorney Acts for Both Parties

Where an attorney acts for both parties to a transaction, no privilege can be invoked in a lawsuit between the two parties (they obviously did not desire and could not expect confidentiality as between themselves in a joint consultation), but the *privilege can be claimed* in a suit between either or both of the two parties and *third persons* (multiple parties can desire and expect confidentiality as against the outside world).

c. Client as Holder of Privilege

The privilege, if it exists, can be claimed by the client, her guardian or conservator, the personal representative of a deceased client, or the successor, trustee, or similar representative of a corporation, association, etc. The person who was the attorney at the time of the communication can claim the privilege, but only on behalf of the client. The attorney's authority to do this is presumed in the absence of any evidence to the contrary.

d. **Duration of Privilege**
The attorney-client privilege applies indefinitely. Termination of the attorney-client *relationship* does not terminate the privilege. The privilege even continues to apply after the client's death. *Rationale:* Knowing that communications will remain confidential even after death encourages the client to communicate fully and frankly with her attorney. [Swidler & Berlin v. United States, 524 U.S. 399 (1998)]

e. **Nonapplicability of the Privilege**
There are three significant exceptions to the application of the attorney-client privilege:

1) **Legal Advice in Aid of Future Wrongdoing**
There is no privilege if the services of the attorney were sought or obtained as an aid in the planning or actual commission of something that the *client knew, or should have known, was a crime or a fraud*.

2) **Claimants Through Same Deceased Client**
There is no privilege regarding a communication relevant to an issue between parties, all of whom claim through the same deceased client—regardless of whether the claims are by testate or intestate succession or by inter vivos transaction.

3) **Dispute Between Attorney and Client**
There is no privilege for a communication that is relevant to an issue of *breach of duty* by the attorney to his client (malpractice) or by the client to her attorney (*e.g.*, client's failure to pay her attorney's fee for professional services).

f. **Waiver of the Privilege**
The privilege belongs solely to the client and she alone can waive it. If the client chooses to waive the privilege, her attorney may be compelled to testify.

g. **Attorney's Work Product**
Documents prepared by an attorney for his *own use* in prosecuting his client's case are not protected by the attorney-client privilege. However, they may be protected by the attorney's "work product" rule. In *Hickman v. Taylor*, 329 U.S. 495 (1947), the United States Supreme Court held that the work product of a lawyer—in that case, statements of interviews with potential witnesses—is not subject to discovery except in cases of necessity.

h. **Limitations on Waiver of Attorney-Client Privilege and Work Product Rule**
Federal Rule of Evidence 502 allows parties to disclose privileged material without risking waiver of the attorney-client privilege and work product rule as to undisclosed material. Additionally, the rule protects against waiver when the disclosure is the result of an innocent mistake.

1) **Disclosure in Federal Proceeding**
A voluntary disclosure of privileged material made in a federal proceeding operates as a waiver of the attorney-client privilege or work product protection *only with respect to the disclosed material*. The waiver *does not* extend to undisclosed privileged material *unless*: (i) the waiver is *intentional*, (ii) both the

disclosed and undisclosed material concern the *same subject matter*, and (iii) fairness dictates that all the material should be considered together *to avoid a misleading presentation of evidence*. [Fed. R. Evid. 502(a)] If the disclosure was *inadvertent* and the holder took reasonable steps to prevent disclosure and rectify the error (*e.g.*, attempting to retrieve the mistakenly disclosed material), then there is *no waiver*. [Fed. R. Evid. 502(a), (b)]

2) Disclosure in State Proceeding

A disclosure of privileged material made in a state proceeding is not an effective waiver in a subsequent federal proceeding if: (i) the disclosure would not operate as a waiver if it had been made in a federal proceeding, or (ii) the disclosure is not a waiver under that state's law. [Fed. R. Evid. 502(c)]

4. Physician-Patient Privilege

The physician-patient privilege is a statutory privilege, which has not been adopted in all jurisdictions. However, in a substantial number of jurisdictions, a physician (and, in some jurisdictions, a dentist or nurse) is foreclosed from divulging in judicial proceedings information that he acquired while attending a patient in a professional capacity, which information was necessary to enable the physician to act in his professional capacity.

a. Elements of Physician-Patient Privilege

1) Professional Member of Relationship Must Be Present

If the professional member of the relationship is not present for purposes of treatment, and that fact is known to the patient, the relationship does not exist and no privilege attaches.

2) Information Must Be Acquired While Attending Patient

The information must be acquired while attending the patient in the course of treatment; the privilege does not apply to information obtained by the professional in some other way.

3) Information Must Be Necessary for Treatment

If information given by the patient deals with a nonmedical matter (*e.g.*, details of an accident), the information is not privileged. Physicians have also been held competent to testify regarding facts that a lay witness might observe which are not induced by the professional relationship, such as the observable fact that the patient was ill, dates of treatment, or description of clothing worn by the patient.

Example: A treating physician who removed the clothing of an unconscious accident victim will be permitted to testify that a heroin packet fell out of the patient's right sock.

b. Nonapplicability of the Privilege

There are many exceptions and implied waivers of the physician-patient privilege, and the privilege is of little importance as a result. The privilege does not apply (or is impliedly waived) in the following situations:

1) Patient Puts Physical Condition in Issue

The physician-patient privilege is not applicable in those situations creating the

largest number of litigated cases, since a person cannot invoke the privilege where he himself has put his physical condition in issue, *e.g.*, where he sues for personal injuries.

2) **In Aid of Wrongdoing**
Like the attorney-client privilege, there is no privilege if the physician's services were sought or obtained in aid of the planning or commission of a crime or tort, or to escape detection or apprehension after the commission of a crime or tort.

3) **Dispute Between Physician and Patient**
There is no privilege regarding a communication relevant to an issue of breach, by the physician or by the patient, of a duty arising out of the physician-patient relationship, *e.g.*, malpractice, failure to pay one's bill.

4) **Agreement to Waive the Privilege**
The patient may agree by contract (*e.g.*, life insurance policy) to waive the privilege.

5) **Federal Cases Applying Federal Law of Privilege**
In cases where state law does not supply the rule of privilege (*i.e.,* most federal question cases), the federal courts do not recognize any physician-patient privilege. They do, however, recognize a psychotherapist-client privilege (*see* below).

c. **Criminal Proceedings**
There is a split of authority as to the applicability of the physician-patient privilege in criminal proceedings. In some states, the privilege applies in both civil and criminal cases. In a number of others, it cannot be invoked in criminal cases generally. In still other states, the privilege is denied in felony cases, and in a few states, it is denied only in homicide cases. Note that where a psychiatrist is involved, however, the applicable privilege is the psychotherapist-client privilege (below), which is more widely accepted in all proceedings than the physician-patient privilege.

d. **Patient Holds the Privilege**
The privilege belongs to the patient, and he may decide to claim or waive it.

5. **Psychotherapist/Social Worker-Client Privilege**
The United States Supreme Court recognizes a federal privilege for communications between a psychotherapist (psychiatrist or psychologist) or licensed social worker and his client. [Jaffee v. Redmond, 518 U.S. 1 (1996)—confidential communications between police officer and licensed social worker following a shooting were privileged] Thus, the federal courts and virtually all of the states recognize a privilege for this type of confidential communication. In most particulars, this privilege operates in the same manner as the attorney-client privilege (*supra*).

6. **Husband-Wife Privilege**
Under the early rule, spouses were absolutely incompetent to testify for or against each other during the period of marriage, and this incompetency had the same effect as the Dead Man Acts—neither spouse could speak out in court if the other spouse was a party. The prohibition against spousal testimony in favor of the party-spouse has been abandoned. However, there remains a rule of spousal immunity whereby a married person may not be compelled to testify *against* her spouse in a criminal case. Apart from this rule, a separate privilege exists

in most jurisdictions that protects confidential communications during marriage. Thus, there are two separate privileges as follows: (i) the privilege not to testify against a spouse in a criminal case—spousal immunity, and (ii) the privilege for confidential marital communications.

a. Spousal Immunity—Privilege Not to Testify in Criminal Cases

When the privilege of spousal immunity is invoked, a married person whose spouse is the defendant in a criminal case *may not be called as a witness by the prosecution*, and a married person *may not be compelled to testify* against his spouse in *any* criminal proceeding. (This second part of the privilege exists even where the spouse is not a defendant, such as in grand jury proceedings.) The purpose of this immunity is to protect the marital relationship from the disruption that would follow from allowing one spouse to testify against the other.

1) Federal Courts—Privilege Belongs to Witness-Spouse

In federal courts, only the witness-spouse may invoke the privilege against adverse spousal testimony. Thus, one spouse *may* testify against the other in criminal cases, with or without the consent of the party-spouse, but the witness-spouse may not be compelled to testify, nor may she be foreclosed from testifying (except as to confidential communications, *infra*). [*See* Trammel v. United States, 445 U.S. 40 (1980)] Some states (*e.g.,* California) follow the federal view.

2) Some State Courts—Privilege Belongs to Party-Spouse

In some state courts, the privilege belongs to the party-spouse. Thus the witness-spouse may not be compelled to testify, and she may be foreclosed from testifying if the party-spouse asserts the privilege.

3) Valid Marriage Required

There must be a valid marriage for the privilege to exist. No privilege exists if the marriage is void (*e.g.,* because it is incestuous, bigamous, or a sham).

4) Immunity May Be Asserted Only During Marriage

The privilege lasts only during the marriage and terminates upon divorce or annulment. If a marriage exists, the privilege can be asserted even as to matters that took place *before* the marriage. Remember, however, that in federal court the privilege belongs to the witness. Therefore, an accused cannot use marriage to silence a federal court witness.

b. Privilege for Confidential Marital Communications

In any civil or criminal case, either spouse, whether or not a party, has a privilege to refuse to disclose, and to prevent another from disclosing, a confidential communication made between the spouses while they were husband and wife. The rationale is to encourage open communication and trust and confidence between husband and wife.

1) Both Spouses Hold Privilege

Both spouses jointly hold this privilege, and either can refuse to disclose the communication or prevent any other person from disclosing the confidential communication.

2) Elements of the Privilege

a) **Marital Relationship**

The communication must be made during a valid marriage. Divorce will *not* terminate the privilege retroactively, but communications after divorce are not privileged.

b) **Reliance upon Intimacy**

The communication must be made in reliance upon the intimacy of the marital relationship. Routine exchanges of a business nature, abusive language, and misconduct directed to the spouse are not privileged. If the communication was made in the *known* presence of a stranger, it is not privileged. The confidential communication need not be spoken but may be made by conduct intended as a communication.

c. **Nonapplicability of Privileges**

Neither the spousal immunity nor the confidential marital communications privilege applies in actions between the spouses or in cases involving crimes against the testifying spouse or either spouse's children (*e.g.*, assault and battery, incest, bigamy, child abuse, etc.).

7. Privilege Against Self-Incrimination

Under the Fifth Amendment of the United States Constitution, a witness cannot be compelled to testify against himself. (For full discussion, *see* Criminal Procedure outline.) Thus, any witness may refuse to answer any question whose answer might incriminate him, and a criminal defendant may use the privilege to refuse to take the witness stand at all. The privilege belongs to the witness; a party cannot assert it on the witness's behalf.

a. **"Incriminating" Defined**

Testimony is incriminating if it ties the witness to the commission of a *crime* or would furnish a lead to evidence tying the witness to a crime; the testimony need not prove guilt. [Hoffman v. United States, 341 U.S. 479 (1951)] A witness cannot refuse to answer because of exposure to civil liability; it must be to avoid *criminal* liability.

b. **When Privilege Applies**

The privilege can be claimed at any state or federal proceeding, whether civil or criminal, at which the witness's appearance and testimony are compelled (*e.g.*, by subpoena). The privilege can be invoked only by natural persons, not corporations or associations.

8. Clergy-Penitent Privilege

A person has a privilege to refuse to disclose, and to prevent others from disclosing, a confidential communication by the person to a member of the clergy in the clergy member's capacity as a spiritual adviser. A member of the clergy can be a minister, priest, rabbi, or other similar functionary of a religious organization, or reasonably believed to be so by the person consulting him. This common law privilege is very similar in its operation to the attorney-client privilege, *supra*.

9. Accountant-Client Privilege

This is a statutory privilege, found in a number of jurisdictions, which is similar to the attorney-client privilege, *supra*.

10. Professional Journalist Privilege

Whether a journalist may be forced to divulge her sources of information has been a much-litigated question and the subject of a trend of statutory authority. The Supreme Court has

held that there is no constitutional protection for a journalist's source of information, so the existence of the privilege is *limited to individual state statutes*, which have been recently growing in number.

Less than half of the states have enacted statutes protecting the journalist's source of information, and the protection ranges from an absolute privilege to one qualified by the need for disclosure in the public interest.

11. Governmental Privileges

a.   Identity of Informer

The federal government, or a state or subdivision of a state, generally has a privilege to refuse to disclose the identity of a person who has furnished to a law enforcement officer information purporting to reveal the commission of a crime.

1)   Privilege Claimed by Government

The privilege can be claimed by an appropriate representative of the government, such as a prosecutor.

2)   No Privilege If Identity Otherwise Voluntarily Disclosed

No privilege exists if the identity of the informer or his interest in the subject matter of his communication has been voluntarily disclosed by a holder of the privilege, such as a prosecutor, or if the informer appears as a witness in the case.

3)   Judge May Dismiss If Informer's Testimony Crucial

If the government elects not to disclose the identity of an informer and there is a reasonable probability that the informer could provide testimony necessary to the fair determination of guilt or innocence, the judge, on his own motion or that of the accused, must dismiss the proceedings.

b.   Official Information

This is a general catch-all privilege that attaches to certain communications made *by or to public officials*. Official information has been defined as information not open to the public, relating to the internal affairs of the government or its subdivisions. It applies to some fairly low-level communications made by or to officials (*e.g.*, a judge's communications to his law clerk).

H.   EXCLUSION AND SEQUESTRATION OF WITNESSES

Upon a party's request, the trial judge will order witnesses excluded from the courtroom so they cannot listen to the testimony of other witnesses. [Fed. R. Evid. 615] The trial judge may also do this on his own motion. However, Federal Rule 615 prohibits the exclusion of: (i) a *party* or a designated officer or employee of a party, (ii) a person whose *presence is essential* to the presentation of a party's case, or (iii) a person *statutorily authorized* to be present.

VII. THE HEARSAY RULE

A.   STATEMENT OF THE RULE

The Federal Rules define hearsay as "a statement, other than one made by the declarant while

testifying at the trial or hearing, offered in evidence to prove the truth of the matter asserted." [Fed. R. Evid. 801(c)] The rule against hearsay is probably the most important exclusionary rule of evidence. If a statement is hearsay, and no exception to the rule is applicable, the evidence must be excluded upon appropriate objection to its admission. [Fed. R. Evid. 802] An out-of-court statement that incorporates other hearsay within it is known as "hearsay on hearsay" or "hearsay within hearsay." Hearsay within hearsay is admissible only if both the outer hearsay statement and the inner hearsay statement fall within an exception to the hearsay rule.

1. Reason for Excluding Hearsay

The reason for excluding hearsay is that the adverse party was *denied the opportunity to cross-examine the declarant*; *i.e.*, the party had no chance to test the declarant's perception (how well did she observe the event she purported to describe), her memory (did she really remember the details she related), her sincerity (was she deliberately falsifying), and her ability to relate (did she really mean to say what now appears to be the thrust of her statement).

a. Cross-Examination of Declarant

Note that it is the declarant who made the statement that the adverse party was not able to cross-examine. Of course, the adverse party can cross-examine the witness who repeats the statement, but this does not help much where all the witness does is repeat a statement as to which the party needs to cross-examine the original declarant.

If W (witness on the stand) testifies as to what D (declarant making out-of-court statement) said about an event, and D's statement is *offered for its truth*, then the opportunity to cross-examine W is not enough. The party against whom W testifies has *no opportunity to test* the perception, the memory, the articulateness, or the veracity of D, the very witness whose account of the event the jury is being asked to believe. Of course, W is available for cross-examination, but W is only repeating what D said, and W is of little help in the attempt to question the accuracy of D's version.

b. Cross-Examination at Time Statement Made

Note too that the *declarant and witness can be the same person*. For example, a witness might state, "I don't remember anything about the accident, but I do remember that later that day I said to my wife, 'the black car went through the red light.'" Since the adverse party could not cross-examine the witness-declarant as to his perception, memory, sincerity, or ability to relate at the time the statement was made, the statement is hearsay. It is *contemporaneous* cross-examination that is required.

2. "Statement"

For purposes of the hearsay rule, a "statement" is (i) an oral or written assertion, or (ii) nonverbal conduct intended as an assertion. [Fed. R. Evid. 801(a)]

a. Oral Statements

"Statement" includes oral statements (*i.e.,* where the witness testifies that somebody said " . . . ").

b. Writings

Any written document that is offered in evidence constitutes a "statement" for hearsay purposes.

c. **Assertive Conduct**

Conduct intended by the actor to be a substitute for words (*e.g.,* the nod of the declarant's head indicating yes) is a "statement" within the meaning of the hearsay rule.

d. **Nonassertive Conduct**

Under the traditional common law definition of hearsay, "statement" included nonassertive conduct—sometimes called "Morgan hearsay." Nonassertive conduct is conduct the declarant ***did not intend as an assertion*** but which is being offered as an assertion. However, under modern codes and the Federal Rules, evidence of nonassertive conduct is not hearsay. The rationale is that the likelihood of fabrication is less with nonassertive conduct than with assertive or verbal conduct.

Examples: 1) Consider the conduct of a deceased sea captain who, after examining every part of a ship, embarked on it with his family, when his conduct is being introduced on the question of the seaworthiness of the vessel. Although the sea captain did not intend his embarking on the vessel to serve as an assertion of anything, his conduct can be used to imply that he thought the ship was seaworthy and, since he knew his business, that the ship was in fact seaworthy.

    2) Similarly, the fact that a doctor treated a person for plague is nonassertive conduct by the doctor that could be used to show that the person had plague.

3. **"Offered to Prove the Truth of the Matter"**

This is the most crucial component of the hearsay rule. The basic reason for rejecting hearsay evidence is that a statement offered to prove that which it asserts is true may not be trustworthy without the guarantees of cross-examination. However, where the out-of-court statement is introduced for any purpose other than to prove the truth of the matter asserted, there is no need to cross-examine the declarant, and so the statement is not hearsay.

Example: The witness on the stand testifies, "On April 2, Decla said to me, 'Yesterday I was in Buffalo.'" If the issue is whether Decla was in Buffalo on April 1, the testimony is hearsay. It is ***not*** hearsay if the issue is whether on April 2, Decla was capable of talking. On the latter issue, it is enough to cross-examine the witness.

The following are other examples of out-of-court statements that are not hearsay.

a. **Verbal Acts or Legally Operative Facts**

There are certain utterances to which the law attaches legal significance (*e.g.,* words of contract, defamation, bribery, cancellation, permission). Evidence of such statements (sometimes called "legally operative facts") is not hearsay because the issue is simply whether the statements were made.

Examples: 1) In an action on a ***contract***, words that constitute the offer, acceptance, rejection, etc., are not hearsay because they are offered only to prove what was said, and not that it was true.

    2) Similarly, in a ***defamation*** action, the statement alleged to be a slander or libel may be admissible as nonhearsay. Thus if D said, "X is a thief," X will introduce D's statement not to show its truth—that he

himself is a thief—but merely to show that the actionable statement was made.

b. Statements Offered to Show Effect on Hearer or Reader

A statement that is inadmissible hearsay to prove the truth of the statement may nevertheless be admitted to show the statement's effect on the hearer or reader.

Examples: 1) In a ***negligence case*** where knowledge of a danger is the issue, a third person's statement of warning is admissible for the limited purpose of showing ***knowledge or notice*** on the part of a listener. Thus, a statement to the defendant driver, "Your tire is about to burst," is admissible to show that the defendant had notice of the possible danger. Of course, it is inadmissible hearsay to show that the statement was true—*i.e.,* that there was in fact a defect or dangerous condition.

2) H is on trial for the stabbing murder of W. H claims the killing was done by a bushy-haired, one-armed man whom H saw fleeing the scene. Policeman, P, testifies for the prosecution that H was arrested immediately after the killing and that a letter was found in H's possession. The letter states, "Your wife has been having an affair with your neighbor, Mr. Gigolo, for the last five years. Wise up!" The letter was signed, "A friend." Prosecutor offers this letter to establish H's motive for killing W. Is the letter hearsay? No! True, the letter is an out-of-court statement of "friend." But it is not offered to prove the truth of its contents. The letter is relevant to the issue of ***motive*** and would still be relevant to motive if, in fact, W had been faithful. The letter, true or not, is offered to show the probable effect it had on H when he read it.

c. Statements Offered as Circumstantial Evidence of Declarant's State of Mind

Statements by a declarant that serve as circumstantial evidence of the declarant's state of mind are not hearsay. Such statements are not offered to prove the truth of the matters asserted but only that the declarant ***believed*** them to be true. The most common examples of this type of nonhearsay are evidence of ***insanity*** and evidence of ***knowledge***.

Examples: 1) In a proceeding where the declarant's sanity is in issue, evidence is offered to show that the declarant had stated out of court, "I am John the Baptist." This statement would not be introduced as proof of its truth, but rather as circumstantial evidence of the declarant's insanity.

2) Evidence that before an accident an automobile driver stated, "My brakes are defective," is not admissible to prove that the brakes were defective, but is admissible to show that the declarant believed the brakes were defective but drove the car anyway.

1) Compare—State of Mind Exception

Statements that reflect directly (rather than circumstantially) on the declarant's state of mind are ***hearsay but are admissible*** under an exception to the hearsay rule (*see* D.1., *infra*). Many courts have used this "state of mind exception" to admit all declarations that reflect on the declarant's state of mind without regard to the fact that many could simply be admitted as nonhearsay. Although the ability

to distinguish the two may be helpful for exam purposes, as a practical matter, the distinction makes little difference because the result (admissibility of the statements) is the same.

4. Nonhuman Declarations

There is no such thing as animal or machine hearsay. Hearsay involves an out-of-court statement by a ***person***. Therefore, a witness who testifies to the time of day (what the clock says) or to radar readings (what the machine says) is not testifying to hearsay. Data that is generated completely electronically is not hearsay. Similarly, the behavior of a drug-sniffing dog in identifying a suspect is not hearsay. The issues presented by these examples are ones of relevance or reliability of the mechanism or animal. For example, a witness may testify to the actions of a drug-sniffing dog in identifying a suspect if there is a foundation showing that the dog was properly trained and is reliable in identifying drug carriers.

5. Illustrations of Hearsay and Nonhearsay

The following are specific examples of the application of the hearsay definition.

a. **Hearsay**

1) On the issue of whether the traffic light was red or green, the witness testifies that he was told by Decla that the light was green. (***Oral*** hearsay.)

2) On the issue of whether a glassine envelope contained heroin, the prosecution offers a crime laboratory report that the envelope contained heroin. (***Written*** hearsay.)

3) On the issue of whether Spano had been a resident of New York for one year prior to commencing his lawsuit, Spano offers the affidavit of Decla that Spano had lived in Buffalo for 10 years. (***Written*** hearsay; under oath, but hearsay nonetheless.)

4) On the issue of whether Yuckl was the child molester, a police officer testifies that when he asked the child-victim whether the perpetrator had a beard, the child nodded his head. (Hearsay by ***assertive conduct***; nodding, which translates, "Yes, the man had a beard.")

5) On the issue of whether the painting sold to Harvey was actually a genuine Picasso, there is offered a dealer's bill of sale describing the painting as a Picasso. (***Written*** hearsay.)

b. **Nonhearsay**

1) In a contract action, the written, executed contract is offered. (Although an extra-judicial writing, it is not offered to prove the truth of matters asserted in it; ***legally operative fact***.)

2) In an action for fraud, on the issue of defendant's good faith in representing to plaintiff that a painting was a genuine Picasso, defendant offers a bill of sale from his art dealer describing the painting as a Picasso. (Offered to prove ***defendant's***

good faith in repeating a representation; not offered to prove that the painting was in fact a Picasso. The evidence, in other words, was offered to show the impact of the dealer's representation on the defendant's state of mind, *i.e.,* his belief.)

3) On the issue of whether landlord knew about a defective stair, a witness testifies that he heard Decla say to the landlord, "The stair is broken." (Offered to prove *notice*, not that the stair was in fact broken.)

4) On the issue of whether the complaining witness had a venereal disease, Grutz testifies for the prosecution that the complaining witness had not been placed in the venereal disease ward upon her admission to the girls' reformatory. (Nonhearsay under the Federal Rules, since it is *nonassertive conduct.*)

5) On the issue of whether a transfer of a share of stock from Decla to Bushmat was a sale or a gift, Bushmat testifies that Decla made a statement at the time of the transfer: "I'm giving you this share of stock as a birthday present." (*Legally operative* words of gift.)

6) Action for personal injuries by a guest in an automobile against its owner. On the issues of contributory negligence and assumption of risk, a witness testifies that an hour before the accident a mechanic said to the owner in the presence of the guest, "The tread on that left front tire is paper-thin. You're likely to have a blowout." (*Notice, knowledge*; not offered to establish that in truth the tread was thin.)

7) Action of P against D. Witness No. 1 testifies for P that D's car was going "over 70 miles an hour." To impeach Witness No. 1, D offers the testimony of Witness No. 2 that Witness No. 1 said a day after the accident that D was going "slowly." (Used solely to cast *doubt on credibility*; not offered to establish the truth of the assertion.)

B. STATEMENTS THAT ARE NONHEARSAY UNDER THE FEDERAL RULES

Federal Rule 801(d) removes from the definition of hearsay certain statements that would be hearsay under the common law definition. Since the following types of statements are not hearsay, when relevant, they are admissible as substantive evidence.

1. Prior Statements by Witness

Certain statements by a person who testifies at the trial or hearing, and is *subject to cross-examination* about the statements, are not hearsay.

a. Prior Inconsistent Statement

A witness's prior inconsistent statement is not hearsay if it was made *under oath* at a prior proceeding or deposition. [Fed. R. Evid. 801(d)(1)(A)] For example, a statement made by the witness during grand jury testimony, if inconsistent with her in-court testimony, would be admissible not only to impeach her credibility (VI.E.3.a., *supra*) but also as substantive proof.

b. Prior Consistent Statement

A prior consistent statement, regardless of whether made under oath, is not hearsay if it is offered to rebut an express or implied charge that the witness is lying or exaggerating

because of some motive. [Fed. R. Evid. 801(d)(1)(B); *see* VI.E.6.c., *supra*] Note that a consistent statement offered for this purpose is admissible only when made *before* the alleged motive to lie or exaggerate came into being; *i.e.,* a prior consistent statement made after the motive to lie arose is not admissible. [Tome v. United States, 513 U.S. 150 (1995)]

c. **Prior Statement of Identification**
A witness's prior statement identifying a person after perceiving him is not hearsay. [Fed. R. Evid. 801(d)(1)(C)] Photo identifications are within the scope of this rule. Note that the prior identification need not have been made at a formal proceeding or under oath, and its admissibility is not limited to rehabilitation of the witness.

2. **Admissions by Party-Opponent**
Although traditionally an exception to the hearsay rule, an admission by a party-opponent is not hearsay at all under the Federal Rules. [Fed. R. Evid. 801(d)(2)] An admission is a statement made or act done that amounts to a *prior acknowledgment* by one of the parties to an action of one of the relevant facts. If the party said or did something that now turns out to be inconsistent with his contentions at trial, the law simply regards him as *estopped* from preventing its admission into evidence. The party who made the prior statement can hardly complain about not having had the opportunity to cross-examine himself. He said it. He is stuck with it. Let him explain it if he can.

a. **In General**
To be an admission, the statement need not have been against interest at the time it was made (compare the statement against interest exception, C.3., *infra*). The statement may even be in the form of an opinion.

1) **Personal Knowledge Not Required**
Lack of personal knowledge *does not necessarily exclude* a party's admission (*e.g.,* president of defendant company said, "My company has investigated the matter thoroughly and the reports indicate that we were negligent"). In fact, an admission may be predicated on hearsay.

2) **Judicial and Extrajudicial Admissions**
Formal judicial admissions (in pleadings, responses to requests to admit, stipulations) are *conclusive*; informal judicial admissions made during testimony *can be explained*; extrajudicial (evidentiary) admissions are *not conclusive and can be explained*. A formal judicial admission in one proceeding may become an extrajudicial or evidentiary admission in another proceeding. (Plea of guilty to traffic infraction admissible in civil action on same facts.) A formal judicial admission that is withdrawn may in that same action become an informal admission (statements in original answer admissible though superseded by amendment). A withdrawn plea of guilty in a criminal case is not, however, admissible against a defendant in any civil or criminal proceeding. [Fed. R. Evid. 410]

3) **Adoptive Admissions**
A party may expressly or impliedly adopt someone else's statement as his own, thus giving rise to an "adoptive admission." [Fed. R. Evid. 801(d)(2)(B)]

Example: Where Plaintiff claims an orthopedic abnormality in a suit against Defendant, Defendant may properly offer against Plaintiff Plaintiff's prior application for a chauffeur's license, which included a doctor's certificate stating that Plaintiff had "no orthopedic abnormality."

a) Silence

If a party fails to respond to accusatory statements where a reasonable person would have spoken up, his silence may be considered an implied admission. For silence to be an admission the following requirements must be met:

(i) The party must have ***heard and understood*** the statement;

(ii) The party must have been ***physically and mentally capable of denying*** the statement; and

(iii) A ***reasonable person would have denied*** the accusation under the same circumstances.

Note that failure to reply to an accusation or statement made by the police in a criminal case can ***almost never*** be used as an implied admission of a criminal act.

b. Vicarious Admissions

An admission is frequently not the statement or act of the party against whom the admission is offered at trial. The question that remains is—what relationship must exist between the declarant and the party to make the former's statement admissible against the latter?

1) Co-Parties

Admissions of a party are ***not receivable against her co-plaintiffs or co-defendants*** merely because they happen to be joined as parties to the action. If there are two or more parties, the admission of one is receivable against her but, in the absence of authority, not against her co-party.

2) Authorized Spokesperson

The statement of a person ***authorized by a party to speak on its behalf*** (*e.g.*, statement by company's press agent) can be admitted against the party as an admission. [Fed. R. Evid. 801(d)(2)(C)]

3) Principal-Agent

Statements by an agent concerning any matter within the scope of her agency, made ***during the existence of the employment relationship***, are admissible against the principal. [Fed. R. Evid. 801(d)(2)(D)] Therefore, if a truck driver-employee has an accident while on the job and admits that she was negligent, this admission may be introduced against her employer even if she was not authorized to speak for the employer.

4) Partners

After a partnership is shown to exist, an admission of one partner, relating

to matters *within the scope of the partnership business*, is binding upon her co-partners since, as to such matters, each partner is deemed the agent of the others.

5) Co-Conspirators

The Supreme Court has held that admissions of one conspirator, made to a third party *in furtherance of a conspiracy to commit a crime or a civil wrong*, at a time when the declarant was participating in the conspiracy, are admissible against co-conspirators. [United States v. Inadi, 475 U.S. 387 (1986)] The thought is that a conspiracy is analogous to a partnership—"partners in crime." The government need not demonstrate the unavailability of a nontestifying co-conspirator as a prerequisite to admission of the co-conspirator's out-of-court statements under Rule 801(d)(2)(E). However, *testimonial* admissions of a conspirator are admissible against a co-conspirator only if there was an opportunity to cross-examine the hearsay declarant. (*See* F.1.a., *infra*.)

6) Privies in Title and Joint Tenants—State Courts Only

Where one person succeeds to the same property rights formerly enjoyed by another, there is often such privity that the rights of the present owner may be affected by admissions of the former owner made before the owner parted with her interest. In most state courts, admissions of each joint owner are admissible against the other, and admissions of a former owner of real property made at the time she held title are *admissible against those claiming under* her (grantees, heirs, devisees, or otherwise). These statements are not considered admissions under the Federal Rules, although they may be admissible under one of the hearsay exceptions (*e.g.*, as a statement against interest).

7) Preliminary Determination of Agency or Conspiracy—Court Must Consider Contents of Hearsay Statement

Before a hearsay statement is admissible as a vicarious admission, the court must make a preliminary determination of the declarant's relationship with the party against whom the statement is being offered. When making a determination of (i) the declarant's authority to make the statement, (ii) the existence and scope of an agency relationship, or (iii) the existence of a conspiracy and participation by the declarant and the party, the *court must consider the contents of the offered statement*, but the statement alone is not sufficient to establish the required relationship or authority. [Fed. R. Evid. 801(d)(2)]

C. HEARSAY EXCEPTIONS—DECLARANT UNAVAILABLE

Certain kinds of hearsay are considered to have special guarantees of trustworthiness and are recognized exceptions to the hearsay exclusion. The Federal Rules treat the exceptions in two groups—those that require the declarant be unavailable, and those under which the declarant's availability is immaterial. This section covers the five important exceptions requiring the declarant's unavailability: (i) former testimony, (ii) statements against interest, (iii) dying declarations, (iv) statements of personal or family history, and (v) statements offered against party procuring declarant's unavailability.

1. "Unavailability" Defined

A declarant is unavailable if:

(i)   He is exempted from testifying by court ruling on the ground of *privilege*;

(ii)   He persists, despite a court order, in *refusing to testify* concerning the statement;

(iii) He testifies to *lack of memory* of the subject matter of the statement;

(iv) He is unable to be present or testify because of *death or physical or mental illness*; or

(v)   He is absent (*e.g.,* beyond the reach of the trial court's subpoena) and the statement's *proponent* has been *unable to procure* his *attendance or testimony* by process or other reasonable means.

[Fed. R. Evid. 804(a)(1) - (5)] Note that a declarant is not unavailable if his "unavailability" was procured by the proponent of the statement or if the statement's proponent did not attempt to procure the declarant's attendance.

2. Former Testimony

The testimony of a now unavailable witness given at another hearing or in a deposition taken in accordance with law is admissible in a subsequent trial as long as there is a sufficient similarity of parties and issues so that the opportunity to develop testimony or cross-examine at the prior hearing was meaningful. [Fed. R. Evid. 804(b)(1)] This exception is the clearest example of hearsay with special guarantees of trustworthiness, since the former testimony was given during formal proceedings and under oath by a witness subject to cross-examination.

a. Identity of Parties

The requirement of identity of parties does not mean that parties on both sides of the controversies must be identical. It requires only that the party *against whom* the testimony is offered or, in civil cases, the party's predecessor in interest was a *party in the former action*. "Predecessor in interest" includes one in a privity relationship with the party, such as grantor-grantee, testator-executor, life tenant-remainderman, joint tenants. The requirement of identity of parties is intended merely to ensure that the party against whom the testimony is offered (or a predecessor in interest in a civil case) had an adequate opportunity and motive to cross-examine the witness.

b. Identity of Subject Matter

The former testimony is admissible upon any trial in the same or another action of the same subject matter. Again, the sole purpose of this requirement is to ensure that the party against whom the transcript of testimony is offered had an adequate opportunity to cross-examine the unavailable witness on the relevant issue. Obviously, the "cause of action" in both proceedings need not be identical. It is enough if the "subject matter" of the testimony is the same. In other words, the party against whom the testimony is offered must have had an opportunity and similar motive to develop declarant's testimony at the prior hearing.

c. Opportunity to Develop Testimony at Prior Hearing

The party against whom the former testimony is offered (or a predecessor in civil cases) must have had the opportunity to develop the testimony at the prior proceeding by direct, cross, or redirect examination of the declarant. Thus, the *grand jury testimony* of an unavailable declarant is *not admissible* as former testimony against the accused at

trial. This is because grand jury proceedings do not provide the opportunity for cross-examination.

d. Under Oath

The former testimony must have been given under oath or sworn affirmation.

e. Use in Criminal Proceedings

It has been argued that the use in a criminal proceeding of former testimony from some prior trial violates the defendant's constitutional *right to confront and cross-examine* all adverse witnesses. However, the Supreme Court has rejected this argument, holding that there is *no violation* of an accused's right of confrontation, as long as:

1) The accused or his attorney was present and *had the opportunity to cross-examine* at the time the testimony was given (*e.g.*, at a preliminary examination or a former trial for the same offense); *and*

2) The witness, whose former testimony is sought to be used, is now *unavailable*, despite bona fide efforts by the prosecution to produce him. [California v. Green, 399 U.S. 149 (1970)] *Note:* A greater showing of "unavailability" is required in criminal cases than in civil cases. For example, a mere showing that a witness is incarcerated in a prison outside the state has been held insufficient to establish "unavailability" (because no showing that he could not be produced by prosecution). [Barber v. Page, 390 U.S. 719 (1968)]

3. Statements Against Interest

A statement of a person, now unavailable as a witness, against that person's pecuniary, proprietary, or penal interest when made, as well as collateral facts contained in the statement, is admissible under the statement against interest exception to the hearsay rule. [Fed. R. Evid. 804(b)(3)]

The reason for this exception lies in the exigency of the declarant being unavailable and the circumstantial probability of trustworthiness (declarant is unlikely to knowingly make a statement against her interest unless the statement is true). The statement against interest differs most significantly from an admission in that, under the statement against interest exception, the statement *must be against interest when made*, and the declarant whose statement is admitted may be a stranger to the litigation rather than a party.

a. Requirements of the Statement

To qualify as an exception to the hearsay rule, a statement against interest must meet the following requirements:

1) The statement must have been *against pecuniary, proprietary, or penal interest when made*.

2) Declarant must have had *personal knowledge of the facts*.

3) Declarant must have been *aware that the statement is against her interest* and she must have had *no motive to misrepresent* when she made the statement.

4) Declarant must be *unavailable as a witness*.

b. Collateral Facts

In addition to the fact against interest, the statement often contains collateral facts not against interest. These connected collateral facts are also admissible.

Example: A written receipt acknowledging payment and specifying date of payment, the person who made payment, and the nature of the claim paid is admissible in its entirety.

c. Risk of Civil Liability

Under the Federal Rules, statements subjecting the declarant to civil liability are specifically admissible. [Fed. R. Evid. 804(b)(3)]

d. Risk of Criminal Liability

Many courts have been reluctant to admit evidence of statements that subject the declarant to penal liability for fear of opening a door to a flood of perjured testimony. The modern trend and the Federal Rules permit statements against penal interest. However, where a criminal defendant wishes to show her own innocence by introducing statements by another admitting the crime, the Federal Rules require that there be *corroborating circumstances* indicating the trustworthiness of such statements. [Fed. R. Evid. 804(b)(3)]

1) Third-Party Confession Allowed

States that do not allow statements against penal interest may not exclude the confession of a third party where to do so would deprive the accused of a *fair trial*. [Chambers v. Mississippi, 410 U.S. 284 (1973)]

2) Co-Defendant's Confession May Not Be Admissible

The confession of a co-defendant *implicating herself and the accused* may not be admissible because of *confrontation* problems.

e. "Statement" Means Single Remark

A "statement" against interest for purposes of the exception means a single self-inculpatory remark, not an extended declaration. Thus, if a person makes a declaration containing statements that are against his interest and statements that are not, the statements that are not against interest are not admissible, even though they are part of a broader narrative that is on the whole against the declarant's interest. [Williamson v. United States, 512 U.S. 594 (1994)]

Example: X confessed to receiving and transporting drugs, but in so doing implicated Y as the owner of the drugs. The statements implicating Y did not contain any information against X's interest, although the confession as a whole was clearly against X's penal interest. X refused to testify at Y's trial. X's statements implicating Y are not within the scope of the hearsay exception for statements against interest and are thus inadmissible. The exception covers only those remarks that inculpate the declarant, not the extended declaration. [*See* Williamson v. United States, *supra*]

4. Dying Declarations—Statements Under Belief of Impending Death

In a prosecution for *homicide or a civil action*, a declaration made by the now unavailable declarant while *believing his death was imminent* that concerns the *cause or circumstances*

of what he believed to be his impending death is admissible. [Fed. R. Evid. 804(b)(2)] The declarant need not actually die, but he must be unavailable (*see* 1., *supra*) at the time the declaration is offered.

Note that under the traditional view, still followed by some states, the declaration was admissible only in homicide prosecutions (not civil actions), and then only if the declarant actually died.

5. **Statements of Personal or Family History**

Statements concerning birth, marriage, divorce, death, relationship, etc., are admissible under an exception to the hearsay rule. Hearsay statements concerning family history are often necessary to prove the facts of people's everyday lives. For example, most people rely on the hearsay statements of others for the knowledge of where they were born, who their relatives are, etc.

a. **Statement Need Not Have Been Made Before Controversy**

In most jurisdictions, the statement must have been made at a time when no controversy existed as to the matters stated—to ensure their reliability. However, the Federal Rules have dropped this requirement on the theory that the time at which the statement was made affects its weight rather than its admissibility. [Fed. R. Evid. 804(b)(4)]

b. **Usually Declarant Must Be a Family Member**

The now unavailable declarant must be a member of the family in question or otherwise intimately associated with the family. Most jurisdictions require that the declarant be related by blood or marriage to the family whose history is involved. Some jurisdictions, and the Federal Rules, have extended this requirement to admit statements by declarants who are so intimately associated with the family that they are likely to have accurate information concerning the matters declared (*e.g.*, the family doctor). [Fed. R. Evid. 804(b)(4)]

c. **Personal Knowledge Required**

The declarant's statements may be based either on her own personal knowledge of the facts involved or on her knowledge of family reputation.

d. **Other Ways to Prove Pedigree**

Personal and family history may be proven by use of other exceptions to the hearsay rule. For example, it may be proven by: vital statistics [Fed. R. Evid. 803(9)]; records of religious organizations [Fed. R. Evid. 803(11)]; marriage certificates and other certificates [Fed. R. Evid. 803(12)]; family records [Fed. R. Evid. 803(13)]; statements in property documents [Fed. R. Evid. 803(15)]; reputation [Fed. R. Evid. 803(19)]; and judgments [Fed. R. Evid. 803(23)]. For these exceptions, the declarant's availability is immaterial.

6. **Statements Offered Against Party Procuring Declarant's Unavailability**

The statements of a person (now unavailable as a witness) *are admissible* when offered against a party who has engaged or acquiesced in wrongdoing that intentionally procured the declarant's unavailability. [Fed. R. Evid. 804(b)(6)] In effect, a party forfeits his right to object on hearsay grounds to the admission of an unavailable declarant's statements when the party's deliberate wrongdoing procured the unavailability of the declarant as a witness.

D. HEARSAY EXCEPTIONS—DECLARANT'S AVAILABILITY IMMATERIAL

The following exceptions do not require that the declarant be unavailable. The admissibility of these declarations proceeds upon the theory that the out-of-court declarations were made under circumstances that make them more reliable and therefore preferable to the actual in-court testimony of the declarant. Included in this group of exceptions are the following:

1. Present State of Mind

A statement of a declarant's then-existing state of mind, emotion, sensation, or physical condition is admissible. [Fed. R. Evid. 803(3)] The exception is based on the need to obtain evidence as to the declarant's internal state of mind or emotion. It must usually be made under circumstances of apparent sincerity. The statement is often offered to establish the *intent* of a person, either as a direct fact to be proved as such (domicile, criminal intent) or as a basis for a circumstantial inference that the intent was probably carried out.

a. Rationale

The rationale is that (i) insofar as the declarant knows her own state of mind, there is no need to check her perception; (ii) since the statement is of present state of mind, there is no need to check her memory; and (iii) since state of mind is in issue, it must be shown some way—and very often, the declarant's own statement is the only way.

b. When Admissible

1) State of Mind Directly in Issue and Material to the Controversy

Declarations of existing state of mind are admissible when the declarant's state of mind is directly in issue and material to the controversy.

Example: In a case where the domicile of Edwina is material, Edwina's statement that "I plan to live in Colorado for the rest of my life" is admissible.

2) Offered to Show Subsequent Acts of Declarant

Declarations of existing state of mind are also admissible when the declarant's state of mind is not directly in issue—if they are declarations of intent offered to show subsequent acts of the declarant; *i.e.,* a declaration of intent to do something in the future is admitted as circumstantial evidence tending to show that the intent was carried out. In *Mutual Life Insurance Co. v. Hillmon*, 145 U.S. 285 (1892), a hearsay written statement was admitted into evidence to prove the declarant did what he said he intended to do.

Examples: 1) The location of X on May 15 is relevant. W may testify that she heard X say on May 8 that "I intend to go to Denver next week."

2) In a prosecution of a husband for murder of his wife, the wife's prior statements that she intended to commit suicide are admissible.

c. Statements of Memory or Belief Generally Not Admissible

The hearsay statement is *not admissible* if it expresses a memory or belief of the declarant, and the statement is offered for the purpose of proving the *truth of the fact remembered or believed.*

Example: Declarant's out-of-court statement, "I think I left the keys in the car," may not be introduced for the purpose of proving that he left the keys in the car.

Statements of memory or belief are **admissible**, however, to prove facts remembered or believed concerning the execution, revocation, identification, or terms of **declarant's will**.

2. Excited Utterances

A declaration made by a declarant during or soon after a startling event is admissible. The declaration must be made under the stress of excitement produced by the startling event. The declaration must concern the immediate facts of the startling occurrence. [Fed. R. Evid. 803(2)] The spontaneousness of such a declaration and the consequent lack of opportunity for reflection and deliberate fabrication provide an adequate guarantee of its trustworthiness.

a. Startling Event Required

There must have been some occurrence startling enough to produce a nervous excitement and thus render the declaration an unreflective and sincere expression of the declarant's impression. The declaration **must relate to the startling event**.

b. Declaration Must Be Made While Under Stress of Excitement

The declaration must have been made while the declarant was under the stress of the excitement (*i.e.*, **before the declarant had time to reflect** upon it). The time element is the most important factor in determining whether the declaration was made under the stress of the excitement. If a declaration is made while the event is still in progress, it is easy to find that the excitement prompted the utterance. Declarations made shortly after the event have sometimes been excluded as mere narrative of past events. But when the declaration is made so near to the time of the occurrence as to negate any probability of fabrication, it is usually admissible.

3. Present Sense Impressions

A present sense impression is admissible as an exception to the hearsay rule.

a. Comment Made Concurrently with Sense Impression

If a person perceives some event that is not particularly shocking or exciting, and it does not in fact produce excitement in the observer, that person may nevertheless be moved to comment on what she perceived at the time of receipt of the sense impression or immediately thereafter. [Fed. R. Evid. 803(1)]

b. Safeguards

Such a comment regarding a situation then before the declarant, *i.e.*, the statement of a present sense impression, does not have the supposed safeguards of impulse, emotion, or excitement, but there are other safeguards of reliability. Statements of present sense impression are **safe from defects in memory**. There is usually little or **no time for calculated misstatement**. The statement will usually have been made to another person—the very witness who reports it—who would have **equal opportunity to observe** and to contradict or correct a misstatement.

Example: Decla said to N, "Look at that car go." W may testify that Decla made the statement in order to prove that the car was speeding.

4. Declarations of Physical Condition

a. Present Bodily Condition—Admissible

Generally, declarations of present bodily condition are admissible as an exception to the hearsay rule, even though they are not made to a physician. They may be made to a spouse, relative, friend, or any other person. Of course, declarations made to a physician are admissible. [Fed. R. Evid. 803(3)] Such declarations relate to symptoms, including the existence of pain. Because they are contemporaneous with the symptoms, they are more reliable than present testimony based upon recollection.

Example: Victim tells friend, "My ankle hurts so much it must be broken." The statement is admissible as a declaration of present pain, although it is not to be used to prove the ankle was in fact broken.

b. Past Bodily Condition—Admissible If to Assist Diagnosis or Treatment

As a general rule, declarations of past physical condition are excluded, since there is no way to check the memory of the declarant by cross-examination and there is a greater likelihood of falsification where the declarant is describing a past condition. However, the Federal Rules, recognizing that a patient has a strong motive to tell the truth when seeking medical treatment, admit declarations of past physical condition *if made to medical personnel to assist in diagnosing or treating the condition*. [Fed. R. Evid. 803(4)] Furthermore, the Federal Rule allows declarations not only of past symptoms and medical history, but also of the *cause or source of the condition* insofar as reasonably pertinent to diagnosis or treatment. Moreover, contrary to the majority state view, Rule 803(4) permits such declarations even when made to a doctor employed to testify.

5. Business Records

Any writing or record, whether in the form of an entry in a book or otherwise, made as a memorandum or record of any act, transaction, occurrence, or event is admissible in evidence as proof of that act, transaction, occurrence, or event, if made in the regular course of any business; and if it was the regular course of such business to make it at the time of the act, transaction, occurrence, or event or within a reasonable time thereafter.

a. Rationale

The rationale for this exception lies in the belief that special reliability is provided by the *regularity* with which business records are kept, their *use and importance* in the business, and the *incentive* of employees *to keep accurate records* or risk employment penalties. If a record qualifies as a business record, it may be admitted without calling the author of the record or the employee with personal knowledge of the recorded event. It makes no difference that the record is self-serving and offered in evidence by the party whose business made the record.

b. Elements of Business Records Exception

Under the Federal Rules and modern statutes, the main requirements for admissibility of a business record are as follows:

1) "Business"

Under the Federal Rules, "business" includes every "association, profession, occupation, and calling of every kind, whether or not conducted for profit." Thus,

the definition would include records made by churches, hospitals, schools, etc. [Fed. R. Evid. 803(6)]

2) Entry Made in Regular Course of Business
It must also appear that the record was made in the course of a regularly conducted business activity, and that it was customary to make the type of entry involved (*i.e.*, that the entrant had a duty to make the entry).

a) Business Activity
The record must have been maintained in conjunction with a business activity.

(1) Hospital Records
Entries in hospital records are generally admissible to the extent that they are ***related to the medical diagnosis or treatment*** of the patient (the primary business of the hospital). For example, a patient's statement that she was injured on X's property would probably be inadmissible because whether she was injured on X's property or someone else's is unrelated to her medical treatment.

(2) Police Reports
Police reports may qualify as business records in civil cases. Generally, police reports are not admissible against a criminal defendant under the business records exception. However, some jurisdictions admit police reports if they contain only routine information rather than observations or opinions of officers.

(3) The Rule of *Palmer v. Hoffman*—Records Prepared for Litigation
A similar aspect of the "business activity" requirement was raised in the case of *Palmer v. Hoffman*, 318 U.S. 109 (1943). In that case, railroad personnel, in accordance with their regular practice, prepared a report concerning an accident in which the railroad was involved. The United States Supreme Court held that the report was not admissible at trial because it was prepared in anticipation of litigation, and railroading, not litigating, was the railroad's primary business.

(a) Narrow Interpretation
Many courts have interpreted the rule of *Palmer v. Hoffman* narrowly. These courts have generally ***excluded*** such a self-serving employee accident report only when the report was prepared ***primarily*** for litigation and the author of the report had a strong motive to misrepresent.

(b) Federal Rules—Court's Discretion
The Federal Rules have dealt with the problem of *Palmer v. Hoffman* by granting the trial court discretion to exclude any business record if the ***source of information*** or other circumstances indicate the record lacks trustworthiness. [Fed. R. Evid. 803(6)]

b) Entrant Under Duty to Record
For a record to have been made in the regular course of a business activity,

the entrant must have had some duty to make the entry as part of her employment (*i.e.*, records kept as a hobby do not qualify). This duty may be either public (statutory, etc.) or private (contractual—including duties imposed by an employer).

3) Personal Knowledge

The business record must consist of matters within the personal knowledge of the entrant *or* within the personal knowledge of someone with a business duty to transmit such matters to the entrant.

a) Recorder Need Not Have Personal Knowledge of Event

Most business records statutes do not require that the person making the entries have personal knowledge of the event. Indeed, where the one who has personal knowledge of the transaction (informant) and the one making the record (recorder) are both employees of the business, there is no problem. Once established as a business record, it is admissible without calling either the informant or the recorder, even though the recorder lacked personal knowledge. The integrity of the special reliability assumption is maintained because the informant was under a ***business duty to report*** accurately and the recorder was under a ***business duty to properly record*** the information.

b) Informant Must Be Under Business Duty to Convey Information

A problem arises, however, when the informant with personal knowledge is an outsider, having little or no connection with the business whose records are being offered in evidence. The well-known case of *Johnson v. Lutz*, 253 N.Y. 124 (1930), engrafted a limitation on the business records exception. It holds that an entry is admissible as a business record only when the record was made by the employee recorder on information obtained directly by him or imparted to him by an informant who was under a business duty to convey such information. Thus, a police report entry by a police officer was held inadmissible where the informant was a third person who was under no "business" duty to convey information (the "business" being law enforcement). The statutory business records exception, in other words, was not intended to permit receipt in evidence of hearsay statements made by third persons not engaged in the business in question or under any duty in connection with it. Thus, the rationale is that the assumed reliability justifying the hearsay exception cannot be maintained if the information in the record was supplied by an outsider who had no business incentive to report accurately.

c) Recorded Statement May Be Admissible Under Other Exceptions

If, as in *Johnson v. Lutz*, the record-maker and the informant are not business related, the recorded statement of the informant may nonetheless be receivable with the help of some other exceptions to the hearsay rule. This involves a two-phase process. The business records exception serves as a vehicle for demonstrating the bare fact that the ***statement was made*** (*i.e.*, it allows the paper record to substitute for the in-court testimony of the employees who received the information); the second phase involves reference to some ***independent ground of admissibility*** of the statement to establish the ***truth***

of assertions contained in it. A police report entry is receivable where the informant was a party and his statement constituted an *admission*. Note too that certain police reports may be admissible under the public records exception (*see* 7.a., *infra*).

4) Entry Made Near Time of Event
The entry must have been made at or near the time of the transaction while the entrant's knowledge of the facts was still fresh.

5) Authentication
The authenticity of the record must be established. The usual method of authentication is to have the custodian or other qualified witness testify to the identity of the record and the mode of its preparation. However, a foundation witness is not necessary to authenticate the record (*i.e.,* the record will be self-authenticating) if the custodian or other qualified person certifies in writing that the record meets the requirements of the business records exception. [Fed. R. Evid. 803(6), 902(11)]

Normally, the original or first permanent record of the transaction must be introduced, but where the records to be introduced are voluminous, summaries or compilations may be admitted.

6) Entrant Need Not Be Unavailable
For the business record to be admissible, the person who made the entry need not be unavailable as a witness.

7) Trustworthiness
The court may exclude an otherwise qualifying business record if the source of information or the method or circumstances of preparation indicate lack of trustworthiness.

c. Use of Business Records as Evidence of No Transaction
At common law, business records were admitted only to prove the facts contained therein. They were not admissible for negative purposes—*i.e.,* to show that no transaction had taken place. However, the modern trend allows business records to be used to prove the nonoccurrence or the nonexistence of a matter if it was the regular practice of the business to record all such matters. [Fed. R. Evid. 803(7)] For example, the lack of any entry showing payment in a business record may be evidence that in fact no payment was made.

6. Past Recollection Recorded
Witnesses are permitted to refresh their memories by looking at almost anything—either before or while testifying. This is called *present recollection revived* (*see* VI.B.3.a., *supra*). However, if the witness's memory cannot be revived, a party may wish to introduce a memorandum that the witness made at or near the time of the event. Use of the writing to prove the facts contained therein raises a hearsay problem; but if a proper foundation can be laid, the contents of the memorandum may be introduced into evidence under the *past recollection recorded* exception to the hearsay rule. The rationale is that a writing made by an observer when the facts were still fresh in her mind is probably more reliable than her testimony on the stand—despite the fact that cross-examination is curtailed. For admissibility requirements, *see* VI.B.3.b., *supra*.

7. Official Records and Other Official Writings

a. Public Records and Reports

The exception for public records and reports is necessary to avoid having public officers leave their jobs constantly to appear in court and testify to acts done in their official capacity, especially since the entrant could probably add nothing to the record. Also, such records are presumed to be trustworthy because officials are under a duty to record properly that which they do.

1) What May Be Admitted

Records, reports, statements, or data compilations, in any form, of a public office or agency are admissible to the extent that they set forth:

(i) The activities of the office or agency;

(ii) Matters observed pursuant to a duty imposed by law (excluding police observations in criminal cases); or

(iii) In civil actions and proceedings and against the government in criminal cases, factual findings (including opinions and conclusions) resulting from an investigation made pursuant to authority granted by law, unless the sources of information or other circumstances indicate lack of trustworthiness.

[Fed. R. Evid. 803(8); Beech Aircraft Corp. v. Rainey, 488 U.S. 153 (1988)]

Examples: 1) A manual prepared by the office that processes Medicare claims, explaining which claims are properly payable under Medicare, is admissible against the defendant in a Medicare fraud case under Federal Rule 803(8)(A).

2) A police officer arrives at the scene of the accident. Several witnesses tell him that Dan drove through a stop sign and hit Vic, who was riding a bicycle. The police officer has had many years' experience in evaluating accident scenes. From the tire marks, he decides that Dan did indeed run the stop sign. In his report he includes the statements of the witnesses and his evaluation of the scene, including his conclusion that Dan ran the stop sign. Everything except the witnesses' statements can be admitted under Federal Rule 803(8)(C), including the officer's conclusion. The witnesses' statements can be admitted only if they fall within some other exception. Remember that the investigative report is admissible only in civil cases and only *against the government* in criminal cases. The report could not be offered against Dan in a criminal prosecution.

3) An Equal Employment Opportunity Commission investigator's report would be admissible in an action against an employer alleging discriminatory employment practices. As with the officer's report above, any hearsay statements will be excised unless they fall within an exception, but the investigator's conclusions and opinions are admissible.

2) Requirements for Admissibility

a) Duty to Record
The writing must have been made by, and within the scope of duty of, the public employee.

b) Entry Near Time of Event
The writing must have been made at or near the time of the act, condition, or event.

c) Trustworthiness
The sources of information and other circumstances must be such as to indicate its trustworthiness.

b. Records of Vital Statistics
Records of births, deaths, and marriages are admissible if the report was made to a public office pursuant to requirements of law. [Fed. R. Evid. 803(9)]

c. Statement of Absence of Public Record
Evidence in the form of a certification or testimony from the custodian of public records that she has diligently searched and failed to find a record is admissible to prove that a matter was not recorded, or, inferentially, that a matter did not occur. [Fed. R. Evid. 803(10)]

d. Judgments
A certified copy of a judgment is always admissible proof that such judgment has been entered. The problem is to what extent the facts adjudicated in the former proceeding can be introduced to prove facts in the present case.

1) Prior Criminal Conviction—Felony Conviction Admissible
The traditional view, still followed by most state courts, is that a judgment of conviction is inadmissible. First, it is merely the "opinion" of the jury, and second, it is hearsay as proof of the fact asserted, *i.e.*, the guilt of the defendant. Of course, under certain circumstances the conviction may be used for impeachment. The Federal Rules, however, specifically provide that judgments of felony convictions are *admissible in both criminal and civil actions to prove any fact essential to the judgment.* For example, if a defendant was convicted of a felony assault, the injured party could use the judgment of conviction in a later civil suit against the same defendant to prove the happening of the assault. In the Rules, felony convictions are defined as crimes punishable by death or imprisonment in excess of one year. [Fed. R. Evid. 803(22)] The convictions that may be used are limited to felonies because persons may choose not to defend misdemeanor charges (*e.g.*, traffic violations).

a) Admissible to Prove Fact Only Against Accused
In a criminal case, the government may use a prior conviction for this purpose only against the accused. Against persons *other than the accused*, the government may use prior convictions *only for impeachment*.

b) Rules Barring Character Evidence Still Apply

The hearsay exception for judgments of prior felony convictions is subject to the general rule that prohibits the admissibility of convictions as character evidence. (*See* II.E., *supra*.) The hearsay exception merely provides a means of proving the facts upon which a conviction is based when such facts are independently admissible either to prove specific acts of misconduct on the issue of a person's motive, intent, absence of mistake, etc., or as proof of prior acts of sexual assault or child molestation in cases alleging sexual assault or child molestation.

2) Prior Criminal Acquittal—Excluded

The exclusionary rule is still applied to records of prior acquittals. The reason is that a criminal acquittal may establish only that the state did not prove the defendant guilty beyond a reasonable doubt, whereas the evidentiary standard is lower in civil cases.

3) Judgment in Former Civil Case

a) Inadmissible in Criminal Proceeding

A civil judgment is clearly inadmissible in a subsequent criminal proceeding because of the differing standards of proof.

b) Generally Inadmissible in Civil Proceeding

The general rule is that civil judgments are also inadmissible in subsequent civil proceedings. However, there are certain statutory *exceptions* to the rule of inadmissibility. For example, under the Federal Rules, a prior civil judgment is admissible as proof of matters of personal, family, or general history, or boundaries of land, if it would be provable by reputation evidence (*e.g.*, X may prove her citizenship by a judgment establishing that X's parents were citizens). [Fed. R. Evid. 803(23)]

8. Ancient Documents and Documents Affecting Property Interests

Under the Federal Rules, statements in *any* authenticated document *20 years old or more* are admissible. [Fed. R. Evid. 803(16)] Moreover, in contrast to the traditional view that only ancient property-disposing documents qualified for the exception, statements in a document affecting an interest in property (*e.g.*, deed, will, etc.) are admissible regardless of the age of the document. [Fed. R. Evid. 803(15)]

9. Learned Treatises

Many courts do not admit statements from standard scientific treatises or authoritative works as substantive proof, limiting admissibility to use as impeachment of the qualifications of the expert witness. The Federal Rules recognize an exception to the hearsay rule for learned treatises. Federal Rule 803(18) provides for the substantive admissibility of a learned treatise if the treatise is:

(i) Called to the attention of the expert witness upon cross-examination or relied upon by her during direct examination; and

(ii) Established as reliable authority by the testimony or admission of the witness, by other expert testimony, or by judicial notice.

Even under the Federal Rules, however, the relevant portion of the treatise is not actually shown to the jury; it is admissible by being read into the record.

10. Reputation

In addition to reputation testimony concerning a person's character [Fed. R. Evid. 803(21)], reputation evidence concerning someone's personal or family history [Fed. R. Evid. 803(19)] or concerning land boundaries or the community's general history [Fed. R. Evid. 803(20)] is admissible hearsay.

11. Family Records

Statements of fact concerning personal or family history contained in family Bibles, genealogies, jewelry engravings, engravings on urns, crypts, or tombstones, or the like are admissible hearsay. [Fed. R. Evid. 803(13)]

12. Market Reports

Market reports and other published compilations (lists, directories, etc.) are admissible if generally used and relied upon by the public or by persons in a particular occupation. [Fed. R. Evid. 803(17)]

E. RESIDUAL "CATCH-ALL" EXCEPTION OF FEDERAL RULES

The Federal Rules provide a general catch-all exception for hearsay statements not covered by specific exceptions. [Fed. R. Evid. 807] There are three requirements for a statement to be admitted under the catch-all exception:

1. "Trustworthiness" Factor

First of all, the statement must have "circumstantial guarantees of trustworthiness" that are equivalent to those of statements admitted under other hearsay exceptions.

2. "Necessity" Factor

The statement must be offered on a *material fact*, and must be *more probative* as to that fact than any other evidence which the proponent can reasonably produce so that the *"interests of justice"* will be served by its admission.

3. Notice to Adversary

Finally, the proponent must give notice in advance of trial to the adverse party as to the nature of the statement (including the name and address of the declarant) so that the adversary has an opportunity to prepare to meet it.

F. CONSTITUTIONAL ISSUES

1. The Confrontation Clause

In criminal cases, it may be argued that the use of hearsay evidence violates the accused's *right to "confront" and cross-examine* the witnesses against him. Note, however, that there generally is no Confrontation Clause problem if the hearsay declarant is present at the trial and is subject to cross-examination at that time.

a. Prior Testimonial Statement of Unavailable Witness

Previously, the Supreme Court ruled that if the prosecution offered a statement that

was made at a prior judicial proceeding and the declarant was not available to be cross-examined by the defendant, the statement would be admissible if it was supported by indicia of reliability. The indicia of reliability requirement could be met by showing that the statement "falls within a firmly rooted hearsay exception" or that it was supported by "a showing of particularized guarantees of trustworthiness." [Ohio v. Roberts, 448 U.S. 56 (1980), *as modified by* United States v. Inadi, 475 U.S. 387 (1986)] However, the Supreme Court has held that the *Roberts* test departed from the intent of the Confrontation Clause. [*See* Crawford v. Washington, 541 U.S. 36 (2004)] Under *Crawford*, prior ***testimonial evidence*** may ***not*** be admitted unless:

(i) The declarant is ***unavailable***; and

(ii) The defendant had an ***opportunity to cross-examine*** the declarant at the time the statement was made.

1) Statements Made in the Course of Police Interrogation
If the primary purpose of police interrogation is to ***enable the police to help in an ongoing emergency***, statements made in the course of the interrogation are ***nontestimonial*** (*e.g.*, statements made during a 911 call describing the circumstances and perpetrator of an ongoing incident of domestic violence). When the primary purpose of the interrogation is to ***establish or prove past events potentially relevant to a later criminal prosecution***, statements are ***testimonial*** (*e.g.*, statements made by victim to police shortly after a domestic violence incident, setting forth details of the incident). [Davis v. Washington, 547 U.S. 813 (2006)]

2) Affidavits Reporting Results of Forensic Analysis
Affidavits that summarize the findings of forensic analysis (*e.g.*, fingerprint or ballistic test results) are testimonial and thus may not be admitted into evidence unless the technician is unavailable and the defendant previously had an opportunity to cross-examine. [Melendez-Diaz v. Massachusetts, 129 S. Ct. 2527 (2009)]

b. Confrontation Clause Rights May Be Forfeited by Wrongdoing
A defendant forfeits his Sixth Amendment right of confrontation by committing a wrongful act that was ***intended to keep the witness from testifying*** at trial. [Giles v. California, 128 S. Ct. 2678 (2008)—unless the defendant killed the victim with the intent to make her unavailable to testify, he did not forfeit his confrontation rights with respect to allegations of domestic violence made by the victim to the police three weeks before he killed her]

c. The Right to Physically Face Witnesses
The Sixth Amendment guarantee of confrontation includes not only the right to cross-examine witnesses, but also the right to physically face them at trial. The Supreme Court held that right to be violated at a child sex abuse trial because a screen was erected in court between the defendant and two youthful complainants so they could not see the defendant as they testified. [Coy v. Iowa, 487 U.S. 1012 (1988)] However, the Court has also held that the right of confrontation is not absolute. A child witness in a sexual abuse case may testify via one-way closed circuit television without violating the defendant's confrontation rights ***if the trial judge makes individual findings of***

probable trauma to the child from testifying in the defendant's presence. [Maryland v. Craig, 497 U.S. 836 (1990)]

2. The Right to a Fair Trial
In addition, the Court has held that state hearsay rules and other exclusionary rules cannot be applied where the effect would be to deprive an accused of her Fourteenth Amendment due process right to a *fair trial* [Chambers v. Mississippi, 410 U.S. 284 (1973)], or deny her right to compulsory process [Rock v. Arkansas, 483 U.S. 44 (1987)].

VIII. PROCEDURAL CONSIDERATIONS

A. BURDENS OF PROOF
The term "burden of proof," as used by judges and lawyers at trial, encompasses two separate meanings or burdens. Thus, burden of proof can mean:

1. Burden of Producing or Going Forward with Evidence

a. Produce Sufficient Evidence to Raise Fact Question for Jury
This defines the burden of one party to introduce sufficient evidence to avoid judgment against her as a matter of law. It is the burden of producing sufficient evidence to create a fact question of the issue involved, so that the issue may appropriately reach the jury. The burden of producing evidence is a critical mechanism for judicial control of the trial. Although the burden is usually cast upon the party who has pleaded the existence of the fact, the burden as to this fact may shift to the adversary when the pleader has discharged her initial duty.

b. Prima Facie Case May Shift Burden of Production
Consider *Plaintiff v. Defendant* in a negligence action. Plaintiff offers evidence in her case-in-chief of Defendant's negligence. Defendant's motion for a nonsuit, made at the conclusion of Plaintiff's case, is denied. This denial reflects a judicial ruling that Plaintiff has made out a prima facie case of Defendant's negligence. Put another way, it means that Plaintiff has met her burden of going forward with evidence on the negligence issue.

Now assume that Defendant rests immediately after Plaintiff's case-in-chief without producing any rebuttal evidence. Plaintiff then moves for a directed verdict in her favor, claiming that Defendant was negligent as a matter of law. If this motion were granted, it would mean that (i) Plaintiff's evidence was sufficiently persuasive, (ii) the burden shifted to Defendant, and (iii) Defendant failed to meet his newly imposed burden of producing evidence of no negligence. If Plaintiff's motion were denied, it would mean only that Plaintiff met her initial burden but that it did not shift to Defendant; and, therefore, the burden of production having dropped out of the case, the matter is now for the jury. Once in the hands of the jury, the question is whether Plaintiff has met her burden of persuasion.

2. Burden of Persuasion (Proof)

a. Determined by Jury After All Evidence Is In
This is what is usually meant when the term "burden of proof" is used. This burden

becomes a crucial factor only if the parties have sustained their burdens of production and only when all the evidence is in. When the time of decision comes, the jury must be instructed how to decide the issue if their minds remain in doubt. There are no tie games in the litigation process. Either the plaintiff or the defendant must win. If, after all the proof is in, the issue is equally balanced in the minds of the jury, then the party with the burden of persuasion must lose.

b.   Jury Instructed as to Which Party Has Burden of Persuasion
The burden of persuasion does not shift from party to party during the course of the trial simply because it need not be allocated until it is time for a decision by the trier of fact. The jury will be told which party has the burden of persuasion and what the quantum of proof should be. The jury is never told anything about the burden of going forward with evidence because that burden is a matter for the judge alone.

c.   Quantum or Measure of Proof
The trier of fact must be persuaded of the truth of disputed facts by one of the following standards, depending upon the nature of the action:

1)   Preponderance of the Evidence
The preponderance of the evidence standard applies in most civil cases. This standard has been defined as meaning that the fact finder must be persuaded by the party to whom the burden on the issue has been allocated that the fact is *more probably true than not true.*

2)   Clear and Convincing Proof
Some civil cases (an oral contract to make a will or issues of fraud) often require proof by "clear and convincing evidence." This standard requires the trier of fact to be persuaded that there is a *high probability* that the fact in question exists.

3)   Beyond a Reasonable Doubt
This is the *highest standard* and applies to criminal cases. In a criminal prosecution, the guilt of the defendant must be established beyond a reasonable doubt.

B.   PRESUMPTIONS

A presumption is a rule that requires that a particular inference be drawn from an ascertained set of facts. It is a form of substitute proof or evidentiary shortcut, in that proof of the presumed fact is rendered unnecessary once evidence has been introduced of the basic fact that gives rise to the presumption. Presumptions are established for a wide variety of overlapping policy reasons. In some cases, the presumption serves to correct an imbalance resulting from one party's superior access to the proof on a particular issue. In others, the presumption was created as a timesaver to eliminate the need for proof of a fact that is highly probable in any event. In other words, the inference from the basic fact to the presumed fact is so probable and logical that it is sensible to assume the presumed fact upon proof of the basic fact. In still other situations, the presumption serves as a social or economic policy device. It operates to favor one contention by giving it the benefit of a presumption and to correspondingly handicap the disfavored adversary.

Example: A common presumption is that the driver of a vehicle is the owner's agent. When plaintiff has been injured by the negligent operation of a vehicle, the nondriving owner-defendant will be liable for the negligence of the driver if the driver is the owner's agent. Plaintiff's burden of proving that the driver was the agent of the

owner is aided by a presumption of agency that arises upon proof of ownership. The justification of this presumption of agency from ownership may be explained in terms of *fairness* in light of defendant's superior access to the evidence; in terms of *probability*, since it is unlikely that defendant's car was stolen by the driver; or in terms of a *social policy* of promoting safety or increasing available compensation for traffic victims by widening the responsibility of owners.

1. **Effect—Shift Burden of Production**

Federal Rule 301 provides that a presumption imposes on the party against whom it is directed the burden of going forward with evidence to rebut or meet the presumption. However, absent a provision otherwise, a presumption generally does not shift to such party the burden of proof in the sense of the risk of nonpersuasion, which remains throughout the trial upon the party on whom it was originally cast.

Example: Plaintiff has the burden of going forward and the burden of persuasion on the issue of Edwina's death. Plaintiff introduces evidence sufficient to support the fact that Edwina has been absent without tidings for a period of seven years. The proof of this basic fact causes a presumption of the presumed fact—Edwina's death. Plaintiff has made out a prima facie case on Edwina's death. More than that, if the defendant is silent and fails to offer proof in rebuttal (either of the presumed fact of death, or the basic fact of absence for a period of seven years), the jury will be instructed that they *must* find Edwina is dead if they believe the absence has been for seven years.

2. **Rebutting a Presumption**

A presumption is overcome or destroyed when the adversary produces some evidence contradicting the presumed fact. In other words, the *presumption is of no force or effect* when sufficient contrary evidence is admitted. This is the federal view adopted by Federal Rule 301, except where state law provides the rule of decision (*see* 6., *infra*).

Example: Plaintiff-victim of automobile driver's negligence sues owner. Plaintiff proves ownership, thus giving rise to the presumption that the driver was the agent of the owner. Defendant-owner testifies that the driver was not his agent, and his evidence could justify a jury finding that the driver was without authority from the owner. At this point, plaintiff's presumption is gone. He will have to sustain the burden of proving by a preponderance of the evidence that the driver was the agent of the owner, or his case will fail.

    a. **Amount of Contrary Evidence Necessary**

    The amount of contrary evidence that must be introduced to overcome the presumption has never been clearly articulated. Some cases require "enough evidence to support a finding of the nonexistence of the presumed fact." Others simply require "substantial evidence."

3. **Distinguish True Presumptions from Inferences and Substantive Law**

The true presumption with its mandatory rebuttable inference should not be confused with inferences and rules of substantive law.

    a. **Permissible Inferences**

    The permissible inference (prima facie case, or sometimes erroneously called

"presumption of fact") will allow a party to meet the burden of production but *will not shift the burden* to the adversary. Examples of situations giving rise to permissible inferences are:

1) Res Ipsa Loquitur
A permissible inference of negligence arises where the instrumentality causing injury was under the exclusive control of the defendant and the accident would not ordinarily occur without negligence.

2) Spoliation or Withholding Evidence
The intentional destruction or mutilation of relevant evidence may give rise to an inference that the destroyed evidence is unfavorable to the spoliator. An unfavorable inference may also arise when a party fails to produce evidence or witnesses within his control which he is naturally expected to produce.

3) Undue Influence
Where the attorney who drafted a will is its principal beneficiary to the exclusion of the natural objects of the testator's bounty, an inference of undue influence may be found.

b. "Presumptions" in Criminal Cases

1) Accused Is Presumptively Innocent
The accused in a criminal case is presumptively innocent until the prosecution proves every element of the offense beyond a reasonable doubt. Accordingly, it is clear that in criminal cases "presumptions" do not shift to the accused the burden of producing evidence, nor of persuading the fact finder. A "presumption" in a criminal case is truly nothing more than a *permissible inference.*

2) Judge's Instructions on Presumed Facts Against Accused
The trial judge in a criminal case is not free to charge the jury that it *must* find a "presumed" fact against the accused. When the existence of a presumed fact is submitted to the jury, the judge shall instruct the jury that it *may* regard the basic facts as sufficient evidence of the presumed fact, but that it is not required by law to do so. If the presumed fact establishes guilt, is an element of the offense, or negates a defense, its existence must be found (proved) beyond a reasonable doubt.

c. Conclusive Presumptions
This form of inference goes beyond the true presumption since it *cannot be rebutted* by contrary evidence. A "conclusive" presumption is really a rule of substantive law.
Example: In some states, it is conclusively presumed that a child under a certain age (*e.g.,* seven years old) cannot commit a crime. No evidence to the contrary can rebut this presumption, and part of the proof of the case requires a showing that the accused is over the minimum age.

4. Specific Presumptions
The following are common rebuttable presumptions:

a. **Presumption of Legitimacy**

The law presumes that every person is legitimate. The presumption applies to all cases where legitimacy is in dispute. The mere fact of birth gives rise to the presumption. The presumption is destroyed by evidence of illegitimacy that is "clear and convincing." For example, the presumption is overcome by proof of a husband's impotency, proof of lack of access, or the negative result of a properly conducted blood grouping test.

b. **Presumption Against Suicide**

When the cause of death is in dispute, a presumption arises in *civil* (not criminal) cases that the death was not a suicide.

c. **Presumption of Sanity**

Every person is presumed sane until the contrary is shown. The presumption of sanity applies in *criminal as well as civil* cases.

d. **Presumption of Death from Absence**

A person is presumed dead in any action involving the property of such person, the contractual or property right contingent upon his death, or the administration of his estate, if:

1) The person is inexplicably absent for a continuous period of *seven years* (death is deemed to have occurred on the last day of the seven-year period); and

2) He *has not been heard from,* or of, by those with whom he would normally be expected to communicate.

e. **Presumption from Ownership of Car—Agent Driver**

Proof of ownership of a motor vehicle gives rise to the presumption that the owner was the driver or that the driver was the owner's agent.

f. **Presumption of Chastity**

There is a presumption that every person is chaste and virtuous.

g. **Presumption of Regularity**

The general presumption is that no official or person acting under an oath of office will do anything contrary to his official duty, or omit anything that his official duty requires to be done.

h. **Presumption of Continuance**

Proof of the existence of a person, an object, a condition, or a tendency at a given time raises a presumption that it continued for as long as is usual with things of that nature.

i. **Presumption of Mail Delivery**

A letter shown to have been properly addressed, stamped, and mailed is presumed to have been delivered in the due course of mail. The presumption is said to be based upon the probability that officers of the government will perform their duty.

j. **Presumption of Solvency**

A person is presumed solvent, and every debt is presumed collectible.

k. **Presumption of Bailee's Negligence**

Upon proof of delivery of goods in good condition to a bailee and failure of the bailee to return the goods in the same condition, there is a presumption that the bailee was negligent.

l. **Presumption of Marriage**

Upon proof that a marriage ceremony was performed, it is presumed to have been legally performed and that the marriage is valid. A presumption of marriage also arises from cohabitation.

5. **Conflicting Presumptions**

If two or more conflicting presumptions arise, the judge shall apply the presumption that is founded on the weightier considerations of policy and logic. For example, where the validity of a later marriage is attacked by evidence of a prior valid marriage, the presumption of the validity of the later marriage is deemed to prevail over the presumption of the continuance of the first marriage.

6. **Choice of Law Regarding Presumptions in Civil Actions**

Under the Federal Rules, the effect of a presumption respecting a fact that is an element of a claim or defense as to which the rule of decision is supplied by state law is also governed by state law.

C. RELATIONSHIP OF PARTIES, JUDGE, AND JURY

1. **Party Responsibility**

Ours is an adversarial adjudicative process, and so the focus is on party responsibility or, perhaps what is more to the point, on lawyer responsibility. Very little happens in the litigation process unless some lawyer makes it happen by filing pleadings and motions, by initiating discovery, by entering into stipulations, by calling witnesses and offering exhibits at trial, or by interposing objections to the admission of evidence. In other words, the parties, through their lawyers, frame the issues in a litigation by making allegations, admissions, and denials in their pleadings, and by entering into binding stipulations. They assume the burden of proving the issues they have raised. And then, by deciding which witnesses to call to the stand and what tangible exhibits to introduce (and by deciding to what they will object), they control the flow of evidence. But the parties and their lawyers are not the only ones to be allocated important responsibilities in the adversary trial process.

2. **Court-Jury Responsibility**

Under our system, the trial court is more umpire than advocate. The trial judge's primary responsibility is to fairly superintend the trial; the judge is not permitted to become a partisan in it. As a general rule, questions of law are for the trial court to deal with, and questions of fact determination are for the jury, although trial judges frequently encounter the necessity of making preliminary fact determinations in connection with such matters as the admission or exclusion of evidence. (Of course, both types of questions—legal and factual—are for the trial court in a nonjury case.)

3. **Preliminary Determination of Admissibility**

In most cases, the existence of some preliminary or foundational fact is an essential condition to the admissibility of proffered evidence. Thus, before a written contract may be

received in evidence, it must be shown that the contract is genuine; and before testimony as to an alleged dying declaration may be admitted into evidence, it must be shown that the declaration was made under a sense of impending death. In some cases, the existence or nonexistence of the preliminary fact is determined by the jury, with the judge merely deciding whether the evidence of the foundational fact is sufficient to allow the jury to find its existence. In other cases, the question of the preliminary fact must be decided by the judge alone—in which case the evidence will not even be heard by the jury unless the judge first finds the preliminary or foundational fact.

a. Preliminary Facts Decided by Jury

The Federal Rules of Evidence distinguish preliminary facts to be decided by the jury from those to be decided by the judge, on the ground that the former questions involve the ***relevancy*** of the proffered evidence, while the latter questions involve the ***competency*** of evidence that is relevant. Rule 104(b) of the Federal Rules of Evidence defines preliminary facts to be decided by the jury as those where the answer to the preliminary question determines whether the proffered evidence is relevant at all. For example, if a statement is proffered to show notice to X, the jury must decide whether X heard it. If X did not, the statement is irrelevant for that purpose; but the decision is left ultimately to the jury, because if the jury does not believe X heard it, they will not use it anyway.

1) Role of the Judge

Before the judge allows the proffered evidence to go to the jury, she must find that the proponent of the proffered evidence has introduced evidence sufficient to sustain a finding of the existence of the preliminary fact. The court may ***instruct the jury*** to determine whether the preliminary fact exists and to disregard the proffered evidence if the jury finds that the preliminary fact does not exist. Such an instruction may be desirable if the trier of fact would otherwise be confused, but with most questions of conditional relevancy the instruction will be unnecessary, since a rational jury will disregard these types of evidence anyway unless they believe in the existence of the foundational fact. If the judge allows the introduction of evidence and then subsequently determines that a jury could not reasonably find that the preliminary fact exists, she must instruct the jury to disregard that evidence.

2) Examples of Preliminary Facts Decided by Jury

a) Agency

If plaintiff sues defendant upon an alleged contract, evidence of negotiations with a third party is inadmissible because it is irrelevant unless the third party is shown to be defendant's agent. However, the evidence of the negotiations with the third party is admissible if there is evidence sufficient to sustain a finding of the agency.

b) Authenticity of a Document

If there is a dispute about whether a note was signed by the defendant (as opposed to a forger), the authenticity of the document is to be left for the jury. In a sense this is merely an issue of relevancy, since the note, if forged, is irrelevant to the liability of the defendant.

c) **Credibility**

When a conviction of a crime is offered to attack the credibility of a witness, the judge must admit the evidence and allow the jury to determine the witness's credibility if there is evidence sufficient to identify the witness as the person convicted.

d) **Personal Knowledge**

The question of whether a witness had personal knowledge can go to the jury if there is sufficient evidence to sustain a finding that the witness had personal knowledge.

b. **Preliminary Facts Decided by Judge**

1) **Facts Affecting Competency of Evidence**

The question of the existence or nonexistence of all preliminary facts other than those of conditional relevance must be determined by the court. In most cases, the questions which must be decided by the judge involve the competency of the evidence or the existence of a privilege. These questions are withheld from the jury because it is felt that, once the jury hears the disputed evidence, the damage will have been done and the instruction to disregard the evidence, if the preliminary fact is not found, will be ineffective.

2) **Requirements for Privilege**

Preliminary facts to establish the existence of a privilege must be determined by the court. This must be so, or else a privilege might be ignored merely because there was sufficient evidence (and this might not be a great deal) for a jury to find it did not exist. Whether or not the jury believed that the facts giving rise to the privilege existed, they would still have heard the privileged evidence, subject only perhaps to a most unrealistic instruction to disregard it if they found the privilege to exist.

3) **Requirements for Hearsay Exceptions**

All preliminary fact questions involving the standards of trustworthiness of alleged exceptions to the hearsay rule must also be determined by the court. For example, the court must decide whether a statement offered as a dying declaration was made under a sense of impending death, or whether a purported business record was made in the regular course of business. The reason for this is that, otherwise, the jury will hear the hearsay evidence where the judge's finding is not that it fell within an exception to the hearsay rule, but only that there was enough evidence for the jury to so find. The jurors, however, once they have heard the hearsay evidence, might ignore the judge's instruction to disregard it unless they found the preliminary fact.

4) **Others**

The above two cases are the most important where the judge must first determine the existence of a foundational fact. However, there are several other major categories.

a) The judge must determine whether a witness is disqualified for *lack of mental capacity*.

    b)   The judge must rule on the qualifications of a witness as *an expert.*

    c)   If a conviction of a crime is offered to attack credibility and the disputed preliminary fact is whether a *pardon* has been granted to the witness so convicted (the pardon rendering the impeaching conviction inadmissible), the judge must make the determination.

    d)   The judge must determine whether a witness is sufficiently acquainted with a person whose sanity is in question in order for him to be *qualified to express an opinion* as to that person's sanity.

    e)   The judge is required to determine the preliminary facts necessary to warrant reception of *secondary evidence of a writing* (*e.g.,* whether original writing was lost or destroyed).

    f)   The judge is required to determine the *voluntariness of a confession* before he allows the jury to hear it. This is a rule of constitutional law. The theory is that otherwise the jury might hear involuntary confessions but rely on them anyway because the jury felt that they were nonetheless trustworthy.

5)   Procedure for Preliminary Fact Determinations by Judge

    a)   What Evidence May Be Considered
    Federal Rule 104(a) permits the trial judge to consider any (nonprivileged) *relevant evidence,* even though not otherwise admissible under the rules of evidence. Thus, the trial judge may consider affidavits or hearsay in ruling on preliminary fact questions. Most state courts, however, hold that the rules of evidence apply in preliminary fact determinations as much as in any other phase of the trial; thus, only admissible evidence may be considered.

    b)   Presence of Jury
    Whether the jury should be excused during the preliminary fact determination is generally within the discretion of the trial judge. However, because of the potential for prejudice to the accused in a criminal trial, the jury *must* be excused during hearings on the "voluntariness" of the accused's confession, or whenever the accused testifies during the preliminary fact hearing and requests that the jury be excused. [Fed. R. Evid. 104(c)]

c.   Testimony by Accused Does Not Waive Privilege Against Self-Incrimination
An accused may testify as to any preliminary matter (*e.g.,* circumstances surrounding allegedly illegal search) without subjecting herself to having to testify generally at the trial. Furthermore, while testifying upon a preliminary matter, an accused is not subject to cross-examination on other issues in the case. [Fed. R. Evid. 104(d)]

d.   Judicial Power to Comment upon Evidence
The trial judge is expected to marshal or summarize the evidence when necessary. However, in most state courts, the trial judge may not comment upon the weight of the evidence or the credibility of witnesses. In federal court, the trial judge has traditionally been permitted to comment on the weight of the evidence and the credibility of witnesses.

e. Power to Call Witnesses

The judge may call witnesses upon her own initiative and may interrogate any witnesses who testify, but may not demonstrate partisanship for one side of the controversy.

f. Rulings

A trial judge has an obligation to rule promptly on counsel's evidentiary objections and, when requested to do so by counsel, to state the grounds for her rulings.

g. Instructions on Limited Admissibility of Evidence

When evidence that is admissible as to one party or for one purpose, but inadmissible as to another party or for another purpose, is admitted, the trial judge, on request, shall restrict the evidence to its proper scope and instruct the jury accordingly, e.g., "Ladies and gentlemen of the jury, the testimony that you have just heard is receivable against the defendant Bushmat only and will in no way be considered by you as bearing on the guilt or innocence of the co-defendant Lishniss." [Fed. R. Evid. 105]

ESSAY EXAM QUESTIONS

INTRODUCTORY NOTE

The essay questions that follow have been selected to provide you with an opportunity to experience how the substantive law you have been reviewing may be tested in the hypothetical essay examination question context. These sample essay questions are a valuable self-diagnostic tool designed to enable you to enhance your issue-spotting ability and practice your exam writing skills.

It is suggested that you approach each question as though under actual examination conditions. The time allowed for each question is 45 minutes. You should spend 10-15 minutes spotting issues, underlining key facts and phrases, jotting notes in the margins, and outlining your answer. *If* you organize your thoughts well, about 30 minutes will be more than adequate for writing them down. Should you prefer to forgo the actual writing involved on these questions, be sure to give yourself no more time for issue-spotting than you would on the actual examination.

The BARBRI technique for writing a well-organized essay answer is to (i) spot the issues in a question and then (ii) analyze and discuss each issue using the "CIRAC" method:

C — State your ***conclusion*** first. (In other words, you must think through your answer ***before*** you start writing.)

I — State the *issue* involved.

R — Give the *rule(s)* of law involved.

A — *Apply* the rule(s) of law to the facts.

C — Finally, restate your ***conclusion***.

After completing (or outlining) your own analysis of each question, compare it with the BARBRI model answer provided herein. A passing answer does ***not*** have to match the model one, but it should cover most of the issues presented and the law discussed and should ***apply the law to the facts*** of the question. Use of the CIRAC method results in the best answer you can write.

EXAM QUESTION NO. 1

After performing routine liposuction surgery on Bob Boyd, Dr. Ann Adams was distressed to discover that the surgery did not achieve the anticipated result. In fact, there were unforeseen complications that resulted in emergency surgery to remove a blood clot. Fortunately, Boyd made a full recovery, but not before enduring a 10-day hospital stay, incurring significant medical bills, and missing two weeks of work.

After the surgery and during Boyd's recuperation, Dr. Adams, who is a very conscientious, compassionate physician, continually met with Boyd and his family; on at least two of these occasions she expressed her sympathy for the situation and her regret that the surgery had not yielded the anticipated result.

Dr. Adams, who remained haunted by Boyd's surgery, spoke on several occasions with her husband about her concern that she may have in some way contributed to Boyd's surgical problems as she had performed the surgery early in the morning, following a night of partying, when she had a severe headache, possibly the result of a hangover. Her husband attempted to reassure Dr. Adams, telling her that all doctors make mistakes and advising her that under no circumstances should she admit any liability. She similarly confided her concerns to her personal physician whom she consulted when she continued to suffer from severe headaches.

Prior to Boyd's full recovery, Dr. Adams met with her accountant to discuss how she might set up some sort of trust or annuity for Boyd's family in the event he did not recover. Because Boyd fortunately did make a full recovery, Dr. Adams did not pursue this idea any further.

After his recovery, Boyd filed a medical malpractice suit against Dr. Adams in Clarke County superior court, alleging that she was negligent in performing the liposuction surgery that resulted in his complications. Among other things, he sought loss of income for the two weeks of work he missed.

Upon being served with the lawsuit, Dr. Adams put her malpractice carrier on notice. Dr. Adams then called her personal lawyer, Lou Lawyer, who agreed to meet with her the very next day, on New Year's Day. Dr. Adams, who was visibly upset about the lawsuit, took her sister Karen (who has always been her best friend and confidante), with her to sit in on the meeting to provide moral support.

The insurance carrier has retained you to represent Dr. Adams in the medical malpractice litigation. You receive a call from Lou Lawyer, who tells you that she is Dr. Adams's personal lawyer and that she, Lawyer, will represent Dr. Adams's personal interests because the interests of Dr. Adams and her malpractice carrier may not always coincide. When you meet with Dr. Adams, she confides her concerns about having conducted the surgery while suffering from a severe headache. Before Dr. Adams leaves your office, she entrusts to your safekeeping her entire personal file on Boyd and his surgery, which contains Boyd's medical charts and related information created on the day of the surgery.

Prior to the date of trial, Boyd's counsel sends you the plaintiff's portion of the pretrial order in which he is required to identify all witnesses, with a brief summary of their anticipated testimony. In this pleading, Boyd's counsel indicates that he intends to call the following witnesses at trial:

Witness: Summary of Testimony

1.   Dr. Adams's physician: Any statements regarding the Boyd surgery which Dr. Adams may have made to her physician.

2.   Dr. Adams's husband: Any statements regarding the Boyd surgery which Dr. Adams may have made to her husband.

3.   Dr. Adams's accountant: Any statements regarding the Boyd surgery which Dr. Adams may have made to her accountant.

4.   Karen: Any statements regarding the Boyd surgery which Dr. Adams may have made to Lou Lawyer during the New Year's Day conference and any advice which Lou Lawyer may have given Dr. Adams during that conference.

5.   Dr. Adams:

(a)   Prior malpractice complaints filed against her.

(b)   Any statements of sympathy, regret, or like statements which Dr. Adams may have made to Boyd or his family after the surgery.

(c)   The existence and extent of her medical malpractice insurance.

(d)   The contents of her file on Boyd and his surgery.

You now must prepare your portion of the pretrial order in which you are required to indicate what objections, if any, you have to each witness identified and the proposed subject(s) of testimony.

(1)   For each witness listed above, please specify what objections, if any, should be made. In each instance, explain your reason(s) for each objection, or your reason(s) for determining that no objection is appropriate. Please direct your response only to the indicated subject matter of testimony.

(2)   Assume that you indicate in your portion of the pretrial order that you intend to introduce evidence of Boyd's insurance policies that provide him with compensation for loss of work (income replacement) in this situation. What objections, if any, do you anticipate from your opposing counsel?

EXAM QUESTION NO. 2

Mom and Daddy are the divorced parents of Angel, their three-year-old daughter. According to Mom, she was bathing Angel after she returned home from a visitation with Daddy, and Angel complained that "it hurt" around her genital area. Mom said she became concerned and questioned Angel about her complaint. She said Angel told her that she and Daddy had a "secret" that Daddy "rubbed" against her and made her hurt.

Mom called the family physician, Dr. Kildare, and reported this to him. Dr. Kildare saw Angel and her mother that night at the emergency room at the local hospital. The hospital records regarding the emergency room visit contain an entry in the nurse's notes from the now deceased Nurse Crockett, indicating that Angel told her "Mommy hurt me" when asked why she was at the hospital. Angel later told Dr. Kildare about the "secret" she and Daddy had after Mom promised Angel a new doll and some ice cream. Then Dr. Kildare examined Angel and found redness and swelling in Angel's genital area. Dr. Kildare concluded that "Angel had been sexually abused by Daddy." He recommended that Angel be seen by a child psychologist, Dr. Feelgood.

Dr. Feelgood saw Angel the following week. After interviewing, testing, and evaluating Angel, he arrived at the opinion that "Angel showed no symptoms or indications of having been sexually abused."

Mom filed an action to terminate Daddy's visitation privileges. The court, *sua sponte*, ordered Mom and Daddy to undergo evaluations by Dr. Marcus Welby, a psychiatrist.

After the evaluations were complete, Dr. Welby opined that the evaluation of Daddy did not reveal any indication of or propensity for sexual child abuse. As to Mom, he opined that she exhibited symptoms of Munchausen Syndrome by Proxy, a psychiatric disorder that results in one harming or injuring a child to obtain sympathy or attention. Dr. Welby began a course of treatment and counseling with Mom. He later arrived at the opinion that Mom could have caused the injury to Angel in an effort to keep Daddy from seeing Angel.

As to the issue of sexual child abuse, *vel non*, the parties contemplate offering into evidence the following:

(1)   The testimony of Mom as to what Angel told her;

(2)   Dr. Kildare's testimony concerning his examination of Angel and his opinion that "Angel had been sexually abused by Daddy";

(3)   Hospital records containing Angel's statement to Nurse Crockett at the emergency room that "Mommy hurt me";

(4)   Dr. Feelgood's testimony and opinion that Angel "showed no symptoms or indications of having been sexually abused";

(5)   Dr. Welby's opinion regarding Daddy's lack of propensity for being a sexual abuser;

(6)   Dr. Welby's opinion that Mom could have caused the injury to Angel and his diagnosis as to Mom of Munchausen Syndrome by Proxy.

As to each of these items of evidence, set out the foundation that should be laid for the admission of the evidence, the appropriate objection(s), if any, the grounds for the said objection(s), and whether the evidence is admissible. In answering this question, rely only on the Federal Rules of Evidence and assume that the doctors are qualified as experts and that all requirements of *Daubert v. Merrell Dow Pharmaceuticals, Inc.* have been met.

EXAM QUESTION NO. 3

Johnson, a longtime farmer, had grown beans for more than 20 years. His large operation, during an average year, yielded annual returns of more than $350,000. The 700 acres that he maintained used all of the latest techniques for fertilizing, planting, and harvesting the crops.

The neighboring farm was operated by the Harolds. They had been in business less than five years and believed cotton grew best on that type of land. However, their inexperience made their farming operations marginal at best.

The Harolds solicited the services of Plane-O, an out-of-state crop dusting company. Plane-O's aircraft was fitted with a unique video camera that would actually film crops as they were being sprayed. Using several of his best pilots, Plane-O sprayed the Harolds' farm for an entire week. They did so following the strict instructions and mapping directions of the Harolds. But less than two days after being given their instructions, the pilots followed their own maps and surveys.

During an inspection of his fields in April of that year, Johnson noticed unusual leaf and stem damage to his beans. He believed that the damage to his crops was caused by the spraying residue that had been blown from his neighbor's fields. The nearest agricultural agent lived 50 miles away and would not come to inspect the crops. Johnson had a grandson who was visiting for the summer. The grandson took several pictures of the plants. These were mailed to the agricultural agent. The agent thought the photographs of the bean field were just like any other pictures. Weeks later, the damage had grown worse, with 80% of the beans affected.

One year later, Johnson has sued the Harolds and Plane-O for his crop loss. Plane-O has refused to come to the state and allow its airplane film or its pilots to be used. They want to settle their claim out of court. Johnson wants the agricultural agent to testify about the crops by using the airplane film and the photographs. The judge has requested a pretrial memorandum as to the evidence in this case. Relying on the Federal Rules of Evidence, please prepare the document for presentation to the court.

EXAM QUESTION NO. 4

Ann was driving towards a stoplight. As she entered the intersection, she was struck from the right by Dan Defendant. Riding in the front seat with Ann was Sally Plaintiff.

After the impact, Wilbert came up to Ann's car to ask if the two ladies were all right. Ann looked at Wilbert and said, "But, the other guy (Dan) ran the light." Wilbert looked back and said, "Yes, I know, because I saw him run the light, also."

George, Wilbert's friend, came up to the car just in time to hear Wilbert make his statement. Wilbert left to go check on Dan while George stayed to talk to the ladies. George told the ladies that he was looking away until after he heard the impact, and he did not see the light. George watched Ann calm Sally down and heard Ann say three or four times, "You'll be OK, Sally, he ran the light and we can sue him." George also heard Sally moan, "My knees hurt so bad!"

In a few minutes Wilbert came back and told Ann, Sally, and George that Dan had told him (Wilbert) that he (Dan) was talking on his cell phone and because he was not looking at the light as he approached the intersection, he (Dan) had no idea what color the light was. Wilbert also said that Dan said that he (Dan) was driving home after celebrating with friends at the Beer Bust Bar. A blood alcohol test did not reveal any alcohol in Dan's blood.

When the police came to investigate, Dan told the police that his light was green and that there was nothing distracting him as he approached the light. This is what the police put in the police report. The police also included George as a witness but failed to include Wilbert as a witness.

At the hospital, Sally told the triage nurse that her neck, back, and knees were hurting. This was put into the medical records, resulting in diagnostic procedures and treatment for Sally's neck, back, and knees.

(1) Sally sues Dan for personal injuries in a jurisdiction that follows the Federal Rules of Evidence. Sally wants to have George and Wilbert testify about Dan's celebration at the Beer Bust Bar. Dan objects. State whether or not the objection will succeed with each witness and why.

(2) Sally wants to have George and Wilbert testify that Dan said he was talking on his cell phone and was not looking at the light as Dan approached the intersection. Dan objects. State whether or not the objection will succeed with each witness and why.

(3) Sally wants to have George and Wilbert testify that Dan ran the red light. Dan objects. State whether or not the objection will succeed with each witness and why.

(4) In her deposition, Sally said that immediately after the impact her neck, back, and knees were hurting badly. Dan wants to have Ann and George testify that Sally did not complain of pain in her neck and back at the scene of the impact. Sally objects. State whether or not the objection will succeed with each witness and why.

(5) In her lawsuit, Sally sues for injuries to her ankles. Dan wants to introduce the triage nurse's notes to show that there was no complaint of ankle injury to the triage nurse. Sally objects. State whether or not the objection will succeed and why.

ANSWERS TO ESSAY EXAM QUESTIONS

ANSWER TO EXAM QUESTION NO. 1

(1)   Hearsay would *not* be an appropriate objection to any testimony regarding Dr. Adams's statements. The issue is whether any of the offered testimony is hearsay or otherwise inadmissible. Hearsay is an out-of-court statement offered to prove the truth of the matter asserted. Voluntary admissions by a party-opponent are admissible nonhearsay. Thus, any statements made by Dr. Adams are admissible.

Dr. Adams's physician: No objection should be made to the testimony by Dr. Adams's physician. The physician-patient privilege prohibits physicians from releasing any medical information concerning a patient. Here, however, statements Dr. Adams made regarding the surgery she performed on Boyd would probably not be considered "medical information" and, therefore, would be admissible.

Dr. Adams's husband: An objection to the testimony of Dr. Adams's husband should be made based on the privilege for confidential marital communications. Communications between a husband and wife are excluded on public policy grounds. For this privilege to apply, the communication must be made during a valid marriage, and the communication must be made in reliance upon the intimacy of the marital relationship. Here, Dr. and Mr. Adams are married, and Dr. Adams expressed her concerns about Boyd to her husband in reliance upon the intimacy of their relationship. Therefore, these statements are privileged and inadmissible.

Dr. Adams's accountant: An objection to the testimony of Dr. Adams's accountant should be made based on the accountant-client privilege if the jurisdiction recognizes this privilege. Communications between an accountant and a client are privileged if they are made in a professional capacity and are within the scope of the representation. Here, Dr. Adams talked to her accountant about potentially setting up a trust or annuity for Boyd's family. She met with the accountant for the purpose of discussing this, so the communications were made in a professional capacity. Setting up a trust or annuity is also within the scope of the accountant's representation of Dr. Adams, and a court would likely find that explaining why she wants to set up such a trust or annuity is also within the scope. Dr. Adams's failure to pursue the matter does not destroy the privilege. Therefore, any statements Dr. Adams made to her accountant regarding Boyd are inadmissible if the jurisdiction recognizes the accountant-client privilege.

Karen: No objection should be made to Karen testifying about statements Dr. Adams made to Lou Lawyer. Confidential communications between an attorney and client, made during professional consultation, are privileged from disclosure. Communications are "confidential" if they were not intended to be disclosed to third persons, other than those to whom disclosure would be in furtherance of the rendition of legal services to the client or those who are necessary for the transmission of the communication (*e.g.*, an interpreter). Communications made in the known presence and hearing of any other third person are not privileged. Here, although Karen attended Dr. Adams's conference with Lou Lawyer to provide moral support, her presence was not necessary to the rendition of legal services or the transmission of communications. Thus, Karen may testify to Dr. Adams's statements made during the New Year's Day conference.

However, an objection to Karen's testimony about any advice which Lawyer may have given during the conference should be made based on hearsay. As discussed above, hearsay is generally inadmissible unless it falls under one of the exceptions to the hearsay rule. Here, Lawyer's unprivileged communications do not fall under any such exceptions and, therefore, are inadmissible.

Dr. Adams: (a) An objection that any prior malpractice claims against Dr. Adams are irrelevant should be made. Evidence of similar occurrences involving the same instrumentality is only admissible if those occurrences happened under the same or similar circumstances, are probative of the material

issue involved, and have a probative value that outweighs the risk that the evidence will confuse the jury or result in unfair prejudice. Here, the facts do not indicate what the other malpractice claims are about, so it is unclear whether they occurred under the same or similar circumstances. If they did not occur under similar circumstances, they are irrelevant and inadmissible. However, if the court finds that the prior claims are similar, then an objection should be made that the probative value of any prior malpractice claims against Dr. Adams are substantially outweighed by their prejudicial effect. Here, because evidence of other similar malpractice claims could cause the jury to confuse them with the Boyd claim, it should be excluded.

(b)   No objection should be made regarding the statements made by Dr. Adams to Boyd and his family. An admission by a party-opponent is a statement made or act done that amounts to an acknowledgment by that party to one of the relevant facts. Admissions are admissible nonhearsay. Here, the statements made by Dr. Adams regarding her regret that the surgery did not achieve the anticipated result is contrary to her intentions at trial and is therefore admissible as an admission.

(c)   An objection that the existence and extent of Dr. Adams's malpractice insurance is inadmissible should be made. Evidence that a person was or was not insured against liability is not admissible to show that she acted negligently or is able to pay a substantial judgment. Therefore, opposing counsel cannot ask Dr. Adams about her malpractice insurance.

(d)   No objection should be made to Dr. Adams's testimony regarding the contents of her file on Boyd and his surgery. The file is admissible under the business records exception to the hearsay rule, which allows admission of any writing or record made in the regular course of business as proof of the recorded act, transaction, occurrence, or event. Note that the physician-patient privilege would not prohibit Dr. Adams's testimony because Boyd would likely provide his written authorization.

(2)   Opposing counsel will likely object to the introduction of evidence of Boyd's insurance policies under the collateral source rule. The collateral source rule states that damages are not reduced or mitigated by benefits that a plaintiff receives from another source, such as insurance. Defendants may not introduce evidence relating to any such financial aid from other sources. Therefore, Dr. Adams will not be able to introduce evidence that Boyd's insurance will compensate him for loss of work because his insurance is a collateral source and cannot be considered.

ANSWER TO EXAM QUESTION NO. 2

(1)   *Mom's testimony:* Mom's testimony regarding the statement made to her by Angel that Daddy was the cause of her injury will be admissible into evidence. To lay the proper foundation for Mom's testimony, it must be shown that her testimony is relevant and that its probative value outweighs any danger of unfair prejudice, confusion of the issues, or undue delay. In this case, Mom's testimony is relevant to the cause of Angel's injury and its probative value outweighs any danger of unfair prejudice, confusion of the issues, or undue delay. The opponent will object that her testimony is inadmissible hearsay. Hearsay is an out-of-court statement offered to prove the truth of the matter asserted. While the statement is hearsay—it is being offered to prove that Daddy caused Angel's injury—it is nevertheless admissible as a declaration of present bodily condition. Under that exception, a declaration of a present bodily condition is admissible when made to another person if it relates to symptoms, including the existence of pain. Here, Angel told Mom that she hurt in the area around her genitals. This is a declaration of a present bodily condition. Thus, Mom's testimony regarding Angel's statement is admissible.

(2)   *Dr. Kildare's testimony:* Dr. Kildare's testimony regarding his examination of Angel is admissible into evidence, but his opinion that Daddy abused her is inadmissible. To lay the proper

foundation for Dr. Kildare's testimony, it must be shown that his testimony is relevant and that its probative value outweighs any danger of unfair prejudice, confusion of the issues, or undue delay. Dr. Kildare's testimony is relevant because it concerns his examination of Angel and identifies the possible aggressor. Additionally, its probative value outweighs any danger of unfair prejudice, confusion of the issues, or undue delay.

The portion of Dr. Kildare's testimony relating to his examination of Angel is admissible as expert opinion and not subject to any objections by the opponents. Generally, expert opinion testimony is admissible if the subject matter requires specialized knowledge, the witness is qualified as an expert, and the opinion is supported by a proper factual basis (*e.g.*, facts made known at trial). Dr. Kildare's testimony is admissible expert opinion testimony because it requires specialized knowledge—special medical knowledge is required to determine whether an individual has signs of sexual abuse. Further, he has been qualified as an expert and his opinion is based on facts in evidence. Thus, the portion of Dr. Kildare's testimony regarding his examination of Angel is admissible.

However, the opponent will object to Dr. Kildare's testimony that Daddy abused Angel because it embraces the ultimate issue in the case—*i.e.*, who caused Angel's injury. Generally, testimony that embraces the ultimate issue in a case is not objectionable if it assists the judge or jury in determining a fact in issue or in understanding the evidence. An expert's conclusion as to the ultimate issue is not helpful to the judge or jury in that sense and is therefore inadmissible. Here, Dr. Kildare's opinion that Daddy abused Angel is conclusory and is not helpful to the judge or jury; thus, it is inadmissible.

(3) *Hospital records:* The hospital records and Angel's statements within the records are inadmissible. To lay the proper foundation for the hospital records, it must be shown that they are relevant and must be authenticated by proof showing that the writing is what the proponent claims it is. Medical records are authenticated if certified by a custodian (*e.g.*, a hospital employee). Thus, a proper foundation can be established because the records are relevant and can be certified by a hospital employee. The opponent, however, will object on grounds that they contain hearsay within hearsay, which is defined as an out-of-court statement that contains other hearsay. Hearsay within hearsay is admissible only if both the outer hearsay (the hospital record) and the inner hearsay (Angel's statements) fall within an exception to the hearsay rule.

The hospital records are admissible under the business records exception to the hearsay rule. Generally, a record is admissible into evidence as proof of an event if made in the regular course of business and it was the regular course of the business to make the record at that time. Entries in hospital records are generally admissible if related to the medical diagnosis or treatment of the patient. The hospital record from Angel's visit to the emergency room is admissible because the record was made in the regular course of the hospital's business and it was the regular course of the hospital's business to make hospital records during an emergency room visit. The entry in the record regarding Angel's statement that "Mommy hurt me," however, is not admissible because it does not relate to her diagnosis or treatment and does not fall within any exception to the hearsay rule. Thus, neither the records nor the statements within the records are admissible.

(4) *Dr. Feelgood's testimony:* The testimony of Dr. Feelgood is admissible as expert opinion testimony. To lay the proper foundation for Dr. Feelgood's testimony, it must be shown that his testimony is relevant and that its probative value outweighs any danger of unfair prejudice, confusion of the issues, or undue delay. Dr. Feelgood's testimony is relevant because it indicates his opinion as to whether Angel was sexually abused and its probative value outweighs any danger of unfair prejudice, confusion of the issues, or undue delay. As stated above, expert opinion testimony is admissible if the subject matter requires specialized knowledge, the witness is qualified as an expert, and the opinion is based on facts in evidence. Dr. Feelgood's testimony is admissible as an expert opinion because it requires his specialized knowledge of psychology and he has been qualified as an expert. Additionally, it is supported by

a proper factual basis. The opponent will object on the ground that Dr. Feelgood's testimony embraces the ultimate issue in the case; however, this objection will be overruled because the statement merely states that Angel showed no signs of sexual abuse and that testimony will be helpful to the judge or jury in determining whether she did in fact suffer sexual abuse. Therefore, Dr. Feelgood's testimony is admissible.

(5) **_Dr. Welby's opinion regarding Daddy:_** Dr. Welby's opinion that Daddy lacks propensity for being a sexual abuser is admissible character evidence and the proponent can establish the proper foundation for Dr. Welby's expert opinion testimony. Opinion testimony is a proper means of proving character. Therefore, Dr. Welby's opinion that Daddy lacks propensity for being a sexual abuser is admissible.

(6) **_Dr. Welby's opinion regarding Mom:_** Dr. Welby's opinion that Mom could have caused Angel's injury and his diagnosis of her disorder is inadmissible. As discussed above, a proper foundation can be established for Dr. Welby's testimony. Further, he is qualified as an expert and his testimony is such that requires the specialized knowledge of psychiatry. However, the opponent will object by asserting the psychiatrist-patient privilege. That objection will be sustained because the privilege protects from disclosure communications between a patient and psychiatrist made during consultation. Dr. Welby consulted with Mom in his professional capacity; thus, the communications are privileged. Therefore, Dr. Welby's opinion is inadmissible.

ANSWER TO EXAM QUESTION NO. 3

The evidence in this case consists of the agricultural agent's testimony based on the airplane film and the grandson's photographs. Under the Federal Rules of Evidence, an expert may testify if the subject matter is one where scientific, technical, or other specialized knowledge will assist the trier of fact in understanding the evidence or determining a fact in issue. In this case, if the agricultural agent's testimony will concern the cause and extent of the bean field damage, one can argue that it is scientific/specialized knowledge that will assist the trier of fact in making a determination as to the Harolds' and Plane-O's liability. Thus, the agricultural agent would be permitted to testify as an expert.

Here, Johnson wants the agricultural agent to base her opinion on the airplane film and his grandson's photographs. An expert may base her opinion on facts inadmissible in evidence if the facts are of a type reasonably relied upon by experts in the particular field. Therefore, the agricultural agent could base an opinion on the airplane film and the photographs and not admit them into evidence if other experts in the field would rely upon them in basing an opinion. Although the facts indicate that Plane-O refuses to allow its film to be used, if Plane-O is subject to the court's jurisdiction, Johnson can obtain the airplane film through discovery. The agricultural agent could then examine the airplane film and the photographs and provide testimony in court.

The airplane film and photographs also could be admitted into evidence if authenticated. Film/photographs are authenticated if identified by a witness as a portrayal of certain facts relevant to the issue and verified by the witness as a correct representation of those facts. The witness need not be the photographer so long as he is familiar with the scene depicted. Consequently, in order for the photographs to be admitted in evidence, Johnson or his grandson would have to testify. In order for the airplane film to be admitted, one of the pilots would probably have to testify. If Plane-O is subject to the court's jurisdiction, his pilots could possibly be subpoenaed to testify about the film. An argument might be made that Johnson could authenticate the film. However, he would have to be familiar with all the scenes depicted in the film, and not just his bean field.

ANSWER TO EXAM QUESTION NO. 4

(1)   The objection will be sustained as to both George and Wilbert because the evidence is irrelevant. Relevant evidence is evidence that has a tendency to make the existence of any fact that is of consequence more probable than it would be without the evidence. Here, evidence that Dan was at the Beer Bust Bar prior to the accident is irrelevant. Such a proposition might be relevant to prove that Dan had been drinking alcohol prior to the accident; however, the blood alcohol test that was performed did not reveal any alcohol in Dan's blood. Thus, neither George nor Wilbert can be called to testify that Dan was celebrating at the Beer Bust Bar. [Note that if the evidence was relevant for other purposes, Wilbert could testify as to the statement as an admission by a party-opponent, but George could not because it is hearsay within hearsay.]

(2)   The objection will be overruled as to Wilbert, but will be sustained as to George.

Wilbert can testify as to Dan's statement because it is the admission by a party-opponent, which is admissible nonhearsay. An admission by a party-opponent is a statement by one of the parties that amounts to a prior acknowledgment of one of the relevant facts. If the party said something that now turns out to be inconsistent with his contentions at trial, the statement is admissible. Here, Dan told Wilbert that he was talking on his cell phone and was not looking at the light. However, his statements to the police indicate that the light was green and nothing was distracting him. Because this is a relevant fact, the statement is admissible as an admission by a party-opponent.

George cannot testify as to what Dan told Wilbert because the statement is hearsay within hearsay. Hearsay within hearsay is admissible only if both the outer hearsay and the inner hearsay statements fall within an exception to the hearsay rule. As stated above, the statement from Dan to Wilbert is admissible. However, the statement from Wilbert to George recounting Dan's statement does not fall within any hearsay exception. Thus, George cannot testify as to Dan's statement to Wilbert.

(3)   The objection will be overruled as to Wilbert, but will be sustained as to George.

Wilbert can testify as to whether Dan ran the red light because the evidence is relevant and because he is a competent witness. As stated above, relevant evidence is evidence that has a tendency to make the existence of any fact that is of consequence more probable than it would be without the evidence. Here, the evidence is relevant to prove Dan's liability. A witness is competent if he has personal knowledge of the matter and he declares that he will testify truthfully. Wilbert is competent because he has personal knowledge as to whether Dan ran the red light—he saw the accident happen. Additionally, if he testifies he will be under oath to tell the truth. Thus, the objection will be overruled as to Wilbert.

George cannot testify as to whether Dan ran the red light because he did not see the accident happen and therefore has no personal knowledge. He is relying on the statement made by Wilbert, which is hearsay not within any exception. Thus, the objection will be sustained as to George.

(4)   The objection will be overruled as to both Ann and George. The purpose of the testimony would be to impeach Sally's credibility as a witness. To impeach a witness, a party can show that the witness has previously made statements that are inconsistent with some material part of her testimony. Here, Ann and George can both be questioned as to whether Sally failed to complain of pain in her back and neck at the scene of the accident. If Sally testifies in accordance with her deposition testimony (that her back and neck did hurt), the testimony of Ann and George can be used to impeach her.

(5)   The objection will be overruled. The triage nurse's notes are admissible under the business records exception to the hearsay rule. Any writing or record made as a memorandum or record of any event is admissible in evidence if made in the regular course of any business. Entries in hospital records qualify under this exception to the extent they are related to the medical diagnosis or treatment of the patient. Here, the notes are admissible because they were made by the nurse in the ordinary course of her business—providing patients with medical care. The document can be authenticated by having

the custodian or other qualified witness testify to the identity of the record or by certifying in writing that the document meets the requirements of the business records exception. Thus, the objection will be overruled and the notes are admissible.

Trusts

TRUSTS

TABLE OF CONTENTS

I. INTRODUCTION

A. TRUST DEFINED

A trust is a fiduciary relationship in which a trustee holds legal title to specific property under a fiduciary duty to manage, invest, safeguard, and administer the trust assets and income for the benefit of designated beneficiaries, who hold equitable title.

B. TYPES OF TRUSTS

Trusts are classified according to the method of their creation: (i) ***express trusts***, which arise from the expressed intention of the owner of property to create the relationship with respect to the property; (ii) ***resulting trusts***, which arise from the presumed intention of the owner of property; and (iii) ***constructive trusts***, which do not depend on intention but rather constitute a useful equitable remedy in cases involving wrongful conduct and unjust enrichment.

C. CATEGORIES OF EXPRESS TRUSTS

Express trusts fall into two categories: private trusts and charitable trusts. These two categories of trusts are distinguished primarily by the identity of their beneficiaries. A ***private trust*** is created for the benefit of certain ascertainable persons; thus, a trust "to T in trust for my husband, and at his death to my children," is a private trust. A ***charitable trust***, on the other hand, is created for the benefit of an indefinite class of persons or the public in general; thus, a trust providing scholarship funds for needy students at a named university is considered a charitable trust.

D. UNIFORM TRUST CODE

Much of trust law is founded on the common law, best represented in the Restatement of Trusts and the basis for this outline. In 2000, the Uniform Law Commission promulgated the first national codification of trust law. The Uniform Trust Code ("UTC"), enacted in nearly half the states, draws on the common law and existing state law, and for some issues incorporates trust law reform. Although for purposes of the bar exam you will need to be familiar with the common law of trusts, references to the UTC will be made throughout this outline to highlight some of these reforms.

II. EXPRESS PRIVATE TRUSTS

A. CHARACTERISTICS OF AN EXPRESS TRUST

A trust is a fiduciary relationship with respect to property in which one person, the ***trustee***, holds the legal title to the trust property, the ***res***, subject to enforceable equitable rights in another, the ***beneficiary*** (cestui que trust). It is basically a device whereby one or more persons manage the property for the benefit of others. The trust must have a valid ***trust purpose***. The trustee ordinarily has legal title to the property and the beneficiaries have equitable title. The testator or grantor who creates an express trust is the trustor or ***settlor***, who must have had the ***intent*** to create the trust. Consideration is not required for the creation of a trust; in fact, trusts are usually created gratuitously.

1. Intention to Create a Trust

a. Manifested by Words, Writing, or Conduct

The settlor's manifestation of intention to create a trust is essential to the existence of an express trust. Except as limited by requirements of the Statute of Wills or Statute

of Frauds (applicable to real property), this intention may be manifested by written or spoken words or by conduct, and it need not be manifested in any particular form of language. An oral trust of personal property is valid in all jurisdictions.

1) Delivery of Deed May Manifest Intent
Although some external expression of trust intent is required, the failure of the settlor to communicate his intention to the beneficiaries or other persons does not prevent the creation of a trust. Delivery *to the trustee* of the deed creating the trust is sufficient.

a) Problem Where Settlor Is Also Trustee
However, where the settlor is also the trustee and does not notify anyone of the trust, the trust may fail for lack of intent to create a trust. When the beneficiaries are not notified, evidence that the settlor-trustee segregated the property and kept separate account books for it is relevant in establishing that a trust was intended.

b. Must Be Manifested While Settlor Owns Property
The intention to create a trust must have been manifested by the settlor at a time when he owned the trust property and prior to its conveyance to another.

1) Must Manifest Intent Prior to Conveyance
One cannot convey property outright and later execute a trust instrument declaring that the transfer was actually one in trust. The conduct of the transferor and the transferee subsequent to the conveyance, however, may be important as evidence of the intention that existed at the time of the conveyance.

2) Must Intend Trust to Take Effect Immediately
The settlor must have intended the trust to take effect immediately and not at some future time (*e.g.,* a promise by A to create a trust when he collects a debt from B does *not* create a trust now).

a) Future Interest May Be Trust Res
However, a presently declared trust can have as the trust res a future interest in property (*e.g.,* A can convey "to B for life and then to C as trustee for D"; C has present duties to protect D's equitable future interest).

b) Effect of Promise to Create Trust
If the settlor promises gratuitously to create a trust in the future, a trust arises in the future only if, at that time, the settlor manifests anew his intention to create the trust. Often this promise will be to hold property in trust when the property is acquired. On the other hand, if the promise is *supported by consideration*, the trust can arise in the future, when the property is acquired, without any further manifestation of intent.

c. Precatory Expressions
Usually a settlor clearly directs the trustee to carry out the intended terms of the trust, but difficulties arise when the transferor merely expresses a hope, wish, or suggestion that the property be used for a certain purpose. A direction such as "to B with the hope

that B will use the property to provide for the support of C" is precatory language. Most courts today infer from such language that **no trust** was intended, but only that the transferor wished his desires to be known so that the transferee could comply with them if willing to do so. This inference may be overcome if:

1) The directions are ***definite and precise***, not vague;

2) The directions are addressed by a decedent to his ***executor*** or ***administrator***, or to one who otherwise occupies the position of a fiduciary under the will;

3) Failure to impose a trust results in an ***"unnatural" disposition*** by a testator (*e.g.,* a close relative takes no interest under the will); or

4) Extrinsic evidence shows that the transferor had been supporting the alleged beneficiary ***prior to executing the instrument***, and the "beneficiary" would not have sufficient means of support absent a finding that a trust was created (*e.g.,* A gives property to B with what appears to be precatory directions to use the property for C's benefit, but evidence shows that A had always supported C, suggesting that A intended to impose enforceable trust obligations on B).

2. Trustee

Although a trustee is essential to the operation of a trust, once a trust is established it will not fail merely because of the trustee's death, incapacity, resignation, or removal. Thus, where a will names X as trustee, the trust does not fail merely because X has predeceased the testator. A successor trustee will be appointed in order to carry out the testator's intention, except in the unusual case where it clearly appears that the trust is to continue only as long as the originally designated trustee continues to serve.

a. Absence of Trustee—Testamentary vs. Inter Vivos Trusts

The refusal of a named trustee to accept an appointment or his failure to qualify, or even the complete failure to name a trustee in a will, does not defeat a ***testamentary trust*** (a trust created by a will). On the other hand, because of the necessity of a present and effective transfer in order to create a ***trust by deed*** (*see* B.1.a., *infra*), the absence of a trustee may result in an attempted ***inter vivos*** trust (a trust created during settlor's lifetime) failing for want of delivery. Such a trust fails because there has been no transfer—not because there was no trustee, for equity would supply the trustee had there been a valid delivery of the deed creating the trust.

Example: O hands $10,000 to X, telling X to invest the $10,000 and pay the income to A for life, remainder to B. X remains silent, but takes the $10,000. The law may presume X's acceptance of the trust from his acceptance of the trust property, although inaction might also be a disclaimer. The particular circumstances and inferences therefrom must be examined. If X accepts delivery of the trust property but refuses to act as trustee, a trust may still have been created if that was O's intent. In such a case, the court will appoint a substitute trustee, thereby preventing the failure of the trust.

b. Trustee Must Have Duties

An "active trust" exists when the trustee has duties. A "passive trust," one where the

trustee has no duties at all, will fail and the beneficiaries will take legal title immediately. However, in many jurisdictions the duty to convey title to the beneficiaries is enough to make the trust "active." If the duties are not spelled out in the trust instrument, the court will imply the trustee's duties if there is (i) an intention to create a trust, (ii) a res, and (iii) an identified beneficiary.

Example: T bequeaths "$600 to X, as trustee for X's child, A; the trust to terminate when A reaches age 18." Nothing is said about the trustee's duties. Therefore, the court will imply that the income is to be accumulated and the accumulated income and principal invested and paid to A at age 18, and the trust will not fail.

c. Qualifications of Trustee

1) Capacity to Acquire or Hold Title for One's Own Benefit
In the absence of a statute, anyone who has capacity to acquire or hold title to property for his own benefit has capacity to take property as a trustee. Unincorporated associations can be trustees only where they can hold title to property for their own benefit. If a partnership cannot hold title to property, a purported transfer to the partnership in trust may be deemed to be a transfer to the partners individually as trustees.

2) Administrative Capacity
Although a party may have capacity to take and hold property as a trustee, he may not have the capacity to administer it. For example, minors or insane persons may take title to property, but because their contracts or acts are usually voidable, they are generally held to lack capacity to administer the trust. Such a trustee will be removed by the court and replaced with a qualified trustee.

3) Statutory Limitations on Right to Serve as Trustee
Statutes sometimes limit the right of some persons or corporations to serve as trustees. This is particularly common in the case of testamentary trusts. Foreign corporations are often denied the right to conduct trust business in states other than their state of incorporation.

Example: T dies a resident of California. Her will bequeaths $10,000 to the Chicago Northern Bank, an Illinois corporation, in trust for B. By statute, the Chicago bank cannot serve as trustee of a testamentary trust in California, so the court will appoint another trustee.

d. Removal of Trustee
A court has the power to remove a trustee or to refuse judicial confirmation of the appointment of a trustee in a will. (Denial of confirmation will be ordered when the named trustee is incompetent or declines to serve.)

1) Grounds for Removal of Trustee
Basically, a court may remove a trustee if his continuation in office would be detrimental to the trust (taking into consideration both the settlor's intent and the interests of the beneficiaries). There are numerous grounds upon which a trustee may be removed, including the following:

a) Commission of a serious **breach of trust**;

b) Legal or practical **incapacity** to administer the trust;

c) **Unfitness** for the position (*e.g.,* habitual drunkenness, commission of a crime involving dishonesty, permanent or long continued absence from the state, or extreme old age or other practical inability);

d) **Refusal to post bond or to account**;

e) The existence of a **significant conflict of interest**;

f) The **trustee's insolvency** if the court feels that this situation jeopardizes the welfare of the trust; and

g) **Extreme friction or hostility** between the trustee and the beneficiaries, where such hostility is likely to interfere with the proper administration of the trust. However, the mere existence of friction that does not interfere with proper administration is not a ground for removal.

2) **Effect of Settlor's Knowledge of Grounds Prior to Appointment**
Circumstances that might constitute grounds for removal, such as the existence of conflicting interests, need not be acted upon by a court where such circumstances were known to the settlor at the time she created the trust. The existence and knowledge of grounds at the time the trust was created, however, are **not conclusive**, and in extreme cases a court may nevertheless proceed to remove the trustee. The terms of the trust are significant, of course, in this regard.

3) **Beneficiaries Cannot Compel Removal Without Grounds**
Absent grounds for removal, the beneficiaries cannot compel the removal of a trustee, **unless this power is granted** to them by the trust instrument. The power to remove a trustee without grounds **may also be reserved by the settlor**.

e. **Disclaimer or Resignation by Trustee**
A trustee who has not accepted the trust—either expressly, by implication, or by contracting in advance to do so—can disclaim and refuse appointment arbitrarily. However, he cannot accept a trust in part and disclaim it in part. Also, after having accepted the trust, the trustee cannot thereafter disclaim; the problem then becomes one of resignation (*see* below).

1) **Relation Back of Acceptance**
The trustee's acceptance of a testamentary trust "relates back" to the settlor's death, because the trust is treated as having been in existence from that date. Thus, it is possible for the trustee, by accepting, to become liable (in his fiduciary capacity) on tort claims arising prior to the time he accepted.
Example: T devises an apartment house to X, in trust for B. P is injured by a defective stairway the day after T's death. X accepts his duties as trustee the following day. By accepting, X becomes liable to P on the tort claim (although as discussed at VI.E.5.b., *infra*, X is entitled

take title, cannot be a trustee, and it is doubtful that it can be the beneficiary of a trust because it is not a legally recognized person.

Example: T bequeaths $100,000 to X in trust for the benefit of the Socialist Labor Party, an unincorporated noncharitable association. The association cannot take equitable title because it is not a legally recognized person, and therefore cannot be the beneficiary of a trust.

b. Incidental and Indirect Beneficiaries

Not every person who stands to benefit from the operation of a trust is to be regarded as a "beneficiary." If the trust operates only incidentally to benefit a person, that person is not a beneficiary and cannot enforce rights thereunder.

Example: If A conveys "to T in trust to pay the creditors of A," even assuming that this is a trust rather than a mere agency (there is a split of authority), it would probably be considered a trust for the benefit of A and not one enforceable by his creditors (except perhaps as third-party beneficiaries under a contract). It would seem that A could terminate the trust because he is its sole beneficiary.

1) Named Attorney Not Deemed Beneficiary

Where a trust requires the trustee to employ a named attorney for the trust, the attorney is not deemed a beneficiary and has no right to enforce a provision for his appointment. The trustee can refuse to employ the attorney, and in fact should do so, when he feels that the best interests of the trust will not be served by the appointment. However, the right to have the named person appointed as the attorney is a term of the trust presumably intended for the benefit of the beneficiaries, and the failure to make the appointment would be actionable by the beneficiaries (rather than by the attorney) if it resulted in a loss to the trust.

c. Notice to and Acceptance by Beneficiary

Notice to the beneficiary that a trust is being created for his benefit is not essential to the validity of the trust. (The failure to give such notice may, however, serve as evidence contesting an alleged present intention to create a trust.) However, the beneficiary must accept his rights under the trust. A ***trust cannot be forced*** on the beneficiary without his acceptance.

1) Acceptance May Be Express or Implied

Acceptance may be express or implied, even by silence or inaction, and the acceptance of a beneficial interest is ***normally presumed***. The acceptance, whether express or implied, relates back to the date the trust was created.

2) Beneficiary May Renounce Before Acceptance

Before acceptance, and within a reasonable time after learning of the creation of the trust, the beneficiary may renounce or disclaim his rights thereunder.

d. Definiteness of Beneficiaries Under Private Trust

To have a private trust, there must be definite beneficiaries. Otherwise, there would be no one to enforce the trust, and the trustee could appropriate the trust property for himself, which is not what the settlor intended.

1)   **Unascertained Beneficiaries**
Beneficiaries need not be identified at the time a trust is created, but they must be *susceptible* of identification by the time their interests are to come into enjoyment.

   a)   **Unborn Beneficiaries**
   An unborn beneficiary may be described in the instrument, and the trust will be valid even as to his interest. Thus, if A conveys to T in trust for B for life, remainder to B's children, the beneficiaries are "definite" even though B had no children at the time of the trust conveyance. It is sufficient that B's children would be susceptible of identification at the time their interests were to come into enjoyment (*i.e.,* on B's death).

   b)   **Determining Identities of Unascertained Beneficiaries**
   The means by which the unascertained beneficiaries are to be determined must satisfy the formal requirements necessary for the creation of a trust. They must be described in a manner that satisfies the Statute of Wills or the Statute of Frauds, although methods such as *incorporation by reference* and *acts of independent significance* may be relied upon in the same fashion that they may be relied upon to complete the terms of a will.

2)   **Class Gifts**
A private trust may exist for the benefit of members of a class, provided the class is one that is sufficiently definite. In fact, as long as the class is a *reasonably definite* one, it is permissible that the members of the class are to be selected by the trustee in his discretion, or that the property is to be held for such members of the class as the trustee finds meet certain requirements. If the class is too broad, however, the trust may be unenforceable; instead the instrument could be construed as an outright gift to the trustee or as a power of appointment.

e.   **Resulting Trust Remedy Where Express Trust Invalid**
If a trust fails for lack of a beneficiary, a resulting trust in favor of the settlor or his successors is presumed.

Example: A transfers to B by written deed, will, or declaration of trust that states A's intention to create a trust but fails to identify the intended beneficiary (or B refuses to act as trustee according to an oral agreement with A naming the beneficiary). B holds upon a resulting trust for A (or his successors). (*See* VIII.B.2., *infra,* concerning resulting trusts.) This is the result because it is clear that B holds in trust, and because the terms of the trust are not provided, the equitable interests are undisposed of and remain in the settlor.

f.   **Charitable Trusts Need Not Have Definite Beneficiaries**
The requirement of definite beneficiaries does not apply to charitable trusts, where the charitable purpose may be quite broad and the beneficiaries left for the determination of the trustee (*e.g.,* "scholarships for needy students"). (*See* III.A., *infra*, on charitable trusts.)

5.   **Trust Purposes**
Trusts may be created for any purpose that is not deemed contrary to public policy. An intended trust or a provision in the terms of a trust is *invalid if*:

    (i)   It is *illegal*;

    (ii)   Its performance involves the commission of a ***criminal or tortious act*** by the trustee; or

    (iii) Its enforcement would be ***contrary to public policy***, even though not involving criminal or tortious conduct by the trustee.

a.   Definition of Acts Contrary to Public Policy

Public policy is violated if the purpose of a trust is to: induce others to engage in criminal or tortious acts; encourage immorality; or induce a person to neglect parental, familial, or civic duties.

Example: T bequeaths a sum in trust "for A for life if he divorces B, remainder to A's children; otherwise, to C." This is probably an ***invalid*** trust purpose because it encourages divorce, which is generally against the public policy favoring marriage.

Compare: T bequeaths a sum in trust to pay for the care of minor black children whose fathers or mothers have been imprisoned as a result of conviction of a crime of a political nature. This was upheld as a ***valid*** trust, and not a trust to induce a breach of the criminal law. [*In re* Estate of Robbins, 371 P.2d 573 (Cal. 1962)]

b.   Effect of Invalidity of Condition

Where a condition is attached to an interest and the condition is held to violate public policy, the consequences of the condition's invalidity depend upon a number of circumstances.

    1)   Provision by Settlor Controls

    If the settlor provides what is to happen in the event a condition is held invalid, that will control.

    2)   Interest Relieved of Illegal Condition Subsequent

    If the settlor has made no alternative provision, and the condition is determined to be a condition subsequent to the interest to which it pertains, the condition is invalidated, but the trust remains valid and the interest is relieved of the condition. Thus, if a person's right to certain benefits would be divested upon a condition subsequent that is invalid, the benefits would continue absolutely and free of the condition.

    3)   Invalid Condition Precedent Stricken

    If the invalid condition is a condition precedent to a certain interest, upon striking out that condition the court may:

        (i)   Hold that the ***interest fails*** altogether, regardless of whether the condition occurs; ***or***

        (ii) Hold that the ***interest is valid***, regardless of what happens in regard to the condition.

The general intent of the settlor will control. Holding the interest valid is the preferred view, unless there is evidence that the settlor's probable intention is to void the beneficiary's interest altogether if the condition is unenforceable.

c. Rule Against Perpetuities

Violations of the Rule Against Perpetuities can arise in creating interests in trust. Pursuant to the common law Rule, a nonvested property interest (*e.g.*, the interest of a beneficiary under a trust) is invalid unless it is certain to vest or fail no later than 21 years after the death of a person who is alive when it is created. However, most states have adopted a wait-and-see approach or an alternative 90-year vesting period that would save the interest. (*See* Multistate Real Property outline.)

B. CREATION OF EXPRESS TRUSTS

A trust is generally created in three ways:

(i) An *inter vivos trust* may be created by a *declaration of trust* by a property *owner*, stating that he holds the property as trustee in trust;

(ii) An *inter vivos trust* (sometimes called a "living trust") is also created by *transfer* of property by the settlor during his lifetime; and

(iii) A *testamentary trust* is created by *will*.

Trusts can also be created by the exercise of a power of appointment or by a promise enforceable under contract law.

1. Inter Vivos Trusts

a. Present Declaration or Present Transfer of Trust Required

1) Declaration of Trust

A person can create a trust by declaring himself trustee for another (*e.g.*, A declares that he holds 100 shares of GM stock in trust for B). Where there is a declaration of trust, no delivery is required because the settlor is the trustee. When the trustee is another person, the property must be delivered to the trustee in order to transfer it in trust.

2) Transfer of Property

A trust can be created by the transfer of property to another as trustee. The *trustee takes legal title* upon delivery of a deed or other document of title, or upon actual delivery of manually transferable property.

3) Delivery Required

Delivery means an act that places *the trust property out of the settlor's control* (unless the settlor is to serve as trustee). A settlor may also deliver to a third person with instructions to that person to deliver to the trustee. As indicated previously, failure to name a trustee or a promise to name one in the future may indicate a lack of present intention and may prevent a delivery of the trust res.

4) Must Manifest Intent When Trust Res Exists

If a trust is not established because there is no trust res, and the subject matter of the trust later comes into the settlor's hands, a trust arises at the subsequent time if, and only if, the settlor manifests an intention **then** to create a trust.

Example: A tells B that she is leaving him $10,000 by will. Before A dies, B declares a trust of this legacy. The trust is invalid because there is no res. However, if after A dies, B in some way manifests an intention to hold the $10,000 in trust, the trust arises at that time.

b. Formal Requirements—Statute of Frauds

1) Writing Required for Trusts of Land

Most states **do not require a writing** for a trust of **personal property**. If, however, the subject matter of an inter vivos trust is **land**, a **written instrument** is commonly required under the Statute of Frauds to make the trust effective. The writing must be signed by the person entitled to impress the trust upon the property. Note that, in certain circumstances, an otherwise invalid oral trust of land may be enforced by way of a constructive trust (an equitable remedy). (*See* VIII.C.5., *infra*.)

2) Parol Evidence Rule

In most jurisdictions, evidence outside the written agreement is permitted for the purpose of showing the true intent of the parties only where the writing is **ambiguous on its face**. A few states, however, will allow the parol evidence even if the writing is unambiguous, holding that the necessary ambiguity may be created by the extrinsic evidence itself.

2. Testamentary Trusts

a. Formalities

To create a trust by will, the intention to create a trust and the other essentials of the trust (identification of the beneficiaries, the trust property, and the trust purposes) must be ascertainable in one of the ways permissible under the applicable Statute of Wills. This means that the trust intent and the **essential terms** of the trust must be **ascertained** from one of the following:

1) The **terms of the will** itself.

2) An existing writing properly **incorporated by reference** into the will (where incorporation by reference is recognized).

Example: In a will executed on July 31, T bequeaths a sum to First National Bank in trust for the purposes set forth in a trust instrument executed by T on June 30 of that same year. No trust came into being on June 30 because no res was put in the trust. T then dies. The June 30 trust instrument is incorporated by reference, and a testamentary trust by reference to that instrument is established.

    If T had amended the trust on September 14, the amendment could not have been incorporated by reference because it was **not in**

existence when the will was executed. Even so, by statute in most states the amendment is given effect under the Uniform Testamentary Additions to Trusts Act or its equivalent.

3) Facts having a substantial, ***independent significance*** apart from their effect on the terms of the will.

    Example: T establishes an inter vivos trust of $100,000 for the benefit of B on June 30. In a will executed on July 31 of that year, T bequeaths $200,000 in trust to be added to the trust established on June 30. T amends the trust on October 17. T then dies. The trust has independent significance (an inter vivos trust of $100,000). Thus, the $200,000 is added to the inter vivos trust ***as amended***, and does not become a separate testamentary trust.

4) The exercise of a ***power of appointment*** created by the will.

    Example: T bequeaths a sum in trust for the benefit of "such persons as A shall appoint by deed or will." The trustee holds on a resulting trust for T's estate until A exercises his power of appointment, and then he holds in trust for the beneficiaries appointed by A.

b. **"Secret" and "Semi-Secret" Trusts**

1) **Absolute Gift But Trust Intended ("Secret Trust")—Constructive Trust May Be Imposed**

    In the case of a secret trust, the will makes a gift, absolute on its face, to a named beneficiary. However, in reality, the gift was made in reliance upon the beneficiary's promise to hold the gift property in trust for another. To prevent the unjust enrichment of the named beneficiary (secret trustee), courts will allow the intended trust beneficiary to present ***extrinsic evidence*** of the agreement. If the agreement can be proved by ***clear and convincing*** evidence, a constructive trust will be imposed on the named beneficiary. The ***Statute of Frauds*** is not a bar because the suit is not to compel enforcement of the trust, but rather to impose a constructive trust to prevent unjust enrichment. The ***Statute of Wills*** is not a bar because the constructive trust does not operate on the will itself, but rather on the property, once it comes into the hands of the named beneficiary.

    Example: T left 14 colleges $1.6 million. Concerned about a statutory restriction on gifts to charities, T executed a codicil giving the residue of his estate to R. The will gave no indication of a trust, or that R was not to have beneficial ownership. On T's death, the gift to the colleges failed and passed to R through the residuary clause. Evidence was offered that R had promised to hold the residuary in trust for the colleges. *Held:* To prevent unjust enrichment, a constructive trust was imposed upon clear and convincing evidence that R agreed to hold the gift in trust. [Trustees of Amherst College v. Ritch, 45 N.E. 876 (N.Y. 1897)]

    a) **Promise Enforceable Whether Made Before or After Will's Execution**
        Unlike the rule applicable to lifetime conveyances (*see infra*), in the case of wills, relief is given whether the agreement to hold in trust is made before

or after the will is executed. In either situation there is ***induced reliance***—if the promise is made after the will's execution, the testator is induced not to change her will. Also, it does not matter whether the person intended to perform the agreement at the time he made his promise. All that matters is that the testator executed her will in reliance on the promise.

    b)   Compare—Attempted Modification of Gift Outside Will
If a testator executes a will making an absolute devise, then writes a note (opened after the testator's death) telling the legatee that she wants the legatee to hold the property in trust for certain enumerated purposes, the Statute of Wills prevents enforcement of the trust. No constructive trust is raised because there is no induced reliance and no unconscionable conduct on the part of the legatee. He cannot be compelled to execute the trust because no trust was created by the will.

2)   Gift "In Trust" Without Beneficiary ("Semi-Secret Trust")—Resulting Trust Implied
In the case of a semi-secret trust, the will makes a gift to a person in trust, but ***does not name the beneficiary***. The testator may have communicated the terms to the "trustee." The majority of courts have taken the position that the trust is unenforceable because of the Statute of Wills. The will does not identify the intended beneficiary, and it would violate the policy of the wills statute to permit identification by parol testimony. The gift fails for want of identification of the beneficiary. The named trustee holds the property on a resulting trust for the testator's heirs.

3)   Different Result in "Secret Trust" and "Semi-Secret Trust" Cases Explained
Why is it that in the secret trust cases (will purports to make absolute disposition) the trust can be proved, but in the semi-secret trust cases it cannot? The answer lies in who the litigants are in the two cases. In the secret trust case, the issue is between the legatee and the beneficiaries of the alleged oral promise; to prohibit proof of the legatee's promise would lead to unjust enrichment. But in the semi-secret situation, the one thing that is clear is that the legatee himself was not intended to take beneficial enjoyment; the disposition to him was "in trust." Thus, the dispute is between the intended but unidentified beneficiaries and the heirs; the "induced reliance-unjust enrichment" element is not present.

III. CHARITABLE AND HONORARY TRUSTS

A. DISTINCTIVE RULES APPLY TO CHARITABLE TRUSTS
Charitable trusts, because of their substantial benefit to society, are granted some special exemptions from the rules that apply to private trusts. In general, charitable trusts are liberally construed. The rules governing charitable trusts differ from those applicable to private express trusts in three important particulars.

1.   Must Have Indefinite Beneficiaries
To be sustained as a charitable trust, the trust, if not for a specified charitable agency, must

be in favor of a reasonably large class of indefinite beneficiaries and cannot be for the benefit of identifiable individuals. By contrast, a private trust must be for definite and ascertainable beneficiaries.

2. Cy Pres Doctrine Applicable

Where it is impossible to give the settlor's intention effect (*e.g.,* the designated charity goes out of existence), the court may redirect the trust to a purpose "as near as possible" to the charitable endeavor initially designated by the settlor.

3. May Be Perpetual

A charitable trust may last forever; it is not subject to the Rule Against Perpetuities. By contrast, all interests in a private trust must "vest" within the period of the Rule Against Perpetuities.

B. TRUST MUST BE FOR CHARITABLE PURPOSES

The purpose of a charitable trust must be one that is considered to *benefit the public.* Charitable purposes include the relief of poverty; the advancement of knowledge, education, or religion; the promotion of health; and the accomplishment of governmental purposes (*e.g.,* parks, museums, playgrounds). A purpose that limits the benefits of the trust to a particular class of the public (*e.g.,* Chicago orphans) may be charitable, but the class may not be so narrowly defined that it designates only a few individuals upon whom the settlor wishes to confer private benefits. A trust for the dissemination of ideas may be charitable even though the ultimate purpose may be to accomplish a change in present law (*e.g.,* a trust to promote the abolition of discrimination against women, tariffs, or capital punishment).

Examples: 1) A trust for disseminating the views of a *particular political movement* qualifies as educational and hence charitable because awareness of political action is deemed to be beneficial to the public. However, a trust for the benefit of a *political party* is not charitable. A fine line is drawn here. For example, a trust for the Socialist Labor Party is not charitable, but a trust to advance the doctrines of socialism is charitable.

2) A trust is charitable if its purpose *benefits the community*, even though some persons not needing charitable assistance will benefit. For example, if the trust is for widows of police officers slain on duty, it is irrelevant that wealthy widows will be entitled to share because the public as a whole is benefited by such protection for police officers' wives. However, a trust for widows of the presidents of the Elks would not be a charitable trust unless limited to needy widows, as the public as a whole is not benefited by such a trust.

3) A trust is also charitable even though *matching funds* are required (*e.g.,* $1 to the Red Cross for every $1 it raises from other sources).

Compare: 1) Where the beneficiary is a *profit-making entity* and the profits are not applied to charity, the trust is not charitable (*e.g.,* if the beneficiary is a private school that pays out profits in dividends to investors, it is irrelevant that the gift also promotes education).

2) Where the beneficiary is *not predominantly devoted to charitable objects*, the trust is not charitable. Thus, where a gift was to a fraternal order (*e.g.,* the Knights

of Columbus), it did not qualify as charitable because, even though the group was involved in charitable endeavors, it was primarily devoted to advancing social and fraternal relations among its members (noncharitable objective).

1. General Terms Acceptable

The charitable purpose may be expressed in very general terms. Thus, a direction to a trustee to apply funds for such "charitable" or "humanitarian" causes as he selects is sufficient. Where the trust was for "benevolent" or "worthy" causes, the English cases and some older cases held the trust void on the theory that "benevolent" meant proceeding from a good motive and did not limit the objects to charitable ones. Many courts now interpret the words "charitable" and "benevolent" to be synonymous, so that a trust for "benevolent purposes" will be limited to charitable objectives and be upheld. Note, however, that if benevolence is not construed to mean charitable, the trust will fail.

Example: A trust to provide gifts of money each Christmas to children in the John Kerr School has been held void because it was not limited to charitable causes; had it been for **needy** children it would have been valid. [Shenandoah Valley National Bank v. Taylor, 63 S.E.2d 786 (Va. 1951)]

2. Effect of Gift Controlling Factor

It is the **effect** of the gift to the public or a portion thereof, **not the motive** of the settlor, that controls. Thus, if S establishes a trust to build public tennis courts on land adjacent to his home, it is irrelevant that his motive was so he could use them. Likewise, it is irrelevant that a school, park, scholarship, etc., created through a trust is required to be named after the donor (*e.g.*, John Jones Memorial Park).

3. Mixed Trust

Where the beneficiaries of a single trust are both charitable and noncharitable, the trust is a "mixed trust," and the special **rules for charitable trusts do not apply**. However, two separate trusts will be found if there is some indication as to (i) how much of the corpus the settlor intended to be applied towards charitable purposes, or (ii) how long the settlor intended the corpus to be applied towards charitable purposes.

Example: T bequeaths $100,000 to trustees to distribute the income "to such educational institutions and worthy individuals as the trustees should select." This is a mixed trust and is not exempt from the Rule Against Perpetuities as charitable trusts are (*see* E., *infra*). It is void because the trustees' discretionary power to distribute income to worthy individuals can be exercised beyond the period of the rule. (*See* Wills outline on Rule Against Perpetuities applied to powers of appointment.)

4. Charitable Trust Implied When Charitable Purpose Clear

A gift "for the needy" implies that a trustee should be appointed to carry out the purpose. A gift "to the Red Cross" implies that the organization takes the property as trustee to apply it to the charitable purposes of the Red Cross. If the charitable organization is an unincorporated association unable to take title, a trustee will be appointed to administer the funds for the benefit of the organization. Of course, the trustee itself need not be a charitable organization (*e.g.*, "to Bank of America as trustee for indigent widows").

C. INDEFINITE BENEFICIARIES

Beneficiaries of a charitable trust must be indefinite. For example, a trust to assist needy migrant

farm workers meets this test, because the permissible recipients are an ***unnamed and changing class***. But if particular individual farm workers were the designated beneficiaries, even if they were very needy, the trust would not qualify as "charitable" because of the absence of an indefinite or changing group of beneficiaries. Note that the indefinite class can be quite small.

Examples: 1) A trust to assist needy children of persons convicted for participating in political demonstrations qualifies as charitable. The entire community benefits when any needy group receives necessary sustenance, education, etc.

                  2) Trusts to aid victims of a certain disaster (*e.g.*, a fire or a hurricane) are charitable even though, in a sense, the beneficiaries are a fixed group.

D.   ENFORCING CHARITABLE TRUSTS

1.   Settlor and Potential Beneficiaries Have No Standing to Sue Charitable Trustee

Because the purpose of a charitable trust is to benefit the community, the courts consider the community at large the beneficiary of a charitable trust rather than the particular individuals who happen to receive benefits from it. The settlor of a charitable trust is deemed to have no greater interest in the performance of a charitable trust than any other member of the community, and therefore may not maintain an action for its enforcement. Nor may any potential recipients of the charitable trust maintain such an action. *Note:* Under the UTC, the settlor and qualified beneficiaries (*i.e.*, current beneficiaries and first-line remaindermen) ***have standing*** to bring suit to enforce a charitable trust. [UTC §§110(d), 405(c)]

Example: S creates a trust to provide scholarships for Spanish-speaking residents of Chicago. S has no standing to bring suit against the trustee concerning administration of the trust, nor does Juanita Hernandez, who lives in Chicago and claims that she has been discriminated against in not receiving a scholarship from the trust.

2.   Charitable Trusts Enforceable by State Attorney General

In many states, the duty to enforce charitable trusts is placed upon the state's attorney general. Thus, in the above example, the settlor or Juanita Hernandez would have to persuade the attorney general to look into the matter.

E.   RULE AGAINST PERPETUITIES

Charitable trusts may be perpetual. The Rule Against Perpetuities does not apply to charitable trusts. Also, under the "charity-to-charity" exception to the Rule, the Rule Against Perpetuities does not apply to transfers where a limitation is used to shift the beneficial interest from one charity to another on the happening of a remote condition. Note carefully, however, that the Rule ***will apply to a limitation shifting the interest*** from a private use to a charitable use or from a charitable use to a private use.

Examples: 1) "To the Cook County YMCA for so long as the premises are used for YMCA purposes, and if the premises shall ever cease to be so used, then to the Cook County United Fund." The gift is valid under the charity-to-charity exception.

                  2) "To the Cook County YMCA, its successors, and assigns; provided, however, that if the premises ever cease to be used for YMCA purposes, then over to Joan Smith, her heirs, successors, and assigns." The gift over violates the Rule; the invalid interest is stricken, and the Cook County YMCA has a fee simple absolute.

3) "To Joan Smith, her heirs, successors, and assigns for so long as the land is used for residential purposes; and if the land ever ceases to be used for residential purposes, then over to the Cook County YMCA." The gift over violates the Rule; Joan Smith has a fee simple determinable and the grantor has a possibility of reverter.

F. CY PRES

Because a trust for charitable purposes may be perpetual, it often happens that the specific charitable purpose indicated by the settlor is accomplished or becomes impracticable. In such a case, where the settlor had a general charitable intent, the court will direct that the trust property be applied to another charitable purpose as close as possible to the original one, rather than permit the trust to fail and become a resulting trust (*see* VIII.B.2.c., *infra*).

1. Rationale

The idea underlying cy pres (translated, it means "as near as possible") is this: The settlor had a general charitable intent as reflected by the trust (such as the curing of disease, the dissemination of knowledge, or the promulgation of a particular religious faith). To carry out her general charitable objective, she selected this particular agency as trustee or as the beneficiary. But her general charitable intent should not be frustrated because this secondary intent (that the named trustee or beneficiary be the agency for carrying out these objectives) can no longer be accomplished. Instead, the court will select another trustee or beneficiary whose work will most closely approximate the general objectives sought by the settlor.

2. Finding of General Charitable Intent Required

Where the specified charitable use is no longer possible or practical, the court must decide whether the settlor intended the trust to fail or would have wished the property devoted to a similar use. Of course, where the settlor has provided for such a contingency, her direction controls. The fact that a gift is given "on condition" that it be used for a specific charitable purpose has not precluded a finding of general charitable intent. Where a specific intent alone is found, the trust fails and passes as a resulting trust to the settlor's successors in title. The fact that a resulting trust would be impractical because through the passage of time those entitled are numerous and would take small shares often influences a court to find a general charitable intent.

3. Selecting a Purpose "As Near As Possible"

In formulating an alternative use for the trust property, the court must determine the settlor's primary purpose, although her other purposes should be taken into account.

Example: Where funds were given to a church to build a memorial hospital for tuberculosis patients, in formulating an alternative use it must be decided which of the settlor's purposes she considered most important: the church as recipient, the memorial nature of the building, or the medical nature of the gift.

4. Compare—Equitable Deviation

Even if the court refuses to apply cy pres—because the purpose of the trust can still be carried out—it can, by exercising its equitable power, authorize equitable deviation from an *administrative term* of the trust.

Example: Assume a trust is created for the benefit of students in Greenville City High School. The city high school district is subsequently consolidated with the county high school district. Equitable deviation may be applied, extending benefits to students in all high schools in the county. (However, there is some

judicial disagreement over whether a geographical limitation is an administrative term of the trust.)

G. HONORARY TRUSTS

An "honorary" trust is a trust that is *not for charitable purposes* and has *no private beneficiaries*. Examples are trusts for maintenance of a cemetery plot and trusts for pets. These are called "honorary" trusts because there is no beneficiary who can enforce the trust by bringing an action against the trustee; the trustee is on her honor to carry out the trust. Even though not enforceable, honorary trusts are upheld in the sense that if the named trustee is *willing* to carry out the terms of the trust, she will be permitted to do so. If, however, she fails or refuses to do so, a resulting trust will be imposed for the settlor or the testator's estate. *Note:* Under the UTC, honorary trusts *are enforceable* up to 21 years by someone named in the trust instrument or appointed by the court. A trust for the care of an animal alive during the settlor's lifetime is *valid*; it terminates when the animal dies. [UTC §§408, 409]

1. Void If It May Continue Beyond Perpetuities Period

Many courts hold that an honorary trust is void if it may continue beyond lives in being plus 21 years. This creates a problem for most honorary trusts. Because the "measuring lives" that can be used for Rule Against Perpetuities purposes must be human lives (cannot use poodles, turtles, or elephants), absent special drafting to avoid the problem, a trust for the care of the settlor's dog may be held invalid. Under the "what might happen" remote possibilities test of the Rule Against Perpetuities, the dog *might* outlive anyone now alive by more than 21 years. Because the named trustee cannot be compelled to carry out the terms of the trust, she is treated as having a power of appointment, which might be exercisable beyond the period of the Rule Against Perpetuities.

2. Constructional Outs Taken to Avoid Perpetuities Problem

To uphold an honorary trust, some courts have taken these constructional "outs" to save the gift:

a. Trust Was Personal to Named Trustee

In a bequest of $5,000 "to my sister Sue, to be used by her to take care of my dear Bowser for the rest of his days," the court might hold that the trust was personal to Sue, such that Sue and only Sue could serve as trustee; when Sue dies, the trust will terminate. Because the likelihood is that Sue will outlive Bowser, the trust purposes can be accomplished, and Sue can be used as the "measuring life" for purposes of the Rule Against Perpetuities.

b. Fund Will Be Exhausted Within Period of Perpetuities

The court might stretch to find that the $5,000 bequeathed to Sue will likely be exhausted (by expenditures for dog food and veterinary bills) within the period of perpetuities; therefore, the trust will not last beyond the life in being plus 21 years.

IV. TRANSFER OF THE BENEFICIARY'S INTEREST

A. ALIENABILITY IN GENERAL

1. **Voluntary Alienation**

   In the absence of some provision in a statute or trust instrument to the contrary (*e.g.*, restriction on alienation of contingent interest), the equitable interest of a trust beneficiary is freely alienable to the extent the beneficiary can transfer other property. The transferee takes the interest subject to all conditions and limitations that would have applied but for the assignment.

2. **Involuntary Alienation**

   Except as otherwise provided by statute or as validly restricted by the terms of the trust instrument, the interest of an insolvent trust beneficiary can generally be reached in appropriate proceedings (such as a creditor's bill in equity) to satisfy the claims of his creditors. However, unless the debtor is the sole beneficiary and can presently demand conveyance of the trust property, the creditor reaches only the interest of the beneficiary and *not the trust property itself*. The basic remedy of the creditor is to sell the beneficial interest and have the proceeds applied to his claim, with the buyer at the sale acquiring the exact interest the debtor held as beneficiary. Because of the sacrifice element involved, a court of equity may refuse to order sale of an income interest and will instead require the trustee to pay the beneficiary's income to the creditor until the debt is satisfied if the creditor will be paid by this method within a reasonable time.

B. RESTRAINTS ON ALIENATION—SPENDTHRIFT TRUSTS

A spendthrift trust is one in which, by statute or more often by virtue of the terms of the trust, the beneficiary is *unable voluntarily or involuntarily to transfer his interest* in the trust. In other words, he cannot sell or give away his right to future income or capital, and his creditors are unable to collect or attach such rights. This type of trust is usually created to provide a fund for the maintenance of the beneficiary that will be secure against his own improvidence.

1. **Rights of Creditors**

   What are the rights of the creditors of an income beneficiary of a spendthrift trust? Creditors cannot reach the beneficiary's interest in the sense of selling it as a means of realizing upon and anticipating his future rights. However, the restraint on alienation does not apply to the income *after it has been paid out* to the beneficiary. Thus, the property in the beneficiary's hands after distribution is no longer protected by the spendthrift clause and is subject to the claims of his creditors. (However, the creditors have to catch the beneficiary before he spends it!)

2. **Restraint on Involuntary Alienation Only—Invalid**

   A restraint that prohibits creditors from reaching a beneficiary's interest, but does not prohibit the beneficiary from voluntarily alienating his interest, *violates public policy*. If the beneficiary could give his interest away, but his creditors could not reach it, it would violate the basic rule that creditors can reach any interest the debtor can alienate. (Nonetheless, in a few cases the restraint on involuntary alienation alone has been upheld.)

3. **Attempted Assignment in Violation of Spendthrift Provision**

   Assume that A, the income beneficiary of a spendthrift trust, has purported to assign his interests to B. An assignee in such a case cannot compel a trustee to pay. Thus, B cannot compel the trustee to pay the income to him, and the trustee may not do so over A's objection. The purported assignment does, however, operate as an *authorization* to the trustee to pay income to B, and as long as the authorization has not been repudiated by A, the trustee may, without liability, make payments to B. Such an authorization generally does not violate

the spendthrift restraint, because the trustee could pay A, who could turn it over to B. But the authorization may be repudiated by A at any time.

4. **Exception—Settlor as Beneficiary**
An important exception to the validity of spendthrift restraints is that the settlor cannot protect his own retained interests from his creditors by the inclusion of a spendthrift provision.
Example: If S transfers to T in trust to pay income to S for life, remainder to B, and the trust includes a spendthrift clause, S's creditors can reach S's right to the income just as if the spendthrift clause had not been included. *Rationale:* If this were not true, debtors could easily avoid their creditors and retain income from their property.

a. **Test for Determining Whether Beneficiary Is Also Settlor**
Sometimes it is not clear whether the beneficiary is also the settlor. *If a person furnishes the consideration for the creation of a trust, he is the settlor*, even though the trust is created by another person.
Example: If in consideration of the conveyance of Blackacre from A to B, B transfers Whiteacre to T in trust for A for life, remainder to A's children, *A* is the settlor of the trust. A's life estate can be reached by his creditors and can be assigned by him, even though the trust contains a spendthrift clause.

5. **Exceptions for Special Classes of Creditors**
Even where spendthrift restrictions are valid, in a number of states the beneficiary's interest is subject to certain types of claims such as the claims of *dependents*, the *government*, and *persons supplying necessities* (*e.g.*, a divorced wife can usually reach the husband's interest to satisfy a claim for alimony; and the federal government can reach the interest to pay taxes owing). In a few states, *tort creditors* can reach the trust assets on the theory that they, unlike contract creditors, have no means of protecting themselves against the beneficiary's actions.

C. DISCRETIONARY TRUSTS
In a discretionary trust, the trustee is given discretion whether to apply or withhold payments of income or principal (or both) to a beneficiary. This discretion relates to more than just the time and manner of payment; it actually limits the extent of the beneficiary's rights to the amounts the trustee decides to give him, with the rest going over to others eventually.

1. **Creditors' Rights**

a. **Before Trustee Exercises Discretion—Interest Cannot Be Reached**
Before the trustee exercises his discretion to make payments to the beneficiary, the beneficiary's interest is not assignable and cannot be reached by his creditors. The theory is that, because the beneficiary has no right to payment that he can enforce against the trustee, there is nothing for the creditors to reach—*i.e.*, the creditors' rights cannot rise above those of the beneficiary.

b. **After Trustee Exercises Discretion—Payments Made to Creditors**
If the trustee exercises his discretion and elects to make payments to the beneficiary, the trustee must make those payments not to the beneficiary but directly to his creditors or assignees if the trustee has notice of an assignment or attachment by the creditors, *unless the beneficiary's interest is protected by a spendthrift restriction.*

Example: T bequeaths a sum in trust to pay the income and principal to B in the trustee's uncontrolled discretion. B's creditors cannot require the trustee to pay the income or principal to them. However, by giving notice to the trustee, they can prevent the trustee from paying B until their claims are satisfied. Of course, if there is a spendthrift clause, they cannot reach B's interest in any way and the trustee can pay B if he chooses to do so.

c.   Creditors May Reach Discretionary Interest Created for Settlor
The few cases on point seem to establish the principle that where a discretionary interest is created for the settlor himself, his creditors can reach the retained interest.

2.   Beneficiary's Rights
The beneficiary cannot interfere with the exercise of the trustee's discretion unless the trustee *abuses his power.* What constitutes abuse depends upon the extent of discretion conferred upon the trustee. If the trust is a "support trust," there is more room for a court's interference because the trust has a specific purpose; but even if the trustee's discretion is uncontrolled, the court will interfere if the trustee acts in bad faith or dishonestly.

D.   SUPPORT TRUSTS
A support trust is one where the trustee is required to pay or apply only so much of the income or principal (or both) as is necessary for the support of the beneficiary.

1.   All Income for Support
A trust to "pay all of the income to A for his support" is not a support trust. When the whole of the income is to be paid to A for his support, the words "for his support" merely state the motive for the transfer. The beneficiary is not limited to amounts necessary for his support.

2.   Not Assignable
Even without a spendthrift clause, the character of a beneficiary's interest in a support trust is such that no one but the beneficiary can enjoy it; his interest is not assignable by definition. His creditors cannot reach it; that would defeat the purpose of the trust.

3.   Effect of Other Resources Available to Beneficiary
Whether the beneficiary of a support trust who has other income or resources that can be used for his support is entitled to support out of the trust fund without taking into account such other resources is a question of the *settlor's intention.* The cases are fairly evenly divided, some inferring that the beneficiary should receive his support from the trust regardless of other resources, and others inferring the opposite.

Example: T bequeaths a fund in trust to pay such income to B as is necessary to support B. It requires $25,000 a year to support B. B has $5,000 of income from other sources. The cases are split as to whether B gets $25,000 from the trust or only $20,000.

V.   MODIFICATION AND TERMINATION OF TRUSTS

A.   TERMINATION OF TRUST BY ITS OWN TERMS
A trust terminates when the duration of the trust as specified by the settlor has expired, or if the instrument specifies no termination time, when the settlor's purposes have been accomplished.

Thereafter, the trustee must wind up the affairs of the trust with reasonable promptness, retaining only such powers as are necessary to preserve the property and to distribute it to the beneficiaries.

B. POWER OF SETTLOR TO REVOKE OR MODIFY

1. Must Reserve Right to Revoke or Modify
In many states, without an *express* reservation by the settlor of a right to revoke or modify the trust, he has no such powers. *Note:* Under the UTC and by statute in several non-UTC states, a trust is *presumed revocable* unless the trust instrument expressly provides that it is irrevocable. [UTC §602(a); Cal. Prob. Code §15400]

2. Power to Revoke Includes Power to Amend
Where the power to revoke exists, it includes the power to amend. If the method of revocation is specified in the trust instrument, it must be followed. If no method is specified, any instrument showing the settlor's intent will suffice. However, an inter vivos trust usually cannot be revoked by will, unless the trust expressly so provides.

C. MODIFICATION OR TERMINATION BY AGREEMENT OF BENEFICIARIES
Most jurisdictions permit modification or termination *only if*:

(i) *All beneficiaries consent* (even a remote contingent interest in an unborn beneficiary is sufficient to preclude termination); *and*

(ii) The modification or termination *will not interfere with a material purpose* of the trust. This is known as the "*Claflin* doctrine."

1. Determining Material Purpose
The settlor's purpose in creating a trust is not always clear from the trust language. The following examples explore the problem of determining what constitutes a material purpose of the settlor:

a. Distribute Principal at Designated Age
Where a testator creates a trust to pay the income to A *until he is 30 years old* and then to distribute the remainder to him, A is the sole beneficiary. (Note, however, had the remainder provision been to A if he is living at a stated age, and if not, then to A's issue, A would *not* be the sole beneficiary.) In this case, should A be allowed to terminate the trust before he reaches age 30? Here, a court would probably say no. The primary purpose of the trust in this situation likely is to keep the principal of the property out of A's hands until he reaches the designated age.

b. Preserve Property for Remainderman
If a testator left property for life to A, remainder to B, and thereafter B died leaving his remainder interest to A, A could probably terminate the trust because it was not anticipated by the settlor at the outset that A would end up with all of the interests in the property. The purpose of the trust was probably *to preserve the property for B*. To allow A to terminate now will not obstruct a purpose of the original trust.

c. Provide for Successive Enjoyment by Life Tenant and Remainderman
The most frequent type of case follows: A has a life interest and B has the remainder,

and A and B join together to compel a termination of the trust. How does one determine what purpose the testator had in mind in creating the trust, unless clearly indicated on the face of the instrument?

Of course, the whole of the instrument and its surrounding circumstances may be considered. The general inference seems to be that a trust such as this one was set up merely for the purpose of providing for successive enjoyment by A and B; therefore, they can terminate the trust if they both agree. If there is no spendthrift provision, A can convey his life estate to B, resulting in B having the equitable fee and being able to terminate the trust. If the parties can terminate the trust by two pieces of paper (A transfers to B; B demands termination), why not let them do it with one piece (A and B demand termination)?

d. Protect Beneficiary from Own Poor Management or Judgment

However, if the settlor established a trust to protect a beneficiary from his own misman-agement or mistakes of judgment, the beneficiary would not be allowed to terminate. In the preceding example, if it is found that the settlor established the trust for A for life because he had no confidence in A's management of the property, a court should refuse termination.

Also, the presence of a spendthrift restriction will preclude the termination of a trust, even if all beneficiaries request it, because the spendthrift clause shows the settlor's purpose and manifests his lack of confidence in the judgment and managerial ability of the beneficiaries.

2. Liability of Trustee

If *all beneficiaries consent* and if the trustee is willing to comply with their request for termination, a termination of the trust and a distribution of the corpus in the agreed fashion among the beneficiaries will almost certainly leave the trustee without any liability. This is so even though the termination of the trust violates an essential purpose of the settlor. The reason for this is that there is *no one to hold the trustee liable* for his act, all beneficiaries being estopped to bring an action against him because of their consent. (However, there is slight authority to the effect that the trustee may remain liable to the beneficiaries in such a case if a spendthrift trust were involved.)

3. Role of Settlor in Terminating Inter Vivos Trust

a. Settlor's Objections May Not Preclude Termination

If the beneficiaries have a right to terminate under the above rules, the settlor's objections will not preclude their terminating the trust. Of course, the settlor's objections might be considered relevant in determining what the purposes of the trust are and whether the termination defeats those purposes.

b. Joinder of Settlor Waives Material Purpose

If under the above rules, all beneficiaries request the termination and termination is precluded only by a material purpose of the settlor, the courts generally agree that the joinder of the settlor in the request for termination will have the effect of waiving that purpose and permitting the beneficiaries to compel termination.

D. JUDICIAL POWER TO TERMINATE OR MODIFY TRUST

1. Premature Termination
A court may terminate a trust prior to the time fixed in the trust instrument where: (i) the trust purposes are *accomplished early*; or (ii) the trust purposes become *illegal or impossible* to carry out. Trusts are not to continue where such continuation will be pointless.

2. Doctrine of Changed Circumstances
A court may authorize or direct a trustee to deviate from the *administrative* terms of a trust (including permitting acts that are not authorized or are even expressly forbidden by trust provisions) if: (i) compliance with the terms of the trust would defeat or substantially impair the accomplishment of the trust purposes; and (ii) the settlor did not know or anticipate the new circumstances.

Example: T devised his *World* newspaper stock in trust for his family and directed the trustee not to sell it. The stock has declined in value over many years and the prospects for recovery are slim. A court should approve the trustee's application to sell the stock. [*In re* Estate of Pulitzer, 139 Misc. 575 (N.Y. 1931)]

a. Doctrine Cannot Change Beneficial Rights of Beneficiaries
The doctrine of changed circumstances cannot be used to change the beneficial rights of beneficiaries. For example, a court cannot permit invasion of principal for the income beneficiary where this has not been provided for expressly or by implication in the terms of the trust instrument—even though the life beneficiary may be in serious need of additional benefits and even though it appears from the circumstances that the settlor would have wished to permit invasion of principal had he anticipated the needs which subsequently arose.

However, a court may strain to find an implied power of invasion in the trust instrument. Statutes in many states give the court the power to invade principal for the income beneficiary if the court finds that support of the income beneficiary was the *primary purpose* of the trust.

b. Court Can Accelerate Vested Rights
Although a court cannot, through the doctrine of changed circumstances, change beneficiaries' beneficial rights, it can accelerate vested rights.

Example: If B is only to receive income until age 25 and then principal at that age, with no requirement of survivorship, principal can be advanced to him earlier if needed.

VI. TRUST ADMINISTRATION

A. POWERS OF THE TRUSTEE

1. Sources of Trustee's Power
The trustee can properly exercise only such powers as are expressly or impliedly conferred upon her. These include:

(i) Powers expressly conferred upon her by the ***terms of the trust***;

(ii) Powers conferred upon her by the ***terms of a statute*** or by ***court decree***; and

(iii) Those powers that are ***"necessary or appropriate to carry out the purposes of the trust*** and are not forbidden by the terms of the trust" [Rest. 2d §186].

Note: The UTC confers broad powers on the trustee, including all powers that an unmarried individual has over her own property. [UTC §815]

2. Joint Powers

Where there are two or more trustees, the traditional position taken by the courts is that all trust powers had to be exercised by ***unanimous*** agreement. However, both the UTC and the Uniform Trustees' Powers Act ("UTPA") provide that any power vested in three or more trustees may be exercised by a ***majority*** of them. Nearly half the states now apply this rule. Of course, under either rule, if there are only two trustees, they must act unanimously. Note that any action taken in contravention of the jurisdiction's rule is voidable. [UTC §703(a); UTPA §6(a)]

3. Personal Powers

Trustees' powers generally attach to the office of trustee and are not personal to the occupants originally named to that office; *i.e.,* powers usually pass to successor trustees. However, powers may be personal to a particular trustee and therefore may not pass to a successor trustee. This may be implied from the terms of the instrument and the surrounding circumstances, but courts are generally reluctant to imply such a result. The mere fact that a power is discretionary is not a sufficient basis to treat it as one personal to the particular trustee named in the instrument. Courts will consider the purposes of the trust, the nature of the power, possible special qualifications that the originally appointed trustee may have, and any other factors that appear relevant.

4. Imperative and Discretionary Powers

a. Imperative Powers

A power is "imperative" (sometimes called a "mandatory" power) where the trust terms require the performance of a particular act—*e.g.,* trustee is absolutely required to "sell all my real estate and hold the proceeds in trust for my grandchildren until they reach age 30."

b. Discretionary Powers

Most powers are discretionary in the sense that the trustee may or may not perform a particular act, as she determines in her judgment to be most appropriate. Exercise of a discretionary power is subject to judicial review to prevent abuse of the trustee's discretion. To the extent that the exercise of such a power involves a ***business judgment*** rather than a question of law or of interpretation, a court will generally refuse to interfere.

1) Effect of Giving Trustee Absolute Discretion

Where the terms of the trust provide that the trustee shall have "sole" or "uncontrolled" discretion, the trustee's power is still not wholly immune from review.

Example: T bequeaths a large fund in trust for the comfortable support of specified relatives and, on their deaths, to charity. T's will provides that the trustee has "sole discretion to determine what amounts are payable and shall not be accountable to anyone." One of the beneficiaries is living in poverty and the trustee gives her $100 a month and accumulated income. When she asks for more income, the trustee cuts her off completely. The beneficiary can sue and receive more income by court order. The clause purporting to relieve the trustee of the legal duty to account is void, insofar as it attempts to deprive a court of jurisdiction, if a beneficiary can show that the trustee is not acting in good faith, or, in some jurisdictions, that the trustee is acting unreasonably.

2) Limitation—Trustee Must Exercise Some Judgment
A court will also intervene where a trustee has completely *failed to exercise judgment* with regard to a discretionary power.

5. Implied Powers
The following powers may be impliedly conferred upon the trustee at common law, but are *expressly conferred* by the UTC. [*See* UTC §816]

a. Power of Sale
Where the trust terms neither confer nor withhold the power to sell trust property, a power of sale is generally quite readily inferred by the courts. In deciding whether to infer a power of sale, courts consider the language of the instrument, the character of the property, the purposes of the trust, and whether the property is to be transferred to the remaindermen on termination of the trust. A power of sale may be more readily inferred in cases involving personal property than in cases involving real property.

1) Directive Not to Sell
Note that the settlor can direct the trustee not to sell certain property transferred into the trust. This directive is valid, and the trustee cannot sell the property without a court order permitting the sale on the grounds that circumstances have changed so much that not selling would put the trust corpus in jeopardy (*see* V.D.2., *supra*).

b. Power to Incur Expenses

1) Necessary and Ordinary Expenses
It is generally implied that a trustee can incur expenses that are appropriate to carry out the trust purposes. She can incur such expenses as are necessary and ordinary in the management of the trust property and in keeping the property in repair, and she can employ agents and advisors where this is prudent or where she cannot reasonably be expected to personally perform certain duties.

2) Improvements on Trust Property
Courts are less willing to infer the power to make improvements on trust property, but generally improvements can be made. Improvements involve some element of investment discretion, and one might consider in relation to the propriety of a

particular improvement whether it will have the effect of concentrating investment in a particular type of property so as to be a violation of the trustee's duty to diversify investments (*see* C.2.b.5), *infra*).

c. Power to Lease
Normally, a trustee has an implied power to lease trust property on such terms and for such periods as are reasonable under the circumstances.

d. No Implied Power to Borrow Money
Under ordinary circumstances, the trustee has no implied power to borrow money on the credit of the trust estate; nor has she power to mortgage or otherwise encumber the trust property. However, in the well-drafted trust instrument, the trustee is usually given the express power to borrow and mortgage.

B. DUTIES OF THE TRUSTEE

1. Standard of Care Required of Trustee
In administering the trust, the trustee must exercise that degree of care, skill, and caution that would be exercised by a ***reasonably prudent person*** in managing her own property. ***Care*** relates to her diligence and to the efforts she makes. ***Skill*** relates to the trustee's capabilities. ***Caution*** is the element of conservatism in administering the trust.

2. Duty of Loyalty—No Self-Dealing
Absent court approval or contrary trust provision, a trustee cannot enter into any transaction in which she is dealing with the trust in her individual capacity. A trustee cannot "wear two hats," and in the same transaction represent both her personal interest and the interests of the trust estate. The concern addressed by the self-dealing rules is not that the trustee might act improperly or take advantage of the situation. Rather, the concern is that the trustee's personal interest might affect her judgment as to whether, *e.g.*, the price is a fair one, or whether the asset should be sold at all. The possible effect on the trustee's judgment as to the wisdom of the action is what makes the self-dealing transaction improper. A trustee owes a ***duty of undivided loyalty*** to the trust and its beneficiaries, and that loyalty might be tainted by her personal interest. No fraud or bad faith need be shown by the beneficiaries, and no excuse can be offered by the trustee to justify the transaction. The self-dealing rules apply to all fiduciaries, including guardians and personal representatives of decedents' estates.

a. Specific Self-Dealing Rules

1) Cannot Buy or Sell Trust Assets
A trustee may not purchase any property owned by the trust even if she pays full value, and may not sell assets to the trust even if the price is a fair one.

Example: The trust's assets include 2,000 shares of Google common stock. Determining that there is a need to diversify the trust's investments, the trustee purchases 1,000 shares of Google stock from the trust, paying the market value as determined by the NASDAQ quotes on the day of the purchase. This is improper self-dealing. If the Google stock later goes up in value, the trust beneficiaries can demand that the trustee return the Google stock to the trust and take back her purchase price without interest. (If the Google stock later goes

down in value, the beneficiaries would ratify the transaction and waive the breach of trust, in effect telling the trustee, "thanks for getting rid of that lousy investment.")

2) **Cannot Sell Assets from One Trust to Another Trust**

A trustee of one trust may not sell property to another trust of which it is also trustee. The concern of this rule is not self-dealing, but the possibility of favoring one trust at the expense of another.

Example: Trust A holds 3,000 shares of Acme common stock. Deciding to diversify the trust's investments, the trustee sells 1,000 shares of the stock to Trust B, of which she is also trustee. Even though the sale price is a fair one, this is a breach of trust—and note that the trustee is in an impossible position. If the Acme stock rises in value, the beneficiaries of Trust A can sue for the lost profits. If the stock declines in value, the beneficiaries of Trust B can sue for the resulting loss.

3) **Cannot Borrow Trust Funds or Make Loans to Trust**

A trustee may not borrow trust funds, no matter how fair the interest rate and how well-secured the loan. A trustee may not loan her personal funds to the trust, and any interest paid on such a loan must be returned to the trust.

4) **Cannot Use Trust Assets to Secure Personal Loan**

A trustee may not use trust assets to secure a personal loan, and the lender does not obtain a valid security interest if she knew or had reason to know that the assets belonged to a trust.

5) **Cannot Personally Gain Through Position as Trustee**

A trustee cannot gain any personal advantage from her position (other than compensation for serving as trustee). The trustee is accountable for any profit arising out of administration of the trust, even if the profit did not result from a breach of trust.

6) **Corporate Trustee Cannot Invest in Its Own Stock**

A corporate trustee cannot invest in its own stock as a trust investment. But it can *retain* its own stock if such stock was a part of the original trust res when the trust was established, provided that retention of the stock meets the prudent investor standard.

7) **Self-Employment Can Constitute Form of Prohibited Dealing**

Generally, self-employment is a form of prohibited self-dealing. However, extraordinary services to the trust on the part of the trustee may entitle the trustee to additional compensation. This problem may arise if the trustee renders *legal services* to the trust that are outside the normal scope of her duties and for which additional compensation is fair and appropriate.

b. **Indirect Self-Dealing—Transactions with Relatives, Business Associates**

The above self-dealing rules apply to sales or loans to a trustee's relative or business associate, and to a corporation of which the trustee is a director, officer, or principal shareholder.

c. **Duty to Account**

The duty to keep and render accounts, and to furnish information to the beneficiary or his agent at the beneficiary's request, is one way of insuring that the trustee is meeting her obligation of loyalty.

d. **Good Faith Irrelevant**

Good faith on the trustee's part or benefit to the trust is irrelevant. (For example, a trustee, acting in complete good faith and to help the trust, loans money to the trust and takes a second mortgage on trust property. When the first mortgage is foreclosed, it turns out that the trustee has made a profit. That profit must be turned over to the trust.) The policy reason for this harsh rule is that personal interest on the part of the trustee opens the door to biased judgments and thus to decisions that may not be in the beneficiary's best interests.

e. **Duty Extends Equally to All Beneficiaries**

The duty of loyalty extends equally to all beneficiaries, unless the trust instrument specifies otherwise. Dealing impartially with the beneficiaries is more difficult when the beneficiaries are entitled to successive benefits; *e.g.*, A receives income for life, B receives the trust corpus at A's death. The trustee has a duty to A to see that the trust property produces income. She violates her duty to A if the property is not income-producing. On the other hand, to carry out her duty to B, the trustee must insure that the trust property will not depreciate in value.

f. **Beneficiary's Rights in Case of Prohibited Transaction**

If a prohibited transaction takes place, the beneficiary may: (i) *set aside* the transaction; (ii) *recover the profit* made by the trustee, reduced by losses arising out of the same transaction (*see* E.1.b., *infra*); or (iii) *ratify* the transaction (which would occur when the transaction has turned out to be advantageous to the trust). Thus, the trustee bears the risk of subsequent loss, and is also required to turn over any profit where the dealings with the trust were advantageous to her.

g. **Restrictions on Self-Dealing Can Be Waived by Settlor**

The settlor of a trust can waive the rules prohibiting self-dealing by expressly conferring upon the trustee the power to act in a dual capacity. If the self-dealing rules are waived by the settlor, the trustee will not be held liable for her conduct unless she has acted dishonestly or in bad faith, or has abused her discretion.

3. **Duty to Separate and Earmark Trust Property—No Commingling**

Trust assets must be kept physically separate from the trustee's personal assets and from the assets of other trusts. (Statutory exceptions in most states permit a corporate fiduciary to hold property of trusts of which it is a trustee in a common trust fund.) In addition, trust property must be titled in the trustee, as trustee for a specific trust. For example, money deposited in a bank account must be deposited in the name of "T as trustee," and not in the name of T personally. If the trustee commingles trust assets with her own, she faces several "heads I win, tails you lose" presumptions:

a. **Property Lost or Destroyed**

If the trustee commingles trust property with her own and some of the property is thereafter lost or destroyed (*e.g.*, casualty loss, or failure of a bank), the presumption is

that the property lost was the trustee's own, and that the property still on hand belongs to the trust.

b. Assets that Rise or Decline in Value

If a portion of the commingled assets increased in value, it is presumed that those belonging to the trust increased in value; if a portion declined in value, it is presumed that those belonging to the trustee, individually, declined in value.

4. Duty to Perform Personally (Prohibition on Delegation of Trust Duties)

A trustee cannot delegate the entire administration of a trust. On the other hand, she may delegate acts that would be unreasonable to require her to perform personally (*e.g.*, mailing letters). There is no clear-cut standard for judging when delegation is proper. Should you have a question that raises an issue of improper delegation, discuss the facts in light of what a reasonably prudent person would do, the degree of discretion delegated, and whether someone with special skill is needed to do the act.

a. Investment and Management Decisions

Under the traditional rule, investment decisions could not be delegated. Under the Uniform Prudent Investor Act ("UPIA"), however, a trustee may delegate investment and management functions that a prudent trustee of comparable skills could properly delegate under the circumstances. [UPIA §9] (For an in-depth discussion of delegating investment and management decisions, *see* C.2.c., *infra*.)

b. Following Advice of Others

The trustee can seek the advice of attorneys and others on matters that she may not delegate. However, the trustee must make the decisions. If she appears to take advice without exercising her independent judgment, she may be held liable on the theory that she improperly delegated her duties.

c. Remedy

If a trustee improperly limits or surrenders her control over trust property, she becomes a *guarantor* of the fund. Her motives or the fact that the loss was not directly caused by the abdication of control will not be considered by the court. The trustee is held liable for the *amount of the actual loss* to the trust.

5. Duty to Defend Trust from Attack

Except when the trustee's examination reveals that an attack against the trust is well founded, she has a duty to defend the trust.

6. Duty to Preserve Trust Property and Make It Productive

There is a basic duty to preserve and protect the trust corpus. From this basic duty, there normally will be implied the duty to make the trust property productive, which includes the duty to invest. The duty to preserve and protect the corpus requires that the trustee exercise reasonable care to do the following (and if she has held herself out as having special skills or has been selected on account of such special skills, she will be held to exercise such skills):

a. *Collect all claims* due the trust.

b. ***Lease land or manage it*** so that it is productive; or sell it if it is not productive (but this does not apply if the trust instrument requires the trustee to convey that land to a beneficiary).

c. ***Record recordable documents*** to protect title; keep securities and funds in safe places; ***pay taxes*** on trust assets to prevent liens thereon; and ***secure insurance*** on trust properties. It is proper for the trustee to obtain insurance on trust property—including liability insurance—even though such insurance protects her individually as well as the trust estate.

d. ***Invest trust funds*** within a reasonable period of time following receipt thereof (and continuously review such investments and sell and reinvest when required). If the trustee fails to invest trust monies, she is chargeable with the amount of income that would normally accrue from appropriate investments.

C. INVESTMENTS

The majority of states have enacted a version of the UPIA, which regulates the investment responsibilities of the trustee. A few states continue to use a statutory "legal list" approach, which establishes approved types of investments for a trust.

1. Uniform Act or Legal List Are Default Rules

No matter which approach to investments a state uses, the trust terms can expand or limit a trustee's powers, including investment powers. Thus, the UPIA or legal list provisions apply ***only if there is no contrary provision in the trust instrument***.

a. Grant of Discretionary Powers

If the trust instrument provides for investments to be made "in the discretion of the trustee," it is a question of interpretation whether the trustee's investment power is enlarged beyond the powers prescribed by the UPIA or legal list.

1) UPIA Jurisdiction

In a UPIA jurisdiction, the trustee's authority to make investments "in her discretion" usually permits only those investments that satisfy the prudent investor standard.

2) Legal List Jurisdiction

In a "legal list" jurisdiction, such language is likely to free the trustee from the list and probably permits investment in a manner similar to that under the UPIA.

3) Language Strictly Construed

There is a tendency to strictly construe language that purports to enlarge the trustee's investment powers.

2. Uniform Prudent Investor Act

a. Standard of Care

Under the UPIA, a trustee must invest and manage trust assets as a prudent investor would, taking into account the purposes, terms, distribution requirements, and other circumstances of the trust. To satisfy this objective standard of prudence, the trustee must exercise ***reasonable care, skill, and caution***. [UPIA §2(a)]

1) Fiduciaries with Special Skills Held to Higher Standard

A trustee with special skills or expertise, or who has represented herself as having such knowledge, has a duty to use those skills or expertise. [UPIA §2(f)]

2) Loyalty and Impartiality

A trustee must act exclusively for the beneficiary when investing and managing trust assets, or she is acting imprudently. [UPIA §5] If there is more than one beneficiary, she must act impartially in investing and managing the trust assets, taking into account the beneficiaries' differing interests. [UPIA §6]

b. Prudence Evaluated as to Overall Investment Strategy

The UPIA is based on the modern portfolio theory of investing. Thus, each investment decision must be evaluated, not in isolation, but in the context of the ***entire trust portfolio*** (corpus) and as part of an ***overall investment strategy*** that has risk and return objectives reasonably suited to the particular trust. [UPIA §2(b)] Under this approach, an investment that might be imprudent standing alone because it is too risky can become prudent if undertaken in relation to other, more conservative trust investments.

1) Investment Performance Measured by "Overall Return"

Under the UPIA, investment returns are measured by the "overall return" concept rather than the production of ordinary income. Historically, trustees invested with the goal of generating income for the trust (*e.g.,* dividends, interest, rental income). In today's investment world, assets that generate a steady income stream (*e.g.,* corporate bonds) may decline in real value due to inflation. In contrast, many investments (*e.g.,* publicly traded common stock, stock in a closely held corporation) generate little or no dividend income, yet produce substantial profits in the form of capital gains. A prudent investor seeks overall return, not merely income. The prudent investor rule recognizes that the most effective way to provide for current income beneficiaries, as well as the trust remaindermen, may be to generate gains through capital appreciation.

2) Risk/Return Curve

Modern investment practices reflect sensitivity to the so-called risk/return curve. Returns correlate strongly with risk, but tolerance for risk varies greatly with the purposes of the trust and the relevant circumstances of the beneficiaries. For example, a trust whose main purpose is to provide support for an elderly retiree of modest means will have a lower risk tolerance than a generation-skipping trust designed to build wealth for the settlor's grandchildren. The UPIA requires the trustee to ***tailor an investment strategy*** that incorporates risk and return objectives ***suited to the particular trust***. [UPIA §2(b)]

3) Any Type of Investment Permitted

The UPIA permits a trustee to invest in ***any kind of property or any type of investment*** "consistent with the standards of this Act"; therefore, no particular type of investment is inherently imprudent. [UPIA §2(e)] The overriding concern is the risk/return objective of the investment, rather than the classification of investments as prudent or imprudent. Depending on the objectives of the trust and the circumstances of the beneficiaries, it may be prudent for a trustee to invest in

recently developed investment vehicles such as derivatives, asset-based securities, options, and commodity futures contracts.

4) **Factors Considered in Making Investment Decisions**
The following circumstances are relevant and must be considered by the trustee in making investment decisions:

(i) General *economic conditions*;

(ii) The possible effect of *inflation or deflation*;

(iii) The expected *tax consequences* of investment decisions or strategies;

(iv) The role that each investment plays within the *overall trust portfolio*;

(v) The expected *total return* from income and the appreciation of capital;

(vi) *Other resources* of the beneficiaries;

(vii) Needs for *liquidity, regularity of income*, and *preservation or appreciation of capital*; and

(viii) An asset's *special relationship* or value to the purposes of the trust or to one or more of the beneficiaries.

[UPIA §2(c)]

a) **Retention and Disposition of Assets**
Within a reasonable time after accepting the trusteeship or receiving trust assets, the trustee must review the trust assets and make and implement decisions concerning their retention and disposition, taking into account the factors listed above. [UPIA §4]

b) **Duty to Investigate**
A trustee is also required to make a reasonable effort to verify information likely to affect the investment and management of the trust's assets (*e.g.*, review audit reports). [UPIA §2(d)]

5) **Diversification of Investments**
A trustee must diversify the investments of the trust unless the trustee reasonably determines that, because of special circumstances, the purposes of the trust are better served without diversification. [UPIA §3]

6) **Reviewing Compliance with Act**
Compliance with the UPIA is determined in light of the facts and circumstances existing *at the time of the trustee's decision or action* and not by hindsight. [UPIA §8] A trustee who acts in substantial compliance with the Act is not liable to the beneficiaries even if the trust estate declines in value or produces less income than anticipated.

c. **Delegation of Investment and Management Functions Permitted**
A trustee may delegate investment and management functions that a prudent trustee of comparable skills could properly delegate under the circumstances. This provision recognizes that the trustee (especially an individual trustee) may have limited investment expertise, and that even an experienced investor may have limited expertise in sophisticated investment vehicles. The trustee must exercise *reasonable care, skill, and caution* in:

(i) *Selecting* an agent;

(ii) *Establishing the scope and terms* of the delegation, consistent with the purposes of the trust; and

(iii) *Periodically reviewing* the agent's actions to monitor the agent's performance and compliance with the terms of the delegation.

[UPIA §9(a)]

1) **Agent's Duty**
The agent has the duty to exercise reasonable care in complying with the terms of the delegation. [UPIA §9(b)]

2) **Trustee's Liability**
If the trustee exercises reasonable care, skill, and caution in selecting, delegating, and reviewing the agent's actions, she is not liable for the decisions or actions of the agent to whom the function was delegated. [UPIA §9(c)]

3. **Statutory Legal Lists**
A state's statutory legal list sets forth approved investments for trust assets. The list usually includes government bonds, first mortgages, and other conservative investments.

a. **Permissive vs. Mandatory Lists**
If the list is deemed to be "permissive," the trustee can invest in securities outside the list but incurs a heavier burden of proving the propriety of each investment when she does so. If the list is "mandatory," the trustee probably commits a breach of trust anytime she invests in properties outside the list, although the cases are not altogether consistent in this regard.

b. **List May Not Be Followed Blindly**
Under either type of statutory list, the trustee cannot blindly follow the list. The fact that a type of investment is permissible does not necessarily mean that the investment is proper. In selecting among permissible investments, the trustee must exercise reasonable care, skill, and caution. All circumstances must be taken into account, including such things as preserving purchasing power in the face of possible inflation, minimizing risks to capital, and the need to obtain a fair return on the investment. The propriety of particular investments is discussed below.

1) **Unsecured Loans and Second Mortgages**
Except for bank deposits bearing interest, an unsecured loan of trust funds is

normally an improper investment. Most states regard an investment in a second mortgage as a breach of trust in the absence of extreme or compelling circumstances.

2) Corporate Stocks
Most statutory lists exclude common and preferred stocks.

3) Land
The courts are divided on whether investment in land is permissible. Acquisition of land or other property for the purpose of resale at a profit is speculation and therefore a breach of trust.

Example: Trustee buys 1,000 acres of unimproved desert land. This is an improper investment. Not only is it speculative, but it produces no income and the trustee has the duty of making the trust property *productive*. Otherwise, the life tenant would lose his income by investments in unproductive property.

4) Mortgage Participations
Mortgage participations, under which large sums are advanced by several trusts administered by the same trustee as loans to property owners in exchange for mortgages, are increasingly upheld as proper investments—mainly because they permit a greater diversification than would be possible if a single trust fund had to make the loan by itself.

5) Investment in Mutual Funds
Historically, a trustee could not invest in mutual funds because doing so was regarded as an improper delegation of the investment duty. However, a mutual fund is a *permissible investment* under the UPIA, and statutes in several states *expressly authorize* investment in mutual funds because this produces *diversification* of investments in smaller trust estates.

6) Testator's Business
Where a testator is engaged in business at the time of his death and leaves all of his property to his executor in trust, the executor cannot properly continue the business unless authorized by the testator. She must dispose of the business and make proper trust investments, and if she fails to do so within a reasonable time, she is liable for any losses that result.

D. SUMMARY—THE FIDUCIARY OBLIGATION
The standards imposed on the trustee are harsh. The policies behind such stringent standards and remedies for their violation are: (i) deterrence of wrongful conduct, and (ii) easing the burden of proving a breach of duty, should that become necessary. Do not overlook mentioning policy reasons in your answer. Watch for a bar exam question regarding *self-dealing, diversification, improper investment*, and *offsetting* gain from one breach against loss from another. You should ask the following questions:

1. Was the act one that the trustee was *authorized* to perform under the terms of the trust and applicable law? If not, there is a breach of trust regardless of the good faith, skill, and diligence with which the trustee performed the act.

2. If the act was proper for the trustee to perform, did the trustee perform in a manner that *satisfies the standard of conduct* required of her? Did she act prudently, diligently, and in good faith, exercising the appropriate amount of care, skill, and caution of a reasonably prudent person under the circumstances?

E. LIABILITIES OF TRUSTEE

1. Enforcement by Beneficiaries
The beneficiaries may seek to have the trustee surcharged (*i.e.,* pay damages suffered by the trust) or removed from office if the trustee breaches her duties. The settlor may sue if he is also a beneficiary, but third parties may not seek to enforce the trust.

a. Prior to Breach
A court of equity will compel the trustee to perform her duties or will enjoin her from committing the breach.

b. After Breach
The trustee is liable to the trust estate for losses resulting from the breach and for any profit that clearly would have accrued to the trust but for the breach, as well as any profit made by the trustee as a result of her breach. The trustee will also be liable for interest on her liability from the time of the breach.

c. Defenses
Equity may not enforce the trust if the beneficiaries expressly or impliedly *consented* to or *joined in the breach* of trust. The beneficiary must sue within a reasonable time after the breach or he will be barred from enforcing the trust by the doctrine of *laches*. Note that the mere failure to object when the trustee commits a breach of trust does not constitute consent.

2. More than One Breach of Trust—Losses Cannot Be Offset
Where a trustee is liable for losses resulting from one breach of trust, she cannot reduce the amount of this liability by offsetting it against a gain resulting from another breach of trust.

Example: Trustee is required by the trust instrument to invest in bonds. She invests one-half the corpus ($50,000) in Green Co. stock and one-half ($50,000) in Purple Co. stock. Purple Co. stock becomes worthless, but Green Co. stock doubles in value; so there is no net loss. Even so, the trustee has been dealing with *different* portions of the trust property. The gain in Green Co. stock *cannot be offset* against the loss in Purple Co. stock. Therefore, Trustee is personally liable for the $50,000 loss in Purple Co. stock.

3. Trustee's Liability for the Acts of Others

a. Agents
A trustee is *not liable* to the beneficiaries for the acts of her agents *unless* the trustee:

1) Directs, permits, or acquiesces in the act of the agent, or conceals the act, or negligently fails to compel the agent to redress the wrong;

2) Fails to exercise reasonable supervision over the agent;

3) Permits the agent to perform duties that the trustee was not entitled to delegate; or

4) Fails to use reasonable care in the selection or retention of her agents.

b. **Co-Trustees**
A trustee is *not liable* to the beneficiaries for a breach of trust committed by a co-trustee *unless* the trustee:

1) Improperly delegated her authority to the co-trustee (one trustee cannot delegate to a co-trustee power to manage the property);

2) Participated, approved, or acquiesced in the breach by her co-trustee, or negligently disregarded her own duties of administration so as to facilitate the breach by her co-trustee; or

3) Concealed the breach or failed to take proper steps to compel redress of it by the co-trustee.

c. **Predecessor Trustees**
A trustee is *not liable* to the beneficiaries for breaches of trust committed by a predecessor trustee *unless* she:

1) Knew or should have known of the breach and failed to take proper steps to prevent further breach or to compel redress of a prior breach; or

2) Negligently failed to determine the amount of property that should have been turned over to her, or otherwise neglected to obtain delivery of the full trust property from the predecessor.

d. **Successor Trustees**
A successor trustee can maintain the same actions as could be maintained by the original trustee. She can sue third persons for damaging trust property before she became trustee, and she can sue predecessor trustees to redress a breach of trust.

4. **Effect of Exculpatory Clauses**
An exculpatory clause is one that attempts to relieve the trustee of liability for breach of duty in the administration of the trust or lowers the standard of conduct required of her. Generally, courts tend to frown upon these clauses and will construe them narrowly. An exculpatory clause designed to absolve the trustee of *all liability* will be held *void* as against public policy. Limited exculpatory clauses are valid except insofar as they: (i) attempt to relieve the trustee from liability for *bad faith, intentional breach of trust, or recklessness*; or (ii) appear in the trust instrument because of the trustee's *abuse of a confidential relationship* with the settlor. [Rest. 2d §222]

Example: The trust agreement authorizes Trustee to continue the settlor's business, and provides that Trustee shall not be personally liable for negligence. A large hole develops in the front steps of the business. Trustee is aware of this and does not remedy it within a reasonable period. Z falls in the hole and is injured. Trustee is liable because his conduct was reckless, not simply negligent.

5. **Trustee's Liability to Third Parties**

a. **Contract Liability**

Unless the contrary is explicitly provided in the contract, the trustee is personally liable to third parties on contracts entered into with them in the course of the trust administration.

1) **Indemnification Rights**

As long as the trustee acted properly in making the contract (*i.e.*, the contract was within her powers, and she acted with reasonable prudence and care), she is entitled to *indemnification*—either by paying the creditor directly from the trust property or by paying the claim herself and obtaining reimbursement from the trust estate.

2) **Reimbursement for Legal Fees**

The trustee is also entitled to reimbursement for legal fees incurred in defending suits brought against her by third parties, unless the suit arises out of a breach of duty or from some fault of the trustee.

b. **Tort Liability**

The trustee is personally liable to third parties for torts to the same extent as would be an *ordinary owner*. She is liable for torts committed by herself or her agents.

1) **Indemnification**

The trustee is entitled to indemnification from the trust if she is not personally at fault and if the tort liability is a risk that is a normal incident of the type of activity in which the trustee was properly engaged.

Example: T holds in trust an apartment house as a proper investment. T does not take out liability insurance, which is a breach of duty. A is injured when a painter negligently leaves a ladder in the hall. T is liable to A in tort. T is not entitled to indemnification from the trust because, although T was not personally at fault, the loss results from T's breach of duty in not insuring.

2) **Creditors**

If the trustee is entitled to indemnification, tort creditors can reach the trust assets to satisfy their claims.

F. **LIABILITY OF THIRD PARTIES TO THE TRUST**

1. **Property Improperly Transferred to Party Who Is Not Bona Fide Purchaser**

The trustee's transactions with third parties that constitute a breach of trust can be set aside by a beneficiary or successor trustee, provided it does not result in taking property from a bona fide purchaser. The third party can be compelled to return the trust property improperly transferred to him or to restore the proceeds or product of that property, if it can be traced into his hands.

2. **Transfer to Bona Fide Purchaser Cuts Off Beneficiaries' Interests**

A third party who acquires the legal title to trust property *for value and without notice of the trust* takes the property free of the equitable interests of the beneficiaries.

a. **Third Party Deemed to Have Notice If Knows Facts Requiring Inquiry**

The third party will be deemed to have notice of the existence of the trust if he knows of facts requiring an inquiry that, if pursued, would have disclosed the existence of the trust. If the third party knows that the property is held in trust (*e.g.*, the existence of the trust appears on the face of a document representing the property), courts have generally held that he has a duty to inquire into the trustee's authority; therefore, he will be charged with such information as a reasonable inquiry would produce. Some cases and many statutes relieve persons dealing with trustees of the duty to inquire into the propriety of the trustee's actions.

b. **Innocent Donee Is Not Liable for Damages**

An innocent donee of trust property must restore the property to the trust but cannot be held liable for damages. If the donee has exchanged the trust property for other property, he can either restore the value of the property when received or its substitute, whichever value is lower.

3. **Participation in Breach of Trust**

Clearly, a third party who ***knowingly*** participates in a breach of trust by the trustee is liable for the resulting loss to the trust estate. One who ***innocently participates*** in a breach of trust is generally not liable to the beneficiaries, except to the extent he is obligated to return property transferred to him when not protected as a bona fide purchaser.

4. **Direct Suit by Beneficiary**

Generally, the beneficiaries of a trust ***cannot*** bring an action in law or in equity against a third party who damages the trust property or is liable to the trustee on a contract. The trustee is the proper person to sue the third party. However, the beneficiaries can sue the trustee for breach of trust. The ***exceptions*** to the general prohibition on a direct suit by the beneficiaries are:

a. **Trustee Participates in Breach**

If the trustee participates with the third party in a breach, the beneficiaries can sue the third party directly. *Rationale:* The third party has directly wronged the beneficiaries by inducing the trustee to commit a breach of trust.

b. **Trustee Fails to Sue**

If the trustee fails to sue a third party liable in tort or contract, the beneficiaries can bring a suit in equity to compel her to perform her duty. To prevent multiplicity of actions, the third party can be joined in this suit.

c. **Trustee Abandons Office**

If the trustee has abandoned her office or has left the jurisdiction and a successor trustee has not been appointed, the beneficiaries can sue the third party in equity without joining the trustee.

G. **ALLOCATION OF RECEIPTS AND EXPENSES BETWEEN INCOME AND PRINCIPAL ACCOUNTS**

Assets received by the trustee must be allocated to either principal or income. For example, suppose a trust is created for A for life, remainder to B. A is to receive the income for life; at A's death, B is to receive possession of the principal. The trustee will usually credit the assets received

to principal, and credit all income earned to income. However, certain receipts are of a mixed nature (both income and principal), depending upon how they are viewed, and certain expenses are made to protect both income and principal. Thus, allocation problems occur.

1. Uniform Principal and Income Act

As previously noted, the majority of states have enacted the UPIA to enable a trustee to make prudent investment decisions without having to realize a particular portion of the portfolio's total return in the form of traditional trust accounting income. To implement adoption of this new investment regime, the majority of states have also enacted the Uniform Principal and Income Act ("UPAIA"). The Act, which applies to all trusts and estates *unless the governing instrument provides otherwise* [UPAIA §103(a)], gives the trustee or personal representative an *adjustment power* to reallocate investment portfolio return [UPAIA §104]. This adjustment power authorizes the trustee to characterize items such as capital gains, stock dividends, etc., as income if the trustee deems it appropriate or necessary to carry out the trust purposes, *e.g.*, where the income component of a portfolio's total return is too small (or too large) because of the investment decisions made by the trustee.

a. Duty of Fairness to All Beneficiaries

The trustee is under a *duty to administer the trust impartially* "based on what is fair and reasonable to all of the beneficiaries," except to the extent that the trust or the will manifests an intent that one or more of the beneficiaries is to be favored over the others. [UPAIA §103(b)]

b. Adjustment Power

If the trust describes the amount that may be distributed to a beneficiary as "income," the starting point is that the trustee must follow traditional trust accounting rules by distributing interest and dividend income, etc., to the beneficiary. If the resulting distribution effectuates the settlor's intent and the purposes of the trust, then nothing further needs to be done. If, however, the trustee determines that by distributing only the trust's "income" she is unable to comply with the requirement that all beneficiaries be treated fairly, the trustee may adjust between principal and income to the extent the trustee considers necessary. [UPAIA §104]

Example: If a trustee decides that the investment portfolio should be composed primarily of financial assets whose total return will result primarily from capital appreciation rather than dividends and interest, the trustee can satisfy its duty of fairness to the beneficiaries by allocating capital gains to the income account. On the other hand, if the trustee decides that the risk and return objectives for the trust are best achieved by a portfolio whose total return includes interest and dividend income that will provide the income beneficiary with an appropriate level of beneficial enjoyment, the trustee can decide that it is unnecessary to exercise the power to adjust.

c. Factors to Be Considered

In deciding whether and to what extent to exercise the adjustment power, the trustee is to consider the following factors:

(i) The *nature, purpose, and expected duration* of the trust;

(ii) The *intent* of the settlor;

(iii) The identity and circumstances of the *beneficiaries*;

(iv) The needs for *liquidity, regularity of income, and preservation and appreciation of capital*;

(v) The nature of the trust's *assets*;

(vi) The *net amount allocated to income* under the other sections of this Act and the increase or decrease in the *value of the principal assets*;

(vii) Whether and to what extent the trust gives or denies the trustee the power to *invade principal or accumulate income*;

(viii) The actual and anticipated effect of *economic conditions* on principal and income and effects of *inflation and deflation*; and

(ix) The *anticipated tax consequences* of an adjustment.

[UPAIA §104(b)]

d. Adjustment Not Permitted If Result Would Be Adverse Tax Consequences
The trustee may not make an adjustment if the trustee is a beneficiary of the trust, as this would give the beneficiary a general power of appointment for estate tax purposes, and the trust assets would be taxed in the beneficiary's estate. Also, an adjustment cannot be made if the adjustment power would disqualify the trust for a federal estate tax marital or charitable deduction or cause the trust's income to be taxed to the trustee under the Internal Revenue Code's "grantor trust" rules. [UPAIA §104(c)]

2. Allocation of Receipts
The Act sets out detailed rules as to how certain receipts and expenses are to be allocated between the income and principal accounts (subject to the trustee's adjustment power). In general, the allocation rules follow traditional accounting rules. Net rental income is income, as is interest on a bond or a certificate of deposit. [UPAIA §405] The proceeds of sale of a trust asset (including any capital gains or profit resulting from the sale) are principal, as are eminent domain awards for the governmental taking of property. [UPAIA §404]

a. Receipts from Entity
Money received from an entity such as a corporation, partnership, or real estate investment trust (*e.g.,* cash dividends, partnership cash distributions) is characterized as income unless the money is characterized as a capital gain for federal income tax purposes, or is received in partial or total liquidation of the entity. *All property other than money* received from an entity (*e.g.*, stock dividends, stock splits) is characterized as principal. [UPAIA §401]

b. Insurance Policies and Other Contracts
Proceeds from a life insurance policy or other contract in which the trust or trustee is named beneficiary are allocated to principal. If a contract insures the trustee against a

type of loss (*e.g.*, loss of profits from a business), the proceeds are allocated to income. [UPAIA §407]

1) Dividends from Insurance Policy
Dividends on an insurance policy are allocated to the account from which the premiums are paid. [UPAIA §407(a)]

c. Deferred Compensation—Ten Percent Default Rule
For periodic receipts from a deferred compensation plan (*e.g.*, pension or profit-sharing plan or individual retirement account), the receipt is income to the extent that the payment is characterized by the payor as income, and the balance is principal. If no part of the payment is characterized as income or as a dividend, 10% of the payment is characterized as income and the balance is principal. [UPAIA §409]

d. Liquidating Assets Such as Patents, Copyrights—Ten Percent Rule
A "liquidating asset" is an asset whose value will diminish over time because the asset is expected to produce receipts over a limited period. Proceeds from such liquidating assets (*e.g.*, patents, copyrights, book royalties) are allocated 10% to income and 90% to principal. [UPAIA §410]

e. Mineral Interests—Ten Percent Rule
For most oil, gas, mineral lease, and water right payments, receipts are allocated 10% to income and 90% to principal. [UPAIA §411]

f. Unproductive Property
Under the former law, if a particular trust asset produced little or no income, on the asset's sale, the income beneficiary was entitled to a portion of the sale proceeds under the principle of "delayed income." The objective was to compensate the beneficiary for the income the asset would have earned had it been invested more productively. Consistent with the UPIA, which looks to total return from the overall portfolio rather than the income from particular assets, the unproductive property rule was repealed except for certain trusts that are intended to qualify for the estate tax marital deduction. [UPAIA §413]

3. Allocation of Expenses

a. Expenses Charged to Income
The following expenses are charged against income: one-half of the regular compensation of the trustee and of any person providing investment advisory or custodial services to the trustee; one-half of all expenses for accountings, judicial proceedings, and other matters affecting both income and remainder interests; the entire cost of ordinary expenses (including interest, ordinary repairs, and regularly recurring taxes assessed against principal); and insurance premiums covering the loss of a principal asset. [UPAIA §501]

b. Expenses Charged to Principal
The following expenses are charged against principal: the remaining one-half of the compensation of the trustee and any person providing investment advisory or custodial services to the trustee; the remaining one-half of all expenses for accountings, judicial

proceedings, and other matters affecting both income and remainder interests; payments on the principal of a trust debt; expenses of a proceeding that concerns primarily an interest in principal; estate taxes; and disbursements related to environmental matters. [UPAIA §502]

VII. WILL SUBSTITUTES

A. IN GENERAL

If a settlor desires to transfer, at the moment of her death, property interests to a trustee and beneficiaries (or merely to a beneficiary), she must do so by a duly executed will. However, it is possible for a settlor to make an *inter vivos transfer* by which economic benefits pass at her death without the formalities of a will. The principal vehicles by which this is done are *revocable inter vivos trusts, life insurance designations*, and *bank arrangements*.

B. REVOCABLE INTER VIVOS TRUSTS

A revocable inter vivos trust avoids the costs and delays of probate and has a number of advantages over a will. The reason why the revocable trust is not a will, and does not have to comply with the Statute of Wills, is that an *interest passes* to the beneficiary *during the settlor's life*; it merely becomes *possessory* on the settlor's death. The interest can be revoked or divested during the settlor's life, but it passes subject to revocation.

1. Determining Whether an Interest Passes

Whether "an interest passes" during the settlor's life is really a conclusion derived from applying the ritual and evidentiary policies of the Statute of Wills. Where a written instrument is delivered to an independent third-party trustee, there is little doubt that these policies are satisfied. Still, certain problems remain with the revocable trust when the court is not satisfied that the policies are met.

a. Where Trustee Given Usual Powers

If a settlor transfers property to another in a revocable inter vivos trust, and the trustee has normal trustee powers, the trust is valid everywhere.

Example: S transfers to T a sum in trust to pay the income to S for life, then on S's death to pay the principal as S directs by will, and if S fails to direct, to pay the principal to C. S retains the right to revoke the trust. This is a valid trust.

b. Where Administrative Powers Retained

If a settlor transfers property in writing to another in a revocable inter vivos trust, but the *settlor retains administrative and investment control over the trustee*, it can be argued that the arrangement is no more than an agency that ceases at the settlor-principal's death. However, almost all modern cases *sustain* a revocable trust of this kind. *Rationale:* The ritual and evidentiary policies of the Statute of Wills are satisfied by the writing and delivery, even though the trustee is not independent.

c. Declaration of Trust

If a settlor declares herself the trustee of a revocable inter vivos trust, the trust might fail on the theory that the settlor is still the owner and no interest has passed to a

beneficiary. Inasmuch as any act by the settlor-trustee could be deemed a revocation of the trust, it is hard to see how any beneficiary would ever have any enforceable right against the settlor-trustee. Nonetheless, such a trust has been upheld in modern cases where the settlor notified third parties or *took some action that made clear her intention to create a trust*.

Example: S declares herself trustee of shares of stock in Bay View Corporation. The income is payable to S; the trust is revocable at any time, but if it remains unrevoked at S's death, the stock is payable to B. S *notifies the corporation* that she is holding the stock under a declaration of trust. The trust is valid.

                     If S merely wrote out a declaration of trust, which she kept in her desk drawer, and did not change the name on the corporation's books or notify anyone, probably no trust would be created.

Comment: The courts want to be sure that S *intended* to make a *binding* transfer, even though revocable. The *witnessing* of a declaration of trust may give that assurance.

2. Advantages of Revocable Trust

A revocable inter vivos trust is widely used in estate planning and has the following advantages:

a. Management of Assets

Harold has retired, and he and his wife, Wanda, do a lot of traveling in their motor home. This makes management and supervision of Harold's investments rather inconvenient, so Harold transfers his investment assets to Central National Bank as trustee of a revocable trust, to pay the income to Harold for life, then to Wanda for her life, then to distribute the principal to their descendants per stirpes. This arrangement provides for effective management of Harold's assets by a bank with investment expertise and provides the other benefits described below.

b. Planning for Incapacity—Avoidance of Guardianship

Suppose that Harold, in the above example, has a stroke and is incapacitated. If Harold had not established the revocable trust (and if Harold had not given Wanda or some other family member a "durable" power of attorney), it would be necessary to have Harold adjudicated an incompetent and a guardian appointed to manage his assets. But because Harold transferred legal title in his investment assets to the bank as trustee, the trust continues to operate for Harold's benefit without the necessity of a guardianship administration.

c. Avoidance of Probate

Suppose Harold dies, survived by Wanda and their children. Because legal title to Harold's investment assets is held by the bank as trustee, the assets are not subject to probate administration. The assets continue to be held for the benefit of Wanda (and the children) without the expenses and delays of a probate administration.

d. Secrecy

A will is a public record, but an inter vivos trust is not recorded anywhere. Secrecy as to assets and beneficiaries is thus available.

e.   **Choice of Law**
The settlor can select as trustee a person living in another state and provide that the law of that other state shall govern the trust. Local restrictions on testation can thereby be avoided—*e.g.*, by choosing a state that permits spendthrift trusts, or permits a spouse's statutory forced share to be avoided by a revocable trust.

f.   **Defeat Spouse's Forced Share?**
In almost all common law states, the surviving spouse is given a forced share (usually one-third or one-half) in the decedent's estate at death. By putting her assets in a revocable trust and removing them from her estate, a person can in *some* states prevent the spouse from sharing in her property. In most states, however, a revocable trust is deemed an *illusory transfer* and can be set aside to the extent of the spouse's forced share.

3.   **"Pour-Over" Gift from Will to Revocable Trust**
Suppose that S has created a revocable trust that will continue after her death for the benefit of her nephews and nieces. By her will, S wants to bequeath her residuary estate in trust for the same nephews and nieces. One approach might be for S's will to create a testamentary trust. However, this would result in two trusts for the same beneficiaries, two sets of trustee's fees, and added complications. Instead, S's will might provide: "I bequeath my residuary estate to the First National Bank, trustee under an instrument of trust executed by me on May 11, 2010, to be added to and administered in accordance with the trust terms, including any amendments thereto." Such a gift to an inter vivos trust (called a *pour-over* gift in practice) is valid under the Uniform Testamentary Additions to Trusts Act ("UTATA"), which has been adopted by most states. The statute thus permits the integrated disposition of testamentary assets with a trust created during the settlor's lifetime. [UTATA §1]

a.   **Trust Must Be in Existence Before or Executed Concurrently with Will**
A pour-over gift from a will to an inter vivos trust is not valid unless the trust was executed prior to or contemporaneously with the will. If the testator's will (making a pour-over gift) is executed on a Monday but the trust is established two weeks later, the pour-over gift is invalid and lapses.

b.   **Trust May Be Amendable and Revocable**
A pour-over gift by will is valid even though the inter vivos trust is amendable and revocable. The gift is to the trust as it exists at the testator's death, including amendments to the trust made after the will was executed.

c.   **Gift Is Valid Even Though Trust Unfunded During Settlor's Lifetime**
The statute authorizes pour-over gifts to a trust that is not funded with any assets during the settlor's lifetime and whose sole purpose is to receive such a testamentary gift. The statute eliminates any basis for challenging the gift on the ground that no valid trust was created during the settlor's lifetime because the trust had no res. Such a devise is valid even though the only res of the trust is the possibility of receiving a devise under a will. Another statute authorizes the payment of life insurance proceeds, employee death benefits, and similar benefits to an unfunded trust whose sole purpose is to receive such benefits on the settlor's death.

C.   **LIFE INSURANCE TRUSTS**
Life insurance trusts are usually one of the following kinds:

1. **Contingent Beneficiary Trust**

   W, owner and insured under a life insurance policy, designates the policy beneficiary as her husband, H; and if H does not survive W, to B to hold in trust for W's children. This is a *valid inter vivos trust*, which becomes effective immediately. The contingent right to the proceeds in W's children is a sufficient res. B has *active duties* in that he waits to see if H dies before W and, if he does, collects the proceeds on W's death. This is not a testamentary trust, even though B receives the proceeds, if at all, only on W's death, because the trust came into being during W's life.

2. **Assignment of Policies**

   A, owner and insured under a life insurance policy, assigns the policy to B to hold in trust for A's children. The trust can be funded (*i.e.*, other funds are transferred to B from which B pays the premiums), or unfunded (*i.e.*, the only trust res is the policy and A continues to pay the premiums). In either event, it is valid as an *inter vivos transfer*.

3. **Payable to Testamentary Trustee**

   A, owner and insured under a life insurance policy, designates as beneficiary "the trustee *named in my will*." In A's will, she names her brother B as trustee of her property for the benefit of her children. Some courts have held that this is a testamentary designation that does not comply with the Statute of Wills and, thus, fails. Others (*e.g.*, California) have held that if A has a will executed *prior* to the change in beneficiary designation, an inter vivos trust arises as soon as the beneficiary designation is made because A so intends. However, if the beneficiary designation is "the trustee *to be named in my future will*," no inter vivos trust would arise at the time of the change of beneficiary, and the attempted designation would fail as a testamentary act. In many states (*e.g.*, California), statutes have been passed *permitting* trustees "to be named in a will" to be designated as insurance beneficiaries without rendering the transaction testamentary.

D. **TOTTEN TRUST BANK ACCOUNTS**

   "Totten trust" is the name given to a bank account in the depositor's name "as trustee" for a named beneficiary (*e.g.*, "A, trustee for B"). Under such a bank account, A, the depositor, retains the passbook and continues to make deposits and withdrawals during her lifetime. B has no beneficial interest in the account during A's lifetime, but succeeds to whatever is on deposit at A's death. It is called a Totten trust because it was first recognized in *In re Totten,* 71 N.E. 748 (N.Y. 1904).

   1. **Trustee-Depositor Has Full Rights During Lifetime**

      A Totten trust is not really a trust because there is no separation of legal and equitable title. The depositor remains the owner of all funds on deposit during her lifetime and can withdraw them at any time.

   2. **Revocation by Other Lifetime Act**

      While Totten trusts are revoked by withdrawals, they can also be revoked by any lifetime act that manifests an intent to revoke.

      Example: A delivered to her attorney a document expressly revoking "all of my 'in-trust-for' accounts." This is a valid revocation, even though the revoking instrument was not delivered to the various banks. Thus, the funds passed under A's will rather than to the designated Totten trust beneficiaries. The fact that A did not comply with the method for changing beneficiaries set out

in the bank signature card was irrelevant; that agreement was solely for the protection of the bank and did not limit A's right to revoke.

3. Revocation by Will

If A leaves a will that says, "I bequeath all funds on deposit in my 'in-trust-for' savings accounts to my friend C," this is a valid disposition. C, and not the beneficiaries named in A's Totten trusts, is entitled to the funds on deposit.

a. Compare—Joint Bank Accounts

By contrast, a joint bank account with survivorship provisions *cannot* be bequeathed by a will.

Example: A deposits funds in a savings account, the signature card for which (signed by A and B) provides that A and B hold "as joint tenants with right of survivorship." A leaves a will that purports to bequeath all of her interest in the bank account to C. The gift to C is ineffective because on A's death the fund passed by right of survivorship to B.

4. Gift upon Delivery of Passbook

Most states hold that if depositor A delivers the passbook to beneficiary B, this constitutes a valid gift to B of the amount on deposit.

5. Subject to Creditors' Claims

Because the depositor has complete control over the deposit during his lifetime, he is treated as the owner insofar as his creditors are concerned. His creditors can reach the deposit while he is living, and can reach it as part of his estate on death.

6. Terminates If Beneficiary Predeceases Depositor

If beneficiary B predeceases depositor A, the trust automatically terminates. The funds on deposit belong to A absolutely and do not pass to B's estate. (The beneficiary must survive the depositor-trustee in order to succeed to the amount on deposit under a Totten trust account.)

E. UNIFORM TRANSFERS TO MINORS ACT

To provide a convenient procedure for making gifts to minors who have no legal capacity to manage or sell property, every state has enacted some version of the Uniform Transfers to Minors Act ("UTMA"), under which property may be transferred to a person (including the donor) as custodian for the benefit of a minor. The transfer may be made to a custodian by an executor, trustee, or guardian under a governing instrument (*e.g.*, will, power of appointment, or deed, for a minor beneficiary). The transfer is in the form, "To [name of custodian] as custodian for [name of minor] under the [name of state] Uniform Transfers to Minors Act." [UTMA §9] Under the UTMA, custodianship terminates when the donee attains age 21. [UTMA §20]

1. Custodian's Powers and Duties

A custodianship is not a trust. The custodian does not hold legal title to the custodial property; legal title is in the minor, subject to the custodian's statutory power. The custodian has statutory powers: (i) to collect, hold, manage, invest, and reinvest the custodial property; (ii) to pay to or on the minor's behalf so much or all of the custodial property as the custodian deems advisable for the minor's use and benefit; and (iii) to the extent not expended, to pay over the property when the minor attains age 21 (or to the minor's estate should she die before age 21). A custodian is a fiduciary and is subject to the standard of care of a prudent person dealing with property of another. [UTMA §§12, 14, 20]

2. Qualifies for Annual Gift Tax Exclusion

A custodial gift made pursuant to the UTMA qualifies for the $13,000 per donee annual federal gift tax exclusion.

VIII. TRUSTS ARISING AS A MATTER OF LAW—RESULTING AND CONSTRUCTIVE TRUSTS

A. IN GENERAL

Resulting and constructive trusts do not arise by a settlor's express declaration of trust. They are *implied* by law or *imposed* by the courts. Resulting trusts involve a *reversionary interest* when the equitable interest in property is not completely disposed of and are based on the presumed intent of the settlor. The doctrine of constructive trusts was developed by equity courts as a means of granting relief where, by a series of events, one person has obtained legal title to property (real or personal) that, the conscience of equity feels, rightfully belongs to another, the purpose being to prevent *unjust enrichment* by the person who has obtained title. Because resulting and constructive trusts are implied by the courts, the Statute of Frauds is inapplicable; no writing is necessary even where real property is involved.

B. RESULTING TRUSTS—WHEN WILL THEY BE IMPLIED?

Resulting trusts are generally of three types: (i) *purchase money resulting trusts*, (ii) resulting trusts arising on *failure of an express trust*, and (iii) resulting trusts arising from an incomplete disposition of trust assets (*i.e.*, *excess corpus*). In resulting trusts, the person who is declared by equity to be the beneficiary of the resulting trust is the one responsible for supplying the trust property (corpus). He has either directly conveyed the property to the person held to be the trustee, or he has supplied the consideration for a transaction through which the other person, the "trustee," acquired title to the property. Thus, the person who holds title did not give consideration. From this fact, equity presumes that he was not intended to have the benefits of ownership and that he should be a trustee for the person who did furnish the consideration or conveyed title to him.

1. Purchase Money Resulting Trusts

In the typical situation, there is a sale of property—real or personal—in which Y obtains legal title from the seller (*e.g.*, a deed names him as grantee; stock certificates list him as owner). But Y, who takes title, did not supply the consideration; another person, X, paid the consideration. Unless X and Y are close relatives (*see* e., *infra*), it is unlikely that X intended a gift. X probably intended to retain some benefit; thus, the courts imply that Y is trustee and X is beneficiary of a resulting trust. ("Resulting" in that it results from X having furnished the consideration.) This resulting trust is dry or passive in that Y, the title holder and trustee, has no management duties. His *sole duty* is to convey his title to X, the beneficiary. The court's decree that there is a resulting trust will likely order him to do so.

a. Form of Consideration Immaterial

The consideration given by X, the beneficiary, is usually money; but it need not be. The resulting trust will arise if the seller asks for consideration in the form of services and X supplies them, or if X gives consideration by canceling a debt owed to him by the seller. The trust will be implied whether X pays the consideration directly to the seller or deposits it with Y, who in turn passes it to the seller and takes title. *But note:*

A resulting trust arises only from consideration *given for actual purchase of the property*. This excludes money furnished by X to pay off a mortgage, to pay taxes on the land, or to build improvements on it.

b. **Time When Consideration Furnished**

For a resulting trust to arise, the beneficiary, X, must supply the consideration *at or before* the time Y takes title (*e.g.*, in the case of real property, at the time of delivery of the deed to Y). It is also sufficient if X obligates himself, prior to or at the time Y takes title, to pay the consideration (*e.g.*, X gives the seller a promissory note). Payments made by X *after* Y has taken title will not give rise to a resulting trust unless X has bound himself to make such payments.

c. **Burden of Proof on One Claiming as Beneficiary**

The burden is on X, the party claiming to be the beneficiary of a resulting trust, to prove by *clear and convincing evidence* that he supplied the consideration. He is entitled to bolster his claim by extrinsic evidence (*i.e.*, evidence outside the contract of sale of the property and the deed or other document of title given to Y) that Y had agreed to hold the property solely for his benefit. Of course, if there is an actual trust agreement between X and Y, and if any applicable Statute of Frauds provision is satisfied, the trust would be an express trust, not a resulting trust.

d. **Rebuttable Presumption of Resulting Trust**

Once X proves that he supplied the consideration, a resulting trust is presumed. However, Y, the title holder and alleged trustee, may rebut the presumption by submitting evidence that no trust was intended and that, to the contrary, the money used as consideration for the purchase was either: (i) a *gift* from X to Y; (ii) a *loan* from X to Y; or (iii) *payment* by X of a *debt owing* to Y.

1) **Presumption Rebutted by Proof of Loan**

If X loans the money to Y to buy the property, there is no resulting trust because the money belonged to Y (who had obligated himself to repay the loan) when the consideration was paid. On the other hand, if X lends money to Y to purchase property and title is taken in the name of X, the lender, there is a resulting trust in favor of Y as beneficiary because he supplied the consideration (funds he had borrowed) and yet did not receive title.

2) **Recitals as to Who Paid Consideration Not Conclusive**

A recital in the contract of sale, deed, or other document of title that X (or Y) paid the consideration is not conclusive. Extrinsic evidence will be received to establish not only how much the consideration for a transfer was, but also who paid it.

3) **Effect of Agreement Between Parties as to Nature of Interest**

The alleged trustee, Y, may *partially* rebut the presumption of a trust by showing, *e.g.*, that X and Y had agreed that X (who paid the consideration) would have only a life estate or some other interest less than a full fee simple absolute in resulting trust.

e. **Major Exception—No Trust Presumption Where Parties Closely Related**

If X (the person supplying the consideration) is a close relative of Y (the one taking

title), *a gift* from X to Y of the funds used for consideration, rather than a resulting trust, is presumed. The close family relationship between X and Y precludes any presumption of a trust.

1)   Relationships Where Gift Is Presumed
A gift, not a trust, is presumed from the following relationships:

a)   *Parent* supplies consideration, title taken in *child's* name.

b)   *Grandparent* supplies consideration, title taken in *grandchild's* name.

c)   *Spouse* supplies consideration, title taken in *other spouse's* name.

2)   Relationships Where Trust Is Presumed
The normal presumption of a trust applies where the person furnishing consideration is the *uncle, aunt, brother, sister, child, or grandchild* of the person receiving title.

f.   Second Exception—Unlawful Purpose
Equity will usually decline to imply a trust where the arrangement under which title is taken in Y's name is for an unlawful purpose, such as:

(i)   X, who supplied the consideration, is trying to keep property from his creditors.

(ii)   X is trying to avoid a tax liability.

(iii)   Y is eligible for financing (*e.g.,* he is a veteran) that X cannot get.

This exception is often justified on the ground that X cannot invoke the equitable resulting trust doctrine because he has "unclean hands." Under modern decisions, however, illegality of purpose may not always bar relief by way of resulting trust, especially where the gravity of the illegal scheme is slight compared to the unjust enrichment that will occur if Y is permitted to keep the property for which he did not pay.

g.   Third Exception—Transferee Obtained Title Wrongfully
For there to be a resulting trust, the placing of title in Y's name must be with the consent of X, the one furnishing consideration. Where Y has taken title without such consent, there is usually fraud or other wrongdoing sufficient to raise a *constructive trust* in favor of X (*see* C.2., *infra*).

h.   Pro Rata Resulting Trusts
Where X pays only *part* of the purchase price, the resulting trust in his favor will be only for a pro rata portion of the title. Thus, if the total price is $8,000 and X paid $2,000 of it, the resulting trust doctrine makes X the equitable owner of an undivided one-fourth interest. He is a co-tenant with the title holder, Y (or perhaps with some other resulting trust beneficiary who paid all or part of the remaining $6,000).

2.   Resulting Trusts Arising on Failure of Express Trust
Typically, S, the settlor, creates an express trust and conveys legal title to T, the trustee. A

problem arises when the beneficiary of the trust cannot be located or is dead, or the trust is unenforceable or void for some other reason (*e.g.*, it violated the Rule Against Perpetuities), and the settlor, S, in creating the trust, did not provide what should be done with the property in this event. Equity implies the answer: The express trust ends and a resulting trust arises in which S is the beneficiary. This resulting trust is dry or passive—T's duty as trustee of the resulting trust is simply to convey title back to S. If S is dead, his estate is the beneficiary. The property will go to his heirs or to those who took under his will.

a. Rationale
The theory of this type of resulting trust is that S must have intended the property to revert to him or his successors if the trust could not be carried out. T was intended only to manage the property and not to have full beneficial ownership. Because the trust has failed, T's duties have ended and he should not be entitled to retain title to the trust property.

b. No Resulting Trust Where Consideration Paid to Settlor
There is no resulting trust in favor of S where he received consideration for his conveyance of the property to the trustee. If someone other than T paid the consideration, a trust may result in favor of that person. If T paid it, T keeps title.

c. On Failure of Charitable Trust
Where the express trust is charitable and the designated beneficiary ceases to exist (*e.g.*, the XYZ Home for the Blind closes down operation), a resulting trust in favor of the settlor is implied *where no general charitable intent* by S appears (so that the cy pres doctrine is inapplicable).

d. Limitation—Illegal Purpose
If the express trust that fails was established by S for an illegal purpose (*e.g.*, to defraud S's creditors), equity may refuse to imply a resulting trust, allowing T to keep title plus the beneficial interest. Modern cases indicate that equity will imply a resulting trust despite the illegal scheme if the gravity of S's wrongdoing is slight compared to the unjust enrichment T would obtain if he were permitted to keep the trust property.

3. Resulting Trust Implied from Excess Corpus
A resulting trust in favor of the settlor also arises when the trust purpose is fully satisfied and some trust property remains (*e.g.*, trust was to construct a lodge building and the project is completed with funds left over). There could be a resulting trust of part of the corpus even where the trust is not completely terminated, if it is clear that the trust property is in excess of the amount needed to carry out the trust purpose.

C. CONSTRUCTIVE TRUSTS—WHEN WILL THEY BE IMPLIED?
A constructive trust is not really a trust at all. Rather, "constructive trust" is the name given to a *flexible equitable remedy* imposed by a court to prevent an unjust enrichment of one person at the expense of another as the result of *wrongful conduct*, such as fraud, undue influence, or breach of a fiduciary duty. The constructive trustee's *only* duty is to convey the property to the person who would have owned it but for the wrongful conduct. This permits the wronged party to receive the very property of which he was deprived. This remedy is especially important where property has increased in value since it was wrongfully acquired.

Proof of the facts necessary to establish a constructive trust must be by *clear and convincing evidence*.

1. **Constructive Trust Arising from Theft or Conversion**
   If Y steals or converts property from X, *title remains in X*, so there is no need to imply a trust to restore title to the owner, X. But if Y uses the proceeds of his theft to buy other property, he takes title to it. X can trace to this new property and have a constructive trust imposed upon it to prevent Y from profiting from his wrong. X is the beneficiary of the constructive trust; Y is the trustee. Y's sole duty is to convey the property to X, for once a constructive trust is declared by a court to exist, it is a dry trust and the trustee has no active management duties.

2. **Constructive Trust Arising from Fraud, Duress, Etc.**
   Where Y, by fraudulent misrepresentation or concealment (*see* Multistate Torts outline), *causes X to convey title to property to him*, X is entitled to a decree that Y holds the property in constructive trust for X's benefit. Moreover, if Y, after defrauding X out of property, sells or exchanges it for other items, the items would be the subject of a constructive trust under the tracing doctrine.

   a. **Property Conveyed to Third Party Who Is Not a Bona Fide Purchaser**
      If Y acquired title from X by fraud and conveyed title to a third party, Z, who is not a bona fide purchaser (*e.g.*, he did not pay value or he knew that Y had acquired title by fraud), the constructive trust could be imposed against Z, requiring him as "trustee" to convey title back to the victim, X.

      Accordingly, where the third party, Z, has given value to Y to acquire X's property and has acquired it with notice of fraud, the victim, X, will have a choice of two possible constructive trusts to pursue (*i.e.,* X can have Z declared constructive trustee of the original property or have Y declared constructive trustee of the proceeds from the sale to Z).

   b. **Circumstances Giving Rise to Constructive Trust**
      As in the case of fraud, a constructive trust will be declared against a party who obtains title to property by *duress, undue influence, or mistake of fact*. (Under modern decisions, even a unilateral mistake of material fact by the owner of property, causing him to convey it, is a sufficient basis for implying a constructive trust.)

   c. **Where Will Is Concealed or Fraudulent**
      Where Y conceals X's true will and takes property under a prior will or by intestacy, he holds the property as constructive trustee for the aggrieved devisees and legatees. Where a party takes title to property under a forged or fraudulent will, he is a constructive trustee for decedent's aggrieved heirs or devisees, even if he was innocent of wrongdoing.

   d. **Interference with Contract Relations**
      The constructive trust remedy is also available against a party who obtains title to property by committing the tort of interference with contract relations.

3. **Constructive Trust Arising from Breach of Fiduciary Duty**

a. **Fiduciary Relationship Defined**

One who stands in a fiduciary relationship to another person owes that person a duty to deal fairly with his property. Examples of the fiduciary relationship are attorney to client, guardian to ward, director to his corporation, trustee to trust beneficiary, executor to estate, etc. The fiduciary's duty prohibits him from taking title to property belonging to the beneficiary (at least not without making full disclosure as to its value, etc.), and from seizing for himself an opportunity to acquire property that comes to him in his capacity as fiduciary. (*See, e.g.,* the Corporations outline on the duty of a director not to "usurp a corporate opportunity.")

b. **Breach of Fiduciary Duty**

If the fiduciary violates this duty, he will be required to hold the property he thereby acquires in constructive trust in favor of the person to whom he owes the duty. Under the same principle, if an attorney advising a client on his will permits the client to leave property to the attorney without the attorney's making full disclosure of all he knows concerning its value, the attorney will, on the client's death, hold title to the property in constructive trust for the estate of the client.

4. **Constructive Trust Arising from Homicide**

If one person kills another and is convicted of murder or manslaughter, he holds any property he acquires from the victim by will or intestacy as constructive trustee in favor of whomever would have taken the property (*e.g.,* a more distant relative of the victim) had the killer predeceased the victim. (*See* Wills outline.)

a. **Where Victim and Killer Held Property in Joint Tenancy**

Where the victim held property in joint tenancy with the killer, the latter obtains full legal title to the property. However, he holds at least one-half interest therein as constructive trustee for the estate of the victim. In some states, he holds the whole fee in constructive trust for the victim's estate, less his own life estate in one-half.

5. **Constructive Trust Arising from Breach of Promise**

a. **General Rule—No Constructive Trust**

Generally, a person's mere breach of a promise is not a sufficient basis for implying a constructive trust. Thus, where A conveys real property to B on B's oral promise either to hold it as trustee for C or to convey it to C, and B later repudiates his promise, there is no constructive trust. (If the rule were otherwise, the purpose of the Statute of Frauds would be frustrated.) However, A may be able to get a constructive trust imposed in his favor. (A growing number of cases and the Restatement (Third) of Trusts say he can.) A can then convey the property directly to C. The theory is that to permit B to keep the property would result in unjust enrichment, which thwarts the purpose of the Statute of Frauds.

1) **Consideration for Promise Irrelevant**

The general principle that a mere breach of promise will not raise a constructive trust uniformly applies even where there was consideration for the promise. A may recover damages and, in some circumstances, obtain specific performance, but a constructive trust will not be imposed.

b. **Exceptions to General Rule**

1) **Breach of Fraudulent Promise—Fraud in the Inception**
   If A conveys land to B on his oral promise to hold it for, or convey it to, C, and if *at the time he made the promise B did not intend to keep it*, there is almost certainly fraud (misrepresentation) and a constructive trust will be imposed against B in favor of C (or perhaps in favor of A, who will then be able to convey directly to C).

2) **Breach of Promise by One in Confidential Relationship**
   Where the grantee who orally promises to hold the property in trust is in a confidential relationship with the grantor (*e.g.,* family relation, attorney-client, business partners), the breach of the grantee's promise is constructively fraudulent and the agreement to hold in trust may be shown for the purpose of imposing a constructive trust for the benefit of the intended beneficiaries. The grantee's promise must be proved by clear and convincing evidence.

   This is the big loophole in the Statute of Frauds. Such a confidential relationship exists not only where there is a fiduciary relationship such as attorney-client, but also where the transferor, because of family relationships or otherwise, is accustomed to being guided by the judgment of the transferee. Very seldom will a person give a deed of land to another on an oral trust where a confidential relationship does not exist.

3) **Breach of Promise Concerning a Will or Inheritance**
   Broken promises to a decedent concerning devolution of his property on death are a major exception to the general rule that a mere breach of promise is an insufficient basis for imposing a constructive trust. This exception appears to stem from the fact that when the promise is broken, the promisee is dead, unable to personally seek enforcement, and thus particularly in need of assistance from equity.

   Examples: 1) H wills all of his property to W in reliance on her oral promise to leave it to H's children at her death. H dies; W takes the property, but on her death wills it to X. X holds title as constructive trustee for H's children. (*See* Wills outline on will contracts.)

   2) A writes his will leaving his property to B (or forgoes changing a prior will in favor of B) in reliance on B's promise to hold the property for C or to convey it to C. A dies; B takes title and does not carry out his promise. The majority rule holds that B is a constructive trustee for C. The same rule applies where A forgoes writing any will and dies intestate in reliance on a promise by his intestate heir, B, to hold for or convey to C. (*See* discussion of secret and semi-secret trusts, II.B.2.b., *supra.*)

   In both examples 1) and 2), the required promise of the constructive trustee can be implied, as where the testator asks him if he will dispose of the inheritance or bequest in a certain manner and he remains silent under the circumstances, suggesting acquiescence.

3) X renders services to Y in reliance on Y's promise to leave property to X, and Y does not do so. Some courts will find the heir or devisee of Y who has taken title on Y's death to be a constructive trustee for X, particularly *where X's services are difficult to value* so that an action for quasi-contract against Y's estate is not an adequate remedy; *or where X would suffer unconscionable injury* because he has been induced to make a detrimental *change of position* in reliance on the oral agreement. Other jurisdictions hold that the Statute of Wills or the Statute of Frauds bars the constructive trust remedy in this context.

4) Promise Causing Debtor to Forgo Bidding at Foreclosure Sale
Some jurisdictions will impose a constructive trust on the promisor where his promise to buy and convey land to the debtor causes the debtor to forgo bidding at the foreclosure sale.

Example: A's land is to be sold in a foreclosure sale. B promises to buy the land for A's benefit; in reliance, A does not bid at the sale. B buys the land but breaks his promise to hold for A or convey to A. A number of jurisdictions will hold B a constructive trustee for A, on condition that A repay B's expenses, particularly where B's actual damages are hard to value. Other jurisdictions hold that the Statute of Frauds bars the constructive trust remedy under such facts.

c. Standard of Proof—Clear and Convincing Evidence
The party seeking to have a constructive trust imposed must prove the facts he relies on (*e.g.*, fraud, breach of confidence, theft) by clear and convincing evidence (*i.e.*, more than a mere preponderance).

D. OBLIGATIONS OF TRUSTEE OF CONSTRUCTIVE OR RESULTING TRUST

1. Duty to Convey Title
From the time the court declares a constructive or resulting trust to exist, *the sole duty of the trustee is to convey legal title to the beneficiary*. If he does not do so, he is responsible for the profits the beneficiary would have earned. This problem is usually avoided by the court decreeing title to be in the beneficiary at the time it finds an implied trust to have arisen.

2. Other Trustee Duties and Liabilities—Constructive Trusts
When a court declares a constructive trust to exist, such a trust is retroactive to the later of: (i) the date the trustee took title; or (ii) the time of the fraud, breach of promise, or other wrongful conduct on which the trust is based.

a. All Profits Taken from Property
From that date, the trustee is accountable to the beneficiary for all profits he has taken from the property and, if he has used it himself, its fair rental value.

b. Profits on Transactions in Breach of Fiduciary Duty
Also, from that date, the trustee owes a fiduciary duty to the beneficiary to deal fairly with the property and to make full disclosure, and he will be accountable for profits made on transactions where he breached this duty.

c. **Liability for Damage to Property**
During this period of time and prior to conveying title to the beneficiary, the trustee will be held liable for damages to the property that he willfully or negligently causes.

d. **No Duty to Invest**
The trustee has no duty to invest the trust property.

3. **Other Trustee Duties and Liabilities—Resulting Trusts**
The rules above are also applicable to trustees of resulting trusts from the date on which they arise:

a. In the case of a resulting trust on failure of an express trust, from the date the express trust becomes void, or from the date it becomes inoperable for lack of a beneficiary;

b. In the case of excess corpus, from the date the trust purpose is completed; and

c. In the case of a purchase money resulting trust, from the date the trustee takes title to the property.

4. **Tracing Assets**
The doctrine of tracing trust assets is fully applicable to dealings by the trustee of a constructive or resulting trust with trust property and the profits from trust property.

E. **APPLICATION OF EQUITABLE PRINCIPLES**
Actions in which a party seeks a declaration imposing a resulting or constructive trust were historically actions in equity. Thus, most equitable principles are applicable.

1. **Party Claiming as Beneficiary Must Not Have "Unclean Hands"**
The party claiming to be the beneficiary of such a trust may be denied relief if he has "unclean hands" (*i.e.*, his conduct regarding the matter at issue has been unlawful or inequitable, *e.g.*, if he has made misrepresentations to other parties).

2. **Party Claiming as Beneficiary Must Be Willing to "Do Equity"**
The party claiming to be the beneficiary of such a trust and seeking relief in equity must himself "do equity." For example, if the alleged trustee has in good faith paid taxes on the property, paid for sewer lines and the like, or constructed improvements on the land, the beneficiary must agree to make reasonable reimbursement to the trustee.

3. **Exception—Adequate Remedy at Law Does Not Preclude Relief**
While most equitable principles apply to actions seeking to impose a resulting or constructive trust, there is one important exception: These remedies are generally available even though the one claiming to be the beneficiary has an adequate remedy at law (*e.g.*, a suit for damages). In answering a question on constructive or resulting trusts, you should expressly state that an adequate remedy at law ordinarily does not preclude such type of equitable relief. However, as noted above, an adequate remedy in damages at law may preclude a constructive trust in two particular instances: (i) breach of oral promise to make a will; and (ii) breach of oral promise to hold property purchased at a foreclosure sale for the benefit of the promisee.

ESSAY EXAM QUESTIONS

INTRODUCTORY NOTE

The essay questions that follow have been selected to provide you with an opportunity to experience how the substantive law you have been reviewing may be tested in the hypothetical essay examination question context. These sample essay questions are a valuable self-diagnostic tool designed to enable you to enhance your issue-spotting ability and practice your exam writing skills.

It is suggested that you approach each question as though under actual examination conditions. The time allowed for each question is 30 minutes. You should spend 10 minutes spotting issues, underlining key facts and phrases, jotting notes in the margins, and outlining your answer. *If* you organize your thoughts well, 20 minutes will be more than adequate for writing them down. Should you prefer to forgo the actual writing involved on these questions, be sure to give yourself no more time for issue-spotting than you would on the actual examination.

The BARBRI technique for writing a well-organized essay answer is to (i) spot the issues in a question and then (ii) analyze and discuss each issue using the "CIRAC" method:

C — State your *conclusion* first. (In other words, you must think through your answer *before* you start writing.)

I — State the *issue* involved.

R — Give the *rule(s)* of law involved.

A — *Apply* the rule(s) of law to the facts.

C — Finally, restate your *conclusion*.

After completing (or outlining) your own analysis of each question, compare it with the BARBRI model answer provided herein. A passing answer does *not* have to match the model one, but it should cover most of the issues presented and the law discussed and should *apply the law to the facts* of the question. Use of the CIRAC method results in the best answer you can write.

EXAM QUESTION NO. 1

Otis loaned Amy $10,000 and Ben $20,000, and took their promissory notes as evidence of the loans.

Three months later, before leaving for an extended trip to Europe, Otis did the following:

•   Mailed a letter to Amy with the promissory notes of Amy and Ben enclosed. In the letter Otis stated that he wanted Amy to hold the two debts ($10,000 and $20,000) in trust for Chloe.

•   Executed and delivered to Don an unattested instrument purporting to transfer to Don in trust for Chloe such Ford Motor stock as Otis should own at the time of his death. (Otis then owned 500 shares of Ford Motor stock.)

•   Validly executed a will that contained these provisions:

1.   I bequeath $30,000 to Xavier hoping that he will let Yolanda have a good part of it.
2.   I bequeath all of my AT&T stock to Don upon trust for such purposes as I have communicated to him.
3.   I give the rest of my property to Rachel.

Prior to the execution of the will, Otis told Don that he wanted him to hold the AT&T stock that he would receive under Otis's will in trust for Chloe.

Otis was killed in an auto accident while in Europe and left no wife or descendants surviving. At Otis's death who is entitled to (1) Amy's debt of $10,000, (2) Ben's $20,000 debt, (3) Otis's 500 Ford Motor shares, (4) Otis's 300 AT&T shares, and (5) the $30,000 bequest contained in the first item in Otis's will? Explain.

EXAM QUESTION NO. 2

In consideration of the payment of $50,000 by Andrew to Beth, Beth transferred Whiteacre to Carl in trust to pay the income from the land to Andrew for his life and then to convey the land to Diane. The trust instrument provided that the interests of Andrew and Diane should not be transferable by them or subject to the claims of their creditors, and expressly authorized Carl to withhold the income.

Subsequently, Beth transferred 500 shares of Google stock to Carl in trust to pay the income to Emily until Emily should reach age 30, and then to transfer the shares to Emily.

The following year, Beth died and by will bequeathed $100,000 to First Bank in trust to pay the income to Frank for life, and then to distribute the corpus to Frank's children.

Answer the following questions:

(1)   May a creditor of Andrew, who sold Andrew a yacht, reach the income from Whiteacre while it is still in Carl's hands?

(2)   May a creditor of Diane, who sold Diane a luxury automobile, reach Diane's trust interest in Whiteacre while Andrew is alive?

(3)   Emily, age 26, asks Carl to terminate the trust of the Google stock and transfer the 500 shares to her. Carl refuses.

(a)   May Emily compel Carl to transfer the stock?

(b)   If Carl decides to transfer the stock to Emily, may Carl incur liability by so doing?

(4)   Frank and his three children, all over 21 and mentally competent, request First Bank to terminate the trust and transfer the $100,000 to them. First Bank refuses. May Frank and his children compel termination of the trust?

EXAM QUESTION NO. 3

By her will, Tara put one-third of her net probate estate into a private, noncharitable trust. Tara's will named Xander, Yvonne, and Zeke (all of whom survived Tara) as trustees. On administration of Tara's estate, Xander, Yvonne, and Zeke received the subject matter of the trust and undertook their duties as trustees. Read the following three *separate, alternative* assumptions of fact, and respond to the questions.

(1) Assets of the trust include a commercial building. Tara's will directed the trustees to sell the building and invest the proceeds of sale in corporate bonds. Xander and Yvonne wish to sell the building and invest in negotiable bonds issued by Innovative, Inc., a commercial corporation. Zeke believes the proposed investment to be imprudent, and refuses to consent to the sale and investment. Can Xander and Yvonne without fear of future liability proceed with the proposed sale and investment on the basis of majority vote?

(2) Assets of the trust at Tara's death include a parcel of unimproved land. Should the trustees retain the land as an investment?

(3) Assets of the trust at Tara's death include items that are properly disposed of by holding a public sale. Xander, one of the trustees, wishes to purchase some artwork at the sale, and tells Yvonne and Zeke that he intends to bid at the sale. What should Yvonne and Zeke do?

Discuss fully.

EXAM QUESTION NO. 4

Hal's will, duly admitted to probate, creates a $750,000 testamentary trust for the benefit of Hal's widow, Wendy. The will provides that all the income of the trust is to be paid to Wendy during her life; thereafter, the principal is to be paid over to Hal's granddaughter, Grace.

Tom has just accepted appointment as trustee of the trust and seeks your advice with respect to the following:

The trust assets include a $500,000 commercial building rented out to tenants. To maintain the property, it is essential that current repairs be made promptly, and it is desirable that certain permanent improvements (*e.g.*, replacement of wood floors with concrete) be undertaken if tenants are to be kept. Tom asks you as his attorney (1) whether costs of current repairs and taxes are chargeable against current receipts; (2) whether it is permissible to make permanent improvements, and if costs of permanent improvements are chargeable against principal; (3) whether Tom may mortgage the building to raise money for making improvements; and (4) whether Tom is personally liable on the contracts he makes as trustee. Advise Tom on the law with respect to these matters. Explain.

ANSWERS TO ESSAY EXAM QUESTIONS

ANSWER TO EXAM QUESTION NO. 1

(1) & (2) **Amy's and Ben's Debts**

The debts of Amy and Ben are held in a valid trust for Chloe. Elements of a valid trust are: a trustee, a beneficiary, trust property, an intention to create a trust, and a valid trust purpose. Here, Chloe is the beneficiary, the debts evidenced by promissory notes are the trust property, the letter to Amy clearly indicates an intent to create a trust, and nothing in the facts indicates a trust purpose that is illegal or against public policy. The issues are whether the debts are the proper subject matter of a trust, and whether Amy can serve as trustee.

The debts are a proper trust res. A trust res may be property of any type—real or personal, tangible or intangible, legal or equitable. Thus, a debt, which is intangible property, is a proper res. Amy cannot, however, be the trustee of the trust that contains her own debt as the trust res. A person cannot be the trustee of her own debt to another. Amy, as trustee, cannot sue herself, as debtor, to collect the debt. Because Amy could not carry out all of the duties of a trustee, she cannot qualify. This fact probably will not cause the trust to fail, however. A basic rule of trust law is that no trust fails for lack of a trustee. The court will appoint someone to serve as trustee, provided all of the other elements and requirements are present. The reason is that the settlor's primary intention was to create a trust to carry out the specified objectives (here to provide something for Chloe); the naming of the specific trustee was incidental to this primary purpose. The mere fact that the named trustee cannot serve is no reason to defeat the settlor's primary intention, so the court will appoint someone else to carry out the trust. There is no reason to believe that Otis intended the trustee powers to be personal to Amy; so there is no impediment to the court's naming a substitute trustee.

There is an argument that the trust of Amy's debt will fail, and thus pass by the residuary clause of Otis's will to Rachel. If, because of Amy's disqualification, Amy is considered absent or dead, the trust, being an inter vivos trust, will fail for lack of a valid delivery. This argument likely will not succeed given the fact that Otis clearly intended title to the property to pass and that it be held in trust for Chloe. The settlor's intent is the crux of the delivery requirement. It seems unlikely that an equity court will conclude that the trust fails because of a technicality; *i.e.*, that Otis did not know that Amy was disqualified from acting as trustee of her own debt.

Thus, the trust will most likely be held valid with respect to both debts, and a new trustee will be named, at least with respect to Amy's debt.

(3)   **500 Ford Motor Shares**

The Ford Motor stock passes to Rachel under the residuary clause of Otis's will. The issue is whether the unattested instrument delivered to Don created a valid trust for Chloe's benefit.

Here, the requisite intent to create a present trust was lacking, and there was no valid delivery of assets so as to create a valid inter vivos trust. Clearly, because Otis stated that he wished the trust to contain all of the Ford stock owned at his death, he intended to create a testamentary trust. A testamentary trust is created by will and must, therefore, comply with the formalities dictated by the Statute of Wills. Because the instrument delivered to Don is unattested, it does not comply with the Statute of Wills and will not qualify as a testamentary trust. Because the trust fails, the stock falls into the residue of Otis's estate, and will pass to Rachel.

(4)   **300 AT&T Shares**

Under the traditional majority view, the AT&T stock will pass to Rachel, the residuary legatee.

(Under the minority view, the AT&T stock would pass to Chloe, the intended beneficiary.) The issue is whether the bequest and prior oral instructions to Don created a valid trust for Chloe's benefit.

This is a semi-secret trust because the trust is clear from the terms of the will, but no beneficiary is named. When this happens and the testator dies, as here, while relying on an oral promise by the intended trustee to hold the property in trust, the property is distributed as follows: The designated trustee, Don, will not take the gift because on the face of the will it is clear he is given no beneficial interest. Most courts follow the rule that a resulting trust is implied for the benefit of the settlor or his estate (here, the residuary legatee). This way it is not necessary to breach the Statute of Wills by hearing extrinsic evidence of the testator's intent. Thus, the stock will be held by Don on a resulting trust for Rachel.

(5) $30,000 Bequest

The $30,000 will pass to Xavier as the absolute owner. Yolanda has no enforceable interest in the $30,000. The issue is whether the phrase "hoping that he will let Yolanda have a good part of it," creates a trust in favor of Yolanda.

Whether precatory words, such as "hope," create a trust or merely reveal what the transferor would like to have done with the property without requiring the transferee to do it, is a question to be determined from the facts. However, most courts infer from such language that no trust was intended, and that the transferor merely wished his desires to be known. This inference may be overcome by: (i) definite and precise directions, (ii) directions addressed to a fiduciary, (iii) the fact that a failure to impose a trust will result in an unnatural disposition, or (iv) the fact that the transferor had been supporting the "beneficiary." Nothing in the facts given indicates the presence of any of these factors that would overcome the inference that no trust was intended. In fact, the directions given are exceptionally vague. Therefore, the court will most likely find that there is no trust, and Xavier takes the $30,000 free and clear.

ANSWER TO EXAM QUESTION NO. 2

(1) Andrew's Creditor

Andrew's creditor can reach the income from Whiteacre while it is still in Carl's hands. The issue is whether a beneficiary who furnished the consideration for the creation of a spendthrift trust can protect his interest in the trust from his creditors.

A spendthrift trust is one in which a valid restraint on alienation is imposed, expressly or impliedly, by the terms of the trust, providing that the beneficiary cannot transfer his interest voluntarily and that his creditors cannot reach it for the satisfaction of their claims. Thus, the beneficiary cannot sell or give away his right to future income, and his creditors cannot reach these rights. However, the settlor of a trust cannot protect his own interests from his creditors by the inclusion of a spendthrift provision. If a person furnishes the consideration for the creation of a trust, he is the settlor, even though the trust is created by another person.

Here, the trust instrument provides that the interests of Andrew and Diane cannot be transferred by them or subject to the claims of their creditors. Thus, this is a spendthrift trust. The facts state that Andrew gave Beth $50,000 in consideration for the creation of this trust. Therefore, Andrew is the settlor of this trust. As settlor, Andrew cannot use an otherwise valid spendthrift provision to protect his own interest. Thus, the spendthrift provision is invalid as it pertains to Andrew, and Andrew's creditor can reach the income of the trust.

(2) Diane's Creditor

Diane's creditor probably cannot reach Diane's interest in the trust while Andrew is alive. The issue is whether a creditor can reach the remainder interest in a spendthrift trust.

The trust in this case states that the income from Whiteacre goes to Andrew for his life, and then Whiteacre passes to Diane. Therefore, Diane has an equitable remainder interest. Because the majority of courts uphold the validity of a spendthrift restriction on an equitable remainder, Diane's creditor probably will not be able to reach Diane's interest in the trust while Andrew is alive.

(3) Termination of Trust by Emily

(a) **Material Purpose:** Emily may not compel Carl to transfer the Google stock to her. The issue is whether Emily, as the sole beneficiary, has the power to terminate the trust.

The majority view permits termination of a trust by a beneficiary only if: (i) all beneficiaries are in existence and consent, and (ii) the termination will not interfere with a material purpose of the settlor. Because Emily is the only beneficiary and she wishes to terminate the trust, clearly the first requirement is satisfied. The next step is to determine Beth's purpose in establishing the trust. When a settlor creates a trust to pay the income to an individual until that individual reaches a designated age and then to distribute the principal to that same person, the court will not allow termination by the sole beneficiary. The reason is that the primary purpose of the trust in this situation must be to keep the principal of the property out of the beneficiary's hands until she reaches the designated age. Because Emily is not to receive the principal of this trust until she reaches age 30, the court will assume that keeping the stock out of Emily's hands until that time was a material purpose of Beth. Thus, Emily will not be able to compel Carl to distribute the stock.

Note that the answer would change if Beth were to join Emily in asking that the trust be terminated. If all beneficiaries request the termination of the trust and termination would be precluded only by a material purpose of the settlor, the courts generally agree that the joinder of the settlor in the request for termination will waive the purpose and permit the beneficiaries to compel termination.

(b) **Carl's Liability:** Carl would not be liable if he transfers the stock to Emily. The issue is whether the trustee is liable for the early termination of the trust.

If all beneficiaries consent and the trustee is willing to comply with their request for termination, a termination of the trust and a distribution of the corpus in the agreed fashion among the beneficiaries will leave the trustee without any liability. This is so even though the termination of the trust would violate an essential purpose of the settlor. Because Emily, the only beneficiary of the trust, wishes to terminate the trust, Carl, the trustee, will not incur liability by so terminating. There is no one to hold the trustee liable for his act, since Emily is estopped from bringing an action because of her consent.

(4) Termination of Trust by Frank and His Three Children

Frank and his now living children cannot compel the termination of the trust. The issue is whether a trust can be terminated without the consent of a possible or unborn beneficiary.

As discussed above, *all* beneficiaries must consent to the termination of the trust. The facts state that the trust will pay income to Frank for life, corpus to Frank's children. Because Frank is still alive, he can have more children. Thus, the possibility of an unborn beneficiary precludes the consent of *all* beneficiaries. Because *all* potential beneficiaries cannot consent to the trust's termination, Frank and his now living children cannot compel the termination of the trust.

ANSWER TO EXAM QUESTION NO. 3

(1) Commercial Building

Whether Xander and Yvonne may without fear of future liability proceed with the proposed sale

and investment on the basis of majority vote depends on the law followed by the jurisdiction regarding the exercise of joint powers.

In many states, investment decisions by co-trustees must be ***unanimous*** unless there is evidence of an intent to the contrary by the settlor. In other states and under the Uniform Trust Code ("UTC"), however, trust powers may be exercised by a ***majority*** of trustees. However, even in states that require unanimity, if a co-trustee's continued presence is hindering the purposes of the trust, the other trustees may be able to obtain a court order removing the co-trustee and appointing a substitute trustee.

Here Tara, as settlor, expressly directed the trustees to sell the commercial building and invest the sale proceeds in corporate bonds. That is exactly what Xander and Yvonne propose to do. Unless Zeke's objection is to these particular bonds, Xander and Yvonne are on firm ground in arguing that Zeke is hindering the purpose of the trust and therefore should be removed.

(2) Unimproved Land

The trustees probably should not retain the parcel of unimproved land as an investment. The issue is whether retaining unimproved land as a trust asset is prudent.

Trustees of a trust are under a duty to maximize the profitability of trust assets. Most states follow some form of the "prudent investor" rule, whereby a trustee must exercise that degree of skill, judgment, and care that persons of prudence would, by considering the purpose, terms, distribution requirements, and other circumstances of the trust.

The trustees have a duty to use reasonable care and skill to provide a reasonable rate of return from each and every trust asset. If land is involved, the trustees are under a duty to lease or manage the property so as to produce income. If the land cannot be made productive (and the trust instrument does not require its retention), the trustees' duty to the income beneficiaries obligates them to sell within a reasonable time and invest the proceeds more prudently.

Here, unless the trust requires the trustees to retain the unimproved land or it is not too speculative to anticipate the unimproved land producing income (*e.g.*, through the lease of mineral interests), retaining the land would be a breach of their duty to make the trust property productive.

(3) Artwork

Yvonne and Zeke must take the appropriate steps to avoid liability for Xander's self-dealing. The issue is trustees' liability to the beneficiaries for a breach of trust committed by a co-trustee.

A trustee has a duty of loyalty, which requires the trustee to administer the trust property according to the interest of the beneficiaries alone. This duty prohibits the trustee from placing himself in a position in which a conflict of interest might arise. Thus, a trustee cannot purchase trust property. A prohibited transaction is not made permissible because it takes place at a public sale. Here, if trustee Xander bids on artwork at the public sale, he breaches his fiduciary obligation to the trust beneficiaries not to engage in self-dealing.

Yvonne and Zeke should try to dissuade Xander from buying the artwork. If that fails, they should refuse to join in any transfer to Xander if Xander is successful in bidding at the sale. A transfer by less than all of the trustees (or in some jurisdictions, less than a majority) is voidable. They could also notify the beneficiaries and the court of Xander's actions. Xander's purchase of trust assets is a breach of trust and, thus, grounds for removal.

If Xander purchases the artwork, the beneficiaries may (i) set aside the transaction, (ii) recover the profit made by Xander, or (iii) affirm the transaction. Yvonne and Zeke are not liable for Xander's breach of trust unless they participate, approve, or acquiesce in the breach; negligently disregard their own duties of administration so as to facilitate the breach; or conceal the breach or fail to seek proper redress by Xander.

ANSWER TO EXAM QUESTION NO. 4

A trustee is under a fiduciary duty in the management of trust assets to insure the security and fairness of its administration. The trustee must use the same degree of judgment, skill, and care as would a "prudent investor" in the management of the trust assets. Unless otherwise stated in the trust instrument, a trustee must not only preserve the trust assets but must also use the trust property in a productive manner. The trustee is responsible for protecting the interest of both the life income beneficiary and the principal beneficiary. Thus, in this case, the trustee, Tom, has a duty to provide income to Wendy and to protect the trust res for Grace.

(1) Current Repairs and Taxes

The expense of making the current repairs and paying the taxes is chargeable to the income interest of the trust. At issue is the allocation of ordinary expenses between the income and principal accounts.

Under the Uniform Principal and Income Act ("UPAIA"), when the trustee incurs "ordinary expenses" in the administration of the res they are chargeable to the income interest. These expenses include ordinary repairs and maintenance, taxes assessed upon the principal, insurance premiums, and the like. While the holder of a life estate is never required to make repairs upon the property of the estate, the same does not hold true for a trustee of a life estate.

Here, the trustee is directed by the trust instrument to provide income to Wendy, a direction that can be followed only if the building is productive, *i.e.*, if the tenants pay rent. If the repairs to the building are not made and the building becomes uninhabitable, then the purpose of the trust is frustrated. The same holds true for the current assessed taxes on the premises during Wendy's life estate. Thus, in order to maintain the purpose of the income trust, ordinary repairs must be made and property taxes must be paid; they are thus chargeable to the income interests. In addition, the rents collected from the tenants in the building are deemed income payable to Wendy under the trust.

(2) Permanent Improvements

The costs of making the permanent improvements to the res are chargeable to the principal. At issue is the allocation of extraordinary expenses between the income and principal accounts.

Under the UPAIA, when extraordinary expenses or repairs are incurred for the purpose of making a capital improvement to the trust property, such costs are chargeable against principal.

In this case, Tom wishes to make improvements to the building that will preserve and possibly increase the value of the property. This is consistent with the duty of the trustee and the intention of the settlor. Accordingly, Tom may make the permanent improvements to the trust property and charge the expense to principal, but if the improvements are likely to depreciate, they are amortized out of income over the expected life of the improvement so that the principal account is paid back. Additionally, Grace is entitled to the full purchase price upon the sale of the property.

(3) Mortgage

With court approval, Tom may mortgage the building to raise money for making improvements. At issue are a trustee's implied powers.

Unless expressly provided by the trust terms, a trustee generally has no power to mortgage trust property. (If the jurisdiction has adopted the UTC, the trustee has the express power to encumber trust assets.) There may be situations where the purposes and circumstances of the trust may make it appropriate to imply the power to mortgage. In these cases, a court may authorize the trustee to mortgage if necessary to preserve the trust estate and it is consistent with the settlor's probable intent. Therefore, the court will probably authorize Tom to mortgage the property if it is necessary to preserve the building and the money for the improvements cannot be obtained in any other way.

(4) Tom's Liability

Tom is personally liable on the contracts he makes as trustee. At issue is a trustee's liability to third parties.

The trustee, as holder of the legal title in the trust property, is personally liable on contracts entered into on behalf of the trust. When the trustee acts in good faith and within the scope of his duties, he is entitled to indemnification from the trust. Thus, Tom is personally liable on all contracts entered into on behalf of the trust because he is the legal owner of the property; however, he may be entitled to indemnification from the trust estate.

Wills

WILLS

TABLE OF CONTENTS

I. INTRODUCTION

A. HISTORICAL BACKGROUND

Historically, real property and personal property were treated differently (the law relating to real property originated with the common law courts, while the law relating to personal property originated with the ecclesiastical courts). The modern trend is to eliminate any differences in the treatment of real and personal property, but some distinctions still exist in many jurisdictions. The vocabulary of intestate succession and wills also has a historical basis.

B. TERMINOLOGY

Although the distinctions between many of these terms have now been blurred (*e.g.*, any dispository clause in a will may be termed a "devise"), the following list of terms is helpful in understanding any discussion of the passing of property at death.

1. When property passes by *intestate succession*:

   a. The decedent is the "intestate";

   b. The person entitled to property is the "heir" (who takes by "descent");

   c. "Issue" and "descendants" are synonymous, both referring to all *lineal descendants* and including adopted offspring; and

   d. The personal representative is the "administrator."

2. When property passes by *will*:

   a. The decedent is the "testator";

   b. The clause directing disposition of land is the "devise";

   c. The person entitled to land is the "devisee";

   d. The clause directing disposition of personal property is a "legacy" as to money and a "bequest" as to other personal property;

   e. The person entitled to personal property is the "legatee"; and

   f. The personal representative is the "executor," where named in the will (otherwise, the "administrator cum testamento annexo," *i.e.*, administrator with the will annexed).

II. INTESTATE SUCCESSION

A. IN GENERAL

Intestate succession is the statutory method of distributing assets that are not disposed of by will. Property may pass by intestate succession where:

(i)   The decedent dies *without having made a will*;

(ii) The decedent's will is *denied probate* (*e.g.,* due to improper execution or successful will contest);

(iii) The decedent's will *does not dispose of all of his property* (resulting in "partial intestacy") either because a gift has failed or because the will contains no residuary clause; or

(iv) The decedent's will *specifies* that his property should pass according to the laws of intestate succession.

At common law, all real property passing by intestate succession went to the decedent's children (the surviving spouse was entitled only to dower or curtesy). Personal property went one-third to the surviving spouse and two-thirds to the surviving children. Today, the distribution of an intestate decedent's property is governed by state statute.

B.   INTESTATE SHARE OF SURVIVING SPOUSE

1.   Descendants Also Survive
If the decedent is survived by a spouse and by descendants, in most states the surviving spouse takes *one-third or one-half of the estate*. Some states give the surviving spouse a specific dollar amount plus the one-third or one-half of the estate. In some states (*e.g.,* states adopting the Uniform Probate Code ("UPC")), however, the surviving spouse takes the entire estate if the decedent is survived by descendants who are all descendants of the surviving spouse and the surviving spouse has no other surviving descendant. [UPC §2-102]

2.   No Descendants Survive
If the decedent is survived by a spouse but no descendants, in most states the surviving spouse takes the *entire estate*. In UPC states, the spouse takes the entire estate only if the decedent is not survived by descendants or parents. [UPC §2-102]
Example: W dies, survived by her husband H and her parents, M and D. In most states, H would inherit the entire estate.

C.   INTESTATE SHARE OF CHILDREN AND OTHER DESCENDANTS
The portion of the estate that does not pass to the surviving spouse, or the entire estate if there is no surviving spouse, passes to the decedent's children and descendants of deceased children. Parents and collateral kin never inherit if the decedent is survived by children or more remote descendants.

1.   Majority Rule—Per Capita with Representation
In most states, the decedent's issue take their shares per capita with representation. Under this pattern of distribution, the property is divided into equal shares at the first generational level at which there are living takers. Each living person at that level takes a share, and the share of each deceased person at that level passes to his issue by right of representation.
Examples: 1) D, a widow, dies intestate survived by: (i) child A, who has a son, W; (ii) X and Y, grandchildren by D's deceased child B; and (iii) grandchild Z, the daughter of D's deceased child C.

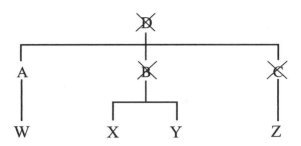

Because there is a living heir at the first generational level, D's estate is divided into three equal shares at that level. A takes one-third. The one-third that B would have inherited had he survived D passes by right of representation to his children, X and Y (one-sixth each). Similarly, Z takes a one-third share. W takes nothing even though he is D's issue because his mother A is alive to inherit.

2) Same family tree as above, except that A also predeceased D. Because there are no living takers at the first generational level, the shares are determined at the second generational level. Each grandchild takes a one-fourth share.

This type of distribution is often called a *"per stirpes"* distribution. Note, however, that this is different from a "strict per stirpes" distribution (followed by only a few states), under which the stirpital shares are determined at the first generational level beyond the decedent even if there are no living takers.

2. **Modern Trend—Per Capita at Each Generational Level**
A growing number of states and the UPC replace the above scheme with a rule under which the distribution is per capita at each generation. Under this scheme, the initial division of shares is made at the first generational level at which there are living takers, but the shares of deceased persons at that level are combined and then divided equally among the takers at the next generational level. Thus, persons in the same degree of kinship to the decedent always take equal shares. [UPC §2-106(b)]

Examples: 1) W, a widow, dies intestate survived by: (i) her son A; (ii) grandchild Q (the child of her deceased son B); and (iii) grandchildren X, Y, and Z (the children of her deceased daughter C).

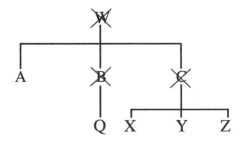

Under a *per capita with representation distribution*, A would take one-third; Q would take one-third; and X, Y, and Z would take one-ninth each, taking by representation the share of their deceased parent. In effect X, Y, and Z were penalized because they came from a larger family than their cousin Q. Under the *per capita at each generational level* scheme, A takes one-third

(because there are three lines of issue). The other two one-third shares are combined into a single share (amounting to two-thirds of the estate) and distributed in equal shares at the next generational level. Q, X, Y, and Z take one-sixth each.

2) Same facts as above, except that A also predeceased W, leaving no issue.

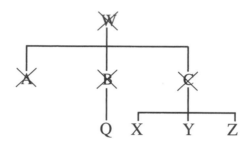

Here, the first generational level at which there are living takers is the grandchild level. The grandchildren take per capita, one-fourth each.

D. SHARES OF OTHER HEIRS

1. Parents
If the decedent is not survived by a spouse or descendants, in most jurisdictions the estate passes to the decedent's parents (one-half each) or surviving parent (who takes all).

2. Descendants of Parents
If the decedent is not survived by a spouse, descendants, or parents, the estate passes to the descendants of the decedent's parents, *i.e.,* the decedent's brothers and sisters and the issue of deceased brothers and sisters.

3. Grandparents
In most states, if the decedent left no spouse, descendants, parents, or descendants of parents, one-half of the estate passes to the decedent's maternal grandparents or their descendants and one-half passes to the paternal grandparents or their descendants.

4. Nearest Kin
If the decedent is not survived by any of the above, most states divide the estate into maternal and paternal shares. One-half goes to the nearest kin on each side of the family, no matter how remotely related to the decedent. Some states, however, have enacted "laughing heir" statutes, which cut off inheritance by persons so remotely related to the decedent that they suffer no sense of loss, only gain, at the news of the death. These statutes usually cut off inheritance rights of persons related to the decedent beyond the descendant-of-the-grandparents level.

5. Escheat
If the decedent does not leave any relative capable of taking the estate, the estate passes to the state. This is called escheat.

E. SPECIAL CASES INVOLVING CHILDREN

1. **Adopted Children**

    a. **As to Adopting Family—Adopted Child Treated Same as Natural Child**
For purposes of intestate succession, an adopted person is treated the same as a natural child of his adopting parents. The adopted child can inherit from and through his adopting parents, and the adopting parents and their kin can inherit from and through the adopted child. A child adopted after the execution of a will is considered to be a pretermitted child within the meaning of a pretermitted child statute (*see* IX.B., *infra*). Similarly, an adopted child is considered to be a lineal descendant within the meaning of an anti-lapse statute (*see* VIII.A., *infra*).

    b. **As to Natural Parents—All Inheritance Rights Cut Off**
Where a child is adopted by a new family, the adopted child and his kin have no inheritance rights from or through the adopted child's natural parents, and the natural parents and their kin have no inheritance rights from or through the natural child who has been put up for adoption.

        1) **Exception—Adoption by Spouse of Natural Parent**
Adoption of a child by the spouse of a natural parent has no effect on inheritance rights between the child and that natural parent or his family. Inheritance rights concerning the other natural parent, however, are severed. Under the UPC, such an adoption has no effect on inheritance rights from or through *either* natural parent. [UPC §2-119(b)] Therefore, under the UPC, an adopted child may inherit from or through both natural parents as well as the adopting parent, whether the marriage of the natural parents was ended by divorce or death. *Note:* The other natural parent, however, may not inherit from or through the adopted child.

           Example: Wanda and Harry have a child (Art). Wanda divorces Harry. Some years later, Wanda marries Sam; Sam adopts Art. For purposes of inheritance, Art is a child of his natural mother Wanda, and is a child of his adoptive father Sam, and any inheritance rights concerning Harry have been severed. Under the UPC, however, Art has three lines from which he can inherit: Wanda and her family, Sam and his family, and Harry and his family.

        2) **Exception—Death of Natural Parent**
Adoption of a child by the spouse of a natural parent who married the natural parent after the death of the other natural parent has no effect on inheritance rights between the child and the family of the deceased natural parent. Also, adoption of a child by a close relative has no effect on the relationship between the child and the families of the deceased natural parents.

           Example: Suppose in the above example, Art's natural father (Harry) died, and Art's natural mother subsequently married Sam, who adopted Art. This second exception simply means that Art continues to have inheritance rights through his deceased natural father (*e.g.,* his natural grandparents—Harry's parents) notwithstanding his adoption by a new father.

2. **Stepchildren and Foster Children**

a. **General Rule—No Inheritance Rights**

Generally, stepchildren and foster children have no inheritance rights.

Example: W, a widow, has a daughter D. W marries H. Thereafter, the three live as a family unit, ***but*** H does not adopt D. There is no legal relationship between H and D. If D dies intestate, H is not a "parent" for inheritance purposes. If H dies intestate, D is not a "child" for inheritance purposes.

b. **Exception—Adoption by Estoppel**

However, under the right facts, in the above example D might be able to establish adoption by estoppel. This equity-type doctrine permits a stepchild or foster child to inherit from or through his stepparents or foster parents as though legally adopted. The doctrine is invoked where stepparents or foster parents gain custody of a child under an ***agreement with the natural parent*** that they will adopt the child. Just as the stepparent or foster parent would be estopped from denying the existence of a valid adoption, so also are those claiming under him on his intestate death.

3. **Posthumous Children**

Generally, one cannot claim as an heir of another person unless he was alive at the other person's death, but an exception is made for a posthumous child. A child in gestation at the decedent's death inherits as if born during the decedent's lifetime.

Example: Sam and his brother Bill die in the crash of a private plane. Bill's wife is three months pregnant, and six months later Bill Jr. is born. For the purposes of distributing ***Bill's*** estate, Bill Jr. is an heir. However, for purposes of distributing ***Sam's*** estate, Bill Jr. is not an heir because he was not alive at his uncle's death and he was not Sam's issue.

4. **Nonmarital Children**

At common law, a nonmarital child could not inherit from either parent, but only from his own issue. Today, all states permit inheritance from the mother, and the modern trend permits inheritance from the father as well, provided paternity is established. [*See* UPC §§2-115(5), -117] In fact, as a result of constitutional litigation expanding rights of nonmarital children, in most states these children can inherit from the natural father if:

a. The father married the mother after the child's birth ("legitimated by marriage");

b. The man was adjudicated to be the father in a paternity suit; or

c. After the man's death, he is proved in the probate proceedings (usually by "clear and convincing evidence") to have been the father of the child.

5. **No Distinction Between Half Bloods and Whole Bloods**

Half bloods are brothers and sisters who have only one common parent. Most jurisdictions, including those that have adopted the UPC, have abolished all distinctions between siblings of the half blood and those of the whole blood. [*See* UPC §2-107] Thus, they inherit equally.

Example: H and W have a daughter A. H dies; W marries H-2, and has two daughters (B and C) by that marriage. H-2 does not adopt A. Then H-2 and W die. A and C are sisters of the half blood: They have only one common parent. By contrast, B and C are siblings of the whole blood: They share two common parents.

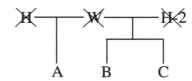

A   B   C

Suppose C dies intestate, unmarried, and without descendants. Her nearest kin are her half sister A and her full sister B. A and B each would take one-half of C's estate.

III. SUBSIDIARY PROBLEMS COMMON TO INTESTACY AND WILLS

A. SIMULTANEOUS DEATH

A person cannot take as an heir or will beneficiary unless he survives the decedent because property cannot pass to a dead person. (*See* discussion of lapse, VIII.A., *infra*.) Because it is often difficult to determine whether a person survived the decedent (*e.g.*, both are fatally injured in same car accident), nearly all states have enacted a statute to deal with simultaneous deaths or deaths in quick succession.

1. Uniform Simultaneous Death Act—Property Passes as Though Owner Survived

Most states have enacted a version of the Uniform Simultaneous Death Act ("USDA"), which provides that when the title to property or its devolution depends on priority of death and there is insufficient evidence that the persons have died otherwise than simultaneously, the property of each person is disposed of as if he had survived. [USDA §1] In other words, the property passes as though the beneficiary or heir predeceased the other decedent.

The purpose of the USDA is to prevent the property of one person from passing to a second person (and then to the second person's beneficiaries), resulting in double administration and possibly double taxation of the same assets in quick succession, even though the second person did not survive long enough to enjoy ownership of the property.

2. USDA Applies to All Types of Transfers

The USDA applies to distributions of property **by any means** (intestacy, will, joint tenancy with right of survivorship, life insurance contract, etc.).

Examples: 1) A is the insured under a life insurance policy that names "B, if he survives the insured," as the primary beneficiary and C as the contingent beneficiary. A has a will that devises Blackacre to B and her residuary estate to the Red Cross. B has no will. A and B die simultaneously in a plane crash.

The life insurance proceeds are distributed as though A, the insured, survived B, the beneficiary. Thus, the proceeds are paid to C. For purposes of construing A's will, A, the testator, is deemed to have survived B, the beneficiary. Thus, the devise to B lapses and (assuming the anti-lapse statute does not apply) Blackacre passes under the residuary clause as undisposed-of property. For purposes of distributing B's intestate estate, B, the property owner, is deemed to have survived A.

2) H and W own real estate as tenants by the entirety. H and W die simultaneously in an automobile accident. "Where there is no sufficient evidence

that two joint tenants or tenants by the entirety have died otherwise than simultaneously the property so held shall be distributed one-half as if one had survived and one-half as if the other had survived." [USDA §3] Thus one-half passes through W's estate as though W survived H, and the other half passes through H's estate as though H survived W. (The point: There is no evidence to trigger the right of survivorship.)

3. USDA Applies Unless Instrument Provides Otherwise

No one is compelled to have the USDA's presumption apply to her estate. Thus, the presumption raised by the USDA does not apply if the decedent's will or other instrument makes a different provision regarding survival. [USDA §6]

Example: W has a $1 million estate; her husband H has little property of his own. W's will provides: "I devise one-half of my estate to my husband H. I devise the remaining one-half of my estate (or my entire estate if H does not survive me) to my descendants per stirpes." If W dies survived by H, the $500,000 given to H will qualify for the federal estate tax marital deduction, and will save substantial taxes in W's estate. But if W and H die simultaneously, and if the USDA presumption applies to her estate, nothing will be deemed to pass to H. W's estate will not qualify for a marital deduction.

In this case, it is common to include a ***marital deduction reverse presumption*** clause: "If my husband and I die under such circumstances that the order of our deaths cannot be established by sufficient evidence, for purposes of this marital deduction gift my husband shall be deemed to have survived me." Now, if W and H die simultaneously, H will be deemed to have survived W. The $500,000 will pass to H (and then through his estate to the couple's descendants). W's estate will qualify for a $500,000 marital deduction, saving taxes in her estate. This "reverse presumption" is valid.

4. Evidence of Simultaneous Death

The USDA applies only if there is "no sufficient evidence" of survival.

Example: Sue has a will that devises her entire estate "to my sister Mary if she survives me; otherwise to my brother Bill." Mary has a will that devises her estate to her husband, Horace. Sue and Mary are in a terrible automobile accident. Sue is pronounced dead at the scene of the accident. Mary, alive but unconscious, is taken to a local hospital where she dies two hours later. Here, there is sufficient evidence that Mary survived Sue. Thus, Sue's entire estate passes under her will to Mary, and then passes under Mary's will to Horace.

a. 120-Hour Rule

To cover the above situation, many states require that a person survive the decedent by 120 hours in order to take as a will beneficiary, intestate heir, life insurance beneficiary, or surviving joint tenant (absent a contrary provision). This is the position of the UPC and the revised version of the USDA. [UPC §2-104; USDA (1993) §§2 - 4]

b. Time-of-Survival Clause

In drafting wills, the technique most commonly used to cover the contingency of simultaneous deaths, or deaths in quick succession, is to make all gifts (other than marital deduction gifts) contingent on surviving the testator by, *e.g.*, 60 days.

B. DISCLAIMERS

1. Disclaimed Interest Passes as Though Disclaimant Predeceased Decedent
No one can be compelled to receive a gift. Therefore, a beneficiary or heir may disclaim any interest that otherwise would pass to the person from the decedent or the decedent's estate, with the consequence that the interest passes as though the disclaiming party predeceased the decedent. Disclaimers are made primarily for tax reasons.

Example: M, who is 75 years old, dies leaving a will that devises her entire estate to her descendants per stirpes. M is survived by her daughter D and her son S, each of whom has several children in college. D is a doctor and has a substantial estate and a substantial income in her own right. The effect of the inheritance will be to aggravate D's own income tax and estate planning problems. If D accepts the inheritance and then makes gifts to her children, there will be gift tax consequences. *Solution:* D disclaims all or a part of her inheritance. (Partial disclaimers are valid under federal tax law.) The result is that the disclaimed interest passes from the decedent to D's children with no gift tax consequences.

In contrast, S is a law professor whose only outside source of income is from fees for giving bar review lectures. Under these economic circumstances, the idea of disclaiming his inheritance does not even cross his mind.

2. Must Be in Writing, Irrevocable, and Filed Within Nine Months
To be effective for federal estate and gift tax purposes, the disclaimer of a gift by will, an intestate share, or life insurance or death benefit proceeds must be (i) in writing, (ii) irrevocable, and (iii) filed within nine months *of the decedent's death*. [I.R.C. §2518(b)] Although some state disclaimer statutes impose additional procedural requirements, most state statutes have been drafted to conform to the federal statute.

a. Beneficiary Under Age Twenty-One
A beneficiary who is under age 21 has until nine months after her 21st birthday to make a disclaimer under the federal statute.

b. Joint Tenants
Under federal law and the UPC, the period in which a surviving joint tenant may disclaim the portion of the tenancy acquired by right of survivorship is nine months *from the other joint tenant's death*. [26 C.F.R. §25.2518-2(c)(4); Estate of Dancy v. Commissioner of Internal Revenue, 872 F.2d 84 (4th Cir. 1989); UPC §2-1107]

c. Future Interests
While some states allow disclaimer of a future interest within nine months of its vesting in possession (*i.e.*, after the life tenant's death), to avoid federal gift tax, the interest must be disclaimed within nine months of its *creation*.

3. Disclaimer May Be Made on Behalf of Infant, Incompetent, or Decedent
A disclaimer may be made by a guardian or personal representative on behalf of an infant, incompetent, or decedent, but the court having jurisdiction of the estate of the incapacitated person or decedent must find that it is in the *best interests* of those interested in the estate of the beneficiary and is not detrimental to the best interests of the beneficiary.

Example: H dies leaving a will that devises "all my property" to his wife W "if she survives me; otherwise to our children." W survives H, but dies four months later. The result is that (because of the unlimited federal estate tax marital deduction) the property is not taxed in H's estate, but the entire property is taxed in W's estate with no marital deduction available. *Solution:* W's executor could disclaim, on behalf of W's estate, one-half of the gift from H, thus eliminating the estate tax on the disclaimed gift, and the property would go directly to the children.

4. Estoppel If Any Benefits Accepted

An interest cannot be disclaimed if the heir or beneficiary has accepted the property or any of its benefits. In other words, a person who, *e.g.*, transfers or encumbers the property or enters into a contract for its sale is estopped from disclaiming the property.

5. Creditors' Claims

In most states, a disclaimer can be used to defeat creditors' claims. Because the effect of the disclaimer is that the property passes as though the disclaimant predeceased the decedent, the disclaimant has no interest that can be reached by creditors. However, a disclaimer cannot be used to defeat a federal tax lien. [Drye v. United States, 528 U.S. 49 (1999)]

6. Disclaimer of Life Estate Accelerates Remainder

Because the disclaimed interest passes as though the disclaimant predeceased the decedent, upon disclaimer of a life estate the remainder is accelerated.

Example: T's will devises property in trust: "Income to A for life, and on A's death, principal to her descendants then living, per stirpes." A makes a timely and valid disclaimer for tax reasons. The will is read as though the disclaimant predeceased the testator, and thus the remainder is accelerated. A's "descendants then living per stirpes" are determined at T's death (not at A's death), and the property is distributed outright to them.

C. DECEDENT'S DEATH CAUSED BY HEIR OR BENEFICIARY

Most courts hold that one who feloniously and intentionally brings about the death of a decedent forfeits any interest in the decedent's estate. The property passes as though the killer predeceased the victim. This result is usually accomplished either through the operation of a specific statute or the imposition of a constructive trust.

1. Rule Applies to All Forms of Transfer and Benefits

The typical statute disqualifies the killer from taking under a will, by intestacy, or as beneficiary of a life insurance policy on the decedent's life. The killer is also disqualified from taking an elective share, a homestead life estate, an exempt personal property set-aside, a family allowance, or as a pretermitted spouse. [*See* UPC §2-803]

Example: Frank's will devises Blackacre "to my son Sam." Sam murders Frank. Frank is survived by Sam (now serving 20 years in the penitentiary) and by Sam's son Gordon. Because the gift of Blackacre passes as though Sam predeceased Frank, Gordon takes Blackacre under most anti-lapse statutes (discussed in VIII.A., *infra*).

2. Joint Ownership—Right of Survivorship Severed

If one joint owner in a joint tenancy, tenancy by the entirety, or joint bank account kills the other, the killer loses the benefits of the right of survivorship.

Example: H and W own Whiteacre as tenants by the entirety. W kills H. The right of survivorship is severed; in effect, the estate is treated as a tenancy in common. H's one-half interest passes under his will (or by intestacy) as though W predeceased him. W continues to own her undivided one-half interest in Whiteacre.

Note: W does not forfeit **her** interest in the property because of the killing. The purpose of the statute is to prevent W from benefiting from her wrongful act by taking H's interest by right of survivorship.

3. Proof of Killing—Evidentiary Standard

A final judgment of conviction of murder in any degree is conclusive for purposes of this type of statute. However, in the absence of a conviction of murder in any degree, the court may determine by a ***preponderance of the evidence*** whether the killing was unlawful or intentional.

Example: M dies under suspicious circumstances. Her daughter D is charged with murder in the first degree, but she is acquitted. Notwithstanding the acquittal, under the typical slayer statute the court could find that D unlawfully and intentionally brought about M's death, and that D forfeited all interests in M's estate. This is because the evidentiary test would be the "preponderance of the evidence," not the "beyond a reasonable doubt" standard of the criminal action.

D. ADVANCEMENT OF INTESTATE SHARE

An advancement is a gift made to a next of kin with the intent that the gift be applied against any share which the next of kin inherits from the donor's estate.

1. Common Law—Lifetime Gift to Child Presumptively an Advancement

At common law, it was presumed that an intestate desired to treat all of his children equally. Consequently, when an intestate made a substantial gift to one child and not to others during his lifetime, the gift was held to be an "advancement" (*i.e.,* an advance payment) of the child's intestate share upon the parent's death.

2. Modern Law—Common Law Presumption Reversed

Most states hold that the advancement doctrine can apply to any heir but reverse the presumption by providing that a lifetime gift is presumptively *not* an advancement unless shown to be intended as such. States that have adopted the UPC approach are even more stringent, requiring a writing to prove an advancement. In those states, no lifetime gift is considered an advancement unless it is: (i) declared as such in a contemporaneous writing by the donor, or (ii) acknowledged as such in writing by the donee. (The donee's writing need not be contemporaneous.) [*See* UPC §2-109]

3. Procedure If Advancement Found

Once it has been determined that an advancement was made, the amount advanced is computed with the net value of the estate for purposes of distribution; or, as the courts say, the amount advanced is brought back into ***hotchpot***. Thus, an heir who has received an advancement has his share reduced by the amount of the advancement. However, if the advancement is greater than the heir's intestate share, he is not responsible for returning the excess.

Examples: 1) In a state that applies the common law doctrine of advancements, Hortense, a widow, gives land worth $50,000 to her son Seth. Several years later, Hortense dies intestate survived by Seth and her daughter Debbie as her nearest kin. Hortense leaves an estate valued at $200,000. The land given to Seth is worth $80,000 at Hortense's death. The gift to Seth is treated as an advancement, *i.e.,* a partial satisfaction of Seth's share of his mother's estate. If Seth wishes to take a share of the estate as heir, he must allow the *date of gift value* to be brought into hotchpot:

$200,000   actual intestate estate
+ 50,000   date of gift value of advancement
$250,000

Seth's share of the estate is $125,000, of which he is deemed already to have received $50,000. Thus, Seth takes $75,000 of Hortense's estate, and Debbie takes $125,000.

2) Same facts, except that the UPC applies. The gift is *not treated as an advancement* unless Hortense so indicated in a writing made at the time the gift was made, or unless Seth made a written declaration that he understood that the gift was intended as an advancement. (The writing by the donor must be *contemporaneous* with the gift, but the writing by the donee can be made at any time after the gift.) If there is no such writing, the gift to Seth is ignored, and the $200,000 estate is divided equally between Seth and Debbie.

4. Advancee Predeceases Intestate
Generally, an advancement is binding upon those who succeed to the estate of the advancee in the event the advancee predeceases the intestate. In states following the UPC approach, however, an advancement is *not binding* on a predeceased heir's successors *unless* the required writing or acknowledgment specifically provides otherwise. [UPC §2-109(c)]

5. Advancement Valued at Time of Gift
The value of an advancement is determined as of the time the gift was made, and any fluctuations in the value of the advanced property will not affect the position of the next of kin.

E. SATISFACTION OF LEGACIES
The same rules apply to lifetime gifts to will beneficiaries as to intestate heirs. Under modern law, a testamentary gift may be satisfied in whole or in part by an inter vivos transfer from the testator to the beneficiary subsequent to the execution of the will, if the testator intends the transfer to have that effect. For obvious reasons, this doctrine does not apply to gifts made prior to execution of the will. In states following the UPC approach, the doctrine does not apply unless the testator provides for satisfaction in the will or a contemporaneous writing or the devisee acknowledges, in writing, the gift as one in satisfaction. [UPC §2-609]

Example: T's will bequeaths $10,000 to A. After executing the will, T transfers $10,000 to A along with a written statement that this is in satisfaction of the bequest in T's will. The bequest to A is satisfied; A takes nothing under T's will.

1. Value of Gifts in Satisfaction
Generally, if a gift is found to be in satisfaction of a testamentary provision, the value of

the gift must be determined as of the time that gift was made. In states following the UPC approach, gifts in satisfaction are valued at the time the devisee comes into possession or enjoyment or at the death of the testator, whichever occurs first. [UPC §2-609(b)]

2. Gift of Specifically Bequeathed Property to the Beneficiary

There is one situation in which satisfaction of a bequest can occur even if not proved to have been so intended. If the testator gives the specifically described property to the beneficiary, there is both a satisfaction of the legacy and an ademption (*see* VIII.B., *infra*).

IV. FORMAL REQUISITES AND EXECUTION OF WILLS

A. WHAT CONSTITUTES A WILL

A will is an instrument, executed with certain formalities, that usually directs the disposition of a person's property at death. A will is revocable during the lifetime of the testator and only operative at his death. Thus, an instrument that is operative during the testator's lifetime (as by presently transferring an interest in property) cannot be a will.

1. Codicil

A codicil is a *supplement* to a will that alters, amends, or modifies the will.

2. Instrument Need Not Dispose of Property to Be a Will

Although most wills dispose of property at death, the disposition of property is not a legal requisite of a will. The term "will" includes an instrument that merely appoints a personal representative or revokes or revises another will.

3. Will Has No Legal Effect Until Testator's Death

A will takes effect only upon the death of the testator. Until that time, the will may be revoked or amended, and the beneficiaries have only an *expectancy* (*i.e.,* they acquire no property rights under the will). Because of the ambulatory nature of a will, it operates upon circumstances and properties as they exist at the time of the testator's death ("a will speaks at the time of death"). In construing the will, however, the circumstances that existed at the time the will was executed are considered to discern what the testator meant by the words he used.

B. TESTAMENTARY INTENT

For a will to be valid, the testator must intend that the particular instrument operate as his will. In the case of a well-drafted will, this issue is rarely in doubt. Testamentary intent is established by the document itself (*e.g.,* "I, Hobie Gates, do hereby declare this instrument to be my Last Will"). The problem cases have involved instruments that contain no such recital and are ambiguous as to whether they were intended to be testamentary in effect. In these cases, testamentary intent will be found only if it is shown that the testator: (i) intended to dispose of the property; (ii) intended the disposition to occur only upon his death; and (iii) intended that the instrument in question accomplish the disposition.

1. Present Intent Required

The intention required is a present testamentary intent. A signed and witnessed statement of an intent to make a will in the future (*e.g.,* "I am going to make a will leaving all my property to you") is not a will, for it shows that the instrument itself was not intended to be a will.

2. Sham Wills

An instrument containing a recital that "this is my Last Will" raises a presumption of testamentary intent, but the presumption is rebuttable. Evidence is admissible to show, *e.g.*, that a person made a will naming his girlfriend as beneficiary to induce her to sleep with him [Fleming v. Morrison, 72 N.E. 499 (Mass. 1904)], or that the instrument was executed as part of a ceremonial initiation into a secret order [Shiels v. Shiels, 109 S.W.2d 1112 (Tex. 1937)].

3. Ineffective Deed Cannot Be a Will

If a deed fails as an inter vivos conveyance (*e.g.*, for want of delivery), it cannot be probated as a will even though it was signed and attested by the required number of witnesses. If the grantor intended the deed to be operative during his lifetime, it cannot be a will.

4. Conditional Wills

A conditional will is one that expressly provides that it shall be operative only if some condition stated in the will is satisfied. However, language that reads like a condition may be interpreted by the court as merely expressing the testator's *motive or inducement* for making the will.

a. Condition Must Be Expressed in Will

Parol evidence is not admissible to show that a will absolute on its face was intended to be conditional. Parol evidence may be admitted to show that the instrument was not meant to have any effect at all (*e.g.*, a sham will), but not to show conditions.

b. Condition vs. Motive

Suppose Mary signs a duly attested instrument that reads, "I am going on a safari to Africa. If anything happens to me on the trip, here is how I want my property disposed of . . . ." Mary returns safely from the trip, but dies five years later. Should her will be admitted to probate? This question has no clear answer, and in your answer you should *argue both ways*. Many courts have held that this language merely reflects that Mary was thinking generally about the possibility of death and the need for a will, which at that moment took the specific shape of not returning from Africa. [Eaton v. Brown, 193 U.S. 411 (1904)] However, on very similar facts, a number of cases have held the will to be conditional on not returning from the particular trip, and have denied probate. [*In re* Pascal's Estate, 152 N.Y.S.2d 185 (1956)] The following factors have been cited by the courts in favor of holding that the will was unconditional:

1) The fact that the testator executed a will is an indication that she *did not intend to die intestate*.

2) The fact that the testator *preserved the document* after returning from the trip is another indication that the will's operation was not intended to be limited.

C. TESTAMENTARY CAPACITY—MUST BE EIGHTEEN AND OF SOUND MIND

In nearly all states, a person who has attained age 18 has the right and power to make a will. If a 16-year-old executes a will and dies 20 years later, the will is not valid because the testator did not have capacity at the time the will was executed. In addition, the testator must be of sound mind. The requirements for establishing testamentary capacity are discussed in X., Will Contests, *infra*.

D. EXECUTION OF ATTESTED WILLS

For a will to be valid and admissible to probate, the testator must meet the formal requirements of due execution imposed by the statutes of the appropriate state. These statutes are often referred to as a state's Statute of Wills. If the statutory requirements are not met, the will is void (not merely voidable), and cannot be admitted to probate even if there is no objection. The formalities required for execution of a will vary from state to state. Most states require the following formalities:

(i)   The will or codicil must be *signed by the testator*, or by another person at the testator's direction and in her presence.

(ii)   There must be *two attesting witnesses*.

(iii)   The testator must sign the will (or acknowledge her previous signature or acknowledge the will) *in each of the witnesses' presence*.

(iv)   The witnesses must sign in the *testator's presence*.

Some states impose one or more of the following additional requirements:

(v)   The testator must *sign at the end* of the will.

(vi)   The testator must *"publish" the will*, *i.e.*, declare to the witnesses that the instrument is her will or otherwise communicate this fact so that the witnesses know they are witnessing a will rather than some other legal document.

(vii)   The *witnesses must sign in the presence of each other*.

1. Signature Requirement

a. What Constitutes a Signature

Any mark affixed by the testator, with the intent that the mark operate as the testator's signature, satisfies the signature requirement. "Betty," "Mom," "J.R.," the X of an illiterate person, and even the testator's fingerprint are all valid signatures. In addition, the testator's signature may be made by another person at the testator's direction and in the testator's presence. In fact, if that person writes the testator's name and then writes his own name, the person can be counted as one of the two needed attesting witnesses.

Example: Goldie, who is illiterate, has a will prepared. In the presence of Herb Miller, Goldie asks Ollie Pinkston to sign her name for her. The will has signature lines for the testator and for only one witness. On the signature line for the testator, Ollie writes "Goldie Lomineck, by Ollie Pinkston." Herb then signs on the witness line. "Ollie Pinkston" counts as the signature of an attesting witness, and the will has been validly executed.

b. Contemporaneous Transaction Doctrine—Order of Signing Not Critical

Suppose that one or more of the witnesses sign the will before the testator signs it (or that the testator and the witnesses sign on the wrong lines). The exact order of signing is not material, as long as all of the signings occurred as a part of a single, contemporaneous transaction.

c. **Placement of Signature**

In most states and under the UPC, a will is valid as long as the testator signs somewhere on the instrument (*e.g.,* on the margin, or in the first clause). [*See* UPC §2-502(a)(2)] In a substantial minority of states, however, a will must be *subscribed* (*i.e.,* signed at the end). In states with this requirement, what happens if additional materials (*e.g.,* clause naming an executor) follow the testator's signature? In many states with this requirement, if anything other than the attestation clause follows the testator's signature, the entire will is void. However, by statute or case decision in several states, everything appearing above the testator's signature is given effect, but any matter following her signature is not considered a part of the will and is disregarded.

1) **Compare—Words Added After Will Executed**

Suppose that, after the will is signed and witnessed, T adds several clauses, making a new gift and naming an executor, underneath her signature. This case does *not* involve the "signature at the end" requirement. Here, the added clauses are not given effect for another reason: They are *unattested words*. Only the words present on the will at the time it was executed are part of the duly executed will.

2. **"Presence" Requirement**

Signing in someone's presence is required under many statutes, although the requirement takes various forms. In most states, each witness must sign in the testator's presence, but not necessarily in each other's presence. In other states, the witnesses must sign in the testator's presence and in the presence of each other. In most states, the testator must sign or acknowledge the will or signature in the presence of each witness, but not necessarily at the same time. Courts have applied various tests to determine when a person is in another's presence.

a. **Majority View—"Conscious Presence" Test**

A majority of courts apply the more liberal "conscious presence" test: The presence requirement is satisfied if each party was conscious of where the other parties were and what they were doing, and the act of signing took place nearby, within the *general awareness and cognizance* of the other parties.

Example: The will is signed in a hospital room. T, lying in bed behind a heavy screen, cannot see the witnesses (and vice versa) because they are standing in the doorway, 20 feet away. Nevertheless, the parties have signed in each other's conscious presence. [Nichols v. Rowan, 422 S.W.2d 21 (Tex. 1967)]

Compare: T and one witness sign the will in Attorney's office. Attorney then excuses himself and takes the will into the office two doors down the hall, where the second witness signs. Here the conscious presence test was *not* satisfied. Merely being in the same suite of offices does not constitute "presence." [Morris v. West's Estate, 643 S.W.2d 204 (Tex. 1982)]

b. **Minority View—"Scope of Vision" Test**

Some courts take the view that the parties must be in each other's scope of vision when they sign. Under this test, a person is present only if he could have seen the signing. (An exception is made for blind persons.) This does not mean that the signing must actually

have been observed, but only that the person was in such close proximity that he ***could have seen the signing had he looked***.

3. Witnesses
Most states require that a will be attested by two competent witnesses.

a. Competency
All jurisdictions require that witnesses be competent. Competency for this purpose generally means that, at the time the will is executed, the witness is mature enough and of sufficient mental capacity to understand and appreciate the nature of the act she is witnessing and her attestation, so that she could testify in court on these matters if necessary. Most states do not impose a minimum age requirement for witnesses.

b. Interested Witnesses
At common law, an attesting witness who was also a beneficiary under the will was not a competent witness, and was barred from testifying as to the will's execution. If one of the two necessary attesting witnesses was a beneficiary, the will could not be probated. This harsh rule has been abolished in every state.

1) Majority Rule—Will Valid, But Bequest to Interested Witness Is Void
In most states, statutes solve the interested witness problem by eliminating the interest: The will is valid, but the gift to the witness-beneficiary is void. These are called ***"purging statutes"*** because they operate to purge the bequest to the witness.

a) Exception—Supernumerary Rule
An exception is made if the witness-beneficiary was a supernumerary witness, *i.e.,* if there were three witnesses, two of whom were disinterested, and the will can be proved by the disinterested witnesses.

b) Exception—Witness-Beneficiary Would Take If Will Had Not Been Admitted to Probate
The statutes also carve out an exception if the interested witness would have taken if the will were not admitted to probate, *i.e.,* if the beneficiary would have been an heir if there were no will, or if the beneficiary was also given a bequest in an earlier will that he did not witness. In such a case, the witness-beneficiary takes the lesser of: (i) the legacy, or (ii) his intestate share (or gift under earlier will).

2) Uniform Probate Code—Interested Witness Rule Abolished
Under the UPC, a will or codicil, or any part thereof, is ***not*** invalid because the will or codicil is signed by an interested witness. [UPC §2-505(b)]
Example: T's will bequeaths $25,000 to Harry, and devises his residuary estate to Sue. Harry signs the will as an attesting witness. In most states, the bequest to Harry would be purged unless: (i) Harry was one of three attesting witnesses, or (ii) Harry would be an heir (or legatee under an earlier will) if the will had not been executed. Under the UPC, Harry takes the $25,000 legacy in any case because the UPC has abolished the interested witness rule.

4. Attestation Clause

A well-drafted will invariably contains an attestation clause. This clause, which appears immediately below the signature line for the testator and above the witnesses' signature lines, recites the elements of due execution.

Example: "On the above date, the testator declared to us, the undersigned, that the foregoing instrument was her last will. She then signed the will in our presence, we being present at the same time. We then signed the will in the testator's presence and in the presence of each other, we and each of us believing the testator to be of sound mind on the date hereof."

An attestation clause is ***prima facie evidence*** of the facts recited therein. Unlike a self-proving affidavit (*see* 5., *infra*), however, an attestation clause does not constitute sworn testimony and cannot serve as a substitute for the courtroom testimony of the attesting witnesses. Attestation clauses can be useful in two situations:

a. Witness with No Memory

Suppose witness A testifies that, although he recognizes his signature on the will, he has no recollection of signing it and thus does not recall whether he signed in the testator's presence. The courts have uniformly held that probate of a will does not turn upon the memory of the attesting witnesses. The void created by the witness's memory lapse is filled by the attestation clause, which is prima facie evidence that the facts as recited therein actually occurred.

b. Witness with Faulty Memory

Suppose witness B testifies that she remembers the execution ceremony very well even though it occurred 10 years before, and that the one thing she especially "remembers" is that the testator was not in the room when she signed the will. A number of cases have upheld probate of the will after a jury finding that the attestation clause, and not the witness on the witness stand, is telling the truth.

5. Self-Proving Affidavit

Many states and the UPC permit a will to be made self-proved at the time it is executed. The testator and the attesting witnesses sign the will, and then sign a sworn affidavit before a notary public reciting that the testator declared to the witnesses that the instrument was her will, and that the testator and the witnesses all signed in the presence of each other. [*See* UPC §2-504] (The affidavit can be executed at any time subsequent to the will's execution, but standard practice is to execute both the will and the self-proving affidavit in one ceremony.)

a. Substitutes for Court Testimony of Attesting Witnesses

The self-proving affidavit serves the same function as a deposition or interrogatory. It is a method by which the witnesses' sworn testimony can be secured at the time the will is executed, eliminating the need to track down the witnesses and arrange for their testimony in probate court after the testator's death. Self-proved wills may be admitted to probate without further proof.

b. Signatures on Affidavit Can Be Counted as Signatures Needed on Will

A few courts have ruled that the signatures on the affidavit cannot be counted as the

signatures needed on the will itself because the affidavit, a procedural document designed to facilitate probate, was not executed with testamentary intent. The better and majority view, however, is that the will is validly executed. Because there is generally no requirement that the witnesses sign at any particular place on the will, the signatures on the affidavit are sufficient for execution.

Example: T signs the will, and then T and the witnesses sign the self-proving affidavit (on a separate page stapled to the will) before a notary public. However, neither witness signs the will itself underneath the attestation clause. Under the majority view, the will has been validly executed because the signatures on the affidavit can be counted as the signatures needed on the will.

6. Attorney Liability for Negligence in Preparation of Will

A growing number of states have discarded the "privity of contract" defense and have held that the attorney owes a duty, not just to the client who contracted for his services, but to the beneficiaries named in the will. Thus, the beneficiaries can sue the attorney for negligence in the preparation of a will or for negligence in supervising its execution. The amount of the recovery can be substantial (*e.g.*, the amount the beneficiaries would have received had the will been admitted to probate).

E. HOLOGRAPHIC WILLS

The UPC and about one-half of the states recognize holographic wills and codicils. [*See* UPC §2-502] A holographic will is one *that is entirely in the testator's handwriting and has no attesting witnesses*. Where recognized, a holographic will usually may be made by any testator with capacity, but a few states limit them to persons serving in the armed forces or mariners at sea.

1. Testator's Handwriting

Generally, to be valid, a holographic will must be *entirely* in the testator's handwriting. However, the UPC and most states that recognize holographic wills accept a will that contains some typewritten text as long as the portion not in the testator's handwriting is not *material* (*i.e.*, the typewritten portion may be disregarded without violating the testator's intent). [*See* UPC §2-502(b)] Note that most states do not require that a holographic will be dated.

2. Testator's Signature

A holographic will must be signed by the testator, but there is no requirement that it be signed at the end of the will. The signature can even be found in the opening caption (*e.g.*, "I, Jane Jones, do hereby declare . . ."). Courts also take a liberal view of what constitutes a signature; most will allow initials, a first name only, or a nickname.

3. Testamentary Intent

A question often arises with respect to documents offered as holographic wills as to whether the document was really intended to be a will. Often a letter or informal memorandum is offered for probate as a holographic will, and the court must make the determination of whether the document was so intended. *The test is whether some future writing was contemplated.* Extrinsic evidence is admissible to establish that an ambiguous document was intended to be a will.

Examples: 1) T's attorney received the following handwritten letter:

C. INCORPORATION BY REFERENCE

In most states, an extrinsic document (not present at the time the will was executed) may be incorporated into the will by reference so that it is considered a part of the will. To incorporate a document by reference, three requirements must be met:

(i) The document must be *in existence* at the time the will was executed;

(ii) The language of the will must *sufficiently describe* the writing to permit its identification; and

(iii) The will must *manifest an intent to incorporate* the document.

1. Document Must Be in Existence at Time of Execution of Will

The requirement for incorporation most strictly adhered to by courts is that the document must be in existence at the time the will is executed. The courts are fearful that if this requirement is not adhered to, a testator could incorporate "a paper to be written which will be placed in my desk drawer," and could later name new beneficiaries by an unattested writing. Obviously, the safeguards of the Statute of Wills would be in serious danger if that were given effect.

Example: If the will executed and attested to on May 1 provides "$1,000 to each of the persons named in a letter that I have written and dated March 1 of this year, which will be found in my safe deposit box at the Acme Bank," and if the letter was in existence at the time the will was executed, the letter is incorporated by reference and the gifts are valid.

Compare: If the will provides "$1,000 to each of the persons named in a letter that will be found in my safe deposit box at the Acme Bank," but it can be shown that the letter was written *after the will's execution*, the letter is *not* incorporated by reference and the intended gifts will fail.

a. Exception for List Disposing of Items of Tangible Personal Property

Sometimes clients seem more concerned about making gifts of personal items of sentimental value (*e.g.,* crystal bowls, Winchester rifles, etc.) than about disposing of their intangible wealth or real estate holdings. Also, division of personal and household effects among the surviving family members can lead to arguments unless the testator has given clear directions as to how these items are to be divided. To provide a convenient mechanism for making gifts of such items, many states and the UPC have enacted statutes carving out an exception to the rule that, to be incorporated by reference, the document must be in existence at the time the will is executed. In those states, a will may refer to a written statement or list to dispose of items of *tangible personal property* (not money, intangible property, or property used in a trade or business) not otherwise specifically disposed of by the will. The writing must be *signed* by the testator and must *describe* the items and the devisees with reasonable certainty. The writing may be referred to as one in existence at the time of the testator's death. It may be prepared before *or after* the execution of the will, and it *may be altered* by the testator after its initial preparation. [*See* UPC §2-513] Note that unless a state has a specific statute addressing this issue, such lists prepared after the execution of the will are invalid.

2. **Identification of Extrinsic Document**

The language of the will must refer to the extrinsic document in such a way as it may be reasonably identified, and the document must correspond to the description given in the will.

Example: M purchased a will form at a stationery store. In the space for naming the beneficiaries of his estate, M wrote: "Attached dated June 7, 2009." After M's death, the will (which was duly executed) was found in an envelope along with a handwritten and signed (but unwitnessed) memorandum dated June 7, 2009. The memo, which was paper-clipped to the will, designated the beneficiaries of M's estate. The will's reference to the date of the memo and its being "attached" were sufficient to incorporate the memo by reference.

D. **ACTS OF INDEPENDENT SIGNIFICANCE**

Under the "acts of independent significance" doctrine (sometimes called the doctrine of "nontestamentary acts"), a will may dispose of property by reference to acts and events that have significance apart from their effect on the dispositions made by the will. Even though the identification of a beneficiary or the amount of a bequest will be determined by some future unattested act, the bequest is nonetheless valid if the act has some lifetime significance other than providing for the testamentary gift.

1. **Identification of Beneficiaries**

The future act may relate to the identification of the beneficiaries.

Example: T's will provides "a legacy of $1,000 to each person who is in my employ at the time of my death." Thereafter, T hires three new employees and fires two longtime employees. Under this doctrine, it is assumed that T would not make employment decisions simply to make or unmake legacies in his will. The act of employment has independent significance apart from its effect on T's will. The gifts are valid.

2. **Identification of Property**

This doctrine also permits identification of the property that is to be the subject matter of a bequest.

Example: T's will bequeaths "my house and its contents to my sister Sarah." Thereafter, T buys new furniture and several valuable paintings, totally redecorating her house. The gift is valid and includes all items of furniture and furnishings that are in T's house at her death, *i.e.,* "those items of tangible personal property which convert an empty building into a habitable dwelling." The gift ***does not include intangible property*** that happened to be stored in the house (stock certificates worth $377,000; savings account passbook covering deposits of $124,000). [Souder v. Johnson, 501 So. 2d 745 (Fla. 1987)]

Compare: T's will bequeaths "the oil paintings in my den to the persons whose names I plan to write on the back of each painting." Thereafter, T writes various names on post-its and sticks them on the back of several paintings in his den. The gifts are ineffective because the tagging has no significance except as a testamentary act.

3. **Acts of Third Persons**

The doctrine of independent significance has been used with regard to acts of third persons

as well as to acts of the testator. The usual situation is where a testator directs that his property be distributed in accordance with the will of another person. If the will is executed, and the other requirements of incorporation are met, the other person's will can be incorporated by reference. The more difficult case is where the testator provides that his property shall be disposed of as provided in the future will of another person.

Example: T executes his will devising the residue of his estate to any charitable trust established by the last will and testament of his brother, Barney Robles. Barney is alive and has no will. Subsequently, Barney executes a will devising all his property to the Robles Trust for Mental Health, a testamentary trust established by his will. Then Barney dies. Then T dies. It is generally held that the doctrine of independent significance applies, and the gift is valid.

E. POUR-OVER GIFT TO INTER VIVOS TRUST

The usual fact situation is like this: T established a revocable inter vivos trust. T then executed his will devising the residue of his estate to the trustees of the inter vivos trust to hold under the terms of the trust instrument as amended on the date of T's death. Subsequently, T amended the trust and then died. Can the residue be poured over into the trust as amended? The amendment could not be incorporated by reference because it was not in existence when the will was executed. Some courts, however, held the amendment had independent significance if the inter vivos trust had a significant amount of property and was set up for lifetime motives. The problem was solved by legislation permitting this very useful estate planning device.

In most states, the Uniform Testamentary Additions to Trusts Act ("UTATA"), or its equivalent, has been enacted. A devise or bequest made to a trustee of an inter vivos trust is valid, notwithstanding the fact that the testator has reserved the power to amend or revoke the trust or has actually amended the trust after executing his will, and further notwithstanding the fact that the trust instrument or any amendment was not executed in accordance with the Statute of Wills. [UTATA §1; *see* UPC §2-511]

F. NONPROBATE ASSETS CANNOT BE DISPOSED OF BY WILL

Only property owned by the decedent at death can be disposed of by will. A will cannot make a gift of "nonprobate assets"—*i.e.,* interests that pass at death other than by will or intestacy. Also, nonprobate assets are not subject to the personal representative's possession for purposes of administering the decedent's estate. There are three principal categories of nonprobate assets.

1. Property Passing by Contract—Life Insurance Proceeds and Employee Benefits

Life insurance proceeds (and death benefits under an employee retirement plan) are payable to the beneficiary designated by the insured (or employee) in his contract with the life insurance company (or retirement plan carrier).

Example: Tom is the insured under a $50,000 Prudential life insurance policy that names Mary as primary beneficiary. Tom dies leaving a will that provides: "I direct that the $50,000 proceeds under my Prudential life insurance policy be paid to my brother Bill rather than to Mary." This will provision is ineffective. Payment of the insurance proceeds is governed by the contract between Tom and Prudential, and the beneficiary can be changed only by complying with the terms of the policy governing beneficiary designations. Mary takes the $50,000 proceeds.

2. **Property Passing by Right of Survivorship**

Property held by the decedent and another person as joint tenants with right of survivorship, and property held by the decedent and his spouse as tenants by the entirety, pass directly to the survivor outside of the probate process.

Example: H and W owned a house as tenants by the entirety. W filed for divorce, and the parties tentatively agreed upon a property settlement under which the house would be awarded to W. In anticipation of this, W executed a will that devised the house to C. However, W died before the hearing on the divorce petition was held. *Held:* W's will was ineffective as to the house because the parties were married at W's death. Title to the house passed to H by right of survivorship. Moreover, there is no basis for impressing a constructive trust in C's favor because no wrongful conduct or unjust enrichment was involved. [Miller v. Miller, 487 A.2d 1156 (D.C. 1985)]

3. **Property Held in Trust**

When an inter vivos trust is established, legal title to the settlor's assets is transferred to the trustee, and if the trust continues in operation after the settlor's death, legal title remains in the trustee.

Example: Sam establishes a revocable self-declaration of trust that names himself as trustee. The trust provides that all income is to be paid to Sam for life. Upon Sam's death or incapacity, Miami National Bank is to become successor trustee. After Sam's death, all trust income is to be paid to Sam's wife, Wilma, for life. On the death of the survivor of Sam and Wilma, the trust principal is to be distributed to Sam's descendants. Sam dies; the trust continues in operation free of the probate process.

VI.   REVOCATION OF WILLS

A.   IN GENERAL

1. **Must Have Capacity to Revoke Will**

A person who has testamentary capacity (*i.e.,* is of sound mind, has the capacity to know the nature of the act he is doing, etc.) may revoke his will at any time prior to death.

2. **Contractual Will May Be Revoked**

Even a testator who has validly contracted not to revoke a will (*see* VII.C., *infra*) may do so, and the will must be denied probate. In this case, however, there may be an action for breach of contract against the decedent's estate, and the remedy may be the imposition of a constructive trust upon the beneficiaries under the will. (*See* Trusts outline.)

3. **Methods of Revocation**

Once validly executed, a will may be revoked only by the methods prescribed by statute or permitted by case law. These methods include revocation by operation of law, by subsequent instrument, and by physical act.

B.   REVOCATION BY OPERATION OF LAW

In many states, a will may be partially or totally revoked by operation of law in the event of

subsequent marriage, divorce, or birth or adoption of children. The theory of the rules providing for such revocation is that it is assumed the testator would not want the will (or the will provision) to operate in view of the changed family situation.

1. Marriage Following Execution of Will—Omitted Spouse

In most states, marriage following execution of a will has *no effect* on the earlier will, even though it makes no provision for the new spouse, on the theory that the new spouse is given adequate protection by the state's elective share statute (or, in community property states, by the community property system). However, in a minority of states and under the UPC, if a person marries after executing a will and the spouse survives the testator, the new spouse takes an intestate share of the testator's estate as an "omitted spouse." In most of these states, the will is only partially revoked, *i.e.,* only to the extent necessary to provide the spouse with an intestate share. In making up the omitted spouse's intestate share, the usual abatement rules (discussed in XI.E., *infra*) apply. Property passing by partial intestacy (if any) is first used, then the residuary estate, then general legacies, demonstrative legacies, and, finally, specific devises and bequests.

Note that even in states with omitted spouse statutes, no revocation occurs and the spouse does not receive the intestate share if: (i) the *will makes provision* for the new spouse; (ii) the will provides that the spouse's *omission was intentional*; or (iii) it appears that the will was made in *contemplation of the marriage*. [*See* UPC §2-301]

2. Divorce Revokes All Provisions in Will or Revocable Trust in Favor of Former Spouse

In most states, by statute, divorce following execution of a will revokes all gifts and administrative appointments in favor of the former spouse. The rest of the will remains valid, and is read as though the ex-spouse predeceased the testator. The UPC extends the application of the rule to provisions in favor of the former spouse's *relatives*. [UPC §2-804]

Examples: 1) Tom's will devises Blackacre "to my wife, Wanda, if she survives me, but if she does not survive me to my brother Ben." The will devises Tom's residuary estate to his son Sam. Wanda divorces Tom; then Tom dies survived by Wanda, Ben, and Sam. The gift to Wanda is revoked and, because the will is read as though Wanda predeceased the testator, Blackacre passes to Ben.

2) Same facts as above, except that the devise of Blackacre was "to my wife, Wanda, if she survives me, but if she does not survive me to my *wife's* brother Ben." Under the UPC, both the gift to Wanda and the alternate gift to Ben are revoked, and Blackacre passes under the residuary gift to Sam.

a. Statutes Do Not Apply to Life Insurance Policies

The statutes apply only to wills and revocable trusts, not to insurance policies.

Example: Suppose, in the first example above, Tom had a $25,000 life insurance policy that named Wanda as primary beneficiary "if she survives me" and Ben as contingent beneficiary. After the divorce, Tom does not change the beneficiary designation. Wanda takes the $25,000 policy proceeds.

b. Statutes Apply Only to Divorce by Testator or Settlor

The only divorce relevant under the statutes is the testator's or settlor's.

Example: T's will bequeaths property "to my brother's wife, Louise Ellstrom." Thereafter, T's brother divorces Louise, and Louise changes her name back to Smith, her maiden name. Louise takes the gift under T's will. The designation of "my brother's wife" was not a condition to the gift, but merely described which Louise T had in mind.

3. Pretermitted Children

Most states have pretermitted child statutes. (*See* IX.B., *infra.*) Under these statutes, if the testator fails to provide in his will for any of his children born or adopted after the will is executed, the child is entitled to a share of the estate equal in value to what he would have received if the testator had died intestate. In making up the child's share, the general rules of abatement apply. Thus, in the ordinary case, the pretermitted child's share comes out of the residuary estate, and the will is revoked to that extent.

C. REVOCATION BY WRITTEN INSTRUMENT

1. Instrument of Revocation Must Be Executed with Testamentary Formalities

A will or any part thereof may be revoked or altered by a subsequently written will, codicil, or other writing declaring such revocation, as long as there is a present intent to revoke and the instrument is executed with the same formalities as are required for the execution of a will. In states that recognize holographic wills, a valid holographic will may revoke a typewritten, attested will.

Example: A revocation can be by a writing that says nothing more than "I revoke my will," provided such writing is executed and attested with proper formalities. However, the usual method of revoking a will is to execute a new will that states: "This is my last will and testament, and I hereby revoke all earlier wills and codicils thereto."

2. Revocation by Implication—Inconsistent Provisions

Suppose that a testator executes a second testamentary instrument that does not contain any express language of revocation of an earlier will. To the extent possible, the two instruments are read together; *i.e.,* the second instrument is treated as a codicil to the will. However, the second instrument revokes the first to the extent of any inconsistent provisions.

Examples: 1) T executes a will that leaves all of her property to John. Later, T executes a second will that leaves all of her property to Dolly, but the will does not contain an express clause revoking the first will. When T dies, Dolly takes T's entire estate, the first will having been revoked completely by the inconsistent provision of the second will.

2) By his first will, T bequeaths his stamp collection to Art and his residuary estate to Ruth. By a later instrument executed with proper formalities, T bequeaths his stamp collection to Jack, his Studebaker convertible to Susan, and $5,000 to Tom. This second instrument contains no words of revocation. The second instrument is treated as a codicil, and revokes the first will only to the extent of inconsistent provisions. Thus Jack (not Art) takes the stamp collection, Susan takes the Studebaker, Tom takes $5,000, and Ruth takes T's residuary estate.

D. REVOCATION BY PHYSICAL ACT

1. **Requirements**

   a. **Physical Act**
   The statutes of each state specifically prescribe the acts sufficient to revoke a will. Typically, these acts are burning, tearing, obliterating, or canceling a material portion of the will. The act must be shown to have had an actual effect on the will or its language.
   Example: T writes "Void. Isadore Berman" at the bottom of each page of a three-page will, not intersecting or coming into contact with any portion of the will. *Held:* The will was not revoked because the writing was: (i) not a revocation by subsequent instrument because it was not signed by attesting witnesses, and the jurisdiction did not recognize holographic wills; and (ii) not a revocation by physical act because no portion of the will was canceled, defaced, or obliterated.

      1) **Burning**
      Burning a material portion of the will's language is sufficient to revoke the will, but merely burning the will's outside cover or singeing the corners is insufficient.

      2) **Tearing**
      Tearing or cutting is sufficient if a material part, such as a dispositive provision or the testator's signature, is cut or torn.
      Example: T cuts her signature off the will with scissors. *Held:* This is a valid revocation by physical act, as this act of canceling or defacing shows a clear intent that T intended to revoke the will in its entirety.

      3) **Obliteration**
      Revocation by obliteration (*e.g.*, inking out or erasing) requires damage to a material part of the will.

      4) **Cancellation**
      Lining out or writing an "X" or the word "void" across a will is sufficient to revoke if the lines touch the words of the will. Thus, writing words of cancellation on the back or in the margin of the will are ineffective to revoke the instrument.
      Example: T's act of writing "Not Valid" across the *face* of each page of a three-page will constitutes a sufficient canceling, defacing, or obliterating to revoke the will.

   b. **Intent to Revoke**
   The intention to revoke must be present *at the time of the physical act* for revocation to be effective.
   Example: Tom's house is badly damaged by a fire. When advised that his will was among the items destroyed by the fire, Tom states: "That's all right; I wanted to revoke it anyhow." The will has not been revoked because the intent to revoke did not accompany the physical act of destruction.

2. **Revocation by Proxy Permitted**
   In most states and under the UPC, a will may be revoked by physical act by a person other

than the testator, provided that the revocation is: (i) *at the testator's direction*, and (ii) in the testator's *presence*. [*See* UPC §2-507(a)(2)]

3. Partial Revocation

Most statutes and the UPC authorize partial, as well as total, revocation by physical act. [*See* UPC §2-507(a)] The problem is in determining whether the testator intended a partial or full revocation. Extrinsic evidence is admissible to make that determination.

    a. Only Residuary Gifts May Be Increased

    Courts are reluctant to give effect to nontestamentary actions that operate to increase the size of a general or specific bequest, but the testator can always increase the size of a residuary gift by canceling or obliterating a general or specific bequest.

    Example: T's will provides: "I devise Blackacre to A for life, remainder to B. The rest and residue of my estate to C." If T attempts to strike the words "for life, remainder to B," thus giving a fee simple absolute to A, the change will not be given effect. Increasing the gift from a life estate to a fee simple is like making a new gift without complying with testamentary formalities.

    Compare: If, in the above example, T struck the entire devise of Blackacre, the change would be valid and the residue would be increased. C would take Blackacre along with the rest of the residue of the estate.

4. Presumptions as to Revocation

    a. Will Not Found After Testator's Death

    Where a will that was last seen in the testator's possession or control cannot be found after the testator's death, a presumption arises that the will was revoked (*i.e.,* the reason the will cannot be located is that the testator destroyed it with the intent to revoke). However, if the will was last seen in the possession of a third person or if a person adversely affected by its contents (*e.g.,* an heir, or a legatee under an earlier will) had access to the will, no presumption of revocation arises.

    b. Will Found After Death in Mutilated Condition

    Where a will last seen in the testator's possession or control is found after his death in a mutilated condition (*e.g.,* torn in two, or crossed out with felt-tip pen), a presumption arises that the testator did the mutilating with the intent to revoke the will.

    c. Evidence to Overcome Presumption of Revocation

    To overcome the presumption of revocation raised in the foregoing situations, extrinsic evidence is admissible to show the testator's intention.

5. Effect of Revocation on Other Testamentary Instruments

    a. Revocation of Will

    The revocation of a will revokes all codicils to that will.

    b. Destruction of Duplicate Will

    Where a will has been executed in duplicate (both original and duplicate are signed and

witnessed), an act of revocation performed by the testator upon *either* copy revokes the will. Both signed copies of the will are of the same legal stature.

However, the destruction of an *unexecuted* copy of the will, accompanied by an intent to revoke, does *not revoke* the will. The act of obliteration, destruction, etc., must be done on the will itself.

c. **Revocation of Codicil**
A physical act of revocation performed on a codicil *revokes only the codicil*, not the prior will. In the absence of evidence to the contrary, it is presumed that in revoking the codicil the testator intended to reinstate the will provisions changed by the codicil as though the codicil had never been executed.

Example: T executed a will, and later executed three separate codicils to the will. Thereafter, T revoked the third and then the second codicil; then T died. *Held:* Read the will and first codicil as though the second and third codicils had never been made.

6. **Lost or Destroyed Will—Contents Must Be Clearly and Distinctly Proved**
Suppose that a will is accidentally destroyed in a fire, or that the will cannot be located after the testator's death, but the presumption of revocation that is raised by such facts is overcome by proof that the testator did not intend to revoke the will. All states permit probate of a lost or destroyed will provided that the following three elements can be proved: (i) *valid execution*; (ii) the *cause of nonproduction* (*i.e.,* that revocation is not the reason for nonproduction); and (iii) the *contents* of the will. The contents are usually proved by the testimony of at least two witnesses or by production of a carbon or photocopy of the will.

E. **REVIVAL OF REVOKED WILLS**
In most states, a will, once revoked, is not revived unless it is reexecuted or republished by codicil. Thus, a will revoked by a subsequent instrument is not automatically revived when the revoking instrument is itself revoked.

Example: T executes Will-1. Sometime later, T executes Will-2, which expressly or impliedly revokes all (or part) of Will-1. T keeps Will-1. If T later revokes Will-2, Will-1 is not revived. Will-1 was revoked immediately upon the execution of Will-2. Thus, Will-1 had no legal existence after that point and could not be resurrected merely by revoking Will-2.

Note that the UPC and a minority of states hold that destruction of the revoking instrument may revive the revoked document depending on the testator's intent as established by the testator's statements and the circumstances surrounding the case. [*See* UPC §2-509]

1. **Reexecution**
A will can be reexecuted with full testamentary formalities or by the testator acknowledging her signature on the will or acknowledging the will and having this attested to by two witnesses.

2. **Republication by Codicil**
Provided the first will is still in physical existence, it may be revived by the valid execution of a codicil that expressly refers to it.

F. DEPENDENT RELATIVE REVOCATION

1. Mistake of Law or Fact as to Validity of Another Disposition

Dependent relative revocation ("DRR") is an equity-type doctrine under which a *court may disregard a revocation* if it determines that the act of revocation was premised on a mistake of law or fact and would not have occurred but for the testator's mistaken belief that another disposition of her property was valid. If the other disposition is ineffective for some reason, the revocation accompanying the attempted disposition also fails and the will remains in force. Necessary to application of DRR is that the disposition that results from disregarding the revocation comes closer to effectuating what the testator tried (but failed) to do than would an intestate distribution.

Examples: 1) Tillie validly executes a will that devises her entire estate to her sister Ann. Later, Tillie executes a second instrument that bequeaths $10,000 to her friend Fred and the remainder of her estate to Ann. However, the instrument is signed by only one attesting witness. Tillie, erroneously believing that the second instrument has been validly executed, tears up the first will. Tillie dies, survived by her sister Ann and her brother Bob as her nearest kin. The second instrument is not admitted to probate because it was not properly attested. On these facts, DRR would be applied so as to disregard the revocation of the first will, which would be admitted to probate upon compliance with the proof of lost wills statute. *Rationale:* Although Tillie revoked the first will by physical act, her act of revocation was based on her mistaken assumption that the second instrument was a valid will. Had Tillie known that the second will was invalid, she would not have revoked the first will. (Of course, if Tillie had known the true situation, she would have properly executed the second will! It's too late for that now, however.) Because Ann was the principal beneficiary under both instruments, disregarding the revocation of the first will comes closer to what Tillie tried (but failed) to do than would an intestate distribution, under which Bob would take one-half of Tillie's estate.

2) Trevor executes a will that devises one-half of his estate to his sister Sue and the other one-half to his son (and sole heir) Steve. Later, Trevor executes a second will that, after expressly revoking the first will, devises one-third of his estate to Sue and two-thirds to Steve. Trevor does not destroy the first will. Trevor then changes his mind once again. He destroys the second will, intending to revoke it and to revive the first will. Under the no-revival rule, the first will is not revived. Now it appears that both wills have been revoked! Here, DRR would be applied to disregard the revocation of the second will. Trevor's act of revoking the second will was based on the mistaken belief (a mistake of law) that, by doing so, he could revive the first will. The courts reason that Trevor would prefer that one-third of his estate pass to Sue under the second will than to have Trevor's entire estate pass to his son by intestacy. Disregarding the revocation comes closer to what Trevor tried but failed to do than would an intestate distribution.

If the second will said "one-third to my friend Hobie Gates and two-thirds to Steve" and the other facts were the same, DRR would *not* be applied. Trevor's

revocation of the second will (in effect, "I do not want Hobie Gates to take anything") would be ***independent*** of his intent to revive the earlier will that made a gift to Sue. To disregard the revocation of the second will would defeat Trevor's intent. On these facts, the conventional rules would be applied and an intestacy would result.

3) Tim's validly executed will includes a bequest of "$2,000 to my niece Nellie." Thereafter, Tim crosses out the "$2,000" and writes in "$5,000" above it, intending thereby to revoke the gift of $2,000 and replace it with a gift of $5,000. The attempt to increase the gift to Nellie is ineffective as an unattested writing. Although Tim's striking of "$2,000" was an effective partial revocation by physical act, DRR will be applied so as to disregard the revocation. Tim would not have revoked the $2,000 bequest but for the erroneous belief that the $5,000 bequest was valid. (But if Tim had attempted to reduce the $2,000 bequest to $500, DRR would not be applied. In this situation, by striking the $2,000 Tim in effect said, "I do not want Nellie to take $2,000." It cannot be assumed that Tim would prefer Nellie to take $2,000 rather than zero.)

Compare: Same facts as in the third example above, except that Tim strikes the entire "$2,000 to my niece Nellie," and writes in above it "$5,000 to my sister Sue." Here, DRR should not be applied. Tim's revocation of the gift to Nellie (in effect, "I do not want Nellie to take anything") would be ***independent*** of his ineffective attempt to make a gift to Sue. To disregard the revocation would defeat Tim's intent. On these facts, the conventional rules would be applied, and the bequest to Nellie would be revoked.

VII. CONTRACTS RELATING TO WILLS; JOINT WILLS

A. CONTRACT TO MAKE A GIFT BY WILL

1. Contract Law Governs
Assuming the usual requirements of a valid contract are met, a contract to make, not to make, or not to revoke a will is valid. Problems in this area are controlled by contract law and not by the law of wills. The contract is not a will; it does not have to be executed with testamentary formalities; it cannot be probated. Likewise, the contract cannot be used to oppose the probate of a properly executed will that is inconsistent with the terms of the agreement. Such a will must be probated. There may be an action for damages or a suit in quasi-contract for the consideration provided, but the usual remedy is for a court of equity to impose a ***constructive trust*** upon the appropriate beneficiaries under the will.

2. Consideration
The promisee does not have any enforceable contract rights unless she provided some consideration for the testator's promise to name her as a will beneficiary. Without consideration, the testator's promise is merely a promise to make a gift in the future and is not enforceable. But note that in a contract to make a gift by will in exchange for a promise by the beneficiary to provide care to the testator, the mere fact that the testator died before the promisee could

provide much in the way of care does not render the contract unenforceable—the promise to provide the care was sufficient consideration.

3. **Formalities**

As a general rule, a contract to make a will or a gift by will need not be in writing unless land is involved. Many states have, however, enacted statutes requiring all such contracts to be in writing. Many follow the lead of the UPC, which states that a contract to make a will or not to revoke a will can be established only by:

(i) *Provisions in the will* stating the material provisions of the contract;

(ii) An *express reference* in a will to the contract and extrinsic evidence proving the terms of the contract; or

(iii) A *writing signed by the decedent* evidencing the contract.

[UPC §2 514]

4. **Remedies for Breach**

a. **During Testator's Life**

Generally, there is no remedy during the testator's life because there is no way of knowing whether the testator will carry out his promise until his death. If the testator repudiates the contract after substantial performance by the promisee, however, the promisee may seek damages, quantum meruit (value of services rendered), or equitable relief.

b. **After Testator's Death**

If the promisor fails to make the promised testamentary gift, the promisee can seek damages equaling the value of the property promised. If the promise was to devise specific property, however, the usual remedy is for the court to impose a constructive trust on the property for the promisee's benefit.

B. JOINT AND RECIPROCAL WILLS

1. **Introduction**

a. **Joint Will**

A joint will is the will of two or more persons executed on the same piece of paper and intended to serve as the will of each. Thus, a joint will is a single instrument executed by two or more testators. A joint will is admissible to probate on the death of each testator; it is as if there were separate pieces of paper. If one of the joint testators should revoke his joint will, the document would still serve and be admissible to probate as the will of the other(s).

b. **Reciprocal Wills**

Reciprocal wills are separate wills executed by two or more testators that contain substantially similar or "reciprocal" provisions. Thus, a reciprocal will is an instrument executed by only one person but which is similar in its provisions to the terms of another testator's will. A *"mutual will"* may refer to a reciprocal will *or* it may refer

to a joint will or a reciprocal will executed in accordance with a ***contract*** ("mutuality" referring to a contract).

> *Example:* H makes a will leaving everything to W if she survives H, and if W does not survive H, everything is to go one-half to W's heirs and one-half to H's heirs. W makes a will leaving everything to H if he survives W, and if H does not survive W, everything is to go one-half to W's heirs and one-half to H's heirs. H and W have reciprocal wills.

2. Revocability
Joint wills or reciprocal wills are revocable at any time during a testator's life in the same manner as any other will. This is true even if the wills are executed pursuant to a contract which provides that the wills shall not be revoked (although such revocation may give rise to a cause of action for breach of contract; *see* below).

3. No Presumption of Contract
The stated majority rule is that the mere execution of joint wills does not raise a presumption that the wills are contractual (*i.e.,* that they were executed pursuant to a promise by each party not to revoke). However, many courts do in fact find that joint wills are contractual. By contrast, an overwhelming majority of courts find that mere execution of reciprocal wills (even when drafted by the same attorney and executed on the same day) does not constitute evidence that the wills are contractual.

C. CONTRACTS NOT TO REVOKE
Just as parties can enter into a contract to make a will or a gift by will, a testator may enter into a contract not to revoke her will. Most of these cases involve a joint will or reciprocal wills (*see* above).

1. Contractual Will Revocable During Both Parties' Lifetimes
Either party may revoke a contractual will provided she gives ***notice*** to the other party to the contract, so that the other party will have a chance to change his will.

2. Relief Denied If First Party Dies in Breach
If one party secretly revokes her will (*i.e.,* does not give notice to the other party to the contract) and predeceases the other party, the survivor has no remedy because he has not been damaged. The survivor is alive and able to change his will so as to avoid sustaining any damage.

3. Constructive Trust Remedy If Survivor Dies in Breach
If the surviving party to a contractual will revokes her will and executes a new one, the new will is admissible to probate. However, because this is a breach of contract, the beneficiaries of the contractual will have a cause of action against the estate. The usual remedy is to impose a constructive trust on the property. The beneficiaries under the new will, which was executed in breach of contract, hold on constructive trust for the benefit of the contract beneficiaries; *i.e.,* their duty as trustee is to convey the property to the contract beneficiaries.

> *Example:* H and W execute a joint will that expressly provides that the will is contractual and that the survivor cannot revoke it after the first party's death. H dies and W probates the will and accepts its benefits. W then executes a new will that revokes the joint will and devises her estate to other beneficiaries. After W's death, both wills are offered for probate.
>
> The joint will cannot be probated because W revoked it by a later will. The second will is admissible to probate because it was W's last will and it was

validly executed. (Wills law controls to this extent.) However, the beneficiaries of the joint will can now bring an action to impress a constructive trust against the beneficiaries of the second will because execution of that will was in breach of W's contract with H.

a. Compare—Remedy for Breach During Survivor's Lifetime
If the surviving party to a contractual will attempts to dispose of property covered by the agreement (*e.g.*, property received from the other contracting party) during his lifetime, the contract beneficiaries may be able to impress a constructive trust upon the property. In contrast, if the surviving party merely revokes his will (no inter vivos transfer or other act of clear repudiation) in breach of the contract, the contract beneficiaries have no cause of action until that party's death.

VIII. CHANGES IN BENEFICIARIES AND PROPERTY AFTER WILL'S EXECUTION

A. LAPSED GIFTS AND ANTI-LAPSE STATUTES

1. Gift Lapses If Beneficiary Predeceases Testator
If a will beneficiary dies during the testator's lifetime, the gift to him lapses; *i.e.*, it fails. A will cannot make a gift to a dead person.

Example: T's will provides: "I bequeath all of my Google stock to my good friend Jim Brown; and I bequeath my residuary estate to my sister Sarah Goode." Jim Brown predeceases T. The gift to Jim Brown lapses, and the Google stock falls into the residuary estate as undisposed-of property.

2. Anti-Lapse Statutes
Nearly all states have anti-lapse statutes that operate to save the gift if the predeceasing beneficiary (i) was in a *specified degree of relationship* to the testator, *and* (ii) *left descendants* who survived the testator. The beneficiary's descendants take by substitution under the anti-lapse statute. The anti-lapse statutes vary as to the scope of beneficiaries covered by them. In many states, the anti-lapse statute applies only when the predeceasing beneficiary is a *descendant of the testator*. Several states and the UPC extend the application of the statute to any predeceasing beneficiary who is *the testator's stepchild, grandparent, or a descendant of the testator's grandparent*. [UPC §2-603] There are a few states with very broad statutes that apply to any relative of the testator or any beneficiary at all.

Example: T's will provides: "I devise Blackacre to my brother William Baxter; and I devise my residuary estate to my husband, John." William predeceases T, leaving a will that bequeaths "all my property to my wife, Wanda"; William is survived by Wanda and by a child, Billy, both of whom also survive T. Under the most restrictive statute, the anti-lapse statute would not apply because William was not T's descendant. Under a UPC-type statute, however, the anti-lapse statute would apply because brother William was a descendant of T's grandparents. Billy would take Blackacre by substitution under the statute.

Note: Blackacre does ***not*** pass to Wanda under William's will. The anti-lapse statute does not save the gift for the predeceasing beneficiary's estate. Instead, it provides substitute takers—here, William's descendant Billy. William, having predeceased T, had no interest in T's estate that he could devise by will.

Compare: Same facts, except that William was not survived by any descendants. Although William (T's brother) was within the scope of the UPC-type anti-lapse statute, the statute does not apply because William left no descendants. The gift of Blackacre lapses; Blackacre falls into the residuary estate and passes to T's husband, John.

3. Anti-Lapse Statute Does Not Apply If Contrary Provision in Will

The anti-lapse statute does not apply if there is a contrary will provision; *i.e.*, the gift is contingent on the beneficiary's surviving the testator.

Example: T's will provides: "I bequeath $25,000 to my daughter Mary if she survives me." Mary dies during T's lifetime, leaving a child (Monica) who survives T. The anti-lapse statute does ***not*** operate in Monica's favor because the will shows a contrary intention. The gift to Mary was, by its terms, contingent on Mary's surviving T. Because Mary predeceased T, the condition to the gift was not satisfied. The gift fails according to its own terms.

4. Statute Applies Only to Gifts by Will

In most states, the anti-lapse statute applies only to testamentary gifts. In some states and under the UPC, however, it also applies to revocable inter vivos trusts, life insurance beneficiary designations, and other nonprobate transfers. [*See* UPC §§2-706, -707]

5. Lapse in the Residuary Gift

a. Common Law—"No Residue of a Residue"

Suppose that a testator devises her residuary estate to two or more beneficiaries, one of the beneficiaries predeceases the testator, and the anti-lapse statute does not apply. At common law and in some states today, the share devised to that beneficiary does ***not*** pass to the remaining beneficiaries (unless the will so provides). Instead, the lapsed residuary gift "falls out of the will" and passes under the intestacy statutes to the testator's heirs. This was called the "no residue of a residue" rule.

Example: T's will devises "all the rest, residue, and remainder of my estate in equal shares to my friend Alan Adams, my Uncle Bill, and my sister Carrie." Alan Adams predeceases T, leaving a child (Alice) who survives T. Because Alan is not related to T, the anti-lapse statute does not apply, and Alan's one-third share lapses. Under the common law rule, the one-third lapsed share falls out of the will and passes by intestacy to T's heirs. Bill and Carrie each take one-third of the residuary estate as provided in the will.

b. Majority Rule—Surviving Residuary Beneficiaries Take

Most states have replaced the "no residue of a residue" rule with a statutory rule under which the residuary beneficiaries who survive the testator take the deceased beneficiary's share of the residuary estate. If the residue is devised to two or more

persons and the share of one of them fails for any reason, absent a contrary will provision, his share passes to the other residuary beneficiaries in proportion to their interests in the residue.

Example: Consider the example immediately above, except that the majority rule applies. Again, Alan Adams predeceases the testator. Because Alan was not related to T, the anti-lapse statute does not apply. Under the "surviving residuary beneficiaries rule," the one-third share devised to Alan passes to the other residuary devisees. Bill and Carrie each take one-half of the residuary estate.

1) Exception If Anti-Lapse Statute Applies

If the predeceasing residuary beneficiary was within the scope of the anti-lapse statute and left descendants, the anti-lapse statute takes precedence over the rule that the surviving residuary beneficiaries take.

Example: Suppose in the previous example that T's Uncle Bill predeceases T, leaving a child (Willette) who survives T. Suppose further that this occurs in a jurisdiction that has adopted a UPC-type anti-lapse statute. Because Bill was a descendant of a grandparent of the testator, the anti-lapse statute applies, and Willette takes the one-third share of the residuary estate that was devised to Bill. The "surviving residuary beneficiaries rule" gives way to the anti-lapse statute when the predeceasing residuary beneficiary is within the scope of the statute *and* leaves descendants who survive the testator.

6. Class Gifts

a. Class Gift Rule—Class Members Who Survive Testator Take Gift

If a will makes a gift to a class of persons ("children," "brothers and sisters," etc.) and a class member dies during the testator's lifetime, those class members who survive the testator take the gift (absent a contrary will provision). The rationale for the class gift rule is that the testator did not want anyone other than members of the designated class to share in the gift. Another explanation for the rule is that the will is read and the takers are determined as of the testator's death, and only those who meet the class description at that time share in the gift. The best way to understand the class gift rule is to contrast it with the courts' treatment of gifts to individually named beneficiaries.

Example: Tom's will bequeaths 600 shares of Xerox stock "to the children of my good friend Homer Hanson," and devises his residuary estate to his sister. At the time the will is executed, Homer has three children: Dan, Fran, and Stan. Dan predeceases Tom, leaving two children who survive Tom. The anti-lapse statute does not apply because Dan was not related to Tom. Because the bequest of the Xerox stock was made to a class, Dan's share of the gift does not fall into the residuary estate. Instead, the class gift rule applies, and the class members who survived the testator share the gift. Thus, Fran and Stan each take 300 shares of Xerox stock.

Compare: Tammy's will devises Blackacre "in equal shares to my good friends, Al Anson, Bill Bryce, and Carol Carter," and bequeaths her residuary estate

to her husband, Fred. Al Anson dies leaving two children; then Tammy dies. The anti-lapse statute does not apply because Anson was not related to Tammy. Because this was a gift of one-third shares to the three named beneficiaries, the share devised to Anson lapses and falls into the residuary estate. Tammy's husband Fred owns one-third of Blackacre along with Bill Bryce and Carol Carter.

b. Exception If Anti-Lapse Statute Applies

As with the "surviving residuary beneficiaries rule," the "class gift rule" gives way to the anti-lapse statute when the predeceasing class member was within the scope of that statute **and** left descendants who survive the testator.

Example: Consider the same facts as in the previous example, except that the gift of Xerox stock was "to the children of my **son** Homer Hanson." Again, Dan predeceases Tom, leaving two children who survive Tom. Because Dan was Tom's descendant, his two children take by substitution under the anti-lapse statute. (This is true under any anti-lapse statute.) They take 100 shares each; Fran and Stan take 200 shares each.

7. Beneficiary Dead When Will Executed—Void Gift

If a will makes a gift to a beneficiary who was dead at the time the will was executed, the gift is void. In most states, the rules that apply to lapsed gifts (anti-lapse statute, "surviving residuary beneficiaries rule") also apply to void gifts.

B. ADEMPTION

Under the doctrine of ademption, when specifically bequeathed property is not in the testator's estate at death (*e.g.*, it was destroyed, sold, given away, or lost), the bequest is adeemed; *i.e.*, it fails. Ademption applies because the property that was to have satisfied the bequest is not in the estate.

1. Applies to Specific Devises and Bequests

Ademption applies **only** to specific devises and bequests. A specific legacy is a gift of property that is particularly designated and is to be satisfied only by the receipt of the particular property described.

Examples: 1) T's will bequeaths "my Rolex watch to my sister Sue." After the will is executed, T sells her Rolex watch and uses the sale proceeds to purchase a Seiko watch. Ademption operates because the testamentary disposition was of a Rolex watch, not a Seiko, and T did not own a Rolex watch at her death.

2) T's will devises Blackacre to his brother Bill. Thereafter, T sells Blackacre for $30,000 and deposits the sale proceeds in a savings account. Unless evidence of T's intent is admissible (*see* below), ademption applies and Bill takes nothing. Neither the proceeds of the sold item nor similar items purchased with the proceeds go to the beneficiary.

a. May Not Apply to Gift of Sale Proceeds

Suppose, in the second example above, that T's will provides: "I direct that my executor sell Blackacre and distribute the sale proceeds to my brother Bill." Most courts hold that ademption does not apply, and that Bill takes the sale proceeds—to the extent that they can be traced. *Rationale:* Because the gift was of the proceeds from the sale, it should

not matter whether Blackacre was sold by T during his lifetime or by the executor after T's death. T's intent can still be effectuated by giving the sale proceeds to Bill. (But if the sale proceeds cannot be traced—if, *e.g.*, T has spent the proceeds—ademption applies.)

b. May Not Apply to Gift of Testator's Interest in Property
If the bequest is of the testator's interest in the property, rather than of the property itself, the gift may not be adeemed.

Example: T's will devises "all of my right, title, and interest in Blackacre to my brother Bill." T sells Blackacre on an installment contract under which the vendee promises to pay T $10,000 per year for 10 years. The contract gives T a vendor's lien. Because the gift was not of Blackacre itself but of T's *interest* in Blackacre, Bill takes T's interest as it exists at T's death. Bill takes the remaining installment payments and T's security interest (the vendor's lien).

2. Testator's Intent

a. Testator's Intent Irrelevant
Most courts apply the "identity" theory of the common law, under which the ademption issue is decided solely on the basis of an objective test: whether the specifically bequeathed property is a part of the testator's estate at her death. Under this approach, the testator's intent is irrelevant. The courts do not speculate on the reasons why the property was not in the estate or what the testator might have intended.

b. Statutory Modifications
Many states have enacted statutes that soften the ademption rule in certain circumstances [*see* UPC §2-606]:

1) Where ***casualty insurance proceeds*** for the loss of the specifically bequeathed property are paid after the testator's death, the beneficiary is entitled to the proceeds.

2) The beneficiary is entitled to the ***condemnation award*** in cases where the specifically devised property is taken by eminent domain before the testator's death, but the award is paid after the testator's death.

3) Where specifically devised property is subject to an ***executory contract*** at the testator's death, the beneficiary is entitled to all of the testator's rights under the contract, including the right to the remaining payments and any security interest retained by the testator.

4) Where a will makes a specific bequest of ***securities*** in one entity, the beneficiary is entitled to securities in another entity owned by the testator as a result of merger, consolidation, reorganization, or other similar action initiated by the entity.

5) If a testator becomes ***incompetent*** and the specifically devised property is ***sold by a guardian*** or a condemnation award or insurance proceeds are paid to the guardian for the property, the devisee is entitled to a general pecuniary legacy equal to the amount of the proceeds.

3. Partial Ademption

Partial ademption applies when, *e.g.*, the testator devises a large tract of land, then sells a portion of the tract. Ademption applies to the portion of the property not in the estate, but the remaining portion in the estate at death passes to the beneficiary.

4. Ademption Does Not Apply to General or Demonstrative Legacies

Ademption applies only to specific devises and bequests. It does not apply to general or demonstrative legacies.

a. General Legacy

A general legacy is a bequest of a dollar amount that is payable out of the general assets of the estate without a claim on any particular source of payment.

Example: "I bequeath the sum of $5,000 to my nephew Ringo." At T's death there is not that much cash in his estate. It does not matter. Ademption does not apply to general legacies. Other property in T's estate must be sold, if necessary, to satisfy Ringo's general legacy. Alternatively, the personal representative could make a "distribution in kind" (*i.e.*, a distribution of assets worth $5,000) in satisfaction of the legacy.

b. Demonstrative Legacy

A demonstrative legacy is a gift of a general amount that identifies a particular asset as the primary source of payment.

Example: "I bequeath $10,000 to my niece Nancy, to be paid out of the proceeds of my 3M stock." Before his death, T sells all of his 3M stock, and there is no such stock in his estate at his death. The $10,000 legacy is not adeemed; the $10,000 must be raised by the sale of other property in T's estate. Ademption does not apply to demonstrative legacies.

c. Bequests of Securities—Special Rules Apply

The courts will construe a bequest of securities as a general legacy, if it is possible to do so, in order to avoid application of the ademption doctrine. The cases turn on whether the testator made a gift of "200 shares" or "*my* 200 shares."

Examples: 1) Tom's will bequeaths "my 200 shares of Acme common stock to my cousin Bill." Thereafter, Tom sells the Acme stock, and does not own any such stock at his death. Because the bequest is of "*my* 200 shares" of Acme stock, this is a *specific bequest* of the shares that Tom owned at the time the will was executed. Ademption applies, and Bill takes nothing.

2) Tom's will also bequeaths "200 shares of Baker common stock to my niece Nora." Thereafter, Tom sells the Baker stock, and does not own any such stock at his death. Here, the courts seize on the absence of a possessive pronoun (he did not say "*my* 200 shares") and conclude that Tom did not intend to make a gift of the 200 shares of Baker stock that he owned. Rather, Tom's will made a *general legacy* of the *value* of 200 shares of Baker stock. Because ademption does not apply to general legacies, Nora is entitled to the date-of-death value of 200 shares of Baker stock. (The courts would reach this result even if Tom owned exactly 200 shares of Baker stock at the time the will was executed!)

The only way this strained "reasoning" can be explained is that the courts want to avoid application of the ademption doctrine in cases such as this.

C. INCREASES TO PROPERTY AFTER EXECUTION OF WILL

1. Increases Occurring Before Testator's Death

Increases to specific gifts occurring during the testator's lifetime are distributed as follows: income on property (*e.g.*, rents and profits) goes into the general estate, but improvements to real property go to the specific devisee. (*See* below for rules regarding stock splits and dividends.)

2. Increases Occurring After Testator's Death

Any increase to specific gifts occurring after the testator's death passes to the specific beneficiary because the beneficiary is deemed to own the property from the time of the testator's death.

3. Stock Splits and Stock Dividends

Suppose that the testator's will makes a specific bequest of shares of stock, and the corporation thereafter declares a stock split or a stock dividend. Most states follow the common law rule: A specific bequest of stock *includes any additional shares produced by a stock split*, but does *not include shares produced by a stock dividend*. However, under the UPC and by statute in several non-UPC states, a specific bequest of stock *also includes* shares of stock produced by a stock dividend. [UPC §2-605]

Examples: 1) T's will includes a bequest of "my 100 shares of Southwest stock to my daughter Carol." Thereafter, Southwest declares a two-for-one stock split, and a stock certificate for an additional 100 shares is issued to T. On T's death, Carol takes all 200 shares of Southwest stock. *Rationale:* T's 200 shares of Southwest stock after the split represented the same proportionate share of ownership in Southwest as the 100 shares before the split. Carol is entitled to the ownership interest that T held when he wrote his will.

2) Same facts, except that T's will bequeathed "100 shares [not "*my* 100 shares"] of Southwest stock to my daughter Carol." Thereafter, Southwest declares a two-for-one stock split. Despite the absence of a possessive pronoun, this was a specific bequest of Southwest stock, and Carol takes the additional 100 shares produced by the stock split. Wait a minute! In the second example under B.4.c., *supra*, when the issue was ademption, a bequest of "200 shares of Baker stock" was classified as a general legacy! How can the same form of bequest be classified as specific when a stock split has occurred? Because, say the courts, different issues are involved. A bequest of stock can be classified as general for one purpose (ademption) and specific for another purpose (stock split).

3) T's will bequeaths "my 200 shares of Acme common stock to my sister Ruth." Thereafter, Acme declares a 10% stock dividend, and a certificate for an additional 20 shares of Acme stock is issued to T. Under the majority rule, Ruth takes only the 200 shares of Acme stock under the theory that stock dividends should be treated the same as cash dividends, and a legatee

of stock is not entitled to stock (or cash) dividends declared during the testator's lifetime. Under the UPC, however, Ruth would also be entitled to the 20 shares of dividend stock.

IX. RESTRICTIONS ON POWER OF TESTATION—PROTECTION OF THE FAMILY

A. PROTECTION OF THE SURVIVING SPOUSE—ELECTIVE SHARE STATUTES

Nearly all states have enacted elective share statutes designed to protect a surviving spouse from disinheritance. These statutes give the spouse an election to take a statutory share (usually one-third or one-half) of the decedent's estate *in lieu of* taking under the decedent's will.

1. Amount of Elective Share
The elective share amount varies from state to state. In most states, the amount is one-third of the net probate estate if the decedent is survived by issue and one-half if the decedent is not survived by issue. In other states, the amount varies based on the duration of the marriage. [*See*, *e.g.*, Mont. Code Ann. §72-2-221]

2. Property Subject to Election
In most states, the share is calculated from the decedent's net estate, which is the probate estate minus the payment of expenses and creditors' claims. In some states, however, the share fraction is applied to the decedent's "augmented estate," which includes certain lifetime transfers (*see* 6., *infra*).

3. Notice Must Be Filed
The right to an elective share is not automatic; the surviving spouse must file a notice of election within a specified period (usually within six months after the will is admitted to probate).

4. Right to Election Is Personal to Spouse
Generally, only the surviving spouse may make the election to take against the will. Election can be made, however, on behalf of a legally incapacitated spouse by a guardian, with court approval, upon a showing that an election is necessary to provide adequate support for the spouse during his or her life expectancy. In contrast, if the spouse dies before the election is made, the election *cannot be made by the spouse's personal representative*. The reason for this is that the statute is intended to protect the surviving spouse against disinheritance, not to provide benefits to the spouse's heirs.

5. Effect of Election on Testamentary Plan
The elective share is paid in the manner causing the least disruption to the testator's testamentary plan. Thus, the elective share is first paid in cash or kind from the assets passing under the will that, but for the election, would have passed to the spouse outright. (Life estates are treated as though the spouse predeceased the testator, and the remainder is accelerated.) To the extent that these assets are insufficient to satisfy the share, the excess is paid pursuant to the abatement rules that apply to creditors' claims (*see* XI.E., *infra*).

6. Lifetime Transfers to Defeat Elective Share
In most states that have addressed this issue by statute, lifetime transfers by the decedent are

subject to the elective share if the grantor-spouse retained the power to *revoke or to invade, consume, or dispose of the principal*. Thus, in these states, revocable trusts may not be used to defeat a spouse's right of election. If it were otherwise, the policy underlying the elective share statute could easily be defeated by these types of transfers. The UPC states, which are included in the above discussion, also include other lifetime transfers in which the decedent retained an interest (*e.g.*, retained life estates, right of survivorship estates) in their concept of the *"augmented estate"* used for purposes of calculating the elective share. [*See* UPC §2-205]

7.   Compare—Dower and Curtesy

At common law, a surviving wife's dower right entitled her to a *life estate in an undivided one-third* of all lands of which her husband was seised during marriage. Dower was *inchoate* during the husband's lifetime and became a possessory estate on the husband's death. Dower applied not only to lands owned by the husband at death, but also to lands conveyed by the husband during his lifetime without the wife's joinder on the deed. A surviving husband's right of curtesy gave him a *life estate in all* (not just one-third) of his wife's lands *if* issue were born of the marriage. Dower and curtesy took precedence over claims by creditors of the deceased spouse. Most states have abolished dower and curtesy in favor of the statutory substitutes discussed, *supra*.

B.   PROTECTION OF CHILDREN—PRETERMITTED CHILD STATUTES

A testator may disinherit her children; *i.e.*, a parent need not bequeath anything to her children. Pretermitted child statutes are not intended to address that issue, but are designed to protect children from being *accidentally omitted* from the will.

1.   Omitted Child Entitled to Intestate Share

In most states, the statute operates so that a child born or adopted *after the will was executed* takes an intestate share of the decedent's estate (*i.e.*, the share he would have taken had the decedent died intestate), provided none of the exceptions below apply. In making up the child's share, the normal abatement rules apply.

2.   Exceptions

Under most statutes, the pretermitted child will not take a share if:

a.   It appears from the will that the *omission was intentional*;

b.   At the time the will was executed, the testator had other children and devised substantially all of his estate to the *other parent* of the omitted child; or

c.   The testator provided for the omitted child by a *transfer outside of the will* with the intent that it was in lieu of a testamentary gift.

3.   Protects Children of Testator Only

In most states, the pretermitted child statute operates only in favor of the testator's children; the testator's grandchildren are not covered.

C.   HOMESTEAD, FAMILY ALLOWANCE, AND EXEMPT PERSONAL PROPERTY

1.   Homestead

Most states have statutes that protect the family residence or farm from creditors' claims.

These statutes usually exempt a certain amount of land from the claims of the decedent's creditors. The amount of land exempted depends on whether the residence is urban or rural. These homestead laws often include a provision that the surviving spouse or minor/dependent children are entitled to occupy the homestead as a residence for as long as they so choose despite the disposition of the residence in the decedent's will.

2. Family Allowance
Nearly all states authorize the payment of a family allowance to the decedent's surviving spouse or minor children. [*See* UPC §2-404] Some states limit the allowance to a specific dollar amount (*e.g.*, $15,000), while others authorize payment of an amount needed to maintain the spouse and children for one year or a "reasonable amount" to be fixed by the court. The purpose of the allowance is to provide funds for support of the spouse and children during the period the decedent's assets are tied up in probate administration. The family allowance, which usually takes precedence over all claims other than funeral and administration expenses, is *in addition to* the amount passing to the spouse (or children) by will, intestacy, or elective share.

3. Exempt Personal Property
In addition to homestead rights and a family allowance, the surviving spouse of a decedent usually is entitled to petition to set aside certain items of tangible personal property listed in the statute. [*See* UPC §2-403] Typically, this exemption applies to household furnishings, appliances, personal effects, farm equipment, and sometimes automobiles. These items are *in addition to* amounts passing to the spouse under the decedent's will, by intestate succession, or under the elective share. If there is no surviving spouse, these items may be set aside for the decedent's minor children. The items are exempt from all claims against the estate except perfected security interests thereon.

D. TESTAMENTARY GIFTS TO CHARITY
Most states do not place any restrictions on charitable devises and bequests. A few do, however, still have Mortmain statutes that restrict charitable bequests by voiding all charitable bequests made in wills executed within a short time before death or by limiting the gifts made within that time to a fixed percentage of the estate. These Mortmain statutes may be unconstitutional. Several courts have found them to violate state and federal Equal Protection Clauses.

X. WILL CONTESTS

A. GROUNDS FOR CONTEST—IN GENERAL
A will contest challenges whether the document offered for probate is a valid will. The contestant may raise any matter tending to show that the will is not valid and should be denied probate. A will may be contested on any of the following grounds:

(i) *Defective execution* (*e.g.*, only one witness when two are required);

(ii) The will offered has been validly *revoked*;

(iii) The testator *lacked testamentary capacity*;

(iv)   The testator *lacked testamentary intent*;

(v)   The will or a gift therein is a product of *undue influence*;

(vi)   The will or a gift therein was procured by *fraud*; or

(vii)   The document was executed or a gift was made as the result of a *mistake*.

Note that most wills are challenged on the grounds of lack of testamentary capacity or undue influence.

B.   PROCEDURAL ASPECTS

1.   Time for Contest
Although the statutory period varies from state to state, in most states, a will contest must be filed within *six months* after the will is admitted to probate.

2.   Proper Contestants
Only *interested parties* have standing to contest a will. To be an interested party, the person must have a direct interest in the estate that would be adversely affected by the admission of the will to probate. Examples of interested parties are intestate heirs and legatees under earlier wills. Creditors do not have standing to contest a will, and neither do executors or testamentary trustees named in earlier wills.

3.   Necessary Parties
In most states, *all legatees under the will and all heirs* are necessary parties to a will contest and must be given notice.

4.   Burden of Proof
The burden of proof is on the will contestant to establish the grounds.

5.   Will May Fail Either Partially or Entirely
A will is void if its execution is procured by undue influence, fraud, duress, or mistake. If only a part of the will was so procured, only that part is void, and the remainder of the will is given effect.

C.   TESTAMENTARY CAPACITY

1.   Must Be Age Eighteen to Make a Will
In most states, a person must be 18 years of age or older to make a will. The requirement is applied as of the *date of execution* of the will, not as of the date of death.

2.   Mental Capacity
The capacity required for making a will is a different and lower standard of capacity than that required to make a contract. To have mental capacity to make a will, the testator must have sufficient capacity to be able to understand:

(i)   The nature of her *act*—*i.e.*, she must actually know that she is executing a will;

(ii)   The *nature and extent of her property*;

(iii) The persons who are the **natural objects of her bounty**; and

(iv) The **nature of the disposition** she is making, *i.e.,* a general understanding of the practical effect of the will as executed.

a. Testator's Capacity Determined at Time of Will's Execution
It is at the making of the will, not at death, that the mental capacity must exist. This being so, all circumstances existing at the time of execution are admissible on the capacity issue, as well as evidence relating to the testator's state of mind shortly before and after the execution of the will. Generally, the more distant in time from the will's execution a particular fact might be, the less significance will be attached to that fact in determining the testator's capacity at the time of execution.

b. Testator with Physical Ailments or Drug Addiction
The fact that the testator was very old, physically frail or ill, that she possessed a failing memory, or was a habitual drinker or addicted to drugs does *not* mean that she lacked the requisite mental capacity and was unable to comprehend the nature of her act.

c. Testator Adjudicated Insane
A person who has been adjudicated insane or for whom a guardian or conservator has been appointed does not necessarily lack testamentary capacity. While such an adjudication is *evidence* of a lack of the required mental capacity, it is *not conclusive* and can be overcome by showing that the testator still met the specific standards set out above.

3. Insane Delusion
"Insane delusion" is a distinct form of incapacity. A person may have sufficient mental capacity to conduct his affairs and to make a will, but may be suffering from an insane delusion so as to require a particular provision in a will to fail on the ground of testamentary incapacity. An insane delusion may invalidate the entire will or only a particular gift.

a. Causation Requirement
A will can be set aside on the ground of insane delusion only if, and to the extent it can be shown that, the delusion *caused* the testamentary disposition. The contestant must show that the testator would not have made the disposition in question *but for* the insane delusion.

b. "Insane Delusion" Defined
An insane delusion is a legal, not a psychiatric, concept. Such a delusion is a belief in facts that do not exist and that no rational person would believe existed.

Example: A belief that all children are spies for Communist China is an insane delusion. A belief that all children are cruel and mean, however, may not be an insane delusion if the testator's life experiences are such that a sane person could come to that conclusion.

1) Unusual Religious Beliefs
Unusual and bizarre religious beliefs ordinarily do not constitute insane delusions, and if they do, it is usually difficult to prove they caused the devise. On the other hand, a belief that Henry Hart, to whom the testator's estate is devised, is God is probably an insane delusion.

2) **False Beliefs**

False beliefs or groundless prejudices of testators with respect to members of their families give rise to difficult cases. Because courts generally do not give relief for mistake in the inducement (*see* F.2., *infra*), disinherited heirs often claim that the testator was suffering from an insane delusion. A groundless belief that the testator's wife is sleeping with other men or that his children are not his has been held to be an insane delusion, but there are cases contra. In these "false beliefs about family members" cases, it is very difficult to predict whether a court will hold that the testator was merely mistaken (and no relief can be granted) or was suffering from an insane delusion. These cases tend to be resolved on their own facts.

4. **Burden of Proof as to Mental Capacity on Contestant**

Whether the testamentary disposition is rational or irrational, many states recognize a presumption that the testator was competent. The burden of introducing evidence to the contrary is on the contestant. If the contestant introduces evidence sufficient, if believed, to warrant a finding of mental incapacity, the presumption drops and the proponent must now introduce evidence of capacity.

D. **UNDUE INFLUENCE**

A will (or a gift in a will) is invalid if it is obtained through the exercise of undue influence. However, mere pleading, cajoling, nagging, or threatening the testator does not constitute undue influence. Influence is not undue unless the free will of the testator is destroyed and the resulting testamentary disposition reflects the desires, not of the testator, but of the party exerting undue influence.

1. **Requirements**

To establish undue influence, the contestants, who have the burden of proof, must establish that:

a. *Influence* was exerted on the testator;

b. The *effect* of the influence was to overpower the mind and free will of the testator; and

c. The *product* of the influence was a will that would not have been executed but for the influence.

2. **Circumstantial Evidence Does Not, By Itself, Establish Undue Influence**

Over half of the appellate cases in which the jury finds undue influence are reversed on appeal because the court finds only circumstantial evidence, and no direct evidence, that influence was exerted. These factors, by themselves, are insufficient to establish undue influence:

a. **Mere Opportunity to Exert Influence**

A will cannot be set aside on proof of facts that, at most, merely show that a party had ample opportunity to exert influence (*e.g.*, she lived next door to her mother, had a key to her mother's house, held a power of attorney to act on her mother's behalf, took care of her mother's financial affairs, etc.).

b. **Mere Susceptibility to Influence Due to Age or Physical Condition**

The fact that the testator was elderly, in poor health, had memory lapses, took Valium,

etc., does no more than indicate that the testator was susceptible to undue influence. This evidence does not establish that the testator's mind was in fact subverted and overpowered at the time the will was executed.

c. **"Unnatural Disposition" that Favors Some Relatives Over Others**
The mere fact that the will makes an unnatural disposition that favors some relatives over others (*e.g.*, two-thirds of the testator's estate to her daughter, one-third to her church, and nothing to her son) is not sufficient to establish undue influence. It is only when all reasonable explanation for the bequests is lacking that the trier of fact may take this as a circumstance showing undue influence.

3. **Presumption of Undue Influence**
A presumption of undue influence may be created by the following facts:

(i)   A *confidential relationship* existed between the testator and the beneficiary who was alleged to have exercised undue influence;

(ii) The *beneficiary participated* in some way in procuring or drafting the will or in some other significant activity relating to the execution of the will; and

(iii) The provisions of the will appear to be *unnatural* and favor the person who allegedly exercised undue influence.

Once these elements appear, the *burden shifts* to the proponent of the will to prove that it was not induced by his undue influence.

a. **Confidential Relationship**
A presumption of undue influence arises when a confidential relationship (*e.g.*, attorney-client, doctor-patient) exists *and* the beneficiary participated in drafting the will. Other relationships in which it is shown that one person relied heavily upon, and placed more than a normal amount of confidence in, another may also suffice to show a confidential relationship.

Example: Granddaughter G, who took care of her 90-year-old blind and bedridden grandmother, cashed her Social Security checks, and paid her bills, was in a confidential relationship. Because G was active in procuring the will (which was written by a notary public who was G's close friend) and there were suspicious circumstances (other relations who were in the house at the time were unaware that the will was being signed by the testator and witnessed by two of G's friends), a presumption of undue influence arose.

1) **No Automatic Presumption Between Spouses**
Although a husband and wife share a confidential relationship, a presumption of undue influence does *not automatically* arise between spouses. This is due in part to the policy of preserving marriages, which an automatic presumption would thwart. In order for a spouse's influence to be "undue," the spouse must have exerted influence over the testator in such a manner that it *overpowered the free will* of the testator and resulted in a *disposition reflecting the desires* of the spouse exerting the influence.

Example: The day after their wedding, Husband drove Wife to his attorney's office where Wife drafted and signed her will. She left half of her estate to Husband's son even though she had never met him. Although Husband and Wife share a confidential relationship, there is not enough evidence to raise a presumption of undue influence.

Compare: After their marriage, Wife isolated Husband from his children by telling him that they were after his money. Husband was involved in a car accident that put him in critical condition. Wife brought a will to the hospital for Husband to sign. The witness stated that Husband wanted to include his children in the will but Wife would not let him. Here, there clearly is undue influence.

b. Procurement of Will
The criteria for determining whether the beneficiary was active in procuring the will can include one or more of the following: (i) the beneficiary's presence when the testator expressed the desire to make a will; (ii) the beneficiary's recommending an attorney to prepare the will; (iii) the beneficiary's giving an attorney instructions as to what the will should contain; (iv) the beneficiary's knowledge of the will's contents prior to its execution; (v) the beneficiary's securing witnesses for the will; (vi) the beneficiary's being present when the will is executed; and (vii) the beneficiary's safeguarding the will after its execution.

c. Unnatural Disposition
A presumption of undue influence may arise, despite the absence of a confidential relationship between the testator and beneficiary, when the execution of a will is surrounded by suspicious circumstances, as where the testator disinherits her children in favor of a stranger. However, the mere fact that a will is unnatural in preferring a stranger over blood kindred is not sufficient to give rise to a presumption of undue influence unless there are other suspicious circumstances.

E. FRAUD
Where the execution of a will or the inclusion therein of a particular gift is the result of fraud, the will or the particular gift is invalid. A finding of fraud requires a showing that the testator has been willfully deceived as to the character or the content of an instrument, as to the extrinsic facts that would induce the will or a particular disposition, or with respect to facts material to a disposition. (Innocent misrepresentation does not constitute fraud, although relief might possibly be available on the ground of mistake.)

1. Causation
Fraud invalidates a will only if the testator was *in fact* deceived by and acted in reliance on the misrepresentation. In other words, a gift is invalid only if the testator would not have made it had she known the true facts.

2. Fraud in the Execution (Fraud in the Factum)
In the case of fraud in the execution, there is a misrepresentation as to the nature of the contents of the instrument.
Examples: 1) Upon hearing a statement by A that the instrument presented to T gives A

a power of attorney to pay T's bills while T is in the hospital, T signs it. In fact, the instrument contains provisions devising all of T's property to A.

2) A tells T that the instrument is T's will, but in fact A has substituted a will containing different provisions.

3. Fraud in the Inducement

In the case of fraud in the inducement, the testator intends to execute the instrument as her will and to include the particular contents of that instrument, but she is fraudulently induced into making this will, or some particular gift therein, by misrepresentations as to facts which influence her motivation. The will or the particular gifts affected by the fraud must be set aside.

Example: Where Lilly tells T that his son, Isaac, is dead, it may be uncertain whether the new will, leaving everything to Lilly, was induced by the belief that Isaac was dead or whether the will would have been made in the same fashion had T known that Isaac was still alive. T might wish to exclude Isaac, from whom he had not heard in many years, in favor of Lilly, who had remained a dutiful daughter.

 Such situations are resolved by inferences drawn from the family circumstances and other extrinsic evidence (excluding T's oral declarations) as to what T's probable intent was.

4. Fraudulent Prevention of Will

Cases occasionally involve a fraudulent prevention of the execution of a will by one or more of the persons who would take by intestate succession. The cases are split as to whether any relief is available.

a. Intestate Succession Laws Apply

Some courts conclude there is no way of granting relief because a court "cannot write a will on behalf of a decedent"; hence, the intestate succession laws apply.

b. Better View Is to Impose Constructive Trust

The better view is that a constructive trust may be imposed against the intestate successors for the benefit of those who would have been beneficiaries of the will that the decedent was fraudulently prevented from executing. Some courts have even imposed constructive trusts in these cases on innocent heirs who were not themselves wrongdoers but who would be unjustly enriched.

F. MISTAKE

1. Mistake in Execution of Will

a. Mistake as to Nature of Instrument—Extrinsic Evidence Admissible

Extrinsic evidence is admissible to show that the testator was unaware of the nature of the instrument she signed (*e.g.,* she believed it to be a power of attorney). Such a mistake relates to the issue of whether the testator had the requisite testamentary intent, without which the will would be invalid.

b. Wrong Will Signed—Courts Divided on Relief Question

In cases where the testator has signed the wrong will, the courts are divided on the

question of whether relief should be granted. Suppose that reciprocal wills are prepared for H and W, under which each devises his or her estate to the other. By mistake, H signs the will prepared for W, and W signs the will prepared for H. Thus, the will signed by H reads, "I, Rose Snide, leave all my property to my husband, Harvey Snide." Some courts have denied relief on the ground that H lacked testamentary intent because he did not intend to execute the document that he signed. [*In re* Pavlinko's Estate, 148 A.2d 528 (Pa. 1959)] However, the better and modern view is that the court should grant relief because both the existence and the nature of the mistake are very obvious. The court should insert "Harvey" for "Rose" and "husband" for "wife" (and vice versa), as appropriate. [*In re* Snide, 52 N.Y.2d 193 (1981)]

2. Mistake in Inducement—No Relief Granted

If the alleged mistake involves the reasons that led the testator to make the will (or the reasons for making or not making a particular gift therein), and the mistake was not fraudulently induced, no relief is granted. *Rationale:* To allow evidence as to the alleged mistake would open the door to fraudulent testimony because the testator is dead and cannot contradict the testimony as to the supposed mistake. Moreover, even if the alleged mistake were shown, this would not establish that the testator would have made a different disposition had the true facts been known.

Example: T's son Ron is a prisoner of war. Assuming that Ron is dead, T revokes a will that left everything in equal shares to Ron and T's other son, Don, and executes a new will leaving everything to Don. After T's death, Ron returns alive. Evidence of the mistake is not admissible, and Don takes T's estate under the second will.

a. Exception If Mistake Appears on Face of Will

The courts have recognized (more often in dictum than in actual holdings) that if the mistaken inducement appears on the face of the will, relief will be granted.

Example: Same facts as above, except that T's new will says, "Because my son Ron is dead, I revoke my earlier will and leave all of my property to my son Don." Several courts have stated in dicta that because the mistake is shown on the face of the will and extrinsic evidence need not be relied on to show the mistake, the court should deny probate of the second will and instead probate the will that benefits Ron.

3. Mistake as to Contents of Will

a. Mistaken Omission—No Relief Granted

Extrinsic evidence is not admissible to show that a provision was mistakenly omitted from a will, or that a provision contained in the will is not what the testator intended. Absent evidence of fraud, duress, or suspicious circumstances, it is conclusively presumed that the testator understood and approved the terms of the new will when she signed it. *Rationale:* The courts are reluctant to have property pass, not pursuant to the terms of a duly executed will, but on the basis of oral testimony.

Example: T executes a will that makes only minor changes from an earlier will (which was revoked by the new will). Unlike the earlier will, the new will does not contain a residuary clause. The attorney who prepared the new will makes a sworn affidavit stating that the omission was inadvertent and was contrary to T's instructions. The affidavit is not admissible,

and the new will must be probated. Because the will is clear as to its meaning and is not ambiguous, extrinsic evidence as to T's intent is inadmissible. Correction would require the addition of a new provision, and *the courts cannot reform a decedent's will*.

b. **Plain Meaning Rule—Evidence Not Admissible to Contradict Plain Language**
If the language of a will is unambiguous, evidence is not admissible to show that the testator made a mistake in describing a beneficiary or the property that was to be the subject of the gift. *Rationale:* The testator signed the will and is conclusively presumed to have read, understood, and intended its contents. To allow oral testimony to contradict the will's plain meaning would open the door to fraud.

Examples: 1) T's will bequeaths "200 shares of Acme stock" to B. Evidence, no matter how compelling, is *not* admissible to show that T actually owned 300 shares of Acme stock and intended to bequeath all 300 shares to B.

2) T's will bequeaths property "to my cousin, John Smith." T had a cousin John Smith whom he had not seen in 10 years. T also had a nephew John Smith of whom he was particularly fond, and T had told third parties that he had made a gift to the nephew in his will. Evidence is *not* admissible to show that T intended to make a gift to his nephew and not to his cousin.

4. **Latent or Patent Ambiguity—Extrinsic Evidence Admissible to Cure Ambiguity**

a. **Latent Ambiguity**
A latent ambiguity exists when the language of the will, although clear on its face in describing a beneficiary or property, results in a misdescription when applied to the facts to which it refers. Extrinsic evidence is admissible to cure the ambiguity. *Rationale:* Reliance on parol evidence does not have the effect of "rewriting" the will or adding to its terms. Instead, the evidence is being received to give meaning to the words the testator actually used. *But note:* If the extrinsic evidence does not resolve the ambiguity, the gift fails.

Examples: 1) T's will devises Blackacre "to my niece Nellie." T has two nieces named Nellie. Parol evidence is admissible to show which niece T intended to benefit.

2) Same facts as above, except that T does not have a niece named Nellie. He does, however, have a niece named Norrie and a cousin named Nellie. Parol evidence is admissible to show whether T intended to make a gift to cousin Nellie or to niece Norrie. But if the evidence does not establish which one T had in mind, the gift fails.

3) A devise of "Lot #6, Square #403," which T did not own, could be shown by extrinsic evidence to pass Lot #3, Square #406, which T did own. [Patch v. White, 117 U.S. 210 (1886)]

4) T's will bequeathed her residuary estate "to Apollo Medical Center as a memorial to my late husband." Apollo was acquired by another corporation, and the hospital's name was changed to Humana Hospital. Thereafter, T executed a new will that repeated the gift to the Apollo Medical

Center. Evidence was admitted to show that T intended the gift for the hospital at which her husband was treated before his death, and that the name change did not defeat the gift. "[T]he misnomer of a devisee will not cause the devise to fail where the identity of the devisee can be identified with certainty." [Humana, Inc. v. Estate of Scheying, 483 So. 2d 113 (Fla. 1986)]

b. Patent Ambiguity

A patent ambiguity exists when the uncertainty appears on the face of the will (*e.g.,* where the will mentions two cousins, Mary Jones and Mary Smith, and then makes a gift "to my cousin Mary"). The traditional view is that extrinsic evidence is not admissible to correct a patent ambiguity, and that the gift fails because of the misdescription. However, the modern and better view is that such evidence is admissible.

Example: T's will bequeathed one-third of his business to A and B, but the will was unclear as to whether A and B were to receive one-third each or whether, instead, the one-third share was to be divided between A and B (giving them one-sixth each). *Held:* This was a patent ambiguity, and extrinsic evidence should be admitted to cure the ambiguity.

G. NO-CONTEST CLAUSES

A no-contest clause (sometimes called an *in terrorem* clause) provides that a beneficiary who contests the will forfeits his interest under the will.

1. Majority Rule—No Forfeiture If Probable Cause for Contesting Will

Under the UPC and in most states, if the beneficiary had probable cause for bringing the will contest (*i.e.,* it was not a suit whose sole purpose was to provoke a settlement), the no-contest forfeiture clause is not given effect. [*See* UPC §2-517] Whether the beneficiary had probable cause is a question of fact. Note that suits objecting to the court's jurisdiction, challenging the appointment of an executor, and asking the court to construe the will are not will contests within the meaning of most no-contest clauses.

Example: Tom dies leaving a will that bequeaths $10,000 to his son Roy, and the rest of his substantial estate to his friend Ruby. The will contains a no-contest clause that reads: "Should any beneficiary named herein contest this will or any of its provisions, he shall forfeit all interests given to him by my will." Roy brings a will contest on grounds of undue influence and lack of capacity. Roy loses the will contest, and Tom's will is admitted to probate. In most states, Roy forfeits the $10,000 bequest.

2. Minority Rule—No-Contest Clause Given Full Effect Regardless of Probable Cause

Some states (*e.g.,* Illinois, Oregon) have not adopted the "probable cause" defense to enforcement of no-contest clauses. A provision that triggers forfeiture if a beneficiary contests the will is given full effect, regardless of whether there was probable cause for challenging the will.

XI. PROBATE AND ESTATE ADMINISTRATION

A. TERMINOLOGY AND OVERVIEW

"Probate" refers to the proceeding in which an instrument is judicially determined to be the

duly executed last will of the decedent (or, if there is no will, the proceeding in which the decedent's heirs are judicially determined). At the probate proceeding, a *personal representative* is appointed to carry out the estate administration. In most states, the personal representative is called an *executor* if named in the decedent's will, and an *administrator* if named by the court.

Testate estates must go through some form of administration. Intestate estates need not be administered if the heirs are able to agree as to the distribution of property; however, they often are administered in order to cut off creditors' claims and to ensure clear title in the heirs.

B. SUMMARY OF RULES AND PROCEDURE
The following is a summary of probate rules and procedure:

1. Any interested person may *file* a petition for probate.

2. The custodian of a will *must produce it within a certain time* (*e.g.*, 30 days) after the death of the testator.

3. The *testator's domicile at the time of death*, not the place of death, determines the place of "primary" administration of the estate (but "ancillary" administration, including probate, is also necessary wherever property to be administered is located).

4. A will *must be offered for probate within a specified number of years*. For example, the UPC requires that a will be probated within three years or the decedent is deemed to have died intestate. [UPC §3-108]

5. A will must be *probated* in order for a person to *take* under its terms.

6. A probated will *cannot be collaterally attacked* (*e.g.*, in a later will contest) when a specified short statute of limitations after probate has run.

7. A *lost or destroyed will* may be probated, provided its contents can be proved.

8. In a probate proceeding, the *following facts must be proved*:

    a. That the testator is dead (this fact is jurisdictional);

    b. That the formalities of execution were observed; and

    c. That the notice requirements for probate have been complied with.

C. PERSONAL REPRESENTATIVE

1. Appointment of Personal Representative
Any person who has *capacity to contract* may serve as personal representative. Thus, an incompetent or a minor cannot serve.

a. How Executor or Administrator Is Appointed
If an "executor" is named in the will, he will be appointed as personal representative unless subject to a particular disqualification. If no executor is named in the will or if

the executor named cannot serve, an "administrator cum testamento annexo" will be appointed as personal representative. If the decedent died intestate, an "administrator" will be appointed as personal representative.

b.   Preference of Appointment
A typical statutory order of preference for appointment of a personal representative would be: (i) the person named as executor in the will; (ii) the surviving spouse, if a will beneficiary; (iii) any will beneficiary; (iv) the surviving spouse; (v) any other heir; and (vi) after 45 days, a creditor.

c.   Authority of Representative
The authority of the personal representative is derived from his court appointment, and he serves as an officer of the court.

d.   Bond Required for Issuance of Letters Testamentary
The personal representative must file a bond for the faithful performance of his duties, unless the testator has provided in his will that no bond shall be required. When the personal representative has filed the required bond, "letters testamentary" (for an executor or administrator cum testamento annexo) or "letters of administration" (for an administrator) are issued certifying his authority to act on behalf of the estate.

2.   Powers and Duties of the Personal Representative
The personal representative has functions generally analogous to those of a receiver of a defunct corporation or a trustee in bankruptcy, and must take whatever steps are necessary to wind up the decedent's affairs. In that respect, the primary functions of the personal representative are to:

(i)   *Give notice* to devisees, heirs, and claimants against the estate;

(ii)   *Discover and collect the decedent's assets* and file an inventory;

(iii) *Manage* the assets of the estate during administration;

(iv)   *Pay expenses* of administration, claims against the estate, and taxes; and

(v)   *Distribute* the property.

Like the trustee, the personal representative serves in a fiduciary capacity. (*See* Trusts outline.) Unlike the trustee, however, the personal representative is primarily a liquidator, rather than a manager, and generally must have court approval for such activities as borrowing money, operating a business, or selling property.

3.   Compensation of Personal Representative
The personal representative is entitled to compensation for his services rendered on behalf of the estate. Rates of compensation may be governed by statute, *e.g.*, based on the estate's value. If there is no controlling statute, the court has discretionary authority to award reasonable compensation. Factors a court might consider in determining reasonable compensation include the amount of time spent performing appropriate services, the degree of difficulty involved, and a reasonable hourly rate.

a. **May Be Provided for by Will**
The testator may provide compensation for the personal representative by means of a gift in the will. However, the personal representative may renounce such a testamentary gift, and take whatever compensation to which he would otherwise be entitled.

b. **May Be Denied for Wrongful Conduct**
The court may deny compensation where the personal representative has engaged in dishonest or fraudulent conduct, or has otherwise acted in bad faith or willful neglect of his duties.

D. CREDITORS' CLAIMS

1. Notice
One of the personal representative's first tasks is to give notice to the creditors of the estate, advising them of the pendency of the administration and when and where claims must be filed. Notice may be accomplished by publication, but the personal representative must mail or personally deliver the notice to creditors who are known or are reasonably ascertainable.

2. Nonclaim Statutes
In most states, creditors' claims must be filed within a specified period of time (*e.g.*, three months after notice) or they are barred. These statutes apply to all claims: liquidated and nonliquidated, matured and contingent, contract and tort.

a. **Exception—Failure to Give Notice**
If notice is not given to creditors in accordance with the statute, claims are barred only after a specified number of *years* have passed since the decedent's death.

3. Priority of Claims
Typically, statutes provide that claims are to be paid in the following order:

a. Administration expenses;

b. Funeral expenses and expenses of the last illness (up to specific dollar amount);

c. Family allowance;

d. Debts given preference under federal law (*e.g.*, tax claims);

e. Secured claims (up to the value of the security interest);

f. Judgments entered against the decedent during his lifetime; and

g. All other claims.

E. ABATEMENT
Abatement is the process of reducing testamentary gifts in cases where the estate assets are not sufficient to pay all claims against the estate and satisfy all bequests and devises. The testator may set out an order of abatement in the will. If there are no contrary provisions in the will, estates in most jurisdictions abate in the following order:

(i) Property passing by intestacy;

(ii) The residuary estate;

(iii) General legacies, which abate pro rata;

(iv) Specific devises and bequests.

[*See* UPC §3-902] Within each category, some states provide that personal property abates before real property.

1. Demonstrative Legacies

To the extent that the property from which the gift was to be satisfied is in the estate at death, demonstrative legacies are treated as specific legacies for abatement purposes. To the extent the fund is insufficient, however, the demonstrative legacy is treated as a general legacy.

F. EXONERATION OF LIENS

At common law and in many states today, if specifically devised property is, at the testator's death, subject to a lien that secures a note on which the testator was personally liable, the beneficiary is entitled to have the lien exonerated (unless there is a contrary will provision). Thus, the beneficiary is entitled to demand payment of the debt out of the residuary estate so that the property passes to him free of any encumbrance. However, the UPC and a growing number of states provide that liens on specifically devised property are ***not*** exonerated unless the will so directs. In these states, a specific devise passes subject to a security interest even if the will contains a general (rather than specific) provision to pay all debts. [*See* UPC §2-607]

G. GUIDELINES WHEN WILL AMBIGUOUS

It is commonly stated that where the language of a will is clear and unambiguous, there is no need for either interpretation or construction. The directions in the will must be followed. Where there is some ambiguity, the court will interpret the will and consider any admissible extrinsic evidence to determine the testator's intent. Only where there is no evidence of the testator's intent is it necessary to use a rule of construction as a presumption concerning that intent. Of course, inevitably the existence of rules of construction will influence a court when it sets out to interpret a will.

1. Interpretation—Testator's Actual Intent

a. Will Clear—Extrinsic Evidence Inadmissible

If the will clearly specifies a particular disposition, it must be carried out, and extrinsic evidence of a contrary intent of the testator, no matter how persuasive, is inadmissible.

b. Will Ambiguous—Extrinsic Evidence Admissible

If a provision in the will is ambiguous, the court should attempt to find the testator's intent within the "four corners" of the instrument. Only if that attempt fails should the court admit certain extrinsic evidence that is probative on the issue of intent. Extrinsic evidence may be used only to explain the meaning of what is written in the will and cannot subtract from the will, add missing provisions, or show some entirely different meaning.

1) Testimony Regarding Surrounding Circumstances Permitted

Testimony regarding the testator's surrounding circumstances at the time of execution is permitted, *e.g.,* the amount and character of his property, the natural objects of his bounty, his relations with his relatives, and their situations and circumstances.

2) Declarations of Testator Not Admissible

What would seem the most probative evidence of the testator's intent—his declaration as to what he meant to do—is generally *not* admissible because of the high chance of perjured testimony.

a) Exception—Equivocation

The only exception to this rule concerns a so-called latent ambiguity (*see* X.F.4.a., *supra*) known as "equivocation." An equivocation is where the description of a beneficiary or of the property describes more than one person or more than one item of property. In such cases, and in those only, testimony of the declarations of the testator is admissible.

Example: T bequeaths $10,000 to "my cousin Bill," but unknown to T he had two cousins named Bill. Testimony that he knew only one of them would be admissible as "surrounding circumstances." In addition, testimony by T's lawyer that T said, "I want $10,000 to go to my cousin Bill Smith of Chicago" is admissible.

c. Intent as of Time of Execution

The intention of the testator should be sought as of *the time of execution* of the will (or of a later codicil that republishes it).

Example: T leaves his estate to his "heirs." Thereafter the statute of descent and distribution is amended. The estate should pass to those who would have been T's heirs under the statute in force at the time the will was executed.

2. Rules of Construction

When there is no evidence of the actual intent of the testator, the court must resort to rules of construction such as those noted below:

a. Favor those who *would take intestate*.

b. Favor the construction *that avoids intestacy*.

c. Favor the construction that is *consistent with the perceived "plan"* of disposition.

d. *Every portion* of the will should be given effect if possible.

e. Between totally inconsistent clauses, the *latter is most likely the final intent*.

3. Beware of Finding Gifts by Implication

As much as the court wants to find that the will disposes of all of the property, however, sometimes there will be a situation that the will does not cover. Do not invent or imply what the testator would have done.

XII. WILL SUBSTITUTES

A. IN GENERAL
Individuals wishing to avoid taxes and to eliminate the cost and inconvenience of probate often turn to various "will substitutes" to transfer their property upon death. Frequently, the decedent's testate or intestate takers argue (usually unsuccessfully) that these forms of transfer constitute "testamentary" transfers and are, therefore, invalid for failure to comply with the required formalities for execution of a will. The following are examples of will substitutes:

1. Life insurance;

2. Joint tenancies or tenancies by the entirety (*see* Multistate Real Property outline);

3. Inter vivos trusts (*i.e.,* trusts created during the settlor's lifetime);

4. Bank arrangements;

5. Deeds;

6. Contracts; and

7. Inter vivos gifts, including gifts causa mortis (*i.e.,* gifts made in contemplation of death).

B. LIFE INSURANCE
Life insurance is probably the most widely used will substitute. Assume that H takes out a life insurance policy on his life, payable to W. H owns the policy and can cash it in or change the beneficiary. The life insurance contract clearly has testamentary effect in the sense that at H's death an economic interest will pass from H to W. Nevertheless, it is not a "will," and the designation of W as beneficiary does not have to be attested by witnesses. Rather, the courts have held that a life insurance policy is a contract, and the disposition is governed by the terms of the contract. (Note that most life insurance policies provide that a change of beneficiaries can be effected by the owner only by notification to the company during the owner's life. Thus, a will cannot change the beneficiary designation, unless the terms of the contract permit this.)

C. BANK ARRANGEMENTS

1. Totten Trusts
A "Totten trust" (named after an early New York case) is a deposit of money in the depositor's own bank account in trust for another person. The majority rule is that such a transfer creates a valid revocable trust, even though the depositor retains complete control over the account during her lifetime and the transfer is complete only upon her death. The trust is revoked to the extent of withdrawals made by the depositor before her death, and may also be revoked by the depositor's will. Creditors of the depositor can reach the funds in the account during her life.

2. Joint or Survivor Accounts
The deposit of money in a bank in the names of two persons "with right of survivorship" is generally held effective to give the survivor the absolute right to all of the money. However, in many states, extrinsic evidence is admissible to show that the dead depositor did not intend

a gift to the survivor, and that the account was only a convenience for paying the depositor's bills. Where the survivor is not the spouse but someone else, this issue has been frequently litigated.

3. Payable on Death Designations

Many courts have held a payable on death ("P.O.D.") designation on a bank account ineffective, on the rationale that no interest of any type is transferred to the designated beneficiary during the depositor's lifetime, and hence the unattested designation violates the Statute of Wills. This result has been criticized by many authorities on the ground that a Totten trust is distinguishable from a P.O.D. designation only by the fact that the depositor has recited that he holds the deposit "in trust," and yet the Totten trust device is upheld. In response to this criticism, a number of states have enacted statutes specifically permitting P.O.D. accounts as valid will substitutes. [*See* UPC §§6-101 *et seq.*]

D. DEEDS

A deed deposited in escrow, with delivery conditioned upon the grantor's death, may be a valid nontestamentary transfer (*see* Multistate Real Property outline). Similarly, if a deed that is by its terms effective only upon the grantor's death has actually been delivered to the grantee, a court may sustain the transfer as nontestamentary by construing the deed as a present transfer of a future interest, subject to a life estate reserved in the grantor.

E. CONTRACTS

A contract that purports to dispose of property upon death is testamentary in nature and must comply with the formalities required for a will in order to be enforceable.

XIII. POWERS OF APPOINTMENT

A. THE TERMINOLOGY OF POWERS—BASIC DEFINITIONS

1. Power of Appointment Defined

A power of appointment is an authority created in or reserved by a person enabling that person (called the *donee* of the power) to designate, within the limits prescribed by the creator of the power (called the *donor*), the persons who shall take certain property and the manner in which they shall take it. When a person reserves a power in herself, she is both donor and donee of the power. Other important terms include the following:

a. The *objects* of the power are the persons in whose favor a power is exercisable.

b. The *appointees* are the persons in whose favor the power is actually exercised.

c. The *appointive property* is the property that is the subject of the power.

d. The *takers in default of appointment* are the persons designated to take the property if the donee fails to effectively exercise his power of appointment.

2. General vs. Special Power of Appointment

While the concept of, and distinction between, general and special powers derive from the

common law, the only definition of importance today is the one set forth in section 2041 of the Internal Revenue Code, which applies the federal estate tax to assets over which the decedent held a general power, but not to assets over which she held a special power.

a. General Power
A general power of appointment is one exercisable in favor of the donee herself, her estate, her creditors, *or* the creditors of her estate.

b. Special Power
A special power of appointment is one exercisable in favor of a specified class of persons, which does *not* include the donee, her estate, her creditors, or the creditors of her estate.

3. Presently Exercisable vs. Testamentary Power
A presently exercisable power of appointment is one exercisable by the donee during her lifetime. A testamentary power is one that is exercisable only by the donee's will.

Examples: 1) T's will devises property "to A for life, and on A's death to such persons as A shall appoint by will; in default of appointment to B." T is the donor of the power of appointment. A is the donee of a *general testamentary power*. It is a general power because the objects of the power ("such persons") include A's estate or the creditors of A's estate. It is testamentary because it is exercisable only by will. B is the taker in default of appointment; B holds a vested remainder subject to total divestment. For purposes of classifying B's interest, the power of appointment is treated as a divesting condition subsequent because B takes *unless* A exercises the power of appointment.

2) T's will devises property "to A for life, and on A's death to such of A's issue as she shall appoint during her lifetime or by will; in default of appointment, to A's issue then living, per stirpes." A is the donee of a *special power of appointment* that is exercisable during A's lifetime or by will. It is a special power because A is limited to appointing among her issue. "A's issue then living" are the takers in default of appointment; there is a contingent remainder in A's issue.

In most states, a presently exercisable power of appointment is also exercisable by the donee's will unless the donor has expressly limited exercise of the power to the donee's lifetime.

B. GENERAL POWERS OF APPOINTMENT

1. Donee Acts as Donor's Agent
The basic theory of powers of appointment (whether general or special) is that the donee is the donor's agent in designating the beneficiaries of the appointive property; she is not the owner of the property. When the donee exercises the power, it is treated as though the donee is "filling in the blanks" in the donor's will or trust. An appointment is deemed to relate back to the donor's will so that the appointee takes title directly from the donor of the power rather than from the donee. This is referred to as the *doctrine of relation back*.

2. Power of Appointment Is Personal to Donee
A power of appointment is personal to the donee. If she dies without having exercised the

power, it terminates; she cannot devise the power by her will. The donee cannot delegate the power to another; nor can she assign it. (She can, however, exercise the power by creating another power in the appointee. This is true in all cases if it is a general power; it is true of a special power in some cases—this is discussed in C., *infra*.)

3. Generally Appointive Property Not Subject to Dower or Elective Share Statute
Dower does not attach to real property over which the husband holds a power of appointment because the husband did not own the property. In many states, a surviving spouse's elective share does not apply to assets over which the deceased spouse held a power of appointment.

4. Generally Creditors Cannot Reach Appointive Assets
Under the theory that the donee does not own the appointive property, if the donee does not exercise her general power (whether presently exercisable or testamentary), her creditors cannot reach the property.

a. If Donee Exercises Power—Creditors Can Reach Those Assets
If the donee exercises the general power, the courts have abandoned the agency theory in favor of a fiction that enables the donee's creditors to reach the property. This is true whether the donee appoints to herself or to some other person. The theory is that the donee, in making the appointment, is exercising a dominion that is practically identical to that exercised by her over her own property, and so her creditors can reach the appointive property as though she were the owner. *Minority rule:* By statute in several states (*e.g.,* California, Michigan), creditors of the donee of a general power can reach the appointive property regardless of whether the power is exercised.

b. If Donee Is Also Donor—Creditors Can Reach Appointive Assets
If the donee of a general power is also the donor, her creditors can reach the appointive assets whether or not she exercises the power. A general power of appointment cannot be used to squirrel away one's assets from her creditors. (This is analogous to the rule that a spendthrift clause in favor of the settlor of a trust is invalid.)

5. Failure to Exercise General Power of Appointment
If the donee of a general power fails to exercise the power and the donor's instrument creating the general power contains no gift in default of appointment, the appointive property reverts to the *donor's estate* and passes according to the residuary clause of the donor's will or by intestacy to the donor's heirs.

C. SPECIAL POWERS OF APPOINTMENT

1. Exclusive vs. Nonexclusive Special Powers
A special power of appointment is *exclusive* if it may be exercised in favor of some objects of the power to the exclusion of others; *i.e.,* the donee can exclude some objects and can appoint unequal shares. A special power is *nonexclusive* if it must be exercised in favor of all of the appointees.

a. Strong Presumption that Special Powers Are Exclusive
Special powers are presumed to be exclusive unless the donor expressly provides otherwise.

Examples: 1) On A's death the trustee shall distribute the corpus *"among* A's children as A shall appoint by will." By traditional analysis, use of the word "among," without any other qualifying words, makes the power *nonexclusive*. However, it is not likely that you will ever see a nonexclusive power, for invariably there is qualifying language, along the lines of the examples that follow, that leads to a finding of "exclusive."

2) "Among *such* of A's children as he shall appoint by will." Although the word "among" has been used, the reference to "such of" A's children clearly indicates that the power is exclusive.

3) "Among A's children as A shall appoint by will, *in such shares and proportions* as A shall determine." The power is exclusive.

b. **Nonexclusive Powers—Illusory Appointment Doctrine**
Suppose A has a special power to appoint *among* his children. He has three children and the special power is deemed to be nonexclusive, meaning that he cannot exclude any of the children in exercising the power. What prevents A from appointing $10 to one child and the rest of the property to the other two children? To resolve this problem, the common law courts developed the "illusory appointment" doctrine.

When a special power is nonexclusive, the donee may not favor some of the appointees by making an "illusory" appointment to the other appointees. He must appoint a "substantial" share to *all* appointees. Most courts have recognized and applied this doctrine despite the difficulties involved in determining what is a "substantial" share. *Note:* Under the Restatement (Third) of Property, each appointee must receive a *reasonable*, rather than substantial, share. [Rest. 3d of Property: Wills & Other Donative Transfers §17.5 cmt. j]

2. **Implied Gift in Default of Appointment**
If the donee of a special power of appointment does not exercise the power *and* there is no gift in default of appointment, a gift to the objects of the special power is implied.
Example: Property is devised to S for life, with a testamentary power to appoint "among his children, if he should have any; and in case he should die not leaving any children, I give and devise the same to the children of my daughter." S is survived by children, but he did not appoint to them by will. The court will imply a gift in default of appointment and direct a distribution among S's children.

3. **Absent Fraud, Creditor of Donee Can Never Reach Appointive Assets**
Under the agency theory of powers of appointment, the creditor of the donee of a special power cannot reach the property *even if the donee exercises the power*. This is true even if the donee of the special power is also the donor, unless the transfer was in fraud of the donor-donee's creditors. This is an extension of the principle that any irrevocable disposition, not made with the intent to defeat creditors' claims, is not subject to challenge by the transferor's creditors.

D. **EXERCISE OF POWERS OF APPOINTMENT**

1. **Any Instrument Can Exercise Power Unless Donor Directs Otherwise**

   Unless the donor directs otherwise, a power of appointment can be exercised by any instrument that is effective to transfer title to property. The donee must have legal capacity to execute an effective instrument of transfer. Of course, if it is a testamentary power, it must be exercised by a will that is validly executed under the laws of the particular jurisdiction.

   If, however, the donor calls for the power's exercise "by an instrument specifically referring to this power," this mandate must be complied with to effectively exercise the power.

2. **Residuary Clause Does Not, By Itself, Exercise Testamentary Power**

   The majority rule is that a residuary clause, by itself, does not exercise any power of appointment held by the testator as donee.

   Example: A, holding a general testamentary power of appointment, dies leaving a will that does not in its terms refer to the power, but contains a residuary clause that devises "all the rest, residue, and remainder of my property, of whatever kind or nature and wherever located," to various persons. Under the majority rule, A's will does not exercise the power of appointment, and the appointive assets pass to the takers in default of appointment named in the donor's will.

3. **"Blanket" Exercise of Power Is Permissible**

   If a person holding a testamentary power executes a will that devises "all the rest, residue, and remainder of my property, *including any property over which I may have a power of appointment*," this "blanket" exercise of any power of appointment will be given effect *unless* the donor called for an appointment by an instrument that specifically refers to the power.

4. **Exercise by Implication**

   The courts will find that a power of appointment (whether general or special) was exercised by implication (i) when the donee purports to dispose of the property as though it were her own, meaning that the disposition can be given effect only if it is treated as an exercise of the power; or (ii) when the disposition cannot be given its intended meaning or any effective meaning unless the donee is treated as having exercised the power. An exercise by implication can be found *unless* the donor called for appointment "by an instrument expressly referring to this power."

   Example: B holds a life estate and a general testamentary power over a group of assets that includes Blackacre. B dies leaving a will that provides: "I devise Blackacre to my son, B Jr." B's general power is exercised with respect to Blackacre (but not as to the other appointive assets), for this is the only way the disposition in B's will can be given effect.

   This will be the result *unless* the donor, in creating the power, called for its exercise by specific reference to the power. In this situation, because B made no explicit reference to the power, it is not exercised. Blackacre (along with the other appointive assets) passes to the takers in default of appointment.

5. **Scope of Power**

   Many states hold that a donee of a power of appointment, even a special power, may exercise the power by creating a trust for the benefit of an object of the power rather than appointing the property outright. [*See* Rest. 3d of Property: Wills & Other Donative Transfers §19.14]

Other states reject this view. There is a similar split of authority as to whether a donee of a special power can grant an object of this power a broader special power than the donee had. Because the donee could appoint the property outright, the better view seems to be that he can create a power in the object broader than his own power.

E. APPLICATION OF RULE AGAINST PERPETUITIES
The common law Rule Against Perpetuities, which requires that an interest vest or fail within a life in being plus 21 years, applies to powers of appointment. (For a detailed discussion of the Rule Against Perpetuities, *see* Multistate Real Property outline.) Generally, a power of appointment raises the following perpetuities issues: the validity of the power itself, the validity of its exercise, and the validity of the gift in default of appointment.

1. Presently Exercisable General Powers
A presently exercisable general power is treated the same as fee simple ownership; thus, if it is certain that the power will become *exercisable* or fail within the perpetuities period, it is valid. The fact that the donee might not actually exercise the power until after the perpetuities period is irrelevant. Note that when a presently exercisable general power is exercised, the perpetuities period begins to run from the date of exercise; therefore, the interests created must vest or fail within 21 years after the death of a life in being on the date of exercise.

a. Gifts in Default of Appointment
Gifts in default of a presently exercisable general power are rarely invalid under the Rule. The perpetuities period begins to run only when the power ceases.

2. Special and Testamentary Powers
If a special or testamentary power *may* be exercised beyond the perpetuities period, which begins to run from the creation of the power, it is void. Thus, unless expressly limited to the perpetuities period, any special or testamentary power given to an unborn person is invalid.

a. Relation-Back Doctrine
Interests created by the exercise of a special or testamentary power are read back into the original instrument creating the power, and the perpetuities period begins on the date that power was created.

b. Second Look Doctrine
Even though the exercise of the power is read back into the donor's instrument, facts and circumstances existing on the date of exercise are taken into account in determining the validity of the interests created by the exercise.

Example: Testator devises property "to Don for life, then as Don appoints by will." Don appoints by his will "to Ed for life, remainder to Ed's children." This is construed as though Testator's will read "to Don for life, then to Ed for life, then to Ed's children." If Ed was alive at Testator's death, the remainder to Ed's children is valid. If Ed was not alive at Testator's death, the remainder to Ed's children is void.

c. Gifts in Default of Appointment
Gifts in default of appointment are subject to the Rule Against Perpetuities, but the second look doctrine also applies to them.

3. **Effect of Invalid Appointment**

If a donee makes an invalid appointment, the property passes to the taker in default of appointment, if any. If none, the property reverts back to the donor's estate. However, if the donee of a *general power* manifests an intent to take the property out of the creating instrument and "capture" it for the donee's estate, the property will pass to the donee's estate.

F. CONTRACTS TO APPOINT

1. **Testamentary Powers—Contract to Appoint Is Invalid**

The donee of a testamentary power cannot contract to make an appointment. Such a contract, if made, cannot be the basis of an action for specific performance or damages. However, the promisee can obtain restitution of the value given by her for the promise unless the donee actually exercised the power pursuant to the contract.

    a. **Basis of Rule—Power to Be Exercised by Will Only**

    Where the donee is given a testamentary power, the donor's intent was that the donee should retain the opportunity to make a judgment as to the power's appropriate exercise until his death. To permit the donee to contract for the power's exercise would defeat this purpose of the donor, and would transform a power that was intended to be testamentary into a presently exercisable power. This applies *whether the testamentary power is special or general*.

2. **Presently Exercisable Powers—Contract to Appoint Is Valid**

The donee of a presently exercisable power can contract to make an appointment. If, however, it is a presently exercisable *special* power, the contract or promised appointment cannot confer a benefit on a nonobject of the power.

    a. **Basis of Rule—Donee Can Appoint to Himself**

    Recognition of the right to contract is simply a recognition that the power is presently exercisable. If the donee has a presently exercisable general power, he could appoint to himself and then give the property in the indicated manner. If he has a presently exercisable special power, he can contract to exercise in favor of an object of the power just as he could directly appoint to the object.

    b. **Contract to Exercise Special Power Cannot Benefit a Nonobject**

    In *In re Carroll's Will*, 274 N.Y. 288 (1937) (a leading case), A had a presently exercisable power to appoint $250,000 "to and among her children or any other kindred who shall survive her and in such shares and manner as she shall think proper." A promised that she would appoint the $250,000 to child C if C would agree to pay $100,000 to A's husband, not a permissible appointee. The court held that the resulting exercise of the power in C's favor was entirely void.

XIV. ADVANCE HEALTHCARE DIRECTIVES: LIVING WILLS AND DURABLE HEALTHCARE POWERS

A. INTRODUCTION

The majority of states have enacted legislation governing the use of advance healthcare directives,

which are instructions concerning what to do regarding an individual's health if he becomes unable to make healthcare decisions in the future. The two most common types of advance healthcare directives are *living wills* and *durable healthcare powers*.

1. **Living Will**

   A living will states an individual's desires, if he becomes *terminally ill* or is in a *persistent vegetative state*, regarding: (i) whether to administer, withhold, or withdraw *life-sustaining procedures*; (ii) whether to provide, withhold, or withdraw *artificial nutrition or hydration*; and (iii) whether to provide treatment to *alleviate pain*.

2. **Durable Healthcare Power**

   A durable healthcare power (sometimes called a "durable power of attorney for healthcare") appoints an agent to make healthcare decisions on behalf of the principal. Unlike an ordinary power of attorney, which normally terminates on the incapacity of the principal, a durable healthcare power does not become effective *until the principal becomes incapacitated* and it remains effective despite the incapacity. Unless expressly limited, a durable healthcare power may extend to any and all healthcare decisions that might arise.

3. **Scope of Advance Directives**

   Generally, a living will is a very limited instrument, dealing only with a terminally ill person and pertaining only to life-prolonging or pain relieving measures. A durable healthcare power usually is much broader, covering all healthcare decisions. However, an individual can define the scope of a living will or healthcare power as broadly or as narrowly as he chooses.

B. **CREATION AND EXECUTION**

Living wills and durable healthcare powers must be: (i) in *writing*, (ii) *signed* by the testator or principal or another at his direction, and (iii) *witnessed* by two adults. The testator or principal must be an adult, and most states require that he be of sound mind.

1. **Capacity Is Presumed**

   An individual is presumed to have capacity to execute a living will or durable healthcare power. Thus, if capacity is challenged, the burden of proof is on the challenger to show that the testator or principal lacked capacity or was unduly influenced.

C. **REVOCATION**

1. **Living Will**

   A living will can be revoked by: (i) obliterating, burning, tearing, or destroying the will; (ii) a written revocation of the will; or (iii) an oral expression of intent to revoke the will. The majority of states allow a living will to be revoked at any time, regardless of the individual's mental or physical condition.

   a. **When Effective**

      The revocation is effective when communicated to the testator's primary physician.

2. **Durable Healthcare Power**

   Generally, a durable healthcare power can be revoked by notifying either the agent or the principal's healthcare provider, and the revocation can be either *oral* or *written*. Some states also allow revocation in the same manner as that for living wills, *supra*.

a. **Revocation of Prior Powers**
Unless otherwise provided, the execution of a valid durable healthcare power revokes any prior durable healthcare powers.

b. **Former Spouse as Agent**
The designation of a principal's spouse as his agent is ***automatically revoked*** if the marriage is annulled or dissolved. Some states also revoke the designation upon legal separation.

D. INDIVIDUALS ELIGIBLE TO ACT AS AGENT UNDER DURABLE HEALTHCARE POWER

A principal can appoint as agent anyone ***except*** an owner, operator, or employee of a healthcare facility at which the principal is receiving care (and that individual may be an agent if she is related to the principal).

E. AUTHORITY OF AGENT UNDER DURABLE HEALTHCARE POWER

The agent has the authority to make any healthcare decisions on the principal's behalf that the principal could have made for himself while having capacity. The authority of the agent is within the discretion of the principal and must be stated in the instrument creating the durable healthcare power. The agent must act in accordance with the principal's expressed instructions and wishes. If specific powers are not expressed or stated in the instrument creating the durable healthcare power, the agent must act in the principal's ***best interest***, as determined by the principal's personal values and by weighing the factors likely to be of importance to him.

1. **Powers**
Some of the powers that the agent has are: (i) the power to consent to or refuse any type of medical care; (ii) the power to admit or discharge the principal from a healthcare facility; and (iii) the power to access the principal's medical records.

2. **Agent's Liability**
The agent is not subject to civil or criminal liability or to discipline for unprofessional conduct relating to healthcare decisions, provided she acted in ***good faith***.

ESSAY EXAM QUESTIONS

INTRODUCTORY NOTE

The essay questions that follow have been selected to provide you with an opportunity to experience how the substantive law you have been reviewing may be tested in the hypothetical essay examination question context. These sample essay questions are a valuable self-diagnostic tool designed to enable you to enhance your issue-spotting ability and practice your exam writing skills.

It is suggested that you approach each question as though under actual examination conditions. The time allowed for each question is 45 minutes. You should spend 10-15 minutes spotting issues, underlining key facts and phrases, jotting notes in the margins, and outlining your answer. *If* you organize your thoughts well, about 30 minutes will be more than adequate for writing them down. Should you prefer to forgo the actual writing involved on these questions, be sure to give yourself no more time for issue-spotting than you would on the actual examination.

The BARBRI technique for writing a well-organized essay answer is to (i) spot the issues in a question and then (ii) analyze and discuss each issue using the "CIRAC" method:

C — State your ***conclusion*** first. (In other words, you must think through your answer ***before*** you start writing.)

I — State the ***issue*** involved.

R — Give the ***rule(s)*** of law involved.

A — ***Apply*** the rule(s) of law to the facts.

C — Finally, restate your ***conclusion***.

After completing (or outlining) your own analysis of each question, compare it with the BARBRI model answer provided herein. A passing answer does ***not*** have to match the model one, but it should cover most of the issues presented and the law discussed and should ***apply the law to the facts*** of the question. Use of the CIRAC method results in the best answer you can write.

EXAM QUESTION NO. 1

Horace and Winona, husband and wife, had two children, Van and Debbie. Horace also had a child, Lois, by a prior marriage. All three children were over 21 when Horace died from a gunshot wound inflicted by Winona during one of their frequent altercations. Winona was sentenced and incarcerated after she pled guilty to murder.

Horace's will, which has now been filed for probate, made the following bequests:

1. All right, title, and interest in his residence on Elm Street to Winona;

2. All right, title, and interest in his 50-acre tract of property in Bibb County to Debbie;

3. All right, title, and interest in his Jaguar and his Bank Two stock to Van;

4. The remainder of his estate to Lois.

At the time of his death, Horace still owned his residence on Elm Street. Three months before Horace's death, Bibb County condemned 10 acres of the 50-acre tract; the county has paid Horace's executor $20,000, the value of the condemned property. Horace had then sold the remaining 40 acres to Mr. and Mrs. Neighbor; he financed the sale for the Neighbors, who gave him a promissory note for $100,000 and a deed to secure debt on the 40 acres to secure the debt obligation. Prior to his death, Horace had purchased a 2010 Jaguar to replace his 1979 Jaguar, which he gave to Van as a graduation gift. After his will was executed, Bank Two was bought by Major Bank so that Horace's Bank Two stock was replaced with Major Bank stock.

(1) Indicate to whom each of the following items of property owned by Horace at the time of his death will be distributed in accordance with the terms of Horace's will, and discuss the basis for each conclusion:

(a) Horace's residence on Elm Street.
(b) The $100,000 note and deed to secure debt executed by the Neighbors.
(c) The $20,000 in condemnation proceeds.
(d) The 2010 Jaguar.
(e) The Major Bank stock.

(2) Assume, for purposes of answering this question only, that Horace was not killed by Winona, but rather both of them were killed in an automobile accident. After finding no pulse on Horace, the paramedic heard Winona whisper, "Help us." Both were pronounced dead at the scene. Winona died intestate. To what extent, if any, would your answer to the preceding question as to the distribution of Horace's estate change under this set of facts? Explain your answer.

(3) Would your answer to question (2) above change if Winona's family offered a *copy* of her will to probate, providing that upon her death Winona's estate would be divided "equally among my husband and my three children"?

EXAM QUESTION NO. 2

Ten years ago on January 1, Tom, a widower with no descendants, executed an inter vivos trust agreement known as Trust A with ABC Bank as Trustee. The agreement provided for payment of income of the trust to himself for his lifetime and for termination and distribution of all assets to his cousin Alice one year after his death. He reserved the right to amend or revoke the agreement at any time during his lifetime.

The following month, Tom properly executed a will which included the following provisions:

> First: I give $20,000 to my friend Fred.
>
> ***
>
> Fifth: I give my farm in McLean County to my cousin Jane.
> Sixth: I give all the rest of my estate to ABC Bank as trustee of the trust known as Trust A under an agreement dated January 1 of this year, as in force at my death.
>
> ***
>
> Tenth: I name XYZ Bank as executor of this will.

Five years later, Tom amended Trust A to provide that upon termination of the trust, all assets were to be distributed to his cousin George. Two years later, he sold and conveyed 200 acres of his 500-acre McLean County farm to a neighbor and also sold the other 300 acres to another neighbor pursuant to a contract for deed providing for principal payments plus interest to be made over a period of 20 years and for delivery of a warranty deed to the purchaser upon payment of the purchase price in full.

Tom died last month, at which time Trust A as amended was in effect as was the contract for deed which had a remaining principal balance of $125,000 to be paid over the next 15 years. When his will was removed from his bank safe deposit box, it was discovered that the words "friend Fred" in paragraph First had a single line drawn through them in ink (although the words were still legible) and the words "American Cancer Society" were written immediately adjacent thereto in Tom's handwriting together with his signature immediately beneath. A note attached to the will in Tom's handwriting indicated that the lining through and addition were made by him shortly after he had a falling out with Fred.

XYZ Bank as executor of Tom's will consults you and asks your opinion as to the following:
(1)   What is the effect of the lining through and addition appearing in paragraph First of the will?
(2)   What, if anything, will Jane take pursuant to paragraph Fifth of the will?
(3)   Does paragraph Sixth constitute a valid devise of the residuary estate to ABC Bank as trustee of Trust A?

What is your advice? Give reasons.

EXAM QUESTION NO. 3

Alice executed her will five years ago. Under the terms of this will, Alice bequeathed 500 shares of ABC common stock to her sister, Betty, and the residue of her estate in trust to pay the income to her daughter, Carrie. The will provided that upon Carrie's death the principal of the residuary trust should be distributed "to Carrie's issue." When the will was executed, Alice owned 500 shares of ABC common stock.

When Alice died last month, her estate consisted of 1,000 shares of ABC common stock and a substantial amount of other property. Alice had acquired the additional 500 shares of ABC common stock as a "stock dividend."

Alice was survived by her sister, Betty; her daughter, Carrie; Carrie's two children, Don and Ellen; Don's three children, Frank, Gail, and Heather; and Ellen's two children, Ida and Joan. Alice also was survived by her husband, Oscar, whom she married two years before her death. Alice's prior husband, Michael, the father of Carrie, had died 30 years ago.

Alice's family tree can be diagrammed as follows:

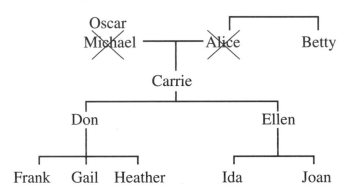

(1) What are Oscar's property rights, if any, in the assets of Alice's estate? Explain.

(2) What are Betty's rights with respect to the 1,000 shares of ABC common stock owned by Alice at the time of her death? Explain.

(3) If Don and Ellen were to predecease Carrie and Carrie was then survived by Frank, Gail, Heather, Ida, and Joan, how should the principal of the trust created under Alice's will be distributed among Carrie's issue at Carrie's death? Explain.

(Examinees in community property states should assume that all of Alice's property is sole and separate property and that the community had no interest in said property and should analyze this problem accordingly.)

EXAM QUESTION NO. 4

Angelo developed a distinct artistic style as a painter of portraits while under the influence of LSD. He obtained the LSD from Vulture. Angelo, while driving under the influence of LSD, is killed in an automobile accident. The autopsy reveals severe brain damage from use of the chemical. This instrument is found in his coat pocket:

5 May 2010

One thousand dollars each to Mary and Lamb. The rest to Val Vulture who has been good to me and anyone who opposes my gift to him loses their interest.

/s/ Mike Angelo

Witnesses:
/s/ Fred Falcon
/s/ Willie Fox

Angelo is survived by Mary and Lamb, his nieces, as his only heirs. Paintings worth $100,000 are in his estate. Vulture offers the instrument of May 5, 2010, for probate as a will, and Lamb comes to you for answers to the following questions:

(1)   If she contests the purported will and loses, will she lose her $1,000?

(2)   She owes Chortle's Mink Salon $10,000 for a mink coat and has no money other than that she might obtain from Angelo's estate. Can Chortle contest the purported will so she will lose nothing if the contest fails?

(3)   What grounds for contest offer the greatest promise for success and why?

Advise and discuss.

ANSWERS TO ESSAY EXAM QUESTIONS

ANSWER TO EXAM QUESTION NO. 1

(1) Distribution Under Horace's Will

(a) Residence: Horace's residence on Elm Street likely will be distributed to Lois. At issue is the effect of a beneficiary's killing the decedent on her interest. A beneficiary who feloniously and intentionally kills the testator forfeits her interest (under the will, by intestacy, etc.), which passes as if the beneficiary predeceased the decedent. A guilty plea to murder is conclusive proof that the killing was felonious and intentional. Here, Winona forfeits her bequest of the Elm Street residence because she pled guilty to the murder of Horace. Thus, the gift lapses and falls into the residuary estate, which will be distributed to Lois. Note that most states' anti-lapse statutes will not save the gift for Van and Debbie because Winona is not Horace's descendant (or stepchild, grandparent, or descendant of a grandparent under the broader Uniform Probate Code ("UPC")). However, if the state is one of the few with a broad anti-lapse statute that apples to **any** beneficiary, Van and Debbie may be substituted as beneficiaries of the residence.

(b) Note and Deed to Secure Debt: The $100,000 note and deed to secure debt executed by the Neighbors will be distributed to Debbie. At issue is the effect of the testator's sale of specifically bequeathed property before his death. When specifically bequeathed property has been sold, given away, lost, or destroyed during the testator's lifetime, the gift is adeemed (*i.e.*, it fails). However, if the bequest is of the testator's interest in the property, rather than of the property itself, the gift may not be adeemed if the testator still retains some interest at death. Here, Horace devised all "right, title, **and interest**" in the 50-acre tract to Debbie. Because the gift was of Horace's interest in the 50-acre tract, Debbie takes Horace's interest as it exists at his death. Thus, she takes the note and deed to secure debt.

(c) Condemnation Proceeds: The $20,000 in condemnation proceeds likely will be distributed to Debbie. At issue is whether the beneficiary of specifically bequeathed property that has been condemned during the testator's lifetime is entitled to the condemnation award. Courts generally apply the ademption doctrine objectively, without regard to the testator's intent, and without regard to why the asset is not in the estate at death. However, in many states and under the UPC, ademption does not apply if the property was taken by eminent domain before the testator's death, but the award is paid after the testator's death. Instead, the beneficiary is entitled to the condemnation award. Here, 10 acres of the 50-acre tract were condemned three months before Horace's death, but the county did not compensate Horace for the taking until after his death. Thus, Debbie is entitled to the $20,000 condemnation award.

(d) 2010 Jaguar: The 2010 Jaguar likely will be distributed to Van. The first issue is whether the bequest of the Jaguar was satisfied by a lifetime gift. In most states, if the testator makes a lifetime transfer of property to a beneficiary that is the subject of a specific gift named in the will, the transfer will not be treated as in satisfaction of that gift unless shown to be intended as such. The UPC requires such evidence of intent in a contemporaneous writing by the donor or a written acknowledgment by the donee. Here, Horace gave the 1979 Jaguar to Van as a graduation gift, but there is no evidence that Horace intended the gift to be a satisfaction of the bequest in his will. Thus, the bequest is probably not satisfied.

The second issue, then, is whether the bequest is adeemed. A will takes effect only upon the death of the testator. Because of the ambulatory nature of a will, it operates upon circumstances and properties as they exist at the time of the testator's death ("a will speaks at the time of death"). Here, Horace specifically bequeathed Van "his Jaguar." Although at the time he executed his will Horace owned a 1979 Jaguar, at the time of his death when his will became operative he owned a 2010 Jaguar. Thus, it appears that Van takes both Jaguars.

(e) **Major Bank Stock:** The Major Bank stock likely will be distributed to Van. At issue is whether a specific beneficiary of stock replaced as the result of an entity acquisition is entitled to the new stock. In many states and under the UPC, where a will makes a specific bequest of securities in one entity, the beneficiary is entitled to securities in another entity owned by the testator as a result of merger, consolidation, reorganization, or other similar action initiated by the entity. Here, the Bank Two stock changed only as the result of Major Bank's acquisition of Bank Two. Thus, Van is entitled to the Major Bank stock.

(2) Distribution If Deaths in Quick Succession

Horace's Elm Street residence likely would be distributed in equal shares to Van and Debbie. At issue is whether Horace and Winona died simultaneously. Under the Uniform Simultaneous Death Act ("USDA"), when the title to property or its devolution depends on priority of death and there is *no sufficient evidence* that the persons have died otherwise than simultaneously, the property of each person is distributed as if he had survived. Here, there is sufficient evidence that Winona survived Horace for at least a moment because she spoke after Horace had no pulse. Thus, the USDA does not apply and the residence passes to Winona's estate. In most states, if an intestate is survived by children but no spouse, her estate passes in equal shares to the children. Thus, Van and Debbie take the Elm Street residence.

(3) Distribution Under Copy of Winona's Will

If the copy of Winona's will can be probated, the distribution of the Elm Street residence would be the same as that set out in (2), *supra*. The first issue is whether and under what circumstances a copy of a will may be admitted to probate. If the original will cannot be found, a copy of the will (clearly proved to be such by subscribing witnesses and other evidence) may be admitted to probate. However, there is a presumption that the will was revoked by the testator, which must be rebutted by a preponderance of the evidence. Here, Winona's family may offer the copy of her will to the probate court, but they must establish that it is her will (as by testimony of the subscribing witnesses) and rebut the presumption of revocation.

The second issue is whether Lois is considered Winona's "child" for purposes of intestacy. Generally, stepchildren have no inheritance rights. However, the doctrine of adoption by estoppel allows a stepchild to inherit from her stepparent as though legally adopted where the stepparent gains custody of a child under an agreement with the natural parent that she will adopt the child. Here, there is no evidence of such an agreement. Thus, although Winona's will purports to include Lois as one of her "three children," Lois will not take under this provision.

ANSWER TO EXAM QUESTION NO. 2

(1) Paragraph First

The effect of the lining through of Fred's name and the addition of the American Cancer Society depends upon whether the will was holographic (unattested and entirely in the testator's handwriting) and whether the state is one of the approximately 25 states that recognize holographic wills. Most states that recognize holographic wills give effect to handwritten changes, such as substituting beneficiaries, made by the testator after the holographic will is completed. Thus, if Tom's will is holographic, the American Cancer Society will take $20,000. These types of interlineations are not usually given effect, however, if made to an attested will unless the changes themselves are sufficient to constitute a

holographic codicil (and the jurisdiction recognizes such codicils). Here, Tom's revisions were signed and together with the handwritten note were probably sufficient to constitute a holographic codicil. Thus, even if the original will was a typewritten, attested will, the interlineation will be given effect if the jurisdiction recognizes holographic codicils.

If the jurisdiction does not recognize holographic instruments, the next issue is whether the lining through caused a revocation. Most states authorize partial, as well as total, revocation by physical act. One method of revocation by physical act is obliteration (as by lining through) of a material portion of the will. When, as here, a particular provision is obliterated, the question is whether the testator intended to revoke the entire will or only that provision. It seems clear from these facts that Tom intended only to change that provision and leave the rest of his will intact. Thus, the gift to Fred was properly revoked. However, because the addition of the American Cancer Society as beneficiary would not be recognized in these jurisdictions, the court must consider whether the doctrine of dependent relative revocation would apply. Under this doctrine, the court may disregard a revocation if it determines that the act of revocation was premised on a mistake of law or fact and would not have occurred but for the testator's belief that another disposition of his property was valid. The disposition that results from disregarding the revocation must come closer to effectuating what the testator tried but failed to do than would an intestate (or residuary) distribution. Here, the court must determine whether the gift to Fred or the $20,000 passing by the residuary clause would come closer to the testator's plan. Given his falling out with Fred, and the alternative residuary beneficiary named in the will, the court would probably find that Fred's gift was revoked and the money passes into the residuary estate.

(2) Paragraph Fifth

Jane receives 300 acres of the farm, subject to the contract of sale. Thus, she receives all remaining payments. At issue is whether the beneficiary of a specific bequest that has been partially conveyed to another and the remainder sold pursuant to an installment contract is entitled to the property or sale proceeds.

Where a will makes a specific bequest of a particular item of property and the item is not in the estate at the time of the decedent's death, the bequest fails (is "adeemed"). The named taker of the specific item does not get the proceeds if the item is sold by the testator before his death. Thus, Jane receives nothing from the 200 acres that were sold and had already been conveyed at Tom's death.

However, where the testator has only *contracted* to sell property, the gift of the item is not adeemed, and the specific devisee takes the property subject to the contract and is entitled to the proceeds of sale. Here, the remaining 300 acres pass to Jane subject to the contract, so that Jane gets the remaining payments.

(3) Paragraph Sixth

Paragraph Sixth constitutes a valid devise of the residuary estate to ABC Bank as trustee of Trust A. At issue is whether paragraph Sixth is a valid pour-over gift.

A will may dispose of property to the trustee of an identified, amendable inter vivos trust (which is in existence at the time of execution of the will), to be held and distributed according to its terms. Property passing under the will is governed by the terms of the trust, even as amended after the execution of the will.

Here, the trust was in existence at the time of execution of the will. Also, the trust is identified in the will. Thus, the will may dispose of property to the trustee (ABC Bank) according to the terms of the trust, notwithstanding that the trust is amendable inter vivos or that the trust was amended five years after execution of the will.

ANSWER TO EXAM QUESTION NO. 3

(1) Oscar's Rights

Oscar is entitled to a forced or elective share. Oscar married Alice three years *after* she executed her will. Thus, the first issue is the effect on the will of the subsequent marriage. The states are divided on the effect of marriage on a previously executed will. Most states have no statute dealing with the effect of marriage on a previously executed will. In these states marriage, by itself, does not affect the will. The new spouse is given adequate protection by dower or an elective share statute. A substantial minority of the states have statutes under which the testator's subsequent marriage has an effect on the will. In most of these states, the will is only partially revoked. The marriage revokes the will only to the extent of providing the new spouse with an intestate share. After distribution of the spouse's intestate share, the will operates to distribute the remaining assets. Thus, depending on whether there is a statute, Oscar will either be entitled to an elective share or an intestate share.

Nearly all of the common law jurisdictions have enacted elective share statutes designed to give the surviving spouse some protection against disinheritance. These statutes give the spouse an election to take a statutory share of the decedent's estate in lieu of taking under the decedent's will. The elective share amount varies from state to state. In most states, the amount is one-third of the decedent's net estate if the decedent was survived by descendants, and one-half if the decedent was not survived by descendants.

In most states, the elective share is first paid in cash or in kind from assets passing under the decedent's will that would have passed outright to the surviving spouse but for the election. To the extent that such assets are insufficient, the elective share is paid pursuant to the abatement rules that apply to creditors' claims. That is, property passing by partial intestacy is first applied; then the residuary estate; then general legacies, demonstrative legacies, and specific bequests are abated (in that order). Here, the entire forced share would be payable from the assets bequeathed to the residuary trust for the benefit of Carrie and her issue.

(2) Betty's Rights

Betty is entitled to all 1,000 shares of ABC common stock if the state has a UPC-type statute, but only 500 shares if the state follows the common law rule. Whether Betty is entitled to the additional 500 shares of ABC common stock that Alice acquired as a stock dividend between the time the will was executed and the time Alice died depends first on whether Alice intended the bequest to be general or specific.

A general bequest is a gift that is payable out of the general assets of the estate and which does not require delivery of any specific asset or satisfaction from any designated portion of the testator's property. If Alice intended the bequest to be general, then Betty is not entitled to the additional 500 shares because this would be a greater share of the total estate than the value of the 500 shares that Alice specified in the will.

A specific bequest is a gift of a particular item of real or personal property that is capable of being identified and distinguished from all other property in the testator's estate. A specific devise or bequest can be satisfied only by the distribution of the specific asset. Ascertaining whether the testator intended a specific bequest depends on what issue the court is deciding. If the issue is deciding whether property is adeemed by extinction (when it is no longer in the estate at the testator's death), courts will construe a bequest of "500 shares of ABC common stock" as a general bequest (which is not adeemed) rather than a specific bequest (which would result in the beneficiary's taking nothing), even if the testator owned exactly 500 shares of that stock when she made the will. In contrast, if the issue is accessions (increases or additions to the property), whether the testator owned the shares that she designated in her will is a critical factor in classifying the bequest as specific rather than general. Here, since Alice's

estate could have satisfied Betty's bequest if Alice had died immediately after the will was executed (because Alice owned 500 shares of ABC stock at that time), the bequest was probably a specific bequest.

In most states, the fact that the bequest of stock is specific does not resolve the issue of Betty's entitlement to the additional shares. While most courts grant a beneficiary of a specific stock bequest any additional shares of stock produced by a *stock split*, most of these courts distinguish stock dividends and conclude that stock dividends do not pass to the beneficiary of a specific bequest of corporate stock. The rationale is that the shares of stock on hand after the stock split represent the same proportionate share of corporate ownership as before the split and therefore a beneficiary of stock subject to a stock split should receive the additional shares. On the other hand, stock dividends are paid out of the earned surplus of the corporation just the same as cash dividends. They should be treated as income on the original capital and not as part of the original capital. Thus, stock dividends paid during the testator's lifetime should be treated the same as cash dividends, and Betty would be entitled to only 500 shares of ABC stock. Some courts and the UPC take the minority position that the value of the original shares is diminished as much by the issuance of a stock dividend as by a stock split, and hence in either case the new shares should go to the legatee of the specific gift.

(3) Distribution Among Carrie's Issue If Don and Ellen Predecease Her

If Don and Ellen were to predecease Carrie and Carrie was then survived by Frank, Gail, Heather, Ida, and Joan, the principal of the trust created under Alice's will would be distributed on a per stirpes or per capita basis depending on state law.

Alice's will states that upon Carrie's death, the principal should be distributed "to Carrie's issue." The word "issue" includes children and grandchildren. While the court will look to the testator's intent to determine how the property should be distributed among Carrie's issue, in the absence of a contrary intent the court will follow the intestacy statute of the state to determine the distribution. When there is at least one taker at the first generational level (*i.e.*, the child level), the shares are divided at the child level. This form of distribution is often called a "per stirpes" distribution. Thus, if Don had survived Carrie, he would have taken a one-half share to the exclusion of his own children, and Ellen's children would have divided in equal amounts the remaining one-half share.

If both Don and Ellen failed to survive Carrie, however, the question becomes how the five grandchildren will divide the property; *i.e.*, are the shares determined at the child level (in which case Frank, Gail, and Heather will take one-sixth and Ida and Joan will take a one-fourth interest) or at the grandchild level (in which case each grandchild will take a one-fifth interest)?

Under the intestacy statute of most states, the shares are determined at the first generational level at which there are living takers. Each descendant at that generational level takes one share, and the share of each deceased person at that generational level is divided among his descendants by representation. This form of distribution is called "per capita with representation." Thus, if both children predecease Carrie, the five grandchildren would each take a one-fifth share of Alice's trust. Note that the same result would be reached in those states following the modern trend, which is a per capita distribution at each generational level. Under that scheme, the initial division of shares is made at the first generational level at which there are living takers, but the shares of deceased persons at that level are combined and then divided equally among the takers at the next generational level. In this case, the result does not change because all of the takers are at the same generational level. Other states apply a "strict per stirpes" rule. Under this rule, the shares are always determined at the first generational level even though there are no living takers at that level. Applying a strict per stirpes distribution to the facts, Don's children would share in the one-half share he would have received. Frank, Heather, and Gail would therefore each take a one-sixth interest. Ida and Joan would share in the one-half interest Ellen would have received and thus each would take a one-fourth interest.

ANSWER TO EXAM QUESTION NO. 4

(1) Lamb's Contest

If Lamb contests the purported will and loses, she likely will not lose her $1,000. At issue is whether Lamb has probable cause to contest the purported will.

No-contest clauses, such as the one in this instrument, are valid and enforceable in most states. Where such a clause is present, the beneficiary who contests the will forfeits her legacy **unless she has probable cause** for bringing the contest. Whether the beneficiary has probable cause is a question of fact. Here, although Lamb is unlikely to succeed in a will contest (*see* below), she almost certainly has probable cause to challenge the will given the medical evidence of Angelo's brain damage. Of course, should she be successful in the contest, the no-contest clause falls with the will, and she will take one-half of Angelo's estate.

(2) Chortle's Contest

Chortle cannot contest the purported will. At issue is whether Chortle has standing to contest the purported will.

Only interested parties have standing to contest a will. To be an interested party, the person must have a direct interest in the estate that would be adversely affected by the admission of the will to probate. Creditors, even creditors of the decedent, do not have standing to challenge a will. Thus, Chortle, a creditor of Lamb's, has no standing to challenge Angelo's will. If, however, Lamb assigns her interest under the will to Chortle, Chortle would be able to challenge the will.

(3) Grounds for Contest

The best possible basis for a will contest is that the influence of the drugs and the damage caused thereby led to a lack of testamentary capacity. This basis is very difficult to prove. The mental capacity required for making a will is a lower standard than that required for making a contract. The testator need only have sufficient capacity to understand: (i) the nature of his act (that he is executing a will); (ii) the nature and extent of his property; (iii) the persons who are the natural objects of his bounty; and (iv) the practical effect of the will. Nothing in the facts indicates that Angelo lacked understanding of any of these facts. In fact, the instrument itself evidences an understanding of some of these factors. For instance, the attesting witnesses and the formality of the document indicate that he understood this was a will, and the gift to his nieces indicates that he knew who were the natural objects of his bounty. The fact that a testator is addicted to drugs does not mean that he lacked the requisite mental capacity and was not able to comprehend the nature of his act. The medical evidence would have to be very substantial to prove that Angelo lacked capacity.

Another challenge could be advanced on the ground that it is not clear that the document was intended as a will; *i.e.*, that the document lacks testamentary intent. For a will to be valid, the testator must intend that the particular instrument operate as his will. Where the instrument lacks a recital that it is a will, testamentary intent will be found only if it is shown that the testator: (i) intended to dispose of property; (ii) intended the disposition to occur only upon his death; and (iii) intended this instrument to accomplish the disposition. It seems clear from the instrument itself that Angelo intended this instrument to dispose of his property. The only question is whether he intended it to occur only upon his death. The attestation and formality of the document indicate that he intended a will. He certainly would not need this type of instrument to give his nieces cash, and would probably not use such a document to transfer his paintings. A court would probably find that he intended the disposition of property to occur only upon his death, and that the requisite testamentary intent was present to make this instrument a valid will.